. . .*all necessary information about facilities, prices, pets, children, amenities, credit cards and the like. Like France's Michelin*. . .
—New York Times

Provides a wealth of the kinds of information needed to make a wise choice. —American Council on Consumer Interests

The entries for each hotel include rates, services and facilities available, as well as a short description of the style and mood of the establishment. —San Francisco Chronicle

The photos put you on the scene while the text and side notes offer explicit answers. —Los Angeles Times

. . .*A page is devoted to each hotel, with a description of the accommodations and facilities plus information on dining, rates, credit cards and other items of interest.* —Chicago Sun

. . .*Little descriptions provide all the essentials: romance, historical landmarks, golf/fishing, gourmet food, or, just as important, low prices. Take your pick!* —National Motorist

. . .*inviting descriptions of each hotel, along with detailed lists of the services offered.* —Milwaukee Journal

The title says it all; this is a comprehensive listing. —Travel Agent

updated. . .a national listing. —Publisher's Weekly

. . .*Lanier's book is very useful and will be popular. Recommended for libraries throughout the United States and other countries. A very good buy.*
—U.S. Government Technical Information Center, Fort Ord

. . .*This is well worth making shelf space in any travel library.*
—Travel Weekly

. . . a seductive volume for window shopping. . . Handsomely illustrated. . . Hotels that provide the atmosphere of a fine residence: beauty in design, color and furnishings, fresh flowers, luxurious toiletries and linens. Other considerations for select business and physical fitness facilities, excellence of cuisine and concierge services.   —Chicago Sun-Times

. . . these hotels lived up to the author's description. Fortunately the author covers a range of rates from affordable to expensive.
                                                              —St. Louis Post-Dispatch

. . . unique places with exquisitely appointed rooms, interesting architecture, luxurious ambience and excellent food and service.
                                                              —Cincinnati Enquirer

The book may give in one volume readers everything they ever wanted to know. . .   —Dallas Morning News

. . . well coded and full of practical information.   —Diversion

. . . Definitive and worth the room in your reference library.
                                                              —Los Angeles

A state-by-state and city-by-city guide. . . researched listings. . an impressive number.   —San Francisco Chronicle

If elegant small hotels are your thing - and whose aren't they? - check out Elegant Small Hotels. Details 168 such establishments, complete with celeb comment on many of them.   —Elle

. . . Lanier, as usual provides good value for the money.
                                                              —USA Technical Information Center

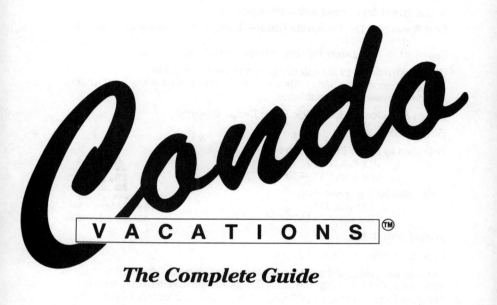

Condo VACATIONS™

The Complete Guide

Pamela Lanier

Lanier Publishing International, Ltd.

Other Books by Pamela Lanier:

The Complete Guide to Bed & Breakfasts, Inns & Guesthouses in the United States and Canada—John Muir Publications

Elegant Small Hotels—John Muir Publications

All-Suite Hotel Guide—John Muir Publications

Alaska in 22 Days—John Muir Publications

Bed & Breakfast Cookbook—Running Press

Golf Resorts—The Complete Guide—Lanier Publishing International, Ltd.

Design & Production John Stick, Cover Design Ken Scott

ISBN: 0-89815-301-8

Published by Lanier Publishing International, Ltd.
        P.O. Box 20429
        Oakland, CA 94620

Distributed by Ten Speed Press
        P.O. Box 7123
        Berkeley, CA 94707

American Hotel
& Motel Association
ALLIED MEMBER

Printed in the U.S.A.

Project Coordinator Diane Last

I wish to acknowledge the following persons and organizations for their help in making this Guide a reality: Raymond C. Ellis, American Hotel Motel Association, Marianne Barth, Paul Gray, Carl Berry, all fifty state Departments of Tourism, Chambers of Commerce and Visitors Bureaus. Special thanks to Mort, Martha and Aaron Liebman and the staff of Copygraphics, Inc., of Santa Fe, New Mexico for their care and dedication in bringing this book to type.

Library of Congress Cataloging-in-Publication-Data
Lanier, Pamela
  Condo Vacations: a complete guide to over 1200 condominiums/by Pamela Lanier.
    p. cm.
  Includes index
  ISBN: 0-89815-301-8
  1. Resorts—United States—Directories. 2. Resorts—Directories. 3. Condominiums—United States—Directories. 4. Condominiums—Directories. I. Title
TX907.2.L36 1989
647'.94—dc19
                                           89-300028
                                             CIP

Contents

VOTE

FOR YOUR CHOICE OF
CONDO OF THE YEAR

Did you find your stay at a Condominium listed in this Guide particularly enjoyable? Use the form in the back of the book or just drop us a note and we'll add your vote for the "Condo of the Year."

The winning entry will be featured in the next edition of **Condo Vacations, The Complete Guide.**

Please base your decision on:
- Helpfulness of the Staff
- Quality of Service
- Cleanliness
- Amenities
- Decor
- Food

Look for the winning Condo in the new **Condo Vacations, The Complete Guide.**

Introduction

You need a vacation. But where are you going to go? Why not take a condo vacation as an alternative to traditional hotels and motels. A new choice which offers greater freedom at lower rates.

What Is A Vacation Condominium?

A vacation condominium is a lodging which features suites, rather than single rooms. Most condos have at least one separate bedroom. Others may have two or three. The vast majority of condos in this Guide have full kitchen facilities. Most of the conveniences of hotels, such as daily maid service are available, as well as individual air conditioning and heat control, and color, often cable TV.

Who Stays In Vacation Condos?

The unique features of condos attract families, couples traveling together, business travelers who want a better working situation, and small business groups that are having meetings.

Why Stay In Vacation Condos?

Freedom! And lower prices. Don't be crowded in a motel room where you can barely get by the TV to the bed. Condominiums, for a comparable price, offer a kitchen, bedroom, living room with a couch that opens up for extra sleeping, and bathrooms with tubs—some even have jacuzzis in the master bath.

If you want to eat out, fine. There may be excellent restaurants in the area, but you can cut costs by eating at home.

Staying at a condo can trim vacation expenses by up to fifty per cent when compared with a stay in a similarly located traditional hotel with all meals taken in a restaurant.

Family Fun!

Renting a condominium is like taking your home with you. The sheets are on the bed, the cable TV is ready, and the kitchen is waiting for you to prepare all the special treats your children love.

The staff at most condo resorts can recommend reliable baby sitters, and offer daily maid service, giving everyone a break. Family reunions are also a natural for condominiums.

Business Meetings

Business groups benefit from the flexible accommodations and added privacy a condo affords, without the distracting hustle and bustle of a conventional resort hotel.

Group Vacations

For a few couples who want to get together for a vacation, why not rent a condominium? Condos are a great bargain for couples traveling together who can split the cost. Condo staffs are expert at arranging everything from ski lift tickets to equipment rental, which means less hassle and more fun for everyone!

Ski Vacations

Ski-area condominiums are especially appealing. Most ski condos offer a ski package which includes lift tickets, and many have ski schools and nurseries for children. Also, many condos are ski/in-ski/out so you can ski home whenever you want to without the tedious job of piling your skis on the car and fighting the traffic home.

Beach Vacations

Rent a condominium on the beach and take the little ones to build sand castles while you relax and get a fantastic tan. Or maybe you're looking for a romantic hide-away for the two of you to celebrate a special occasion. Condos offer a couple the boon of extra space and privacy—something we can all appreciate!

Whatever your vacation desire, a condominium vacation can fill it, and if you have specific ideas in mind, such as a spa where you can be pampered, special lessons from a golf or tennis pro, guided deep sea fishing, helicopter, skiing, or peace, quiet and seclusion — it's all there waiting for you.

Pamela Lanier
San Francisco
April, 1989

Guide Notes

Prices

Our rate code reflects the most current information available beginning with the least expensive condominiums off season. Generally, the rates are for the condo based on an average occupancy of up to 4 in a one-bedroom, or 6 in a two-bedroom. We give price codes as follows:

$	- to $50	Some places charge for extra
$$	- $51 to $100	persons in the room. Usually
$$$	- $101 to $150	nominal.
$$$$	- $151 to $399	
4$	- $400 to $499	5$ - $500 to $599, etc.
10$	- anything over $1,000	

These codes are designed to provide you with a *general* idea of the rates. Be sure to check for exact prices when you reserve.

Credit Cards And Checks

We make note of the credit cards which are accepted — other cc means other credit cards are accepted. Generally, personal checks are accepted with some restrictions. Be sure to inquire about this.

Reservations

The more popular condominiums fill up fast for peak season. Six months ahead is not too soon to reserve your place in the Hawaiian sun for Christmas; and Aspen area slopes are often booked by summer's end, so be sure to reserve early. However, last minute travelers are sometimes able to take advantage of last minute openings. When you make your reservation, be sure to confirm the availability of the amenities and services you require.

Pets, Smoking and Handicapped Access

We make note if you can bring your pet (it must be on a leash); however, some condominiums which allow pets limit the size, so if Bonzo is a Great Dane, be sure to check.

We make note where there are non-smoking rooms for the convenience of our readers who can't tolerate cigarette smoke.

We also make note of condominiums which have units accessible to the handicapped. Such rooms fill up early so be sure to reserve well in advance, and double check to make sure the facilities meet your requirements.

Maps

We include a map for each state to assist you in your planning. Also, at the back of the guide is a list of tourism offices. We recommend that you contact the tourist offices to get the general travel information before you go. It is a valuable free resource!

Deposit Policy

Generally, one or two nights' rate is required in advance, by check or credit card. Some condominiums have flat fees.

Cancellation Policy

Some places keep a percentage of the deposit, no matter when the cancellation is made. Deposits are usually refunded when cancellation is made by a specified time, anywhere from 72 hours to 2 months, depending on the resort's policy. Holiday seasons require a longer cancellation notice. Cancellation policies can be quite stringent, so be sure to check.

Check-in And Check-out

The most popular check-out time tends to be noon, but can be as early as 10:00 a.m. Check-in times vary — 2, 3 or 4 p.m. Please confirm check-in and check-out times when you make your reservation. If you have special time requirements, the condominium staff may be able to accommodate you.

Maid And Linen Service

Most condominiums have maid service; in some, included in the rate. For others it is an extra charge. Linens are generally provided as is kitchen equipment — often gourmet! It is important to check what service is provided when you book. Many beach properties request that you bring your own beach towels.

Hotel Amenities And Business Facilities

In our feature listing, we note which condominiums have full hotel services, i.e., front desk, message center, bell men, etc. Condominiums are increasingly popular for business meetings so we make note of conference facilities, conference room capacity and business services available which generally means on-site FAX, Xerox, message center, etc.

Recreational Facilities

We provide data on the full gamut of recreational facilities available, from pool and sauna to nearby golf courses.

Room Amenities

Most condominiums these days feature over-size beds, king or queen. We make note of kitchen facilities, individual air conditioning and heating, TV, cable TV and VCR. Many condominiums have more facilities and amenities than we have space to note. We recommend that you narrow your choices to two or three condominiums and then write or call for their brochures and request information about your exact requirements.

Children

Most condominiums are very well prepared for family visits. Many make a special point of offering childrens activities, such as play grounds, kiddie pool, movies, arts and crafts and ski nursery and other supervised activities. Usually, the condominium staff can recommend a reliable baby sitter. Cribs and high chairs and extra cots are generally available at no extra charge. If you require children's equipment, be sure to reserve it in advance. In most condominium complexes there are plenty of families with kids, which means extra fun for everyone.

Location

In our feature listing, we note the distance to downtown, to airport, whether the property is beach front, and proximity to ski lifts.

Restaurant-Bar

We make note of the presence on site of restaurants or bar when available.

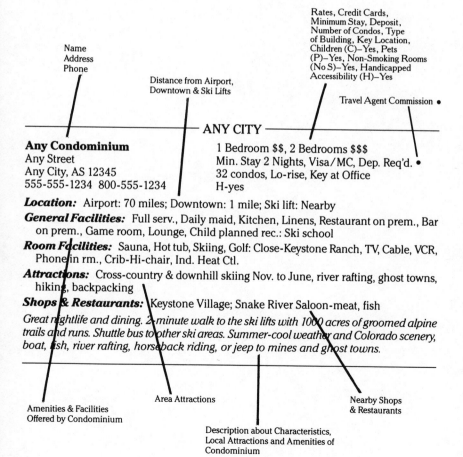

Name
Address
Phone

Distance from Airport,
Downtown & Ski Lifts

Rates, Credit Cards,
Minimum Stay, Deposit,
Number of Condos, Type
of Building, Key Location,
Children (C)–Yes, Pets
(P)–Yes, Non-Smoking Rooms
(No S)–Yes, Handicapped
Accessibility (H)–Yes

Travel Agent Commission •

━━━━━━━━━━━━━ ANY CITY ━━━━━━━━━━━━━

Any Condominium
Any Street
Any City, AS 12345
555-555-1234 800-555-1234

1 Bedroom $$, 2 Bedrooms $$$
Min. Stay 2 Nights, Visa/MC, Dep. Req'd. •
32 condos, Lo-rise, Key at Office
H-yes

Location: Airport: 70 miles; Downtown: 1 mile; Ski lift: Nearby
General Facilities: Full serv., Daily maid, Kitchen, Linens, Restaurant on prem., Bar on prem., Game room, Lounge, Child planned rec.: Ski school
Room Facilities: Sauna, Hot tub, Skiing, Golf: Close-Keystone Ranch, TV, Cable, VCR, Phone in rm., Crib-Hi-chair, Ind. Heat Ctl.
Attractions: Cross-country & downhill skiing Nov. to June, river rafting, ghost towns, hiking, backpacking
Shops & Restaurants: Keystone Village; Snake River Saloon-meat, fish
Great nightlife and dining. 2-minute walk to the ski lifts with 1000 acres of groomed alpine trails and runs. Shuttle bus to other ski areas. Summer-cool weather and Colorado scenery, boat, fish, river rafting, horseback riding, or jeep to mines and ghost towns.

Amenities & Facilities
Offered by Condominium

Area Attractions

Nearby Shops
& Restaurants

Description about Characteristics,
Local Attractions and Amenities of
Condominium

Alabama

Dadeville •

Gulf Shores

DADEVILLE

Still Waters
1000 Still Water Dr.
Dadeville, AL 36853
205-825-7021 800-633-4954

1 Bedroom $$, 2 Bedrooms $$$, Villas
Pool, Kitchen, Linens

Attractions: Montgomery attractions: Zoo, Planetarium, Fine Arts Museum, azalea trail,
   historic sights, Weight room, bicycles, Tennis, Golf

*Individually appointed villas with lake or golf views, and decks with grills, in a resort that
meets your every vacation requirement. Marina, lakeside beach, cabana and cafe. Active
games and sports, theme parties, special social activities, boat rentals, stables.*

GULF SHORES

Compass Point
1516 Sandpiper Lane
Gulf Shores, AL 36542
205-948-6411 800-344-8122

1 Bedroom $$, 2 Bedrooms $$, 3 Bedrooms $$
1 Bedrm/week $$$$, 2 Bed/week 4$,
   3 Bed/week 5$
Min. Stay 2 Nights, Visa/MC, Dep. Req'd.
25 condos, Hi-rise, Key at Office

Location: Airport: 1 hour; Downtown: 1 mile; Need car

General Facilities: Conf. rm., Kitchen, Linens

Room Facilities: Pool, Putting green, Cable, Ind. AC Ctl., Ind. Heat Ctl.

Attractions: Charter boat rentals, 24 acre water park, sandy beaches, beach horseback
   riding

Shops & Restaurants: Tourist shops, Liz Claiborne-Ralph Lauren outlets; Nolans-
   variety

*Surrounded by live oaks and oleanders, these units offer breathtaking views and master
bedrooms with private bath and balcony. Heated swimming pool, fishing pier, boat ramp
and putting green. History buffs will enjoy visiting Fort Morgan with its museum, gift shop
and restaurant, or tour the historic districts of Mobile and Pensacola. The Lagoon has safe
shallow waters for children and is perfect for water sports. Shopping, dining and nightlife
are nearby, or take a stroll on the landscaped grounds.*

Cabo Regis

GULF SHORES

Seabreeze Condominiums
West Beach Blvd., Rt. 1, Box 1994
Gulf Shores, AL 36542
205-948-6411 800-344-8122

2 Bedrooms $$
Min. Stay 2 Nights, Dep. Req'd.
Lo-rise, Key at Compass Pt. office

Location: Airport: 1 hour; Downtown: 1 mile; Need car

General Facilities: Daily maid, Kitchen, Linens

Room Facilities: Pool, Cable, Ind. AC Ctl., Ind. Heat Ctl.

Attractions: Naval Air Museum, Bellingrath Gardens, Fort Morgan, Mobile Bay Ferry,
Country Club golfing

Shops & Restaurants: Rivera, Liz Claiborne, Ralph Lauren outlets; Fine seafood
restaurants

*Relax on the beautiful sandy beaches only steps away for a peaceful vacation, or for the
more athletically inclined, try horseback riding on the beach or golf at the Country Club.
Shopping, restaurants and many historical areas in Pensacola and Mobile, which also
have greyhound racing. The Mobile Bay Ferry takes you to Fort Morgan, defended by
David Farragut in the Battle of Mobile Bay.*

Village By The Gulf
W. Beach Blvd., P.O. Box 2079
Gulf Shores, AL 36542
205-948-6832 205-948-6833

Arizona

Flagstaff
Lake Havasu
Pinetop
Carefree
Paradise Valley
Phoenix • Scottsdale
Mesa
Tuscon

CAREFREE

Boulders Resort
34631 N. Tom Darlington, Box 2090
Carefree, AZ 85377
602-488-9099 800-223-7636

120 condos

Location: Downtown: nearby

General Facilities: Conf. rm. cap. 175, Kitchen, Restaurant on prem., Bar on prem., Lounge, Baby-sitter

Room Facilities: Pool, Tennis, Fitness Center, Golf: 3 courses

Attractions: Day trips and Grand Canyon flights, desert jeep tours, Taliesen West, ballooning, horses

Shops & Restaurants: Scottsdale shopping; Latilla Room, Palo Verde Room

120 Casitas blending in with the Sonoran desert north of Scottsdale. Contemporary in feeling, yet a place to unwind amid Indian handicrafts and regional art. Dining room menus feature innovative dishes and natural ingredients. You can be as active or as lazy as your spirit moves you.

FLAGSTAFF

Fairfield Flagstaff Comm. Club
1900 N. Country Club Dr., Box 1208
Flagstaff, AZ 86002
602-526-3232 800-526-1004

1 Bedroom $$, 2 Bedrooms $$$, Hi-rise
Pool, Kitchen, Linens

Attractions: Grand Canyon-80 miles, Sedona red rocks, Meteor Crater, Painted Desert-100 miles, Stables, mini golf, Tennis, Golf

Tastefully decorated units in the Arizona hill country. Sharpen your golf and tennis skills, swim in the pools or Lake Elaine, horseback ride through Coconino National Forest. 14 miles to Snowbowl winter skiing. Sunburst Lounge for late night dancing.

HOT SPRINGS

Willow Beach Lakefront Condos
Route 3, Box 122
Hot Springs, AZ 71913
501-525-4398

1 Bedroom $$, Lo-rise
Pool, Kitchen, Linens, Phone in rm.

Attractions: Lake, Oaklawn Race Track

9,000 acres of water sports on Lake Hamilton. Completely furnished lakefront view units with grill on balcony. Fishing docks, covered boat slips and a nearby marina.

──────────────── LAKE HAVASU CITY ────────────────

Nautical Inn Resort & Conf.　　AmEx/Visa/MC •
Center　　　　　　　　　　　　16 condos
1000 McCulloch Blvd.　　　　　　No S-yes
Lake Havasu City, AZ 86403
602-855-2141 800-892-2141

Location: Airport: 4 minutes; Downtown: 4 min.; Beach front

General Facilities: Conf. rm. cap. 150, Kitchen, Restaurant on prem., Bar on prem.

Room Facilities: Pool, Sauna, Hot tub, Tennis, Golf: Nautical Inn course, TV, Phone in rm.

Attractions: London Bridge, complimentary round trips to Laughlin, Nevada, entertainment

Shops & Restaurants: London Bridge & K-Mart shopping centers, Bayless; Versaille/Fr., Capt's Table

Located on beautiful Lake Havasu and right across from the London Bridge. Captain's Table restaurant has a wide variety of cuisine and specializes in cakes and pies. Dance floor.

──────────────── LAKE HAVASU ────────────────

Inn at Tamarisk　　　　　Studio $$, 1 Bedroom $$, 2 Bedrooms $$
3101 London Bridge Road　　1 Bedrm/week 9$, 2 Bed/week 10$
Lake Havasu, AZ 86403　　　Dep. Req'd.
602-764-3044　　　　　　　　Lo-rise

General Facilities: Kitchen

Room Facilities: Pool, Tennis, Croquet, table tennis, TV

Attractions: World OutBoard Classic, Sailboat Regattas, Ski tournaments, International Jet Ski Race

Shops & Restaurants: English Village quaint shops under London Bridge; French, continental, American

Quiet desert oasis, a short walk to Lake Havasu beach. Comfortable condominiums, pool, barbecues and cabana area. Families also enjoy shuffleboard, horseshoes and the putting green. Scheduled free bus trips with fun packet to Laughlin, Nevada, casinos. English village along the water with unique shops beneath the London Bridge.

──────────────── MESA ────────────────

Arizona Golf Resort & Conf.　　1 Bedroom $$, 2 Bedrooms $$$
Center　　　　　　　　　　　　AmEx/Visa/MC, Dep. 1 Night
425 South Power Road　　　　　　6 condos, Lo-rise
Mesa, AZ 85206　　　　　　　　　P-yes
602-832-3202 800-528-8282

Location: Airport: Phoenix 30 minutes; Downtown: 10 min.

General Facilities: Conf. rm. cap. 1000, Kitchen, Linens, Restaurant on prem., Bar on prem., Lounge

Room Facilities: Pool, Sauna, Hot tub, Tennis, Bikes, volleyball, Golf: Championship course, TV, Cable, Phone in rm., Ind.AC Ctl., Ind. Heat Ctl.

Attractions: Apache Trail & Tri Lakes Region, Champion Fighter Museum, Mormon Temple, Rockin R Ranch, entertainment

Shops & Restaurants: Fiesta Mall, VF Factory Outlet; Annabelle's/prime rib

One of Arizona's best golf resorts with a complete range of activities. Dance in the lounge after dinner at Anabelle's.

PARADISE VALLEY

Hermosa Inn Resort
5532 N. Palo Cristi Rd.
Paradise Valley, AZ 85253
602-955-8614

1 Bedroom $$$, Villas
Pool, Kitchen

Attractions: Putting green, Tennis, Golf

Comfortable seclusion and quiet elegance in Arizona's Valley of the Sun. Villas with mini-kitchens, private patios and Spanish-style beehive fireplaces. Peaceful relaxation by the pool. Play tennis, practice on the putting green, or play a full 18 holes of golf.

PHOENIX

The Wigwam
Litchfield Park
Phoenix, AZ 85340
602-935-3811

Dep. Req'd.
Lo-rise

Location: Airport: Sky Harbor; Downtown: 15 miles

General Facilities: Restaurant on prem., Bar on prem., Lounge

Room Facilities: Pool, Tennis, Trap skeet shooting, Ind. AC Ctl.

Attractions: Phoenix attractions, entertainment

Shops & Restaurants: Phoenix shops; Terrace Dining Room-on-site

Wigwam limousines meet you at the airport. Three championship golf courses, tennis courts, horseback riding, skeet shooting. Evening entertainment, dining under the stars. 60 acres of manicured lawns and flower gardens.

PINETOP

Roundhouse Resort
Buck Springs Rd., P.O. Box 1468
Pinetop, AZ 85935
602-369-4848

Studio $$, 1 Bedroom $$, 2 Bedrooms $$$$
AmEx/Visa/MC, Dep. 1 Night •
59 condos, Lo-rise, Key at Reserv. desk
H-yes

Location: Airport: Phoenix/Tucson 4 hrs; Downtown: 2 miles; Need car; Ski lift: 24 miles

General Facilities: Daily maid, Kitchen, Restaurant on prem., Bar on prem., Game room, Lounge, Baby-sitter

Room Facilities: Pool, Hot tub, Golf: ½ mile, TV, Cable, Phone in rm., Crib-Hi-chair, Ind. AC Ctl., Ind. Heat Ctl.

Attractions: Rodeos, parades, art shows, Petrified Forest Nat. Park, Painted Desert, Old West history, entertainment

Shops & Restaurants: Shops, boutiques and trading posts; Roundhouse-Southwest dining

Situated on the edge of the Sitgreaves National Forest in a natural setting. Outstanding athletic facilities and unlimited recreation and sightseeing. Barbecue and picnic area next door to the heated pool. Indoor handball and racquetball court, exercise room, basketball gymnasium and game room. On-site restaurant and various entertainment throughout the year. For stay-at-homes, the resort provides cards, board games and puzzles. 24 miles to skiing at Sunrise's 60 trails and 3 mountains.

Please mention *Condo Vacations the Complete Guide* when you reserve your condominium.

SCOTTSDALE

Hyatt Regency Scottsdale   7 condos
Scottsdale, AZ

Location: Downtown: nearby

General Facilities: Conf. rm., Kitchen, Restaurant on prem., Bar on prem., Child planned rec.: Kamp Kachina

Room Facilities: Pool, Hot tub, Tennis, Health spa, Golf: 3 9-hole courses

Shops & Restaurants: Shopping adjacent to the resort; Two on-site restaurants

Units with a southwestern feeling. Unforgettable pool with swim-up bar, four water slides and a subterranean grotto whirlpool. Two restaurants and a high-energy lobby bar. Bicycle, jogging and walking paths. Kamp Kachina for children ages 5 to 12. Numerous area adventures and excellent shopping adjacent to the resort for the non-golfers.

Scottsdale Camelback Resort   Studio $$, 2 Bedrooms $$, 3 Bedrooms $$$
& Spa   2 Bedrms/week 5$, 3 Bed/week 6$
6302 E. Camelback Rd.   Min. Stay 2 Nights, Visa/MC, Dep. Req'd. •
Scottsdale, AZ 85251   79 condos, Villas, Key at Front desk
602-947-3300

Location: Airport: 8 miles; Downtown: 1 mile; Need car

General Facilities: Conf. rm. cap. 80, Daily maid, Kitchen, Linens, Restaurant on prem., Baby-sitter, Child planned rec.: Summer activities

Room Facilities: Pool, Sauna, Hot tub, Tennis, Racketball, putting, Golf: 2 miles, TV, Cable, Phone in rm., Crib-Hi-chair, Ind. AC Ctl., Ind. Heat Ctl.

Attractions: Sedma, Grand Canyon, Rawhide, entertainment

Shops & Restaurants: Fashion Square, Old Town, Scottsdale, 5th Ave.; Avanti-Northern Italian

Luxurious, completely equipped villas nestled at the base of Camelback Mountain. Minutes from golf, fine dining and world-famous Fifth Avenue shops. Complimentary tennis clinics Wednesday and Saturday. A vacation experience!

Stouffer Cottonwoods Resort   2 Bedrooms $$$$
6160 N. Scottsdale Road   34 condos, Lo-rise
Scottsdale, AZ 85253
602-991-1414 800-468-3571

Location: Airport: Sky Harbor 20 min.; Downtown: minutes

General Facilities: Full serv., Conf. rm. cap. 350, Kitchen, Linens, Restaurant on prem., Bar on prem., Lounge

Room Facilities: Pool, Hot tub, Tennis, Putting green, Golf: Championship nearby, TV, Cable

Attractions: Grand Canyon, Casa Grande National Momument, Hoover Dam, Montezuma's Castle

Shops & Restaurants: Borgata designer and specialty boutiques; The Moriah, on-site

Southwestern-style rooms with wood-beamed ceilings, mini-bar and beehive fireplace. Each unit has its own whirlpool spa on a private walled patio accented by flowers. Call room service for your breakfast, then off to tennis, putting green practice or shuffleboard. Take a romantic walk or bicycle ride among the desert greenery, flowers and scenic trails. Jogging trails, pool, spa. Next door is the Borgata with its unique shops.

Villa Serenas
8111 E. Broadway
Tucson, AZ 85710
602-886-6761 800-345-3449

Studio $$, 1 Bedroom $$
AmEx/Visa/MC, Dep. Req'd. •
Hi-rise, Key at Leasing office
H-yes

Location: Airport: 12 miles; Downtown: 5 miles; Need car; Ski lift: Mt. Lemon

General Facilities: Conf. rm. cap. 50, Daily maid, Kitchen, Linens, Game room, Lounge

Room Facilities: Pool, Sauna, Hot tub, Tennis, Exercise, badminton, Golf: Putting greens, TV, Cable, Phone in rm., Crib-Hi-chair, Ind. AC Ctl., Ind. Heat Ctl.

Attractions: Old Tucson Amusement Park, Desert Museum, Colossal Cave, Saguaro Monument, Sabino Canyon, entertainment

Shops & Restaurants: Park Mall, Tucson Mall (all major dept. stores); The Tack Room/continental

Tucson's largest resort—award-winning landscaping, pools, fountains, spas, ponds and unmatched recreational facilities. Lounges, clubrooms, boat and trailer parking. Condominiums decorated in contemporary furnishings in soft desert colors. Everything under the sun for your vacation enjoyment.

Our listings—supplied by the managements—are as complete as possible. Many of the condos have more features than we list. Be sure to inquire when you book.

Arkansas

Lost Bridge
Village, Garfield
Holiday Island
• Siloam Springs   • Cherokee Village
Fairfield Bay • • Drasco
Higden, Greers Ferry
• Arkadelphia
• Hot Springs
Mount Ida

CHEROKEE VILLAGE

Los Indios
P.O. Box 840
Cherokee Village, AR 72714
501-257-2469

2 Bedrooms $$
Pool, Kitchen

Attractions: Pea Ridge Battlefield, ES&NA railroad, Passion Play, Beaver Lake, Arkansas football, Tennis

Two bedroom, two bath condomiums with fully equipped kitchens, microwave, laundry facilities and deck with barbecue. Master bath has jacuzzi.

DRASCO

Tyrolese Condominiums
P.O. Box 83
Drasco, AR 72530
501-362-3075

Lo-rise
Pool, Kitchen

Attractions: Boat ramp, horseshoes, Tennis

Tyrolese condominiums, Alpine Village in the Ozarks on Greers Ferry Lake. Lakeside decks, near pool, tennis courts and Cafe St. Clair. Badminton, shuffleboard, horseshoes, picnic area, boat ramp.

FAIRFIELD BAY

Fairfield Bay
P.O. Box 3008
Fairfield Bay, AR 72088
501-884-3333 800-643-9790

1 Bedroom $$, 2 Bedrooms $$, Villas
Kitchen, Linens

Attractions: Ozark Folk Center, Blanchard Springs Caverns, white river rafting, marina, bowling, Exercise complex, Tennis, Golf

Foothills of the Ozarks on Greers Ferry Lake, two championship golf courses, tennis, water sports paradise, Racquet Club memorable dining-dancing, skiing. Pre-1920 Ozark Folk Center and Blanchard Springs Caverns.

Shadow Mountain Resort

───────────── HIGDEN, GREERS FERRY ─────────────

Devil's Fork Resort & Dock
Rt. 1, Box B
Higden, Greers Ferry, AR 72067
501-825-6240

2 Bedrooms $
2 Bedrms/week $$$$
Dep. Req'd.
Lo-rise, Key at Office

Location: Downtown: 35 miles; Need car
General Facilities: Kitchen, Linens, Child planned rec.: Playground
Room Facilities: TV, Cable, Crib-Hi-chair, Ind. AC Ctl.
Attractions: Sugar Loaf Mountain nature and hiking trails accessible only by water
Shops & Restaurants: Grocery, pharmacy, laundromat, hardware

A fisherman's paradise. Boat dock, ramp, boat slips, fishing supplies and free use of a fishing boat. Fish cleaning facilities and large freezers for storage. Water sport lovers will enjoy the pollution-free lake with its swimming area, ladder and float. Outdoor ball sports and indoor table games. Brick cottages have covered patios and fish cookers.

───────────── HOLIDAY ISLAND ─────────────

Table Rock Landing On Holiday
1 Landing Dr.
Holiday Island, AR 72632
501-253-7561

1 Bedroom $$
Pool

Attractions: Recreation Center, Tennis, Golf

Comfortable, roomy, spaciously designed—two-story living room, mirrored whirlpool bath, grass-covered hillside leading to Table Rock Lake. Recreation Center, variety of activities, Eureka Springs sightseeing. Quiet, luxury living.

---------------------------------- HOT SPRINGS ----------------------------------

Belvedere Resort
317 Belvedere Drive
Hot Springs, AR 71901
501-624-4488

2 Bedrooms $$
Pool, Kitchen, Linens

Attractions: Pool table, exercise, Tennis, Golf

Escape from the pressures of everyday life to a special retreat in the Ouachita hills. Take lessons from the golf pro before trying the challenging course. Condos furnished with elegance and comfort in mind. Restaurant, lounge, art deco bar and antique pool table.

Buena Vista Resort
Route 3, Box 175
Hot Springs, AR 71913
501-525-1321 800-255-9030

Studio $, 1 Bedroom $, 2 Bedrooms $$,
   3 Bedrooms $$
Dep. Req'd.
Lo-rise

General Facilities: Kitchen, Game room, Child planned rec.: Fenced play-yard

Room Facilities: Pool, Tennis, Mini-golf, volleyball, TV, Phone in rm., Crib-Hi-chair, Ind. AC Ctl., Ind. Heat Ctl.

Attractions: Seasonal horse racing, bathhouses, Magic Springs, Mid-America Museum, observation tower

Shops & Restaurants: Mini store on grounds

Units on ten wooded acres on the shores of 22-mile Lake Hamilton. Your children can play in the fenced play-yard with slide and merry-go-round while you watch from the covered sitting dock, or help them feed the ducks and squirrels. Many recreational activities, including a summer game room with pool table, table tennis, video games, and pinball machines. Hot Springs is within a National Park and has many area attractions and lakes.

Emerald Isle Condominiums
7005 Central Ave.
Hot Springs, AR 71913
501-525-3696

2 Bedrooms $$$, Lo-rise
Pool

Attractions: Championship golf, Derby week, Hot Springs attractions, lakes, dinner/dance cruises, Spa, minature golf, tennis, golf

Just bring your suitcase and your food. Lakeside fun on the beach with floating platform, bank fishing, cookouts, boat docks, paddle boats. Bridges over the lake lead to the pool and gazebos with gas grills. Children enjoy the playground, splash pool and mini golf.

Los Lagos
P.O. Box 1600
Hot Springs, AR 71902
501-922-0200

2 Bedrooms $$
Pool, Kitchen

Attractions: Sailing, swimming, water sports, hiking, fishing, tennis, golf, Mini golf, shuffleboard

Pamper yourself in this year-round vacation resort. November to March temperatures are perfect for all sports and provide the best fishing. Natatorium and Fitness Center to keep you busy all day. Cortez Beach for swimming and picnics.

─────────────────── HOT SPRINGS ───────────────────

Sheraton Hot Springs Lakeshore 2 Bedrooms $$$, Hi-rise
3501 Albert Pike   Pool, Kitchen
Hot Springs, AR 71914
501-767-5511 800-426-3184

Attractions: Hot Springs Mountain Tower, Oaklawn, Mid-America Museum Complex, Exercise room, docks, Tennis

Views of Lake Hamilton and the Ouachita Mountains from almost anywhere on the property. Private sandy beach, atrium pool and jacuzzi, and boat dockage with water sports equipment rentals. Dine at Hanford's, dance at Champagne Alley, have a romantic evening by the Lake.

SunBay Resort & Condominiums 1 Bedroom $$, 2 Bedrooms $$$, Villas
6110 Central Avenue   Pool, Kitchen
Hot Springs, AR 71913
501-525-4691 800-847-0090

Attractions: Thoroughbred racing, Bathhouse Row, fishing, boating, water skiing, Athletic Club, Tennis

Exquisitely furnished condominiums on the shores of Lake Hamilton in the midst of carefully planned, colorful landscaping. Some units have jacuzzis, fireplaces, wet bars and private balconies. For a rigorous, fitness vacation, there's water sports, jogging and tennis.

The Wharf   2 Bedrooms $$$, Lo-rise
408 Long Island Drive   Pool, Kitchen, Linens
Hot Springs, AR 71913
501-525-4604

Attractions: Oaklawn Race Meet, Jan. 29 thru Apr. 23, Tennis

Wood and stone exteriors highlight these two-bedroom, two-bath condominiums with walkways down to the lake. Oversized whirlpool bath and glass-enclosed decks. Have fun fishing, skiing, boating or swimming in Lake Hamilton, surrounded by tall pines.

─────────────── LOST BRIDGE VILLAGE, GARFIELD ───────────────

Beaver Lake Lodge Resort
Route #1, 1653 Lodge Dr.
Lost Bridge Village, Garfield, AR 72732
501-359-3201

─────────────────── MOUNT IDA ───────────────────

Mountain Harbor Resort & Condo 2 Bedrooms $$, Lo-rise
P.O. Box 807   Pool, Daily maid, Kitchen, Linens
Mount Ida, AR 71957
501-867-2191

Attractions: Quachita Mountains, Hot Springs National Park quartz crystal dig, marina, playground, tennis

Individually decorated units nestled in a lush forest on the shores of Lake Ouachita. Coves for bass fishing, hiking trails, East Cove and Lodge Restaurants. Complete marina, breathtaking views, wildflowers, wildlife. Your needs carefully considered.

---————— SILOAM SPRINGS —————---

Smith's Landing Golf & Racquet   2 Bedrooms $
Siloam Springs, AR 72761   Pool, Kitchen

Attractions: Tennis, Golf

Townhouses with natural stone fireplaces, bedroom lofts and modern, complete kitchens. Golf, tennis and swimming in beautiful surroundings.

---————— ARKADELPHIA —————---

Iron Mountain Lodge & Marina   2 Bedrooms $$$, Lo-rise
25 IP Circle   Daily maid, Kitchen, Linens
Arkadelphia, AR 71923
501-246-4310

Attractions: De Gray Lake, Marina rentals

New log-style cottages among the oaks and hickories at the base of Iron Mountain. Boat storage, launching ramp, marina. Exceptional fishing and water sports.

Enter your favorite condo in our "Condo of the Year" contest (entry form is in the back of the book).

California

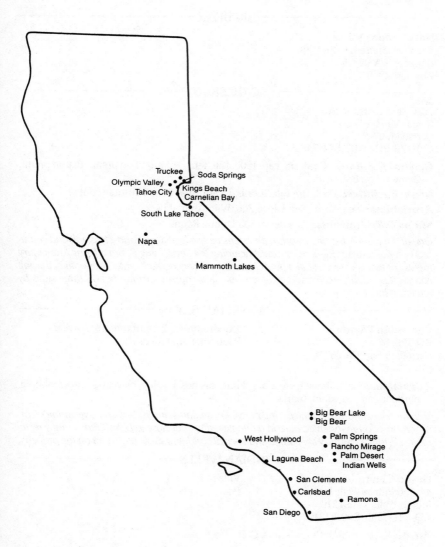

Truckee
Soda Springs
Olympic Valley
Kings Beach
Tahoe City
Carnelian Bay

South Lake Tahoe

Napa

Mammoth Lakes

Big Bear Lake
Big Bear

West Hollywood
Palm Springs
Rancho Mirage
Laguna Beach
Palm Desert
Indian Wells

San Clemente

Carlsbad
Ramona

San Diego

―――――――――――――― BIG BEAR LAKE ――――――――――――――

Teola Pines Lodge
P.O. Box 1746, 547 Main Street
Big Bear Lake, CA 92315
714-866-2720

―――――――――――――― BIG BEAR ――――――――――――――

North Shore Villas
39237 N. Shore Dr., Box 306
Big Bear, CA 92315
714-866-4948

―――――――――――――― CARLSBAD ――――――――――――――

La Costa Hotel & Spa
Costa Del Mar Road
Carlsbad, CA 92009
619-438-9111 800-544-7483

General Facilities: Conf. rm. cap. 1000, Kitchen, Restaurant on prem., Bar on prem.,
   Game room, Baby-sitter
Room Facilities: Pool, Hot tub, Tennis, Health spa, Golf: 2 18-hole courses
Attractions: Sea World, San Diego Zoo, Wild Animal Park
Shops & Restaurants: Brasserie, Spa Dining Room

One of the world's leading resorts with extensive spa facilities. World-class golf and count-less other amenities. Eight restaurants including the Spa Dining Room offering low-calory meals. 23 tennis courts. Heated pools featuring a lovely aquatic center overlooking the golf course. Two highly acclaimed eighteen-hole golf courses surrounded on three sides by towering hills.

―――――――――――――― CARNELIAN BAY ――――――――――――――

Carnelian Woods
P.O. Box 62
Carnelian Bay, CA 95711
916-546-5547

1 Bedroom $$, 2 Bedrooms $$, Lo-rise
Pool, Kitchen, Linens

Attractions: Lake Tahoe recreation, skiing, casinos, jogging, bicycling, snowmobiling,
   outdoor gym, recroom, tennis

Townhouses among the whispering pines, firs, willows and alders on Lake Tahoe's Car-nelian Bay. Family-oriented units in a private setting, but close to Lake Tahoe's many recre-ations. 2-mile x-country ski course and special children's snow play area on the property.

―――――――――――――― INDIAN WELLS ――――――――――――――

Grand Champions
44-600 Indian Wells Lane
Indian Wells, CA 92210
619-341-1000 800-843-9241

Villas
Pool

Attractions: Health Club, Tennis, Golf

Moorish-style architecture and European elegance in the California desert. Enter the lobby with its monumental columns and abundance of fresh flowers. Units have sitting areas for entertainment and conversation. Dine at one of three restaurants.

──────────── INDIAN WELLS ────────────

Indian Wells Racquet Club Resort   1 Bedroom $$$, 2 Bedrooms $$$, Lo-rise
46-765 Bay Club Drive   Pool, Kitchen
Indian Wells, CA 92210
619-345-2811

Attractions: Tennis, Golf

Nestled in a cove below the Santa Rosa mountains, your attractively styled townhouse has a private patio from which you can enjoy the desert flowers and sculptured landscape. Trained tennis instructors, golf across the street, and 8 private swimming pools.

──────────── KINGS BEACH ────────────

Brockway Springs Resort   1 Bedroom $$$, 2 Bedrooms $$$, 3 Bedrooms
P.O. Box 276 $$$
Kings Beach, CA 95719   1 Bedrm/week 8$, 2 Bed/week 10$,
916-546-4201   3 Bed/week 10$
                                                 Min. Stay 2 Nights, Visa/MC, Dep. Req'd.
                                                 Hi-rise, Lo-rise

Location: Need car; Beach front; Ski lift: 7 areas

General Facilities: Conf. rm. cap. 25, Kitchen, Linens, Child planned rec.: Wading pool

Room Facilities: Pool, Sauna, Tennis, Hot Springs, dock

Attractions: Truckee, Virginia City, casinos, seaplane rides, gliders, guided Forest Service outings

Shops & Restaurants: Truckee shops, Tahoe City shops

Lakefront units and crescent townhouse clusters on the lawn, on a wooded pine peninsula on the North Shore. Tahoe's only historic hot springs are here and they indirectly heat the pool. Wading pool, beach, tennis, fishing dock, shore boat and breakwater. Let the public shuttles take you to one of the 7 ski areas. Summer sports and sunbathing. Half mile to Stateline's casinos, dancing and entertainment.

Kings Wood   Lo-rise
P.O. Box 1919   Pool, Kitchen, Linens
Kings Beach, CA 95719
916-546-2501

Attractions: Volley, Badminton, Tennis

All season condominium living at Lake Tahoe. Two-to four-bedroom units with BBQ's, fireplaces, wood supplies, redwood paneling, beam ceilings and large decks. Pool, tennis, volleyball, horseshoes, badminton and foursquare hopscotch (in summer).

McKinney's Landing Townhouses   2 Bedrooms $$$, Lo-rise
P.O. Box 206   Daily maid, Kitchen
Kings Beach, CA 95719
916-546-4074

Attractions: 12 ski areas within easy driving distance, casinos, night spots, Boating

Individually decorated redwood townhouses set in pine and fir groves on the north shore of Lake Tahoe. Private 225-foot pier for boat docking and fishing and private beach swimming. Close to casinos, nightclubs and fine restaurants.

LAGUNA BEACH

Twin Palms
136 Cliff Drive
Laguna Beach, CA 92651
714-497-4773

1 Bedroom $$, 2 Bedrooms $$$
1 Bedrm/week 5$, 2 Bed/week 6$
Dep. Req'd.
Lo-rise

Location: Downtown: 5 min.

General Facilities: Kitchen, Linens

Room Facilities: TV

Attractions: Art festivals, Museum of Art, theatre, ballet, lawn bowling, parks, shuffleboard

Shops & Restaurants: Markets, village shops, art galleries, cafes

Located 1 block from beach, downtown Laguna, Art Festival. Easy gracious living close to beach, restaurants, shopping. Private balcony, barbecue. Attractively decorated, sheltered units.

MAMMOTH LAKES

1849 Condominiums
Box 835
Mammoth Lakes, CA 93546
619-934-7525 800-421-1849

Hi-rise
Pool, Kitchen

Attractions: Exercise equipment, Tennis

Luxury condominium units under the snow-capped Sierras. Summer serenity with cool mountain breezes. Pool, spas, tennis, exercise, endless activities. Friendly, courteous staff.

The Bridges
P.O. Box 1452
Mammoth Lakes, CA 93546
619-934-8919 800-654-1143

2 Bedrooms $$, Lo-rise
Kitchen, Linens

Private gated community with modern, beautifully furnished condominiums, half mile above Chairs 15 and 24. Ski home to a roaring fire, some TV watching, and retiring under designer sheets. Free local magazines, towel service to your door daily, and limo to airport.

Forest Creek Village
P.O. Box 7054
Mammoth Lakes, CA 93546
619-934-8372 800-325-8415

2 Bedrooms $$$, Lo-rise
Kitchen, Linens

Two master bedroom suites and three full baths. Kitchens with wet bars and trash compactors. After a day of skiing you'll be happy you have your own private spa under a greenhouse solarium.

─────────────── MAMMOTH LAKES ───────────────

Mammoth Mountain Inn   Lo-rise
P.O. Box 353
Mammoth Lakes, CA 93546
619-934-2581 800-228-4947

Location: Ski lift: Nearby

General Facilities: Conf. rm., Kitchen, Restaurant on prem., Bar on prem., Game room, Lounge, Child planned rec.: Summer/winter care

Room Facilities: TV, Phone in rm.

Attractions: Tennis, waterskiing, golf, gondolas, sightseeing, horses, skiing, fishing, hiking

Shops & Restaurants: Gift shop and sports shop

Majestic mountains, beautiful forest, local flora, John Muir Wilderness area, winter skiing, special events, day care center, wine tasting room, shuttle service, indoor spas and game room. Be as active or as lazy as you want. Bed and breakfast getaway and complete day care facilities, winter or summer.

Meadow Ridge   1 Bedroom $$$, 2 Bedrooms $$$, Lo-rise
P.O. Box 8290   Pool, Kitchen, Linens, Phone in rm.
Mammoth Lakes, CA 93546
619-934-3808 800-468-5364

Attractions: Tennis

Located near Mammoth Mountain's chair 15 for easy access to downhill skiing. Complete comfort and relaxation with custom modern kitchens, fireplaces and stereos. For a special holiday.

Snowcreek   1 Bedroom $$, 2 Bedrooms $$$, 3 Bedrooms
P.O. Box 1647 $$$$
Mammoth Lakes, CA 93546   1 Bedrm/week 5$, 2 Bed/week 8$,
619-934-3333 800-544-6007   3 Bed/week 10$
                                  Min. Stay 2 Nights, Visa/MC, Dep. Req'd.
                                  150 condos, Villas, Key at Rental office, No S-yes

Location: Airport: 3 miles; Downtown: 2 miles; Need car; Ski lift: Mammoth

General Facilities: Kitchen, Linens

Room Facilities: Sauna, Hot tub, Tennis, Athletic Club (fee), TV, Cable, Ind. Heat Ctl.

Attractions: Alpine and x-country skiing, hiking, fishing, horses, bikes, water skiing

Shops & Restaurants: Shopping malls and boutiques; Roget's/continental

Year-round resort living at its best. 1-4 bedroom condominiums with x-country skiing outside your door. Free shuttle to ski area. Vast open spaces and majestic mountain views. Fee Athletic Club with tennis, racquetball, swimming and aerobics.

Winterset Townhomes   2 Bedrooms $$$, Lo-rise
P.O. Box 7054   Pool, Kitchen, Linens
Mammoth Lakes, CA 93546
619-934-8372 800-325-8415

Lavish interiors in luxurious townhomes with stone fireplaces. Shuttle to ski area. Summer swimming pool and barbecue area.

--- NAPA ---

Silverado Country Club & Resort   Lo-rise
1600 Atlas Peak Road
Napa, CA 94558
707-257-0200 800-532-0500

Location: Need car
General Facilities: Conf. rm. cap. 500, Kitchen, Restaurant on prem., Baby-sitter
Room Facilities: Pool, Jogging, Golf: 2 courses
Attractions: Winery tours, mud baths, Calistoga geyser, Napa Valley Wine Library, bicycle
tours
Shops & Restaurants: Yountville shops; Vintner's Court, Royal Oak

*All of Silverado centers around a historic mansion which was designed to incorporate
adaptations of Italian and French architecture. Individual studios and suites are private,
low-rise clusters around gardens and swimming pools. Twenty Plexipaved tennis courts,
screened for privacy. An hour's jog takes you past as many as twenty wineries. Stop at a
local market for picnic edibles; shop at Vintage 1870 Yountville; tour the area on a bicycle; go on a winery tour, or play the two 72-par golf courses.*

--- OLYMPIC VALLEY ---

Squaw Valley Lodge   1 Bedroom $$$, Lo-rise
P.O. Box 2364   Pool, Daily maid, Kitchen, Linens
Olympic Valley, CA 95730
800-922-9970 800-992-9920

Attractions: Skiing, gambling casinos, nightlife, quaint Truckee, Exercise Room, Tennis

*Wake up in your custom designed condominium under your goose down comforter to a
continental breakfast. 84 steps from your front door is the Squaw Valley tram. Year-round
paradise resort. 15 miles to casinos. Covered parking, daily maid.*

Squaw Valley Townhouses   Studio $, 1 Bedroom $$, 2 Bedrooms $$$,
1604 Christy Hill Lane, Box 2008   3 Bedrooms $$$
Olympic Valley, CA 95730   Min. Stay 2 Nights, Dep. Req'd. •
916-583-3451   40 condos, Lo-rise, Key at 1604 Christy Hill
                                   H-yes

Location: Ski lift: Squaw
General Facilities: Conf. rm., Daily maid, Kitchen, Linens
Room Facilities: Tennis, Horseback riding, TV, Cable, Phone in rm., Ind. Heat Ctl.
Attractions: Squaw Valley skiing

Most units are two bedroom with ski area mountain views.

─────────────── OLYMPIC VALLEY ───────────────

Tavern Inn Condominiums
P.O. Box 2741
Olympic Valley, CA 95730
916-583-1504

1 Bedroom $$$, 2 Bedrooms $$$$, 3 Bedrooms
$$$$
Lo-rise

Location: Airport: Reno; Ski lift: Squaw
General Facilities: Kitchen
Room Facilities: Pool, Hot tub, Tennis, Activity area, TV, Cable, Phone in rm.
Attractions: Skiing, casinos, scenic drives and walks, golf, boating, fishing
Shops & Restaurants: Tahoe City, Truckee shops; River Ranch

European, Alpine architecture among the pines with scenic views of the Sierra Nevada mountains. Free shuttle to Squaw Valley skiing, minutes to 15 other ski areas. Be at Lake Tahoe's year-round playground in 10 minutes for boating, fishing, nightlife, casinos and sightseeing. Units have Jennair cooktop ranges, generous storage space, ceramic tile baths and fireplaces. Most units have skylights, wet bars and greenhouse bay windows.

─────────────── PALM DESERT ───────────────

Ironwood Country Club
49-200 Mariposa Drive
Palm Desert, CA 92260
619-346-0551

1 Bedrm/week 8$, 2 Bed/week 10$,
3 Bed/week 13$
Min. Stay 7 Nights, Visa/MC, Dep. Req'd.
200 condos, Lo-rise, Villas, Key at Office
No S-yes

Location: Airport: 13 miles; Downtown: 2 miles; Need car
General Facilities: Full serv., Conf. rm. cap. 130, Daily maid, Kitchen, Linens, Restaurant on prem., Bar on prem., Lounge, Baby-sitter
Room Facilities: Pool, Hot tub, Tennis, Golf: 2 championship courses, TV, Cable, VCR, Phone in rm., Crib-Hi-chair, Ind.AC Ctl., Ind. Heat Ctl.
Attractions: Palm Springs Aerial Tramway, 100+ golf courses, entertainment
Shops & Restaurants: El Paseo Avenue, 2 shopping malls, Palm Springs; Clubhouse/elegant dining

Choose from four villa complexes with desert, mountain or garden views, all offering convenience and privacy. Golf and tennis privileges extended to guests. Swimming pools and whirlpools. Perfect relaxation spot, especially in the winter.

The Lakes Country Club
75-300 Country Club Drive
Palm Desert, CA 92260
619-345-5695

1 Bedroom $$$, 2 Bedrooms $$$$
Kitchen, Linens, Phone in rm.

Attractions: Tennis, Golf

Condominiums with every modern convenience and luxury. 15 tennis courts, 8 lighted, surrounded by park-like grounds, and a clubhouse with pro shop and lounge overlooking the center court. 6,500-yard 18-hole golf course, two putting greens, chipping green.

Blue Sea Lodge

PALM DESERT

Monterey Country Club
75-300 Country Club Drive
Palm Desert, CA 92260
619-345-5695

1 Bedroom $$$, 2 Bedrooms $$$$
Pool, Kitchen, Linens, Phone in rm.

Attractions: Tennis, Golf

Early California condominiums in adobe brick with red tiled roofs, patios or courtyards. 27 hole championship golf course, 19 tennis courts and 39,000-square-foot clubhouse. Swimming pools and whirlpools, separate locker room facilites.

PGA West
76-300 Country Club Drive
Palm Desert, CA 92260
619-345-5695

1 Bedroom $$$, 2 Bedrooms $$$$, Lo-rise
Pool, Kitchen, Linens, Phone in rm.

Attractions: Tennis, Golf

20 miles southeast of Palm Springs, nestled against the Santa Rosa Mountains. Contemporary and Mediterranean condominiums with fairway or lakeside location. Patio furniture and BBQ. Tennis pro shop, lounge and observation tower.

Palm Desert Resort
77-333 Country Club Drive
Palm Desert, CA 92260
800-472-3712 800-662-4387

1 Bedroom $$

Spacious villas on 320 acres, a lush oasis in the desert. Clean air and sunny days for golf, tennis, sightseeing and shopping. 20 swimming pools and spas. Clubhouse restaurant, scenic views, commitment to quality.

──────────── PALM DESERT ────────────

Palm Valley Country Club
76-200 Country Club Drive
Palm Desert, CA 92260
619-345-7802

1 Bedroom $$$, 2 Bedrooms $$$$, 3 Bedrooms
  $$$$
Visa/MC, Dep. Req'd.
95 condos, Lo-rise

Location: Airport: Palm Springs 20 min.; Downtown: 3 miles

General Facilities: Conf. rm. cap. 300, Daily maid, Kitchen, Linens, Restaurant on prem., Bar on prem., Lounge, Baby-sitter

Room Facilities: Pool, Sauna, Hot tub, Tennis, Racquetball Club, Golf: 36 holes, TV, Cable, Phone in rm., Crib-Hi-chair, Ind. AC Ctl.

Attractions: Annenberg Center for Health Sciences, balloon rides, horseback riding, theaters, entertainment

Shops & Restaurants: Shops at Palm Desert Town Center; Seasonal dining room

Comfort, efficiency and beauty along lush fairways and crystal clear lakes. Walk to pools and spas. Weight room, exercise classes, cushioned jogging trail, beauty salon. Mediterranean-style condominiums on the golf course with front patios, gas barbecues and patio furniture. Some units have fireplaces and wet bars.

Shadow Mountain Resort
45750 San Luis Rey
Palm Desert, CA 92260
619-346-6123 800-472-3713

Studio $$, 1 Bedroom $$$, 2 Bedrooms $$$$
Min. Stay 1 Night, Visa/MC, Dep. Req'd. •
125 condos, Lo-rise, Key at Lobby front desk
No S-yes/H-yes

Location: Airport: 13 miles; Downtown: 3 blocks

General Facilities: Full serv., Bus. fac., Conf. rm. cap. 250, Daily maid, Kitchen, Linens, Restaurant on prem., Bar on prem., Lounge, Baby-sitter, Child planned rec.: Tennis clinics

Room Facilities: Pool, Sauna, Hot tub, Tennis, Paddle ten-volley, TV, Cable, Phone in rm., Crib-Hi-chair, Ind. AC Ctl., Ind. Heat Ctl.

Attractions: Palm Springs Aerial Tram, Living Desert Wildlife Preserve, Joshua Tree National Park, entertainment

Shops & Restaurants: Boutiques, specialty shops, P. Springs Fashion Mall; La Casuelas Nuevas-Mexican

A relaxed condominium resort and racquet club on 21 beautifully landscaped acres. This is one of the top 50 tennis resorts in the U.S., offering extensive tennis clinics. Enjoy theme buffets and barbecues by the spectacular 165' figure-eight swimming pool. Just steps away is the El Paseo shopping area and Bob Hope Cultural Center.

──────────── PALM SPRINGS ────────────

The Desert Princess
28-555 Landau Blvd., Box 2064
Palm Springs, CA 92263
610-325-5011 800-356-7527

1 Bedroom $$$, 2 Bedrooms $$$$, Villas
Pool, Daily maid, Kitchen, Linens

Attractions: Palm Springs dining and shopping, Health Club, Spa, Tennis, Golf

Classic high ceilings, rich carpets, walk-in closets and private covered patios with golf course or moountain views. 40 swimming pools and spas, 10 lighted tennis courts and championship golf among the lakes. Health Club with professional staff for facials and massages.

PALM SPRINGS

Azure Sky Resort
1661 Calle Palo Fierro
Palm Springs, CA 92264
619-325-9109

Studio $$, 1 Bedroom $$
1 Bedrm/week 4$
Min. Stay 2 Nights, Visa/MC, Dep. 1 Night •
11 condos, Villas, Key at On-site office

Location: Airport: 6 miles; Downtown: 2 miles

General Facilities: Full serv., Daily maid, Kitchen, Linens, Lounge

Room Facilities: Pool, Hot tub, Tennis, TV, Cable, Phone in rm., Crib-Hi-chair, Ind. AC Ctl., Ind. Heat Ctl.

Attractions: Palm Springs Tramway, celebrity tour, golf courses, Indian Canyons, Sunshine

Shops & Restaurants: Palm Springs Fashion Plaza; Robbie Reeds/continental

Just minutes from the famous Palm Springs strip, this is a small, intimate resort, ideally suited for a private getaway. All units have fully equipped kitchens, walled patios for private sunbathing, television with HBO and gas barbecues. Decor is southwestern.

Casa Loma
275 Lugo Road, 225 Cahulla Road
Palm Springs, CA 92262
619-325-5281

Studio $, 1 Bedroom $
Dep. Req'd.
Lo-rise, Key at Mt. View Inn
P-yes

Location: Airport: 10 minutes; Downtown: 2 blocks

General Facilities: Kitchen, Linens

Room Facilities: Pool, Sauna, TV, Cable, Phone in rm., Ind. AC Ctl., Ind. Heat Ctl.

Attractions: Celebrity tour, tram to mountaintop, Desert Museum

Shops & Restaurants: Bullocks, Saks, Gucci, I. Magnin; Le Vallarius/Fr.-Cedre Creek

Professionally decorated condominiums at the foot of Mt. San Jacinto. Two blocks from the center of town in the quiet and exclusive tennis club resort, offering Old World charm at reasonable rates. Casa Loma prefers adults.

Cathedral Canyon Resort
34567 Cathedral Canyon Drive
Palm Springs, CA 92264
619-321-9000 800-542-4253

1 Bedroom $$
AmEx/Visa/MC •
160 condos
No S-yes/H-yes

Location: Airport: 6 miles; Downtown: 8 miles

General Facilities: Conf. rm. cap. 500, Daily maid, Kitchen, Linens, Restaurant on prem., Bar on prem.

Room Facilities: Pool, Hot tub, Tennis, Golf: 18-hole PGA rated course, TV, Cable, Phone in rm., Ind.AC Ctl., Ind. Heat Ctl.

Attractions: Oasis Waterpark, Oasis Health Club, Agua Caliente Band of Palm Springs Indians, entertainment

Shops & Restaurants: Desert Fashion Plaza, Palm Desert Town Center; Las Caselas Nuevos/Mexican

Cathedral Canyon Resort lies in the heart of a beautiful desert oasis. Spacious guest suites with luxurious in-room amenities, walk-in closets, two color TV's and complete room service. Patio or balcony overlooking the fairways and mountains. Full service restaurant and patio offering American cuisine. Casual evening dining with the sounds of Sonny Evaro on the keyboard. Friendly, personalized service.

PALM SPRINGS

La Mancha
444 Avenida Caballeros, Box 340
Palm Springs, CA 92263
619-323-1773   800-854-1298

1 Bedroom $$$
Lo-rise, Villas

General Facilities: Daily maid, Kitchen, Linens, Restaurant on prem., Bar on prem.

Room Facilities: Pool, Sauna, Tennis, Gym, croquet, Golf: Nearby, TV, Cable, VCR, Phone in rm.

Attractions: Scenic touring, day trips, tennis

Shops & Restaurants: Dining room/continental-Amer.

Step into your private pool screened from view by high walls, dine in the Don Quixote room or take advantage of the international take-out menu. Complimentary convertibles for local use. Day field trips planned and picnic lunches prepared. Special packages include European Club breakfast and champagne and fruit basket in your villa upon arrival.

Palm Springs Marquis
150 South Indian Avenue
Palm Springs, CA 92262
619-322-2121

Location: Airport: Palm Springs 5 min.; Downtown: 2 blocks

General Facilities: Full serv., Kitchen, Restaurant on prem., Bar on prem.

Room Facilities: Pool, Tennis, Golf: 20 courses nearby

Attractions: Hot air ballooning, polo matches, championship golf, shopping

Shops & Restaurants: Saks, I. Magnin, Gucci

Elegantly contemporary villas with fireplaces and wet bars beneath the mountains in the desert. Spend your time being a sun worshiper by the pool. Play tennis on one of two championship courses, or have the hotel staff arrange your golf date and transportation to one of Palm Springs' many courses. A grand resort oasis in the wilderness.

Sundance Villas
303 Cabrillo Road
Palm Springs, CA 92262
619-325-3888

2 Bedrooms $$$$, 3 Bedrooms $$$$
2 Bedrms/week 10$, 3 Bed/week 10$
Min. Stay 2 Nights, AmEx/Visa/MC,
   Dep. Req'd. •
19 condos, Villas, Key at Manager's office
No S-yes/H-yes

Location: Airport: 3 miles; Downtown: 2 miles; Need car

General Facilities: Daily maid, Kitchen, Linens, Baby-sitter

Room Facilities: Pool, Sauna, Hot tub, Tennis, Golf: Palm Springs C.C.-1 mile, TV, Cable, VCR, Phone in rm., Crib-Hi-chair, Ind. AC Ctl., Ind. Heat Ctl.

Attractions: Aerial tramway, Indian bingo, Desert museums, Waterpark, Indian canyons, home tours

Shops & Restaurants: Loehmann's, Saks, I. Magnin, Bullocks, Dansk; Bono's/So. It., Riccio's/No. It.

Quiet, romantic four-star villas, each with unique, comfortable designer furnishings. Every villa has a private pool and spa enclosed by 6-foot fences. Minutes away from the Aerial Tramway, exciting restaurants and world-famous shopping. Champagne and welcome basket of tempting snacks, arrival morning continental breakfast. Manicure, massage, breakfast in bed, tea time or dinner reservations—just give a call.

RAMONA

San Vicente Country Club
1306 Main Street
Ramona, CA 92065
619-789-8678

1 Bedroom $$, 2 Bedrooms $$$, Villas
Kitchen, Linens, Phone in rm.

Attractions: Golfing, tennis, swimming

RANCHO MIRAGE

Rancho La Palmas Country Club
41000 Bob Hope Drive
Rancho Mirage, CA 92260
619-568-2727   800-228-9290

1 Bedroom $$$, 2 Bedrooms $$$$
Pool, Kitchen, Linens, Phone in rm.

Attractions: Athletic field, Tennis, Golf

Two-to three-bedroom single-story condominiums. Outsides are rough textured stucco, wood accented with exposed beams and tile roofs. Golf and tennis with pro shops and large clubhouse. Athletic field has children's playground, sandbox and pool.

SAN CLEMENTE

Blarney Castle
509 Monterey Lane
San Clemente, CA 92672
714-492-7576

2 Bedrooms $$$$
2 Bedrms/week 5$
Min. Stay 3 Nights, Dep. Req'd. •
3 condos, Lo-rise, Key at Manager's Apt.

Location: Airport: 45 min. John Wayne; Downtown: 10 min.; Need car

General Facilities: Kitchen, Linens

Room Facilities: TV, Cable, Ind. Heat Ctl.

Attractions: 40 minutes-Disneyland, Knott's Berry Farm, baseball, football, Sea World, Zoo

Shops & Restaurants: Local small shops, 15 miles to Mall; Delaney's/Charthouse/ Casa Marie

Small, quiet, homelike atmosphere with only 4 units in the complex. White walls, earthtone furnishings with views of the ocean. Close to every type of sport activity. A good place to come in winter to get away from the ice and snow and enjoy the San Clemente climate.

San Clemente Inn
2600 Avenida Del Presidente
San Clemente, CA 92672
714-492-6103

1 Bedroom $$, 2 Bedrooms $$$
96 condos, Key at Front desk

Location: Downtown: 2 blocks

General Facilities: Full serv., Conf. rm. cap. 50, Kitchen, Restaurant on prem., Child planned rec.: Play area

Room Facilities: Pool

Attractions: Beach, fishing, entertainment

Shops & Restaurants: San Clemente shops; Swallows Cove on-site/gourmet

Executive suites for 1 to four persons. The Inn borders the State Park and is only a three block walk to the beach, or use the pool on the property. Children's play area and weekly barbecues. Gourmet restaurant on-site.

--------------------------- SAN CLEMENTE ---------------------------

Sea Horse Inn
602 Avenida Victoria
San Clemente, CA 92672
714-492-1720

1 Bedrm/week $$$$
AmEx/Visa/MC, Dep. Req'd.
P-yes

General Facilities: Daily maid, Kitchen, Linens

Room Facilities: TV

Attractions: Mexico, San Diego-1 hour, Disneyland-30 minutes, City park

Shops & Restaurants: Fisherman's Seafood

Located in San Clemente, the "Spanish Village by the Sea" near miles of beautiful beaches. 60 minutes to San Diego, 30 minutes to Disneyland. Beach, children's playground, surfing, golfing, smog-free.

Villa Del Mar Inn
612 Avenida Victoria
San Clemente, CA 92672
714-498-5080

1 Bedroom $$, 2 Bedrooms $$
1 Bedrm/week 4$, 2 Bed/week 5$
AmEx/Visa/MC, Dep. Req'd.
Key at Office

Location: Airport: Orange—35 min.; Downtown: ½ mile; Need car; Beach front

General Facilities: Daily maid, Kitchen, Linens

Room Facilities: Beach playground, TV, Cable, Phone in rm., Crib-Hi-chair, Ind. Heat Ctl.

Attractions: San Clemente pier, Dana Point Harbor, Disneyland, Sea World, Newport Beach

Shops & Restaurants: Safeway, Albertson, Lucky's; Fisherman's-seafood

Villa Del Mar Inn located on the beautiful Pacific Coast offers an ideal location with perfect four season climate. For those who want a quiet vacation relaxing and sunning on the beach.

---------------------------- SAN DIEGO ----------------------------

Blue Sea Lodge
707 Pacific Beach Dr.
San Diego, CA 92109
619-483-4700 800-528-1234

Studio $$$, 1 Bedroom $$$$
AmEx/Visa/MC, Dep. 1 Night •
48 condos, Lo-rise, Key at Front desk
H-yes

Location: Airport: 7 miles; Downtown: 7 miles; Need car; Beach front

General Facilities: Daily maid, Kitchen, Linens, Baby-sitter

Room Facilities: Pool, Hot tub, TV, Cable, Phone in rm., Crib-Hi-chair, Ind. Heat Ctl.

Attractions: Sea World, San Diego Zoo, Cabrillo National Momument, Mission Bay Park

Shops & Restaurants: Promenade Center, boutiques and specialty shops; McCormick & Schmick-seafood

Contemporary beachfront condominiums decorated in peach and blue. Situated directly on the Pacific Ocean, across the street from Mission Bay Park with a full range of water sports. A fishing pier is a short walk away. Sea World, the San Diego Zoo and Cabrillo National Momument are all a short drive away.

────────────────── SODA SPRINGS ──────────────────

Soda Springs Station
Old Highway 40
Soda Springs, CA 95728
916-622-3666

At the base of the Soda Springs ski area offering wide open skiing. Ski school and rental equipment available.

────────────────── SOUTH LAKE TAHOE ──────────────────

Bavarian Village Rentals
P.O. Box 709, 1140 Herbert
South Lake Tahoe, CA 95705
916-541-8191 800-822-5922

1 Bedroom $$, 2 Bedrooms $$, 3 Bedrooms $$
1 Bedrm/week 4$, 2 Bed/week 5$,
   3 Bed/week 5$
Min. Stay 2 Nights, Dep. 1 Night •
72 condos, Lo-rise, Key at 1140B Herbert Ave.
H-yes

Location: Airport: 5 miles; Downtown: 1¼ mile; Need car; Ski lift: Heavenly
General Facilities: Kitchen, Linens, Baby-sitter
Room Facilities: Pool, TV, Phone in rm., Crib-Hi-chair, Ind. Heat Ctl.
Attractions: The Lake, boating, swimming, water skiing, skiing, casinos
Shops & Restaurants: Crescent shopping, 1 mile, Safeway 5 blocks;

Clean, quiet, large condominiums with barbecues. Centrally located for beach enjoyment and Stateline casinos. Ski at Heavenly Valley in winter, or water ski in summer. A year-round recreation area for the entire family.

───

Inn by the Lake
P.O. Box 849, 3300 Lake Tahoe Blvd.
South Lake Tahoe, CA 95705
916-542-0330 800-535-0330

1 Bedroom $$$$, 2 Bedrooms $$$$, Lo-rise
Pool, Kitchen, Phone in rm.

Two miles from Stateline casinos, free shuttle service, minutes from Heavenly Valley ski and Lake Tahoe's beach. Continental breakfast, sauna, jacuzzis, and heated brick walkways through the pines. Convenience and comfort by the Lake.

───

Lakeland Village Beach Resort
3535 Highway 50, P.O. Box 705002
South Lake Tahoe, CA 95705
916-541-7711 800-822-5969

Studio $$, 1 Bedroom $$, 2 Bedrooms $$$,
   3 Bedrooms $$$
AmEx/Visa/MC, Dep. 1 Night •
215 condos, Key at 24-hour front desk

Location: Airport: 7 miles; Downtown: 1½ miles; Beach front; Ski lift: Nearby
General Facilities: Full serv., Conf. rm. cap. 75, Daily maid, Linens, Restaurant on prem., Game room
Room Facilities: Pool, Sauna, Hot tub, Tennis, TV, Phone in rm., Crib-Hi-chair, Ind. Heat Ctl.
Attractions: Tahoe Queen paddlewheel boat 2 hour daily cruise. 1½ miles to casinos.
Shops & Restaurants: Casual and fine restaurants

Ideally located to experience all that Lake Tahoe offers. Heavenly Valley skiing 1.5 miles away. 19 secluded acres on 1,000 feet of private beach. Boat rental, parasailing, fishing, sailboards. Complimentary casino and ski shuttle. Within minutes are 24-hour casinos offering gaming, entertainment and fine restaurants.

─────────────── SOUTH LAKE TAHOE ───────────────

Tahoe Beach and Ski Club
P.O. Box 1267, 3601 Tahoe Blvd.
South Lake Tahoe, CA 95705
916-541-6220 800-822-5962

1 Bedroom $$, 2 Bedrooms $$$$
Pool, Kitchen, Phone in rm.

Designer decorated with oak, cedar and imported tile. Ski Kirkwood or Heavenly Valley, take the complimentary shuttle to the casinos, relax in your in-suite whirlpool tub. In summer, sunbathe and swim on 400 feet of private beach.

Tahoe Tyrol
P.O. Box A, 3351 Pine Hill Road
South Lake Tahoe, CA 96702
916-544-6017

2 Bedrooms $$$, Villas
Pool, Kitchen, Linens, Phone in rm.
Shuffleboard

Individual wood trimmed Bavarian mountain chalets below Heavenly Valley. Two-story villas with lake and mountain views from the open decks. Free shuttle service to skiing and casinos. Community center clubhouse with fireplace and kitchen.

Tahoe Valley Motel and Condos
P.O. Box 7702, Hwy. 50/Tahoe Keys
South Lake Tahoe, CA 95731
916-541-0353 800-822-5922

Studio $$, 1 Bedroom $$$, 2 Bedrooms $$$,
   3 Bedrooms $$$
1 Bedrm/week 7$, 2 Bed/week 8$,
   3 Bed/week 9$
Min. Stay 2 Nights, Dep. Req'd.
50 condos, Lo-rise, Key at Tahoe Valley Motel

Location: Airport: 5 miles; Downtown: 7 miles; Need car; Beach front; Ski lift: 3 nearby
General Facilities: Daily maid, Kitchen, Linens, Baby-sitter
Room Facilities: Pool, Hot tub, Tennis, Putting green, marina, TV, Cable, Phone in rm., Crib-Hi-chair, Ind. AC Ctl., Ind. Heat Ctl.
Attractions: Casinos, scenic & nature drives and walks, skiing, bicycles, horses
Shops & Restaurants: Local shops; Fresh Ketch-Tw. Panda-Sw. Chalet

Most condominiums are in the Tahoe Keys area with panoramic views of the Sierras and Lake Tahoe. Olympic size swimming pool, beaches, tennis courts, putting green and basketball court. Ski packages available. Cruise Lake Tahoe on the Tahoe Queen with breakfast onboard, to Squaw Valley or Alpine Meadows, and have dinner on the return cruise with live music and dancing.

─────────────── SQUAW VALLEY ───────────────

Christy Hill Resort Rentals
1604 Christy Hill Lane, Box 2449
Squaw Valley, CA 95730
916-583-3451

Studio $, 1 Bedroom $$, 2 Bedrooms $$$,
   3 Bedrooms $$$
Min. Stay 2 Nights, Dep. Req'd. •
32 condos, Lo-rise, H-yes

Location: Airport: 45 minutes; Downtown: 5 miles; Need car; Ski lift: Squaw
General Facilities: Conf. rm., Daily maid, Kitchen, Linens, Child planned rec.: Ski lessons
Room Facilities: Tennis, Riding, TV, Cable, Phone in rm., Ind. Heat Ctl.
Attractions: Lake Tahoe, Squaw Valley Mountain Ski area, gaming casinos
Shops & Restaurants: Sportswear shops, art galleries, housewares; Le Petite/French

Beautifully decorated condominiums in a glorious mountain and meadow setting. Convenient to all winter and summer sports. Many fine restaurants, excellent sportswear shopping, and casino nightlife nearby.

─────────────── TAHOE CITY ───────────────

Granlibakken Resort
P.O. Box 6329
Tahoe City, CA 95730
916-583-4242 800-543-3221

1 Bedroom $$$

Four season resort in a private valley on Lake Tahoe's North Shore. Tennis, pool, wading pool, sauna, spas, nature trails. Breathtaking surroundings. Friendly atmosphere. Ski packages.

O'Neal Associates, Inc.
P.O. Box 802
Tahoe City, CA 95730
916-583-7368 800-222-5758

1 Bedroom $$, 2 Bedrooms $$$, 3 Bedrooms $$$
1 Bedrm/week 4$, 2 Bed/week 5$,
   3 Bed/week 6$
Min. Stay 2 Nights, Dep. Req'd. •
100 condos, Lo-rise, Key at 1877 N. Lake Blvd.
No S-yes/P-yes/H-yes

Location: Airport: South Shore 30 miles; Downtown: ½ mile; Need car; Beach front; Ski lift: Nearby

General Facilities: Conf. rm. cap. 30, Daily maid, Kitchen, Linens, Game room, Baby-sitter

Room Facilities: Pool, Sauna, Hot tub, Tennis, Volleyball, skiing, Golf: Tahoe City, TV, Cable, VCR, Phone in rm., Crib-Hi-chair, Ind. Heat Ctl.

Attractions: Skiing, boating, horseback riding, sailing, swimming, casinos

Shops & Restaurants: Specialty shops; Le Petit Pier-French

Fully furnished condominium units on Tahoe's beautiful north shore. Units on the lake, or with lake or forest views, all with decks. Lake Tahoe is a winter wonderland, a summer paradise, and a relaxing place to spend a spring or fall vacation.

Tahoe Marina Lodge
P.O. Box 92
Tahoe City, CA 95730
916-583-2365

1 Bedroom $$, 2 Bedrooms $$
1 Bedrm/week 6$, 2 Bed/week 8$
Min. Stay 2 Nights, Visa/MC Dep. Req'd.
Lo-rise

Location: Airport: Reno; Downtown: 3 blocks; Beach front; Ski lift: 6 miles

General Facilities: Kitchen, Linens

Room Facilities: Pool, Tennis, TV, Phone in rm.

Attractions: Casinos, skiing, lake activities

Shops & Restaurants: Tahoe City shops; La Cheminee/French

Lakeside condominiums with private decks or patios and native stone fireplaces. Summer (tennis courts, pool, beach and pier) and winter (shuttle buses to skiing) vacation enjoyment. 10 miles for casino entertainment.

We want to hear from you—any comments regarding the condos or our publication may be noted on the form at the end of the book.

Northstar-at-Tahoe

TRUCKEE

Donner Lake Village Resort
15695 Donner Pass Road, Box 11109
Truckee, CA 95737
916-587-6081

Studio $$, 1 Bedroom $$, 2 Bedrooms $$$
1 Bedrm/week 5$, 2 Bed/week 7$
AmEx/Visa/MC •
51 condos, Lo-rise, Key at Front desk, H-yes

Location: Airport: 5 miles; Downtown: 3 miles; Need car; Beach front; Ski lift: 6 areas

General Facilities: Bus. fac., Conf. rm. cap. 75, Daily maid, Kitchen, Linens, Bar on prem., Lounge, Baby-sitter

Room Facilities: Boating, fishing, Cable, Phone in rm., Crib-Hi-chair, Ind. Heat Ctl.

Attractions: Skiing, hiking, boating, museum, gambling, snowmobiling, biking, water-skiing

Shops & Restaurants: Historic downtown Truckee with specialty shops; The Left Bank/French

A great place for a Tahoe vacation. 51 units on Donner Lake for just relaxing or boating, fishing, swimming and hiking. For winter skiing drive to Boreal, Squaw Valley, Tahoe Donner, Northstar, Sugar Bowl, and Alpine, all within 15 minutes. Browse or shop in downtown Truckee, stop at the soda shop, have a gourmet dinner, or buy your own groceries and cook at home.

——————————————————— TRUCKEE ———————————————————

Northstar at Tahoe
P.O. Box 129
Truckee, CA 95734
916-562-1010 800-533-6787

Studio $$, 1 Bedroom $$, 2 Bedrooms $$,
3 Bedrooms $$$
225 condos, Lo-rise

Location: Airport: Truckee 3 miles; Downtown: 6 miles; Ski lift: Nearby

General Facilities: Conf. rm., Restaurant on prem., Bar on prem., Lounge

Room Facilities: Pool, Sauna, Tennis, Bikes-horses-weights, Golf: Northstar at Tahoe

Attractions: Golf, tennis, horses, biking, swimming, skiing, weight room, Lake Tahoe
activities, entertainment

Shops & Restaurants: Outpost Store (video), gift shop, general store; Schaffer's Mill,
Deli, Pizza

*The 2,560 Northstar resort features golf, tennis, horseback riding, swimming, bike riding,
volleyball and hayrides. Summer fun includes a jazz and brunch in the Village, art show,
running race, food and wine festival and musical reviews. Minors' Camp is offered for children two through ten. A full-service alpine and cross-country ski resort with limited daily
lift passes. Ski to the lifts from your condo or take the shuttle. All the attractions you need
for your vacation.*

——————————————— WEST HOLLYWOOD ———————————————

Sunset Marquis Villas
1200 North Alta Loma Road
West Hollywood, CA 90069
213-657-1333 800-858-9758

1 Bedroom 4$, 2 Bedrooms 5$, Villas
Pool, Daily maid, Kitchen, Linens, Phone in rm.

Attractions: Century City, Hollywood, Beverly Hills, Pacific Design Center, Los Angeles,
Exercise room

*One-half block south of Sunset Boulevard, luxurious Mediterranean villas with private gar-
den patios. 24-hour room service, valet, shoe shine, exercise room, limousine service, pool,
spa, sauna, jacuzzi and concierge to take care of your every need.*

Our goal is to provide as *complete* a listing of condo vacation properties as
possible. If you know of a condo we don't list, please send us their name and
address on the form at the back of this Guide.

Colorado

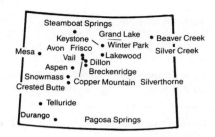

Steamboat Springs
Keystone
Grand Lake • Beaver Creek
Mesa • Avon Frisco • Winter Park Silver Creek
Vail • Lakewood
Aspen • Dillon
Snowmass • Breckenridge
Crested Butte • Copper Mountain Silverthorne
• Telluride
Durango • Pagosa Springs

ASPEN

Alpine Peaks   Pool, Daily maid, Kitchen, Linens
P.O. Box 3123
Aspen, CO 81612
303-925-7820

Attractions: Skiing, Health Spa with massages, steam, sauna, aqua exercise, Health Spa, Tennis

Spacious, individually owned apartments and personalized service. You don't have to be a skier to enjoy Aspen Alps. The desk will be happy to assist you with restaurant reservations, shopping, rental automobiles and ticket information.

Aspen Club Lodge   1 Bedroom $$$
709 E. Durant   Pool, Daily maid, Linens
Aspen, CO 81611
303-925-6760 800-882-2582

Attractions: Tennis

At the base of Aspen Mountain next to Gondola. Many amenities: airport shuttle, underground parking, continental breakfast and guest privileges at the Aspen Health and Racquet Club.

Aspen Silverglo Condominiums   1 Bedroom $$
940 Waters Avenue   Min. Stay 4 Nights, Dep. Req'd.
Aspen, CO 81611   24 condos, Lo-rise
303-925-8450

Location: Airport: Grand Junc. 2 hours; Downtown: 3 blocks; Ski lift: Aspen Mt.
General Facilities: Kitchen, Game room
Room Facilities: Phone in rm.
Attractions: Aspen Music Festival, Aspen Institute for Humanistic Studies, art galleries
Shops & Restaurants: Aspen shops; Restaurants/variety

Warm, intimate, with frontier congeniality. Beam ceilings, rock fireplaces, wood paneling. Convenient to ski areas. Summer wildflowers-hiking, fishing, golf, mountain climbing.

───────────────── ASPEN ─────────────────

Aspen Ski Lodge
101 W. Main St.
Aspen, CO 81611
800-356-6559

1 Bedroom $$, 2 Bedrooms $$$$, Lo-rise
Pool, Kitchen

Small, intimate with a friendly staff. Continental breakfast, weekly champagne gathering, California wine tasting. An unforgettable holiday in a skier's paradise.

Durant Condominiums
718 South Galena Street
Aspen, CO 81611
303-925-7910 800-321-7025

1 Bedroom $$
Pool, Daily maid, Kitchen

Fireplaces and panoramic views, 1.5 blocks from Aspen Mountain Gondola and the center of town. Free shuttle bus to three other ski areas.

Fasching Haus
747 Galena Street
Aspen, CO 81611
303-925-5900 800-321-7025

Studio $$, 1 Bedroom $$, 2 Bedrooms $$$,
   3 Bedrooms $$$$
AmEx, Dep. Req'd. •
30 condos, Lo-rise, Key at Front desk

Location: Airport: 5 miles; Downtown: 2 blocks; Ski lift: Aspen Mt.

General Facilities: Full serv., Conf. rm. cap. 30, Daily maid, Kitchen, Linens, Baby-sitter

Room Facilities: Pool, Sauna, Hot tub, TV, Cable, Phone in rm., Crib-Hi-chair, Ind. Heat Ctl.

Attractions: Music festival, Ballet Aspen, skiing, balloon rides, river rafting, horses, jeep tours, entertainment

Shops & Restaurants: Small boutiques, Esprit Store; Chart House/steak-seafood

Fully furnished, newly remodeled 1-3 bedroom condominiums and lodge rooms in Aspen's best location, 200 yards from the Aspen Mountain Gondola. Pool, jacuzzi, sauna and exercise room. Four mountains for beginners to experts to ski with groomed trails and Rocky Mountain powder. Discover "The Town" for apres-ski. Summer Aspen has music, ballet, art & film festivals, golf and tennis. Housemen on call. Lack of snow refund policy.

Fifth Avenue
747 South Galena
Aspen, CO 81611
303-925-7397 800-321-7025

1 Bedroom $$$, 2 Bedrooms $$
Pool, Daily maid, Kitchen, Phone in rm.

1.5 blocks from the gondola at Aspen mountain, one-to four-bedroom condominiums with fireplaces. Swimming, jacuzzi, sauna and guest laundry facilities.

────────────── ASPEN ──────────────

Inn at Aspen
21646 W. Hwy. 82
Aspen, CO 81611
303-925-1500 800-952-1515

Studio $$, 1 Bedroom $$
AmEx/Visa/MC, Dep. Req'd.
Lo-rise

Location: Ski lift: Buttermilk

General Facilities: Full serv., Conf. rm., Daily maid, Kitchen, Restaurant on prem., Bar on prem., Lounge

Room Facilities: Pool, Sauna, TV, Cable

Attractions: Aspen Music Festival, ballet, Snowmass Repertory Theater, arts and crafts fairs, entertainment

Shops & Restaurants: Victorian Aspen, art galleries; Barrington's Restaurant

Stay in pampered luxury in this comfortable, casual inn. Complimentary shuttle service to Aspen, Snowmass and the airport. The perfect getaway amid spectacular scenery in all seasons.

The Prospector at Aspen
301 E. Hyman
Aspen, CO 81611
303-920-2030 800-522-4525

1 Bedroom $$, Lo-rise
Daily maid, Kitchen, Linens

Attractions: The Crystal Palace, Wheeler Opera House, skiing, cultural attractions, Aspen Club facility, Tennis

Four-season resort high in the Rockies. Two blocks to Aspen's Lift 1A. One bedroom designer suites with stereos, VCR, wet bars and microwaves. View the mountain from your private sun deck with jacuzzi and sauna.

The Gant
P.O. Box K-3 610 S. Westend St.
Aspen, CO 81612
303-925-5000 800-345-1471

1 Bedroom $$, 2 Bedrooms $$$, 3 Bedrooms $$$
AmEx/Visa/MC, Dep. Req'd. •
112 condos, Lo-rise, Key at Gant office
H-yes

Location: Airport: 2 miles; Downtown: 3 blocks; Ski lift: 2 blocks

General Facilities: Full serv., Conf. rm. cap. 225, Daily maid, Kitchen, Linens, Baby-sitter

Room Facilities: Pool, Sauna, Hot tub, Tennis, Ski, golf, horses, rafts, Golf: Aspen 1 mile, Cable, Phone in rm., Crib-Hi-chair, Ind. Heat Ctl.

Attractions: Maroon Bells-wilderness, Gondola, Music festival, Ashcroft-old mining town

Shops & Restaurants: Ralph Lauren, Esprit, Benetton; French-Mex.-Chinese-It.-Cont.

The Gant is a self-contained retreat on five beautifully landscaped acres near the base of Aspen Mountain. Hiking trails lead from the forest and mountains in moments. Complimentary van service is available to shuttle guests on request. 5 tennis courts with a resident tennis pro, 2 pools, 3 jacuzzis, saunas. Ski Aspen, raft the Colorado, attend the Aspen Music Festival-Ballet, and the Wheeler Opera House. The perfect blend of relaxation and stimulation.

———————————————— AVON ————————————————

Avon Center at Beaver Creek　　Hi-rise
100 W. Beaver Creek Blvd., Box 964　Kitchen
Avon, CO 81620
303-949-6202

Attractions: Skiing, golf, tennis, ice-skating, x-country touring, hunting, rafting, fishing,
　Exercise spa

*Traditionally furnished comfortable condominiums. Park your car in the underground
garage and forget it. Shuttle buses at the entrance take you to all points in the area. On-
site restaurants, shops, jacuzzi spa and exercise room.*

Beaver Creek West　　　1 Bedroom $$, 2 Bedrooms $$, 3 Bedrooms $$$
P.O. Box 5290　　　　　Min. Stay 2 Nights, AmEx/Visa/MC,
Avon, CO 81620　　　　　　Dep. Req'd. •
303-949-4840 800-222-4840　124 condos, Hi-rise, Lo-rise, Key at Front desk
　　　　　　　　　　　　　H-yes

Location: Airport: Denver 100 miles; Downtown: 2 blocks; Ski lift: Vail

General Facilities: Daily maid, Kitchen, Linens, Baby-sitter, Child planned rec.: Vail
　Associates

Room Facilities: Pool, Sauna, Hot tub, Tennis, By public lake, Golf: 10 miles—4 courses,
　TV, Phone in rm., Crib-Hi-chair, Ind. Heat Ctl.

Attractions: Snowmobiling, jeep tours, sleigh rides, concerts, weekend events, horses,
　fishing

Shops & Restaurants: Ralph Lauren, Gucci, Benetton, Golden Bear, Vail; Mirabelles/
　Fr.-Legends/seafood

*Comfortable, generously sized affordable lodging near Vail Mountain, home of the 1989
World Alpine Championships. Use the outdoor heated pool, sauna and hot tubs, or pic-
nic on the public park and lake. All units have fireplaces and full baths for each bedroom.
After a busy day try one of the many restaurants and clubs in Vail or Beaver Creek, or stay
in your condo for a quiet family dinner and satellite TV watching.*

The Christie Lodge　　　1 Bedroom $$$, 2 Bedrooms $$$
0047 E. Beaver Creek Bl., Box 1196　Pool, Kitchen, Linens
Avon, CO 81620
303-949-7700 800-331-8076

Attractions: White river rafting, golf, canoeing, horseback riding, ice skating

*A winter and summer wonderland, ten minutes west of Vail. Year-round sports, elegant
dining, nightspots and European boutiques for shopping. Units open onto a glass-domed
atrium among lush foliage.*

─────────────── BEAVER CREEK ───────────────

Park Plaza Lodge
P.O. Box 36, 46 Avondale Lane
Beaver Creek, CO 81620
303-845-7700 800-525-2257

2 Bedrooms $$$, 3 Bedrooms $$$$
Min. Stay 7 Nights, AmEx/Visa/MC,
 Dep. Req'd. •
36 condos, Hi-rise, Key at Front desk

Location: Airport: 2½ miles; Need car; Ski lift: Vail

General Facilities: Full serv., Conf. rm. cap. 500, Daily maid, Kitchen, Linens, Restaurant on prem., Bar on prem., Lounge, Baby-sitter, Child planned rec.: Nursery-Pre-school

Room Facilities: Pool, Sauna, Hot tub, Tennis, Horses, rafting, fish, Golf: B.C. Golf Course-near, Cable, Phone in rm., Crib-Hi-chair, Ind. Heat Ctl.

Attractions: Skiing, rafting, hiking, golf, fishing, ballooning, Orvis Flyfishing School, entertainment

Shops & Restaurants: International selection of shops in Vail Village; Legends/seafood-LeRoy's/Amer.

Five-star condominiums just steps away from the ski slopes, adjacent to an 18-hole golf course. Indoor pool, jacuzzi, steam room, special programs for children and pop and classical concerts for adults. Units have mountain and valley views, and are furnished in blues and rusts with brass, crystal and wood appointments. Continental breakfasts, golf and tennis tournaments and bike races.

Poste Montane at Beaver Creek
76 Avon Dale Lane, Box 36
Beaver Creek, CO 81620
303-845-7500 800-525-2257

Studio $$, 1 Bedroom $$, 2 Bedrooms $$$
Min. Stay 7 Nights, AmEx/Visa/MC,
 Dep. Req'd. •
24 condos, Hi-rise, Key at Front desk

Location: Airport: 2½ miles; Ski lift: Nearby

General Facilities: Full serv., Conf. rm. cap. 500, Daily maid, Kitchen, Linens, Restaurant on prem., Bar on prem., Lounge, Baby-sitter, Child planned rec.: Nursery, Kid's Spot

Room Facilities: Sauna, Hot tub, Tennis, Horses, Rafting, Golf: Beaver Creek Golf Course, Cable, VCR, Phone in rm., Crib-Hi-chair, Ind. Heat Ctl.

Attractions: Skiing, rafting, hiking, golf, fishing, ballooning, Orvis Flyfishing school, entertainment

Shops & Restaurants: International shops Vail Village, specialty shops; Legends/seafood-LeRoy's/Amer.

European mountain lodge, Laura Ashley wallpaper, rose and green color scheme. Children's ski school, theatre and petting zoo. Continental breakfast, steps from the ski lifts and adjacent to 18-hole championship golf course. Hot tub, sauna, bike racing and the 1989 host for the World Alpine Ski Championships.

We want to hear from you—any comments regarding the condos or our publication may be noted on the form at the end of the book.

—————————— BEAVER CREEK ——————————

The Charter at Beaver Creek
120 Offerson Rd., P.O. Box 5310
Beaver Creek, CO 81620
303-949-6660 800-824-3064

Studio $$, 1 Bedroom $$$, 2 Bedrooms $$$$,
  3 Bedrooms $$$$
Min. Stay 2 Nights, AmEx/Visa/MC,
  Dep. Req'd. •
156 condos, Hi-rise, Key at Front desk

Location: Airport: Denver 110 miles; Ski lift: Beaver Cr

General Facilities: Full serv., Conf. rm., Daily maid, Kitchen, Linens, Restaurant on
  prem., Bar on prem., Game room, Lounge, Baby-sitter

Room Facilities: Pool, Sauna, Hot tub, Tennis, Indoor lap pool, Golf: Beaver Creek PGA
  Golf, TV, Cable, Phone in rm., Crib-Hi-chair, Ind. Heat Ctl.

Attractions: Golf, scenic chairlift rides, jeep tours, fishing, outdoor concerts, hiking, bik-
  ing, entertainment

Shops & Restaurants: General store, sports shop, Beaver Creek Village; Terrace/
  casual-First Season

*Quiet mountain retreat at the base of Beaver Creek Mountain. 200 feet to golf, walking dis-
tance to tennis and horseback riding. Surrounded by aspen and spruce-beautiful smog-
free air. Weight-aerobics room. Full breakfast included with winter rates. Piano player in
lounge.*

—————————————————————————————————

The Inn at Beaver Creek
P.O. Box 36, 10 Elk Track
Beaver Creek, CO 81620
303-845-7800 800-525-7800

Studio $$
Min. Stay 7 Nights, AmEx/Visa/MC,
  Dep. Req'd. •
39 condos, Lo-rise, Key at Front desk
H-yes

Location: Airport: 2½ miles; Need car; Ski lift: Beaver

General Facilities: Full serv., Conf. rm. cap. 500, Daily maid, Kitchen, Linens, Bar on
  prem., Lounge, Baby-sitter, Child planned rec.: Preschool/Kid's Spot

Room Facilities: Pool, Hot tub, Tennis, horses, rafting, fish, Golf: B.C. Golf Course-near,
  Cable, Phone in rm., Crib-Hi-chair, Ind. Heat Ctl.

Attractions: Orvis Flyfishing School, skiing, rafting, hiking, golf, ballooning, fishing,
  entertainment

Shops & Restaurants: Vail Village international shops, specialty shops; Golden
  Eagle/game-Mirabelles

*Quaint mountain lodge, 20 feet from chairlift, outdoor pool, hot tub, sauna, steam room,
lounge, underground parking. Pop and classical concerts, bike races, golf and tennis tournaments, 1989 World Alpine Ski Championships. For the children, nursery, preschool,
Small World, kid's spot, theatre and petting zoo. Units are furnished in blues and cranberry
and continental breakfast is offered.*

BRECKENRIDGE

Beaver Run
P.O. Box 2115
Breckenridge, CO 80424
303-453-6000 800-525-2253

Studio $$, 1 Bedroom $$, 2 Bedrooms $$$,
3 Bedrooms $$$$
AmEx/Visa/MC, Dep. Req'd. •
500 condos, Hi-rise, Key at Front desk, H-yes

Location: Airport: 81 miles; Downtown: ¼ mile; Need car; Ski lift: Nearby

General Facilities: Full serv., Conf. rm. cap. 800, Daily maid, Kitchen, Linens, Restaurant on prem., Bar on prem., Game room, Lounge, Baby-sitter

Room Facilities: Pool, Sauna, Hot tub, Tennis, Ski-in/ski-out, TV, Cable, Phone in rm., Ind. Heat Ctl.

Attractions: Historic area, mines, museums, ski areas, lakes, entertainment

Shops & Restaurants: Resort town shopping; Over 120 in town

Modern, comfortable, contemporary suites in a fully self-contained resort. Ski to Breckenridge ski area or visit the historic town of Breckenridge. Live entertainment in the modern lounge. All summer outdoor activities.

Blue River Condominiums
P.O. Box 1942
Breckenridge, CO 80424
303-453-2260

2 Bedrooms $$, 3 Bedrooms $$
2 Bedrms/week $$$$, 3 Bed/week $$$$
AmEx/Visa/MC, Dep. Req'd.

Location: Downtown: 5 min.; Ski lift: Breckenridge

General Facilities: Kitchen, Linens

Room Facilities: TV, Cable

Attractions: Alpine Slide, tennis, golf, jeep tours, hunting, skiing

Shops & Restaurants: Breckenridge shops, boutiques

In a quiet valley, surrounded by a national forest, with one of the state's largest ski mountains for beginners to expert. Three more challenging ski areas are close. Summer brings warm days and cool nights, area activities and the charming town of Breckenridge.

Four Seasons Lodging, Inc.
835 Broken Lance Dr. Box 1356
Breckenridge, CO 80424
303-453-1403 800-848-3434

Studio $$, 1 Bedroom $$$, 2 Bedrooms $$$$
1 Bedrm/week 8$, 2 Bed/week 10$,
3 Bed/week 10$
Min. Stay 2 Nights, Visa/MC, Dep. Req'd. •
55 condos, Lo-rise, Key at 805 S. Columbine Rd.

Location: Airport: 90 miles; Downtown: 2 blocks; Ski lift: Nearby

General Facilities: Daily maid, Kitchen, Linens

Room Facilities: Pool, Hot tub, Golf: 5 miles Breckenridge, TV, Cable, VCR, Phone in rm., Crib-Hi-chair, Ind. Heat Ctl.

Attractions: Skiing, ice skating, golf, tennis, horses, hiking, fishing, jeep tours

Shops & Restaurants: Small novelty shops; Spencers-International

Deluxe accommodations in this "four seasons" resort. Winter-ski, ice skate, snowmobile, or ride through the snow in a horse-drawn sleigh. Spring-Hike to where the first flowers peer from the tundra, golf, tennis, or fly-fish the trout streams. Summer-horseback riding, marathons, rafting and four wheeling to ghost towns. It's a season of festivals-music, theatre and film. Fall-golden aspen, teal blue skies, crisp, clear days and star-studded nights.

BRECKENRIDGE

Gold Point Condominiums
169 N. Fuller Placer Road-Box 568
Breckenridge, CO 80424
303-453-1910   800-231-3780

1 Bedroom $$, 2 Bedrooms $$, 3 Bedrooms $$
Min. Stay 2 Nights, AmEx/Visa/MC,
   Dep. Req'd. •
36 condos, Lo-rise, Key at On site office
H-yes

Location: Airport: 80 miles; Downtown: 3 miles; Need car; Ski lift: Nearby

General Facilities: Daily maid, Kitchen, Linens, Baby-sitter

Room Facilities: Hot tub, Athletic club, Golf: Breckenridge Golf Club, TV, Cable, Crib-Hi-chair, Ind. Heat Ctl.

Attractions: Hiking, skiing, sailing, jeep rides, bike trails, gold mines

Shops & Restaurants: Breckenridge Victorian town, Vail; 60 restaurants in Breckenridge

For those who want the best, Gold Point offers quality accommodations with spacious townhouses and penthouses. Garages with automatic door openers, private balconies overlooking spectacular panoramic mountain views, and fully equipped kitchens. Hot tub, party room, Athletic Club with swimming, racquetball, nautilus, steam sauna, dining room and bar.

Lake Cliffe
160 East La Bonte
Breckenridge, CO 80424
303-468-2301

1 Bedroom $$, 2 Bedrooms $$$
Pool, Daily maid, Kitchen, Linens

Attractions: National forest, golf, tennis, fishing, art shows, rodeos, craft fairs, film festivals

Views of Lake Dillon and the Ten Mile Range from these spacious lakefront units. Amenities include a clubhouse with pool, sauna and jacuzzi. Ski at five mountains, nearby golf, tennis, lake fishing, hiking, horseback riding and rafting for the rest of the year.

Pine Ridge Condominiums
P.O. Box 473
Breckenridge, CO 80424
303-453-6946

Ski home at day's end to your individually decorated condominium, enjoy a steam bath and relax in front of the fireplace while other skiers are still in the parking lot. Helpful, friendly staff to assist you all year long.

Rockridge
49 Atlantic Lode
Breckenridge, CO 80424
303-453-1758

——————————————— BRECKENRIDGE ———————————————

Ski Hill Condominiums
250 Ski Hill Road
Breckenridge, CO 80424
303-453-2262 800-525-3882

Studio $$$, 1 Bedroom $$$, 2 Bedrooms $$$
AmEx/Visa/MC, Dep. Req'd. •
280 condos, Hi-rise, Key at 11072 N. Highway 9
No S-yes/H-yes

Location: Airport: 85 miles; Ski lift: Breckenridge

General Facilities: Kitchen, Linens, Baby-sitter, Child planned rec.: Ski lessons/day care

Room Facilities: Hot tub, Winter ski resort, Golf: Breckenridge—3 miles, Cable, VCR, Phone in rm., Ind. Heat Ctl.

Attractions: Skiing, snowmobile, sleigh ride, ice skating, horses, biking, fishing, boating

Shops & Restaurants: Over 300 shops, restaurants and bars

Deluxe one-and two-bedroom condominiums located in the heart of Breckenridge, one block to shops and restaurants and 2 blocks to the ski lifts and one block to free shuttle. Indoor hot tubs, central laundry facilities, covered parking and elevators. Spectacular alpine summers with sunny days and crisp nights, wildflowers, clear streams for fishing or just lazing in the sun until the cool of the evening.

The Gant

──────────── BRECKENRIDGE ────────────

Summit Ridge Lodgings
11072 US Hwy. 9
Breckenridge, CO 80424
303-453-2262 800-525-3882

Trails End Condominiums
455 West Village Road
Breckenridge, CO 80424
303-968-2626 800-624-4242

1 Bedroom $$, 2 Bedrooms $$$
Pool, Daily maid, Kitchen, Phone in rm.

Long a Breckenridge favorite, Trails End's tastefully appointed condominiums are within easy walking distance to Breckenridge's recreational facilities. Ski-in/ski-out, ski lockers, covered parking.

The Village At Breckenridge
P.O. Box 8329
Breckenridge, CO 80424
303-453-2000 800-332-0424

1 Bedroom $$$, 2 Bedrooms $$$$
Pool, Daily maid, Kitchen, Phone in rm.

Attractions: Health club, steam

You'll be treated with style and friendly service at this resort situated on the shore of historic Maggie Pond. Waterfront promenade and views of Colorado's great outdoors. The Village provides everything you need for a complete summer or winter vacation.

──────────── COPPER MOUNTAIN ────────────

Carbemate Property Management Co.
Box 3216
Copper Mountain, CO 80443
303-968-6854 800-526-7737

Studio $, 2 Bedrooms $$, 3 Bedrooms $$
AmEx/Visa/MC •
56 condos
H-yes

Location: Airport: Denver—15 miles; Downtown: 10 miles; Need car; Ski lift: Copper Mt.
General Facilities: Daily maid, Kitchen
Room Facilities: Sauna, Hot tub, Tennis, Hiking, fishing, spa, Golf: Nearby, TV, Phone in rm., Ind. Heat Ctl.
Attractions: Skiing, hiking, fishing
Shops & Restaurants: Frisco shops

Condominiums in a quiet, cool mountain setting. Southwestern motifs done in naturals with accents of mauve. Most units have mountain views and fireplaces. Free use of Athletic Club.

COPPER MOUNTAIN

Copper Mountain Inn
P.O. Box 3003
Copper Mountain, CO 80443
303-968-6477 800-525-3891

Studio $$, 1 Bedroom $$, 2 Bedrooms $$$,
  3 Bedrooms $$$$
1 Bedrm/week 5$, 2 Bed/week 7$,
  3 Bed/week 10$
Min. Stay 3 Nights, AmEx/Visa/MC,
  Dep. Req'd.; Lo-rise, No S-yes/H-yes

Location: Airport: 2 hours; Downtown: 1 block; Ski lift: Copper Mt

General Facilities: Daily maid, Kitchen, Linens, Baby-sitter, Child planned rec.: Day care

Room Facilities: Pool, Sauna, Hot tub, Tennis, Ice skating, Golf: Copper Creek Golf Club, TV, Cable, Phone in rm., Crib-Hi-chair, Ind. AC Ctl., Ind. Heat Ctl.

Attractions: Summer and winter activities

Shops & Restaurants: Ski shops, clothing, bookstores, kitchen, T-shirt; Japanese and Italian

Close to ski slopes, shops and restaurants. Fantastic scenery. All summer and winter sports for a great vacation any time.

Copper Mountain Resort
I-70 & US Hwy 91, Box 3001
Copper Mountain, CO 80433
303-968-2882 800-458-8386

Studio $$, 1 Bedroom $$, 2 Bedrooms $$$, 3
  Bedrooms $$$$
AmEx/Visa/MC, Dep. Req'd. •
415 condos, Hi-rise, Lo-rise, Key at Mt. Plaza
  Guest Reg., No S-yes/H-yes

Location: Airport: 75 miles; Downtown: 75 miles; Ski lift: Copper Mt

General Facilities: Full serv., Bus. fac., Conf. rm. cap. 300, Daily maid, Kitchen, Linens, Restaurant on prem., Bar on prem., Game room, Lounge, Baby-sitter, Child planned rec.: 4-14 ranch program

Room Facilities: Pool, Sauna, Hot tub, Tennis, Racquet, athletic club, Golf: Copper Creek Golf Club, TV, Cable, Phone in rm., Crib-Hi-chair, Ind. Heat Ctl.

Attractions: Arts and crafts shows, Copper Mountain Country Fair, Best of the West Fest, Bicycle Classic

Shops & Restaurants: Village ski-golf shops, gifts, art, florist; Plaza/Amr.-Rackets restaurant

After a day of skiing relax in the jacuzzi, work out in the Athletic Club, pamper yourself with a massage, or relax and enjoy the view of snow-covered mountains from your condo. A family resort with nursery and children's programs. Sleigh rides through the woods, helicopter skiing, summer biking, golf, horseback riding, family picnics, flyfishing or shop in the Village amid flower-lined walkways.

Foxpine Inn
P.O. Box 3296
Copper Mountain, CO 80443
303-968-2600 800-426-7400

1 Bedroom $$, 2 Bedrooms $$, Hi-rise
Pool, Daily maid, Kitchen, Linens

Attractions: Trail rides, tennis, hiking, biking, rafting, golf, skiing, Lake Dillon

30 paces to the ski lifts from your units, or drive to three other major ski areas. Ski home to your condominium and curl up in front of the warm fireplace. Summer brings lake boating, Colorado River rafting and hiking, biking or riding in beautiful mountain scenery.

――――――――――――――――― CRESTED BUTTE ―――――――――――――――――

San Moritz Condominiums
P.O. Box 169
Crested Butte, CO 81224
303-349-5150

1 Bedroom $, 2 Bedrooms $$, Lo-rise
Kitchen, Linens, Phone in rm.

Attractions: Skiing, year-round vacation recreation

Ski-in, ski-out condominiums for an unforgettable winter vacation. Rock fireplaces and spectacular views. Hot tubs and saunas to ease stiff muscles unused to skiing. Friendly staff will be happy to arrange ski rentals, local transportation and grocery shopping.

The Columbine Condominiums
Drawer C, 51, Whetstone Road
Crested Butte, CO 81225
303-349-2448 800-821-3718

1 Bedroom $$, 2 Bedrooms $$, 3 Bedrooms $$
AmEx/Visa/MC, Dep. 50% •
30 condos, Lo-rise, Key at Three Seasons Condos

Location: Airport: 30 miles; Downtown: 3 miles; Ski lift: Nearby

General Facilities: Daily maid, Kitchen, Linens, Baby-sitter, Child planned rec.: Kids ski school

Room Facilities: Sauna, Hot tub, Golf: Skyland Resort-6 miles, TV, Cable, Phone in rm., Crib-Hi-chair, Ind. Heat Ctl.

Attractions: Skiing, ski-in, ski-out, Crested Butte National Historic District

Shops & Restaurants: Handmade items, souvenirs and pottery; Le Basquet-gourmet French

Casual, comfortable condominiums with magnificent mountain views from your balcony. Put your skis on and head for the chairlifts of Crested Butte. Three miles away is the National Historic District of Crested Butte where plenty of shopping and restaurants are available. For summer visitors, there's river rafting, jeeping, fishing, hiking, tennis, biking, kayaking and horseback riding.

――――――――――――――――――― DILLON ―――――――――――――――――――

Buffalo Village
89400 Ryan Gulch Road
Dillon, CO 80435
303-468-6509

1 Bedroom $$, 2 Bedrooms $$
Pool

Attractions: Tennis

Nestled in the woods of Wildernest Mountain, 3 miles northwest of Dillon, in the heart of ski country. Rock fireplace, oak trim, large closets, tile baths. The best in Rocky Mountain living.

Chateau Claire Condos
240 E. Labonte, Box 539
Dillon, CO 80435
303-468-2760 800-521-0531

1 Bedroom $$, 2 Bedrooms $$, Lo-rise

Completely equipped condominiums in the Rockies. Great skiing, trout fishing, tennis, hiking, pool, hunting, golf, sailing on Lake Dillon. Close to shops, theatres, restaurants and parks.

──────────────── DILLON ────────────────

Orofino
P.O. Box C
Dillon, CO 80435
303-468-5484 800-433-2815

2 Bedrooms $$, Lo-rise
Kitchen, Phone in rm.

Attractions: Skiing, sailing, windsurfing, fishing, golf, horses, tennis, boating, white
water rafting

Year-round sports and recreation in Summit County. Two story townhouses with washer/
dryer and woodburning stove. Choose from four major ski areas. Minutes to shops, restaur-
ants and nightlife. 3 hot tubs open all year.

Snowdance Condominiums
Box 41 Montezuma Rte.
Dillon, CO 80435
303-468-5178 800-228-6138

1 Bedroom $$, 2 Bedrooms $$$
Min. Stay 2 Nights, Visa/MC, Dep. Req'd. •
32 condos, Lo-rise, Key at Office
H-yes

Location: Airport: 70 miles; Downtown: 1 mile; Ski lift: Nearby

General Facilities: Full serv., Daily maid, Kitchen, Linens, Restaurant on prem., Bar
on prem., Game room, Lounge, Child planned rec.: Ski school

Room Facilities: Sauna, Hot tub, Skiing, Golf: Close-Keystone Ranch, TV, Cable, VCR,
Phone in rm., Crib-Hi-chair, Ind. Heat Ctl.

Attractions: Cross-country & downhill skiing Nov. to June, river rafting, ghost towns,
hiking, backpack

Shops & Restaurants: Keystone Village; Snake River Saloon-meat, fish

Summer or winter, Keystone Village and Summit County have great nightlife and dining.
2-minute walk to the ski lifts with 1000 acres of groomed alpine trails and runs. Shuttle bus
to other ski areas. Summer-cool weather and Colorado scenery, boat, fish, river rafting,
horseback riding, or jeep to mines and ghost towns. Hiking, backpacking, and big game
hunting. Night skiing.

Spinnaker at Lake Dillon
317 Labonte Street, Box 2519
Dillon, CO 80435
303-468-8001

Studio $, 1 Bedroom $, 2 Bedrooms $$,
    3 Bedrooms $$
1 Bedrm/week $$$$, 2 Bed/week $$$$,
    3 Bed/week 4$
Dep. Req'd.
28 condos, 15, Villas, Key at Office/lobby lockbox
H-yes

Location: Airport: 85 miles; Downtown: 3 blocks; Need car; Ski lift: Nearby

General Facilities: Daily maid, Kitchen, Linens, Baby-sitter

Room Facilities: Pool, Sauna, Hot tub, TV, Cable, Crib-Hi-chair, Ind. Heat Ctl.

Attractions: Alpine slide, train rides, ghost towns, 5 ski areas, 4 golf courses, jeep trails

Shops & Restaurants: Surplus outlets-Hanes, Van Heusen, Claiborne, Nike; St. Bernard Inn/lt-Keystone

In the heart of Summit County overlooking Lake Dillon, minutes away from five ski areas,
these pleasant condominiums have 2 TVs, Rockies' view from the balconies, fireplaces and
southwestern furnishings. Winter and Spring skiing, or Summer and Fall sailing, boating,
golf, biking, jogging, rafting, or just relaxing under the abundant sunshine.

─────────────────────── DILLON ───────────────────────

Swan Mountain Resort
59 Soda Ridge Road, Box 95
Dillon, CO 80435
303-468-6595

1 Bedroom $$, 2 Bedrooms $$, Lo-rise
Pool, Kitchen, Linens

Attractions: Tennis, Golf

High in the Rockies, a four-season adventureland with exciting summer and winter sports. Pool, hot tub, barbecue, fireplace, microwave oven, balconies and patios.

Yacht Club Condominiums, Inc.
410 Tenderfoot Box 397
Dillon, CO 80435
303-468-2703 800-999-2123

Studio $$, 1 Bedroom $$, 2 Bedrooms $$$,
  3 Bedrooms $$$
AmEx/Visa/MC, Dep. Req'd. •
40 condos, Lo-rise, Key at Office
H-yes

Location: Airport: 1½ hours Denver; Downtown: 3 miles; Need car; Ski lift: Keystone
General Facilities: Kitchen, Linens
Room Facilities: Sauna, Hot tub, Tennis, Sailing, boating, TV, Cable, Crib-Hi-chair, Ind. Heat Ctl.
Attractions: Summer: sailing, fishing, bicycle trails, hiking; Winter: 5 ski areas

Comfortable condominiums on the shore of Lake Dillon individually decorated with tasteful furnishings. Pick your season and enjoy the fabulous outdoor activities that surround you.

─────────────────────── DURANGO ───────────────────────

Cascade Village Resort
P.O. Box 2867, 50827 Hwy 550 N.
Durango, CO 81301
303-259-3500 800-525-0896

Studio $, 1 Bedroom $$, 2 Bedrooms $$,
  3 Bedrooms $$
1 Bedrm/week $$$$, 2 Bed/week 4$,
  3 Bed/week 5$
Min. Stay Ask, AmEx/Visa/MC, Dep. 1 Night •
125 condos, Lo-rise, Key at Benchmark Building

Location: Airport: 45 miles; Downtown: 30 miles; Need car; Ski lift: Nearby
General Facilities: Full serv., Conf. rm. cap. 100, Daily maid, Kitchen, Linens, Restaurant on prem., Bar on prem., Game room, Lounge, Baby-sitter
Room Facilities: Pool, Sauna, Hot tub, Tennis, Adjacent ski area, Golf: Durango-25 miles, TV, Cable, Phone in rm., Crib-Hi-chair, Ind. Heat Ctl.
Attractions: Durango/Silverton Narrow Gauge RR, Mesa Verde Nat. Park, Purgatory Theater, entertainment
Shops & Restaurants: Country store at Cascade, Historic Durango shops; Cafe Cascade-seafood, steaks

Luxury condominiums located in the two million acre San Juan National Forest adjacent to Purgatory ski area. Tennis lessons, horseback riding, river rafting, hiking, fishing, Alpine slide and trout pond. All this plus an indoor pool and jacuzzi make Cascade Village a wonderful summer or winter vacation spot.

─────────────── DURANGO ───────────────

Ferringway
6 Ferringway Circle
Durango, CO 81301
303-247-0441 800-624-9714

1 Bedroom $$, 2 Bedrooms $$$
1 Bedrm/week 4$, 2 Bed/week 5$
AmEx/Visa/MC, Dep. 1 Night •
50 condos, Lo-rise, Key at Front desk, P-yes

Location: Airport: 20 miles; Downtown: ½ mile; Need car; Ski lift: 26 miles

General Facilities: Full serv., Conf. rm. cap. 50, Daily maid, Kitchen, Linens, Game room, Lounge, Baby-sitter

Room Facilities: Pool, Sauna, Hot tub, 2 ski lifts 15-26 mi, Golf: Hillcrest Golf Course, TV, Cable, Phone in rm., Crib-Hi-chair, Ind. Heat Ctl.

Attractions: Durango/Silverton Railroad, winter skiing, fall changing colors, lake fishing

Shops & Restaurants: Boutiques, Main Avenue shops; Sweeny's Grubsteak-duck, fish

Escape the summer heat in the cool air of the mountains. Ride the railroad or alpine slide. Clubhouse has pool, jacuzzi, dressing rooms, sauna and indoor entertaining facilities. Winter skiing at Purgatory for beginners, 2 half-day free learn-to-ski lessons, to advanced. These are the only nightly condominiums in Durango, set on a mesa overlooking the city.

─────────────── DURANGO ───────────────

The Needles
46850 Hwy. 550 N., 10 Eolus Circle
Durango, CO 81301
303-259-5960

2 Bedrooms $$, Lo-rise
Kitchen, Linens

Attractions: Narrow Gauge RR, Indian ruins at Mesa Verde Nat. Park, Ouray hot springs, Pugatory skiing

Homelike townhomes with furnishing from well-known manufacturers. Vaulted ceilings, skylights, bay windows, ceiling fans, and private balcony and whirlpool bath in the master bedroom. Wood cabinetry, tile-hearth fireplace, plush carpeting and modern kitchens.

The Charter at Beaver Creek

DURANGO

Purgatory-Village
175 Beatrice St., P.O. Box 666
Durango, CO 81302
303-247-9000 800-247-9000

Studio $$, 1 Bedroom $$$, 2 Bedrooms $$$$,
  3 Bedrooms $$$$
Min. Stay 2 Nights, AmEx/Visa/MC,
  Dep. Req'd. •
148 condos, Hi-rise, Key at Village Center desk
No S-yes

Location: Airport: 44 miles south; Downtown: 25 miles; Ski lift: Nearby

General Facilities: Full serv., Bus. fac., Conf. rm. cap. 100, Kitchen, Restaurant on prem., Lounge, Baby-sitter, Child planned rec.: Skiing and day care

Room Facilities: Pool, Sauna, Hot tub, Tennis, Skiing, Golf: Tamarron Resort, TV, Cable, VCR, Phone in rm., Crib-Hi-chair, Ind. Heat Ctl.

Attractions: Narrow gauge train, Mesa Verde Nat Park, Big Top Theatre, Alpine Slide, biking, skiing, entertainment

Shops & Restaurants: Village shops and Durango shops; Seafood and Mexican

Choose from units with heavy oak furniture, southwestern design or modern decor with deckside living or views of Needles Mountains. The best skiing in the West, 50 yards from base-area chairlifts with 630 acres of skiable terrain, plus cross-country trails. Beautiful summer surroundings for exploring the high country on foot or horseback, raft trips, Alpine Slide and nightime entertainment at the Repertory Theatre or Big Top Tent.

The Ranch Townhomes
33800 Highway 550
Durango, CO 81301
303-247-0762 800-525-0892

2 Bedrooms $$
Kitchen

Attractions: Bowling, golf, Mesa Verde National Park, fishing, skiing, narrow gauge train, Fishing, golf, chipping, Tennis

Townhomes located on a 500-acre working ranch in the Animas Valley. Exceptionally large, beautifully planned units. Guests enjoy fishing and use of the wooded acres for hiking, picnics and wildlife observation. 15 miles to the north is Purgatory for winter skiing.

Tamarron
P.O. Box 3131
Durango, CO 81302
303-259-2000 800-525-5420

Studio $$, 1 Bedroom $$, 2 Bedrooms $$$,
  3 Bedrooms $$$$
AmEx/Visa/MC, Dep. Req'd. •
Lo-rise, Key at Registr. desk, H-yes

Location: Airport: 33 miles; Downtown: 17 miles; Ski lift: Purgatory

General Facilities: Full serv., Conf. rm. cap. 500, Daily maid, Kitchen, Linens, Restaurant on prem., Bar on prem., Game room, Lounge, Baby-sitter, Child planned rec.: Program for 4 to 11

Room Facilities: Pool, Sauna, Hot tub, Tennis, Health spa, volleyball, TV, Cable, Phone in rm., Crib-Hi-chair, Ind. AC Ctl., Ind. Heat Ctl.

Attractions: Mesa Verde National Park, Durango & Silverton narrow gauge train trip, sightseeing tours, entertainment

Shops & Restaurants: Seven shops on property, art galleries; Palace-continental

Deluxe townhouses set amidst the spectacular San Juan Mountains. An award-winning luxury retreat with restaurants, lounges, shopping arcade, health spa, fishing, riding, tours, sleigh rides, snowmobile and nightly live music in the bar.

─────────────── FRISCO ───────────────

Antlers Realty & Lodging Company
Box 2176, 1890
Frisco, CO 80443
303-668-5076 800-662-2203

Min. Stay 3 Nights, AmEx/Visa/MC,
Dep. 2 Nights •
50 condos, Lo-rise, Villas, Key at 916 Summit Blvd.

Location: Airport: 1½ hours; Downtown: 1 hour; Ski lift: Nearby

General Facilities: Kitchen, Linens, Game room, Lounge, Baby-sitter

Room Facilities: Pool, Sauna, Hot tub, Tennis, TV, Cable, Phone in rm., Crib-Hi-chair, Ind. Heat Ctl.

Attractions: Winter ski areas, ice skating, x-country skiing, rafting, sailing, fishing, hiking, bikes

Shops & Restaurants: Small privately owned retail shops; All types

Beautifully furnished condos from economy to luxury with hot tubs, pools and all the extras. The free shuttle will pick you up right near your door and take you to three world class ski areas. Balconies with mountain or lake views. Summer activities include rafting, sailing, fishing, hiking and biking. Three condominiums to choose from, Lagoon, Mountain Side and Meadow Creek Villas.

───────────────────────────────────────

Cedar Lodge
First and Granite, P.O. Box 2130
Frisco, CO 80443
303-668-0777 800-782-7699

1 Bedroom $$
Kitchen

Attractions: Skiing, rafting, fishing, hiking, sailing, golf, tennis, hunting, horses, sleigh rides

European style condotel resembling a country inn. Free shuttle service to Breckenridge, Keystone and Copper Mountain. Shuttle to Vail, 25 miles away. Suites feature tile entries, oak doors and trim, kitchenettes, covered garage and ski storage.

───────────────────────────────────────

Cross Creek Condominiums
223 Creekside Dr., Box 1966
Frisco, CO 80443
303-668-5175

2 Bedrooms $$$, Lo-rise
Pool, Kitchen, Linens

Attractions: Bikepaths

Tall pines and aspen groves overlook Ten Mile Creek. Warm, natural surroundings for total freedom and enjoyment winter or summer. Unhurried western informality, easy access to Denver, historic park, quaint shops.

Be sure to call the condo to verify details and prices and to make your reservation.

FRISCO

Tenmile Creek Condominiums Resort
200 Granite St., P.O. Box 543
Frisco, CO 80443
303-668-3100

2 Bedrooms $$, 3 Bedrooms $$
Min. Stay 3 Nights, AmEx/Visa/MC,
   Dep. Req'd. •
60 condos, Lo-rise, Key at Office
No S-yes

Location: Airport: 70 miles Denver; Downtown: 2 blocks; Ski lift: Nearby

General Facilities: Conf. rm. cap. 50, Kitchen, Linens

Room Facilities: Pool, Sauna, Hot tub, TV, Cable, Phone in rm., Crib-Hi-chair, Ind. Heat Ctl.

Attractions: Downhill and x-country skiing, snowmobiling, sleigh rides, bikes, boats, fish, windsurfing

Shops & Restaurants: Wal-Mart, Safeway, varied small shops; Golden Annies/Mesquite-Mexican

After a day of powder snow skiing, relax by the fireplace and watch TV or enjoy the fine dining and nightlife of Frisco and Dillon. Pool, jacuzzi, sauna and party room. Endless variety of summer and winter fun.

GRAND LAKE

Soda Springs Ranch Resort
9921 U.S. Highway 34
Grand Lake, CO 80447
303-627-3486

1 Bedroom $$, 2 Bedrooms $$$
Kitchen, Linens

Attractions: Racquetball, putt. green, Tennis

Newly built, commpletely furnished condominiums 5 miles south of Grand Lake. Well-marked trails for every level of skier through meadows and pines. Athletic club, racquetball court, weight room, restaurant. Summer-pool, fishing, jogging, horses.

KEYSTONE

Hearthstone Mountain Homes
239099 U.S. Hwy. 6
Keystone, CO 80435
303-468-9291

———————————————— KEYSTONE ————————————————

Keystone Resort   AmEx/Visa/MC, Dep. Req'd.
Box 38
Keystone, CO 80435
303-534-7712 800-222-0188

Location: Airport: 68 miles Denver; Ski lift: Nearby

General Facilities: Bus. fac., Conf. rm. cap. 110, Daily maid, Kitchen, Linens, Restaurant on prem., Bar on prem., Lounge, Baby-sitter, Child planned rec.: Nursery-programs

Room Facilities: Pool, Sauna, Hot tub, Tennis, Fitness center, Golf: 18-hole course, TV, Cable, Phone in rm.

Attractions: Sailing, bicycling, hayride dinners, western melodrama, summer music festival, tours, entertainment

Shops & Restaurants: Pedestrian mall-gifts, clothing, arts and crafts; Garden Room/cont.-Bighorn Stk.

Condominiums have fireplaces with wood supply and television with HBO. Winter ski activities, and something for everyone in the summer. Tennis staff for instructions, golf course among pines, meadows and 9-acre lake. Golf clinics and Ranchhouse restaurant for lunch and dinner. Nursery for two months and up, picnics, crafts and pony rides for preschoolers and activity programs for older children. Hayrides to a cattle ranch for dinner. Guided tours to Old Keystone and Montezuma. Western melodrama.

Ski Run/Snowdance Manor
Keystone, CO 80435
303-468-9243

———————————————— LAKEWOOD ————————————————

Raintree Inn
3500 S. Wadsworth St.
Lakewood, CO 80235
800-824-3662

———————————————— MESA ————————————————

Goldenwoods Condominiums   Studio $$$, 1 Bedroom $$$$, 2 Bedrooms $$$$
Mesa, CO 81647   AmEx/Visa/MC, Dep. Req'd. •
303-242-5637 800-876-9337   78 condos, Lo-rise, Key at Powderhorn front dsk

Location: Airport: 40 miles; Downtown: 45 miles; Ski lift: Ski in

General Facilities: Full serv., Conf. rm., Daily maid, Kitchen, Linens, Restaurant on prem., Bar on prem., Game room, Lounge

Room Facilities: Sauna, Hot tub, TV, Cable, VCR, Phone in rm., Crib-Hi-chair

Attractions: Sleigh rides, torchlight parade, Colorado historian campfire, hiking, biking, entertainment

Shops & Restaurants: Resort convenience store, small town stores-6 mile; Fajita Willy's/Southwestern

Spectacular scenic playground for year-round activities. Breathtaking views of the valley, alpine and nordic skiing in the winter. Mountain bike touring in the summer. VIP service with a versatile arena for summer and winter activities.

─────────────── MOUNT CRESTED BUTTE ───────────────

Out Run Condominiums
721 Gothic Road
Mount Crested Butte, CO 81224
303-349-2800 800-821-7613

3 Bedrooms $$
3 Bedrms/week 5$
Min. Stay 3 Nights, AmEx/Visa/MC,
   Dep. Req'd. •
36 condos, Lo-rise, Key at Out Run, Birch Bldg.

Location: Airport: 30 miles; Downtown: 3 miles; Ski lift: Nearby

General Facilities: Conf. rm. cap. 30, Kitchen, Linens, Baby-sitter, Child planned rec.:
Nature walks, arts

Room Facilities: Sauna, Hot tub, Tennis, Golf: Golf—4 miles, TV, Cable, Phone in rm.,
Crib-Hi-chair, Ind. Heat Ctl.

Attractions: Snowmobile 8 miles to remote lodge for dinner, Black Canyon, Gunnison
boat tours

Shops & Restaurants: Small, locally owned shops; Soupcon-French/Penelope's

*Modern three-bedroom condominiums in the Rocky Mountains. Wonderful summer and
winter activities in a sparsely populated area that has the perfect blend of climate, scenery and recreation. A variety of children's activities so that parents can have time to themselves. Ski in the winter, golf in the summer, or just read and enjoy the scenery.*

───

The Plaza at Woodcreek
11 Snowmass Road, P.O. Box 5159
Mt. Crested Butte, CO 81224
303-349-6611 800-221-5228

2 Bedrooms $$

Location: Ski lift: Crested B

General Facilities: Kitchen, Restaurant on prem., Game room

Room Facilities: Sauna, Hot tub, Tennis, TV, Cable, Phone in rm.

Attractions: Summer Shakespeare, wildflower festival, Crested Butte Victorian village

Shops & Restaurants: Crested Butte shops; The Black Bear

*A bottle of champagne in your unit is your arrival greeting at this picturesque mountain
resort offering endless year-round recreational opportunities. Continental breakfast served
daily during ski season. Spectacular scenery, pure air, majestic mountains.*

─────────────── PAGOSA SPRINGS ───────────────

Fairfield Pagosa
Hwy. 160, P.O. Box 4040
Pagosa Springs, CO 81157
303-731-4141 800-523-7704

Studio $$, 1 Bedroom $$, 2 Bedrooms $$,
  3 Bedrooms $$
1 Bedrm/week 4$, 2 Bed/week 5$,
  3 Bed/week 6$
AmEx/Visa/MC, Dep. 1 Night •
125 condos, Lo-rise, Key at Registr. desk
No S-yes/H-yes

Location: Airport: Pagosa Springs-2 Mi.; Downtown: 3 miles; Ski lift: Nearby

General Facilities: Full serv., Bus. fac., Conf. rm. cap. 350, Daily maid, Kitchen, Linens, Restaurant on prem., Bar on prem., Game room, Lounge, Baby-sitter, Child planned rec.: Sunburst program

Room Facilities: Pool, Sauna, Hot tub, Tennis, skiing, Golf: Fairfield Pagosa Pines, TV, Cable, VCR, Phone in rm., Crib-Hi-chair, Ind. AC Ctl., Ind. Heat Ctl.

Attractions: Indian Ruins, Durango-Silverton Train, entertainment

Shops & Restaurants: Small shops; South Face-Continental

Fairfield Paagosa is a four-season resort. A host of activities from ice fishing and cross-country skiing to trout fishing and mountain climbing. Located on 18,000 acres with seven lakes for canoeing and paddle-boating. Sunburst Kids program for children ages 4-12 offers adventures and crafts. Tennis and golf are also available. Escape to the Colorado wilderness, but have all the amenities of contemporary living.

─────────────── SILVER CREEK ───────────────

Mountainside at Silver Creek
P.O. Box 4104, 96 Mountainside Dr
Silver Creek, CO 80446
303-887-2571 800-223-7677

1 Bedroom $$, 2 Bedrooms $$
Min. Stay 2 Nights, AmEx/Visa/MC, Dep. 2
  Nights •
90 condos, Lo-rise, Key at Front office

Location: Airport: 90 miles; Need car; Ski lift: Nearby

General Facilities: Full serv., Daily maid, Kitchen, Linens, Baby-sitter, Child planned rec.: Childrens Ski School

Room Facilities: Pool, Hot tub, Tennis, TV, Cable, Phone in rm., Crib-Hi-chair, Ind. Heat Ctl.

Attractions: Silver Creek & Winter Park Skiing, Rocky Mt. & Arapahoe Nat. Park areas

Shops & Restaurants: Gasthaus Eichler-German

The Mountainside at Silver Creek affords endless recreational opportunities or "doing nothing" in a picturesque Colorado setting. In the winter there is excellent skiing for beginners and intermediates at Silver Creek, or Winter Park for the advanced. Summertime brings tennis, golf, horseback riding, lake activities or river rafting. Al units have queen beds, rock fireplaces and in-room jacuzzis.

SILVER CREEK

Inn at Silver Creek
Box 4222
Silver Creek, CO 80446
303-887-2131 800-526-0590

Studio $, 1 Bedroom $$, 2 Bedrooms $$,
3 Bedrooms $$$
AmEx/Visa/MC, Dep. Req'd. •
342 condos, Lo-rise, Key at Front desk
P-yes/H-yes

Location: Airport: 90 miles Denver; Downtown: 85 miles; Need car; Ski lift: Nearby

General Facilities: Full serv., Conf. rm. cap. 700, Daily maid, Kitchen, Linens, Restaurant on prem., Bar on prem., Game room, Lounge

Room Facilities: Pool, Sauna, Hot tub, Tennis, Racquetball, bikes, Golf: Near-Pole Creek/Grnd Lake, TV, Cable, Phone in rm., Crib-Hi-chair, Ind. Heat Ctl.

Attractions: Ski Winter Park and Silver Creek, gateway to Rocky Mtn. Nat. Park, lakes, mountains, entertainment

Shops & Restaurants: Grand Lake, Granby, Winter Park; Gausthouse Eichler/ German

4 season resort and conference center located in the heart of the Colorado Rockies. Moss rock fireplaces, baths with jacuzzi jets and steam closets. Disc Jockey in Winchester Saloon Friday and Saturday nights. VCR and video rentals, gift shop, liquor store, pantry, deli and athletic club. Poolside lounging, summer and winter.

SILVERTHORNE

Paradise Condominiums
221 Summit Blvd., Box 587
Silverthorne, CO 80498
303-468-5846 800-922-2590

1 Bedroom $, 2 Bedrooms $$, 3 Bedrooms $$
Min. Stay 3 Nights, AmEx/Visa/MC,
Dep. 40% •
30 condos, Lo-rise, Key at Main office
No S-yes

Location: Airport: 65 miles; Need car; Ski lift: Nearby

General Facilities: Daily maid, Kitchen, Linens, Game room, Baby-sitter

Room Facilities: Pool, Sauna, Hot tub, Skiing, Golf: 3 miles, TV, Cable, Phone in rm., Crib-Hi-chair, Ind. Heat Ctl.

Attractions: Alpine/Nordic skiing, 4 golf courses, flyfishing, big game hunting, sail

Shops & Restaurants: Western and Indian art galleries, ski shops; Keystone Ranch-Nouvelle/Amr.

Contemporary mountain condominiums furnished in earthtones with interiors detailed with fine woods, rock fireplaces and paintings. Four major ski areas, plus miles of cross-country trails, ice skating and snowmobiling. Summer has tennis, fishing, rafting, horseback riding and sailing on Lake Dillon. Music festivals, dining and dancing, or just relax in the hot tub before the fireplace.

SILVERTHORNE

Wildernest Lodging
P.O. Box 1069, 200 Ryan Gulch Rd.
Silverthorne, CO 80424
303-468-6291

Min. Stay Ask, Visa/MC, Dep. 33% •
200 condos, Lo-rise, Key at Wildernest office
H-yes

Location: Airport: 70 miles; Need car; Ski lift: Nearby

General Facilities: Conf. rm. cap. 30, Kitchen, Linens, Restaurant on prem., Bar on prem., Game room, Lounge

Room Facilities: Pool, Sauna, Hot tub, Tennis, Skiing, boating, hike, Golf: 2 miles-Eagles Nest, TV, Phone in rm., Crib-Hi-chair, Ind. Heat Ctl.

Attractions: 3 ski areas in 15 mile radius, Dillon Lake-1 mile, hiking and bicycle trails

Shops & Restaurants: Breckenridge; Antonias-Italian

Fully equipped condominiums, centrally located in Summit County, just 65 miles west of Denver and only minutes from Copper, Keystone and Breckenridge ski areas and Lake Dillon, home of the world's highest yacht club. Reasonable prices and friendly staff in this historical area.

SNOWMASS VILLAGE

Chamonix at Woodrun
Box 6286, 0476 Wood Road
Snowmass Village, CO 81615
303-923-5543 800-635-7480

2 Bedrooms $$$, 3 Bedrooms $$$$
Min. Stay 1 Night, AmEx/Visa/MC,
Dep. 1 Night •
27 condos, Hi-rise, Key at Front desk
H-yes

Location: Airport: 12 miles; Downtown: ¼ mile; Ski lift: Snowmass

General Facilities: Full serv., Bus. fac., Conf. rm. cap. 30, Daily maid, Kitchen, Linens, Baby-sitter, Child planned rec.: Ski school/day care

Room Facilities: Pool, Hot tub, Slopeside access, Golf: Snowmass Club, TV, Cable, VCR, Phone in rm., Crib-Hi-chair, Ind. Heat Ctl.

Attractions: Skiing, sleighs, dog sleigh rides, ballooning, Aspen Music Festival, rafting, hiking

Shops & Restaurants: Ski/sport shops, designer shops in Aspen; Chez Crandmere/French

Located in the heart of the Elk Mountains of the Rockies with spectacular National Forest surroundings, having direct ski access in winter with complete staff to make a truly relaxed vacation. Lots of natural light, oak trim, high ceilings, individually designer decorated with lots of southwest colors. Balconies with slope and valley view.

The Crestwood
P.O. Box 5460
Snowmass Village, CO 81615
303-923-2450

1 Bedroom $$$, 2 Bedrooms $$$$
Pool, Daily maid, Kitchen, Linens

Attractions: Golf

Call from the Aspen Airport and be picked up and have your groceries waiting for you, plus a complimentary bottle of wine. Mountain setting, flower boxes, stream through the property. Beamed ceilings, fireplaces, balconies, barbecues, HBO.

SNOWMASS VILLAGE

Snowmass Club
P.O. Drawer G-2
Snowmass Village, CO 81615
303-923-5600 800-925-0710

1 Bedroom $$$, 2 Bedrooms $$$$, 3 Bedrooms $$$$
AmEx/Visa/MC, Dep. Req'd. •
55 condos, Lo-rise, Key at Front desk
H-yes

Location: Airport: Aspen/Snowmass; Downtown: 15 min.; Need car; Ski lift: Snowmass

General Facilities: Full serv., Conf. rm. cap. 200, Daily maid, Kitchen, Linens, Restaurant on prem., Bar on prem., Lounge

Room Facilities: Pool, Sauna, Hot tub, Tennis, Health Club, Golf: 18-hole championship, TV, Cable, Phone in rm., Ind. Heat Ctl.

Attractions: Aspen Music Festival, Repertory Theatre, Anderson Ranch Arts Center, dog sled rides, entertainment

Shops & Restaurants: Snowmass Village Mall, Aspen pedestrian mall; Four Corners on-site

Complimentary shuttle greets you at the Aspen/Snowmass Airport to take you to your condominium where you'll find a welcoming bottle of champagne. Read the morning newspaper before you start your skiing day. Afterwards, relax in front of the lobby's massive rock fireplace or cocktail lounge with its piano bar. When the snow melts, activities change to hiking, rafting, fishing, horseback riding, biking, hot air ballooning and gliding. Athletic Club has daily aerobics, massages, gym, pool and raquetball.

The Enclave
360 Wood Rd., P.O. Box B-2
Snowmass Village, CO 81615
303-923-4310 800-525-4200

2 Bedrooms $$$, 3 Bedrooms $$$
Visa/MC,Dep. Req'd. •
40 condos, Lo-rise, Key at Check-in desk
H-yes

Location: Airport: 7 miles; Downtown: 12 miles; Ski lift: Snowmass

General Facilities: Full serv., Daily maid, Kitchen, Linens, Baby-sitter

Room Facilities: Pool, Hot tub, Skiing, Golf: Nearby, TV, Cable, Phone in rm., Crib-Hi-chair, Ind. Heat Ctl.

Attractions: Maroon Bells, trout fishing, hiking, Alpine-Nordic skiing, Aspen, entertainment

Shops & Restaurants: Aspen and Snowmass shops; Krabloonik-game/Chez Grandmere

Located on the ski slopes and bordered on three sides by a national forest, these professionally decorated units have microwaves, Jenn-Air grills and all the kitchen equipment you need. Elevators, covered parking and ski storage. On-mountain winter parties one day during the week. Summer fishing, hiking and mountain attractions.

SNOWMASS VILLAGE

Top of the Village
855 Carriageway Rd., P.O. Box 5629
Snowmass Village, CO 81615
303-923-3673 800-525-4200

2 Bedrooms $$$, 3 Bedrooms $$$
Visa/MC,Dep. Req'd. •
111 condos, Lo-rise, Key at Check-in desk

Location: Airport: 7 miles; Downtown: 12 miles; Ski lift: Snowmass

General Facilities: Full serv., Bus. fac., Conf. rm. cap. 50, Daily maid, Kitchen, Linens, Baby-sitter

Room Facilities: Pool, Sauna, Hot tub, Skiing, Golf: Nearby, TV, Cable, VCR, Phone in rm., Crib-Hi-chair, Ind. Heat Ctl.

Attractions: Mountain attractions, fishing, hiking, skiing

Shops & Restaurants: Aspen and Snowmass shops; Krabloonik-game/Chez Grandmere

Above Snowmass Village, ski to the chairlifts and back to your heated condominium in the afternoon. Oversized closets, ski storage, heated pool and jacuzzi with changing rooms, showers and sauna. Free shuttle service throughout Snowmass Village. Condominiums are warm and bright with light color schemes. Views of mountain and aspen groves.

Woodrun Place Condominiums
Box 6027, 0425 Wood Road
Snowmass Village, CO 81615
303-923-5392 800-635-7480

1 Bedroom $$$, 2 Bedrooms $$$, 3 Bedrooms $$$$
Min. Stay 3 Nights, AmEx/Visa/MC, Dep. Req'd. •
54 condos, Lo-rise, Villas, Key at Front desk
H-yes

Location: Airport: 12 miles; Downtown: ¼ mile; Ski lift: Snowmass

General Facilities: Full serv., Bus. fac., Conf. rm. cap. 120, Daily maid, Kitchen, Linens, Baby-sitter, Child planned rec.: Ski school/day care

Room Facilities: Pool, Sauna, Hot tub, Ski rent/tuning, Golf: Snowmass Club, TV, Cable, VCR, Phone in rm., Crib-Hi-chair, Ind. Heat Ctl.

Attractions: Wednesday night summer rodeos, horses, white water, Aspen Music Festival, sleigh rides.

Shops & Restaurants: Aspen designer shops and ski and sport shops; Krabloonik/gourmet-game

Each unit is designer decorated with a predominant southwest-French country flair with lots of natural light and windows and pastel colors. An enchanting setting surrounded by 14,000' peaks with ski slope access in winter and quiet high country settings in summer with complete guest service. Microwaves, washer/dryers, built-in humidifiers and barbecues.

STEAMBOAT SPRINGS

Bear Claw Condominiums
P.O. Box 774928
Steamboat Springs, CO 80477
303-879-6100

1 Bedroom $$$, 2 Bedrooms $$$
Pool, Daily maid, Kitchen, Linens

Attractions: Skiing, hike the Continental Divide, fishing

Ski to the gondola from your condominium and ski back for a luncheon bowl of soup. Overstuffed furniture and classic wood tables in units with private balconies and fireplaces. Take time out to use the pool, sauna or jacuzzi. Serene summers ideal for hiking.

Ski Hill Condos

STEAMBOAT SPRINGS

Bronze Tree
1855 Ski Time Square Drive
Steamboat Springs, CO 80487
303-879-8811 800-228-2458

2 Bedrooms $$$, 3 Bedrooms $$$$
Min. Stay Ask, Visa/MC, Dep. 2 Nights •
30 condos, Hi-rise, Key at Torian Plum lobby

Location: Airport: 8 miles; Downtown: 3 miles; Ski lift: Steamboat

General Facilities: Full serv., Conf. rm. cap. 15, Daily maid, Kitchen, Linens, Baby-sitter, Child planned rec.: Ski free program

Room Facilities: Pool, Sauna, Hot tub, TV, Cable, Phone in rm., Crib-Hi-chair, Ind. Heat Ctl.

Attractions: Mountain scenery, cross country and night skiing, dog sled rides, ski jumping

Shops & Restaurants: Unique gift shops, gourmet candies, fur shop; Cipriani's/Italian

Traditional, upholstered furniture, oak trim, tile and carpet throughout. Chairlift above, village below. Children 12 and under ski free when parents purchase a five-day ski ticket, one child per parent. Stone fireplaces are stocked with native pine. Individual ski lockers, covered parking and private balconies. Summer hikes among the wildflowers, fishing, white water rafting and ballooning.

STEAMBOAT SPRINGS

Dulany Condominiums
P.O. Box 2995
Steamboat Springs, CO 80477
303-879-7900 800-525-5502

2 Bedrooms $$$, 3 Bedrooms $$$
2 Bedrms/week $$$$, 3 Bed/week $$$$
Min. Stay 7 Nights, AmEx/Visa/MC,
  Dep. 1 Night •
20 condos, Hi-rise, Key at Front desk
H-yes

Location: Airport: Stolpt 7 miles; Downtown: 3 miles; Ski lift: Nearby

General Facilities: Full serv., Bus. fac., Conf. rm. cap. 75, Daily maid, Kitchen, Linens, Baby-sitter

Room Facilities: Hot tub, Golf: Sheraton Steamboat, TV, Cable, Phone in rm., Crib-Hi-chair, Ind. Heat Ctl.

Attractions: Ranching, hiking, hunting, skiing

Shops & Restaurants: Numerous retail stores-Old Town Steamboat; 50 restaurants-varied cuisine

Each of the Dulany condominiums has a personality & character distinctly its own. The wood and tile kitchens, private balconies, and fireplace areas open on a magical view of the mountains and forest trails. Dulany's condominiums nestle on the banks of Burgess Creek, a few easy glides from Mt. Werner's base gondola. You'll experience an exhilarating sense of Steamboat's special style of personal freedom at Dulany.

Four Seasons at Steamboat
2315 Apres Ski Way
Steamboat Springs, CO 80487
303-879-4445 800-492-8466

2 Bedrooms $$
Pool, Kitchen, Phone in rm.

Summer or winter, condominium vacationing at its best. After a day of skiing, take a romantic evening sleigh ride or a dip in the hot tub or pool. The rest of the year brings warm days, cool nights and clear skies for water sports, hiking, and wilderness backpacking.

Golden Triangle Condo Resort
P.O. Box 774847
Steamboat Springs, CO 80477
303-879-2931 800-822-7669

AmEx/Visa/MC, Dep. 1 Night •
24 condos, Lo-rise, Key at Front desk

Location: Airport: 5 miles; Downtown: 2 miles; Ski lift: Nearby

General Facilities: Full serv., Conf. rm. cap. 80, Daily maid, Kitchen, Linens, Lounge, Baby-sitter, Child planned rec.: Ski free program

Room Facilities: Pool, Sauna, Hot tub, Racquetball, steam room, Golf: Sheraton Golf—2 miles, TV, Cable, Phone in rm., Crib-Hi-chair, Ind. Heat Ctl.

Attractions: Winter-dinner steak sleigh rides, natural hot springs, powder, downhill & x-country skiing

Shops & Restaurants: Mattie Silks/French American

Condominiums are minutes away from the Steamboat ski area. The bus to town is one block from the property for dining, entertainment and shopping. Spa facilities, two jacuzzis, steam room sauna, indoor and outdoor pools.

--------- STEAMBOAT SPRINGS ---------

Kutuk
P.O. Box 2995
Steamboat Springs, CO 80477
303-879-6605 800-525-5502

2 Bedrooms $$, 3 Bedrooms $$$
2 Bedrms/week $$$$, 3 Bed/week $$$$
Min. Stay 7 Nights, AmEx/Visa/MC,
    Dep. 1 Night •
32 condos, Lo-rise, Key at Front desk

Location: Airport: Stolpt 7 miles; Downtown: 3 miles; Ski lift: Nearby

General Facilities: Full serv., Bus. fac., Daily maid, Kitchen, Linens, Baby-sitter

Room Facilities: Hot tub, Golf: Sheraton Steamboat, TV, Cable, Phone in rm., Crib-Hi-chair, Ind. Heat Ctl.

Attractions: Ranching, fishing, hiking, skiing

Shops & Restaurants: Numerous retail stores-Old Steamboat and ski area; 50 restaurants-varied cuisine

Situated at the base of Mount Werner, Kutuk Condominiums are adjacent to the Christie Lifts and the many specialty shops, restaurants and night spots of Ski Time Square. All units are uniquely decorated with magnificent views of Mount Werner. Bright, open, spacious, with large outdoor hot tubs and enormous sun deck. Complimentary bottle of wine on arrival.

La Casa at Steamboat
P.O. Box 2995
Steamboat Springs, CO 80477
303-879-6036 800-525-5502

2 Bedrooms $$$, 3 Bedrooms $$$
2 Bedrms/week $$$$, 3 Bed/week $$$$
Min. Stay 7 Nights, AmEx/Visa/MC,
    Dep. 1 Night •
24 condos, Lo-rise, Key at Steamboat Lodge

Location: Airport: Stolpt 7 miles; Downtown: 3 miles; Ski lift: Nearby

General Facilities: Full serv., Bus. fac., Conf. rm. cap. 75, Daily maid, Kitchen, Linens, Baby-sitter

Room Facilities: Hot tub, Golf: Sheraton Steamboat, TV, Cable, Phone in rm., Crib-Hi-chair, Ind. Heat Ctl.

Attractions: Winter sports, fishing, hiking, hunting, golf.

Shops & Restaurants: Old Town Steamboat and ski area retail shops; 50+ restaurants

La Casa's striking sense of urban sophistication is at ease at the base of Steamboat's uncrowded ski runs. Two bubbling, soothing hot tubs, surrounded by pines and aspens, a secluded retreat from the neighboring gondolas, shops and nightlife of Ski Time Square. La Casa—for those who know that excellence is a matter of taste, not cost. A distinctly individual choice for your Steamboat vacation.

Meadows at Eagle-Ridge
Steamboat Springs, CO 80487
303-879-8811 800-228-2458

The Moraine at Steamboat
P.O. Box 771441
Steamboat Springs, CO 80488

2 Bedrooms $$$
Kitchen, Phone in rm.

Quietly elegant, meticulously appointed townhomes—private one-level spa/whirlpool hot tub, sauna, steam bath and dressing area. Mexican tile foyer, stereo intercom, heated garage, door opener. Idyllic spots for fishing, sailing, rafting. Wilderness.

—————————— STEAMBOAT SPRINGS ——————————

Pine Grove Village
P.O. Box 2995
Steamboat Springs, CO 80477
303-525-5502 800-332-5533

1 Bedroom $$, 2 Bedrooms $$
Min. Stay 7 Nights, AmEx/Visa/MC •
29 condos, Lo-rise, Key at Front desk
H-yes

Location: Airport: Stolpt 7 miles; Downtown: 3 miles; Ski lift: Steamboat
General Facilities: Daily maid, Kitchen, Linens, Baby-sitter
Room Facilities: Hot tub, Golf: Sheraton Steamboat-near, TV, Cable, Phone in rm., Crib-Hi-chair, Ind. Heat Ctl.
Attractions: Ranching, fishing, hunting town nestled to the world famous Steamboat ski area.
Shops & Restaurants: Retail stores in old town Steamboat and ski area; 50+ restaurants-varied cuisine

Friendly, neighborly mountain home with contemporary Western furnishings, clean-lined wood accented by earth and sky-tones. Pine Grove is midway between town and ski area with free city shuttle to ski area. Walk to neighboring stores and restaurants. Two new hot tubs and cozy club room.

———————————————————————————————————

Ptarmigan House Condominiums
P.O. Box 3626
Steamboat Springs, CO 80477
303-525-5502 800-332-5533

Studio $$, 1 Bedroom $$, 2 Bedrooms $$,
  3 Bedrooms $$
1 Bedrm/week $$$$, 2 Bed/week $$$$,
  3 Bed/week $$$$
Min. Stay 7 Nights, AmEx/Visa/MC,
  Dep. 1 Night •
24 condos, Lo-rise, Key at Front desk, H-yes

Location: Airport: Stolpt 7 miles; Downtown: 3 miles; Ski lift: Nearby
General Facilities: Full serv., Bus. fac., Daily maid, Kitchen, Linens, Baby-sitter
Room Facilities: Pool, Hot tub, Golf: Sheraton Steamboat, TV, Cable, Phone in rm., Crib-Hi-chair, Ind. Heat Ctl.
Attractions: Ski-in, ski-out locations. A short stroll to village shops, & restaurants
Shops & Restaurants: Retail stores, Old Steamboat and at ski area; 50+ restaurant-varied cuisine

Ptarmigan House reflects the Old World heritage of Steamboat's first skiers. Built at Mt. Werner's base, it sits on one of the Mountain's finest ski-in/ski-out locations. The condominiums reflect a quiet grace and dignity with lustrous wood detailing welcoming warmth and windows and light fixtures sparkling in the fireplace light. A short stroll away are the ski village shops, clubs, restaurants and public transit to downtown Steamboat Springs.

———————————————————————————————————

The Rockies
P.O. Box 881120
Steamboat Springs, CO 88048
303-879-8300

1 Bedroom $, 2 Bedrooms $$, Lo-rise
Pool, Daily maid, Kitchen, Phone in rm.
Golf

The firewood is stacked and ready in your Rockies vacation home, 500 yards from the base of the mountain and the Ski Time Square shopping area with restaurants and bars. Go down to the hot tubs and heated year-round pool, or stay at home and watch HBO.

STEAMBOAT SPRINGS

Ski Trails Condominiums
P.O. Box 881120
Steamboat Springs, CO 88477
303-879-2135

1 Bedroom $, 2 Bedrooms $, Lo-rise
Daily maid, Kitchen

Warm, cozy, quiet condominiums, country wallpaper and plenty of wood for the brick fireplace. Located on Headall ski run, you have ski-in, ski-out convenience. Summer nature walks on Mt. Werner. Take the Silver Bullet Gondola to the top.

Snow Flower Condominiums
P.O. Box 4406
Steamboat Springs, CO 80477
303-879-5104 800-822-7669

AmEx/Visa/MC, Dep. 1 Night •
36 condos, Lo-rise, Key at Front desk
H-yes

Location: Airport: 5 miles; Downtown: 3 miles; Ski lift: Nearby

General Facilities: Full serv., Conf. rm. cap. 80, Daily maid, Kitchen, Linens, Lounge, Baby-sitter, Child planned rec.: Ski free program

Room Facilities: Pool, Hot tub, Tennis, Golf: 2 miles Sheraton Golf, TV, Cable, Phone in rm., Crib-Hi-chair, Ind. Heat Ctl.

Attractions: Winter-dinner steak sleigh rides, natural hot springs, powder cat, downhill, x-country ski

Shops & Restaurants: Mattie Silk's/French-American

Ski down and warm yourself in the fireside lobby accented with special country touches, and relax in all that Snow Country has to offer. Light and airy condominiums highlighted by one-of-a-kind country treasures and works of art, gas fireplaces and balcony views of the valley or ski area. Ski out to the "Silver Bullet," Steamboat's high speed passenger gondola and all the base area lifts. Just steps away you'll find dining, entertainment from western to jazz, and unique boutiques.

Storm Meadows Townhomes
2135 Burgess Creek Road
Steamboat Springs, CO 80487
800-332-5942 800-525-5921

Daily maid, Kitchen, Linens, Phone in rm.

Attractions: Athletic Club

Adjacent to the ski slopes of Mt. Werner, overlooking Yampa Valley. Completely furnished townhomes with mountain-lodge fireplaces and view balconies. Warm, friendly staff—laid-back Western hospitality.

SubAlpine
P.O. Box 881120
Steamboat Springs, CO 80488
800-654-7654 800-525-7654

2 Bedrooms $
Kitchen, Linens

Beautiful view of the Yampa Vallley highlight these quiet, affordable condominiums. Half mile from the base of Steamboat ski area with free shuttle to the slopes. Summer scenic walks and relaxing days after fishing, riding, or hot air ballooning.

STEAMBOAT SPRINGS

The Lodge At Steamboat
P.O. Box 2995
Steamboat Springs, CO 80477
303-525-5502 800-332-5533

1 Bedroom $$, 2 Bedrooms $$, 3 Bedrooms $$$
2 Bedrms/week $$$$
Min. Stay 7 Nights, AmEx/Visa/MC,
   Dep. 1 Night •
120 condos, Lo-rise, Key at Front desk
H-yes

Location: Airport: Stolpt 7 miles; Downtown: 3 miles; Ski lift: Nearby

General Facilities: Full serv., Bus. fac., Conf. rm. cap. 75, Daily maid, Kitchen, Linens, Baby-sitter

Room Facilities: Pool, Sauna, Hot tub, Tennis, Skiing, Golf: Sheraton Steamboat, TV, Cable, Phone in rm., Crib-Hi-chair, Ind. Heat Ctl.

Attractions: Ranching, fishing, hiking, hunting, skiing, tennis, nightlife

Shops & Restaurants: Numerous retail stores-Old Steamboat and ski area; 50 restaurants-varied cuisine

Newly remodeled, private condominiums with floor to ceiling windows. Continuous daytime shuttle service to and from the Gondola. Hourly nighttime round-trip shuttle to shopping and entertainment. A full bathroom for every bedroom. Complimentary coffee and donuts in the Gathering Place. Large sauna, whirlpool and convenient changing rooms.

The Ranch at Steamboat
1 Ranch Road
Steamboat Springs, CO 80487
303-525-2002 800-237-2624

1 Bedroom $$, 2 Bedrooms $$, 3 Bedrooms $$$
Dep. Req'd.
Lo-rise, Key at Front desk

Location: Ski lift: Steamboat

General Facilities: Full serv., Bus. fac., Conf. rm. cap. 200, Daily maid, Kitchen, Linens, Bar on prem., Game room

Room Facilities: Pool, Sauna, Hot tub, Tennis, Nautilus-aerobic, Golf: Sheraton Steamboat, TV, Cable

Attractions: Natural hot mineral springs, rodeos, gondola rides, NASTAR ski racing, night ski, sleighs

Shops & Restaurants: Boutiques; Gourmet restaurants

Leave your car in the locked garage and let us chauffeur you through the complex or to the town of Steamboat Springs. Whether your dream is a winter ski vacation or a relaxing summer choosing your own activities, you'll enjoy the complimentary continental breakfast and daily Denver newspaper. Private balconies with electric barbecues and views of the Mt. Werner ski area.

Our goal is to provide as *complete* a listing of condo vacation properties as possible. If you know of a condo we don't list, please send us their name and address on the form at the back of this Guide.

─────────────── STEAMBOAT SPRINGS ───────────────

Timber Run
P.O. Box 2995
Steamboat Springs, CO 80477
303-879-7000 800-525-5502

1 Bedroom $$, 2 Bedrooms $$, 3 Bedrooms $$
2 Bedrms/week $$$$, 3 Bed/week $$$$
Min. Stay 7 Nights, AmEx/Visa/MC,
    Dep. 1 Night •
80 condos, Lo-rise, Key at Front desk, H-yes

Location: Airport: Stolpt 7 miles; Downtown: 3 miles; Ski lift: Steamboat

General Facilities: Bus. fac., Conf. rm. cap. 75, Daily maid, Kitchen, Linens, Baby-sitter

Room Facilities: Pool, Hot tub, Tennis, Skiing, Golf: Sheraton Steamboat-near, TV, Cable, Phone in rm., Crib-Hi-chair, Ind. Heat Ctl.

Attractions: Steamboat ski area with all winter sports. Summertime fishing, hunting, and hiking.

Shops & Restaurants: Many retail stores in the ski area and Steamboat; Many fine restaurants

Three level timber-sided buildings in tawny wood tones and deep cushioned furniture under angled red roofs. Swimming pool, hot tubs and sauna to soothe your muscles, or take the shuttle to the base area, grocery store, gift shops and nightlife. If you prefer to just relax and stay at home, there is grocery delivery and complimentary coffee and donuts.

───

Torian Plum
1855 Ski Time Square Drive
Steamboat Springs, CO 80487
303-879-8811 800-228-2458

1 Bedroom $$$$, 2 Bedrooms $$$$, 3 Bedrooms
    $$$$
Min. Stay Ask, Visa/MC, Dep. 2 Nights •
45 condos, Hi-rise, Key at Torian Plum Lobby
No S-yes

Location: Airport: 8 miles; Downtown: 3 miles; Ski lift: Nearby

General Facilities: Full serv., Daily maid, Kitchen, Linens, Restaurant on prem., Bar on prem., Baby-sitter, Child planned rec.: Ski area nursery

Room Facilities: Pool, Sauna, Hot tub, Tennis, Athletic Club, TV, Cable, Phone in rm., Crib-Hi-chair, Ind. Heat Ctl.

Attractions: Winter sports-ballooning-indoor tennis-rodeos-soccer-rugby-art/music shows

Shops & Restaurants: LaPage-French

Traditional furnishings in pastel colors, oak trim, brass accessories, all with balconies overlooking the ski area. Ski lockers next to each condominium and underground parking. In summer, white water rafting, horseback riding on mountain trails, steak-fry, hayrides, rodeo, or leave it all behind in the basket of a hot air balloon.

Tamarron

STEAMBOAT SPRINGS

Trappeurs Crossing
1855 Ski Time Square Drive
Steamboat Springs, CO 80487
303-879-8811 800-228-2458

2 Bedrooms $$, 3 Bedrooms $$$
Min. Stay Ask, Visa/MC, Dep. 2 Nights •
34 condos, Lo-rise, Key at Torian Plum Lobby

Location: Airport: 9 miles; Downtown: 4 miles; Ski lift: Nearby

General Facilities: Full serv., Conf. rm. cap. 200, Daily maid, Kitchen, Linens, Baby-sitter, Child planned rec.: Kids ski free

Room Facilities: Pool, Sauna, Hot tub, Tennis, Golf, horses, rafting, TV, Cable, Phone in rm., Crib-Hi-chair, Ind. Heat Ctl.

Attractions: Winter sports-spa facility-indoor/outdoor pool, racquetball, squash

Shops & Restaurants: Mattie Silks-Continental

Special touches at Trappeur's Crossing include gourmet kitchen and wet bar, private balconies, fireplaces, heated parking and an emphasis on rich oak trim, brass and soft colors. Carve up Steamboat's powdery slopes on over 90 different runs for all levels of skiing. Or discover the pleasures of the warm months in the Rocky Mountains with sparkling summer days, just right for hikes among the wildflowers and other outdoor activities.

--------------------- STEAMBOAT SPRINGS ---------------------

Waterford Townhomes
P.O. Box 2995
Steamboat Springs, CO 80477
303-879-7000 800-525-5502

3 Bedrooms $$$
3 Bedrms/week 4$
Min. Stay 7 Nights, AmEx/Visa/MC,
    Dep. 1 Night •
28 condos, Lo-rise, Key at Front desk
H-yes

Location: Airport: Stolpt 7 miles; Downtown: 3 miles; Ski lift: Nearby

General Facilities: Full serv., Bus. fac., Conf. rm. cap. 75, Daily maid, Kitchen, Linens, Baby-sitter

Room Facilities: Pool, Hot tub, Golf: Sheraton Steamboat, TV, Cable, Phone in rm., Crib-Hi-chair, Ind. Heat Ctl.

Attractions: Winter sports, fishing, hiking, hunting, sightseeing.

Shops & Restaurants: Old Town Steamboat and ski area retail stores; 50+ restaurants-varied cuisine

The Waterford's timber-beamed ceilings, massive stone fireplaces, enclosed by wood-paneled walls are reminiscent of a secluded mountain lodge. Tradition blends harmoniously with contemporary convenience. The townhomes overlook the ski village and the Yampa Valley. Complimentary bottle of wine, private outdoor swimming pool in summer, guest bus service and grocery delivery on request.

West Condominiums
Steamboat Springs, CO 88477

Whistler Village on the Creek
Steamboat Springs, CO 88477

Winterwood Townhomes
P.O. Box 2995
Steamboat Springs, CO 80477
303-879-6605 800-525-5502

2 Bedrooms $$
2 Bedrms/week $$$$
Min. Stay 7 Nights, AmEx/Visa/MC,
    Dep. 1 Night •
16 condos, Lo-rise, Key at Res. Mgrs. Condo
H-yes

Location: Airport: Stolpt 7 miles; Downtown: 3 miles; Ski lift: Nearby

General Facilities: Daily maid, Kitchen, Linens, Baby-sitter

Room Facilities: Hot tub, Golf: Sheraton Steamboat-near, TV, Cable, Phone in rm., Crib-Hi-chair, Ind. Heat Ctl.

Attractions: Winter sports, fishing, hiking and hunting

Shops & Restaurants: Old Town Steamboat and ski area—retail shops; 50+ restaurants-varied cuisine

Private, multi-level townhomes sheltered from the outside world by towering stands of spruce and pine. An intimate mountain hideaway, tucked away in a secluded forest glen by a crystal stream. The master bedroom suite features window seats, large, multi-drawered polished wood furnishings, queen-size bed and glass-enclosed private spa. A very personal, elegant greenhouse retreat to enjoy with your complimentary bottle of wine.

─────────────────── TELLURIDE ───────────────────

Riverside of Telluride
460 S. Pine
Telluride, CO 81435
303-728-4311 800-852-0015

1 Bedroom $$, 2 Bedrooms $$, 3 Bedrooms $$
1 Bedrm/week 4$, 2 Bed/week 5$,
  3 Bed/week 6$
AmEx/Visa/MC, Dep. Req'd. •
20 condos, Lo-rise, Key at 250 South Fir
H-yes

Location: Airport: 5 miles; Downtown: 3 blocks; Ski lift: Telluride

General Facilities: Full serv., Daily maid, Kitchen, Linens, Child planned rec.: Learn
   to ski

Room Facilities: Hot tub, TV, Cable, Phone in rm., Hi-chair, Ind. Heat Ctl.

Attractions: Telluride Ski area, historic town of Telluride, mountain scenery

Shops & Restaurants: Resort town gift shops and art galleries; La Marmotle-French

*One-level or townhouse with oak trim and oak dining furniture decorated in muted colors.
On the San Miguel River, 2.5 blocks from the ski lift and the heart of historic Telluride. All
the creature comforts in these spacious units. Year-round activities and summer music festivals.*

─────────────────── VAIL ───────────────────

Antlers At Vail
680 West Lionshead Place
Vail, CO 81657
303-476-2471 800-843-8245

Studio $$, 1 Bedroom $$, 2 Bedrooms $$$,
  3 Bedrooms $$$
1 Bedrm/week 5$, 2 Bed/week 8$,
  3 Bed/week 9$
AmEx/Visa/MC, Dep. 1 Night •
70 condos, Hi-rise, Key at Front desk, P-yes

Location: Airport: 8 miles; Downtown: 40 yards; Ski lift: Vail

General Facilities: Full serv., Bus. fac., Conf. rm. cap. 150, Daily maid, Kitchen, Linens,
   Bar on prem., Lounge, Baby-sitter

Room Facilities: Pool, Sauna, Hot tub, Tennis, Skiing, TV, Cable, VCR, Phone in rm.,
   Crib-Hi-chair, Ind. Heat Ctl.

Attractions: Entertainment

Shops & Restaurants: Art galleries, International, Polo, Cartier, Fila; Left Bank-French

Located in Lionshead on the banks of Gore Creek, walk to Vail's only gondola for unsurpassed skiing. Summer relaxation by the pool or your private balcony. Warmth and friendship surround you in this intimate mountain getaway, renowned for its hospitality and ideal location.

─────────────────── VAIL ───────────────────

Apollo Park Lodge
P.O. Box 2157
Vail, CO 81658
303-476-5881 800-872-8281

1 Bedroom $$, 2 Bedrooms $$$
AmEx/Visa/MC, Dep. Req'd.
Lo-rise, Key at Front desk

Location: Airport: Avon-winter pickup; Downtown: 3 blocks; Ski lift: Vail
General Facilities: Full serv., Daily maid, Kitchen, Linens
Room Facilities: Pool, Golf: 18-hole championship near, TV, Crib-Hi-chair
Attractions: Vail Mountain, Apres-ski, hiking, gondola rides, fishing, horses, concerts
Shops & Restaurants: 100-plus Vail Village shops and boutiques; 85 restaurants

Delightful, tastefully furnished units in the heart of Vail Village with balcony views of the mountain and Gore Creek. 19 lifts for all levels of skiing ability with minimum waits. Ski school class lessons to improve your skills. Day and night ice skating, winter or summer. Lift tickets can be ordered 3 weeks prior to your arrival. Outstanding summer activities, cultural events and concerts.

───

Bighorn Condominium
P.O. Box 400
Vail, CO 81658
303-476-5532

1 Bedroom $$
Min. Stay 4 Nights, AmEx/Visa/MC,
   Dep. Req'd. •
60 condos, Key at 4327 Steamside, H-yes

Location: Airport: 2 hours; Ski lift: Vail
General Facilities: Daily maid, Kitchen, Linens, Baby-sitter
Room Facilities: Pool, Sauna, Hot tub, Golf: Vail Golf Course near, TV, Cable, Phone in rm., Ind. Heat Ctl.
Attractions: Cross-country skiing, snowmobiling, ice skating, hiking, biking, rafting
Shops & Restaurants: Cartier, Polo, Benetton; Left Bank/French

Privately owned clean and comfortable condominiums with views of the woods and open fields. The shuttle takes you to the village or ski area in just 15 minutes. Winter ice skating. Summer hiking, biking, rafting and swimming.

───

Coldstream Condominiums
1476 Westhaven Drive
Vail, CO 81657
303-476-6106

1 Bedroom $$$, 2 Bedrooms $$$$, 3 Bedrooms
   $$$$
1 Bedrm/week 5$, 3 Bed/week 8$
Min. Stay 2 Nights, AmEx/Visa/MC,
   Dep. Req'd. •
35 condos, Lo-rise, Key at Office

Location: Airport: 2 hours Denver; Downtown: 1 mile; Ski lift: Nearby
General Facilities: Daily maid, Kitchen, Linens, Baby-sitter
Room Facilities: Pool, Sauna, Hot tub, Tennis, Racquetball, TV, Cable, VCR, Phone in rm., Crib-Hi-chair, Ind. Heat Ctl.
Attractions: Colorado Mountain College, Cascade Club, Cascade Village, movies
Shops & Restaurants: Vail is known internationally for its shopping and food

Creekside setting offers guests a special kind of solitude and privacy. Custom designed accommodations are appealingly furnished, fireplaces, electric kitchens, covered parking, private balconies and patios with view of the Rockies and within walking distance of a host of summer and winter activities, in the heart of Cascade Village.

―――――――――――――――― VAIL ――――――――――――――――

Fallridge at Vail
1650 E. Vail Valley Dr.
Vail, CO 81657
303-476-1163 800-742-8245

1 Bedroom $$, 2 Bedrooms $$$, 3 Bedrooms $$$$
Min. Stay 4 Nights, Dep. 1 Night •
50 condos, Hi-rise, Key at Front desk, H-yes

Location: Airport: Avon 9 miles; Downtown: 2 miles; Ski lift: Nearby

General Facilities: Conf. rm. cap. 60, Daily maid, Kitchen, Linens, Baby-sitter

Room Facilities: Pool, Sauna, Hot tub, Cross country skiing, Golf: Vail Golf Course, TV, Cable, Phone in rm., Crib-Hi-chair, Ind. Heat Ctl.

Attractions: Winter sports-hiking-biking-ballooning-gondola rides-rafting-photography

Shops & Restaurants: European import shops, upscale American shops, ski; Tyrolean Inn-Continental

Fallridge has been planned for relaxation and privacy. It has beautiful, unobstructed views of Vail Valley from private sun decks. Fallridge is located on the first tee of Vail's 18-hole PGA championship golf course to challenge golfers from mid-May through October, and providing an ideal touring area for cross-country skiers in winter. At day's end, gaze at the setting sun or the splendor of the alpenglow on the Gore Range.

Holiday Inn At Vail/Holiday House
13 Vail Road
Vail, CO 81657
303-476-5631 800-872-7221

1 Bedroom $$, 2 Bedrooms $$$, 3 Bedrooms $$$
Dep. Req'd.
21 condos, Hi-rise, Key at Front desk

Location: Airport: Avon 10 miles; Downtown: 2 min.; Ski lift: Vail

General Facilities: Full serv., Daily maid, Kitchen, Linens, Restaurant on prem., Bar on prem., Lounge

Room Facilities: Pool, Sauna, Hot tub, Golf: Vail 18-hole courses, TV

Attractions: Colorado Ski Museum/Ski Hall of Fame, craft fairs, bicycle race, pro-circuit tennis, fish, entertainment

Shops & Restaurants: Vail Village shops; Gold Rush Restaurant-at Inn

Condominiums ranging in size from one to five bedrooms set in a charming European-style village. All units have fireplaces, balconies, jacuzzis, underground, heated parking and laundry facilities. Skiing and winter play in the fresh, cold air, endless summer fun. Gold Rush Restaurant, Fondue Stube, Fireside Bar. Free shuttle buses throughout Vail Village.

Homestake Condominiums
1081 Vail View Drive
Vail, CO 81657
303-476-3950

1 Bedroom $, 2 Bedrooms $$, Lo-rise
Kitchen, Phone in rm.

Attractions: Skiing, Ski Museum

Condominiums in the Sandstone Lionsridge area of Vail. Studios and one bedrooms with lofts to sleep two. Underground parking, kitchenettes, superb mountain views and fireplaces with wood provided. Sandstone Shuttle to Village and ski mountain.

—————————— VAIL ——————————

Lion Square Lodge
660 W. Lion Head Place
Vail, CO 81657
303-476-2281 800-525-5788

Studio $$, 1 Bedroom $$$, 2 Bedrooms $$$$, 3
  Bedrooms $$$$
AmEx/Visa/MC, Dep. Req'd.
90 condos, Hi-rise, Key at Front desk
H-yes

Location: Downtown: 1 block; Ski lift: Vail

General Facilities: Full serv., Conf. rm. cap. 400, Daily maid, Kitchen, Linens, Restaurant on prem., Lounge

Room Facilities: Pool, Sauna, Hot tub, Tennis, Golf: Vail Golf Course, TV, Cable, Crib-Hi-chair

Attractions: Jerry Ford Invitational Golf Tournament, World Forum, music and theatrical performances

Shops & Restaurants: Vail shopping; KB Ranch Company/steak, seafood

An Alpine village 100 miles west of Denver offering an endless variety of year-round activity. Luxurious accommodations enhancing your memorable vacation in Vail's international atmosphere.

Lodge at Vail/Towers
174 E. Bore Creek Dr.
Vail, CO 81659
800-231-0136

Manor Vail Lodge
595 East Vail Valley Drive
Vail, CO 81657
303-476-5651 800-525-9165

Studio $, 1 Bedroom $$$, 2 Bedrooms $$$$
Min. Stay 7 Nights, AmEx/Visa/MC,
  Dep. Req'd. •
170 condos, Lo-rise, Key at Front desk
No S-yes/H-yes

Location: Airport: 100 miles; Downtown: 1 block; Ski lift: Vail

General Facilities: Full serv., Bus. fac., Conf. rm. cap. 600, Daily maid, Kitchen, Linens, Restaurant on prem., Bar on prem., Lounge, Baby-sitter, Child planned rec.: Day care, ski school

Room Facilities: Pool, Sauna, Hot tub, Tennis, Skiing, Golf: Vail Golf Club, TV, Cable, Phone in rm., Crib-Hi-chair, Ind. Heat Ctl.

Attractions: Gerald Ford Amphitheater, ski, Vail Village, winter/summer mountain activities

Shops & Restaurants: Vail Village-European style pedestrian village; Lord Gore Terrace

Unique personalized units with moss rock fireplaces, ideally located to enjoy the entire Vail resort, walk to ski lifts, amphitheatre, tennis, fish Gore Creek for trout, rent a bicycle, or take a gondola ride to the top of the mountain. In summer, attend art festivals, music concerts, ballet and community theater. Discos, bars, rock and roll, and quiet lounges. Ski accessories and equipment rental are available.

─────────────────── VAIL ───────────────────

Montaneros Condominiums in Vail
641 W. Lionshead Circle
Vail, CO 81657
303-476-2491 800-523-6327

1 Bedroom $$, 2 Bedrooms $$$, 3 Bedrooms $$$$
Min. Stay 2 Nights, AmEx/Visa/MC,
Dep. 3 Nights •
42 condos, Hi-rise, Key at Front desk

Location: Airport: Avon 10 miles; Downtown: 1 block; Ski lift: Vail

General Facilities: Full serv., Bus. fac., Conf. rm. cap. 100, Daily maid, Kitchen, Linens

Room Facilities: Pool, Sauna, Hot tub, Golf: Vail Golf course 3 miles, TV, Cable, Phone in rm., Crib-Hi-chair, Ind. Heat Ctl.

Attractions: Glenwood Hot Springs, Aspen, Leadville, Estes Park, Breckenridge-all within 2 hours

Shops & Restaurants: Ski shops, Ralph Lauren, Cartier, Gucci, novelty; Chanticler/con.-Tyrolean/Aus.

Located on the Lionshead Mall, Montaneros is close to Vail's boutiques and restaurants, yet steps away from the gondola and chairlift. You'll enjoy the heated outdoor pool, whirlpool, sauna and hot tub. Picnics after golf, tennis, hiking or riding. All condominiums are privately owned and decorated differently in colonial, southwestern and contemporary.

───

Mountain Haus at Vail
P.O. Box 1748
Vail, CO 81658
303-476-2434 800-237-0922

Studio $$$$, 1 Bedroom $$$$, 2 Bedrooms $$$$, 3 Bedrooms $$$$
Dep. Req'd.
Hi-rise, Key at Front desk

Location: Airport: Avon 10 miles; Downtown: 1 block; Ski lift: Vail

General Facilities: Full serv., Conf. rm. cap. 100, Daily maid, Kitchen, Linens, Restaurant on prem., Bar on prem., Game room

Room Facilities: Pool, Sauna, Hot tub, Golf: PGA courses near, TV

Attractions: Hiking, gondola rides, stream and lake fishing, horseback riding, river rafting

Shops & Restaurants: Vail elegant shops; Alain's/French country-on-site

Next to the covered bridge, these condominiums are all casually decorated by individual owners. Fireplace, balcony, color TV and all the services found in the best hotels. Superior service in a prime location. Winter enchantment of powder snow and ice skating at the Olympic Ice arena. Summer golf, tennis, fishing, hiking, horseback riding, river rafting, dining at one of Vail's patio restaurants, and shopping.

─────────────────── VAIL ───────────────────

Raintree Inn
2211 N. Frontage Road W.
Vail, CO 81657
303-476-3890 800-543-2814

1 Bedroom $$, 2 Bedrooms $$$, 3 Bedrooms $$$
Min. Stay 2 Nights, AmEx/Visa/MC,
Dep. Req'd. •
19 condos, Hi-rise, Key at Front desk
No S-yes/H-yes

Location: Airport: Denver-100 miles; Downtown: 2 miles; Ski lift: Vail

General Facilities: Full serv., Bus. fac., Conf. rm. cap. 120, Daily maid, Kitchen, Linens, Restaurant on prem., Bar on prem., Game room, Baby-sitter, Child planned rec.: Ski area

Room Facilities: Pool, Sauna, Hot tub, Horseshoes, volleyball, Golf: 10 minutes to 6 courses, TV, Cable, Phone in rm., Crib-Hi-chair, Ind. Heat Ctl.

Attractions: Skiing, hiking, rafting, shopping, biking, tours, sleigh rides, nightlife, golf, entertainment

Shops & Restaurants: Vail Village, Lionshead, shopping center next door; Pepi's/European-German

100 miles west of Denver within 10 minutes of Vail and Beaver Creek ski areas. Cozy, southwestern decor with fireplaces, decks and lofted bedrooms. Live guitar on weekends. Full shuttle service to enjoy the variety of winter and summer activities. Complimentary continental breakfast. Cozy lobby with fireplace. Football game parties in the lounge on Sundays.

───

Simba Resort
1100 N. Frontage Rd.
Vail, CO 81657
303-476-0344 800-321-1489

1 Bedroom $$, 2 Bedrooms $$
Min. Stay 2 Nights, AmEx/Visa/MC,
Dep. 25% •
70 condos, Hi-rise, Key at Front desk
No S-yes

Location: Airport: Denver-100 miles; Downtown: 1.2 miles; Ski lift: Nearby

General Facilities: Full serv., Conf. rm. cap. 20, Daily maid, Kitchen, Linens, Game room, Lounge, Baby-sitter, Child planned rec.: Day care, game room

Room Facilities: Pool, Sauna, Hot tub, Tennis, Racquetball, exercise, Golf: Vail golf course-3 miles, TV, Phone in rm., Crib-Hi-chair, Ind. Heat Ctl.

Attractions: Nordic and alpine skiing, white water rafting, golf, fishing, sightseeing, entertainment

Shops & Restaurants: Vail Village-handmade jewelry-western art; Mexican and Steaks

Sunny one-and two-bedroom condominiums decorated in earth tones and navy, green or maroon. Take a 1 mile walk to Vail Village or take the courtesy van. There is a 60' indoor pool, jacuzzi, steam room and sauna. Simba offers year-round beauty, diversified recreational activities, hospitality and charm. The resort atmosphere and privacy are quietly apart from the activity of the village.

VAIL

Sonnenalp Hotel
20 Vail Road
Vail, CO 81657
303-476-5656 800-654-8312

1 Bedroom $$$$, 2 Bedrooms 4$
Pool, Kitchen

Attractions: Guided bicycle rides, hiking, jeep trip to Colorado ghost town, white-water rafting, Cosmetique Spa, Tennis, Golf

Lobby with hand-crafted woodwork and Bavarian decor. Suites are furnished in an Alpine motif with down comforters and plush terry robes for your nightly comfort. Plenty of sunshine, clear, warm air and dry temperatures. Year-round sports activities and cultural events.

Streamside at Vail
2264 S. Frontage Rd.
Vail, CO 81657
303-476-6000 800-223-8245

Studio $, 1 Bedroom $, 2 Bedrooms $$,
   3 Bedrooms $$$
Min. Stay 2 Nights, AmEx/Visa/MC,
   Dep. 20% •
109 condos, Lo-rise, Key at Front desk
No S-yes/H-yes

Location: Airport: Avon-5 miles; Downtown: 3 miles; Ski lift: Nearby
General Facilities: Full serv., Bus. fac., Conf. rm. cap. 45, Daily maid, Kitchen, Babysitter, Child planned rec.: Nightly movies
Room Facilities: Pool, Sauna, Hot tub, Racquetball, handball, TV, Cable, Phone in rm., Crib-Hi-chair, Ind. Heat Ctl.
Attractions: Winter sports-Narrow Gauge RR-whitewater rafting-hot springs-backpacking, entertainment
Shops & Restaurants: Polo Ralph Lauren-Esprit-Bogner-Cartier-Crabtree; Left Bank-Fr. Ore House-stks

Tastefully appointed southwestern condominiums in earth tone colors on an open, wooded hillside. Streamside offers guests the quieter side of the mountains, the relaxing beauty of a serene wooded setting, the sounds of Gore Creek, and vistas of distant forests and snowy peaks. Nightly wine and cheese parties and movies. Shuttle service, indoor/outdoor pool, racquet-handball courts and exercise equipment.

The Lodge At Lionshead
P.O. Drawer 1868 380 E. Lionshead
Vail, CO 81658
303-476-2700

Studio $$, 1 Bedroom $$, 2 Bedrooms $$, 3
   Bedrooms $$$$
Min. Stay 2 Nights, AmEx/Visa/MC,
   Dep. 3 Nights •
54 condos, Lo-rise, Key at Mgt. Office

Location: Airport: Denver 100 miles; Ski lift: Vail
General Facilities: Daily maid, Kitchen, Linens, Baby-sitter
Room Facilities: Pool, Sauna, Golf: Vail Golf Club nearby, TV, Cable, Phone in rm., Crib-Hi-chair, Ind. Heat Ctl.
Attractions: Skiing, golf, tennis
Shops & Restaurants: Vail Village & Lionshead, shops, boutiques; Tea Room, Vail Valley dining

Situated along scenic Gore Creek, amid aspen and pines, providing a unique combination of seclusion and convenience. Family-oriented for summer and winter vacation experiences. Ski-in/ski-out. Shuttle to golf, tennis, hiking and bike trails.

─────────────────────── VAIL ───────────────────────

The Lodge at Vail
174 East Gore Creek Drive
Vail, CO 81657
303-476-5011 800-223-6800

1 Bedroom $$$$, 2 Bedrooms 5$, 3 Bedrooms 7$
Dep. Req'd.
Lo-rise, Key at Lobby

Location: Airport: 100 miles; Downtown: 1 block; Ski lift: Vail

General Facilities: Full serv., Kitchen, Linens, Restaurant on prem., Bar on prem., Baby-sitter

Room Facilities: Pool, Sauna, Hot tub

Attractions: Golf, tennis, horseback riding, hiking, fishing white water, vintage car races, ballooning

Shops & Restaurants: Vail shops, Lodge—15 shops; Wildflower Inn

European in commitment to service and elegance, attendant to take your skis before you check your dinner reservations or use the jacuzzi or pool. Swiss chalet style condos. Summer celebrity tournaments, vintage car races, hot air ballooning.

───

The Wren Condominiums
500 South Frontage Road, #116
Vail, CO 81657
303-476-0052 800-345-5415

Studio $$, 1 Bedroom $$$, 2 Bedrooms $$$$
Min. Stay 3 Nights, AmEx/Visa/MC,
Dep. 3 Nights
Hi-rise, Key at Front desk

Location: Airport: Stapleton; Downtown: 2 blocks; Ski lift: Vail

General Facilities: Kitchen

Room Facilities: Pool, TV, Cable, Phone in rm., Crib-Hi-chair

Attractions: 2 ski mountains, 4 18-hole golf courses, 60 tennis courts, ice skating, horses

Shops & Restaurants: Vail shops; Vail Village restaurants

All units designed for maximum privacy and unobstructed mountain views. Vail Valley winter and summer sports. Nature trails next door to your condominium. Friendly staff makes you feel at home.

───

Vail Hotel and Athletic Club
352 East Meadow Drive
Vail, CO 81657
303-476-0700 800-822-4754

Studio $$$$, 2 Bedrooms $$$$
AmEx/Visa/MC, Dep. Req'd. •
38 condos, Lo-rise, Key at Front desk

Location: Airport: 10 miles; Downtown: 50 yds.; Ski lift: Nearby

General Facilities: Full serv., Conf. rm. cap. 55, Daily maid, Kitchen, Linens, Restaurant on prem., Bar on prem., Lounge, Baby-sitter, Child planned rec.: Nursery

Room Facilities: Pool, Sauna, Hot tub, Athletic club, Golf: Vail Golf Club, TV, Cable, Phone in rm., Crib-Hi-chair, Ind. Heat Ctl.

Attractions: World-famous ski resort. Four 18-hole golf courses, tennis, shopping, dining, entertainment

Shops & Restaurants: Large amount of shops within walking distance; 352 East/Nouvelle American

Small, distinctive, elegant with full service spa and athletic club on the premises. Most rooms face the mountain. Complete amenity package in room, robes, newspapers. Band entertainment in the bar and restaurant. Golf and tennis nearby, and excellent skiing.

───────────── VAIL ─────────────

Vail International
300 E. Lionshead Circle, Box 877
Vail, CO 81658
303-476-5200

1 Bedroom $$, 2 Bedrooms $$, 3 Bedrooms $$$
Min. Stay 2 Nights, Visa/MC, Dep. Req'd. •
56 condos, Hi-rise, Key at Front desk
H-yes

Location: Airport: 7 miles; Downtown: 10 min.; Ski lift: 400 yds

General Facilities: Daily maid, Kitchen, Linens, Baby-sitter

Room Facilities: Pool, Sauna, Hot tub, Ski Vail, Golf: Vail Golf Course, TV, Cable, Phone in rm., Crib-Hi-chair, Ind. Heat Ctl.

Attractions: Vail Mountain, ice skating, cross-country skiing, snowmobiling

Shops & Restaurants: Vail's famous shops; Left Bank/French

For the family planning a ski vacation. 400 yards to "Born Free" express and gondola. Walk to Vail for shops, restaurants and nightlife. Contemporary furnishings in fully equipped condominiums with fireplaces and mountain views.

Copper Mountain Resort

———————————————————— VAIL ————————————————————

Vail Racquet Club
4690 Vail Racquet Dr., Box 1437
Vail, CO 81657
303-476-4840

1 Bedroom $$, 2 Bedrooms $$, 3 Bedrooms $$$
Min. Stay 1 Night, AmEx/Visa/MC,
 Dep. 1 Night •
Key at R. Club sales office
H-yes

Location: Airport: Avon 20 miles; Downtown: 4 miles; Ski lift: Vail

General Facilities: Conf. rm. cap. 110, Daily maid, Kitchen, Linens, Restaurant on prem., Bar on prem., Game room, Lounge, Baby-sitter, Child planned rec.: Swimming, hiking

Room Facilities: Pool, Sauna, Tennis, Ski Vail, Golf: Vail golf course-1 mile, TV, Cable, Phone in rm., Crib-Hi-chair, Ind. Heat Ctl.

Attractions: World-class ski area, golfing, tennis

Shops & Restaurants: Clothing, sportswear; Vail Racquet Club-French-Amr.

Fully equipped condominiums and townhouses with fireplaces and kitchens. Full health facility with indoor/outdoor jacuzzis, 25 meter lap pool, Olympic outdoor pool, Kaiser and Nautilus equipment, and 18 tennis courts, three of them indoors. All of this in beautiful Gore Range, 4 miles from Vail Village on free bus route.

———

Vail Run Resort
1000 Lions Ridge Loop
Vail, CO 81657
303-476-1500

Studio $$, 1 Bedroom $$, 2 Bedrooms $$$,
 3 Bedrooms $$$$
Min. Stay 2 Nights, AmEx/Visa/MC,
 Dep. 1 Night •
54 condos, Hi-rise, Key at Registr. desk

Location: Airport: 10 miles; Downtown: 1 mile; Ski lift: Vail

General Facilities: Full serv., Daily maid, Kitchen, Linens, Restaurant on prem., Game room, Baby-sitter

Room Facilities: Pool, Sauna, Hot tub, Tennis, Nautilus, TV, Cable, Phone in rm., Crib-Hi-chair, Ind. Heat Ctl.

Attractions: Rafting, horseback riding, jeep tours, fishing, hiking, tennis, golf, entertainment

Shops & Restaurants: Boutique shops throughout the village; Mataam Fez-Moroccan

Be in the middle of what's happening throughout the valley. Summer activities during cool, sunny days. World class skiing in winter. Vail's Alpine Village for shopping and dining. Free shuttle bus. Furnishings are contemporary in this complete resort with nautilus, tanning bed, indoor tennis, pool and 3 restaurants. In-room movies. Sunday keg parties.

Enter your favorite condo in our "Condo of the Year" contest (entry form is in the back of the book).

──────────── VAIL ────────────

Vail Spa   2 Bedrooms $$$$, 3 Bedrooms $$$$
710 West Lionshead Circle   Dep. Req'd.
Vail, CO 81657   Hi-rise
303-476-0882

Location: Airport: Avon; Downtown: 2 blocks; Ski lift: Vail

General Facilities: Daily maid, Kitchen, Linens, Restaurant on prem.

Room Facilities: Pool, Sauna, Hot tub, Exercise, weight room, TV, Crib-Hi-chair

Attractions: Sleigh rides, snowshoe treks, snowmobiling, ice skating

Shops & Restaurants: Vail specialty shops, stores, services; On-site restaurant

Ski Vail and Beaver Creek on a single lift ticket by taking the shuttle bus service. The Spa offers a courtesy van to and from Avon Airport, and one to Safeway twice daily. Condominiums with washer/dryer, fireplaces and a Briggs Spa whirlpool bathtub. If you're not too tired after skiing, use the outdoor pool, indoor lap pool, heated whirlpool, or steam and dry heat saunas. For non-skiers who want to stay in shape there is an exercise and weight room. Go out to dinner at the Spa or Vail restaurants.

───────────────────────────────

Village Inn Plaza Condominiums   Studio $$$$, 1 Bedroom $$$$, 2 Bedrooms
100 East Meadow Drive $$$$, 3 Bedrooms 5$
Vail, CO 81657   Min. Stay 7 Nights, AmEx/Visa/MC,
303-476-5622 800-445-4014   Dep. 2 Nights •
                                     45 condos, Hi-rise, Key at Front desk at Inn

Location: Airport: Avon-20 miles; Downtown: 1 block; Ski lift: Vail

General Facilities: Full serv., Bus. fac., Conf. rm. cap. 50, Daily maid, Kitchen, Linens, Restaurant on prem., Bar on prem., Lounge, Baby-sitter, Child planned rec.: Ski classes

Room Facilities: Pool, Sauna, Hot tub, Golf: Vail golf course-2 miles, TV, Phone in rm., Ind. Heat Ctl.

Attractions: Snowmobiling, day/night sleigh rides with lunch or dinner, nature walks

Shops & Restaurants: All types of shops in the on-site Plaza; Ambrosia-cont/ Alpenpose-Ger.

In the center of Vail Village, a block and a half from the Vista-Bon high speed quad chair, charming Alpine style condominiums with all the creature comforts. Non-skiers enjoy ice skating, snowmobiling, sleigh rides, shopping, dining, museums and art galleries throughout the village. Summer outdoor sports including gondola rides and western cookouts. Year-round heated pool and sun deck. Winter movies for the children. Continental breakfast.

--- VAIL ---

Westwind At Vail
548 South Frontage Road
Vail, CO 81657
303-476-5031 800-852-9378

1 Bedroom $$, 2 Bedrooms $$, 3 Bedrooms $$$
AmEx/Visa/MC, Dep. 1 Night •
35 condos, Lo-rise, Key at Front office
No S-yes/H-yes

Location: Airport: 9 miles; Downtown: 200 ft.; Ski lift: Nearby

General Facilities: Daily maid, Kitchen, Linens, Lounge, Baby-sitter, Child planned rec.: Day facilities

Room Facilities: Pool, Sauna, Hot tub, Ski lift, TV, Cable, VCR, Phone in rm., Crib-Hi-chair, Ind. Heat Ctl.

Attractions: Skiing, golf, tennis, rafting, horses, jeeps, ice skating, gondolas, concerts, art gallery

Shops & Restaurants: Polo Ralph Lauren, Gucci, Bullocks; Left Bank/French

Vail is a year-round resort below the peaks of the Gore Range. Although famous for skiing, there are summer activities too, golf, tennis, concerts, bicycling, kayaking, backpacking, hiking and four wheeling. Units are individually owned and warmly appointed with scenic views of Vail from private balconies on award-winning floral grounds. Free shuttle bus to over 100 shops, 75 restaurants, Beaver Creek skiing. Two outdoor hydro-spa hot pools, intimate sauna in open air courtyard, and heated pool.

The Willows Condominiums
74 E. Willow Road, P.O. Box 759
Vail, CO 81658
303-476-2233 800-826-1274

1 Bedroom $$$, Lo-rise
Daily maid, Kitchen, Linens
Golf

At the base of Vail Mountain, fully furnished condominiums central to Vail's recreation, shops and restaurants. Party lounge, sauna and whirlpool on the lodge property.

--- WINTER PARK ---

Beaver Village Condominiums
50 Village Drive, P.O. Box 3154
Winter Park, CO 80482
303-726-8813 800-525-3304

1 Bedroom $, 2 Bedrooms $$, 3 Bedrooms $$
1 Bedrm/week $$$$, 2 Bed/week 4$,
  3 Bed/week 5$
Visa/MC,Dep. 1 Night •
201 condos, Lo-rise, Key at Clubhouse, H-yes

Location: Airport: 67 miles; Downtown: 1½ blocks; Ski lift: Nearby

General Facilities: Full serv., Bus. fac., Conf. rm. cap. 210, Kitchen, Linens, Lounge, Baby-sitter, Child planned rec.: Kids' Ski School

Room Facilities: Pool, Sauna, Hot tub, TV, Cable, VCR, Phone in rm., Crib-Hi-chair, Ind. Heat Ctl.

Attractions: Winter sports, sleigh rides, tubing, hay rides, horses, fishing, biking

Shops & Restaurants: Small mountain retail shops, Safeway-3 miles; Gasthaus Eichler-German

Enter your Beaver Village condominium and notice the bag of potpourri on your vanity. Firewood is right outside your door. Nearby is the Amenity Center where you can take a soothing hot tub or play a game of backgammon. Get updates on current ski conditions and take complimentary transportation from your doorstep to the slopes. Go home with memories of fantastic skiing, crackling fires, wonderful dining and sincere personal attention.

--- VAIL ---

Hi Country Haus Resort
P.O. Box 3095
Winter Park, CO 80482
303-726-9421 800-228-1025

1 Bedroom $$, Lo-rise
Pool, Kitchen, Phone in rm.

Attractions: Tennis, swimming, hiking, rodeos, Alpine Slide, golf

Just a short 15 minute walk to downtown Winter Park's shops, restaurants and nightlife. Secluded condominiums adjacent to all activities. All the comforts of home, plus swimming pool, hot tub and sauna.

Iron Horse Resort Retreat
P.O. Box 1286, 257 Winter Park Dr.
Winter Park, CO 80482
303-726-8851 800-621-8190

Studio $$, 1 Bedroom $$$, 2 Bedrooms $$$$
Min. Stay 2 Nights, AmEx/Visa/MC,
  Dep. 2 Nights •
126 condos, Hi-rise, Key at Lobby check-in desk
H-yes

Location: Airport: 67 miles Denver; Ski lift: Winter Pk

General Facilities: Full serv., Conf. rm. cap. 120, Daily maid, Kitchen, Linens, Restaurant on prem., Bar on prem., Lounge, Baby-sitter, Child planned rec.: 5 & under ski free

Room Facilities: Pool, Sauna, Hot tub, Golf: Pole Creek-drive, TV, Cable, VCR, Phone in rm., Crib-Hi-chair, Ind. Heat Ctl.

Attractions: Jeep tours, Winter Park

Shops & Restaurants: Cooper Creek Square, Safeway Shopping Mall

Set in the rugged beauty of the Colorado Rockies, this unique vacation resort offers a perfect setting for a romantic retreat or family vacation. Magical moments in every season. Ski-in/ski-out to two mountains. Picnic at Alpine Meadows among the wildflowers or changing fall colors. Trout streams, lakes, trails for walking or riding. Friendly staff and luxury vacation homes with all the amenities.

Lookout Village Condominiums
P.O. Box 3157
Winter Park, CO 80482
303-726-8821 800-443-2781

1 Bedroom $$, 2 Bedrooms $$
1 Bedrm/week $$$$, 2 Bed/week $$$$
Dep. Req'd.
13 condos, Villas, Key at The Summit #10

Location: Airport: 67 miles; Downtown: 3 miles; Ski lift: Winter Pk

General Facilities: Daily maid, Kitchen, Linens

Room Facilities: Sauna, Hot tub, Tennis, Exercise equipment, Golf: Pole Creek 7 miles, TV, Cable, Phone in rm., Crib-Hi-chair, Ind. Heat Ctl.

Attractions: Snow tubing, alpine slide, rafting, bike trails, sleigh rides, horses, hiking, Nat. Park

Shops & Restaurants: Yellow Front, Ben Franklin, Safeway, ski, gifts; Lani's Place/ Mex-Gasthaus/Ger.

Vaulted ceilings, oak cabinetry and woodwork, upholstered furniture custom decorated in earthtones and oak on landscaped grounds with views of pines, aspens and mountain peaks. Five minute walk to Ridge Club for tennis, swimming, racquetball, game room, restaurant and lounge.

─────────────────── WINTER PARK ───────────────────

Silverado II Resort
380 Alpine Vista Lane, POB 3368
Winter Park, CO 80482
303-726-5753 800-654-7157

1 Bedroom $$, 2 Bedrooms $$$$, Lo-rise
Pool, Kitchen

No matter what the season, this is the place for fun. Learn to ski, or improve your technique. For warmer weather, raft the Colorado, backpack, hike or ride. Outdoor pool, sauna, jacuzzi, recreation room, ski shop, restaurant and bar.

The Summit
P.O. Box 3157
Winter Park, CO 80482
303-726-8834 800-443-2781

Studio $$, 1 Bedroom $$, 2 Bedrooms $$,
   3 Bedrooms $$$
Dep. Req'd.
10 condos, Lo-rise, Key at Office Summit #10
No S-yes

Location: Airport: 67 miles; Downtown: 3½ miles; Ski lift: Winter Pk

General Facilities: Daily maid, Kitchen, Linens

Room Facilities: Horseshoes, Golf: Pole Creek Golf 7 miles, TV, Cable, Phone in rm., Crib-Hi-chair, Ind. Heat Ctl.

Attractions: Grand Lake/Lake Granby recreational area, Rocky Mt. National Park, summer festivals, bikes

Shops & Restaurants: Safeway, 7-11, video, ski, gift shops, drug store; Lani's Pl/Mex.-Gasthaus Eichler

A family vacation for summer in the Rockies. Warm, bright days and cool nights. Mountain trails for hiking or biking, jazz festival, rodeos, art fair. Fully furnished and equipped condominiums nestled in the pines in a secluded wooded area. Picnic areas and vista points right out the back door. 5 minutes to the activity, yet away from it all. World-class skiing a free shuttle ride away.

Winter Park
P.O. Box 36
Winter Park, CO 80482
303-726-5587 800-453-2525

1 Bedroom $$

Never a dull moment in the friendliest valley in the Rockies. Children's center with specially trained instructors during ski season. Wildflowers covering the landscape in summer with fishing, rodeo, rafting, golf and hiking. Unpretentious hospitality.

Delaware

South Bethany
Beach

SOUTH BETHANY BEACH

King's Grant
Route 1
South Bethany Beach, DE
301-524-1200 800-437-7600

Lo-rise
Pool, Kitchen

Oceanfront and bayfront condominiums with European-styled gourmet kitchens, lofts, garden baths and fireplaces, one and a half miles between Bethany Beach, Delaware and Ocean City, Maryland. Three and four bedroom units with sun decks and jacuzzis.

Florida

AMELIA ISLAND

Amelia Island Plantation
Box 758, Highway A1A South
Amelia Island, FL 32034
904-261-6161   800-874-6878

1 Bedroom $$$$, 2 Bedrooms $$$$, 3 Bedrooms
$$$$
AmEx/Visa/MC, Dep. 1 Night •
549 condos, Villas
H-yes

Location: Airport: Jacksonville-35 min.; Downtown: 4 miles; Beach front

General Facilities: Conf. rm., Daily maid, Kitchen, Linens, Restaurant on prem., Bar on prem., Game room, Lounge, Baby-sitter, Child planned rec.: Seasonal 3-12 years

Room Facilities: Pool, Sauna, Tennis, Golf: Amelia Links & Long Point, TV, Cable, Phone in rm., Crib-Hi-chair, Ind. AC Ctl., Ind. Heat Ctl.

Attractions: Fernandina Beach, local historic shrimping village, Disney World, St. Augustine, entertainment

Shops & Restaurants: Jacksonville shopping malls; Dune Side Club, Verandah

Villa complexes with your choice of views. Boardwalk to the beach from oceanfront villas. Honeymoon villas with private indoor pools. Wake up to the morning sounds of Amelia, have breakfast and grab your golf clubs, tennis racquet, fishing gear or bathing suit to start your day. Children love the playground, kiddie pool, their own fishing pond and the Coop's fast food. 5 restaurants, ranging from romantic to casual, the Beach Club, dancing, Admiral's Lounge, music, cocktails. Too much to do to list.

─────────────── AMELIA ISLAND ───────────────

Amelia Surf & Racquet Club
800 Amelia Parkway S.
Amelia Island, FL 32034
904-261-0511 800-323-2001

1 Bedroom $$, 2 Bedrooms $$$, 3 Bedrooms $$$
1 Bedrm/week 4$, 2 Bed/week 5$,
    3 Bed/week 6$
Hi-rise

Location: Airport: Jacksonville-35 min.; Beach front

General Facilities: Kitchen

Room Facilities: Pool, Tennis, Surf fishing, Golf: Nearby, TV, Cable, Crib-Hi-chair

Attractions: Horseback riding, deep-sea fishing, wind surfing, sightseeing, cultural events, golf

Shops & Restaurants: Fernandina Beach shops

Professional decorated villas with spacious balconies or patios. Self-contained resort with oaks, palms, dunes and tropical flowers. Improve your tennis on the soft clay courts with lessons from the teaching professional. Wide variety of year-round sports and cultural events.

───

Oceans Of Amelia
382 S. Fletcher Road
Amelia Island, FL 32034
904-261-4013

2 Bedrooms $$, Hi-rise
Pool, Kitchen

Attractions: Walt Disney and Sea World, Jacksonville theatre, night spots and sports

Tastefully decorated units with seaside balconies. Start your day on the beach or at the pool, then go sightseeing in the seaport town of Fernandina with its restauranats and nightly music. Also available nearby are tennis courts, golf, and ocean pier.

─────────────── BOCA RATON ───────────────

La Boca Casa by the Ocean
365 North Ocean Boulevard
Boca Raton, FL 33432
407-392-0885

1 Bedrm/week $$
Min. Stay 7 Nights, AmEx/Visa/MC,
    Dep. Req'd. •
19 condos, Lo-rise, Key at Office by the pool

Location: Airport: 20 miles; Downtown: 1/3 mile; Need car

General Facilities: Kitchen, Linens

Room Facilities: Pool, Hot tub, Golf: Executive Golf/4 blocks, TV, Cable, Phone in rm., Crib-Hi-chair, Ind. AC Ctl., Ind. Heat Ctl.

Attractions: Superior restaurants, shopping, jai alai, polo, racing, golf, cruises, snorkeling

Shops & Restaurants: Saks, Lord & Taylor, Bloomingdales, Burdine's; La Vielle Maison-5-star

Earth tones, wicker and plants decorate these 1 bedroom condos. Prestigious Boca Raton offers polo matches, five-star dining and exceptional shopping. Just steps away from a quiet beach, surrounded by bicycling and jogging paths, or use the heated swimming pool and jacuzzi. Nearby are tropical parks and reefs for snorkeling. Thoroughbred and harness racing, or one-day cruises to the Bahamas.

Bronze Tree

BONITA SPRINGS

Bonita Beach Resort
26395 Hickory Boulevard
Bonita Springs, FL 33923
813-992-2137

Studio $, 1 Bedroom $
1 Bedrm / week $$$$
Lo-rise

Location: Airport: Southwest Florida

General Facilities: Kitchen, Linens

Room Facilities: Fishing

Attractions: Beaches, dog track, golf course, Thomas Edison Lab., Shell Factory, Everglades Gardens

Shops & Restaurants: Fort Myers and Naples shopping

An original Florida fishing camp, now a comfortable resort. Tropical plants and palm trees shade the children's play area and picnic tables. Boat ramp and docks behind the apartments, lighted for night fishing. Beach with a 5 mile unbroken shoreline for swimming and boating, or look for some of the 300 varieties of shells found on the beach and sand bars.

---------------------------- CAPE HAZE ----------------------------

Palm Island Resort
7092 Placida Road
Cape Haze, FL 33946
813-697-4800 800-824-5412

1 Bedroom $$, 2 Bedrooms $$$$, 3 Bedrooms $$$$+
1 Bedrm/week 5$, 2 Bed/week 7$, 3 Bed/week 9$
Min. Stay 2 Nights, AmEx/Visa/MC, Dep. Req'd. •
160 condos, Lo-rise, Key at Reception-Mainland

Location: Airport: Sarasota-45 miles; Downtown: 6 miles; Need car; Beach front

General Facilities: Full serv., Bus. fac., Conf. rm. cap. 100, Kitchen, Linens, Restaurant on prem., Bar on prem., Lounge, Baby-sitter, Child planned rec.: Fishing poles, bikes

Room Facilities: Pool, Hot tub, Tennis, Charter Fishing, Golf: 3 Golf courses-10 miles, TV, Cable, Phone in rm., Ind. AC Ctl., Ind. Heat Ctl.

Attractions: Sarasota-1 hr., John Ringling and Thomas Edison Museum, Jungle Gardens, St. Armands Circle, entertainment

Shops & Restaurants: Boca Grande Boutiques, Venice: Avenue of Boutiques; Garfields, The Pink Elephant

Deluxe accommodations located on an island with no bridges or causeways from the mainland, no cars and no crowds, quiet and unspoiled surroundings, all Gulf-front views with 3 miles of shell-laden beach. Private club launch between island and mainland for guests only, open air tram continually circles resort. Great place for couples/honeymooners, families and small groups. Florida's only true out-island resort. Golf carts, tandem bikes and canoes available for rent.

------------------------- CAPTIVA ISLAND -------------------------

South Seas Plantation
13000 Plantation Road, Box 194
Captiva Island, FL 33924
813-472-5111 800-237-3102

Lo-rise
Pool, Kitchen

Attractions: Water sports, sailing school, cruises to Cabbage Key, Useppa Island, Pine Island Sound, Tennis, Golf

Choose a unit in one of four separate, small, intimate complexes, two overlooking the golf course, one with bay and yachting vistas, and one with beachfront living. Miles of private beach for swimming and strolling, deep water yacht harbor, and golf pro shop.

─────────────── COCOA BEACH ───────────────

Ocean Landings Resort
900 North Atlantic Avenue
Cocoa Beach, FL 32931
407-783-9430

Studio $, 1 Bedroom $$, 2 Bedrooms $$
AmEx/Visa/MC, Dep. 1 Night •
228 condos, Hi-rise, Lo-rise, Key at Front lobby
H-yes

Location: Airport: 50 miles-Orlando; Downtown: 1 mile; Need car; Beach front

General Facilities: Full serv., Bus. fac., Daily maid, Kitchen, Linens, Restaurant on prem., Bar on prem., Game room, Lounge, Baby-sitter

Room Facilities: Pool, Sauna, Hot tub, Tennis, Racquetball, nautilus, TV, Cable, Phone in rm., Crib-Hi-chair, Ind. AC Ctl., Ind. Heat Ctl.

Attractions: EPCOT, Kennedy Space Center, Port Canaveral cruises, deep-sea fishing, equipment rentals, entertainment

Shops & Restaurants: Ron Jon's Surf Shop, Malls; Cocoa Cabana/continental

95 oceanfront units in contemporary, casual style. A complete resort with tennis, racquetball, 2 pools, heated spa, sauna, exercise equipment, barbecues, aerobics classes and get-together breakfasts. The closest beach to Disney World and a perfect alternative to the crowded Orlando scene.

Seagull Beach Club
4440 Ocean Beach Boulevard
Cocoa Beach, FL 32931
407-783-4441

1 Bedroom $$, 2 Bedrooms $$
1 Bedrm/week $$$$, 2 Bed/week 4$
Dep. Req'd. •
36 condos, Lo-rise, Key at Office

Location: Airport: 1½ hours; Need car; Beach front

General Facilities: Kitchen, Linens

Room Facilities: Cable, Phone in rm., Crib, Ind. AC Ctl., Ind. Heat Ctl.

Attractions: Kennedy Space Center, Disney Sea World, Brevard Art Museum

Shops & Restaurants: Basic grocery, Ron Jon's Surf Shop; Bernard's Surf/Italian

Basic beach style one and two bedroom suites in earth tones located directly on the Atlantic Ocean in Cocoa Beach. Swimming pool, beach, and rooftop observation deck. Within walking distance of Cocoa Beach's finer restaurants and shops, and the closest beach to Disney World, Kennedy Space Center and EPCOT Center.

─────────────── CRYSTAL BEACH ───────────────

Sutherland Crossing
962 Seaview Circle, P.O. Box 883
Crystal Beach, FL 34681
813-786-2287

3 Bedrooms $$
3 Bedrms/week 6$
Min. Stay 2 Nights, Visa/MC, Dep. 25% •
Villas, Key at Clubhouse

Location: Airport: 35 minutes; Downtown: 10 min.; Need car

General Facilities: Daily maid, Kitchen, Linens, Restaurant on prem., Game room, Lounge, Baby-sitter

Room Facilities: Pool, Hot tub, Tennis, Mini golf, TV, Cable, Phone in rm., Crib-Hi-chair, Ind. AC Ctl., Ind. Heat Ctl.

Attractions: Busch Gardens, EPCOT Center, entertainment

Shops & Restaurants: Countryside and Clearwater Malls, Burdines, Sears; Jesse's Dockside-seafood

Single-family, "tree house style" villas in a natural, quiet setting, beautifully furnished in blues, mauve and green. Heated pool, jacuzzi, mini-golf, tennis, basketball and trips to "Honeymoon Island" via the Sutherland Express pontoon boat.

─────────────── DAYTONA BEACH SHORES ───────────────

Dolphin Beach Club   Pool, Kitchen, Phone in rm.
3355 South Atlantic Avenue
Daytona Beach Shores, FL 32018
904-761-8130

Attractions: Daytona International Speedway, Shuffleboard

Water activities during the sunny days, glorious sunsets and the many activities of Daytona Beach. Efficiency and 1 bedroom units with complete kitchens.

Fantasy Island Resort II   Pool, Kitchen, Phone in rm.
3175 S. Atlantic Ave.
Daytona Beach Shores, FL 32018
904-756-9446

Attractions: Daytona International Speedway

Beautiful weather and many water activities make this a favorite family resort. Barbecue grills and picnic areas for casual meals. Daytona Beach nightlife.

Seven Seas Resort Condo
2433 S. Atlantic Ave.
Daytona Beach Shores, FL 32018
904-257-1180

Sunglow   1 Bedroom $$, 2 Bedrooms $$$, Hi-rise
3647 S. Atlantic Avenue   Pool, Kitchen
Daytona Beach Shores, FL 32019
904-756-4005 800-225-3396

Attractions: Jai alai, greyhound racing, ten golf courses, Daytona Speedway

A luxury condominium for the price of a hotel room on Florida's picturesque coastline. Professionally decorated with all the comforts of home and close to Florida's major attractions. Game room, pool, jacuzzi, sauna. Oceanfront.

─────────────── DEERFIELD BEACH ───────────────

Avalon   Lo-rise
735 South A1A   Pool, Kitchen
Deerfield Beach, FL 33441
305-427-6611 800-424-1943

Attractions: Golf, tennis, fishing, boating, surfing, shuffleboard, put. green

A place to relax, soak up the sun and change to a leisurely life-style. Many area activities, a few miles to Boca Raton and Fort Lauderdale.

Emerald Seas   1 Bedroom $$, 2 Bedrooms $$$, Lo-rise
660 N. Ocean Blvd.   Pool, Daily maid, Kitchen
Deerfield Beach, FL 33441   Shuffleboard
305-427-1300

On Florida's Gold Coast, large beach, almond/blue designer kitchens, restful furnishing accentuating the colors of the outdoors. Two pools, unsurpassed fishing, charter boats, spectator sports, nightlife. A pleasurable experience in a tranquil setting.

─────────────── DEERFIELD BEACH ───────────────

Inn At Deer Creek Racquet Club
9 Deer Creek Road, A105
Deerfield Beach, FL 33442
305-421-7800 800-327-1699

Studio $, 1 Bedroom $$
1 Bedrm/week 4$
AmEx/Visa/MC, Dep. Req'd. •
25 condos, Villas, Key at Front desk
H-yes

Location: Airport: Ft. Lauderdale; Downtown: 3 miles; Need car

General Facilities: Full serv., Bus. fac., Conf. rm. cap. 160, Daily maid, Kitchen, Linens, Restaurant on prem., Lounge, Child planned rec.: Tennis clinic

Room Facilities: Pool, Tennis, Golf: Deer Creek Country Club, TV, Cable, Phone in rm., Crib, Ind. AC Ctl., Ind. Heat Ctl.

Attractions: Nearby golf, beaches, water ski, Everglades, airboats, Ocean World, cruises

Shops & Restaurants: Bloomingdales, Lord & Taylor, Boca Town Center; Sea Watch/ seafood/continental

Villas with lofts, private jacuzzis, and balconies set among palms, lakes, fountains and tropical landscaping. Play an early morning set of tennis, round of golf, or dip in the pool, then lunch at the Matchpoint Lounge or have a poolside snack. Atlantic Ocean beaches are minutes away. 15 minutes to entertainment, parks, shopping, sports and restaurants. Golf Club dining room offers gourmet meals.

─────────────── DEL REY BEACH ───────────────

Spanish River Resort
1111 E. Atlantic Blvd.
Del Rey Beach, FL 33483
800-453-7946

1 Bedroom $$, 2 Bedrooms $$$, Hi-rise
Pool, Daily maid, Kitchen, Linens

Attractions: Sightseeing Cruises, Fishing, Horse/Dog racing, Trotters, jai alai, Spr. Training, Everglades, Volleyball, Tennis

─────────────── DELRAY BEACH ───────────────

The Berkshire
1775 South Ocean Boulevard
Delray Beach, FL 33483
407-272-1100

1 Bedroom $$, Lo-rise
Pool, Kitchen

One bedroom condominiums on a private beach. Cabanas, heated pool, putting green and shuffleboard.

Dover House Beach Resort
110 S. Ocean Blvd.
Delray Beach, FL 33444
305-276-0309

1 Bedroom $$, Lo-rise
Pool, Kitchen

Bermuda style buildings with white railings and pool furniture, green lawns, palms and shubbery. Units have wall-to-wall windows for the marvelous ocean view, two cable televisions, ceiling fans, music/intercom system, and whirlpool tubs.

The Hamilton House
1213 S. Ocean Blvd.
Delray Beach, FL 33444
305-276-5890

──────────── DELRAY BEACH ────────────

International Tennis Resort
651 Egret Circle
Delray Beach, FL 33444
305-272-4126 800-327-1160

1 Bedroom $, 2 Bedrooms $$
1 Bedrm/week $$$$, 2 Bed/week 4$
AmEx/Visa/MC
Hi-rise

Location: Downtown: 2 min.

General Facilities: Full serv., Daily maid, Kitchen, Linens, Restaurant on prem., Bar on prem.

Room Facilities: Pool, Tennis, Fitness Ctr. Racquet, Golf: Nearby, TV, Cable, Phone in rm., Ind. AC Ctl., Ind. Heat Ctl.

Attractions: Jai alai, polo, dog and thoroughbred racing, deep-sea fishing, Gold Coast beaches

Shops & Restaurants: Linton International Shopping Plaza; Tree Tops

A tennis player's paradise with 44 courts, instruction, clinics and year-round camps. 100 beautifully landscaped acres with biking, jogging trails. 3 swimming pools, 2 racquetball courts, walk to the beach, shopping plaza or Palm Beach gym. Comfort and privacy in tastefully decorated suites with everything you need for living and entertainment. Close to boutiques, art galleries, theaters, cafes, restaurants and night clubs. World-class resort amenities.

Spanish River Resort & Beach Club
1111 E. Atlantic Ave.
Delray Beach, FL 33483
407-243-7946 800-543-7946

Studio $$, 1 Bedroom $$, 2 Bedrooms $$$
1 Bedrm/week $$$$, 2 Bed/week 6$
AmEx/Visa/MC, Dep. Req'd. •
72 condos, Hi-rise, Key at Desk in Lobby
H-yes

Location: Airport: W. Palm Beach 15 mi.; Downtown: 3 bolcks; Beach front

General Facilities: Full serv., Bus. fac., Conf. rm. cap. 50, Daily maid, Kitchen, Linens, Restaurant on prem., Bar on prem., Game room, Lounge, Baby-sitter

Room Facilities: Pool, Sauna, Tennis, Volleyball, TV, Cable, VCR, Phone in rm., Crib-Hi-chair, Ind. AC Ctl., Ind. Heat Ctl.

Attractions: Sightseeing cruises, Fishing, Horse/Dog Races, Horses, jai alai, Spring Training, Everglades

Shops & Restaurants: Worth Ave., Lord & Taylor, Bloomingdales, Saks; Banana Boat-Seafood

Affordable, luxurious 11-story hi-rise with balconies and breathtaking views overlooking public beach and intercoastal waterway. Nestled in quaint shopping district midway between Palm Beach and Boca Raton. Traditionally furnished with the most modern kitchen conveniences for stay-at-home dinners. Call ahead for limo pickup from the airport.

―――――――――――――――――― DESTIN ――――――――――――――――――

Beach House Condominiums
4800 Highway 98 East
Destin, FL 32541
904-837-6131 800-874-8914

1 Bedroom $$
Min. Stay 3 Nights, Visa/MC, Dep. Req'd. •
106 condos, Hi-rise, Key at Beach House

Location: Airport: Elgin 25 miles; Downtown: 7 miles; Need car; Beach front

General Facilities: Full serv., Kitchen, Linens, Game room, Child planned rec.: Easter
to Labor Day

Room Facilities: Pool, Tennis, Shuffleboard, volleyball, Golf: 6 miles two courses, TV,
Cable, VCR, Phone in rm., Crib-Hi-chair, Ind. AC Ctl., Ind. Heat Ctl.

Attractions: Sailing, fishing, diving, scuba, swimming, golf, tennis, water skiing.

Shops & Restaurants: Shoreline Village Mall, Downtown Destin, Shores; Marina Cafe-
Flamingo Cafe

*Gulf-front condominiums on the quiet side of Destin, away from the crowds, yet close to
vacation pleasures. Swimming pool, gazebo, kiddie pool, teen room, tennis, organized
summer recreation. Something for the whole family.*

Breakers East
1010 Highway 98 East
Destin, FL 32541
800-338-4418

*Summer or winter, a great vacation. Shopping, golf, fishing, dining within a two-mile
radius. Improve your tan by the Gulfside pool or on the sand dune beach. New con-
dominiums with two lighted tennis courts.*

Cabana Club
Hwy. 98 East
Destin, FL 32541
904-837-4853 800-874-8914

1 Bedroom $$

*Overlooking the sparkling blue-green waters of the Gulf of Mexico. Perfect vacation retreat
for beach lovers. Relax in your private jacuzzi, enjoy a cool drink on your balcony while
watching the sunset, spend a day on the uncrowded beach.*

Coral Reef Club
Hwy 98 East
Destin, FL 32541
904-837-4853 800-874-8914

1 Bedroom $$

*East of Henderson Beach State Park, two miles from Destin, new condominiums close to
golf and fishing. Enjoy beach activities or sunbathe by the covered, heated pool.*

Crystal Villas
2850 Hwy. 98 East
Destin, FL 32541
904-837-4853 800-874-8914

1 Bedroom $$

*Watch your children build sandcastles or swim in the shallows and tidal pools of this quiet
beach. Shopping, fishing, golf, restaurants are all close. Enclosed heated pool and beach
service.*

DESTIN

Destin Beach Club
1150 Hwy. 98 East
Destin, FL 32541
904-837-3985

1 Bedrm/week $$$$
Min. Stay 3 Nights, AmEx/Visa/MC, Dep.
Req'd.
47 condos, Lo-rise

Location: Airport: Destin Airport; Downtown: 5 min.; Beach front
General Facilities: Kitchen
Room Facilities: Pool, Hot tub, TV
Attractions: Destin Racquet Club, Bayou Golf Course, fishing charters
Shops & Restaurants: Shores Shopping Center; Seafood

Enjoy Florida's romantic sunsets in this beachfront getaway paradise. Contemporary designed units set in a fishing village atmosphere. 10:00 p.m. to 10:00 a.m. quiet time.

Destin Towers Condominiums
1008 Highway 98 East
Destin, FL 32541
904-837-7002 800-338-4418

2 Bedrms/week $6
Min. Stay 7 Nights, Dep. Req'd.
Hi-rise

Location: Airport: Destin Airport; Beach front
General Facilities: Kitchen, Linens
Room Facilities: Pool, Tennis, Golf: Indian Bayou Golf l mile
Attractions: Indian Bayou Golf and Country Club, fishing, sailing, surfing

Take one of two elevators to your condominium in the 16-story Destin Towers. Full balcony overlooking the pool, clubhouse and gulf. Beach service rental of Hobie Cats, cabanas, chairs and umbrellas. Protected walkway from covered parking to the Towers. Family oriented, convenient to Destin activities and entertainment.

Destin Yacht Club
320 Hwy 98 East
Destin, FL 32541
904-837-4853 800-874-8914

Panoramic views of Destin Harbor and the Gulf, boat docks, large balconies. Master bath jacuzzi, second bath sauna. Pool, restaurant and bar. 5 minute drive to beach.

East Pass Towers
100 Gulfshore Drive
Destin, FL 32541
904-837-4191 800-541-4191

Studio $$, 2 Bedrooms $$, 3 Bedrooms $$$
Min. Stay 3 Nights, Visa/MC, Dep. Req'd. •
55 condos, Hi-rise, Key at Office

Location: Airport: 2.5-3 miles; Downtown: 2.5 mile; Beach front
General Facilities: Bus. fac., Daily maid, Kitchen, Linens
Room Facilities: Pool, Hot tub, Marine facility, TV, Cable, VCR, Phone in rm., Crib-Hi-chair, Ind. AC Ctl., Ind. Heat Ctl.
Attractions: Sport fishing, snorkeling, diving trips, golf courses
Shops & Restaurants: Shores Shopping Center, Shoreline Mall; Marina Cafe

On the tip of Holiday Isle, breathtaking views from large balconies, miles of fine sugar-white beaches to enjoy and explore. Pool, jacuzzi, exercise room, marina, beach service, security. Minutes from downtown. Diving and fishing trips. Boat slip available with power, phone, TV cable. Large boats welcome.

DESTIN

Edgewater Beach Condominium　1 Bedroom $$, 2 Bedrooms $$, 3 Bedrooms $$$
5000 Highway 98 East　1 Bedrm/week 4$, 2 Bed/week $5,
Destin, FL 32541　3 Bed/week 6$
904-837-5800 800-322-7263　Min. Stay 3 Nights, Visa/MC, Dep. Req'd.
Hi-rise, Key at Office

Location: Downtown: 5 min.; Beach front

General Facilities: Kitchen, Linens, Restaurant on prem.

Room Facilities: Pool, Tennis, TV, Cable, Phone in rm.

Shops & Restaurants: Edgewater shopping

The French Riviera in Florida. Unique condominiums with cultured marble baths, mirrored closets, hanging gardens on your private balcony. Lush landscaping with three pools fed by a waterfall, illuminated at night. Private beach in a natural paradise.

Emerald Towers　2 Bedrooms $$
1044 Highway 98 East　Min. Stay 3 Nights, Visa/MC, Dep. Req'd.
Destin, FL 32541　82 condos, Hi-rise, Key at Office
904-837-6575 800-874-8914

Location: Airport: 20 miles; Downtown: 1 mile; Beach front

General Facilities: Full serv., Daily maid, Kitchen, Linens, Child planned rec.: Mem. Day-Labor Day

Room Facilities: Pool, Sauna, Tennis, TV, Cable, VCR, Phone in rm., Crib-Hi-chair, Ind. AC Ctl., Ind. Heat Ctl.

Attractions: Fishing charters, sailing, waterpark, golf, beach service, skiing, tennis, entertainment

Shops & Restaurants: Gayfers, McRae's, Penney, Sears, Shoreline Mall; Marina Cafe/Capt. Dave's/Pier98

Two and three bedroom units with private steam, sauna and whirlpool. Pool, tennis, beach service, exercise rooms. Walk to shopping, restaurants. Luxury and quality for your season in the sun.

Gulf Terrace Condominiums
Hwy. 98 East
Destin, FL 32541
904-837-4720 800-992-4720

Holiday Beach Resort—Destin　1 Bedroom $, 2 Bedrooms $$, Lo-rise
U.S. 98 East, P.O. Box 125　Pool, Kitchen, Linens
Destin, FL 32541
904-932-4298 800-874-0402

Attractions: Spa, Tennis

Emerald gulf waters and white sugar sand beach to get rid of your everyday cares. Boardwalks, pool, spa, tennis.

Trappeur's Crossing

──────────── DESTIN ────────────

Holiday Surf & Racquet Club   Hi-rise
510 Gulf Shore Drive   Pool, Kitchen
Destin, FL 32541
904-837-6108 800-833-6108

Attractions: Shuffleboard, Volleyball, Tennis

Your family will love the summer here, while spring and fall are ideal times for adults. Pool, tennis, health clubs, shuffleboard, volleyball, barbecues, swing sets and miles of beautiful, white beach.

───────────────────────────

Huntington by the Sea   1 Bedroom $$
Hwy. 98 East   Min. Stay 3 Nights, Visa/MC, Dep. Req'd.
Destin, FL 32541   21 condos, Hi-rise, Key at Office
904-837-7811 800-874-8914

Location: Airport: 20 miles; Downtown: 6 miles; Need car; Beach front

General Facilities: Full serv., Kitchen, Linens

Room Facilities: Pool, TV, Cable, VCR, Phone in rm., Ind. AC Ctl., Ind. Heat Ctl.

Attractions: Deep-sea fishing, charters for sailing, golf, tennis, swimming

Shops & Restaurants: Shoreline Village Mall, The Market, downtn Destin; Marina Cafe-Flamingo-Scampi's

If you want privacy and seclusion, this is for you. Like being on a tropical island. Swim in the gulf or pool, or take a quiet walk. Barbecues, gazebo, private view balconies. All units individually furnished with modern decor.

─────────────────────── DESTIN ───────────────────────

Inlet Reef Club
506 Gulf Shore Drive
Destin, FL 32541
904-837-6100

2 Bedrooms $$, Hi-rise
Pool, Kitchen

Attractions: Sport fishing, Exercise room, Tennis, Golf

Large apartments with Gulf view private terraces on architecturally designed property. Separate utility rooms, wet bar and pass-through, covered parking. Beach, tennis, pool, sauna and exercise room.

The Islander Condominium
502 Gulf Shore Drive
Destin, FL 32541
904-837-1000

2 Bedrooms $$, Hi-rise
Pool, Kitchen, Linens, Phone in rm.

Attractions: Tennis

On Holiday Isle, a short drive to 5 golf courses and the deep-sea fishing fleet. Beachside cabanas with barbecue, picnic tables, palm trees. Carefree vacation living.

Jetty East Condominium Assoc.
500 Gulf Shore Dr.
Destin, FL 32541
904-837-2141 800-368-0222

Hi-rise
Pool, Kitchen, Linens, Phone in rm.

Attractions: October festivals, sailing, fishing, windsurfing, scuba, snorkeling, tennis, golf

Water sports for everyone and the world's luckiest fishing fleet. Personally decorated completely furnished units. Pool, tennis, 900 feet of beach.

Mainsail
5100 Hwy 98 East
Destin, FL 32541
904-837-7711 800-874-8914

Studio $$, 2 Bedrooms $$, 3 Bedrooms $$$
Min. Stay 3 Nights, Visa/MC, Dep. Req'd. •
189 condos, Hi-rise

Location: Airport: 25 miles; Downtown: 5 miles; Need car; Beach front

General Facilities: Full serv., Daily maid, Kitchen, Linens, Game room, Child planned rec.: Mem.Day-Labor Day

Room Facilities: Pool, Sauna, Hot tub, Tennis, Shuffleboard, TV, Cable, Phone in rm., Crib-Hi-chair, Ind. AC Ctl., Ind. Heat Ctl.

Attractions: Charter fishing, sailing, water sports, tennis, water skiing, windsurfing

Shops & Restaurants: Destin, Shoreline Village Mall, The Market; Marina Cafe-Pier 98-Scampi's

Eight miles east of Destin's Main Street on a 15-acre tract on the Gulf. 4 tennis courts, 2 pools, 2 kiddie pools, walk to 3 shopping centers. Unforgettable combination of sand, sun and surf. Units with wet bars, jacuzzis and ceiling fans.

Sailfish Yacht Club
504 Hwy. 98 East
Destin, FL 32541
904-837-6027

──────────── DESTIN ────────────

Sandestin Beach Resort
Emerald Coast Parkway
Destin, FL 32541
904-267-8000 800-874-3950

1 Bedroom $$$, 2 Bedrooms $$$, 3 Bedrooms $$$
1 Bedrm/week 5$, 2 Bed/week 6$,
3 Bed/week 7$
175 condos, Hi-rise

Location: Airport: Pensacola; Beach front

General Facilities: Bus. fac., Conf. rm. cap. 600, Kitchen, Restaurant on prem., Bar on prem., Game room, Lounge, Child planned rec.: Organized day camps

Room Facilities: Pool, Sauna, Tennis, Health facilities, Golf: 2 18-hole courses

Attractions: Golf, tennis, fishing, marina, October Destin Fishing Rodeo and Seafood Festival, entertainment

Shops & Restaurants: Complete array of clothing and specialty shops; Elephant Walk, Babe's Seafood

Choose from villas or tower units in this award-winning 2800-acre resort with 7.5 miles of waterfront. Golf and tennis packages, lessons and pro shops. Fishing charters, freshwater fishing in stocked lakes, marina for your boat. Water sport rentals available on the beach for Hobie catamarans, sailboards, Aqua Trikes or lie in the sun and get a golden tan. Four restaurants, on-site shopping. Honeymoon package with champagne, decorative glasses, fruit basket, dinner for two and half-day bicycle rental.

Sandestin High Rise
Highway 98 E
Destin, FL 32541
904-267-8000 800-874-3900

Sandpiper Cove Resort
Hwy. 98 Box 158
Destin, FL 32541
904-837-9121 800-874-0448

1 Bedroom $$, 2 Bedrooms $$, Villas
Pool, Kitchen

Elegant condominium living on 43 acres—tennis, 9-hole golf, 4 pools, boat ramp, waterfront restaurant and lounge, beachside pavilion with refreshment center.

Sealoft
3460 Hwy. 98 East
Destin, FL 32541
904-837-4853 800-874-8914

2 Bedrooms $$

Adjacent to State Wayside Park overlooking the Gulf of Mexico. Fireplace, jacuzzi, washer/dryers. For the vacationer who wants a relaxing beach vacation.

Seascape
100 Seascape Drive
Destin, FL 32541
904-837-9181 800-874-9106

1 Bedroom $$, 2 Bedrooms $$$, Lo-rise, Villas
Pool, Kitchen

Attractions: Gulfarium Zoo, Roller Skating, Indian Museum, Biking, hiking, Tennis

Located on Florida's Emerald Coast, 18-hole golf course, 8 tennis courts, both with pro shops, lessons, clinics and tournaments, 5 pools, 1500 feet of unspoiled beach with unmatched solitude and beach club. Freshwater lakes, subtropical vegetation.

--- DESTIN ---

Shoreline Towers & Townhomes
P.O. Box 1006
Destin, FL 32541
904-837-9163   800-874-0162

2 Bedrooms $$, Hi-rise
Pool, Kitchen

Attractions: Golf, sailing, tennis, scuba, charter fishing, Racquetball

Towers have large two and three bedroom condos on the Gulf of Mexico with Clubhouse, tennis, racquetball and pool. Townhomes with parquet floors, carpeting, cathedral ceilings, marble fireplaces and private access to the beach.

Summer Breeze
Hwy. 98 East
Destin, FL 32541
904-837-4853   800-874-8914

1 Bedroom $$

Affordable vacation in a low-density project away from traffic noise. Close to shopping, restaurants and entertainment. Pool, jacuzzi and barbecue.

SunDestin
1040 Hwy. 98 East
Destin, FL 32541
904-837-7093   800-874-8914

1 Bedroom $$
AmEx/Visa/MC, Dep. Req'd. •
280 condos, Hi-rise, Key at Front desk
H-yes

Location: Airport: Destin 2 miles; Downtown: 1 mile; Beach front

General Facilities: Daily maid, Kitchen, Linens, Restaurant on prem., Game room, Lounge, Baby-sitter, Child planned rec.: May thru Labor Day

Room Facilities: Pool, Sauna, Hot tub, Shuffeboard, TV, Cable, Phone in rm., Crib-Hi-chair, Ind. AC Ctl., Ind. Heat Ctl.

Attractions: Sailing, fishing, swimming

Shops & Restaurants: Marina Cafe, Flamingo Cafe

Less than 5 minutes from shopping, golf and Destin airport. Room service, restaurant and lounge. Organized activities and babysitting for children. Outdoor and indoor pool, fitness center, shuffleboard, 24-hour front desk.

Sunchase Townhouses
Hwy. 98 East
Destin, FL 32541
904-837-4853   800-874-8914

1 Bedroom $$

Intimate townhouse complex with spectacular view and beach at your back door. Away from the crowds, yet convenient to shopping, restaurants and deep-sea fishing.

Our listings—supplied by the managements—are as complete as possible. Many of the condos have more features than we list. Be sure to inquire when you book.

─────────────────── DESTIN ───────────────────

Surfside Resort
4701 Highway 98 East
Destin, FL 32541
904-837-4700 800-432-7882

Studio $$, 1 Bedroom $$, 2 Bedrooms $$$,
    3 Bedrooms $$$
1 Bedrm/week 5$, 2 Bed/week 6$,
    3 Bed/week 8$
AmEx/Visa/MC, Dep. 1 Night •
117 condos, Hi-rise, Key at Front desk

Location: Airport: Ft. Walton 30 miles; Beach front

General Facilities: Full serv., Bus. fac., Conf. rm. cap. 100, Daily maid, Kitchen, Linens, Restaurant on prem., Bar on prem., Game room, Lounge, Baby-sitter, Child planned rec.: Rainy day program

Room Facilities: Pool, Sauna, Tennis, Exercise room, picnic, Golf: Seascape, TV, Cable, Phone in rm., Crib-Hi-chair, Ind. AC Ctl., Ind. Heat Ctl.

Attractions: All water sports, fishing, access to 4 championship golf courses, entertainment

Shops & Restaurants: Sandestin Village; Flamingo Cafe, L. Laniappe

Angular rooms with high ceilings and contemporary pastel furnishings. Pool, wading pool, whirlpool, saunas, tennis and skywalk to the beach. Balconies with safety glass railings to block the winds. Casual living at its best. Hotel Services plans volleyball and beach activities. Children's rainy day activity program.

Waterview Towers
150 Gulf Shore Dr.
Destin, FL 32541
904-837-6333 800-874-8914

2 Bedrooms $$
Min. Stay 3 Nights, Visa/MC, Dep. Req'd. •
33 condos, Hi-rise, Key at Office

Location: Airport: Eglin 20 miles; Need car

General Facilities: Full serv., Daily maid, Kitchen, Linens, Baby-sitter, Child planned rec.: Easter-Labor Day

Room Facilities: Pool, Hot tub, Tennis, Shuffleboard, Golf: 5 miles to courses, TV, Cable, Phone in rm., Crib-Hi-chair, Ind. AC Ctl., Ind. Heat Ctl.

Attractions: Water Park, golf, miniature golf, water sports, jet ski, board sailing

Shops & Restaurants: Fort Walton Beach mall; Marina Cafe-Beachside Cafe

Snorkel at the Jetties, watch the fishing fleet, try deep-sea fishing, or simply enjoy the magnificent view of Destin's East Pass Harbor and the Gulf from your large private balcony. Pool, jacuzzi, beach service and covered parking.

─────────────────── DUCK KEY ───────────────────

Hawk's Cay Resort and Marina
Mile Marker 61
Duck Key, FL 33050
305-743-7000 800-826-4061

Pool, Linens

Attractions: Tennis

Coconut palms and sandy beaches on this private island. West Indies style resort greeting you in a comfortable living room setting. Lavish breakfast buffet, two heated jacuzzis on pool deck, marina, dolphin swims, saltwater lagoon, tennis, charters.

─────────────────── ENGLEWOOD ───────────────────

The Castaways Condominiums   Lo-rise
2240 N. Beach Road   Pool, Kitchen
Englewood, FL 33533
813-474-4078

On beautiful Manasota Key, these condominiums are on 300 feet of private beach for shelling, boating, swimming or fishing. Unusual architecture in these modern, round units.

───────────────────────────────────────

El Galeon Condominium Resort   Lo-rise
1770 Gulf Boulevard   Pool, Kitchen
Englewood, FL 33533   Golf
813-474-2709

New villas on the lower west coast of Florida fronting the Gulf of Mexico and Lemon Bay, which has private fishing and boat dock. A great beach for shelling and superior fishing.

───────────────────────────────────────

Englewood Beach & Yatch Club   Pool, Kitchen
1815 Gulf Boulevard
Englewood, FL 34223
813-474-7761

Attractions: Deepwater marina, sailing, windsurfing, fishing, boat docks, fishing
Condominiums on a private Gulf of Mexico beach, fully furnished down to books and games. Lounge by the pool and watch the sailboats. Dock your boat and be ready for early morning fishing and afternoon water sports.

───────────────────────────────────────

Fantasy Island Condominiums   2 Bedrooms $$
2765 N. Beach Road   2 Bedrms/week 5$
Englewood, FL 34223   Dep. Req'd.
813-475-2108   20 condos, Lo-rise, Key at Office

Location: Airport: 40 minutes; Downtown: 1 mile; Need car
General Facilities: Kitchen, Linens
Room Facilities: Pool, Golf: 3 mile radius, TV, Phone in rm., Ind. AC Ctl., Ind. Heat Ctl.
Attractions: Island outings, home of Edison, Busch Gardens, Ringling Museum
Shops & Restaurants: 3 shopping centers for daily needs, Mall; Greek/Italian/fish
28 large, 2-bedroom, 2-bath units, enclosed 2-car garages, two balconies, private entranceway and lots of storage space. Screened balconies overlook Lemon Bay, and across the street is access to the Gulf of Mexico. A peaceful, relaxing atmosphere.

───────────────────────────────────────

LaCoquina Beach Condominium   Lo-rise
2800 North Beach Road   Pool, Kitchen, Linens
Englewood, FL 33533
813-474-0846

Attractions: Fishing, boat-docks
Condominiums available for weekly rentals in April, Easter, Thanksgiving and Christmas only. 2 story condominiums on the Gulf of Mexico with screened lanais.

ENGLEWOOD

Sandpiper Key Condominium Assoc.
1601 Beach Road
Englewood, FL 34223
813-475-3108

2 Bedrms/week $$$$, 3 Bed/week 4$
Dep. Req'd.
215 condos, Hi-rise, Key at Rental office
No S-yes

Location: Airport: Sarasota 1 hour; Need car

General Facilities: Kitchen, Linens

Room Facilities: Pool, Golf and tennis nearby, TV, Cable, Phone in rm., Ind. AC Ctl., Ind. Heat Ctl.

Attractions: Englewood is located on the Gulf of Mexico. Ringling Museum, Jungle Gardens, Edison Home, entertainment

Shops & Restaurants: Quaint boutiques, art galleries, St. Armands Circle; Barnacle Bill's-seafood

Waterfront condominiums within walking distance to Gulf beaches. A mangrove-fringed tropical paradise surrounded by tranquil emerald waters, so bring your own boat since boat docks are available. Indulge yourself in this elegant resort. Swim, fish, shell or just relax listening to the chirping of crickets, splashing of fish or the gentle rolling of the waters.

Torian Plum

─────────────── ENGLEWOOD ───────────────

SunBurst Condominiums   1 Bedroom $, 2 Bedrooms $$
2450 N. Beach Road   1 Bedrm/week $$$$, 2 Bed/week 4$
Englewood, FL 34223   Min. Stay 2 Nights, Dep. Req'd.
813-474-0096   30 condos, Lo-rise, Key at Office

Location: Airport: 45 miles; Downtown: 1 mile; Need car; Beach front
General Facilities: Kitchen, Linens
Room Facilities: Pool, TV, Cable, Crib-Hi-chair, Ind. AC Ctl., Ind. Heat Ctl.
Attractions: Charter boats
Shops & Restaurants: Small area shops; Seafood and Italian

This is a small complex located on the Bay and Gulf. Each unit is individually furnished and decorated. Heated swimming pool, boat and fishing dock. Conveniently located to attractions on Florida's West Coast.

Tamarind Gulf & Bay Condominium Hi-rise
Manasota Key   Pool, Kitchen
Englewood, FL 34223
813-475-2275

Attractions: Golf, swimming, boating, water skiing, sailing, fishing, boat ramp, dockage

Units have roof deck, patios or screened lanai and sheltered parking spaces. Bayfront living with easy access to all water activities, dining, golfing and shopping. Tropically landscaped. Boat ramp and docking facilities on Lemon Bay.

─────────────── FORT LAUDERDALE ───────────────

Bahia Cabana Beach Resort   1 Bedroom $$, 2 Bedrooms $$
3001 Harbor Drive   AmEx/Visa/MC, Dep. 1 Night
Fort Lauderdale, FL 33316
305-524-1555 800-BEACHES

Location: Airport: Ft. Lauderdale 5 mi.
General Facilities: Daily maid, Kitchen, Linens, Restaurant on prem., Bar on prem.
Room Facilities: Pool, Hot tub, Marina, TV, Ind. AC Ctl., Ind. Heat Ctl.
Attractions: Cruise ships, 3½ hrs. Disney World, Swimming Hall of Fame, Ocean World
Shops & Restaurants: Dockside Bar/dining room

Owner-operated resort almost entirely surrounded by water. One and two bedroom apartments with private terraces, tropical grounds, sheltered sun decks and unmatched views. Marina with yacht dockage, miles of beach and picnic area. Food served dockside at the Patio Bar from 11:30 a.m.

Banyan Marina   1 Bedroom $$, 2 Bedrooms $$$, Lo-rise
111 Isle of Venice   Pool, Daily maid, Kitchen, Linens
Fort Lauderdale, FL 33301
305-524-4430

Modern, nicely furnished units on an island, just a few blocks to the beach. Tropical landscaping by the pool and sun deck, large outdoor barbecue. Sit under the shade of the banyan tree. Dockage for 8 yachts.

─────────────────── FORT LAUDERDALE ───────────────────

Coconut Bay Resort Hotel
919 N. Birch Rd.
Fort Lauderdale, FL 33304
305-563-4229

Studio $$, 1 Bedroom $$, 2 Bedrooms $$$
1 Bedrm/week 4$, 2 Bed/week 6$
Lo-rise, Key at Front desk

General Facilities: Full serv., Daily maid, Kitchen, Linens
Room Facilities: Pool, Hot tub
Attractions: Jai alai, Indian reservations, Planetarium, zoo, Sea & Disney World
Shops & Restaurants: Galleria Plaza, Saks, Neiman Marcus

Unpack your suitcase and start to relax and enjoy this waterfront paradise. Walk to most daytime activities. Designer decorated condominiums, kitchens with microwaves. Well-kept recreation areas and tropical gardens.

Inverrary House
3363 Spanish Moss Terrace
Fort Lauderdale, FL 33319
305-731-9278

1 Bedrm/week $$$$, 2 Bed/week 4$,
    3 Bed/week 5$
Min. Stay 7 Nights, Dep. Req'd. •
6 condos, Lo-rise, Key at At building

Location: Airport: 8 miles; Downtown: 8 miles; Need car
General Facilities: Kitchen, Linens, Restaurant on prem., Lounge
Room Facilities: Pool, Sauna, Tennis, Golf: Inverrary C.C. 3 courses, TV, Crib-Hi-chair, Ind. AC Ctl., Ind. Heat Ctl.
Attractions: Ocean World, jai alai, Horse racing, Everglades, Coral reefs, diving, fishing, cruises
Shops & Restaurants: Galeria Mall/Coral Square Mall/department stores; By Word of Mouth/gourmet

Six spacious luxury apartments on a private lake in the heart of Inverrary, steps to pool-fine dining and theaters nearby. 24-hour security gate for privacy in a tropical setting. Tropical print sofas, rattan, glass tables and screened patios with lounge furniture. There are 30 tennis courts, 8 lighted, 3 challenging golf courses, pool and restaurant.

Radisson Ocean Resort
4040 Galt Ocean Drive
Fort Lauderdale, FL 33308
305-566-7500 800-333-3333

Studio $$, 1 Bedroom $$$, 2 Bedrooms $$$$
AmEx/Visa/MC, Dep. 1 Night •
60 condos, Hi-rise, Key at Front desk
No S-yes/H-yes

Location: Airport: 8 miles; Downtown: 6 miles; Beach front
General Facilities: Full serv., Bus. fac., Conf. rm. cap. 225, Daily maid, Kitchen, Linens, Restaurant on prem., Bar on prem., Game room, Lounge, Baby-sitter, Child planned rec.: Game room-pool games
Room Facilities: Pool, Rental catamaran, Golf: American Golf Course, TV, Cable, Crib-Hi-chair, Ind. AC Ctl., Ind. Heat Ctl.
Attractions: Deep-sea fishing and diving arrangements, tennis, entertainment
Shops & Restaurants: Galleria & Coral Square Malls, Shoppes on the Galt; Yesterday's-continental, Amer.

Most suites have a predominant pink and burgundy color scheme, individually decorated with ocean facing balconies that can be enclosed during stormy weather. Directly on the beach. Weekend barbecues, lounge entertainment and weekend brunches. Rent a catamaran or windsurfer while the children are enjoying volleyball, or games in the pool.

――――――――――――― FORD LAUDERDALE ―――――――――――――

Silver Seas   AmEx/Visa/MC •
101 N. Atlantic Blvd.   27 condos, Key at Front desk
Fort Lauderdale, FL 33304   H-yes
305-522-8723

Location: Airport: 12 miles; Downtown: 15 miles; Need car; Beach front

General Facilities: Daily maid, Kitchen, Linens

Room Facilities: Pool, TV, Cable, Phone in rm., Crib-Hi-chair, Ind. AC Ctl., Ind. Heat Ctl.

Shops & Restaurants: Galleria Malls; French, Italian, Continental

Ocean beach, sailing, boating, snorkeling, diving and parasailing.

―――――――――――――――――――――――――――――

The Breakers of Fort Lauderdale   Studio $$, 1 Bedroom $$
909 Breakers Ave.   1 Bedrm/week 10$
Fort Lauderdale, FL 33304   Min. Stay 3 Nights, AmEx/Visa/MC,
305-566-8800 800-525-2535   Dep. 1 Night •
                                       210 condos, Hi-rise, Key at Front desk, H-yes

Location: Airport: 15 minutes; Downtown: 1 block; Beach front

General Facilities: Full serv., Bus. fac., Conf. rm. cap. 150, Daily maid, Kitchen, Linens, Restaurant/Bar on prem., Lounge, Baby-sitter, Child planned rec.: Games by social dir.

Room Facilities: Pool, Sauna, Hot tub, Tennis, Fishing, boats, swim, TV, Phone in rm., Crib-Hi-chair, Ind. AC Ctl., Ind. Heat Ctl.

Attractions: Public tours at Bonnett Estate, State Park at Northside, one block to beach, entertainment

Shops & Restaurants: Nieman Marcus, Lord & Taylor, Jordan Marsh, Mall; La Ferme-French/Martels Place

Pastel colors of these suites tantalize your senses and prepare you for a relaxed vacation. Dining and dancing go hand in hand, as the Brass Monkey Lounge features piano bar entertainment and late night jazz. Weekends, the Breakers Playhouse offers buffets dinners and musical revues. Motto: hospitality. Goal: Satisfied guest.

――――――――――――――― FORT MYERS BEACH ―――――――――――――――

The Boardwalk Caper   Pool, Kitchen, Phone in rm.
1301 San Carlos Boulevard
Fort Myers Beach, FL 33931
813-466-3500

Townhouses located on a deep 200' wide waterway 5 minutes to the Gulf of Mexico and a 3 minute drive to Estero Island's beach. "Vacation equipped" units with choice of water, pool or garden views. 4 swimming pools, 2 tennis courts and spa.

―――――――――――――――――――――――――――――

The Boathouse Beach Resort   1 Bedroom $$, Hi-rise
7630 Estero Blvd.   Pool, Kitchen
Fort Myers Beach, FL 33931
813-481-3636 800-237-8906

You'll think you are on your own yacht with these nautically themed "cabins." Signal flags fly outside the brass and teak fittings of your cabin. Master stateroom, twin bunk berths, galley kitchen and screened terrace.

───────────────── FORT MYERS BEACH ─────────────────

Caribbean Beach Club   Lo-rise
7600 Estero Blvd.   Pool, Kitchen
Fort Myers Beach, FL 33931
813-463-6111

Located on the Gulf side of Estero Island, overlooking a lagoon, just off the beach. One bedroom apartments viewing the Gulf or tropical courtyard and pool area.

Estero Island Beach Club   Lo-rise
1840 Estero Boulevard   Pool, Kitchen
Fort Myers Beach, FL 33931
813-463-6116

This complex offers two styles of one bedroom apartments. Within walking distance to all beach activities.

Island Towers   Hi-rise
4900 Estero Blvd.   Pool, Kitchen
Fort Myers Beach, FL 33931   Shuffleboard
813-463-5795

One bedroom units for one to five persons with king-size bed, queen sofa-sleeper and twin bed lounge chair. On property laundry facilities, grills and bicycles.

Kahlua Beach Club   Hi-rise
4950 Estero Boulevard   Pool, Kitchen
Fort Myers Beach, FL 33931
813-463-5751

One bedroom apartments facing the Gulf of Mexico with beach view balconies.

Lahaina Inn Resort   Lo-rise
5580 Estero Blvd.   Pool, Kitchen, Phone in rm.
Fort Myers Beach, FL 33931
813-463-4414

Attractions: Thomas Edison's winter home and laboratory, Jungle Larry's African Safari Park, Golf

A bit of old Hawaii in Florida. Laze in the sun and soak up Lahaina Inn's Southern hospitality or pursue the endless recreational possibilities. On-site swimming, fishing, volleyball, shelling on the island's seven miles of beach.

Marina Village at Snug Harbor   2 Bedrooms $$$, Hi-rise
645 San Carlos   Pool, Kitchen
Fort Myers Beach, FL 33931
813-463-3949

Attractions: Nautilus gym

Attractively decorated 2 bedroom, 2 bath units, washer/dryers, microwaves and waterfront balconies amid garden boardwalks, tropical gardens and palms. Work out at the Nautilus gym, sunbathe on the rooftop with dining gazebos and Jacuzzi, or boating.

---------- FORT MYERS BEACH ----------

Mariner's Boathouse Beach
Resort
7630 Estero Boulevard
Fort Myers Beach, FL 33931
813-463-8787 800-237-8906

1 Bedroom $$
1 Bedrm/week 4$
Min. Stay 2 Nights, AmEx/Visa/MC,
Dep. 1 Night •
22 condos, Lo-rise, Key at Office on property

Location: Airport: 20 miles; Downtown: 30 min.; Need car; Beach front

General Facilities: Daily maid, Kitchen, Linens, Game room, Baby-sitter

Room Facilities: Pool, Hot tub, Golf: across street, Cable, Phone in rm., Crib-Hi-chair, Ind. AC Ctl., Ind. Heat Ctl.

Attractions: Edison winter home & laboratory, Everglades National Park, wildlife refuges

Shops & Restaurants: Boutiques, Edison Mall, Maison Blanche, Sears; Mucky Duck/seafood

Nautically themed resort, with brass and teak fittings for sun-seekers who want the pleasures of a cruise without leaving land. Units resemble a luxury yacht with screened terrace overlooking the pool, spa and private beach. Boat launching ramps, fishing and deep sea charters, tennis and golf across the street. A short drive to shopping, restaurants and attractions. Perfect for families with small children.

Pointe Estero
6640 Estero Blvd.
Fort Myers Beach, FL 33931
813-765-1155 800-237-5141

1 Bedroom $$, 2 Bedrooms $$
1 Bedrm/week 5$, 2 Bed/week 6$
Min. Stay 2 Nights, AmEx/Visa/MC,
Dep. 2 Nights •
60 condos, Hi-rise, Key at Front desk
H-yes

Location: Airport: 20 miles; Downtown: 25 miles; Need car; Beach front

General Facilities: Conf. rm. cap. 30, Daily maid, Kitchen, Linens, Baby-sitter

Room Facilities: Pool, Hot tub, Tennis, Volleyball, Golf: Bay Beach Club ½ mile, Cable, VCR, Phone in rm., Crib-Hi-chair, Ind. AC Ctl., Ind. Heat Ctl.

Attractions: Thomas Edison Winter Home, Naples-Ft. Myers dog track, Shell Factory, cruises, theatre

Shops & Restaurants: Villa Santini Plaza, Edison Mall, Bell Tower; Veranda-Tuscany's-Chadwicks

Luxury and quality with oversized marble jacuzzi tubs in every master suite and screened balconies overlooking the Gulf of Mexico. Tiki Hut, eating areas, footbridges and a romantic gazebo overlooking a lush, tropical pond. Short distance from grocery stores, shopping, boat rentals, fishing charters, a golf course and several excellent restaurants.

──────────────── FORT MYERS BEACH ────────────────

Royal Beach Club   1 Bedrm/week $$$$, 2 Bed/week $$$$,
800 Estero Blvd.   3 Bed/week 4$
Fort Myers Beach, FL 33931   Min. Stay 3 Nights, Dep. Req'd.
813-463-9494   27 condos, Lo-rise, Key at 800 Estero Blvd.

Location: Airport: 13 Miles; Downtown: 16 miles; Beach front

General Facilities: Kitchen, Linens, Lounge, Baby-sitter

Room Facilities: Pool, Hot tub, TV, Cable, Phone in rm., Crib-Hi-chair, Ind. AC Ctl., Ind. Heat Ctl.

Attractions: Edison House, Shell Factory, Everglades, Deep-sea fishing

Shops & Restaurants: Edison Mall, Metro Mall; Pelican, Mucky Duck, C. Browns

Charming townhouse unit decorated in earth tones and wicker surround the courtyard with its heated pool, and hot tub, shuffleboard and picnic area. All units fully equipped. Tan on the beach right out front.

Tropical Sands Resort   2 Bedrooms $$, Lo-rise
7785 Estero Blvd.   Pool, Kitchen
Fort Myers Beach, FL 33931
813-463-1133

Attractions: Exercise, video room

Nautically decorated condominiums to accommodate six adults with wet bar, ceiling fans and two color T.V.'s with Atari computer. Tropically landscaped grounds surround the pool area, chickee huts and gas grills. Adjacent health spa and recreation complex and beach access.

Windward Passage Resort   1 Bedroom $$, 2 Bedrooms $$, Hi-rise
418 Estero Boulevard   Pool, Kitchen, Phone in rm.
Fort Myers Beach, FL 33931
813-463-1194

Attractions: Volleyball, Shuffleboard, Tennis, Golf

For those who love the beach and all it has to offer. . .calm, warm water and white sand beach. These fine accommodations also have a pool, spa and tennis court and are close to shops, restaurants, charter fishing and golf.

──────────────── FORT MYERS ────────────────

Bahama Beach Club   1 Bedroom $$, Lo-rise
5370 Estero Blvd.   Pool
Fort Myers, FL 33931
813-463-3148

Affordable, spacious condominiums on the Gulf of Mexico. One bedroom units have gulf front screened porches; two bedrooms have poolside front and back porches. Park your car in the covered parking area, put on your suit and enjoy the seawalled private beach.

———————————— FORT MYERS BEACH ————————————

Cane Palm Beach Club
600 Estero Blvd.
Fort Myers, FL 33931
813-463-3222

Hi-rise
Pool, Kitchen, Linens

Attractions: Dog racing, baseball spring training, fishing, championship golf, shuffleboard

If you're a sun worshiper, this is the place to stay. Private white sand beach guarded by palms, heated freshwater pool, outdoor barbecues and screened patios. Nearby activities for young and old, or relax and enjoy your leisure time.

Gulfview Manor Club
6530 Estero Blvd.
Fort Myers, FL 33931
813-463-4446

Hi-rise
Pool, Kitchen

Attractions: Charter fishing, golf, tennis, dog racing, Sanibel & Captive Islands, Everglades trips, shuffleboard

Watch the sunset over the Gulf of Mexico from your private, screened balcony. Swim on the "front door" sands of Ft. Myers beach, collect shells, or sunbathe in the warm sun. Heated pool in a tropical setting. Take a romantic walk along the water's edge of Ft. Myers.

Seawatch On The Beach
6550 Estero Blvd.
Fort Myers, FL 33931
813-463-4469

1 Bedroom $$, 2 Bedrooms $$$, Hi-rise
Pool, Kitchen

You know you are in Florida when you enter the modern building and see the tropical atrium. Open kitchens, screened terraces, washer/dryers and microwaves. Wide beach, pool, spa and tennis court.

Smugglers Cove Condominiums
5100 Estero Blvd.
Fort Myers, FL 33931
813-463-4128

Hi-rise
Pool, Kitchen, Linens

Attractions: Shuffleboard

Headquarters for your tropical vacation on the Gulf of Mexico. Freshwater pool and outdoor barbecues on the premises. Island sailing, fishing, water-jet skiing, para-sailing, tennis and golf are all available on the Island.

Sonesta Sanibel Harbor Resort
15610 McGregor Blvd.
Fort Myers, FL 33908
813-466-4000 800-343-7170

Pool, Kitchen

Attractions: Spa & Fitness Center, Tennis, Golf

Relax by the pool or beach, pamper yourself with health and beauty treatments, work out in the weight room, improve your tennis, then unwind at Jimmy's restaurant for drinks, dinner and live entertainment, and retire to your condo and view San Carlos Bay.

FORT WALTON BEACH

Breakers
381 Santa Rosa Blvd.
Fort Walton Beach, FL 32548
904-244-9127

1 Bedroom $, 2 Bedrooms $$, Hi-rise
Pool, Kitchen, Phone in rm.

Attractions: Destin fishing fleet, water sports, golf, Exercise facilities, Tennis

Suites with balconies, satellite T.V.s and washer/dryers. Four passenger elevators, plus two for beach, pool and service. Beauty salon, video store and game arcade.

El Matador Condominiums
909 Santa Rosa Blvd.
Fort Walton Beach, FL 32548
904-244-3299

2 Bedrooms $$, Hi-rise
Pool, Kitchen, Linens, Phone in rm.

Very large condominium complex with well-designed, individually decorated one and two bedroom units. Serene beachfront living above the sand dunes. Two pools, two tennis courts, game room and private white sand beach. 24-hour security. Rentals limited to families only.

Island Echoes Condominiums
676 Nautilus Ct.
Fort Walton Beach, FL 32548
904-837-4853 800-874-8914

1 Bedroom $$

On the sugar white beaches of Okaloosa Island, this popular vacation getaway features pool, tennis, shuffleboard, beach service and is close to family entertainment attractions, shopping, golf and restaurants.

Marina Bay Resort
80 Miracle Strip Pkwy
Fort Walton Beach, FL 32548
904-244-5132

Pirates Bay Condominium & Marina
214 Miracle Strip Pkwy.
Fort Walton Beach, FL 32548
904-243-3154 800-356-1861

Studio $, 1 Bedroom $$
1 Bedrm/week $$$$
AmEx/Visa/MC, Dep. 1 Night •
120 condos, Hi-rise, Key at Front desk
H-yes

Location: Airport: 12 miles; Downtown: 1 mile

General Facilities: Full serv., Bus. fac., Daily maid, Kitchen, Linens

Room Facilities: Pool, Boating, TV, Cable, Phone in rm., Crib-Hi-chair, Ind. AC Ctl., Ind. Heat Ctl.

Attractions: Gulf intercoastal waterway, marina facility, water slide for children

Shops & Restaurants: Santa Rosa Mall, The Sound-seafood/steaks

Pirates Bay is within walking distance of the area's most popular restaurants. Every unit overlooks the Gulf Intracoastal Waterway, the marina and two free-form swimming pools. These comfortable condos are set among lovely grounds, fully equipped kitchens with refrigerator, icemaker and microwave. Free coffee provided every day for coffee maker. Laundry facilities are located on each floor.

─────────────── FORT WALTON BEACH ───────────────

Sandcastle
461 Abalone Ct.
Fort Walton Beach, FL 32548
904-837-4853   800-874-8914

Secluded beach-front vacationing for the sun-loving, beach-loving family. Fully furnished three bedroom duplexes convenient to downtown Fort Walton Beach.

Sea Oats Resort Condominium   2 Bedrooms $$, Hi-rise
1114 Santa Rosa Blvd.   Pool, Kitchen, Linens, Phone in rm.
Fort Walton Beach, FL 32548
904-244-5200   800-451-2343

Attractions: Okaloosa Island fishing pier, Gulfarium, picnic parks, amusement parks, golf, Shuffleboard, Tennis, Golf

Security entrance to Sea Oats ideal location on the Gulf beach. Each unit has energy efficient windows, tile baths and oversized view balconies. A short walk or bike ride to the amusement parks, picnic parks, fishing piers and golf courses on "The Playground."

Seaspray Condominium   1 Bedroom $$, 2 Bedrooms $$$, 3 Bedrooms
1530 U.S. Highway 98 East $$$
Fort Walton Beach, FL 32548   1 Bedrm/week 4$, 2 Bed/week 6$,
904-244-1108   800-428-2726   3 Bed/week 8$
                                          Min. Stay 2 Nights, Visa/MC, Dep. Req'd.
                                          100 condos, Lo-rise, Key at front office
                                          P-yes

Location: Airport: 5 miles; Downtown: 1 mile; Need car; Beach front

General Facilities: Conf. rm. cap. 50, Daily maid, Kitchen, Linens, Game room, Baby-sitter

Room Facilities: Pool, Sauna, Athletic Club, TV, Cable, Phone in rm., Crib-Hi-chair, Ind. AC Ctl., Ind. Heat Ctl.

Attractions: 9-hole nearby golf course, fishing, Gulfarium, water slide, beach

Shops & Restaurants: Unlimited shopping malls; Seafood and steak house

Townhouse condominium units complete with color cable 32 channel and movie channel TV. These two story units offer a grass courtyard, uncrowded beach, parking at each unit, and no elevators. Stroll the beach, picnic in the park, exercise in the fully equipped athletic club, relax in the sauna, or take a cool dip in the pool. Seaspray is just a short walk to Okaloosa Island Fishing Pier or four miles from Destin, "The World's Luckiest Fishing Village."

——————— FORT WALTON BEACH ———————

Steamboat Landing
161 S.E. Brooks Street
Fort Walton Beach, FL 32548
904-244-1391

1 Bedroom $$
1 Bedrm/week 5$
Visa/MC,Dep. Req'd.
18 condos, Lo-rise, Key at Office

Location: Airport: 12 miles; Downtown: 1 block

General Facilities: Kitchen, Linens, Game room

Room Facilities: Pool, TV, Cable, Phone in rm., Ind. AC Ctl., Ind. Heat Ctl.

Attractions: Sport fishing, charter parties, surf-casting, amusements centers, zoo, museum

Shops & Restaurants: Unlimited shopping malls, souvenir shops; The Seagull-seafood

Completely furnished condominiums on the Intercoastal Waterway with living room and bedroom color T.V. Recreational activities include an Amenity Building, pool table, indoor heated pool, ping pong, large screen T.V./VCR, jacuzzi, basketball, horseshoes, badminton and outdoor pool. Gas grills are available for your favorite barbecued feast.

Surf Dweller Condominiums
554 Coral Court
Fort Walton Beach, FL 32548
904-664-1113 800-338-4418

Hi-rise
Pool, Kitchen

Large, luxurious beachside units with fully equipped kitchens. 30-foot balcony with unmatched gulf view. Pool, kiddie pool, tennis, family recreation and evening entertainment.

——————— FORT WALTON ———————

Sea Oats
1114 Santa Rosa Boulevard
Fort Walton, FL 32548
904-244-5200 800-451-2343

——————— GRENELEFE ———————

Grenelefe Resort
3200 State Road 546
Grenelefe, FL 33884
813-422-7511 800-237-9549

General Facilities: Conf. rm. cap. 2000, Kitchen, Restaurant on prem., Bar on prem., Game room, Baby-sitter

Room Facilities: Pool, Tennis, Fishing, sailing, Golf: West, east, south courses

Attractions: Disney World, Cypress Gardens, Sea World, EPCOT Center

Shops & Restaurants: Convenience store; Tuck's Table, Grene Heron

At the center of Florida's wonderland of world-famous attractions is the quiet community of Grenelefe. The resort embraces 1,000 lush, wooded acres along the shores of Lake Marion. 13 world-class tennis courts, five pools and plentiful water sports and fishing on Lake Marion. Non-sport activities include arts and crafts, cooking schools and bridge tournaments. Daily shuttle bus service to Disney World/EPCOT Center and Cypress Gardens. Championship golf on three meticulously landscaped courses.

The Summit

GULFSTREAM

Gulfstream Manor
3901 N. Ocean Blvd. (A-1-A)
Gulfstream, FL 33444
305-272-6300

1 Bedroom $$, Lo-rise
Pool, Kitchen, Linens, Phone in rm.

Attractions: Shuffleboard, BBQ, Golf

Located directly on the ocean, one bedroom units accommodate 4 people. 2 televisions, microwave and washer/dryer. Close to tennis, golf, shopping and restaurants.

HILLSBORO BEACH

The Barefoot Mailman Resort
1061 Hillsboro Mile
Hillsboro Beach, FL 33062
305-941-0100 800-327-1584

Lo-rise
Pool, Kitchen

Clean air, low pollen count, private beach, manicured lawns, palm trees and large pool make for a most relaxing vacation in sunny Hillsboro Beach.

HOLLYWOOD

Enchanted Isle Resort
1601 S. Surf Rd.
Hollywood, FL 33019
305-922-1508

1 Bedroom $$, 2 Bedrooms $$, Lo-rise
Pool, Kitchen, Phone in rm.

Attractions: Shuffleboard

Four condominium buildings surrounding a pool and courtyard. Oceanfront lawn terrace and private beach. Plan to relax in the quiet atmosphere.

──────────────── HOLLYWOOD ────────────────

Hollywood Beach Hotel Tower   1 Bedroom $$, Hi-rise
301 Harrison Street   Pool, Kitchen
Hollywood, FL 33019
305-920-5133

Unwind at the beach or heated pool. Enjoy cocktails, fine dining, late night snacks and nightly entertainment. Over-sized units with two color T.V.'s and living room convertible queen size sofa.

Hollywood Beach Resort   Studio $$, 1 Bedroom $$$
101 N. Ocean Dr.   AmEx/Visa/MC •
Hollywood, FL 33019   360 condos, Hi-rise, Key at Front desk
305-921-0990 800-331-6103   P-yes/H-yes

Location: Airport: 11.2 miles; Downtown: 1 mile; Beach front

General Facilities: Full serv., Bus. fac., Conf. rm. cap. 50, Daily maid, Kitchen, Linens, Restaurant on prem., Bar on prem., Game room, Lounge, Baby-sitter

Room Facilities: Pool, Hot tub, Spa, TV, Cable, Phone in rm., Crib-Hi-chair, Ind. AC Ctl., Ind. Heat Ctl.

Shops & Restaurants: Oceanwalk Grill/continental

Completely refurbished historical, art deco building, suites done in pastel colors. Relax in your private suite, shop the exciting mall, enjoy the beach. Fun for families or great for romance. Pick your own atmosphere for the best of all worlds.

Neptune Hollywood Beach Club   Studio $, 1 Bedroom $$
2012 N. Surf Rd.   1 Bedrm/week 4$
Hollywood, FL 33019   Min. Stay 3 Nights, AmEx/Visa/MC,
305-922-0459   Dep. 2 Nights
                                       29 condos, Lo-rise, Key at Office

Location: Airport: Miami 15 miles; Downtown: 15 min.; Need car; Beach front

General Facilities: Daily maid, Kitchen, Linens, Baby-sitter

Room Facilities: Pool, Sauna, TV, Phone in rm., Crib-Hi-chair, Ind. AC Ctl., Ind. Heat Ctl.

Attractions: Island cruises, gambling, Metro Zoo, Oceanworld, jai alai, horse races, fishing

Shops & Restaurants: Aventura Mall-Neiman Marcus-Macy's-Saks-Galleria; Martha's/European

Directly on the ocean bordered by the promenade of Hollywood. Tropical parks and carefully tended gardens surround these luxuriously furnished units done in modern earth tones. Short drive to entertainment and elegant shops.

─────────────────── HOWEY-IN-THE-HILLS ───────────────────

Mission Inn Golf & Tennis Resort   Location: Airport: Orlando
Box 441
Howey-In-The-Hills, FL 32737
904-324-2101 800-874-9053

General Facilities: Conf. rm. cap. 350, Kitchen, Restaurant on prem., Bar on prem., Game room, Baby-sitter, Child planned rec.: Children's program

Room Facilities: Pool, Tennis, Sailing, fishing, Golf: 18-hole golf course

Attractions: Disney World/EPCOT, Sea World, Cypress Gardens, cocktail cruises, Lake Harris

Shops & Restaurants: Orlando; El Conquistador/continental

A country-inn hideaway, 45 minutes from Walt Disney World in the foothills of Orlando. Spanish in style reminiscent of Florida's early days with fountains, gardens, birds and waterfalls lining the covered walkways. Work out in the spa, fish, sail, and speedboat on Lake Harris, play tennis and swim. Hilly 18-hole golf course with varied landscaping.

─────────────────── HUTCHINSON ISLAND, STUART ───────────────────

Plantation Beach Club   1 Bedroom $$$, 2 Bedrooms $$$, Hi-rise
329 N.E. Tradewind Lane   Pool, Kitchen
Hutchinson Island, Stuart, FK 34996
813-481-3636 800-237-8096

Attractions: Golf, tennis, water sports

A resort within a resort away from the city, yet only a short distance to Palm Beach activities. Oceanfront suites have screened porches, bathtubs with whirlpools and home entertainment centers. Gas grill and picnic area for outdoor cooking, pool, hot tub and sauna.

─────────────────── HUTCHINSON ISLAND ───────────────────

Indian River Plantation Resort   1 Bedroom $$$, 2 Bedrooms $$$$
555 N.E. Ocean Blvd.   AmEx/Visa/MC, Dep. 1 Night •
Hutchinson Island, FL 34996   56 condos, Lo-rise, Key at Registr. desk
407-225-3700 800-327-4873   H-yes

Location: Airport: 45 minutes; Downtown: 3 miles; Beach front

General Facilities: Full serv., Conf. rm. cap. 525, Daily maid, Kitchen, Linens, Restaurant on prem., Bar on prem., Lounge, Baby-sitter, Child planned rec.: Daily activities

Room Facilities: Pool, Hot tub, Tennis, Golf, boating, TV, Cable, Phone in rm., Crib-Hi-chair, Ind. AC Ctl., Ind. Heat Ctl.

Attractions: Elliott Museum, House of Refuge, sailfish capital of the world, entertainment

Shops & Restaurants: Treasure Coast Mall-Jordan Marsh, Lord & Taylor; Benihana of Tokyo/Japanese

56 oceanfront suites on this 200-acre resort, with golf, lighted tennis court and a marina with 77 slips for boats with maximum 6-foot draft MLT, water and electrical hook-ups, onboard yacht telephone service and cable TV. Entertainment and dancing at one of the three lounges. Ideal year-round weather. Golf and tennis pros for clinics, lessons or tournaments. Outdoor spa and cabana bar.

INDIAN HARBOUR BEACH

Oceanique
2105 Highway A1A
Indian Harbour Beach, FL 32937
305-777-6512

2 Bedrooms $$$, Lo-rise
Pool, Kitchen

Attractions: Disney World, Spaceport U.S.A., tennis, golf, sailing, fishing

Midway between Jacksonville and Miami, in a quiet residential community, yet close to Florida's major tourist attractions. Private beach club and pool.

INDIAN ROCKS BEACH

Bay Shores Yacht & Tennis Club
19451 Gulf Blvd.
Indian Rocks Beach, FL 34635
813-595-9313

1 Bedroom $$, 2 Bedrooms $$, Lo-rise
Pool, Kitchen, Linens

Attractions: Disney World, Busch Gardens, Tiki Gardens, deep-sea fishing, jai alai, Sunken Gardens, Putting green, Shuffleboard, Tennis, Golf

Hi-rise condominiums with view balconies for your complete Florida vacation. Boat docks, fishing and barbecue grills.

INDIAN SHORES

Holiday Villas II
P.O. Box 738, 19610 Gulf Blvd.
Indian Shores, FL 33535
813-595-7392

1 Bedroom $$, 2 Bedrooms $$, Lo-rise
Pool, Kitchen, Linens

Attractions: Disney World, Busch Gardens, Sea World, Cypress Gardens, Circus World, Golf

Luxury apartments with terraces. Swim, fish, look for shells or run barefoot through the white sands. Many local amenities including tennis, golf, restaurants and after-hour entertainment. Small, well-trained, non-shedding dogs permitted in some units.

Holiday Villas III
18610 Gulf Blvd.
Indian Shores, FL 34635
813-595-2335

1 Bedroom $$, 2 Bedrooms $$, Hi-rise
Pool, Kitchen, Linens

Attractions: Disney World, EPCOT Center, tennis, golf, Dock, fishing pier

Great family vacation living on one of Florida's major boating areas. Play volleyball on the beach, have an evening cookout or daytime picnic at the barbecue area, or relax with a game of pool. All ages like to play the video machines. Free green fees.

─────────────── INDIAN SHORES ───────────────

Sand Dollar Resort
18500 Gulf Blvd.
Indian Shores, FL 34635
813-595-8109

1 Bedroom $$, 2 Bedrooms $$, 3 Bedrooms $$
1 Bedrm/week 5$, 2 Bed/week 6$,
  3 Bed/week 6$
Min. Stay 3 Nights, AmEx/Visa/MC,
  Dep. Req'd. •
50 condos, Lo-rise, Key at Front desk
No S-yes/H-yes

Location: Airport: 30 miles; Downtown: 10 min.; Beach front

General Facilities: Full serv., Daily maid, Kitchen, Linens, Baby-sitter

Room Facilities: Pool, Hot tub, Sailing, windsurfing, Golf: Nearby, TV, Cable, Phone in rm., Crib-Hi-chair, Ind. AC Ctl., Ind. Heat Ctl.

Attractions: Busch Gardens, Dali Museum, Wagon Wheel Flea Market, charter boats, Walt Disney World

Shops & Restaurants: Maas Brothers, Burdines, boutiques, shopping plaza; Wine Cellar/variety

Gulf-front condominiums with private balconies. Beautiful sunsets and a white sandy beach for bathing and long moonlit walks. Swimming pool, jacuzzi and surfside cabanas. A few minutes to discos, clubs, shopping and restaurants. If you like to gamble, there is pari-mutuel betting: greyhounds, horses and jai alai not far away.

─────────────── ISLAMORADA ───────────────

Caloosa Cove Resort
Mile Mrk 73.8-73801 OversHwy. US#1
Islamorada, FL 33036
305-664-8811

1 Bedroom $$$, Lo-rise
Pool, Kitchen, Linens

Attractions: Sports, Back Country Fishing, scuba diving, snorkeling, reefs, Shuffleboard, marina, tennis

Thoughtfully furnished units with personalized custom details. Full service marina with dockage for boating and fishing pleasure. Beach for barbecueing and relaxing, solar heated pool. Cocktails at the Safari Lounge with authentic African artifacts.

Morada Wells Resort & Club
M.M. 80½, P.O. Box 1361
Islamorada, FL 33036
305-664-8849

Villas
Pool, Kitchen, Linens

Attractions: Therapy spa, racquetball

Hidden behind tropical trees in natural woodlands are these fully furnished villas and townhouses. Walk along the boardwalk and nature trail, swim, fish, dock your boat for water sports.

─────────────── ISLAMORADA ───────────────

Ocean 80 Resort　　　　　　　　1 Bedroom $$, 2 Bedrooms $$$
U.S. 1, Mile Marker 80, Box 949　　Pool, Daily maid, Kitchen
Islamorada, FL 33036
305-664-4411

Attractions: Handball, badminton, Tennis

Choice of studio, one or two bedroom units with bar unit, entertainment center and ceiling fans. Adult recreational center with two jumbo TV screens, children's pool and playground. Boat dockage and launching facilities, sailboats, jet skis and bicycles.

─────────────── JENSEN BEACH ───────────────

Turtle Reef II　　　　　　　　2 Bedrooms $$, Hi-rise
10740 So. Ocean Drive A1A　　Pool, Kitchen, Linens
Jensen Beach, FL 34957
305-229-9200

Attractions: Disney World, Cape Canaveral, Tennis, Golf

Fully furnished units with split floor plans. Large balconies, dining rooms adjoining breakfast bar and master bath oversized Roman tub. The beach, pool and tennis are just outside your door. Deep sea and surf fishing in the carefree atmosphere of Hutchinson Island.

─────────────── JUPITER ───────────────

Jupiter Bay Resort & Tennis Club　1 Bedroom $$$, 2 Bedrooms $$$$
350 S. US Highway 1　　　　　　1 Bedrm/week 6$, 2 Bed/week 8$
Jupiter, FL 33477　　　　　　　AmEx/Visa/MC, Dep. Req'd. •
407-744-0210 800-228-5152　　224 condos, Lo-rise, Key at Front desk

Location: Airport: 25 Minutes; Downtown: 2 Miles; Need car; Beach front

General Facilities: Full serv., Conf. rm. cap. 125, Daily maid, Kitchen, Linens, Restaurant on prem., Bar on prem., Baby-sitter

Room Facilities: Pool, Hot tub, Tennis, TV, Cable, Phone in rm., Crib-Hi-chair, Ind. AC Ctl., Ind. Heat Ctl.

Attractions: Cruises to Bahamas, Deep-sea fishing, Burt Reynolds Theater, Boating

Shops & Restaurants: Worth Avenue and six large malls

Park-like environment, one block walk to the beach. Jogging heart trail with scenic views of lake and waterfalls.

Jupiter Reef Club　　　　　1 Bedroom $$$, 2 Bedrooms $$$
1600 S. Ocean Dr.　　　　　Pool, Daily maid, Kitchen, Linens
Jupiter, FL 33477
407-747-7788

Attractions: Burt Reynolds Dinner Theater, water sports

Units decorated by Roland Lee and the firm of Childs Dreyfus with at least one view deck. Jupiter Reef Club has private beach access, oceanside pool and spa. Patio area with gazebo and deck chairs graced by tropical greenery.

─────────────── KEY LARGO ───────────────

Marina Del Mar
P.O. Box 1050
Key Largo, FL 33037
305-451-4107 800-451-3483

1 Bedroom $$$, 2 Bedrooms $$$$, Hi-rise
Pool, Kitchen

Attractions: John Pennekamp Coral Reef State Park, Key Largo Marine Sanctuary, Everglades, Fitness, dive center, Tennis

Located on a deep water marina, complete lodging, entertainment and water sports base. Ocean Divers dive center and full service marina make this an ideal spot for fishing, scuba and snorkeling enthusiasts. Pool, sun deck, tennis and fitness center.

Anchorage Resort & Yacht Club
107500 Overseas Highway
Key Largo, FL 33037
305-451-0500

1 Bedroom $$
1 Bedrm/week 6$
AmEx/Visa/MC, Dep. Req'd. •
28 condos, Hi-rise, Key at Front desk

Location: Airport: Miami 55 miles; Need car; Beach front

General Facilities: Bus. fac., Daily maid, Kitchen, Linens, Game room, Baby-sitter

Room Facilities: Pool, Hot tub, Tennis, Shuffleboard, boats, TV, Phone in rm., Crib-Hi-chair, Ind. AC Ctl., Ind. Heat Ctl.

Attractions: Bayside water shuttle, John Pennekamp Coral Reef State Park, Everglades, entertainment

Shops & Restaurants: Coral Gables, Bayside, 1 hr. Key West, 2 hours; Quay Rest-Fisherman-Sundowners

Balmy year-round weather, tropical sunsets, casual dress. Tropically decorated one bedroom units. Fine restaurants, glassbottom boat tours of John Pennekamp Coral Reef Park, as well as scuba and snorkeling excursions. All water sports. Furnished in bright, airy Florida rattan. Relaxed island ambience, yet 1 hour from Miami's culture and nightlife.

Moon Bay Condominium
4700 Overseas Highway
Key Largo, FL 33130
305-451-4161

2 Bedrooms $$
2 Bedrms/week 6$
Dep. Req'd.
Lo-rise

Location: Airport: Miami 55 miles; Downtown: 60 miles; Need car

General Facilities: Daily maid, Kitchen, Linens, Game room, Lounge

Room Facilities: Pool, Sauna, Tennis, TV, Phone in rm., Crib-Hi-chair, Ind. AC Ctl., Ind. Heat Ctl.

Attractions: Scuba diving, snorkeling, windsurfing, deep-sea fishing, jet, water skiing, Coral Reef

Shops & Restaurants: Cutler Ridge Mall, Lord & Taylor, Burdines; Quay/gourmet seafood

Beautiful waterfront resort with magnificent seascapes and spectacular sunsets. Completely equipped for pleasure and comfort. Clubhouse, marina and private boat slip. Tropical island landscaping with stunning views from nearly every room.

Lookout Village

KEY WEST

1800 Atlantic   Pool, Kitchen
1800 Atlantic Blvd.
Key West, FL 33040
305-294-0878

Attractions: Hemingway's house, Conch Train, theaters, sailing, windsurfing, parasailing, Recreation center, Golf

1657-square-foot condominiums with oversized sunken tub, mirrored dressing area, oversized closets, kitchen pantry and breakfast area. Pool and spa set in a tropical garden. Fitness, exercise room and sauna in the recreation center with its party kitchen.

Bay Villas
32 Hilton Haven Road
Key West, FL 33040

Galleon Marina & Beach Resort   1 Bedroom $$$$
617 Front St., P.O. Box 409   Kitchen
Key West, FL 33040
800-544-1010 800-544-3030

Tropical furnishings in seaside colors furnished with everything you need. Pool, private beach, exercise club, water sports. Key West offers exotic gardens, wild orchids, night spots, international cuisine, museums, art galleries, plays and musicals.

─────────────── KEY WEST ───────────────

The Galleon
617 Front St.
Key West, FL 33040
305-296-7711 800-544-3030

1 Bedroom $$$$, 2 Bedrooms $$$$, Hi-rise
Pool, Kitchen

Attractions: Exercise club

Airy rooms with tropical furnishings in seaside pastel colors. Relax in your private jacuzzi or with your complete entertainment system, VCR, tape deck, stereo and cable TV. Even games are provided. Explore Key West's Victorian homes, museums, and art galleries.

La Brisa Condominium
1901 S. Roosevelt Blvd.
Key West, FL 33040
305-294-4770

1 Bedroom $$, 2 Bedrooms $$$, Hi-rise
Pool, Kitchen, Linens, Phone in rm.

Attractions: Recreation Center, Tennis

Just west of the airport on the ocean, opulent master suites, contemporary kitchens, panoramic views. Complete recreational complex. Overlooking protected nature preserve for native wildfowl. Traditional setting.

Pelican Landing
915 Eisenhower Drive
Key West, FL 33040
305-296-7583 800-527-8108

AmEx/Visa/MC •
16 condos, Hi-rise, Key at Office on premises

Location: Airport: 1½ miles; Downtown: 1 mile
General Facilities: Full serv., Daily maid, Kitchen, Linens, Baby-sitter
Room Facilities: Pool, TV, Cable, Phone in rm., Crib, Ind. AC Ctl., Ind. Heat Ctl.
Attractions: Tour train of city, many historical sites
Shops & Restaurants: Souvenir shops, clothing shops; Numerous and varied

Luxury condominiums at affordable prices, balconies with harbor views, catering primarily to boating, fishing, diving, and water sports. Dockage available. Convenient location on the outskirts of Old Town. Tennis, golf, water sports, and shopping all close by.

Reflections On Key West
O Duval St.
Key West, FL 33040
305-296-7701

Enter your favorite condo in our "Condo of the Year" contest (entry form is in the back of the book).

KEY WEST

The Banyan Resort
323 White Head Street
Key West, FL 33040
305-294-9573 800-225-0639

Studio $$, 1 Bedroom $$$, 2 Bedrooms $$$
AmEx/Visa/MC, Dep. 1 Night •
38 condos, Key at Front desk

Location: Airport: 1½ miles; Downtown: 1 block

General Facilities: Conf. rm. cap. 30, Daily maid, Kitchen, Linens, Bar on prem.

Room Facilities: Pool, Hot tub, TV, VCR, Phone in rm., Ind. AC Ctl., Ind. Heat Ctl.

Attractions: Diving, fishing, swimming, boating, charters, museums, art galleries, theaters, biking, entertainment

Shops & Restaurants: Fast Buck Freddies, J. Byrons, food stores; The Battery

A compound of eight restored Victorian houses with all modern interiors surrounded by lush tropical gardens. Decorated in tropical wicker with ceiling fans and french doors. 2 pools, 2 jacuzzis, conveniently located in old town for walking to shopping, restaurants, nightlife and museums. Brunches, aerobics and a Tiki bar by the pool, serving sandwiches, beer and wine.

KISSIMMEE

Club Sevilla
4646 W. Irlo Bronson Memorial Hwy
Kissimmee, FL 32741
305-396-1800

1 Bedroom $$, 2 Bedrooms $$
1 Bedrm/week 5$, 2 Bed/week 5$
Dep. Req'd.
Lo-rise

General Facilities: Kitchen, Linens, Bar on prem., Lounge, Child planned rec.: Playground

Room Facilities: Pool, Tennis, TV, Cable

Attractions: Disney World, Sea World, Wet 'N Wild, Spaceport U.S.A., Circus World, Busch Gardens

Shops & Restaurants: Kissimmee-St. Cloud shopping

Club Sevilla is located in the middle of the Kissimmee-St. Cloud resort area. Accommodations with a Spanish feeling and designer decor. Pool, and children's playground.

Fortune Place Resort
1475 Astro Lake Dr.
Kissimmee, FL 32743
407-348-0330 800-624-7496

1 Bedroom $$, 2 Bedrooms $$$, 3 Bedrooms $$$$
1 Bedrm/week $$, 2 Bed/week $$$,
3 Bed/week $$$$
AmEx/Visa/MC, Dep. 1 Night •
46 condos, Villas, Key at desk, P-yes/H-yes

Location: Airport: 14 miles; Downtown: 20 miles; Need car

General Facilities: Full serv., Daily maid, Kitchen, Linens, Baby-sitter

Room Facilities: Pool, Tennis, Pad-Rac-VB-Shuffleboard, Golf: Buena Ventura Lakes, TV, Cable, VCR, Phone in rm., Crib-Hi-chair, Ind. AC Ctl., Ind. Heat Ctl.

Attractions: Disney World, EPCOT, Sea World, Gatorland, baseball, entertainment

Shops & Restaurants: Florida Mall-largest mall in Florida; Murphy's Lobster House

The luxury and privacy of a modern villa close to Disney World, EPCOT, Sea World and other area attractions, but removed from traffic congestion and noise. A large fenced playground, gas grills and picnic tables. Complimentary breakfast, Saturday evening barbecue and free daily newspaper. Vacationing families with children are especially welcome.

————————— KISSIMMEE —————————

High Point World Resort
2951 High Point Blvd.
Kissimmee, FL 32741
407-396-9600 800-637-8893

2 Bedrooms $$$
Min. Stay 2 Nights, AmEx/Visa/MC,
Dep. 1 Night •
108 condos, Key at Front desk

Location: Airport: 30-40 minutes; Downtown: 15 miles; Need car

General Facilities: Daily maid, Kitchen, Linens, Baby-sitter

Room Facilities: Pool, Hot tub, Tennis, TV, VCR, Phone in rm., Crib-Hi-chair, Ind. AC Ctl., Ind. Heat Ctl.

Attractions: Disney World/EPCOT, Sea World, Cypress Gardens, Busch Gardens, Space Cntr.

Shops & Restaurants: Florida & Oscgola Malls, Belz Factory Outlet; Townsend Plantation/Olive Grdn

Luxury townhomes and villas exquisitely furnished in navy and earth tones. Guest services committed to maximum hospitality; just one mile from Disney World entrance in the heart of vacationland.

Lago Vista Vacation Resort
180 Royal Palm Drive
Kissimmee, FL 32743
305-348-5246

2 Bedrooms $$, Lo-rise
Pool, Kitchen

Attractions: Disney World, Wet 'N Wild, Sea World, Houston Astros Training Camp, EPCOT, Golf

Complete condominiums away from traffic noise and congestion. Pool and lakefront beach for bass and bream fishing, just outside your apartment. The Country Club with golf, tennis and dining is down the street. Ocean beaches can be reached in an hour's drive.

Lifetime of Vacations Resort
7770 W. Irlo Bronson Memorial Hwy
Kissimmee, FL 32741
407-396-3000 800-527-9132

1 Bedroom $$, 2 Bedrooms $$, 3 Bedrooms $$$
Visa/MC
100 condos

Location: Airport: Orlando 30 minutes; Downtown: 25 min.; Need car

General Facilities: Kitchen, Child planned rec.: Playground

Room Facilities: Pool, Boat dock, horseshoes, Golf: Lake Buena Vista nearby, TV

Attractions: Disney World, EPCOT, Sea World, Cypress Gardens, Boardwalk and Baseball

Shops & Restaurants: Florida Mall, Altamonte Mall

Each unit overlooks Lake Wilson with its white sand beach, picnic, barbecue area and children's playground. Moor your boat at the boat dock to be ready for bass fishing and boating. Comfortably furnished units even have a table for cards and games. Bedroom with jacuzzi and steam/sauna shower. Housekeeping available.

─────────────── KISSIMMEE ───────────────

Magic Tree Resort   Pool, Kitchen, Linens
2795 State Road 545 S.
Kissimmee, FL 32741
305-396-2300

Attractions: Walt Disney World, Circus World, Sea World, rapids at River Country, Sea
  World, Shuffleboard, bikes, Tennis

*Visit Walt Disney World and then come back to the relaxation of Magic Tree for a swim
or to unwind in the whirlpool spa. Kiddie pool, playground, game room, bicycling, shuffleboard and Tiki Gazebos. Have a drink at the Patio Bar and cook dinner on the gas barbecue grills.*

Orange Lake Country Club   2 Bedrooms $$
8505 W. Space Coast Pkwy., Rt 192W   Dep. 1 Night
Kissimmee, FL 32741   Villas, Key at Front desk
305-239-0000 800-327-4444

General Facilities: Kitchen, Restaurant on prem., Bar on prem., Game room, Lounge,
  Baby-sitter, Child planned rec.: Pool/playground/bike
Room Facilities: Pool, Sauna, Tennis, Racquetball, Golf: 27-hole course, Crib-Hi-chair
Attractions: 4½ miles west of The Magic Kingdom Entrance, Orange Lake
Shops & Restaurants: General store; Citrus Room, Coffee Shop

*Luxury accommodations on 400 acres. Championship golf and golf school, tennis courts,
sauna, jacuzzis, pools, racquetball, basketball. 80-acre Orange Lake for water sports and
fishing. Children are special here, kiddie pool, playground, bicycling, miniature golf,
shuffleboard, video game room and a movie theatre. On-site restaurant and coffee shop,
exercise room, and even a beauty shop.*

Orbit One Vacation Villas   Villas
2950 Entry Point Blvd.   Pool, Kitchen
Kissimmee, FL 32741
407-396-1300

Attractions: Horseshoes, Tennis

*Enjoy fresh orange juice from fruit picked outside your condominium. White architecture
among palm trees, flower-lined pathways, sculptured ponds with a wooden bridge and
waterfalls. Ceramic tile entryways, wicker and rattan furniture, stereo units, and 5 by 7 tub.*

Polynesian Isles Resort   1 Bedroom $$, 2 Bedrooms $$$, Lo-rise
3045 Polynesian Isles Blvd.   Pool, Kitchen
Kissimmee, FL 32741
305-396-1622

Attractions: EPCOT, Sea World, Wet 'n Wild, Space Center, Busch Gardens, Cypress
  Gardens, Shuffleboard, Tennis

*Located in the heart of Central Florida among palms, tropical gardens, lagoons, water-
falls and orange trees. Native wood and coral rock exteriors. Suites with designer furnish-
ings, full dining rooms, tinted windows and covered balconies.*

KISSIMMEE

Resort World Of Orlando
2738 Poinciana Blvd.
Kissimmee, FL 32741
305-396-8300 800-327-9154

Lo-rise
Pool, Kitchen, Linens

Attractions: Disney World, EPCOT, Racquetball, Tennis

Award-winning decorated villas, some with whirlpool baths and built-in stereos. Tennis, racquetball, giant pool, spa and sauna. Video games and exercise room. Minutes to the many area attractions.

Westgate Vacation Villas
2770 Old Lake Wilson Rd.
Kissimmee, FL 32741
407-351-3351 800-992-2990

Villas
Pool, Kitchen, Linens

Attractions: Walt Disney, Sea World, EPCOT Center, Tennis

Villas on a lake amidst 170 acres of orange groves. Living room with 27" T.V. and mirrored wet bar, master bedroom with king-size bed, 19" T.V., mirrored closets, double jacuzzi and separate shower, extra bedroom with 19" T.V. and double access bathroom.

LAKE BUENA VISTA

Fantasy World Club Villas
2935 Hart Blvd., P.O. Box 22193
Lake Buena Vista, FL 32830
305-396-1808 800-874-8047

2 Bedrooms $$$
AmEx/Visa/MC, Dep. 1 Night
280 condos, Lo-rise, Villas, Key at Front desk

Location: Airport: 20 miles; Need car

General Facilities: Full serv., Daily maid, Kitchen, Linens, Restaurant on prem., Bar on prem., Lounge, Baby-sitter, Child planned rec.: Playground

Room Facilities: Pool, Hot tub, Tennis, TV, Cable, VCR, Phone in rm., Crib-Hi-chair, Ind. AC Ctl., Ind.Heat Ctl

Attractions: Disney World, Sea World, Cypress Gardens, Kennedy Space Center, Busch Gardens

Shops & Restaurants: Convenience store on premises; Olive Garden Restaurant

A family swim and tennis resort minutes away from the entrance to Walt Disney World. Facilities include three heated pools, jacuzzi, playgrounds and 7 lighted tennis courts with a tennis professional to help you with your game. Cook in your fully equipped kitchen, or eat at the Olive Garden Restaurant and Lounge. Transportation arranged to Disney, EPCOT Center and Sea World for a nominal fee.

Isle of Bali
17777 Bali Boulevard, Box 22175
Lake Buena Vista, FL 32830
407-239-5000 800-634-3119

2 Bedrooms $$, Villas
Pool, Kitchen

Attractions: Disney World, Sea World, O'Grady's Goodtime Emporium, Medieval Times and Arabian Nights, Spa, outdoor games, Tennis

Two bedroom vacation villas in Central Florida. Year-round attractions and sports by the lagoon.

———————— LAKE BUENA VISTA ————————

Vistana Resort
13800 Vistana Dr., P.O. Box 22051
Lake Buena Vista, FL 32830
407-239-3100 800-327-9152

2 Bedrooms $$$
AmEx/Visa/MC, Dep. 1 Night •
560 condos, Lo-rise, Villas, Key at Registr. desk
H-yes

Location: Airport: 15 miles; Downtown: 17 miles

General Facilities: Full serv., Daily maid, Kitchen, Linens, Restaurant on prem., Bar on prem., Game room, Baby-sitter, Child planned rec.: Full-time activities

Room Facilities: Pool, Sauna, Hot tub, Tennis, Basketball, Shuffleboard, Golf: Walt Disney courses-1 Mi., TV, VCR, Phone in rm., Crib-Hi-chair, Ind. AC Ctl., Ind. Heat Ctl.

Attractions: 1 mile from Disney World Complex, Sea World, Wet & Wild, Kennedy Space Ctr., entertainment

Shops & Restaurants: Disney World Shopping, Church St. Exchange; Several in area

Spacious, deluxe, designer furnished, contemporary villas. Vistana Resort places its guests in a hub of limitless vacation opportunities. There are two types of accommodations-villas and townhomes. The townhomes offer a two-story living room with floor to ceiling windows. Villas have two color TVs, video players and oversized whirlpool tub. Be as active as you like, or just sit back and "reenergize."

———————— LAUDERDALE-BY-THE-SEA ————————

Driftwood Beach Club
4417 El Mar Drive
Lauderdale-By-The-Sea, FL 33308
305-776-4441

Studio $, 1 Bedroom $$, 2 Bedrooms $$$
Dep. Req'd.
40 condos, Lo-rise

Location: Beach front

General Facilities: Daily maid, Kitchen, Linens, Baby-sitter

Room Facilities: Pool, Shuffleboard, horseshoes

Attractions: Fishing pier, marina, tennis courts, Water Kingdoms, Bahama Islands, Everglades, golf, entertainment

Shops & Restaurants: Lauderdale gift shops, take-out, service stores

Monday morning orange juice wake-ups with coffee and donuts, Wednesday night chicken and ribs barbecues and manager's informal talk about the area are some of the weekly happenings here. Use the private beach with its shuffleboard courts and horseshoe pits or walk two blocks to fishing pier and marina. Pool, grills and large patio—close to tennis and playground.

───────────────── LAUDERDALE-BY-THE-SEA ─────────────────

Howard Johnson Resort and Villas
4660 N. Ocean Drive
Lauderdale-By-The-Sea, FL 33308
305-776-5660 800-327-5919

Studio $$, 1 Bedroom $$, 2 Bedrooms $$$
Dep. 1 Night
Villas, Key at Front desk
No S-yes/H-yes

Location: Airport: Ft. Lauderdale; Beach front

General Facilities: Full serv., Conf. rm., Kitchen, Linens, Restaurant on prem., Bar on prem., Lounge, Child planned rec.: Activities Director

Room Facilities: Pool, Health Club, TV, Cable, VCR, Phone in rm., Ind. AC Ctl., Ind. Heat Ctl.

Attractions: Jai alai, horse/dog racing, Ocean World, Cruise Harbor, State parks, nightclub circuit

Shops & Restaurants: Sea Ranch Shopping Village, On-site gift shop; Howard Johnson restaurant

Check into your Villa and sip the complimentary Perrier. Complimentary coffee and newspaper to start your day before you head for the beach, pools or exercise and steam rooms. Children have their own pool as well as craft classes and supervised activities. Movies and entertainment in the lobby lounge, Oceanfront Patio Bar with BBQ, and family-priced Howard Johnson's restaurant. 5 minute walk to the ocean pier. The staff will be happy to arrange your visit to area attractions.

───

Morningstar Condominium
223 Marine Court
Lauderdale-By-The-Sea, FL 33308
305-771-5924

1 Bedroom $$, 2 Bedrooms $$
Min. Stay 7 Nights, Dep. Req'd.
11 condos, Lo-rise, Villas, Key at Apt. 206
H-yes

Location: Airport: 7 miles; Need car

General Facilities: Kitchen, Linens

Room Facilities: Pool, Tennis, TV, Cable, Crib-Hi-chair, Ind. AC Ctl., Ind. Heat Ctl.

Attractions: Paddlewheel Queen, Jungle Queen, sightseeing, Ft. Lauderdale

Shops & Restaurants: Shopping malls; Raindancer Wharf, Benihana

Completely furnished apartments in modern decor. The beach is just around the corner. Tropical patio, small pool, shuffleboard, laundry facilities and free parking. 10 minute walk to stores, restaurants, post office and nightlife.

───

Villas By The Sea
4500 Ocean Drive
Lauderdale-By-The-Sea, FL 33308
305-722-3550 800-247-8963

1 Bedroom $$, Villas
Pool, Daily maid, Kitchen, Linens, Phone in rm.

Attractions: Fitness room, Tennis

Six adjoining properties, four of which are on the beach. All but one property have their own pools. Free weekly continental breakfast. Monthly calendar of events with various activities, games and parties. Weekly bingo and monthly barbecue.

─────────────── LEHIGH ───────────────

Lehigh Resort Club
225 East Joel Blvd.
Lehigh, FL 33936
813-369-2121 800-843-0971

Studio $$, 1 Bedroom $$, 2 Bedrooms $$$
1 Bedrm/week 5$, 2 Bed/week 6$
AmEx/Visa/MC, Dep. 1 Night •
140 condos, Lo-rise, Key at Front desk
H-yes

Location: Airport: 20 miles; Downtown: 20 miles; Need car

General Facilities: Full serv., Conf. rm. cap. 200, Kitchen, Linens, Restaurant on prem., Bar on prem., Game room, Lounge, Baby-sitter, Child planned rec.: Recreation director

Room Facilities: Pool, Hot tub, Tennis, Shuffleboard, Basketball, Golf: 36-holes on property, TV, Cable, Phone in rm., Crib-Hi-chair, Ind. AC Ctl., Ind. Heat Ctl.

Attractions: Thomas Edison winter home, golf, tennis, entertainment

Shops & Restaurants: Burdines, Robinsons, Mass Brothers, Jacobsons

Complete golf and tennis resort, bordering two 18-hole championship golf courses. Four lighted tennis courts and a recreational director with planned activities for all ages. Nightly entertainment in the lounge.

─────────────── LIDO BEACH, SARASOTA ───────────────

Sarasota Sands
2150 Benjamin Franklin Dr.
Lido Beach, Sarasota, FL 34236
813-388-2138

1 Bedroom $$, 2 Bedrooms $$, Hi-rise
Pool, Kitchen, Linens, Phone in rm.

Attractions: Ringling Museum, Jungle Gardens, Lionel Train and Seashell Museum, V. Wezel Performing Arts, Basketball, racquetball, Tennis

Relaxed, casual, informal atmosphere. Professionally furnished gulf-front condominiums on Lido Beach. Recreation facilities include tennis, racquetball, basketball, shuffleboard, pool, sauna and hot tub.

─────────────── LONGBOAT KEY, SARASOTA ───────────────

Veranda Beach Club
2509 Gulf Of Mexico Drive
Longboat Key, Sarasota, FL 34228
813-383-5511

Hi-rise
Pool, Kitchen, Linens

Attractions: White Sox spring training, Sarasota Kennel Club, deep-sea fishing, Busch Gardens, Health & exercise center, Tennis, Golf

Spacious 38-foot covered porches with Gulf and Bay views span each unit. Each unit is built around a central landscaped courtyard with wrought-iron and a bubbling fountain. Your complete vacation home has a private, furnished, ceramic floored terrace.

─────────────────── LONGBOAT KEY ───────────────────

Four Winds Beach Resort
2605 Gulf Of Mexico Drive
Longboat Key, FL 34228
813-383-2411

1 Bedrm/week 5$, 2 Bed/week 7$
Min. Stay 7 Nights, Visa/MC, Dep. Req'd.
Lo-rise, Key at Desk

Location: Airport: Sarasota 17 miles; Downtown: 6 miles; Beach front

General Facilities: Daily maid, Kitchen, Linens, Restaurant on prem.

Room Facilities: Pool, Hot tub, Tennis, Shuffleboard, Golf: Drive to 30 courses, TV, Cable, Phone in rm.

Shops & Restaurants: Bay Isles Shopping Plaza across the street; French/Cont. restaurant on-site

Minutes away from Sarasota and an easy drive to Florida's major attractions. Tennis, shuffleboard, jacuzzi, pool and barbecues among tropical landscaping. Elegant French restaurant for your dining pleasure.

Gulf Tides of Longboat Key
3008 Gulf of Mexico Dr., Box 8059
Longboat Key, FL 34228
813-383-5595

1 Bedrm/week 4$, 2 Bed/week 5$
Dep. Req'd.

Location: Airport: Sarasota 8 miles; Beach front

General Facilities: Kitchen, Linens, Game room

Room Facilities: Pool, Tennis, Shuffleboard, Golf: Drive to 30 courses, TV, Cable, Phone in rm.

Attractions: Bellm's Cars and Music of Yesterday, Ringling Museums, Jungle Gardens, State theater

Shops & Restaurants: Longboat Key and Sarasota shops

Decorator furnished and color coordinated condominiums, spacious closets with mirrored doors, jacuzzis in master bath and central vacuum systems. A host of recreational activities, including the beach, lighted tennis court, gas grills and solar heated pool.

Little Gull
5330 Gulf of Mexico Drive
Longboat Key, FL 34228
813-383-8818

1 Bedrm/week $$$$, 2 Bed/week 4$, 3 Bed/week 6$
Dep. Req'd.
16 condos, Lo-rise

Location: Airport: Sarasota 12 miles; Need car; Beach front

General Facilities: Kitchen

Room Facilities: Pool, Bicycles, Golf: Area courses, TV, Cable, Phone in rm., Ind. AC Ctl.

Attractions: Busch Gardens, Ringling Museums & Residence, Asolo Theater, Bellm's Cars, Dixie cruise

Shops & Restaurants: Sarasota specialty shops and stores; Longboat Key restaurants

Follow the red brick path to your vacation home hidden among foliage of Australian pine and Spanish dagger. Understated elegance in these condominiums with fireplaces, located on the water. Boat dock and private beach make for a perfect water sport vacation.

Longboat Key Club

LONGBOAT KEY

Longboat Bay Club
3200 Gulf of Mexico Dr.
Longboat Key, FL 33548
813-383-9561

Pool, Kitchen, Linens

Attractions: Sarasota's artistic and cultural activities, golf, art galleries, theatres, Tennis

Enjoy vacation days and nights in your condominium with state of the art kitchen appliances, breakfast nook, 6-ft jacuzzi and telephone-controlled security. Sheltered, deepwater marina on Sarasota Bay with dockage and easy access to Gulf beaches.

Longboat Key Club
301 Gulf Of Mexico Drive
Longboat Key, FL 34228
813-383-8821   800-237-8821

Studio $$$, 1 Bedroom $$$, 2 Bedrooms $$$$,
    3 Bedrooms $$$$
AmEx/Visa/MC, Dep. 1 Night •
221 condos, Hi-rise, Key at Recep. Center, H-yes

Location: Airport: 15 minutes; Downtown: 10 min.; Need car; Beach front

General Facilities: Full serv., Bus. fac., Conf. rm. cap. 200, Daily maid, Kitchen, Linens, Restaurant/Bar on prem., Lounge, Baby-sitter, Child planned rec.: Nature walks, movies

Room Facilities: Pool, Sauna, Hot tub, Tennis, Full service marina, Golf: Islandside on-site, TV, Cable, Phone in rm., Crib-Hi-chair, Ind. AC Ctl., Ind. Heat Ctl.

Attractions: John Ringling Home, Asolo Theatre, Performing Arts Hall, Marie Selby Botanical Gardens, entertainment

Shops & Restaurants: St. Armands Circle shops; Plaza on Longboat Key

Elegant vacation suites, light tropical colors, contemporary styling, balconies with views of the Gulf, lagoons or golf course. A family resort with games, nature walks, tours and movies for the children, four restaurants on-site and a harpist in the Orchid Room.

—————————— LONGBOAT KEY ——————————

White Sands of Longboat Lo-rise, Villas
5114 Gulf of Mexico Drive Pool, Kitchen, Linens
Longboat Key, FL 34228 Putting green, Tennis
813-383-2428

Bermuda-style villa, or gracious townhouse overlooking gardens, the Gulf or Bay. Professionally designed interiors with whirlpool tubs, screened and open porches, even board games. Bay-front fishing and boat dock for your complimentary dory.

———————— MARATHON SHORES, FLORIDA KEYS ————————

Key Lime Resort & Marina Club Lo-rise
P.O. Box 3267 Pool, Kitchen, Linens
Marathon Shores, FL 33052
305-743-3505

Island living in a tropical setting. Pool, tennis and jacuzzi. Parking for boat trailers. Saturday happy hour, bingo one night, cookout one night. Other featured specials such as pot-luck dinners and hors d'oeuvres.

—————————— MARATHON ——————————

Buccaneer Resort & Yacht Club 2 Bedrooms $$$$, Villas
2600 Overseas Highway Pool, Daily maid, Kitchen, Linens
Marathon, FL 33050
305-743-9071

Attractions: Charter boats, windsurfing, sailing, paddleboats, Rental boats, Tennis, Golf

Villas with jacuzzis, two T.V.'s and fully equipped kitchens on a tropically landscaped 10-acre resort on the Gulf. Private beach and dock with boat rentals and instruction. Exotic drinks at the Polynesian Pub and nightly specials in the dining room.

Casa Cayo Condominiums Hi-rise
12690 Overseas Highway Pool, Kitchen
Marathon, FL 33050
305-743-7562

Attractions: Gulf of Mexico, golf, tennis, fishing, boating, diving, Dockage

16-unit condominium on a private peninsula with 270 degree views. Security gates at entrance and free dockage. Access to Gulf and Atlantic waters.

Cocoplum Beach & Tennis Club 2 Bedrooms $$
109 Cocoplum Dr. 2 Bedrms/week 6$
Marathon, FL 33050 Min. Stay 2 Nights, Dep. Req'd. •
305-743-0240 800-228-1587 20 condos, Villas, Key at Main office

Location: Airport: 2 miles; Downtown: 6 miles; Need car; Beach front
General Facilities: Kitchen, Linens, Baby-sitter
Room Facilities: Pool, Hot tub, Tennis, TV, Cable, Crib-Hi-chair, Ind. AC Ctl., Ind. Heat Ctl.
Attractions: Old town Key West, scuba, snorkeling, state parks
Shops & Restaurants: Unique shopping in the the islands; The Quay-French

Two-bedroom, two-bath villas on the southernmost point of the USA. Stuffed furniture in muted mauves, pinks and beiges, glass top dining table, large screened porch. Take an excursion boat or a drive to Key West, or just relax and enjoy the pool or beach.

─────────────── MARATHON ───────────────

Gulfpointe
12690 Overseas Hwy.
Marathon, FL 33050
305-743-9088

Lo-rise
Pool, Kitchen

Attractions: Golf, shopping, boating, beach, water sports, Boat dockage, Tennis

Island life-style and tropical climate for a relaxed vacation. Two-bedroom, two-level con-
dominiums have 1400 square feet of living space and wraparound six-foot-wide terraces
off the living room and master bedroom. Ceramic tile through the lower levels and baths.

───────────────────────────────────────

The Hawks Nest
One Kyle Way South
Marathon, FL 33050
305-743-6711

1 Bedroom $$, 2 Bedrooms $$, Hi-rise
Pool, Daily maid, Kitchen, Linens

Attractions: Bay and deep-sea fishing, snorkeling, diving, water skiing, Boat docking,
Tennis

Functional spacious units with golf or ocean views from the terrace. Bring your boat or rent
a canoe or power boat. Snorkel, swim and dive and explore the reef. Catch your dinner
in the Keys water and barbecue it for dinner at the picnic facility.

───────────────────────────────────────

Marathon Key Beach Club
4590 Overseas Highway
Marathon, FL 33050
305-743-6522

Lo-rise
Pool, Daily maid

Attractions: Hemingway haven, treasure reefs, historic homes, theater, golf, helicopter rides, Boat ramp, bicycles, Tennis

Leave your business suit at home for this casual resort. No telephones to disturb you, just
many water sports, tennis and the largest pool in the Keys. Tropical grounds have barbecue
pit and picnic area. Screened patios, laundries, carport and three dining areas.

───────────────────────────────────────

The Reef at Marathon
6800 Overseas Highway
Marathon, FL 33050
305-743-7900 800-327-4836

1 Bedroom $$$, 2 Bedrooms $$$, Lo-rise, Villas
Pool, Kitchen

Attractions: Boat slip, ramp, tennis

Villas on 6 acres of Florida Bay. Small private boat marina with ramp, small, pebble beach
and slip included with villa. Complimentary canoes, paddle boats, sailboats and wind-
surfers. Tennis, pool and grills.

————————————— MARATHON —————————————

Sombrero Resort & Lighthouse　1 Bedroom $$$
19 Sombrero Blvd.　　　　　　　　1 Bedrm/week 7$
Marathon, FL 33050　　　　　　　AmEx/Visa/MC, Dep. 1 Night •
305-743-2250 800-433-8660　　105 condos, Lo-rise, Key at Front desk
　　　　　　　　　　　　　　　　　H-yes

Location: Airport: 2 Miles; Downtown: 1 mile; Beach front

General Facilities: Full serv., Conf. rm. cap. 100, Daily maid, Kitchen, Linens, Restaurant on prem., Bar on prem., Lounge

Room Facilities: Pool, Sauna, Tennis, Golf: Sombrero Country Club, TV, Cable, VCR, Phone in rm., Crib, Ind. AC Ctl., Ind. Heat Ctl.

Attractions: Bahia Honda State Park, Sombrero Beach, 7-Mile Bridge, Dolphin Research Ctr, entertainment

Shops & Restaurants: K-Mart, Grocery store, Eckerd Drugs; Kelseys-Gourmet

Lounging at pool, fishing, dining. Lovely one-bedroom suites, live entertainment, lush tropical grounds; family oriented; deep water protected marina; tennis pro shop.

————————————— MARCO ISLAND —————————————

Beach Club Of Marco　　　　1 Bedroom $$, 2 Bedrooms $$
901 S. Collier Blvd.　　　　　　1 Bedrm/week 4$, 2 Bed/week 5$
Marco Island, FL 33937　　　　AmEx/Visa/MC, Dep. 1 Night •
813-394-8860 800-323-8860　52 condos, Hi-rise, Key at Registr. desk

Location: Airport: Naples 20 miles; Downtown: 3 miles; Need car

General Facilities: Daily maid, Kitchen, Linens, Restaurant on prem., Bar on prem., Lounge, Baby-sitter

Room Facilities: Pool, Racquetball, TV, Cable, Phone in rm., Crib-Hi-chair, Ind. AC Ctl., Ind. Heat Ctl.

Attractions: Everglades boat tours, seashelling trips, paddle boat tours, charter boat fishing trips, entertainment

Shops & Restaurants: Sears, Maison Blanche, grocery, boutiques, K-Mart; French/Italian/German/Mexican

Gracious, Florida-style furnishings with private balconies. Spend a calm, leisurely vacation or take advantage of the abundant sporting life. Margo 11 trolley takes you on an island historical tour and to island shops. 3.5 miles to the beach. Heated pool, shuffleboard, racquetball, gazebos with barbecue. Ensign's Quarters Restaurant and nightly entertainment in the Upper Deck Lounge.

———————————————————————————————

Charter Club of Marco Beach　Hi-rise
700 S. Collier Blvd.　　　　　　Pool, Kitchen, Linens
Marco Island, FL 33937
813-394-4192 800-237-4411

Attractions: Putting green, fitness center, Tennis

On Marco Island, a bridge away from the mainland, condominiums overlooking the Gulf of Mexico. Enter the round-robin tennis tournaments held twice weekly. Fitness room instructors, sailing lessons, social building, pools and barbecue pavilion.

MARCO ISLAND

Club Regency of Marco Island
500 South Collier Boulevard
Marco Island, FL 33939
813-394-8197 800-237-4171

2 Bedrooms $$$, Villas
Pool, Kitchen, Phone in rm.

Attractions: Everglades, Wootens Airboat tours, Tiki boat tours, Safari Park, Seminole State Park, Tennis

Comfortably furnished with rattan and glass with balconies overlooking the Gulf or lush poolside gardens. White sand beach, pool, jacuzzi, two sun decks with barbecues. Grass play area for children and two tennis courts. All types of sporting activities.

Eagle's Nest
410 S. Collier Blvd.
Marco Island, FL 33937
813-394-5167

1 Bedroom $$$, 2 Bedrooms $$$$, Lo-rise
Pool, Kitchen

Attractions: Exercise room, Tennis, Golf

Villas around a tropical garden with pool and spas. Terra-cotta tiles, wood cabinetry, wicker with tropical prints and French doors to the screened terraces. Walk to restaurants and entertainment. Golf, shopping and water sports are nearby.

Marco Bay Resort
1001 N. Barfield Dr.
Marco Island, FL 33937
813-394-8881 800-228-0661

1 Bedroom $$, 2 Bedrooms $$
1 Bedrm/week $$$$, 2 Bed/week 4$
AmEx/Visa/MC, Dep. 1 Night •
200 condos, Hi-rise, Key at Front desk
H-yes

Location: Airport: Ft. Meyers-55 min.; Downtown: 1 mile; Need car

General Facilities: Full serv., Bus. fac., Conf. rm. cap. 250, Daily maid, Kitchen, Linens, Restaurant on prem., Bar on prem., Baby-sitter, Child planned rec.: Activities director

Room Facilities: Pool, Hot tub, Tennis, Golf: Nearby, TV, Cable, Phone in rm., Crib-Hi-chair, Ind. AC Ctl., Ind. Heat Ctl.

Attractions: Shelling, Sunset cruises, paddlewheeler, Island trolley and Everglades tours

Shops & Restaurants: Port of Marco shopping village; Old Marco Inn-European

Light, airy suites with ample dockage for your boat. Explore the many secluded islands nearby, or charter a fully equipped boat with a licensed captain for serious fishing. The Chickee Bar is at water's edge, and the Hawk's Nest cafe is at poolside. Relax by the pool or take provided transportation to Tigertail Beach. Planned recreational activities for children, plus a video arcade. Marco Bay Resort is a "suite treat."

Sea Winds Beach Resort
890 S. Collier Blvd.
Marco Island, FL 33937
813-642-6262 800-237-4155

Hi-rise
Pool, Kitchen

Attractions: Exercise room, Tennis

Magnificently furnished 2 bedroom condominiums on 3.5 miles of crescent beach. Amenities include pool, whirlpool, tennis, sauna, exercise room, poolside bar and barbecue.

─────────────── MARCO ISLAND ───────────────

Sunrise Bay Resort & Club
10 Tampa Place
Marco Island, FL 33937
813-394-5280

1 Bedroom $$
1 Bedrm/week 5$
Visa/MC,Dep. Req'd. •
20 condos, Hi-rise, Key at Front desk

Location: Airport: Ft. Myers 40 miles; Downtown: 1 mile; Need car; Beach front

General Facilities: Kitchen, Linens

Room Facilities: Pool, Hot tub, Bikes, boat rentals, TV, Cable, Phone in rm., Crib, Ind. AC Ctl., Ind. Heat Ctl.

Attractions: Rosie O'Shea Paddlewheel, Island trolley tours, charter fishing, entertainment

Shops & Restaurants: Island boutiques, Naples 15 miles, 3rd St. South; O'Shea's/seafood, variety

Peaceful, tropical area in historic Marco. Units are partially encircled in walls of mirrors and windows including screened balconies with table and chairs. Shades of blue, brown, wood grains, brass and tweed enhance the nautical theme of this boating and fishing resort. Largest privately owned fishing pier on the Island, with slip space, Seminole-built "chickee hut," pool, spa, bikes, and grills in picnic area. Just a few minutes to sports, dining, shopping and entertainment. Sunday aft. dock parties.

───────────────────────────────────

The Surf Club of Marco
540 S. Collier Blvd.
Marco Island, FL 33937
813-642-5800

2 Bedrooms $$$, Hi-rise
Pool, Kitchen, Linens

Attractions: Charter fishing, shelling, bike rentals, parasailing, water skiing, sailing, Tennis, Golf

Located on Marco Island's crescent beach, two-bedroom, two-bath suites with everything you need for your vacation. Tennis, pool with patio and deck, spa.

─────────────── MIAMI BEACH ───────────────

Golden Strand Ocean Resort
17901 Collins Avenue
Miami Beach, FL 33160
305-931-7000 800-327-4008

Studio $$, 1 Bedroom $$, 2 Bedrooms $$$
Villas

Location: Beach front

General Facilities: Kitchen, Restaurant on prem., Bar on prem., Lounge

Room Facilities: Pool, Hot tub, Spa, gym, putt green

Attractions: Deep-sea fishing, sailing, surfing, golf, jai alai, horse/dog racing

Shops & Restaurants: Aventura Mall, Bal Harbour-Saks, Gucci's, Neiman M; Ocean View, Terrace Cafe

Unusual attention to service, private and exclusive. Villas decorated with meticulous attention to detail. Tile floors, skylights, wet bars. Full service spa, evaluation, exercise program and diet planned especially for you. Yoga, aerobics, weight-training instructors. Pool and putting green for those who prefer a less strenuous vacation.

──────────────── MIAMI BEACH ────────────────

Roney Plaza   1 Bedroom $$, 2 Bedrooms $$$, Hi-rise
2301 Collins Ave.   Pool, Kitchen, Linens
Miami Beach, FL 33139
305-531-8811 800-432-4317

Attractions: Art Deco district, theatre, museums, galleries

Ideally located in fabulous Miami Beach with its many attractions and activities. Olympic-sized pool, restaurant, lounge. Do it all, or do nothing.

Seacoast Towers Apartment Hotel 1 Bedroom $$, 2 Bedrooms $$$, Hi-rise
5151 Collins Avenue   Pool, Daily maid, Kitchen, Linens
Miami Beach, FL 33140
305-865-5152 800-523-3671

Attractions: Marina, Tennis, Golf

Commitment to excellence in the designer decorated suites, equipped with video players, mini-bars and walk-in closets. 600-foot stretch of beach and private marina. Courteous, hospitable staff provides maid service and valet parking.

Marco Bay Resort

MIDDLEBURG

The Inn at Ravines
2932 Ravines Road
Middleburg, FL 32068
904-282-2843

1 Bedroom $$, 2 Bedrooms $$, 3 Bedrooms $$
Visa/MC •
50 condos

Location: Airport: 50 miles; Downtown: 45 miles

General Facilities: Conf. rm. cap. 75, Kitchen, Restaurant on prem., Bar on prem.

Room Facilities: Pool, Tennis, Putting course, Golf: Ravines, TV, Cable, Ind.AC Ctl., Ind. Heat Ctl.

Attractions: St. Augustine, Jacksonville Landing

Shops & Restaurants: Orange Park Mall (15 miles) 120 stores; Hilltop/continental, Ravines'

Warm, comfortable condominiums on 450 acres of planned beauty. The natural terrain of the area has steep hills that rise some 90 feet above sea level with drastic drops of more than 60 feet to the ravine bottom. There are many species of wildlife and more than 50 varieties of trees. All the diversions you could ask for with the ambience of a country inn.

N. REDINGTON BEACH

Emerald Isle
17334 Gulf Blvd.
N. Redington Beach, FL 33708
813-397-0441

2 Bedrooms $$, 3 Bedrooms $$$
2 Bedrms/week 6$, 3 Bed/week 6$
Min. Stay 7 Nights, AmEx/Visa/MC,
   Dep. Req'd.
Hi-rise, Key at Office, No S-yes/H-yes

Location: Airport: 30 miles; Downtown: 10 min.; Beach front

General Facilities: Daily maid, Kitchen, Linens, Baby-sitter

Room Facilities: Pool, Sailing, windsurfing, TV, Cable, Phone in rm., Crib-Hi-chair, Ind. AC Ctl., Ind. Heat Ctl.

Attractions: Busch Gardens, Dali Museum, charter boats, Disney World, St. Petersburg pier, Flea market

Shops & Restaurants: Small shopping plaza, Maas Brothers, Burdines; Wine Cellar/wide variety

Located directly on the Gulf of Mexico between St. Petersburg and Clearwater. Private terraces overlooking the beach, large closets and fully equipped kitchens.

Redington Ambassdor
16900 Gulf Blvd.
N. Redington Beach, FL 33708
813-391-9646

2 Bedrooms $$, Hi-rise
Pool, Kitchen

Built directly on the Gulf of Mexico, within walking distance to shops, stores, restaurants and Redington fishing pier. Two-bedroom, two-bath units with ceiling fans and abundant storage. Recreational deck area, pool, jacuzzi and inside atrium with walk.

NAPLES

Beachcomber Club
290 Fifth Avenue South
Naples, FL 33940
813-262-8112

1 Bedroom $$, 2 Bedrooms $$, Lo-rise
Pool, Kitchen

Mostly efficiencies and one bedroom units with screened porches, cable color TV, telephones, heated pools, landscaped patios.

─────────────── NAPLES ───────────────

Charter Club of Naples Bay
1000 10th Ave. S
Naples, FL 33940
813-261-5559 800-445-3623

2 Bedrooms $$
2 Bedrms/week 6$
Min. Stay 3 Nights, Dep. Req'd.
Lo-rise

General Facilities: Kitchen, Bar on prem., Child planned rec.: Kiddie pool
Room Facilities: Pool, Badminton, Horseshoes, TV

Polynesian motif exteriors and light rattan interiors for casual, comfortable vacation living. King-size bed and color TV in the master bedroom. 30 ft. screened lanai covers the master bedroom and living room for Naples Bay views. Rolling terrain with tropical landscaping, winding paths and shade trees. Bicycles, fishing poles, badminton, horseshoes, pool and kiddie pool. Boat rental at the Marina, or slip for boats up to 18 feet. 8 blocks to the beach.

Edgewater Beach Hotel
1901 Gulfshore Blvd. N.
Naples, FL 33940
813-262-6511 800-821-0196

1 Bedroom $$, 2 Bedrooms $$$
AmEx/Visa/MC
124 condos, Hi-rise

Location: Airport: Naples-10 miles; Downtown: 5 miles; Beach front
General Facilities: Conf. rm. cap. 100, Kitchen, Restaurant on prem., Bar on prem.,
  Lounge
Attractions: Tennis, golf, sailing, boating, sightseeing, fishing, shelling excursions
Shops & Restaurants: Olde Naples shops; Crystal Parrot on-site

Concerned professionals greet you as you enter the imported Italian marble lobby. When you are settled, walk to the beach or swim in the heated pool with its gulfside bar. Exercise room, nearby golf and tennis, trolley outside the lobby for trips to Olde Naples for browsing and shopping. Two lounges, gift shop and view dining in the Crystal Parrot. 4:00 p.m. Happy Hour with hors d'oeuvres. Daily newspaper delivered to your suite.

Golden Isle Apartments
430 Fourth Ave. S.
Naples, FL 33940
813-261-8104

1 Bedroom $$, 2 Bedrooms $$
1 Bedrm/week 4$, 2 Bed/week 5$
MC,Dep. 25%
18 condos, Hi-rise, Key at Office

Location: Downtown: 1 block
General Facilities: Kitchen, Linens
Room Facilities: TV, Cable, Ind. AC Ctl., Ind. Heat Ctl.
Attractions: Naples beach, fishing, charter boats, Jungle Larry's, Everglades
Shops & Restaurants: Grocery, drug and specialty stores; Kelly's, Red Lobster, Chinese

Golden Isle is a small place appealing to couples and families who appreciate a quiet environment among congenial neighbors. Free use of bicycles and 16' Sunfish sailboat. 3 blocks to Naples beach and fishing pier. Public tennis and golf courses are nearby. The simple design of the furnishings create a relaxed atmosphere for vacation enjoyment.

NAPLES

Naples Bath & Tennis
4995 Airport Rd. N.
Naples, FL 33942
813-261-5777 800-225-9692

1 Bedroom $$, 2 Bedrooms $$$, 3 Bedrooms $$$
1 Bedrm/week 6$, 2 Bed/week 7$,
    3 Bed/week 9$
AmEx/Visa/MC, Dep. Req'd. •
80 condos, Lo-rise, Key at Resort office, No S-yes

Location: Downtown: 4 miles; Need car

General Facilities: Full serv., Bus. fac., Conf. rm. cap. 450, Daily maid, Kitchen, Linens, Restaurant on prem., Bar on prem., Lounge, Baby-sitter

Room Facilities: Pool, Sauna, Hot tub, Tennis, Health Club, Golf: Naples Beach & Vineyards, TV, Cable, Phone in rm., Crib-Hi-chair, Ind. AC Ctl., Ind. Heat Ctl.

Attractions: Everglades cruise, deep-sea fishing, dinner cruise, African Safari, Edison Home, entertainment

Shops & Restaurants: Burdines, Maas Bros. Third Street boutiques; Villa Pescatore/George & Dragon

Premier tennis resort community, official home of the 1987-88 Tennis Grand Masters. The place to go if you really care about improving your tennis. 160 acres of tropical paradise. Lakes, pools, jacuzzi, health clubs, planned barbecues, dances, tennis tournaments, aerobics, bridge, recreational activities, shopping, sports, and a nearby beach—all for a complete family vacation.

Park Shore Resort
4535 Tamiami Trail North
Naples, FL 33940
813-481-3636 800-237-8096

1 Bedroom $$, 2 Bedrooms $$, Lo-rise
Pool, Kitchen

Attractions: Golf, fishing, water sports, beach, Racquetball, Tennis

13 acres of lush, tropical landscaping. Lake with an island in the center housing a pool with sparkling waterfall and the Island Club lounge and restaurant. Suites with private patios and sleeper sofas in the living area.

Sandrift Club Condominium
613 E. Lake Dr.
Naples, FL 33940
813-261-2380

Lo-rise
Pool, Kitchen, Phone in rm.

Attractions: Cambier Park, Candy Cane Park, Naples Recreation Center

Heated pool with deck area and self-service poolside bar, jacuzzi, and gas grills surrounded by lawns, tropical flowers and carpeted walkways. Color-coordinated mahogany, period furniture, large-screen color television, and private patio or balcony.

White Sands Resort Club
260 Third St. So.
Naples, FL 33940
813-261-4144

1 Bedroom $, 2 Bedrooms $$, Lo-rise
Pool, Kitchen, Linens, Phone in rm.

Attractions: Water sports, deep-sea fishing, scuba diving, golf, tennis, Shuffleboard

2.5 blocks from the Gulf of Mexico. Units overlook green courtyard with palm trees and umbrella covered tables by the heated pool and spa. Chickee bar, shuffleboard court, and grills. Ride one of the free bicycles to the beach. Quiet, private atmosphere.

──────────────── NAPLES ────────────────

World Tennis Center
4800 Airport Road
Naples, FL 33942
813-263-1900 800-292-6663

2 Bedrooms $$
2 Bedrms/week 4$
Min. Stay 2 Nights, Visa/MC, Dep. Req'd. •
160 condos, Lo-rise, Villas, Key at Rental office
P-yes

Location: Airport: Naples-3 miles; Downtown: 5 miles; Need car

General Facilities: Bus. fac., Daily maid, Kitchen, Linens, Restaurant on prem., Bar on prem.

Room Facilities: Pool, Sauna, Hot tub, Tennis, TV, Cable, Phone in rm., Crib, Ind. AC Ctl., Ind. Heat Ctl.

Attractions: Dog racing, hot air balloon festival, African Safari park, airboat rides, Indian villages, entertainment

Shops & Restaurants: Fifth Avenue South and 3rd Street, Olde Naples; Chef's Garden-continental

1100-square-foot condominiums, white stucco exteriors and Mediterranean-style architecture with rattan furnishings. 11 clay, 5 hard tennis courts, 10 of them lighted. Poolside cafe/bar, Pro Shop, beach three miles away. A family resort for tennis and non-tennis players alike.

──────────────── NAVARRE BEACH ────────────────

Beach Resort
8459 Gulf Blvd.
Navarre Beach, FL 32561
904-939-2324 800-344-7368

1 Bedroom $$
1 Bedrm/week 5$
Min. Stay 3 Nights, Dep. Req'd.
30 condos, Hi-rise, Key at Realty office onsite
H-yes

Location: Airport: 30 miles; Downtown: 15 miles; Need car; Beach front

General Facilities: Daily maid, Kitchen, Linens, Restaurant on prem., Bar on prem.

Room Facilities: Pool, Hot tub, Tennis, TV, Cable, Phone in rm., Ind. AC Ctl., Ind. Heat Ctl.

Attractions: Zoo, Pensacola historical district, Fort Pickens, Air Force/Navy & Indian museums

Shops & Restaurants: Shopping Malls, McRae's, Gayfers, Parisian; Navarre Orleans, Destinees

Secluded family oriented island living. Bedroom has two queen-size beds, living room with sofa sleeper, balcony and private Gulf beach. Barbecue grills, party room and excellent seafood restaurant on property; Pensacola's historic district and deep-sea fishing just 30 minutes away.

Beachview
8425 Gulf Blvd.
Navarre Beach, FL 32561

NAVARRE BEACH

Emerald Surf
8245 Gulf Boulevard
Navarre Beach, FL 32561
904-939-3450 800-331-0540

2 Bedrooms $$
2 Bedrms/week 5$
Min. Stay 2 Nights, Visa/MC, Dep. Req'd.
33 condos, Hi-rise, Key at In office

Location: Airport: 35 miles; Downtown: 25 miles; Need car

General Facilities: Conf. rm., Kitchen, Linens

Room Facilities: Pool, Activities room, TV, Cable, Ind. AC Ctl., Ind. Heat Ctl.

Attractions: Charter boats for rent in Pensacola or Fort Walton, entertainment

Shops & Restaurants: Gift shops; Pensacola/Fort Walton

Enjoy the sun, sea and rolling dunes on this tranquil barrier island to the Gulf Islands National Seashore. Gulf-front suites with whirlpool tubs and private balconies in an unsurpassed water sports playground. Covered shuffleboard court, VCR and tape rental, beach service for chairs, umbrellas, and sailboats. Minutes away from historic Pensacola and fun-loving Ft. Walton. Area tennis courts and golf, plus our magnificent sunsets.

Sundunes Condominiums
7979 Gulf Blvd.
Navarre Beach, FL
904-939-2994 800-262-8224

NEW SMYRNA BEACH

Islander Beach Club Resort
1601 S. Atlantic Ave.
New Smyrna Beach, FL 32069
904-427-3452 800-872-3452

1 Bedroom $$, 2 Bedrooms $$, Hi-rise
Pool, Kitchen, Phone in rm.

Attractions: Disney World, Sea World, Kennedy Space Center, Blue Springs State Park, ocean cruises

Far from the crowds, but an hour's drive to most Florida attractions. Tastefully furnished condominium apartments. Friday and Saturday entertainment at The Islander Lounge, 4-8 p.m. happy hour, poolside food and cocktail service.

NICEVILLE

Bluewater Bay
2000 Bluewater Blvd., P.O. Box 247
Niceville, FL 32578
904-897-3613 800-874-2128

Studio $$, 1 Bedroom $$$, 2 Bedrooms $$$,
  3 Bedrooms $$$
1 Bedrm/week 6$, 2 Bed/week 7$,
  3 Bed/week 8$
AmEx/Visa/MC, Dep. Req'd., Lo-rise, Villas

Location: Airport: Ft. Walton 15 min.; Downtown: 6 miles; Beach front

General Facilities: Daily maid, Kitchen, Linens, Restaurant on prem., Game room, Lounge, Baby-sitter, Child planned rec.: Activity programs

Room Facilities: Pool, Tennis, Recreation Center, Golf: 3 9-hole championship, TV, Phone in rm.

Shops & Restaurants: Merchants Walk area of Bluewater Bay, Niceville; La Fontana/Italian

A variety of superb accommodations-villas and townhouses-to choose from. The whole family will enjoy the many recreational opportunities. Summer youth activity program, evening activities, game room and putt-putt golf. 120-slip marina, private beach, health club and Racquetball Center. Two restaurants, lounge and snack bar.

───────────── NORTH REDINGTON BEACH ─────────────

Ram Sea I and Ram Sea II
17200 Gulf Blvd.
North Redington Beach, FL 33708
813-397-0441

1 Bedroom $$, 2 Bedrooms $$$, 3 Bedrooms $$$
1 Bedrm/week 5$, 2 Bed/week 6$,
  3 Bed/week 6$
Min. Stay 3 Nights, AmEx/Visa/MC,
  Dep. Req'd.
60 condos, Hi-rise, Key at Front desk
No S-yes/H-yes

Location: Airport: 30 miles; Downtown: 10 min.

General Facilities: Full serv., Daily maid, Kitchen, Linens, Baby-sitter

Room Facilities: Pool, Hot tub, Windsurfing, sailing, Golf: Nearby, TV, Cable, Phone in rm., Crib-Hi-chair, Ind. AC Ctl., Ind. Heat Ctl.

Attractions: Busch Gardens, Dali Museum, Disney World, Sunken Gardens, Flea market, pier

Shops & Restaurants: Beach boutiques, small shopping plaza, Burdines; Wine Cellar/variety

Uniquely furnished units overlooking the Gulf. Bathe in the pool, jacuzzi or Gulf, or relax in a surfside cabana. Tour Disney World or go deep-sea fishing, windsurfing or sailing. Shops and restaurants within minutes.

───

Redington Ambassador Resort
16900 Gulf Blvd.
North Redington Beach, FL 33708
813-391-9646

2 Bedrooms $$
2 Bedrms/week 5$
Min. Stay 5 Nights, Visa/MC, Dep. Req'd. •
20 condos, Hi-rise, Key at At resort
H-yes

Location: Beach front

General Facilities: Kitchen, Linens, Baby-sitter

Room Facilities: Pool, Hot tub, TV, Cable, Phone in rm., Crib-Hi-chair, Ind. AC Ctl., Ind. Heat Ctl.

Attractions: Redington fishing pier

Shops & Restaurants: Redington Beach shops

Spacious, modern units carefully planned and decorated. Swimming pool with recreational deck area, jacuzzi and inside atrium with walks and landscaping. Built directly on the beach for those who want to splash in the surf. Walk to shops, restaurants and Redington Fishing Pier. Come to the Ambassador and enjoy the "suite life."

Please mention *Condo Vacations the Complete Guide* when you reserve your condominium.

─────────────── ORLANDO ───────────────

Florida Condominiums
2035 Ludlow Lane
Orlando, FL 32779
407-425-2999 800-247-2999

1 Bedroom $$, 2 Bedrooms $$, 3 Bedrooms $$$
1 Bedrm/week $$$$, 2 Bed/week 4$,
3 Bed/week 5$
AmEx/Visa/MC, Dep. Req'd. •
22 condos, Villas, Key at Office on site
H-yes

Location: Airport: 20 minutes; Downtown: 10 min.; Need car

General Facilities: Conf. rm. cap. 30, Kitchen, Linens, Game room, Baby-sitter

Room Facilities: Pool, Sauna, Tennis, TV, Cable, Phone in rm., Crib-Hi-chair, Ind. AC Ctl., Ind. Heat Ctl.

Attractions: Disney World, EPCOT, Sea World, Church St. Station, Wet'N Wild

Shops & Restaurants: International Drive, Florida Mall; Gary's-steak-seafood

The luxury of beautifully furnished living quarters, plus the convenience of easy access to all of Central Florida's attractions. The pleasure of outstanding recreational features, economy of kitchen and laundry facilities—all this is yours when Florida Condominiums is your vacation headquarters.

Orlando International Resort
5353 Del Verde Way
Orlando, FL 32819
407-351-2641 800-222-6472

2 Bedrooms $$
2 Bedrms/week 4$
AmEx/Visa/MC, Dep. Req'd. •
63 condos, Lo-rise, Key at Mgt. office
H-yes

Location: Airport: 9 miles; Downtown: 6 miles; Need car

General Facilities: Daily maid, Kitchen, Linens

Room Facilities: Pool, Tennis, TV, Phone in rm., Crib-Hi-chair, Ind. AC Ctl., Ind. Heat Ctl.

Attractions: Disney World, EPCOT, Wet 'N Wild, Sea World

Shops & Restaurants: Beltz factory outlet; Townsend's/Florida seafood

Two bedroom luxury units with balconies and washer/dryer on Orlando's popular International Drive. Heated pool, lighted tennis courts and gas barbecue grills. Minutes away from Disney World.

Sonesta Village Hotel-Sand Lake
10000 Turkey Lake Road
Orlando, FL 32819
305-352-8051

Villas
Pool, Kitchen

Attractions: Disney World, Tennis

Villas on Sand Lake featuring lakefront beach, pool, water sports, tennis and play area for children. Just 10 minutes from Walt Disney World.

--------- ORLANDO ---------

The Enclave
6165 Carrier Dr.
Orlando, FL 32819
407-351-1155 800-457-0077

Studio $$, 2 Bedrooms $$$
AmEx/Visa/MC, Dep. 1 Night •
321 condos, Hi-rise, Key at Front desk
H-yes

Location: Airport: 15 minutes; Downtown: 10 min.

General Facilities: Full serv., Conf. rm. cap. 75, Daily maid, Kitchen, Linens, Restaurant on prem., Bar on prem., Baby-sitter

Room Facilities: Pool, Sauna, Hot tub, Tennis, Exercise room, Golf: 2 miles, TV, Cable, Phone in rm., Crib-Hi-chair, Ind. AC Ctl., Ind. Heat Ctl.

Attractions: Wet-N-Wild Water Amusement Park, Sea World, Disney/EPCOT, entertainment

Shops & Restaurants: Belz Factory Outlet, Florida Mall; Royal Orleans/Vespucci/Beach

Peach and green Floridian decor. Full hotel services, two outdoor pools, indoor pool, exercise room, sauna, steam room and jacuzzis. Nightly entertainment in the Enclave's restaurant. Be at Disney/EPCOT in 10 minutes, or walk to the water amusement park.

The Villas of Grand Cypress   Villas
One North Jacaranda
Orlando, FL 32819
407-239-4700 800-835-7377

Location: Airport: Orlando-18 miles

General Facilities: Full serv., Bus. fac., Conf. rm. cap. 200, Daily maid, Kitchen, Linens, Restaurant on prem., Bar on prem., Lounge

Room Facilities: Tennis, Lake, Equestrian Center, Golf: 45-hole Nicklaus designed, TV

Attractions: Walt Disney's EPCOT, Sea World, entertainment

Shops & Restaurants: Black Swan, Ballybunion

Get on the turn-of-the-century Belgian trolley for a scenic 7-mile drive throughout the resort while you decide which activities you prefer-45 hole Nicklaus designed golf course and Academy of Golf with special programs, tennis, racquetball, volleyball, water sports on Lake Windsong, 45-acre nature area for jogging/biking, or the Equestrian Center. Mediterranean Villas, sunlit interiors, vaulted ceilings, morning newspapers, evening turn-down service and twice daily housekeeping-a truly luxurious resort.

────────────────── ORLANDO ──────────────────

Ventura
3100 Raper Dairy Road
Orlando, FL 32822
407-273-8770 800-247-8417

1 Bedrm/week $$$$, 2 Bed/week 4$,
  3 Bed/week 5$
Min. Stay 7 Nights, Visa/MC, Dep. Req'd.
350 condos, Lo-rise, Villas, Key at 3100 Raper
  Dairy Rd.
H-yes

Location: Airport: 6 miles-Orlando; Downtown: 5 miles; Need car

General Facilities: Kitchen, Linens

Room Facilities: Pool, Hot tub, Tennis, Golf: Ventura, TV, Cable, Phone in rm., Ind. AC Ctl., Ind. Heat Ctl.

Attractions: Disneyland, Sea World, Boardwalk, Baseball, Space Center, Rosie O'Grady, entertainment

Shops & Restaurants: Florida, Fashion, Altamonte & Beltz Outlet Malls; Barneys-Steak/South Seas

Live like a Floridian in garden condominiums, modern, furnished in rattan. Unwind with golf or tennis, or jog, bike or stroll down walks alive with oleanders and tropical foliage. Sunbathe on a tropical beach, splash in the Clubhouse pool, or spend the day on the shores of Lake Ventura. Symphony, ballet, opera and first-run New York shows are at Bob Carr Auditorium. Most vacation attractions are within an hour's drive. Your passport to fun and sun.

────────────────── ORMOND BEACH ──────────────────

Aquarius Ocean Front Condominiums
1575 Ocean Shore Boulevard
Ormond Beach, FL 32074
904-441-2050

Ocean East Resort Club
867 S. Atlantic Ave
Ormond Beach, FL 32074
904-677-8111

1 Bedroom $$, 2 Bedrooms $$, Hi-rise
Pool, Kitchen, Linens

Attractions: Exercise rooms

A complete family vacation resort that even supplies family games in your suite. Cook in your condo or dine at one of the restauranats on the property. Splash in the Atlantic or the pool, play beach volleyball, use the exercise room, jacuzzis and sauna.

Oceanfront Condominiums
1575 Ocean Shore Blvd.
Ormond Beach, FL 32074
904-441-2050

Daily maid, Kitchen

A quiet complex of two-bedroom, two-bath units sleeping 6 with full kitchens, living room, dining room and roomy balconies.

Indian River Plantation Resort

--- ORMOND BEACH ---

Seascape & Sunrise
Condominiums
2290 Ocean Shore Boulevard
Ormond Beach, FL 32074
904-441-1058

2 Bedrms/week 4$
Min. Stay 7 Nights, Dep. Req'd. •
39 condos, Hi-rise, Key at Office

Location: Airport: 5 miles; Downtown: 2 miles; Need car; Beach front
General Facilities: Kitchen, Linens, Game room
Room Facilities: Pool, Sauna, TV, Cable, VCR, Phone in rm., Crib, Ind. AC Ctl., Ind. Heat Ctl.
Attractions: 1½ hours to Disney, 1 hr. St. Augustine, 1 hr. to Cape Canaveral
Shops & Restaurants: Mall with grocery, drug, clothing—2 miles; Captain Coty's

Large vistas of glass enhance the panoramic view of the Atlantic Ocean from the living room and master bedroom. Units are complemented by lush tropical landscaping. Walk to the beach, swim in the pool, relax in the sauna. Minutes to places of interest.

Traders Inn Beach Club
1355 Ocean Shore Boulevard
Ormond Beach, FL 32074
904-441-1111

1 Bedroom $
Pool, Kitchen

A neighboring community of Daytona Beach, convenient to area attractions, malls, restaurants and speedway. Units are oceanfront and sleep 4.

─────────────── ORMOND-BY-THE SEA ───────────────

Ocean Beach Condominiums
2220 Ocean Shore Boulevard #106
Ormond-By-The Sea, FL 32074

─────────────── PALM BEACH GARDENS ───────────────

PGA National Club Cottages   Villas
300 Avenue Of The Champions   Pool, Kitchen, Linens
Palm Beach Gardens, FL 33418
305-627-3000 800-325-3535

Attractions: Palm Beach, jai alai, polo, horse and greyhound racing, deep-sea fishing,
 sailing, Health & Racquet Club, Tennis, Golf

*Single-level, two and three bedroom villas with Mediterranean architecture. Vaulted ceil-
ings, master suites with marble baths and oversized sliding glass doors opening onto
screened view patios. European flavor landscaping with tiered fountains.*

─────────────── PALM BEACH SHORES ───────────────

Ocean Club of Palm Beach   1 Bedroom $$, Lo-rise
155 Ocean Ave.   Linens, Phone in rm.
Palm Beach Shores, FL 33404
407-842-9966

Attractions: Golf, tennis, swimming

Sand Dunes Shores   1 Bedroom $$, 2 Bedrooms $$, Lo-rise
165 Ocean Ave.   Pool, Kitchen
Palm Beach Shores, FL 33404
407-848-2581

Attractions: Amusement Center, scuba, snorkeling, fishing, charters, jai alai, Lion
 Country Safari, Bicycles

*Oceanfront condominiums on Singer Island, which has some of the widest beaches in the
State. Pool, spa, grills and bicycles. Amusements, sports, shopping, dining and entertain-
ment within half mile.*

─────────────── PALM BEACH ───────────────

Palm Beach Resort-Beach Club   Lo-rise
3031 South Ocean Blvd.   Pool, Kitchen
Palm Beach, FL 33480
800-826-1943 800-424-1943

Attractions: Fishing, golf, tennis, polo, private boat dock

*Fully equipped units between the Intracoastal Waterway and the Atlantic Ocean on Lake
Worth. One block from the beach, private boat dock. The place for a leisurely vacation on
the lake.*

─────────────── PANAMA CITY BEACH ───────────────

Casa Blanca Resort   Pool, Kitchen, Phone in rm.
11115 U.S. Hwy 98 W   Exercise room
Panama City Beach, FL 32407
904-234-5245

*The beach is right outside the door of these one bedroom units. Pool, sauna, spa, hot tubs,
games and party rooms on the property.*

———————————— PANAMA CITY BEACH ————————————

Landmark Holiday Beach Resort
17501 U.S. Highway 98 W.
Panama City Beach, FL 32407
904-235-3100 800-433-7059

1 Bedroom $, 2 Bedrooms $$, 3 Bedrooms $$
1 Bedrm/week $$$$, 2 Bed/week 4$,
  3 Bed/week 4$
Min. Stay 2 Nights, AmEx/Visa/MC,
  Dep. Req'd. •
95 condos, Hi-rise, Key at At the resort

Location: Airport: 15 miles; Downtown: 5 miles; Beach front

General Facilities: Full serv., Kitchen, Game room, Lounge, Baby-sitter, Child planned rec.: Ice cream social

Room Facilities: Pool, Sauna, Hot tub, Golf: Nearby, TV, Cable, Phone in rm., Crib-Hichair, Ind. AC Ctl., Ind. Heat Ctl.

Attractions: Amusement Park, miniature golf, water slides, cruise ships with dining/dancing, state park, entertainment

Shops & Restaurants: Promenade Mall, Panama City Mall; The Lighthouse/seafood

Warm, inviting white sand beaches; unsurpassed boating and fishing; manicured golf courses; tennis and water sports. Condominiums overlook the Gulf of Mexico and white sands beach, and are designer decorated with tropical touches. Wine and cheese parties, bingo, continental breakfast, and children's ice cream social.

The Landmark Holiday Beach Resort
17501 US Highway 98
Panama City Beach, FL 32407
904-235-1118

Quality accommodations created for your vacation fun. Hi-rise condominium with gulf front view from private balconies. Spa, sauna, indoor pool and tennis.

Largo Mar
5715 Thomas Drive
Panama City Beach, FL 32407
904-234-5750 800-645-2746

1 Bedroom $$, 2 Bedrooms $$$, 3 Bedrooms $$$$
1 Bedrm/week 5$, 2 Bed/week 6$,
  3 Bed/week 10$
Min. Stay 3 Nights, Visa/MC, Dep. Req'd. •
72 condos, Lo-rise, Key at Office-from security

Location: Airport: 8 miles; Downtown: 15 miles; Need car; Beach front

General Facilities: Kitchen, Linens, Game room

Room Facilities: Pool, Sauna, Hot tub, TV, Cable, Phone in rm., Ind. AC Ctl., Ind. Heat Ctl.

Attractions: Fishing, pleasure cruises, dining, dancing, gambling, Shipwreck Island

Shops & Restaurants: Alvins Island & Panama City Malls, gift shops; Capt. Anderson's, Hamilton's

A family place located on the Gulf of Mexico. Golfing, swimming, sailing, boating, sunning-it's all here. Full-time security and the greatest sunsets on the world's most beautiful beaches.

PANAMA CITY BEACH

Latitude 29
21703 W. Hwy. 98
Panama City Beach, FL 32407
904-234-5583

1 Bedroom $$, Lo-rise, Villas
Pool, Kitchen

Versatile one-bedroom units become two by using the living room as a bedroom at night. Architecturally attractive condominiums with large pool and private beach. Minutes drive to golf, tennis, fishing, restaurants and amusements.

Mariner East & West Condominiums
6211-6213 Thomas Drive
Panama City Beach, FL 32407
904-234-9468

1 Bedroom $$, Hi-rise
Pool, Daily maid, Kitchen, Linens

Convenience and comfort in a fine resort. Swim or sunbathe by the pool, collect shells along the beach, play tennis or shuffleboard. Game room with pool table, video games and ping pong. Lounge area, exercise room, saunas.

Moondrifter
8815 Thomas Drive
Panama City Beach, FL 32407
904-234-5564 800-232-6636

1 Bedroom $$, 2 Bedrooms $$
1 Bedrm/week $$$$, 2 Bed/week 4$
Min. Stay 2 Nights, AmEx/Visa/MC,
Dep. Req'd., Hi-rise, No S-yes/H-yes

Location: Airport: 15 miles; Downtown: 7 miles; Need car; Beach front

General Facilities: Full serv., Bus. fac., Kitchen, Linens, Game room, Lounge, Baby-sitter

Room Facilities: Pool, Sauna, Hot tub, Tennis, Shuffleboard, Golf: Near Signal Hill, TV, Cable, VCR, Phone in rm., Crib-Hi-chair, Ind.AC Ctl., Ind. Heat Ctl.

Attractions: Gulf World, glass bottom boats, deep-sea fishing, snorkeling

Shops & Restaurants: Shopping center, food, gifts; Capt. Anderson/seafood

View the crystal clear waters of the Gulf of Mexico from your private balcony. Swim in the pool or beach, sail, fish, play tennis or shuffleboard.

Moonspinner Condominiums
4425 Thomas Dr.
Panama City Beach, FL 32407
904-234-8900 800-223-3947

2 Bedrooms $$$, 3 Bedrooms $$$
2 Bedrms/week 6$, 3 Bed/week 9$
Min. Stay 3 Nights, AmEx/Visa/MC,
Dep. Req'd.
162 condos, Hi-rise, Key at Reserv. office

Location: Airport: 5 miles; Downtown: 12 miles; Beach front

General Facilities: Conf. rm. cap. 100, Daily maid, Kitchen, Linens, Game room, Baby-sitter

Room Facilities: Pool, Sauna, Hot tub, Tennis, TV, Cable, Phone in rm., Crib-Hi-chair, Ind. AC Ctl., Ind. Heat Ctl.

Attractions: Beach resort activities, dog track, cruises, fishing

Shops & Restaurants: Gayfers, Sears, Penney; Capt. Andersons, Boars Head

Complex with full-time security staff and friendly personnel to serve you. Oceanfront pool, rental sailboats, beach service which even provides tanning lotion. Shuffleboard, day and night tennis. Adjacent to St. Andrew State Park and minutes to Panama City Beach.

—————————— PANAMA CITY BEACH ——————————

Nautical Watch Condominiums
6205 Thomas Dr.
Panama City Beach, FL 32407
904-234-6876 800-621-2462

1 Bedroom $, 2 Bedrooms $$, 3 Bedrooms $$
1 Bedrm/week $$$$, 2 Bed/week $$$$,
  3 Bed/week $$$$
Min. Stay 3 Nights, Visa/MC, Dep. Req'd.
81 condos, Lo-rise, Key at Nautical Watch

Location: Airport: 5 miles; Downtown: 1.5 mi.; Need car; Beach front
General Facilities: Kitchen, Linens
Room Facilities: Pool, TV, Cable, Ind. AC Ctl., Ind. Heat Ctl.
Attractions: Trips to Shell Island, dinner cruises from Capt. Anderson's, summer-the Miracle Strip
Shops & Restaurants: Promenade Mall, Panama City Mall, St. Thomas square; Captain Anderson's/seafood

Beautifully furnished condominiums with beach or pool views. Close to fine restaurants and entertainment. Take a trip to Shell Island or enjoy a dinner cruise.

Ocean Terrace Condominiums
8618 Surf Dr.
Panama City Beach, FL 32407
904-234-5631

1 Bedroom $, 2 Bedrooms $$, Lo-rise
Pool, Daily maid, Kitchen

Attractions: Kiddie pool

A small complex catering to family groups. Sun deck with gazebo and kiddie pool, large pool overlooking the gulf, barbecues, cable and HBO. The ideal place for a quiet, peaceful vacation.

Ocean Towers Beach Club
11211 West Highway 98
Panama City Beach, FL 32407
904-235-4050

Hi-rise
Pool, Kitchen, Phone in rm.

Attractions: Exercise room, Golf

Twin towers of this complex border on the clubhouse with enjoyment for the whole family. Free golf and tennis nearby, bicycles, barbecue and heated pool.

Oceanna Condominiums
8000 Surf Dr.
Panama City Beach, FL 32407
904-234-9384

1 Bedroom $$, Lo-rise
Pool, Daily maid, Kitchen, Linens

Attractions: Amusement Parks, deep sea fishing, golf, Shuffleboard

Fully furnished units on the beach away from congestion. Courtyard with gazebo overlooking the pool with picnic tables and barbecue grills.

The Beach Club

PANAMA CITY BEACH

Panama City Resort & Club
16709 W. Hwy 98
Panama City Beach, FL 32407
904-235-2002

Studio $, 1 Bedroom $$$$
1 Bedrm/week $$
Min. Stay 2 Nights, Visa/MC, Dep. Req'd. •
40 condos, Hi-rise, Key at At resort

Location: Airport: 17 miles; Downtown: 20 miles; Need car; Beach front

General Facilities: Full serv., Kitchen, Linens, Game room, Baby-sitter

Room Facilities: Pool, Hot tub, Tennis, Free golf, Golf: 3 miles east, TV, Cable, Phone in rm., Crib-Hi-chair, Ind. AC Ctl., Ind. Heat Ctl.

Attractions: Gulf World Dolphin Show, Casino & Dolphin cruises, two amusement parks, entertainment

Shops & Restaurants: Shops at Edgewater, Magic Mountain; Capt.Andersons-seafood

Friendly, informal atmosphere in this family resort located on the beach. Play golf, tennis, fish, swim, sail, horse races and jai alai. Welcome breakfast on Saturday, potluck lunch, bingo, scavenger hunt and crazy hat contest. Varied pleasures in this year-round playground-relaxed or active, exotic or romantic, peaceful or lively, or a combination of all these.

———————————— PANAMA CITY BEACH ————————————

Pelican Walk
6905 Thomas Drive
Panama City Beach, FL 32407
904-234-9255

1 Bedroom $$, 2 Bedrooms $$, 3 Bedrooms $$$
1 Bedrm/week 4$, 2 Bed/week 6$,
   3 Bed/week 7$
Min. Stay 2 Nights, AmEx/Visa/MC,
   Dep. Req'd. •
Hi-rise
No S-yes/P-yes/H-yes

Location: Airport: 15 miles; Downtown: 7 miles; Need car; Beach front

General Facilities: Full serv., Bus. fac., Kitchen, Linens, Game room, Lounge

Room Facilities: Pool, Sauna, Hot tub, Tennis, Racquetball, Shuffleboard, Golf: Near Signal Hill, TV, Cable, VCR, Phone in rm., Crib-Hi-chair, Ind.AC Ctl., Ind. Heat Ctl.

Attractions: Gulf World, amusement parks, glass bottom boat, deep sea fishing, wind-surfing

Shops & Restaurants: Shopping center, food, gifts; Capt. Anderson/seafood

Four spacious floor plans with contemporary furnishings, ideally located. Two level club-house, social lounge, racquetball, saunas, glass enclosed whirlpool solarium, tennis and 2 beachside pools.

Pinnacle Port Condominiums
23223 W. Hwy. 98
Panama City Beach, FL 32407
904-234-8813 800-874-8823

1 Bedroom $$, 2 Bedrooms $$, Hi-rise
Pool, Kitchen, Phone in rm.

Attractions: Golf, amusement attractions, shopping, Shuffleboard, Tennis

Jutting out into the blue-green waters of the Gulf of Mexico and surrounded by natural land-scaping, Pinnacle Port has half mile of secluded beach. Leave your boat at the dock so you're ready for water-skiing, sailing or fishing. Use the beach, two pools.

Portside Resort
17620 West Alt. Hwy. 98
Panama City Beach, FL 32407
904-235-0244 800-443-2737

2 Bedrooms $$
Pool, Kitchen, Linens

Attractions: Shuffleboard, Tennis

Palms, evergreens and flowering plants surround the tennis courts, clubhouse, shuffleboard and pools. The main pool features a Polynesian thatched palapa surrounded by two free-form pools and a cascading waterfall. Decorator furnished two-story townhomes.

——————————— PANAMA CITY BEACH ———————————

Ramsgate Harbour
23011 W. Hwy. 98-A Alternate
Panama City Beach, FL 32407
904-235-2667　800-423-1889

2 Bedrooms $$$
2 Bedrms/week 6$
Min. Stay 3 Nights, Visa/MC, Dep. Req'd. •
66 condos, Lo-rise, Key at On-site office
No S-yes

Location: Airport: 30 minutes; Downtown: 30 min; Beach front

General Facilities: Daily maid, Kitchen, Linens, Game room

Room Facilities: Pool, Shuffleboard, Golf: Bay Point Lagoon 20 min., TV, Cable, Phone in rm., Ind. AC Ctl., Ind. Heat Ctl.

Attractions: Miracle Strip Amusement Park-Shipwreck Island Water Park-Shell Island-Casino cruise ship

Shops & Restaurants: Panama City Mall, Promenade Mall, outdoor market; Captain Anderson's/seafood

Stucco and weathered grey cedar, enclosed stairwells and covered balconies with Gulf views set among lighted tropical landscaping. Private beach, sun deck, pool and clubhouse with refrigerator, sink and rest rooms. Carpeted condominiums with quarry tile in kitchen, baths and foyer. Washer and dryer, ceiling fans.

Sand Castles West Condominiums
17214 Scenic Highway 98
Panama City Beach, FL 32407
904-234-0833

Lo-rise
Pool, Kitchen

Attractions: Beach activities, Shuffleboard

Completely furnished units for easy beach living. Close to restaurants and shopping areas. Relax at the beach, in the sauna or pool.

Seachase Condominiums
17351 W. Scenic Highway 98
Panama City Beach, FL 32407
904-235-1300　800-457-2051

2 Bedrooms $$
2 Bedrms/week 5$
Min. Stay 2 Nights, AmEx/Visa/MC,
　Dep. Req'd. •
64 condos, Hi-rise, Key at Office on property
H-yes

Location: Airport: 15 miles; Downtown: 15 miles; Beach front

General Facilities: Daily maid, Kitchen, Linens

Room Facilities: Pool, TV, Cable, Phone in rm., Crib-Hi-chair, Ind. AC Ctl., Ind. Heat Ctl.

Attractions: Amusement parks, golf, Putt-Putt golf, Gulf World. "The world's most beautiful beaches," entertainment

Shops & Restaurants: Individual shops, grocery, gifts, pharmacy, liquor; Boars Head—Prime Rib/Seafood

Luxurious condos, directly on the beach with view from ceiling to floor of the world's most beautiful beaches. Excellent seafood restaurants and beach shopping within walking distance. A family oriented condominium. Colors vary from peach and seafoam green to misty mauve and blues. Airy modern wicker furniture.

———————————— PANAMA CITY BEACH ————————————

Southwind Condominiums
17670 W. Hwy. 98
Panama City Beach, FL 32407
904-234-6303

1 Bedroom $, 2 Bedrooms $
Pool, Kitchen
Shuffleboard

Custom designed cabinets, marble vanities, plush carpeting and large private decks. Pool, beach access and clubhouse.

Sugar Beach
8727 Thomas Drive
Panama City Beach, FL 32407
904-234-2102   800-457-8427

1 Bedroom $$, 2 Bedrooms $$, Lo-rise
Pool, Kitchen, Phone in rm.
Tennis

Family size units wrapped around an interior courtyard of grass, tropical plantings and the lake. Directly on the beach and only minutes away from the many beach entertainments and activities. Clubhouse with fireplace, TV, pool and ping pong.

Summer House
6505 Thomas Drive
Panama City Beach, FL 32407
904-234-1112   800-354-1112

1 Bedroom $$, 2 Bedrooms $$, Hi-rise
Pool, Kitchen, Linens
Shuffleboard, Racquetball

Continuously upgraded units, clean and well-kept on a pearly white beach. Beautifully landscaped grounds, friendly personnel and security guards to ensure your privacy. Lounge by one of the pools near the gazebo, play tennis or games in the lobby gameroom.

The Summit
8743 Thomas Drive
Panama City Beach, FL 32407
904-234-7890   800-824-5048

1 Bedroom $$, Hi-rise
Pool, Kitchen, Phone in rm.
Weight rooms, Tennis

Gulfside high-rise condominiums with 24-hour security. Tennis, pools, weight rooms, whirlpools, hot tubs and snack bar.

Sunbird
8850 S. Thomas Drive
Panama City Beach, FL 32407
904-235-4300   800-433-8240

1 Bedroom $$, Hi-rise
Pool, Kitchen, Phone in rm.
Shuffleboard

Contemporary-style furnishings in gulf-front condominiums. Five different one-bedroom floor plans. Three pools, large deck, clubhouse and game room.

Top of the Gulf
8817 S. Thomas Dr.
Panama City Beach, FL 32407
904-234-6561

1 Bedroom $$, Hi-rise
Kitchen, Linens, Phone in rm.
Golf

─────────────── PANAMA CITY BEACH ───────────────

Tropical Breeze
1701 W. Hwy. 98
Panama City Beach, FL 32407
904-234-2228

─────────────────── PANAMA CITY ───────────────────

Bay Point Yacht and Country Club   1 Bedrm/week $$$$, 2 Bed/week $$$$,
100 Delwood Beach Rd., Box 314   3 Bed/week 4$
Panama City, FL 32407   Min. Stay 7 Nights, AmEx/Visa/MC,
904-234-1618 800-543-3307   Dep. Req'd.
                                       557 condos, Lo-rise, Key at Bay Pt. office

General Facilities: Conf. rm. cap. 44, Daily maid, Kitchen, Linens, Restaurant on prem., Bar on prem., Lounge, Baby-sitter

Room Facilities: Pool, Sauna, Tennis, Health club, bikes, Golf: 2 18-hole courses, TV, Cable, Phone in rm.

Attractions: Shell Island, Gulf of Mexico fishing, marina, deep sea/sailing charters, entertainment

Shops & Restaurants: The Terrace Court/nouvelle

Privately owned villas meeting the high decor and equipment standards of the Club. 5 minute drive to public beaches, or launch to undeveloped, isolated beaches. Marina with 154 slips, children's play area, driving range, tennis, golf and health club. There is always music someplace at the Club, fashion shows and theme parties. Proper golf or tennis attire must be worn on the course and courts. An outstanding resort combining casual luxury with southern charm and service by an experienced staff.

─────────────── PENSACOLA BEACH ───────────────

Holiday Beach Resort   2 Bedrooms $$, Lo-rise
19 Via Deluna   Pool, Kitchen, Linens
Pensacola Beach, FL 32561
904-436-4500

Attractions: Spa, Tennis

On the quiet side of Pensacola Beach for a beach vacation and sightseeing in historic Pensacola. Fishing pier, pool, beach, spa, tennis and whirlpool tubs.

───

Palm Beach Club Condominiums
1390 Fort Pickens Rd.
Pensacola Beach, FL 32561
904-932-1399 800-932-6667

───

Sabine Yacht & Racquet Club   1 Bedroom $$, 2 Bedrooms $$
330 Fort Pickens Rd.   Pool, Kitchen, Phone in rm.
Pensacola Beach, FL 32561
904-932-7290 800-343-0344

Attractions: Exercise room, Tennis

1, 2, and 3 bedrooms units on the azure waters of Sabine Bay. Pool, exercise room, boat dock, tennis, large balconies.

———————————— PENSACOLA BEACH ————————————

San De Luna
1350 Fort Pickens Road
Pensacola Beach, FL 32561
904-932-5337 800-874-9243

Tristan Towers	2 Bedrooms $$, 3 Bedrooms $$
1200 Fort Pickens Rd.	2 Bedrms/week 4$, 3 Bed/week 5$
Pensacola Beach, FL 32561	Min. Stay 3 Nights, Visa/MC, Dep. Req'd.
904-932-9341 800-826-0614	90 condos, Hi-rise, Key at Office

Location: Airport: 10 miles; Downtown: 5 miles

General Facilities: Kitchen, Linens

Room Facilities: Pool, Tennis, Putting green, TV, Cable, Phone in rm., Crib-Hi-chair, Ind. AC Ctl., Ind. Heat Ctl.

New beautiful 15-story white building with blue trim on the beach. Tennis, Olympic-size pool, Clubhouse with fireplace, lighted tennis courts, putting green. Residences have washer/dryers and large closets. Boardwalk to beach gazebo, picnic tables and barbecues on a grassy area by the private beach.

Windjammer Condominium
14 Via de Luna Dr.
Pensacola Beach, FL 32561
904-932-5331

———————————— PENSACOLA ————————————

Perdido Towers	1 Bedroom $$, 2 Bedrooms $$
16785 Perdido Key Dr.	Pool, Kitchen, Linens
Pensacola, FL 32507	
904-492-2809	

Attractions: Tennis

All the comforts of home with resort amenities. 28-slip boat dock and launching ramp on Old River. Pool, tennis, racquetball, views. Quiet complex, excellent security.

———————————— PERDIDO KEY, PENSACOLA ————————————

Vista Del Mar Condominiums	1 Bedrm/week $$$$, 2 Bed/week $$$$,
13-333 Johnson Beach Road	3 Bed/week 4$
Perdido Key, Pensacola, FL 32507	Min. Stay 4 Nights, Dep. Req'd.
904-492-0211	64 condos, Hi-rise, Key at Office on property

Location: Airport: 40 Minutes; Downtown: 9 miles; Need car; Beach front

General Facilities: Kitchen, Linens

Room Facilities: Pool, Tennis, Cable, Phone in rm., Crib-Hi-chair, Ind. AC Ctl., Ind. Heat Ctl.

Attractions: Gulf Islands Nat. Seashore, jet ski, sailing, boating, para-sailing, fish.

Adjacent to the Gulf Islands National Seashore with 20 miles of rolling dunes. Excellent surf fishing, plus sailing, jet skiing, wind surfing, speed boating and para-sailing. Several championship golf courses are nearby. Historic Pensacola is just 15 minutes away with many museums and gourmet dining.

PERDIDO KEY

Sandy Key Condominiums
13575 Perdido Key Dr.
Perdido Key, FL 32507
904-492-3084   800-351-8266

2 Bedrooms $$, Hi-rise
Pool, Kitchen

Attractions: Exercise facility, Tennis, Golf

Casually furnished, sliding glass doors to oversize balcony with its tables and chairs for dining or relaxing, whirlpool tub in master bath. Adjacent to Gulf Islands National Seashore. On-site tennis, spa, health facililty, volleyball, basketball, steam room, and pool.

Sea Spray Luxury Condominiums
16287 Perdido Key Dr.
Perdido Key, FL 32507
904-492-2200   800-824-2231

2 Bedrooms $$, Hi-rise
Pool, Kitchen, Linens

Attractions: Exercise room, Tennis

Get ready for beach fun or launch your boat at the marina. Three buildings with 2 and 3 bedroom units. Complete use of all amenities inclluding pools, spa, tennis, exercise and rec room.

Shipwatch Condominium
16787 Perdido Key Dr.
Perdido Key, FL 32507
904-492-0111   800-228-3732

2 Bedrooms $$, Hi-rise
Pool, Kitchen, Linens, Phone in rm.

Attractions: Health club, Tennis

Make the Gulf your personal playground, or try Old River for water skiing and fishing. High ceillings, marble vanities, recessed lighting. Pool, tennis, health club, greenhouse with spa, sauna.

Sundown Condominium
16470 Perdido Key Dr.
Perdido Key, FL 32507
904-492-1816

Pool, Kitchen, Linens, Phone in rm.

Attractions: Tennis, Golf

Exceptionally spacious units halfway between Gulf Shores and Pensacola. Close to the Gulf and Perdido Bay for sailing, fishing and shrimping. Pool and tennis. Minutes to golf.

————————————— POMPANO BEACH —————————————

Canada House Beach Club
1704 North Ocean Boulevard
Pompano Beach, FL 33062
305-942-8200

Studio $, 1 Bedroom $$
Min. Stay 2 Nights, AmEx/Visa/MC,
   Dep. Req'd. •
88 condos, Hi-rise, Key at Front desk
H-yes

Location: Airport: 12 miles; Need car; Beach front

General Facilities: Full serv., Daily maid, Kitchen, Linens, Restaurant on prem., Baby-sitter

Room Facilities: Pool, Hot tub, Minature golf, TV, Cable, Phone in rm., Crib-Hi-chair, Ind. AC Ctl., Ind. Heat Ctl.

Attractions: Cruises from local port (Everglades), fishing, golf, tennis facilities available nearby, entertainment

Shops & Restaurants: Pompano Fashion Square, Burdines, Penny; Sea Watch-Harris-Chinese

Uncluttered, homelike atmosphere with modern style rattan furnishings. Two swimming pools, shuffleboard, putting green, barbecue facilities, bicycles, paddle boats, and Wednesday night cook-outs. Full-time activities director on staff. Game fishing in the Gulf Stream or Bahamas, horse racing, nightlife, or just bask in the sun and enjoy a memorable Florida vacation.

La Costa Beach Club Resort
1504 N. Ocean Blvd.
Pompano Beach, FL 33062
305-942-4900

1 Bedroom $$, 2 Bedrooms $$
Pool, Kitchen, Phone in rm.

Attractions: Ex. room, shuffleboard

All new furnishings in these individually owned condominiums. If the weather should turn cold, use the indoor pool and jacuzzi. Beach and outdoor pool for the usual sunny days.

Ocean Ranch and Villas
1110 South Ocean Boulevard
Pompano Beach, FL 33062
305-941-7100

1 Bedroom $, Lo-rise
Pool, Daily maid, Kitchen, Linens, Phone in rm.

Attractions: Putting green

You'll have access to 250 feet of private beach when you stay at Ocean Ranch with its pool, whirlpool, rental cabanas, exercise room and putting greens. Dining room, piano lounge and glass-enclosed patio bar for relaxation after a day at the beach. Nightclub tours.

Palm Ocean Villas
1430 South Ocean Boulevard
Pompano Beach, FL 33062
305-941-7330

1 Bedroom $$, Lo-rise
Pool, Kitchen

Attractions: Tennis

Let the staff make all arrangements for the many sports and entertainment facilities, or stay at your Villa and do nothing except swim in the ocean or pool. If you bring your boat, there is free boat dockage.

─────────────── POMPANO BEACH ───────────────

Sea Garden
615 N. Ocean Blvd.
Pompano Beach, FL 33062
305-943-6200 800-327-8920

Studio $$, 1 Bedroom $$, 2 Bedrooms $$
1 Bedrm/week 4$, 2 Bed/week 5$
AmEx/Visa/MC, Dep. 1 Night •
40 condos, Lo-rise, Key at Front desk
H-yes

Location: Airport: 10 miles; Downtown: 4 miles; Need car; Beach front

General Facilities: Full serv., Bus. fac., Conf. rm. cap. 300, Daily maid, Kitchen, Linens, Restaurant on prem., Bar on prem., Lounge, Baby-sitter

Room Facilities: Pool, Hot tub, Tennis, Volleyball, Golf: Pompano Municipal close, TV, Cable, Phone in rm., Crib-Hi-chair, Ind. AC Ctl., Ind. Heat Ctl.

Attractions: One day Bahama cruises, Everglades, Jungle Queen & Paddlewheel Queen tours, jai alai, entertainment

Shops & Restaurants: Pompano Fashion Square, Galleria & Town Cntr. Malls; Rinaldo's/It-Le Vieulle Maison

Tropical settinng and lush gardens set on 7.5 acres with 300 feet of beachfront. Restaurant and lounge, two bars with piano entertainment, two pools and fourteen tennis courts.

Sea Side Beach Club
501 Briny Ave.
Pompano Beach, FL 33062
305-941-7650

1 Bedroom $$, 2 Bedrooms $$
Pool, Kitchen

Attractions: Jai alai, dog races, golf, tennis, concerts, discos

Designer coordinated suites for contemporary living. Lay on the beach or by the pool for complete relaxation, or be active and participate in area sports. 5 minute walk to fishing pier, and a short drive to Fort Lauderdale nightlife.

Surf Rider Resort Condominium
1441 S. Ocean Blvd. (AIA)
Pompano Beach, FL 33062
305-785-8991

1 Bedroom $$, 2 Bedrooms $$
Pool, Kitchen, Phone in rm.

Attractions: 200-foot dock, Tennis

Intimate villa hideaways with designer furnishings. Private beach, olympic pool, tennis, docking facilities. Gold Coast restaurants, nightlife and boutiques.

─────────────── PUNTA GORDA ───────────────

Burnt Store Marina Resort
3150 Matecumbe Key Road
Punta Gorda, FL 33955
813-481-3636 800-237-8906

1 Bedroom $$, 2 Bedrooms $$$, Lo-rise
Pool, Kitchen

Attractions: Sailing, boating, fishing, tennis, golf, Marina

Complete resort with 400 wet slip marina and fuel dock. Emphasis on marine recreation, but there is also golf, tennis and a heated pool. Condominiums and lanais overlooking the marina, golf course or pool. Live entertainment in the lounge and property restaurant.

──────────── PUNTA GORDO ────────────

Fishermen's Village Resort Club   1 Bedroom $$, Lo-rise
1200 W. Retta Esplande   Pool, Kitchen
Punta Gorda, FL 33950
813-639-8721

Attractions: Tennis

Apartments with king-size bed in master bedroom, den sleeper sofa and loft area with two twin beds. Above 30 fashion, gift, and specialty shops and 8 restaurants. Balconies overlook the harbor with its 98-slip yacht basin. Pool and tennis.

──────────── REDINGTON BEACH ────────────

Suncoast Resort Rentals
16401 Gulf Blvd.
Redington Beach, FL 33708
800-237-6586

Dune House Condominiums

─────────────────── REDINGTON SHORES ───────────────────

San Remo
18320 Gulf Blvd.
Redington Shores, FL 33708
813-398-5591

2 Bedrms/week 5$, 3 Bed/week 6$
Min. Stay 7 Nights, AmEx/Visa/MC,
Dep. Req'd. •
87 condos, Hi-rise, Key at On-site office
P-yes/H-yes

Location: Airport: Tampa 30 minutes; Beach front

General Facilities: Daily maid, Kitchen, Linens

Room Facilities: Pool, Hot tub, Tennis, Volleyball, Golf: Nearby, TV, Cable, Phone in rm., Crib-Hi-chair, Ind. AC Ctl., Ind. Heat Ctl.

Attractions: Disney World, Sea World, Sunken Gardens, Busch Gardens, Wax Museum, Tiki Gardens

Shops & Restaurants: Tyrone shopping mall, Seminole Mall, other shops; Wine Cellar/Ger.-Amer.-French

Very large units that look like houses, high ceilings, lots of windows and large porches. Tennis across the street, storage for bikes, skateboards, surf and sailboards. Laundry rooms in units. Walk to shops, parks, fishing and restaurants.

─────────────────── SANIBEL ISLAND ───────────────────

Caribe Beach Resort
2669 W. Gulf Dr., P.O. Box 158
Sanibel Island, FL 33957
813-472-1166

Studio $, 1 Bedroom $
1 Bedrm/week $$$$
Visa/MC, Dep. 1 Night
27 condos, Lo-rise, Key at Office
H-yes

Location: Airport: 25 miles; Downtown: 1 mile; Need car; Beach front

General Facilities: Daily maid, Kitchen, Linens

Room Facilities: Pool, Hot tub, Horseshoes, volleyball, TV, Cable, Phone in rm., Crib-Hi-chair, Ind. AC Ctl., Ind. Heat Ctl.

Attractions: Wildlife refuge, underdeveloped surroundings for shelling and boating

Shops & Restaurants: Unique shops all over the Island; Casual seafood restaurants

When you want to get away from it all. Relax on the beach in the Florida sunshine and work on your tan. Collect shells, go biking, or explore the wildlife refuge. When you're ready to eat retire to the lovely groove area with picnic tables and charcoal grills for easy barbecueing right on the edge of the beach. Pool, spa, horseshoes, shuffleboard and volleyball, if you must exercise.

───

Casa Ybel Resort
2255 W. Gulf Dr., P.O. Box 167
Sanibel Island, FL 33957
813-481-3636 800-282-8906

1 Bedroom $$, 2 Bedrooms $$$, Villas
Pool, Daily maid, Kitchen, Linens

Attractions: Shuffleboard, volleyball, Tennis, Golf

Condominiums surround the award-winning Thistle Lodge restaurant recreating the home that the first Sanibel settler built for his daughter as a wedding gift. Suites overlook the Gulf of Mexico. In the center of the resort are the pool with waterslides.

SANIBEL ISLAND

Hurricane House
2939 W. Gulf Drive
Sanibel Island, FL 33957
813-481-3636 800-237-8906

2 Bedrooms $$$, Villas
Pool, Kitchen, Linens

Attractions: Tennis, golf, swimming

Opened in 1987, townhouses with modern kitchens, screened terraces and washer/dryers. Pool, tennis court, and beach for sunning and beachcombing.

Sanibel Cottages
2341 W. Gulf Drive
Sanibel Island, FL 33597
813-481-3636 800-237-8906

2 Bedrooms $$$, Villas
Pool, Kitchen

Attractions: Tennis

Victorian elegance and "Old Florida" style architecture and decor in these two bedroom vacation retreats. Bay windows, window seats and huge tubs with whirlpool jets in the master bath. Green lawn with footbridge and gazebo. Golf, water sports, and dining are nearby.

Sanibel Siesta Condominiums
1246 Fulger Street
Sanibel Island, FL 33957
813-472-4117

2 Bedrooms $$
2 Bedrms/week 5$
Min. Stay 4 Nights, Dep. Req'd. •
62 condos, Hi-rise, Lo-rise, Key at Complex office
P-yes/H-yes

Location: Airport: 27 miles; Downtown: 20 miles; Need car; Beach front

General Facilities: Kitchen, Linens, Baby-sitter

Room Facilities: Pool, Tennis, Shuffleboard, Golf: Beachview public course, TV, Cable, VCR, Phone in rm., Crib-Hi-chair, Ind. AC Ctl., Ind. Heat Ctl.

Attractions: Deep sea & bay fishing, bay shelling, trolley tour of Sanibel/Captiva Isles.

Shops & Restaurants: 30 boutiques and gift shops; Mc T's Shrimp House and Pub

Sanibel Siesta is an island paradise in the shimmering Gulf of Mexico, enjoying a tropical climate, clothed with lush tropical vegetation, and an abundance of shells, birds and other wildlife. A beachfront condominium with shuffleboard, heated pool and wheelchair ramp to the beach. Tennis courts are available and golf course is a block away. For those who seek the carefree life in surroundings of unparalleled natural beauty and privacy.

Song of the Sea
863 E. Gulf Drive
Sanibel Island, FL 33957
813-472-2220 800-237-8906

1 Bedroom $$, Lo-rise
Pool, Kitchen

Attractions: Tennis, golf, shelling, boating, fishing, bird watching

Efficiency units with kitchenettes and terraces, casually decorated one bedroom apartments overlooking the Gulf of Mexico, all in an Old World Inn with whitewashed walls and red tile roofs. Palm trees and shrubbery surround the walkways and parking.

--------- SANIBEL ISLAND ---------

Sundial Beach & Tennis Resort
1451 Middle Gulf Drive
Sanibel Island, FL 33957
813-472-4151 800-237-4184

1 Bedroom $$, 2 Bedrooms $$$, 3 Bedrooms
$$$
AmEx/Visa/MC, Dep. 1 Night •
215 condos, Lo-rise, Key at Front desk
No S-yes/H-yes

Location: Airport: 21 miles; Need car; Beach front

General Facilities: Full serv., Conf. rm. cap. 250, Daily maid, Kitchen, Linens, Restaurant on prem., Bar on prem., Game room, Lounge, Baby-sitter, Child planned rec.: Recreation Dept.

Room Facilities: Pool, Tennis, Bike and boat, Golf: Dunes—2 miles, TV, Cable, Phone in rm., Crib-Hi-chair, Ind. AC Ctl., Ind. Heat Ctl.

Attractions: Ding Darling Wildlife Refuge, Shelling beaches, windsurfing, bikes, entertainment

Shops & Restaurants: Unique specialty shops and boutiques; Thistle Lodge Chadwicks

Sundial Beach Resort is located on Sanibel Island, just off the southwest coast of Florida. Sundial is the only full service resort and conference facility on Sanibel. Walk to cool tropical breezes stirring the native palms and gentle waves lapping the beaches. Stroll barefoot on the shell-strewn beach under the morning sun, or witness the brilliant sunset and gaze at the blanket of stars above the tranquil surf.

Tortuga Beach Club
959 E. Gulf Drive
Sanibel Island, FL 33957
813-481-3636 800-237-8906

2 Bedrooms $$$, Lo-rise
Pool, Kitchen

54 lavish townhouse suites in a Caribbean style island resort. Three-story cluster buildings for those who need privacy. Or socializing at the game room/clubhouse, pool or beach for the gregarious.

--------- SANTA ROSA BEACH ---------

One Seagrove Place
Route 2, Box 650
Santa Rosa Beach, FL 32459
904-231-5032 800-368-9100

2 Bedrooms $$, Hi-rise
Pool, Kitchen

Attractions: Tennis, Golf

You'll feel you're on a secluded island at this family resort with its white sand beach, pool and tennis court, yet you're close to golf, dining, shopping and recreation. Complete electric kitchens with breakfast bar pass-throughs, wide balconies, washers and ceiling fans.

--------- SARASOTA ---------

Calini Beach Club
1030 Seaside Dr.
Sarasota, FL 34242
813-349-2500

2 Bedrooms $$, Hi-rise
Pool, Kitchen, Linens

Two-bedroom, two-bath condominiums with luxurious modern furnishings, marble baths, Italian ceramic floor tile, decorator linens, ceiling fans, mirrored walls and private veranda with gulf or garden views.

—————————————— SARASOTA ——————————————

Limetree Beach Resort
1050 Ben Franklin Drive
Sarasota, FL 34236
813-388-2111

1 Bedrm/week 5$, 2 Bed/week 7$
Min. Stay 3 Nights, Visa/MC, Dep. Req'd.
67 condos, Lo-rise, Key at Office
H-yes

Location: Airport: 7 miles; Downtown: 5 miles; Need car; Beach front

General Facilities: Kitchen, Linens, Game room

Room Facilities: Pool, Hot tub, Tennis, Exercise room, TV, Cable, Phone in rm., Crib-Hi-chair, Ind. AC Ctl., Ind. Heat Ctl.

Attractions: Sarasota Jungle Gardens, Ringling Museum, deep-sea fishing, Disney World, Busch Gardens

Shops & Restaurants: St. Armand's Circle; Charley's Crab

Warm weather, beautiful pool and right on Lido Beach, Limetree Beach Resort is within walking distance to St. Armand's Circle, one of Florida's finest shopping and dining areas. Visit the Jungle Gardens or Ringling Museum, or take an hour's drive to Busch Gardens, or just lie around the pool.

Sea Club V
6744 Sara Sea Circle, Siesta Key
Sarasota, FL 34242
813-349-1176

1 Bedrm/week 7$, 2 Bed/week 8$
Min. Stay 7 Nights, AmEx/Visa/MC,
    Dep. Req'd. •
41 condos, Lo-rise, Key at Front office
H-yes

Location: Airport: 15 miles; Downtown: 10 miles; Need car; Beach front

General Facilities: Full serv., Kitchen, Linens

Room Facilities: Pool, Hot tub, TV, Cable, Phone in rm., Crib-Hi-chair, Ind. AC Ctl., Ind. Heat Ctl.

Attractions: Ringling Estate and Museum, Bellm's Cars & Music of Yesterday, Sarasota Jungle Gardens, entertainment

Shops & Restaurants: St. Armand's Circle, Maas Brothers, Burdines; Miguel's/Fr.-Sugar&Spice/Amish

Sea Club V gives you a private, white sand beach which slopes to the Gulf of Mexico. You can wander out hundreds of feet in these clear waters. Hobie cats, sunfish, wind surfers, sun canoes, snorkeling gear, rafts and beach cabanas are at your doorstep. Nearby is Sarasota with sports from baseball to dog racing, plus many cultural attractions and fine restaurants and shopping.

Suntide Island Beach Club
850 Ben Franklin Dr.
Sarasota, FL 34236
813-388-2151

1 Bedroom $$, 2 Bedrooms $$, Lo-rise
Pool, Kitchen, Linens

Attractions: Jungle Gardens, Botanical Gardens, Busch Gardens, Van Wezel Theatre, Cypress Gardens

All the comforts of home in your tropically furnished condominium surrounded by palms. Pool, jacuzzi and beach. Monday night barbecue with live entertainment.

SARASOTA

The Meadows Golf & Tennis Resort
3101 Longmeadow
Sarasota, FL 34235
813-378-6660 800-428-0808

Studio $$
AmEx/Visa/MC, Dep. 1 Night •
12 condos, Villas, Key at Resort check-in
H-yes

Location: Airport: 5 miles; Downtown: 6 miles; Need car

General Facilities: Daily maid, Kitchen, Linens, Restaurant on prem., Bar on prem., Lounge, Baby-sitter

Room Facilities: Pool, Sauna, Tennis, 3 golf courses, Golf: Meadows, Highlands, Grove, TV, Cable, Phone in rm., Crib-Hi-chair, Ind. AC Ctl., Ind. Heat Ctl.

Attractions: White beaches, theatre and art, Ringling Museum, entertainment

Shops & Restaurants: St. Armand's Circle; Cafe L'Europe/continental

Located minutes from the cultural delights of Sarasota and the white sands of the Gulf Beaches, The Meadows offers world class golf, a professional tennis centre, swimming pools and an abundance of lakes. Three restaurants and four bars on the property. Various planned social events for your entertainment.

Tivoli By The Sea
625 Beach Road, Siesta Key
Sarasota, FL 34242
813-349-5544

2 Bedrooms 4$, Hi-rise
Pool, Daily maid, Kitchen, Linens, Phone in rm.

Attractions: Florida Symphony, Ringling Museum of Art, Jungle Gardens, greyhound racing, Ca'd 'Zan, Putting green, Tennis, Golf

Situated on semi-tropical Siesta Key and linked by two bridges to Sarasota for shopping, entertainment and sightseeing. Dramatically styled two bedroom split-plan apartments with 26-foot balconies and washer/dryers, facing the powdery sands of Siesta Beach and the Gulf.

SATELLITE BEACH

Las Olas Beach Club
1215-25 Highway A1A
Satellite Beach, FL 32937
407-777-3224

2 Bedrooms $$$
2 Bedrms/week 6$
Min. Stay 3 Nights, Visa/MC, Dep. Req'd. •
40 condos, Hi-rise, Key at Reception desk
H-yes

Location: Airport: Melborne-20 minutes; Downtown: 1 hour; Need car; Beach front

General Facilities: Kitchen, Linens, Baby-sitter

Room Facilities: Pool, Hot tub, TV, Cable, Phone in rm., Crib-Hi-chair, Ind. AC Ctl., Ind. Heat Ctl.

Attractions: Kennedy Space Center and easy access to all Orlando attractions, entertainment

Shops & Restaurants: Large indoor mall as well as shopping villages; Italian, French, Seafood

Come to lovely Las Olas and enjoy Central Florida beaches. All units afford gorgeous oceanfront views from private balconies. Welcome continental breakfast, wine & cheese parties and weekly potluck cook-out. Very family oriented, weekly get-togethers and activities organized by the staff, such as volleyball and sand castle building.

─────────────── SEAGROVE BEACH ───────────────

Beachside Condominiums   1 Bedroom $$
Highway 365   1 Bedrm/week 4$
Seagrove Beach, FL 32459   Dep. Req'd.
904-231-4205 800-443-3146   3 condos

Location: Airport: 25 miles; Downtown: 10 miles; Need car

General Facilities: Kitchen, Linens

Room Facilities: Pool, Cable, Ind. AC Ctl., Ind. Heat Ctl.

Attractions: Beach activities

Shops & Restaurants: Destin, Panama City

This is the place to get away from it all and forget your cares by relaxing at the beach or sunbathing by the pool.

Beachwood Villas
Route 2, Box 640
Seagrove Beach, FL 32459
904-231-4031 800-537-5387

All units face the two kidney shaped pools set among attractive, spacious, landscaped common areas. 2 tennis courts, clubhouse, direct beach access. On-site office.

Cassine Gardens   2 Bedrooms $$
Route 2, Box 658, Highway 30-A   2 Bedrms/week 4$
Seagrove Beach, FL 32459   Min. Stay 3 Nights, Dep. Req'd. •
904-231-4851 800-346-0128   72 condos, Lo-rise, Key at On site office
                                    No S-yes

Location: Airport: 40 miles; Downtown: 30 miles; Need car

General Facilities: Kitchen, Linens

Room Facilities: Pool, Tennis, Nature/fitness trail, TV, Cable, Phone in rm., Crib-Hi-chair, Ind. AC Ctl., Ind. Heat Ctl.

Attractions: Gulf of Mexico-Emerald Green Waters, world's whitest beaches

Shops & Restaurants: Santa Rosa/Panama City Mall, Village at Sandestin; Capt.' Andersons/Daves/Bayou Bill

Cassine Gardens is 1 mile east of Seagrove Beach on a 25-acre site. Walk miles crunching in the beach sand looking for shells, or picnic on your private dune. Bicycle down the scenic coastal highway, or jog through two miles of nature trails among cyress groves and estuaries. Take a short walk to White Sand Gulf Beach, or play tennis or volleyball, or sun and swim at the pool.

──────────────── SEBRING ────────────────

Resorts of Sun 'n Lake
4101 Sun 'n Lake Blvd.
Sebring, FL 33872
813-385-2561 800-237-2165

AmEx/Visa/MC
115 condos, Lo-rise, Villas
H-yes

Location: Airport: 86 miles-Olando; Downtown: 7 miles

General Facilities: Conf. rm. cap. 250, Restaurant on prem., Bar on prem.

Room Facilities: Pool, Tennis, Bikes, horseshoes, TV, Cable, Phone in rm., Ind. AC Ctl., Ind. Heat Ctl.

Attractions: Highlands Hammock State Park, Cypress Swamp, wildlife, guided tours & museum, entertainment

Shops & Restaurants: Penney, Byrons, Beall's, Zayre's, Wal & K-Mart; Pierre's/Fr.-Candlelight/Amr.

This small condominium resort is nestled within a residential community in the "unspoiled" heart of Florida, offering the comforts of home with fully furnished, totally equipped one and two bedroom villas and townhouses, all with semi-private pool. Experience complete comfort, sincere hospitality and friendly service. Great for a secluded "getaway."

───────────────────────────────────────

Sun'n Lake Estates—Linkside
4101 Sun 'N Lake Blvd.
Sebring, FL 33872
813-385-2561 800-237-2165

1 Bedroom $, 2 Bedrooms $$
1 Bedrm/week $$$$, 2 Bed/week 4$
Min. Stay 2 Nights, AmEx/Visa/MC,
    Dep. Req'd. •
115 condos, Lo-rise, Villas, Key at Registr. desk

Location: Airport: 86 miles-Orlando; Downtown: 7 miles; Need car

General Facilities: Full serv., Conf. rm. cap. 250, Kitchen, Linens, Restaurant on prem., Bar on prem., Lounge, Baby-sitter

Room Facilities: Pool, Tennis, Shuffleboard, Horseshoes, Golf: Sun 'n Lake of Sebring, TV, Cable, Phone in rm., Crib-Hi-chair, Ind. AC Ctl., Ind. Heat Ctl.

Attractions: Highlands Hammock State Park, Cypress Swamp, guided tours, entertainment

Shops & Restaurants: Penney, Byrons, Beall's, Zayre's, Wal-Mart, K-Mart; Candlelight-Amr./Pierre's-Fr.

Tastefully decorated villas and townhouses nestled within a residential community in "unspoiled" south central Florida. Family recreation and relaxation for get-togethers or secluded getaways. Complete comfort, hospitality and friendly service.

Our goal is to provide as *complete* a listing of condo vacation properties as possible. If you know of a condo we don't list, please send us their name and address on the form at the back of this Guide.

--------- SIESTA KEY, SARASOTA ---------

House Of The Sun
6518 Midnight Pass Road
Siesta Key, Sarasota, FL 34242
813-349-4141

2 Bedrms/week 4$
Min. Stay 7 Nights, Dep. Req'd.
58 condos, Hi-rise, Key at Office

Location: Airport: 10 miles; Downtown: 5 miles; Need car; Beach front

General Facilities: Kitchen, Linens

Room Facilities: Pool, Tennis, TV, Cable, Phone in rm., Crib-Hi-chair, Ind. AC Ctl., Ind. Heat Ctl.

Attractions: Mote Marine-Longboat Key, Jungle Gardens, Myakka State Park, Public golf courses

Shops & Restaurants: Publics grocery, Gulf Gate Mall, Sarasota Square; Italian, French, seafood

Sliding glass doors in the living/dining area lead to your private terrace for partying as you watch the sunset over the Gulf. Frost-free refrigerator freezer with ice maker, kitchen pass-thru snack bar, separate beverage bar in dining area. Underground parking, two elevators. Tennis on the beach with heated swimming pool and game room directly on the water. Walking distance to points of interest, shopping and dining.

Island Colony

—————————————————— ST. AUGUSTINE BEACH ——————————————————

Anastasia Condominiums   2 Bedrms/week $$$$, 3 Bed/week 4$
2 Dondanville Road   Hi-rise
St. Augustine Beach, FL 32084
904-471-2800 800-458-7345

Location: Beach front
General Facilities: Daily maid, Kitchen, Linens
Room Facilities: Pool, Tennis, TV

Oversized rooms on a choice location overlooking St. Augustine Beach. Total-electric kitchens even have trash compactors. Lounge by the pool and patio area or enjoy the miles of sandy beach.

—————————————————————— ST. AUGUSTINE ——————————————————————

Beach Club At St. Augustine   1 Bedroom $$, 2 Bedrooms $$, Hi-rise
Beach   Pool, Kitchen, Linens, Phone in rm.
A1A at 2 Ocean Trace Rd.
St. Augustine, FL 32084
904-471-2626

Attractions: Walt Disney EPCOT, Sea & Circus Worlds, Kennedy Space Center, Daytona Speedway, Dog Track, Exercise room, bikes, Tennis

Appealing, comfortable, designer selected furnishings in one and two bedroom units with shower massages, hair dryers and family games. A planned environment along the beach for fun and leisure. Pro shop, clubhouse, and snack bar.

The Beach Club
2 Ocean Trace Road
St. Augustine, FL 32084
904-471-2626

Beachers Lodge
6970 A1A South
St. Augustine, FL 32084
904-471-8849

Captain's Quarters   Pool, Kitchen, Linens
Route 5
St. Augustine, FL 32084
904-471-0712 800-824-2867

Attractions: Tennis, Golf

Drive into your parking space, step into the elevator to your apartment with walk-in closets and glass walled living room. Pool tennis, beach. Minutes to market, mall and St. Augustine.

──────────────── ST. AUGUSTINE ────────────────

Colony Reef Club
4670 A1A South
St. Augustine, FL 32084
904-471-2233

Villas
Pool, Kitchen

Attractions: Marineland, jai alai, historic St. Augustine, Tennis

All family members will find something to do at this complete seaside resort. Tennis, pool, indoor lap pool, kiddie pool, jungle gym, exercise room, health club, racquetball, jogging trail through garden settings, and, of course, miles of white sand beach.

Four Winds Condominiums
8130 A1A South
St. Augustine, FL 32086
904-471-0683

Lo-rise
Pool, Kitchen, Linens

Attractions: Marineland, Ocala National Forest, Disney World, Kennedy Space Center

Ideally located apartments on a crescent shaped beach. Heated pool for non-beach lovers. Swimming, sunbathing, beachcombing and saltwater fishing in a tranquil setting for full Florida vacation enjoyment.

Ocean Village Club
4250 Route A1A South
St. Augustine, FL 32084
904-471-9329 800-447-0004

1 Bedroom $$, 2 Bedrooms $$
1 Bedrm/week $$$$, 2 Bed/week $$$$
Min. Stay 2 Nights, Visa/MC, Dep. Req'd. •
348 condos, Lo-rise, Key at Rental office/site
No S-yes/H-yes

Location: Airport: 45 minutes; Downtown: 10 Min; Need car

General Facilities: Kitchen, Linens

Room Facilities: Pool, Hot tub, Tennis, TV, Cable, Phone in rm., Crib-Hi-chair, Ind. AC Ctl., Ind. Heat Ctl.

Attractions: Many guided tours, horse and carriage rides, Marineland-15 minutes

Shops & Restaurants: Cobblestone streets closed to traffic-many shops; Salt Water Cowboys/seafood

Oceanfront properties with washers and dryers and small kitchen appliances in each unit. 10 minutes from the historic downtown area of St. Augustine with its many fine restaurants. Swimming pool and hot tub, with North Florida's finest beaches at your door.

Ponce Landing
3100 South A1A
St. Augustine, FL 32084
904-471-1217

2 Bedrooms $$$$, Lo-rise
Pool, Kitchen, Linens

Two-level, two-bedroom townhomes with second-story balcony and sun deck, private patio surrounding two swimming pools. Enclosed garage. Walkway to ocean for sun worshipers, or spend the day in historic St. Augustine.

———————————————— ST. AUGUSTINE ————————————————

Ponce de Leon Resort & Conf. Ctr.   AmEx/Visa/MC
4000 US 1 North   30 condos, Villas, Key at Hotel lobby
St. Augustine, FL 32085
904-824-2821 800-824-2821

Location: Airport: Jacksonville 50 mi.; Downtown: 2 miles; Need car

General Facilities: Conf. rm. cap. 480, Kitchen, Restaurant on prem., Bar on prem.

Room Facilities: Pool, Tennis, Fishing, sailing, Golf: Ponce de Leon course, TV, Cable, Phone in rm., Ind.AC Ctl., Ind. Heat Ctl.

Attractions: St. Augustine, Marineland, greyhound racing, sailing, deep-sea fishing, entertainment

Shops & Restaurants: Historic district shops, sundries shop; Michaels/seafood and steaks

Resort on 350 landscaped acres, adjacent to the inland waterway. Villas are traditionally furnished in pastel colors. Some have whirlpools and sleeping lofts. Six Deco Turf II tennis courts, huge pool and 18-hole putting course with hazards disguised as fountains. Area tours, deep-sea fishing, sailing and water skiing are easily scheduled through the resort.

———

Sand Dollar Condominiums   3 Bedrms/week 5$
8050 South AIA Street   Min. Stay 7 Nights, Dep. Req'd.
St. Augustine, FL 32086   166 condos, Hi-rise
904-471-1733   No S-yes/H-yes

Location: Airport: 1½ hour; Downtown: 11 miles; Need car; Beach front

General Facilities: Kitchen, Linens

Room Facilities: Pool, Tennis, TV, Cable, Phone in rm., Crib-Hi-chair, Ind. AC Ctl., Ind. Heat Ctl.

Attractions: St. Augustine—the nation's oldest city, sightseeing of historical areas, Marineland, tours, entertainment

Shops & Restaurants: Fiddlers Green/seafood

These large, 1700-square-foot units overlook the Atlantic Ocean and Intercoastal Waterway. Miles of white beach, pools and tennis on beautiful spacious grounds. Winter entertainment includes coffee hour, bridge and social events. Eleven miles to St. Augustine.

———

Sea Place Condominiums   2 Bedrooms $$, 3 Bedrooms $$$
4400 A1A South   2 Bedrms/week $$$, 3 Bed/week 6$
St. Augustine, FL 32084   Min. Stay 2 Nights, AmEx/Visa/MC, Dep. Req'd. •
904-471-3881 800-242-7999   42 condos, Lo-rise, Key at Rental office
                             No S-yes/H-yes

Location: Airport: Jacksonville; Downtown: 10 miles; Need car; Beach front

General Facilities: Kitchen, Linens, Baby-sitter

Room Facilities: Pool, Hot tub, Tennis, Racquetball, TV, Cable, Phone in rm., Crib-Hi-chair, Ind. AC Ctl., Ind. Heat Ctl.

Attractions: Historical St. Augustine, Marineland, Alligator Farm

Shops & Restaurants: Ponce de Leon Mall, St. Augustine shops & boutiques; Salt Water Cowboy's/seafood

Centrally located villas with private patios. Step outside your door on paths set in a manicured lawn and swim, surf, sun and sail. Pool, tennis, racquetball and jacuzzi.

ST. AUGUSTINE

Spanish Trace
1 Ocean Trace Road
St. Augustine, FL 32084
904-471-2535

Lo-rise
Pool, Kitchen, Linens

Attractions: Disney World, Sea World, Circus World, Kennedy Space Center, Marineland, Shuffleboard, Tennis

South of St. Augustine, right on the ocean with view of the landscaped courtyard, ocean and dunes. Individually furnished units. Safe ocean swimming, pool, tennis and shuffleboard.

St. Aug. Beach and Tennis Club
4 Ocean Trace Road
St. Augustine, FL 32084
904-471-2880

2 Bedrms/week $$$$, 3 Bed/week $$$$
Min. Stay 7 Nights, Dep. Req'd.
96 condos, Hi-rise, Key at Office
No S-yes/H-yes

Location: Airport: 50 miles; Downtown: 5 miles; Need car; Beach front

General Facilities: Kitchen, Linens, Bar on prem., Baby-sitter

Room Facilities: Pool, Sauna, Tennis, TV, Cable, Phone in rm., Crib-Hi-chair, Ind. AC Ctl., Ind. Heat Ctl.

Attractions: Scenic carriage rides, boat excursion, historical sights, Marineland, Disney World

Shops & Restaurants: Fiddlers Green/seafood

Modern, comfortable, homelike units furnished to the owners' preference. Walk on the beach, keep fit at the health and fitness center, or relax in the jacuzzi after your tennis game.

Summerhouse
8550 A1A South-Anastasia Island
St. Augustine, FL 32086
904-471-1503 800-334-2160

2 Bedrooms $$, 3 Bedrooms $$
2 Bedrms/week 4$, 3 Bed/week 5$
Min. Stay 2 Nights, Visa/MC, Dep. Req'd. •
256 condos, Lo-rise, Key at Site rental office
H-yes

Location: Airport: 45 minutes; Downtown: 15 min.; Need car; Beach front

General Facilities: Conf. rm. cap. 50, Daily maid, Kitchen, Linens

Room Facilities: Pool, Tennis, Racquetball, TV, Cable, Phone in rm., Crib-Hi-chair, Ind. AC Ctl., Ind. Heat Ctl.

Attractions: River cruises, horse carriage tours, Marineland sea shows, oldest USA city

Shops & Restaurants: Anastasia shopping mall, tourist shops; Conch House-seafood, steaks

Tropical rattan in summer colors make for a truly relaxed vacation in these two and three bedroom condominiums. 4 swimming pools, 6 tennis courts and 6 racquetball courts with courtyard or ocean views from the balconies. 2 miles from Marineland, less than two hours to Disney World, discount privileges available for nearby golf courses.

――――――――――――――― ST. AUGUSTINE ―――――――――――――――

The Coquina　　　　　　　　2 Bedrms/week 4$
7900 A1A South　　　　　　　　Dep. Req'd.
St. Augustine, FL 32086　　　　42 condos, Lo-rise
904-471-0055

Location: Downtown: 10 miles; Beach front
General Facilities: Kitchen, Linens, Child planned rec.: Wading pool
Room Facilities: Pool, Tennis, Golf: Nearby, TV, Cable, Ind. AC Ctl., Ind. Heat Ctl.
Attractions: Disney World, Marineland, Daytona Beach, Old Fort, Alligator Farm
Shops & Restaurants: Historical Restoration Area shops, St. Augustine

Well-decorated units in V-shaped construction. Pool and wading pool on the oceanfront by the sea wall with steps leading to the wide, hard sand, unspoiled beach. Friendly, quiet, refined atmosphere.

Tradewinds Condominiums　　1 Bedroom $, 2 Bedrooms $$, Hi-rise
7750 South A1A　　　　　　　　Pool, Kitchen, Linens
St. Augustine, FL 32084
904-471-0113

Attractions: Disney World, Jacksonville, Daytona Beach, Tennis

Family-oriented condominiums with private pier and secured boat storage, on fourteen miles of unbroken white sand beach. Tennis, pool and clubhouse.

―――――――――――― ST. PETERSBURG BEACH ――――――――――――

Breckenridge Resort Beach Club　Studio $$, 1 Bedroom $$$
5700 Gulf Blvd.　　　　　　　　　AmEx/Visa/MC, Dep. 1 Night •
St. Petersburg Beach, FL 33706　200 condos, Hi-rise, Key at Front desk
813-828-3371　800-237-3371　　No S-yes/H-yes

Location: Airport: 35 minutes; Downtown: 15 min.; Beach front
General Facilities: Full serv., Bus. fac., Conf. rm. cap. 250, Daily maid, Kitchen, Linens, Restaurant on prem., Bar on prem., Game room, Lounge, Baby-sitter
Room Facilities: Pool, Tennis, Golf: Pasadena Country C. 5 min, TV, Cable, Phone in rm., Crib-Hi-chair, Ind. AC Ctl., Ind. Heat Ctl.
Attractions: Busch Gardens Theme Park and Zoo, SeaEscape 1 day cruise/casino, museums, entertainment
Shops & Restaurants: Boutiques, resort wear, outlet mall; Wine Cellar/European

Gulf-front studios in mauve color scheme, dinette area, mirrored closet doors, built-in cabinetry. A guitarist to entertain you during the day, and evening comedian/pianist in the lounge. Have fun on the beach or join in the many water sports available on the premises. Two tennis courts, game room and pool.

---------------------- ST. PETERSBURGH BEACH ----------------------

Camelot
1801 Gulf Way, Pass-A-Grille Bch
St. Petersburg Beach, FL 33706
813-360-6988

1 Bedrm/week $$$$, 2 Bed/week 4$
Dep. Req'd.
Lo-rise

Location: Downtown: 5 minute

General Facilities: Kitchen

Room Facilities: Pool, Sauna, Hot tub, Bikes, Shuffleboard, Golf: Nearby, TV, Phone in rm., Ind. AC Ctl.

Attractions: Tennis, golf, water activities

Shops & Restaurants: Convenience market—5 minutes

Two-story resort condominium with friendly, southern style atmosphere. Fully carpeted with designer coordinated furnishings overlooking the beach. Lounge around the pool, tan on the sun deck or picnic on the beach.

Coral Reef Beach Resort
5800 Gulf Blvd.
St. Petersburg Beach, FL 33706
813-360-0821 800-553-6599

1 Bedroom $$, 2 Bedrooms $$$, Hi-rise
Pool, Kitchen

Look out at night at the beautiful, lighted, unusually shaped pool under walkways and surrounded by umbrella covered tables. This five acre resort has a private beach and its own restaurant and deluxe one and two bedroom units.

Hideaway Sands Resort
3804 Gulf Blvd.
St. Petersburg Beach, FL 33706
813-367-2781

1 Bedroom $$, 2 Bedrooms $$, Hi-rise
Pool, Kitchen, Phone in rm.

Attractions: Disney World, Busch Gaardens, dog/horse racing, NASL soccer, jai alai, Exercise room, Golf

Located directly on the beach and convenient to shopping and dining, these units have washer/dryers, microwaves and private balconies. Pool, jacuzzi, billiards and exercise room, BBQ grills, covered pavilion on beach side and complimentary membership to the golf club.

Mariner Beach Club
4220 Gulf Blvd.
St. Petersburg Beach, FL 33706
813-367-3721

1 Bedroom $$, 2 Bedrooms $$$, Lo-rise
Pool

Overlooking the Gulf of Mexico, one and two bedroom condominiums with special touches such as track lighting, ceiling fans, games, books and a daily newspaper. Swimming pool, two jacuzzis and barbecue.

--------------------------------- STUART ---------------------------------

Bay Harbor Club
3954 S.W. Old St. Lucie Blvd.
Stuart, FL 33494
305-287-3111

Lo-rise
Pool, Kitchen, Linens, Phone in rm.

Attractions: Boating, tennis, golf, swimming, Docks

The Bay Harbor Club is situated on the St. Lucie River. Boat slip rentals available. Units are one bedroom with one or two baths, two color televisions and private balconies. Three blocks from golf and three miles from the ocean.

Harbor Ridge Golf Club
13400 NW Gilson Road, Box 2451
Stuart, FL 34995
407-336-1800

2 Bedrooms $$$, Lo-rise
Pool, Daily maid, Kitchen, Phone in rm.

Attractions: Fishing, sailing, swimming, tennis, golf, sailing

Large apartments in a golf and tennis resort have screened terraces, utility rooms, dining rooms and eat-in kitchen. A short walk to the first tee and Swim and Tennis Club. Community has scenic interior lakes, protected mangroves and bald eagle nests.

--------------------------- TARPON SPRINGS ---------------------------

Innisbrook
P.O. Drawer 1088
Tarpon Springs, FL 34688
813-942-2000 800-237-0157

1 Bedroom $$, 2 Bedrooms $$$
Dep. Req'd.
Key at Reception Center
H-yes

Location: Airport: Tampa--25 minutes
General Facilities: Kitchen, Linens, Restaurant on prem., Bar on prem., Child planned rec.: Zoo Crew ages 4-12
Room Facilities: Pool, Sauna, Tennis, Health club, bikes, Golf: 3 on-site courses
Attractions: Disney World, Sea World, Kennedy Space Center, Busch Gardens, Circus World, Weeki Wachee, entertainment
Shops & Restaurants: Le Market Place on-site, gifts, sundries, liquors; 6 restaurants, 2 snack bars

World class golf with 35 clinics and summer junior program. Terry Addison's Australian Tennis Institute with 2 clinic programs and summer junior program. Rich flowering wooded acres with gleaming lakes, citrus groves, pine trees and a wildlife preserve. Zoo Crew activities program for 4-to 12-year-olds. 6 pools, lake or sport fishing, beach shuttle service, bicycle or jog. Day trips arranged to attractions. Dress for dining at the Island Clubhouse and Copperhead nightclub, or relax with room service.

--------------------------- TREASURE ISLAND ---------------------------

Jamaican On The Gulf
11660 Gulf Blvd.
Treasure Island, FL 33706
813-360-6981

1 Bedroom $$, 2 Bedrooms $$$, Hi-rise
Kitchen

Contemporary resort with one and two bedroom suites directly on the Gulf of Mexico. Beach level sun deck and rooftop patio for sunbathing.

—————————————— TREASURE ISLAND ——————————————

Land's End Resort
7500 Bayshore Drive
Treasure Island, FL 33706
813-367-7859 800-382-8883

Lo-rise
Pool, Kitchen

Attractions: Tennis

A beachfront hideaway for a leisurely, relaxing vacation. On a peninsula surrounded by tranquil, blue water. Pool, tennis, gazebos. Be pampered at this romantic, Mediterranean style resort. Close to shopping, restaurants and nightlife.

Nordvind
12700 Gulf Blvd.
Treasure Island, FL 33706
813-360-7037 800-237-5897

1 Bedroom $$, 2 Bedrooms $$, Hi-rise
Kitchen, Linens

Quality, craftsmanship and Scandinavian detail with ceramic tile and oak cabinetry. Lawn and beach views from every suite.

Sand Pebble Resort
12300 Gulf Blvd.
Treasure Island, FL 33706
813-360-1845

Studio $, 1 Bedroom $$, 2 Bedrooms $$,
    3 Bedrooms $$$
1 Bedrm/week 5$, 2 Bed/week 5$,
    3 Bed/week 7$
Min. Stay 2 Nights, AmEx/Visa/MC,
    Dep. Req'd. •
45 condos, Lo-rise, Key at Front desk, H-yes

Location: Airport: 40 minutes; Downtown: 15 min.; Need car; Beach front

General Facilities: Daily maid, Kitchen, Linens, Baby-sitter, Child planned rec.: Activity Director

Room Facilities: Pool, Hot tub, Tennis, Golf: 1 mile, TV, Cable, Phone in rm., Crib-Hi-chair, Ind. AC Ctl., Ind. Heat Ctl.

Attractions: John's Pass Fishing Village, Busch Gardens, Adventure Island, sailing, deep-sea fishing, entertainment

Shops & Restaurants: John's Pass Village, Tyrone Square Mall; Wine Cellar/Lobster Pot/Pompano

Sand Pebble was designed with families in mind and is situated on the Gulf of Mexico on the white sand beach of Treasure Island. Full activity schedule for all ages, swimming pool, in-ground spa and barbecue. Fine shops, restaurants, sailing fishing and spring training baseball camps are all close.

Treasure Island Beach Club
11750 Gulf Blvd.
Treasure Island, FL 33706
813-360-7096

1 Bedroom $$, 2 Bedrooms $$
Pool, Kitchen, Linens, Phone in rm.

Attractions: Disney World, EPCOT, Busch Gardens, major league teams spring training

Units with ultra-modern kitchens, tile baths and convenience appliances. Most have balconies. Beach, pool and in-ground spa for passive fun. Game room with pool table and video games. Dinner cruises and fishing charters available.

────────────── TREASURE ISLAND ──────────────

Treasure Shores
10360 Gulf Blvd.
Treasure Island, FL 33706
813-367-5989

1 Bedroom $$, Lo-rise
Pool, Kitchen

Decorator accessories in these units with video disc players and on-site laundry facilities. If you tire of the beach, try the pool and jacuzzi. Barbecue area. Tennis and golf nearby.

Voyager Beach Club
11860 Gulf Blvd.
Treasure Island, FL 33706
813-360-5529

1 Bedroom $$, 2 Bedrooms $$
Pool, Kitchen, Linens, Phone in rm.
Putting green, Tennis

Enjoy the sunsets over the Gulf of Mexico from your private balcony. All your favorite water sports, heated pool, jacuzzi and rooftop sun deck with shuffleboard. Jog on the beach, and then retire to your condominium for a relaxing jacuzzi.

────────────── VANDERBILT BEACH, NAPLES ──────────────

Vanderbilt Beach & Harbour Club   Pool, Kitchen, Linens
9301 Gulfshore Drive
Vanderbilt Beach, Naples, FL 33940
813-597-5098 800-331-4941

Attractions: Jungle Larry's, sailing, golf, tennis, theatres, Ritz-Carlton, Greyhound racing, Exercise room, bikes

Spacious, airy units furnished with everything you need for your vacation. Eating table in kitchen, screened in, furnished balcony, dining table, washer/dryers. All of this plus lush landscaping, pools, jacuzzis, sauna, exercise room, and bicycles.

Waikiki Beach Tower

———————————————— VERO BEACH ————————————————

Coralstone Club   Lo-rise, Villas
9025 North Highway A1A   Pool, Kitchen, Linens
Vero Beach, FL 32963
305-234-1400 800-634-4566

Attractions: Fitness center, Tennis, Golf

Villas and townhouses architecturally reminiscent of a Bermuda Village, all with screen-enclosed tropical garden patios, private garages, cathedral ceilings, skylights, 6' custom whirlpool baths and even hair dryers. Art Deco clubhouse.

Driftwood Inn Resort   1 Bedroom $$$, 2 Bedrooms $$$
3150 Ocean Dr.
Vero Beach, FL 32963
305-231-0550

Limited number of units for rent, some with full kitchens and some with kitchenettes, i.e., microwaves rather than ranges. Earthtone color schemes with warm accent colors. Clean, uncrowded beaches and tropical landscaping.

Sea Oaks   1 Bedrm/week 4$, 2 Bed/week 6$
8850 North A1A   Min. Stay 7 Nights, Dep. Req'd.
Vero Beach, FL 32963   47 condos, Lo-rise, Key at Office/guard house
407-231-5656 800-231-6227   No S-yes/H-yes

Location: Airport: 45 minutes; Downtown: 10 min.; Need car; Beach front

General Facilities: Daily maid, Kitchen, Linens, Restaurant on prem., Bar on prem., Baby-sitter, Child planned rec.: Tennis clinics

Room Facilities: Pool, Sauna, Hot tub, Tennis, Marina, TV, Cable, Phone in rm., Crib-Hi-chair, Ind. AC Ctl., Ind. Heat Ctl.

Attractions: Vero Beach attractions, L.A. Dodgers spring training, museums, libraries, Riverside Theater, entertainment

Shops & Restaurants: Boutiques, Worth Avenue in Palm Beach; Ocean Grill/seafood-cont.

Five-star tennis and beach resort community bordering the Atlantic Ocean on the east and Indian River on the west. Elegant, old-Florida style architecture on a secluded beach. Gourmet dining in the Oak Room, piano bar, and casual dining in the Beach Club Lounge. Water sports in the Gulf Stream and fishing in the Indian River. Protected, wooded trails along the river's edge for strolling, biking, jogging or bird watching.

Please mention *Condo Vacations the Complete Guide* when you reserve your condominium.

─────────────── VERO BEACH ───────────────

The Reef Ocean Resort
3450 Ocean Drive
Vero Beach, FL 32963
407-231-1000

Studio $, 1 Bedroom $$
1 Bedrm/week 5$
Min. Stay 2 Nights, AmEx/Visa/MC,
  Dep. Req'd.
60 condos, Villas, Key at Office
H-yes

Location: Airport: 1 hour; Downtown: walk; Need car; Beach front

General Facilities: Full serv., Daily maid, Kitchen, Linens, Restaurant on prem., Bar on prem., Lounge

Room Facilities: Pool, Hot tub, Tennis, Putting green, Paddle tennis, TV, Cable, Phone in rm., Crib-Hi-chair, Ind. AC Ctl., Ind. Heat Ctl.

Attractions: Disneyworld-90 min, Cape Canaveral-45 min, Dodgertown, jai alai, Riverside Theatre

Shops & Restaurants: Ocean Drive shops and boutiques, Pennys, Byrons; Black Pearl-Charlie Browns

Dramatic interior design of earth-tones, grass cloth and mirrors. Attention to accessories, such as best-selling novels and party games. Spacious, landscaped grounds for seclusion, Riverside Park for tennis, jogging and exercise, Vero Beach for sun and swimming. On-site barbecues, picnic areas, putting green, paddle tennis, pool, sun deck, restaurant and lounge. Small town atmosphere, but close to major cities for added enjoyment.

─────────────── WEST PALM BEACH ───────────────

Palm Beach Polo & Country Club   135 condos, Lo-rise
13198 Forest Hill Blvd.
West Palm Beach, FL 33414
407-798-7000 800-327-4202

General Facilities: Full serv., Conf. rm. cap. 60, Kitchen, Restaurant on prem., Babysitter

Room Facilities: Pool, Handball, polo, spa, Golf: 45-holes

Attractions: Polo, equestrian center, golf, tennis, rowing clinics, bicycle rentals, racquetball

Shops & Restaurants: Worth Avenue shops; Four dining rooms on-site

Guests stay in contemporary Florida-style condominiums with fairway or lake views and have use of a tennis center with 24 courts, and a full health spa. Three clubhouses scattered about the grounds house four dining rooms. The ocean is a half-hour away, and the concierge will be happy to arrange a deep-sea fishing excursion. Two croquet lawns, numerous swimming pools, rowing clinics, squash and racquetball. Professionally designed golf courses.

———————————— WINTER GARDEN ————————————

Windtree Villas
12 Windtree Ln.
Winter Garden, FL 32787
407-656-1577 800-423-7498

2 Bedrooms $$
2 Bedrms/week 5$
Min. Stay 4 Nights, AmEx/Visa/MC,
   Dep. Req'd. •
186 condos, Lo-rise, Villas, Key at Office
No S-yes/P-yes/H-yes

Location: Airport: 24 miles; Downtown: 2 miles; Need car

General Facilities: Full serv., Conf. rm. cap. 150, Kitchen, Linens, Restaurant on prem., Baby-sitter

Room Facilities: Pool, Tennis, TV, Phone in rm., Crib-Hi-chair, Ind. AC Ctl., Ind. Heat Ctl.

Attractions: Disney World, EPCOT, Wet 'N Wild, Sea World, Orlando

Shops & Restaurants: Reginal Mall, Zayres, small shops, EPCOT shops; Christini's-Lake Buena Vista

Wintree Villas are all two-bedroom, two-bathroom condos, furnished with custom-made furniture in an art deco feeling in shades of mauve, black and peach. Windtree Villas are just 20 minutes from Disney World and 15 minutes from Sea World. Private patios or terraces to enjoy the beautiful Florida sunsets. Pool and tennis are also included on this 16-acre resort.

Georgia

Dillard
Ellijay • • Helen

• Pine Mountain

Tybee Island
Sea Island
St. Simons Island

DILLARD

Sky Valley Resort
Dillard
Dillard, GA 30537
404-746-5301

2 Bedrooms $$, 3 Bedrooms $$$
Lo-rise, Key at Front desk

Location: Airport: Atlanta; Need car; Ski lift: Nearby

General Facilities: Kitchen, Restaurant on prem., Lounge, Child planned rec.: Playground-day camp

Room Facilities: Pool, Tennis, Fishing, hiking, Golf: 18-hole course

Attractions: Tallulah Gorge, Rabun Bald, Black Rock Mountain State Park, river rafting, hiking

Shops & Restaurants: Full-service grocery store, antiques and crafts; The Chateau at SV / nouvelle

Located in the foothills of the Blue Ridge Mountains, fully equipped chalets and condominiums with fireplaces, two to four bedrooms. Wilderness trails for hiking and horseback riding, clean, public beaches for water lovers, mountain streams for fishing. A variety of things to do for the active sportsperson; pool swimming and communing with nature for the less ambitious. Winter skiing. Summer day camp and teen center. Friendly, homespun atmosphere with real Southern hospitality.

ELLIJAY

Blue Ridge Mountain Marina Resort
100 Beaver Lake Dr., Carters Lake
Ellijay, GA 30540
404-276-4891

1 Bedroom $$, Lo-rise
Kitchen

Attractions: Smoky Mountains, Carters Lake, Marina, boat rentals

Cabins on Carters Lake's sixty-two miles of shoreline. The only commercial facility on the Lake. Marina and convenience store with everything for the boater and fishing equipment rental.

---------------------------------- HELEN ----------------------------------

Loreley
1 Bruckenstrasse, P.O. Box ll6
Helen, GA 30545
404-878-2236 800-631-6291

1 Bedroom $$, 2 Bedrooms $$
1 Bedrm/week 4$, 2 Bed/week 4$
Min. Stay 2 Nights, AmEx/Visa/MC,
  Dep. Req'd.
93 condos, Lo-rise, Key at Manager's office
H-yes

Location: Airport: 95 miles Atlanta; Downtown: 2 miles; Need car; Ski lift: Sky Vly.

General Facilities: Kitchen, Linens, Game room, Lounge

Room Facilities: Pool, Sauna, Hot tub, Tennis, Indoor pool, Golf: Innsbruck Golf, TV, Cable, VCR, Crib-Hi-chair, Ind. AC Ctl., Ind. Heat Ctl.

Attractions: The beauty and serenity of Georgia mountains, cascading waterfalls, lakes, rivers & parks, entertainment

Shops & Restaurants: Outlet Mall, recreated Bavarian Village; Chef Hans/German & American

Southern hospitality mixed with Alpine charm, set along the Chattahoochee River. Activities Director plans trips, bingo, dancing, rafting, horseback riding, cook-outs, panning for gold and games for children. Helen's year-round festivities include Octoberfest, Fasching Carnival, Mayfest, hot air balloon race, and canoe and kayak sprints. Tennis, golf, badminton, volleyball, horseshoes, plus safety, security and a good time for family fun.

---------------------------- PINE MOUNTAIN ----------------------------

Calloway Gardens
US Highway 27
Pine Mountain, GA 31822
404-663-2281 800-282-8181

Studio $$$, 1 Bedroom $$$$, 2 Bedrooms $$$$,
  3 Bedrooms $$$$
Dep. 1 Night •
200 condos, Villas, Key at Front desk

Location: Airport: Atlanta 1 hour; Downtown: 2 miles; Need car

General Facilities: Full serv., Conf. rm. cap. 1000, Daily maid, Kitchen, Linens, Restaurant on prem., Bar on prem., Baby-sitter, Child planned rec.: Summer day camp

Room Facilities: Pool, Sauna, Hot tub, Tennis, Trap & skeet range, Golf: Callaway Garden 4 courses, TV, Phone in rm., Crib-Hi-chair, Ind. AC Ctl., Ind. Heat Ctl.

Attractions: Calloway Gardens, Warm Springs, FDR Little White House, entertainment

Shops & Restaurants: Tennis, golf shops, country store on property; Hamilton House/continental

Award-winning resort with lakes, scenic trails, rare azaleas, and wildlife woodlands. John A. Sibley Horticultural Center and Cecil B. Day Butterfly Center. Elegantly furnished villas with stone fireplaces and private patios. A wealth of recreational opportunities and five restaurants to choose from. Evening live entertainment, music and dancing. Fishing and sailing on Mountain Creek Lake, 4 golf courses, 17 tennis courts and 3 pools.

--------------------------------- SEA ISLAND ---------------------------------

The Cloister   Location: Beach front
Sea Island, GA 31561
912-638-3611 800-732-4752

General Facilities: Conf. rm. cap. 450, Kitchen, Restaurant on prem., Bar on prem.,
   Game room, Lounge, Baby-sitter

Room Facilities: Pool, Tennis, Croquet, trap-skeet, Golf: 54-holes

Attractions: Historic retreat plantation, artists' colony, horseback riding, boating

Shops & Restaurants: Area shops; Restaurants on property

A massive fireplace and grand piano set in a romantic Spanish-style lounge with chandeliered high ceiling and stained glass windows greets your arrival at this island resort. Azaleas, a quaint covered bridge and lagoons guard the fairways of The Cloister's 54 holes of legendary golf. Listen to the Sea Island singers Friday at plantation supper.

----------------------------- ST. SIMONS ISLAND -----------------------------

River Watch Inn   Studio $$, 1 Bedroom $$$, 2 Bedrooms $$$$
1 Marina Drive   AmEx/Visa/MC
St. Simons Island, GA 31522   33 condos, Lo-rise, Key at Froont office
912-638-4092   H-yes

Location: Airport: 15-20 minutes; Downtown: 2 miles; Need car

General Facilities: Kitchen, Linens, Restaurant on prem., Bar on prem.

Room Facilities: Pool, Marina, Golf: Close by, TV, Cable, Phone in rm., Crib-Hi-chair,
   Ind. AC Ctl., Ind. Heat Ctl.

Attractions: Fort Frederica, Christ Church, Lighthouse, Okefenokee Swamp, Sapelo
   Island tours, entertainment

Shops & Restaurants: 25 gift and specialty shops, Marina Village; Emmeline & Hessie/seafood-steaks

View St. Simons Sound, the Marshes of Glynn, and inland waterways from the rooftop swimming pool. 25 gift and specialty shops and 3 great restaurants. Full service marina-charter fishing, sailing cruises and lessons, tour boats. Sandy beach, horses, biking.

Sea Palm Resort Golf Club   1 Bedroom $$$, 2 Bedrooms $$$$, Villas
5445 Frederica Rd.   Pool, Kitchen
St. Simons Island, GA 31522
912-638-3351 800-841-6268

Attractions: Pier, lighthouse, Museum of Coastal History, Bloody Marsh, Christ Church,
   tours, Health Club, jogging, Tennis, Golf

Choose a golf course villa set among the oaks or condominium with marsh view, both elegantly decorated. Located in the center of St. Simons Island with its many specialty shops and fine restaurants. 27 holes of chammpionship golf, 12 tennis courts, 2 pools.

------------------------------- TYBEE ISLAND -------------------------------

Trbrisa Beach Resort   Villas
1 15th St., P.O. Box 26   Pool, Kitchen, Linens
Tybee Island, GA 31328   Sun, sailing, fishing, beach, tennis
912-786-4080

Relax in the master suite jacuzzi, have a romantic dinner on your balcony, enjoy the holiday pleasures of the beach or pool. Two-bedroom, two-bath fully equipped villas, with bicycles on the property for touring Tybee Island.

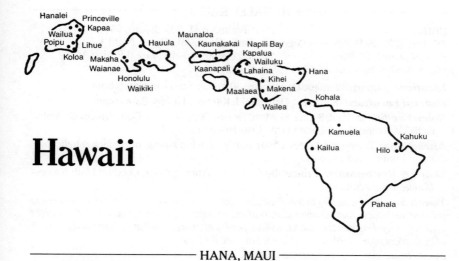

Hawaii

————————— HANA, MAUI —————————

Hana Kai Maui Resort
P.O. Box 38
Hana, Maui, HI 96713
808-248-8426 800-346-2772

Studio $$, 1 Bedroom $$
AmEx/Visa/MC, Dep. 100% •
13 condos, Lo-rise, Key at Office

Location: Airport: 2 hours 10 min.; Downtown: 2 blocks; Need car; Beach front

General Facilities: Daily maid, Kitchen, Linens, Baby-sitter

Room Facilities: Crib-Hi-chair

Attractions: Hiking, swimming, snorkeling, horseback, Seven Sacred Pools, Hana Ranch

Shops & Restaurants: Hasegawa General Store, grocery store; 1 restaurant

Tucked away in a sheltered cove amidst lush foliage leading to the blue Pacific. Spend lazy days at the beach or explore waterfalls, caves, unspoiled picnic areas, cliff enclosed red sand beaches, or swim in the Seven Sacred Pools, once the bathing spot of kings and queens. A unique, lovely and very special part of the Islands.

————————— HANALEI, KAUAI —————————

Albert Road House
P.O. Box 1109
Hanalei, Kauai, HI 96714
808-826-9833

Alii Kai I
P.O. Box 1109
Hanalei, Kauai, HI 96714
808-826-9833 800-367-8047

———————————— HANALEI, KAUAI ————————————

Cliffs
P.O. Box 1005, 3811 Edwards Road
Hanalei, Kauai, HI 96714
808-826-6219 800-367-6046

1 Bedroom $$, 2 Bedrooms $$$
AmEx/Visa/MC, Dep. 1 Night •
100 condos, Lo-rise, Key at Registr. lobby
H-yes

Location: Airport: 30 miles; Downtown: 30 miles; Need car; Beach front

General Facilities: Full serv., Daily maid, Kitchen, Linens, Baby-sitter

Room Facilities: Pool, Sauna, Hot tub, Tennis, Putting green, Golf: Princeville Makai Golf; TV, Cable, VCR, Phone in rm., Crib-Hi-chair

Attractions: Zodiac coast rides, whale watching, windsurfing, horseback & helicopter rides, hiking, entertainment

Shops & Restaurants: Princeville & Kukui Shopping Cntrs, Coconut Mall; Nobles-Mirage-Princeville

There is a unique tranquility in these spacious villas with luscious surroundings. Ten minute drive to the beach, four tennis courts, barbecue facilities, putting green and Friday night cocktail party. Private recreation pavilion, pool and jacuzzis. All units furnished in rattan with tropical printed fabrics and lanai furniture for four.

Hale Moi Resort
P.O. Box 1185
Hanalei, Kauai, HI 96714
808-826-9602 800-367-7042

Studio $$, 1 Bedroom $$
1 Bedrm/week 5$
Min. Stay 2 Nights, AmEx/Visa/MC,
   Dep. 1 Night •
40 condos, Lo-rise, Key at Front office

Location: Airport: Princeville-3 miles; Downtown: 30 min.; Need car

General Facilities: Kitchen, Linens, Baby-sitter

Room Facilities: Golf: Princeville's Oceans; TV, Phone in rm., Crib-Hi-chair

Attractions: Hanalei Town, water sports, Princeville Racquet and Health Club

Shops & Restaurants: Princeville Center; Beamreach-casual fine dining

Tropical, Hawaiian, modern furnishings with natural tones and mountain and waterfall views, and an abundance of outdoor activities.

Hanalei Bay Resort
P.O. Box 220
Hanalei, Kauai, HI 96714
808-826-6522 800-367-7040

Studio $$, 1 Bedroom $$$, 2 Bedrooms $$$$
Min. Stay 2 Nights, AmEx/Visa/MC,
   Dep. 1 Night •
200 condos, Key at Front desk

Location: Airport: 32 miles; Downtown: 1 mile; Need car

General Facilities: Full serv., Restaurant on prem., Bar on prem., Game room, Lounge, Baby-sitter

Room Facilities: Pool, Sauna, Hot tub, Tennis, Golf: Princeville; TV, Cable, Crib-Hi-chair

Attractions: Hanalei Bay, Kaulaulau Valley

Shops & Restaurants: Princeville shopping center; Nobel's

Tropical furnishings in these l, 2 and 3 bedroom units. Babysitting, ice machines, safety deposit boxes, wake-up calls, tennis pro shop, recreation room, bar on property, and nearby shopping center, bank and restaurants.

——————————— HANALEI, KAUAI ———————————

Hanalei Colony Resort
P.O. Box 206
Hanalei, Kauai, HI 96714
808-826-6235 800-367-8047

2 Bedrooms $$
2 Bedrms/week 5$
Min. Stay 3 Nights, AmEx/Visa/MC,
  Dep. Req'd. •
49 condos, Lo-rise, Key at At office

Location: Airport: 6 mi. Princeville; Need car; Beach front

General Facilities: Daily maid, Kitchen, Linens, Restaurant on prem., Bar on prem., Baby-sitter

Room Facilities: Pool, Hot tub, Golf: Golf 6 mi. S. Princeville; Crib-Hi-chair

Attractions: Napali Coast, boat & helicopter rides, whale watching, snorkling, Tropical Gardens, surf

Shops & Restaurants: Mall 35 miles, small unique shops from Haena south; Dolphin, Lanai, Shell, Tahiti

Secluded two-bedroom condos on beachfront property, located two miles from the beautiful Napali coastline. Swimming, snorkeling, fishing and hiking. Golf is 6 miles away. Fine restaurants and shops. For honeymooners and families.

Pali Ke Kua at Princeville
P.O. Box 899
Hanalei, Kauai, HI 96714
808-826-9066 800-367-7042

1 Bedroom $$, 2 Bedrooms $$
1 Bedrm/week 4$, 2 Bed/week 6$
Min. Stay 2 Nights, AmEx/Visa/MC,
  Dep. 1 Night •
98 condos, Lo-rise, Key at Central office

Location: Airport: Princeville-3 miles; Downtown: 30 min.; Need car

General Facilities: Kitchen, Linens, Restaurant on prem., Baby-sitter

Room Facilities: Pool, Hot tub, Putting green, Golf: Princeville's Oceans; TV, Phone in rm., Crib-Hi-chair

Attractions: Hanalei Town, water sports, Princeville Racquet Club and Health Club

Shops & Restaurants: Princeville Center; Beamreach-casual fine dining

For the best golf in Hawaii, come to Pali Ke Kua with its tropical Hawaiian furnishings. Seaside picnic pavilion and private beach cove with breathtaking views.

Paliuli Cottages
P.O. Box 351
Hanalei, Kauai, HI 96714
808-826-6264

Lo-rise
Pool

Attractions: Golf

Unusual cottages on a knoll adjacent to Princeville's golf course and surrounded by mountain and ocean scenery. Split-level two-bedroom, two-bath units with a foyer looking over a bannister into the beamed-ceiling sunken living room.

Waikiki Sunset

HANALEI, KAUAI

Pu'U Po'A
P.O. Box 1185, Ka Haku Road
Hanalei, Kauai, HI 96714
808-826-9602 800-367-7042

2 Bedrooms $$$
2 Bedrms/week 6$
Min. Stay 2 Nights, AmEx/Visa/MC,
   Dep. 1 Night •
56 condos, Hi-rise, Key at Central office

Location: Airport: Princeville-3 miles; Downtown: 30 min.; Need car

General Facilities: Kitchen, Linens, Baby-sitter

Room Facilities: Pool, Hot tub, Tennis, Putting green, Golf: Princeville's Oceans; TV, Phone in rm., Crib-Hi-chair

Attractions: Hanalei Town, golf, tennis, water sports, Princeville Racquet and Health Club

Shops & Restaurants: Princeville Center; Beamreach-casual fine dining

Two-bedroom condominiums, tropically furnished, set high on the cliffs of Princeville. Secluded, white sand beach, spectacular sunsets, next to world-famous Princeville's Oceans Golf Course.

Puamana
P.O. Box 1109
Hanalei, Kauai, HI 96714
808-826-9833 800-367-8047

─────────────────── HAUULA ───────────────────

Pat's at Punaluu Condo
53-567 Kamehameha Highway
Hauula, HI 96717
808-293-8111

Studio $, 1 Bedroom $$, 3 Bedrooms $$
Visa/MC,Dep. 1 Night
40 condos, Hi-rise, Key at Front desk
H-yes

Location: Airport: 45 minutes; Downtown: 32 miles; Need car; Beach front

General Facilities: Bus. fac., Conf. rm. cap. 20, Kitchen, Linens, Restaurant on prem., Bar on prem., Lounge

Room Facilities: Pool, Sauna, TV, Crib-Hi-chair

Attractions: Polynesian Cultural Center, Pipe Line surfing area

Shops & Restaurants: 2 small shopping centers, IGA, Pay-N-Save; Turtle Bay Hilton/continental

On the windward north shore side of Oahu-beautiful beach with tropical country living. Nearby golf, tennis, Waikiki nightlife, Diamond Head, Punalulu Beach. Complimentary happy hour hors d'oeuvres, restaurant, convenience store, clothing and gift shops. All units are self-contained with ocean view and sandy beach frontage with sheltered reef.

─────────────────── HILO ───────────────────

Waiakea Villas
400 Hualani Street
Hilo, HI 96720
808-961-2841 800-367-7042

1 Bedroom $
1 Bedrm/week $$$$
AmEx/Visa/MC, Dep. 1 Night •
155 condos, Lo-rise, Key at Front desk, H-yes

Location: Airport: Hilo Airport—1 mile; Downtown: 5 min.; Need car

General Facilities: Full serv., Daily maid, Kitchen, Linens, Restaurant on prem., Bar on prem.

Room Facilities: Pool, Tennis, TV, Crib-Hi-chair, Ind. AC Ctl., Ind. Heat Ctl.

Attractions: Volcano National Park, Wailoa State Park, Liliuokalani Gardens & Rainbow, Akaka Falls, entertainment

Shops & Restaurants: Prince Kuhio Plaza; Harrington's-seafood

Admidst l4 acres of exotic plants, trees, flowers, rolling lawns and beautiful waterways. Borders Wailoa pond freshwater reserve, black sand beaches, and snow-capped mountains. Tropical, wicker and rattan furnishings in earth tones. Live entertainment in the lounge.

─────────────────── HONOLULU, OAHU ───────────────────

Waikiki Beach Tower
2470 Kalakaua Avenue
Honolulu, Oahu, HI 96815
808-926-6400 800-922-7866

1 Bedroom $$$$, 2 Bedrooms $$$$
AmEx/Visa/MC, Dep. 2 Nights •
98 condos, Hi-rise, Key at Front desk

Location: Airport: 25 minutes; Downtown: 5 min.; Beach front

General Facilities: Full serv., Conf. rm., Daily maid, Kitchen, Linens, Baby-sitter

Room Facilities: Pool, Sauna, Hot tub, Tennis, Golf: Ala Wai; TV, Cable, Phone in rm., Crib-Hi-chair, Ind. AC Ctl.

Attractions: Bishop Museum, International Marketplace, Waikiki, Diamond Head, Polynesian Cultural Center

Shops & Restaurants: Ala Moana Center, International Marketplace

A special experience for discerning guests in Waikiki's best neighborhood. Richly furnished 1 and 2 bedroom/2 bath condominiums with unsurpassed views and private lanais overlooking Waikiki Beach. Only four suites per floor.

─────────────── HONOLULU ───────────────

Colony Surf Hotel
2895 Kalakaua Ave.
Honolulu, HI 96815
808-923-5751 800-367-8047

Hi-rise
Daily maid, Kitch

On the beautiful sandy beach at Diamond Head, minutes from the heart of Waikiki, separated by parks and beaches. Suites overlook the ocean. Complimentary newspaper, travel agency, beauty salon.

Diamond Head Beach Hotel
2947 Kalakaua Ave.
Honolulu, HI 96815
808-922-1928 800-367-6046

Hi-rise
Daily maid, Kitchen, Line

On Diamond Head Beach, a few steps away from the Outrigger Canoe Club. Studios and one bedrooms, full kitchen, lanais, in European style hotel. The oceanside Veranda hosts coffee and rolls every morning. Opposite Kapiolani Park and 10 minute walk to Waikiki.

Fairway Villa
2345 Ala Wai Bvld.
Honolulu, HI 96815
808-923-1364

Pool, Kitchen, Linens

Private condominiums with full kitchens, washer/dryers and private lanais. Sun deck and pool on the roof with views of Diamond Head, ocean and Ala Wai Golf Course.

Imperial Hawaii Resort
205 Lewers Street
Honolulu, HI 96815
808-923-1827 800-367-8047

1 Bedroom $$, 2 Bedrooms $$$$, Hi-rise
Pool, Daily maid, Kitchen, Linens, Phone in rm.

Attractions: Golf, tennis, zoo, aquarium, nightlife, Waikiki attractions

Located a half-block from Waikiki Beach and convenient to shopping, entertainment and recreation. Spacious, family units in a security-controlled facility. Enjoy the view from the rooftop pool, sun deck and saunas. 24-hour coffee shop.

Island Colony
445 Seaside Ave.
Honolulu, HI 96815
808-923-2345 800-922-7866

Studio $$, 1 Bedroom $$
AmEx/Visa/MC, Dep. 2 Nights •
434 condos, Hi-rise, Key at Front desk

Location: Airport: 25 minutes; Downtown: 10 min.

General Facilities: Full serv., Daily maid, Kitchen, Linens, Restaurant on prem., Bar on prem., Lounge, Baby-sitter

Room Facilities: Pool, Sauna, Golf: Ala Wai; TV, Cable, Crib-Hi-chair, Ind. AC Ctl.

Attractions: Bishop Museum, Diamond Head, Waikiki, Kapiolani Park, Waikiki Concert Shell, Zoo, Aquarium

Shops & Restaurants: Ala Moana Center, International Marketplace

Spacious rooms, tropically decorated, with wet bars, under-the-counter refrigerators, and complete kitchens. Just three short blocks from Waikiki Beach where you can tan, surf and swim, or take advantage of the many fine shops and restaurants in the area.

─────────────── HONOLULU ───────────────

Kaimana Villa   1 Bedroom $$
2550 Kuhio Ave.
Honolulu, HI 96815
808-923-3833 800-367-2373

Located in the garden spot of Waikiki within easy walking distance to shopping, restaurants, night spots, Waikiki Beach, Kapiolani Park, Waikiki Shell and Honolulu Zoo. Private lanais, in-room safes, sun deck and jacuzzi.

Maile Court   Studio $, 1 Bedroom $$
2058 Kuhio Ave.   AmEx/Visa/MC, Dep. 1 Night
Honolulu, HI 96815   508 condos, Hi-rise
800-947-2828 800-367-6046

Location: Beach front

General Facilities: Daily maid, Kitchen, Linens

Room Facilities: Pool, Crib-Hi-chair

Attractions: Waikiki beach and shopping

Shops & Restaurants: International Marketplace, Waikiki Shopping Plaza

Beautifully appointed accommodations with mountain, ocean or city views. Swimming pool, jacuzzi, sun deck. Nearby golf and tennis. Walk to shops, restaurants and nightclubs.

Nahua—444   1 Bedroom $$
444 Nahua St.
Honolulu, HI 96815
312-771-3999

Simply furnished units with rooftop swimming pool, sauna, showers, recreation area and barbecues. Conveniently located amidst the scenic and active life of Waikiki.

Pacific Monarch   Studio $$, 1 Bedroom $$
142 Uluniu Ave.   1 Bedrm/week 5$
Honolulu, HI 96815   AmEx/Visa/MC, Dep. 1 Night •
808-923-9805 800-367-6046   140 condos, Hi-rise, Key at Front desk

Location: Airport: 7 miles; Downtown: 5 miles

General Facilities: Full serv., Daily maid, Kitchen, Linens, Bar on prem., Lounge, Baby-sitter

Room Facilities: Pool, Sauna, Hot tub, 2 blocks to beach, TV, Phone in rm., Crib-Hi-chair, Ind. AC Ctl.

Attractions: Zoo, beach, tennis, golf

Shops & Restaurants: Ala Moana, King's Village, International Mkt Place; Hy's/steak, Hyatt/variety

One bedroom units two blocks from Waikiki Beach. Recreation area, pool, sun deck, jacuzzi and sauna. Walk to restaurants and shopping.

───────────── HONOLULU ─────────────

Royal Kuhio
2240 Kuhio Ave.
Honolulu, HI 96815
808-923-2502 800-367-5205

1 Bedroom $$
Dep. 3 Nights •
389 condos, Hi-rise, Key at Front office
H-yes

Location: Airport: 10 miles; Downtown: 1 block

General Facilities: Kitchen, Linens, Game room, Child planned rec.: Swings, jungle gym

Room Facilities: Pool, Sauna, Shuffleboard, putting green, TV, Cable, Crib-Hi-chair, Ind. AC Ctl.

Attractions: Waikiki, Paradise Park, Sea Life Park, Polynesian Cultural Center, beaches

Shops & Restaurants: Ala Moana Shopping Center, Waikiki shopping; Matteo's-Italian

Completely furnished one-bedroom apartments with twin beds and queen pullout sleeper sofa in the living room. Large swimming pool, paddle tennis, basketball court, putting green, sauna, shuffleboard, and Waikiki beach two blocks away.

Waikiki Banyan
201 Ohua Ave.
Honolulu, HI 96815
808-922-0555 800-367-8047

1 Bedroom $$
876 condos, Hi-rise, Key at Front desk

Location: Beach front

General Facilities: Full serv., Daily maid, Kitchen, Linens, Game room, Baby-sitter, Child planned rec.: Children's play area

Room Facilities: Pool, Sauna, Tennis, Golf: Ala Wai—nearby; TV, Crib-Hi-chair, Ind. AC Ctl.

Attractions: Honolulu Zoo, Kapiolani Park, Ala Wai Golf, shopping, entertainment

Each one-bedroom suite is beautifully furnished with accommodations for four. Spacious recreation deck with pool, tennis court, barbecue, children's play area, sauna, locker room, game room, snack bar and minimart. Full hotel services, valet, laundry, babysitting. One block from Waikiki Beach on a quiet street. Diamond Head views.

Waikiki Lanais
2452 Tusitala St.
Honolulu, HI 96815
808-923-0994 800-367-7042

1 Bedroom $$, 2 Bedrooms $$
1 Bedrm/week 4$, 2 Bed/week 5$
AmEx/Visa/MC, Dep. 1 Night •
160 condos, Hi-rise, Key at Front desk
H-yes

Location: Airport: 12 miles; Downtown: 5 miles; Need car

General Facilities: Kitchen, Linens, Baby-sitter

Room Facilities: Pool, Sauna, Hot tub, Exercise room, TV, Phone in rm., Crib-Hi-chair, Ind. AC Ctl., Ind. Heat Ctl.

Attractions: Zoo, Aquarium, Kapiolani Park, beach

Shops & Restaurants: Royal Hawaiian Shopping Plaza, Ala Moana Center; Hy's Steakhouse

In the heart of Waikiki, tucked away in a garden setting, not far off the beaten track, are the Waikiki Lanais with views of the mountains and ocean. There is a rooftop recreation area, swimming pool, mini-gym and Waikiki Beach, Diamond Head, and the Honolulu Zoo are right outside your door. Units feature tropical, Hawaiian decor so you know you are really in Hawaii.

HONOLULU

Waikiki Sunset
229 Paoakalani Ave.
Honolulu, HI 96815
808-922-0511 800-922-7866

1 Bedroom $$, 2 Bedrooms $$$$
AmEx/Visa/MC, Dep. 2 Nights •
310 condos, Hi-rise, Key at Front desk

Location: Airport: 25 minutes; Downtown: 10 min.

General Facilities: Full serv., Conf. rm., Daily maid, Kitchen, Linens, Restaurant on prem., Game room, Baby-sitter

Room Facilities: Pool, Sauna, Tennis, Shuffleboard, Golf: Ala Wai; TV, Cable, Phone in rm., Crib-Hi-chair, Ind. AC Ctl.

Attractions: Bishop Museum, Honolulu Zoo, Aquarium, Kapiolani Park, Diamond Head, Waikiki Shell

Shops & Restaurants: Ala Moana Center, International Marketplace

On the picturesque Diamond Head side of Waikiki, 2 blocks from Kapiolani Park, the Honolulu ZooSpacious 1 and 2 bedroom suites with private lanais and charming poolside cafe. Play unlimited free tennis, shuffleboard, swim, or relax in the sauna. Cook out on the barbecue grills, or dine on varied continental cuisine. A great view—a great location!

KAANAPALI, LAHAINA, MAU

International Colony Club
2750 Kalapu Drive
Kaanapali, Lahaina, Maui, HI 9676
808-661-4070 800-367-8047

1 Bedroom $$, 2 Bedrooms $$, 3 Bedrooms $$$
Min. Stay 4 Nights, Dep. Req'd. •
45 condos, Lo-rise, Key at Manager's office
H-yes

Location: Airport: 30 miles; Downtown: 3 miles; Need car

General Facilities: Kitchen, Linens

Room Facilities: Pool, Shuffleboard, Golf: Royal Kaanapali; TV, Cable, Phone in rm.

Attractions: All ocean activities, thrill craft, fishing, snorkeling, tours, luauas, tropical gardens

Shops & Restaurants: Whaler's Village, hotel shops; Bay Club/Bar & Grill/Veranda.

Hawaiian decor with use of rattan and wicker furniture in a private area, with fruit trees and beautiful landscaping. Each cottage is unique. Relaxed carefree living by the pools, but close to beaches, water sports, shops and dining.

Maui Eldorado Resort
2661 Kekaa Drive
Kaanapali, Lahaina, Maui, HI 96761
808-661-0021 800-542-6825

1 Bedroom $$$, 2 Bedrooms $$$$, Lo-rise
Pool, Daily maid, Kitchen, Linens

Attractions: Golf, tennis, beach recreation, Lawn Bowl, shuffleboard

In the midst of the Royal Kaanapali Golf Course, accented by colorful tropical flowers and palms. Sit on the lanai and be refreshed by the tropical tradewinds. Swim in the Pacific or one of three freshwater pools. Private beach cabana.

─────────────── KAANAPALI, MAUI ───────────────

Kaanapali Alii
50 Nohea Kai Dr.
Kaanapali, Maui, HI 96761
808-667-1400 800-642-6284

1 Bedroom $$$$, 2 Bedrooms $$$$
Min. Stay 3 Nights, AmEx/Visa/MC,
    Dep. 3 Nights •
264 condos, Hi-rise, Key at Front desk
H-yes

Location: Airport: West Maui—l5 min.; Downtown: 3 miles; Beach front

General Facilities: Full serv., Conf. rm. cap. 14, Daily maid, Kitchen, Linens, Baby-sitter, Child planned rec.: Hawaiian handicrafts

Room Facilities: Pool, Sauna, Hot tub, Tennis, Beach activities, Golf: Royal Kaanapali; TV, Phone in rm., Crib-Hi-chair, Ind. AC Ctl., Ind. Heat Ctl.

Attractions: Swimming, snorkeling, golfing, scuba diving, catamaran cruises, helicopter rides, horses

Shops & Restaurants: Whaler's Village, Old Lahaina Town, hotels; La Bretagne-French

Comfortable elegance reflecting the spirit of Hawaiian hospitality. Beachfront on Kaanapali Beach for swimming in the warm Pacific, freshwater pools, jacuzzi, saunas, and exercise room. Watch the whales spout or take a ride on the Sugar Cane Train. Fine restaurants and shopping within walking distance, full hotel services including Concierge and beach activities.

─────────────── KAHUKU ───────────────

Kuilima Estates
P.O. Box 899
Kahuku, HI 96731
808-293-2494 800-367-7040

Studio $, 1 Bedroom $$, 2 Bedrooms $$$
Min. Stay 2 Nights, AmEx/Visa/MC,
    Dep. 1 Night •
80 condos, Lo-rise, Key at Kahuku Sugar Mill

Location: Airport: 1½ hours; Downtown: 1 hour; Need car

General Facilities: Kitchen, Linens, Baby-sitter

Room Facilities: Sauna, Tennis, Golf: Kuilima at Turtle Bay; TV, Cable, Phone in rm., Crib-Hi-chair

Attractions: Polynesian Cultural Center, Kahuku Sugar Mill, surfing, water sports, polo, horses

Shops & Restaurants: Haleiwa Town; The Mill

A wind-surfing paradise near famous beaches, just an hour away from Waikiki. Situated on an 18-hole championship golf course with pools and tennis courts, these tropically furnished units are within walking and driving distance to shopping and dining. The perfect Hawaiian vacation on the "other side."

——————————— KAILUA, KONA ———————————

Keauhou Resort Condominiums   1 Bedroom $, 2 Bedrooms $$
78-7039 Kamehameha III Rd.   1 Bedrm/week $$$$, 2 Bed/week 5$
Kailua, Kona, HI 96740   Min. Stay 5 Nights, Dep. Req'd. •
808-322-9122 800-367-5286   48 condos, Lo-rise, Key at Front office
                                     H-yes

Location: Airport: 12 miles; Downtown: 6 miles; Need car

General Facilities: Kitchen, Linens

Room Facilities: Pool, Golf: Kona Country Club; TV, Cable, VCR, Phone in rm., Crib-Hi-chair

Attractions: Golf, island tours, charter fishing, snorkeling, diving, swimming

Shops & Restaurants: Keauhou shopping village

A cluster of one-and two-level townhouses, nestled in a 5-acre tropical garden. Most units have ocean views with one or two lanais flowering with bougainvillea. Drowse and laze by the pool, or delight in the brilliant treasure trove of marine life in the underwater world of the sparkling waters of the Kona Coast. Glass-bottom viewing boats, charter fishing and dinner sails. Golf at your doorstep.

———————————————————————————————————

Kona Alii   1 Bedroom $$
75-5782 Kuakini Highway   1 Bedrm/week $$$$
Kailua, Kona, HI 96740   Min. Stay 3 Nights, Dep. Req'd. •
808-329-2000 800-553-5035   70 condos, Hi-rise, Key at Office on site
                                     H-yes

Location: Airport: 7 miles; Downtown: 1 block; Beach front

General Facilities: Kitchen, Linens

Room Facilities: Pool, Golf: Kona Golf Course—close; TV, Cable

Attractions: Snorkeling, swimming, sightseeing, volcano, fishing, parasailing

Shops & Restaurants: Tourist shops; Various cuisines

Kona Alii overlooks the Kona coast and is located on Kailua Bay's rugged lava rim. Each one bedroom suite has two baths and sleeps up to six. Large pool and barbecues on the grounds, and tennis courts next door. Walk to Kailua Village with its many fine shops and restaurants. Kona, the largest and youngest island, is famous for black sand beaches, rain forests, volcanoes, and a year-round temperature of 72.

———————————————————————————————————

Kona Bali Kai   155 condos
76-6246 Alii Dr.
Kailua, Kona, HI 96740
800-272-3282 800-243-2992

An intimate resort situated between quaint Kailua-Kona and the Keauhou resort area. Oceanfront suites with sweeping views of Kona Coast on meticulously landscaped grounds surrounding a freshwater swimming pool, jet spa, and sandy sunning area. Kailua-Kona is the capital of deep-sea fishing and the site of the Ironman Triathlon. Arrangements can be made for daily excursions to all the historical sites of the Big Island, or just lie back and relax at Kona by the Sea.

--------------------------- KAILUA, KONA ---------------------------

Kona Billfisher
Alii Drive
Kailua, Kona, HI 96740
808-329-9393 800-553-5035

1 Bedroom $$, 2 Bedrooms $$
1 Bedrm/week $$$$, 2 Bed/week 4$
Min. Stay 3 Nights, Dep. Req'd. •
65 condos, Lo-rise, Key at On site office
H-yes

Location: Airport: 7 miles; Downtown: 1 block

General Facilities: Full serv., Kitchen, Linens, Game room

Room Facilities: Pool, Golf: Near Kona Golf Course; TV, Cable, Ind. AC Ctl., Ind. Heat Ctl.

Attractions: Activity desk, fishing, snorkeling, boating, volcano sightseeing

Shops & Restaurants: Tourist shops, Kailua Village; Various restaurants

Located on the largest of the Hawaiian Islands, the Kona Billfisher is a low-rise project of 65 tastefully appointed units. Deep-sea fishing for billfish and blue marlin. The Ironman Triathlon brings athletes from all over. Active volcano, lush forests and lava deserts bring a variety of sights and activities. Black lava rock coast against the clear blue waters.

Kona By The Sea
75-6106 Alii Drive
Kailua, Kona, HI 96740
808-329-0200 800-922-7866

1 Bedroom $$$, 2 Bedrooms $$$
AmEx/Visa/MC, Dep. 2 Nights •
80 condos, Hi-rise, Key at Front desk

Location: Airport: 10 minutes; Downtown: 10 Min.; Need car; Beach front

General Facilities: Full serv., Daily maid, Kitchen, Linens, Restaurant on prem., Baby-sitter

Room Facilities: Pool, Hot tub, Golf: Nearby; TV, Cable, Phone in rm., Crib-Hi-chair, Ind. AC Ctl.

Attractions: The location is just south of historic Kailua-Kona, circle island trips, volcano visiting.

Spacious privacy with designer furnishings. Every room is an oceanfront suite with views of the Kona Coast.

Kona Reef Condominiums
75-5888 Alii Dr.
Kailua, Kona, HI 96740
808-329-4780 800-367-7040

1 Bedroom $$, 2 Bedrooms $$$
Min. Stay 2 Nights, AmEx/Visa/MC,
Dep. 1 Night •
72 condos, Lo-rise, Key at Front desk

Location: Airport: 10 miles; Downtown: 1 mile; Need car; Beach front

General Facilities: Full serv., Daily maid, Kitchen, Linens, Lounge, Baby-sitter

Room Facilities: Pool, Sauna, TV, Cable, Crib-Hi-chair, Ind. AC Ctl.

Attractions: Volcano, Parker Ranch, Fishing

Shops & Restaurants: Kailua Village; Restaurants featuring fish

Distinctive architecture and meticulously groomed grounds highlight this elegantly furnished resort. Free-form oceanfront pool, spa and pavilion for your day or night relaxing. A short walk takes you to historical sites, shopping, dining, nightlife and the many active pursuits on the big island of Hawaii.

Royal Sea Cliff

KAILUA, KONA

Kona White Sands
Box 594
Kailua, Kona, HI 96745
808-329-9393 800-553-5035

Studio $, 1 Bedroom $
1 Bedrm/week $$$$
Min. Stay 3 Nights, Dep. Req'd. •
10 condos, Lo-rise, Key at on-site office
H-yes

Location: Airport: 9 miles; Downtown: 5 miles; Need car; Beach front
General Facilities: Kitchen, Linens
Room Facilities: TV, Cable
Attractions: Boat and fishing trips, volcano sightseeing, many nearby golf courses
Shops & Restaurants: Tourist shops

Located four miles from Kailua Village, twelve miles from Kona Airport, the ten fully equipped kitchenette suites in a two-story building have private lanais overlooking white sands beach. Golf, tennis, swimming, body-surfing, snorkeling, scuba-diving and fishing are close by. Relax while viewing palms, surf, sparkling blue seas and memorable sunsets.

KAILUA, KONA

Royal Sea Cliff Resort
75-6040 Alii Dr.
Kailua, Kona, HI 96740
808-329-8021 800-922-7866

Studio $$, 1 Bedroom $$$, 2 Bedrooms $$$
Dep. 2 Nights •
148 condos, Hi-rise, Key at Front desk

Location: Airport: 10 minutes; Downtown: 10 min.; Need car

General Facilities: Full serv., Daily maid, Kitchen, Linens, Baby-sitter

Room Facilities: Pool, Sauna, Hot tub, Tennis, TV, Cable, VCR, Phone in rm., Crib-Hi-chair, Ind. AC Ctl.

Attractions: Trips around the Island and to the volcano.

Handsome units furnished in Hawaiian style. Lovely grounds with fresh and salt water pools. Lanais with oceanfront or garden views.

Sea Village
75-6002 Alii Dr.
Kailua, Kona, HI 96740
808-329-1000 800-367-5205

1 Bedroom $, 2 Bedrooms $$
Min. Stay 3 Nights, AmEx/Visa/MC,
Dep. 3 Nights •
131 condos, Lo-rise, Key at Front desk
H-yes

Location: Airport: 10 miles; Downtown: 1 mile; Need car; Beach front

General Facilities: Kitchen, Linens

Room Facilities: Pool, Hot tub, Tennis, TV, Crib-Hi-chair

Attractions: Historic Mokuaikauna Church, Hulihee Palace, Captain Cook Monument, Painted Church

Shops & Restaurants: Kona Coast and Lanihau Shopping Center; Uncle Billy's/steak-seafood

One-and two-bedroom units with completely furnished kitchens with washer and dryer. Spacious patio area, view lanais, oceanside pool, therapeutic jacuzzi, picnic area with barbecues, tennis courts and all water sports. Hawaii's special place in the sun.

White Sands Village
74-6469 Alii Dr.
Kailua, Kona, HI 96740
808-329-6402

2 Bedrooms $$
2 Bedrms/week 4$
Min. Stay 3 Nights, AmEx/Visa/MC,
Dep. Req'd.
108 condos, Lo-rise, Key at Office on grounds
H-yes

Location: Airport: 20 miles; Downtown: 4 miles; Need car

General Facilities: Daily maid, Kitchen, Linens, Bar on prem., Game room, Lounge, Baby-sitter

Room Facilities: Sauna, Tennis, Golf: 3 miles; TV, Cable, Crib-Hi-chair, Ind. AC Ctl.

Attractions: Volcanoes National Park, para-sailing, snorkeling, big-game fishing

Shops & Restaurants: Keauhou Shopping Village, grocery, retail outlets; Dorian's By the Sea/steak-sea

Charm and friendliness away from big cities, sun-filled days, freedom from wind. Take the elevator down to the tennis courts and pool area. Game room with pool table and barbecue. Crescent, white sand beach. Comfortable, roomy family condominiums with air conditioning, modern decor and lanais open to garden or pool. Beach is directly across the street.

———————————— KAILUA, KONA ————————————

Hale Kai O Kona
Alii Drive
Kailua, Kona, HI 96740
714-497-4253 800-854-8843

Hale Kona Kai   Studio $$
75-5870 Kahakai Rd.   Min. Stay 3 Nights, Dep. Req'd.
Kailua, Kona, HI 96740   39 condos, Lo-rise, Key at Condominium office
808-329-2155   No S-yes

Location: Airport: 7 miles; Downtown: 1 mile; Need car; Beach front
General Facilities: Kitchen, Linens
Room Facilities: Pool, TV, Cable, Ind. AC Ctl.
Attractions: Whale watching and coast cruises, charter fishing boats, diving, snorkeling
    Hulihee Palace
Shops & Restaurants: 2 village shopping complexes, gift and small shops; Galley/fish,
    Hugo's/fish

A rare find at ocean's edge, each unit has a private lanai overlooking the sparkling poolside terrace and the gentle waves of Kailua Bay. Casual dress is appropriate is the mid-70's year-round temperatures. The beach is only ten minutes away from your home by the sea.

Kanaloa at Kona   1 Bedroom $$
78-261 Manukai St.
Kailua, Kona, HI 96740
808-322-2272 800-367-6046

Charming Hawaiian village architecture in these low-rise condominiums. Large lanais with wet bars and jacuzzis in oceanfront suites. 3 pools, 1 adults only, 2 tennis courts, recreation center, adjacent 18-hole golf. Abundant palm trees above the calm Pacific.

Kona Bay Hotel, Uncle Billy's
75-5739 Alii Drive
Kailua, Kona, HI 96740
808-329-1393 800-367-5102

Kona Islander Inn
P.O. Box 1239, 75-5776 Kuakini Hwy
Kailua, Kona, HI 96740
808-329-3181 800-367-5124

Kona Magic Sands   Lo-rise
77-6452 Alii Dr.
Kailua, Kona, HI 96740
808-329-9177

All units are oceanfront studios with full kitchens. Informal and relaxed vacationing, sunning by the pool while watching the playful dolphins. White sand beach next door.

KAILUA, KONA

Kona Mansions
Alii Dr.
Kailua, Kona, HI 96740
714-497-4253   800-854-8843

Pacific Island Bed & Breakfast
P.O. Box 391025
Kailua, Kona, HI 96740
808-325-1000

Alii Villas   1 Bedroom $, 2 Bedrooms $$, Lo-rise
75-6016 Alii Drive   Pool, Kitchen
Kailua, Kona, HI 96740
808-329-6488   800-367-5168

Attractions: Swimming, beach, surfing, snorkeling

Individually owned and decorated 1 and 2 bedroom units with private lanais above the ocean. Large swimming pool with spacious lounging area, barbecue recreational area with gas grills, dressing rooms and showers. Coco-palms, blossoms and lush foliage.

Casa De Emdeko   1 Bedroom $$, 2 Bedrooms $$, Lo-rise
75-6082 Alii Drive   Pool, Kitchen
Kailua, Kona, HI 96740
808-329-4155

Attractions: Deep-sea fishing, golf, beachcombing, surfing, snorkeling, tennis

Very modern oceanfront condominiums. Saltwater pool and freshwater pool, man-made beach areas and cabana for parties or large gatherings.

KAMUELA, HAWAII

Villas At Mauna Kea
P.O. Box 218
Kamuela, Hawaii, HI 96743
808-882-7222   800-228-3000

KAMUELA

Puako Beach Condominiums   1 Bedroom $$
3 Puako Beach Dr.
Kamuela, HI 96743
808-882-7711

A variety of vacation adventures await you on the Island of Hawaii. Visit an early Hawaiian fishing village, investigate an ancient temple, take a trip to Volcano National Park, Akaka Falls and Parker Ranch, explore Puako's petroglyphs.

─────────────────── KAMUELA ───────────────────

Waikoloa Villas
Box 3066 Waikoloa Village Station
Kamuela, HI 96743
808-883-9588 800-367-7042

1 Bedroom $$, 2 Bedrooms $$, 3 Bedrooms $$$
1 Bedrm/week 4$, 2 Bed/week 5$,
  3 Bed/week 6$
Min. Stay 2 Nights, AmEx/Visa/MC,
  Dep. 2 Nights •
40 condos, Lo-rise, Key at Administration
No S-yes/H-yes

Location: Airport: 30 miles; Downtown: 20 miles; Need car

General Facilities: Conf. rm. cap. 30, Kitchen, Linens

Room Facilities: Pool, Hot tub, On golf course, Golf: Waikoloa Golf Course; TV, Cable, Crib-Hi-chair

Attractions: Home of Parker Ranch, Volcano National Park, Snow on Mauna Kea often, two beaches-15 min.

Shops & Restaurants: Waimea-20 miles-nontourist shops, supermarket; Edelweiss-German

These condominiums are on 7 luxuriously landscaped acres fronting the Waikoloa Golf Course. Fully equipped units for all meals or just snacks; lanais feature wet bars and ocean or garden views. Outside are two pools, whirlpools, cabanas and gazebo area. Golf, riding stables and two beaches are nearby, while tennis is just across the street.

─────────────────── KAPAA, KAUAI ───────────────────

Pono Kai
1250 Kuhio Hwy.
Kapaa, Kauai, HI 96746
808-822-9831 800-922-7866

1 Bedroom $$, 2 Bedrooms $$$
AmEx/Visa/MC, Dep. 2 Nights •
66 condos, Lo-rise, Key at Front desk
H-yes

Location: Airport: 30 minutes; Need car; Beach front

General Facilities: Full serv., Daily maid, Kitchen, Linens, Baby-sitter

Room Facilities: Pool, Sauna, Hot tub, Tennis, Snorkel, volleyball, Golf: Wailua Golf Course-near; TV, Cable, Phone in rm., Crib-Hi-chair, Ind. Heat Ctl.

Attractions: Quaint Kapaa village, Coconut Plantation Marketplace, Wailua Golf Course

Shops & Restaurants: Coconut Plantation Marketplace

Fronting a mile-long white sand beach, near quaint Kapaa village, Pono Kai has charming one-and two-bedroom condominiums in contemporary Polynesian motifs. View the tropical gardens or ocean from the deck. Shuffleboard, volleyball and putting green on the grounds. Fine dining and shopping at Coconut Plantation . . . easy access to championship Wailua Golf Course.

KAPAA, KAUAI

Kapaa Sands
P.O. Box 3292, 380 Papaloa Road
Kapaa, Kauai, HI 96746
808-822-4901 800-222-4901

Studio $$, 2 Bedrooms $$
Min. Stay 3 Nights, Dep. Req'd. •
24 condos, Lo-rise, Key at Dining room table

Location: Airport: 7 miles; Downtown: 5 miles; Beach front

General Facilities: Daily maid, Kitchen, Linens, Baby-sitter

Room Facilities: Pool, TV, Cable

Attractions: Opaeka's Falls, hike up the Sleeping Giant, ski on the Wailua River

Shops & Restaurants: Plantation Marketplace includes shops/restaurants

A secluded private paradise tucked away on the famed Coconut Coast. Walk to the sea from your oceanfront unit. A low-key vacation hideaway within walking distance to shopping and restaurants. Centrally located between road ends of the island's only highway-70 miles along the coast, ending at the rugged Na Pali mountain range.

Lanikai
390 Papaloa Road
Kapaa, Kauai, HI 96746
808-822-7456 800-367-6046

Pool, Daily maid, Kitchen, Phone in rm.

Superbly furnished two-bedroom, oceanfront condominiums on the ocean's edge between Coco Palms Resort and The Marketplace. Beach, pool, barbecue. Wailua State Park Beach for surfing.

Plantation Hale
484 Kujia Hwy.
Kapaa, Kauai, HI 96746
808-822-4941 800-367-6046

1 Bedroom $$
AmEx/Visa/MC, Dep. 1 Night
160 condos, Lo-rise

Location: Airport: Lihue-7 miles; Need car; Beach front

General Facilities: Daily maid, Kitchen, Linens

Room Facilities: Pool, Shuffleboard, Put. green, Golf: Nearby; TV, Phone in rm., Crib-Hi-chair, Ind. AC Ctl.

Attractions: Fern Grotto, Opaekaa Falls, Waimea Canyon

Shops & Restaurants: Plantation Marketplace, Foodland Supermarket

Located in the Coconut Plantation 50 feet from the island's second largest shopping center. Surfing, swimming, pools. Family-sized units with ample closet space.

Lae Nani
410 Papaloa Rd.
Kapaa, Kauau, HI 96746
808-822-4938 800-367-6046

1 Bedroom $$$

One-and two-bedroom richly decorated condominiums in a setting of natural beauty. Tennis, pool, beach. Next door to shopping, restaurants and entertainment at The Market Place.

KAPALUA, MAUI

Kapalua Bay Hotel & Villas
One Bay Dr.
Kapalua, Maui, HI 96761
800-367-8000 800-669-5656

1 Bedroom $$$$
Dep. 1 Night
Villas

Location: Beach front

General Facilities: Full serv., Daily maid, Kitchen, Linens, Restaurant on prem., Bar on prem., Lounge, Baby-sitter

Room Facilities: Pool, Tennis, Aerobics, volleyball, Golf: 2 18-hole courses; TV, Phone in rm.

Shops & Restaurants: 5 on-site-Village course cafe

Villas grouped in clusters, each complex with its own pool, barbecue and sink facilities. Impeccable, personal service. Water activities, tours of the grounds, sailing, scuba and windsurfing lessons. Scheduled events throughout the year, plus daily children's programs and Hawaiian classes. Ideal place for a honeymoon to remember.

KAUNAKAKAI, MOLOKAI

Molokai Shores
Star Route, Box 1037 Kamehameha H
Kaunakakai, Molokai, HI 96748
808-553-5954

1 Bedroom $$, 2 Bedrooms $$
1 Bedrm/week 4$, 2 Bed/week 5$
AmEx/Visa/MC, Dep. 1 Night •
102 condos, Lo-rise, Key at Front desk

Location: Airport: 7 miles; Downtown: ¼ mile; Need car; Beach front

General Facilities: Kitchen, Linens

Room Facilities: Pool, Putting green, TV, Crib-Hi-chair

Attractions: Kalaupapa Mule Ride, Molokai Ranch wildlife safari, horseback riding, water sports

Shops & Restaurants: Kaunakakai Town; Hotel Molokai/casual.

Quiet and peaceful condominiums, tucked away in a sheltered cove. Oriental furnishings in shades of blue and green. Long, white, sandy beach.

KIHEI, MAUI

Hale Pau Hana Resort
2480 S. Kihei Rd.
Kihei, Maui, HI 96753
808-879-2715 800-367-6036

1 Bedroom $$
Min. Stay 3 Nights, Dep. Req'd. •
82 condos, Hi-rise, Lo-rise, Key at Office on Premises
H-yes

Location: Airport: 14 miles; Downtown: 14 miles; Need car; Beach front

General Facilities: Daily maid, Kitchen, Linens

Room Facilities: Pool, Golf: Near 3 Golf courses; TV, Cable, Phone in rm., Ind. AC Ctl.

Attractions: Tour to Hana, Trip to Haleakala Crater, Snorkel trip to Molakini

Shops & Restaurants: Gift Shops, Bakery, General Store, Restaurants; Outrigger/seafood-prime rib

On one of Maui's finest beaches, all condominiums are on the beach with unobstructed ocean view. Excellent swimming and snorkeling. Tennis courts and golf courses nearby. Many shops and restaurants across the street. Coffee served every morning at 10:00 am. Papu party every Thurs. at 5:30 pm. Barbecues available for guest use.

———————————— KIHEI, MAUI ————————————

Kamaole Sands   1 Bedroom $$$
2695 S. Kihei Rd.
Kihei, Maui, HI 96753
808-879-0666 808-523-0411

In the center of shopping and dining, along a nine-mile chain of beaches, Polynesian elegance, roomy private lanais. Tennis and pool.

Kana'i A Nalu Condo   Lo-rise
Maalaea Bay   Pool, Kitchen
Kihei, Maui, HI 96753
808-244-7684 800-367-5234

Spacious, modern two-bedroom apartments. Fountain-fed pool with lounges surrounded by lawn and palms. Swim in the warm waters of Maalaea Bay.

Kealia Condominium   Studio $$, 1 Bedroom $$, 2 Bedrooms $$$
191 N. Kihei Rd.   Min. Stay 4 Nights, Dep. Req'd. •
Kihei, Maui, HI 96753   50 condos, Hi-rise, Key at Registr. office
808-879-0952 800-367-5222

Location: Airport: 10 miles; Downtown: 3 miles; Need car

General Facilities: Kitchen, Linens

Room Facilities: Pool, Golf: Silver Sword 2 miles; TV, Cable, Phone in rm., Ind. AC Ctl.

Attractions: Deep-sea fishing, whale watching, diving, snorkeling, golf, jogging, sightseeing

Shops & Restaurants: Various shops

Located on scenic Maalaea Bay, this central location is within easy reach of Maui's recreational facilities, businesses, sightseeing centers, shops and restaurants. Units feature cable color television, washers and dryers, lanais with ocean views, barbecues and picnic tables. Swim, sail, fish, jog on the beach, or just relax and enjoy the beauty of Maui.

Kona By The Sea

--- KIHEI, MAUI ---

Kihei Alii Kai
2387 S. Kihei Rd, P.O. Box 985
Kihei, Maui, HI 96753
808-879-6770   800-888-6284

1 Bedroom $$, 2 Bedrooms $$, 3 Bedrooms $$
Min. Stay 3 Nights, Visa/MC, Dep. Req'd. •
127 condos, Hi-rise, Key at Front office

Location: Airport: 20 minutes

General Facilities: Kitchen, Linens

Room Facilities: Pool, Sauna, Hot tub, Tennis, Golf: Silver Sword 1½ mile; TV, Cable, Phone in rm., Crib-Hi-chair

Attractions: Ocean activities, luaus, tours of island

Shops & Restaurants: Foodland, ABC store, Kihei town center; Kihei prime rib & seafood

300 feet to one of the largest beaches on Maui. Spacious units with ocean and mountain views from the balconies. Pool and jacuzzi surrounded by a flower-covered fence. Two tennis courts when you feel the need for more strenuous activity. Fine restaurants within walking distance, or barbecue your dinner at "home."

Kihei Bay Surf
715 S. Kihei Rd.
Kihei, Maui, HI 96753
714-497-4253   800-854-8843

KIHEI, MAUI

Kihei Beach Resort
36 S. Kihei Rd.
Kihei, Maui, HI 96753
808-879-2744 800-367-6034

1 Bedroom $$, 2 Bedrooms $$$
Min. Stay 3 Nights, Dep. 3 Nights •
53 condos, Hi-rise, Key at Office in lobby

Location: Airport: Kahului-15 minutes; Downtown: 2 miles; Need car; Beach front
General Facilities: Daily maid, Kitchen, Linens, Baby-sitter
Room Facilities: Pool, TV, Cable, Phone in rm., Crib-Hi-chair, Ind. AC Ctl.
Attractions: Haleakala Crater, IAO Needle, Hana, Lahaina
Shops & Restaurants: Lahaina, Kahului, Sears, Liberty House; Wailea Steak House/ fish-steak

Accommodations with all the essentials, including maid service to get you away from home housekeeping. Daily coffee in the lobby. Family oriented resort with an excellent climate, fine swimming beach for walking, shelling and snorkeling. Settle down on your lanai overlooking the pool and ocean with a good book. Area restaurants, 15 minutes to the Kahului airport, Maui's major seaport and a great place for shopping.

Kihei Kai
61 N. Kihei Rd.
Kihei, Maui, HI 96753
808-879-2357 800-367-8047

1 Bedroom $
Min. Stay Ask, Dep. Req'd. •
24 condos, Lo-rise, Key at Office

Location: Airport: 30 minutes; Downtown: 2 miles; Need car; Beach front
General Facilities: Kitchen, Linens
Room Facilities: Pool, TV, Cable, Phone in rm., Crib-Hi-chair, Ind. AC Ctl.
Attractions: Snorkeling, windsurfing, surfing, scuba diving, boogie boards, boat trips, sightseeing
Shops & Restaurants: Shopping center 20 minutes away; Seafood-steaks-Chinese

A small resort right on the beach on the leeward shore of the verdant "Valley Island." Ocean views from the private 16-foot lanais. From the beach to the 10,000-foot dormant crater of Haleakala-an hour and a half drive through the ever-changing landscape. Warm., clear days and cool nights. Peace and quiet for a relaxing vacation.

Kihei Sands
115 North Kihei Road
Kihei, Maui, HI 96753
808-879-2624 800-882-6284

1 Bedroom $$, 2 Bedrooms $$
Min. Stay 3 Nights, Dep. Req'd. •
30 condos, Lo-rise, Key at Manager
H-yes

Location: Airport: 20 minutes; Downtown: 3 miles; Need car; Beach front
General Facilities: Kitchen, Linens, Baby-sitter
Room Facilities: Pool, TV, Cable, Phone in rm., Crib-Hi-chair, Ind. AC Ctl.
Attractions: Lahaina, IAO Needle, Hana, Haleakala Crater, snorkeling, boogie boards, windsurfing, swim.
Shops & Restaurants: Rainbow Mall, Azeka's Market; Eriks Seafood-Kihei Prime Rib

Stay at Kihei Sands on the tranquil and beautiful island of Maui. Freshwater pool in a tropical Polynesian setting overlooks the beach and offshore islands of Kahoolawe and Molokini. Centrally located for sightseeing to Lahaina, Hana, Iao Valley, Haleakala, and the Seven Sacred Pools. Ten miles of golden sand beaches are a 2-minute walk.

─────────── KIHEI, MAUI ───────────

Kihei Surfside Resort
2936 South Kihei Road
Kihei, Maui, HI 96753
808-879-1488 800-367-5240

1 Bedroom $$, 2 Bedrooms $$$
Min. Stay 3 Nights, AmEx/Visa/MC,
  Dep. 3 Nights •
83 condos, Hi-rise, Key at Office-Unit 105
H-yes

Location: Airport: 16 miles; Downtown: 1 mile; Need car; Beach front

General Facilities: Daily maid, Kitchen, Linens, Baby-sitter

Room Facilities: Pool, Shuffleboard, Golf: Wailea; TV, Cable, Phone in rm., Crib-Hi-chair

Attractions: Ocean excursions, tours to Molokai, luaus, pineapple plantation tours, Haliakala, fishing

Shops & Restaurants: Wailea tourist shopping, Kihei shopping centers; Continental-Oriental-Hawaiian

Delightful accommodations with rattan furnishings, adjacent to an uncrowded swimming beach, for swimming, skin diving or beach-bumming. Explore the green grottoes and coral caves. . .delight in the tropical blossoms, volcanic mountains and waterfalls. Charter boats are available for blue marlin fishing, or cast from the shore. A great place for a family vacation.

Laulea Maui Beach Club
980 S. Kihei Rd.
Kihei, Maui, HI 96753
808-879-5247 800-367-7040

1 Bedroom $$, 2 Bedrooms $$, 3 Bedrooms $$$
Min. Stay 2 Nights, AmEx/Visa/MC,
  Dep. 1 Night •
60 condos, Lo-rise, Key at Front desk, H-yes

Location: Airport: 11 miles; Downtown: 1 mile; Need car; Beach front

General Facilities: Full serv., Daily maid, Lounge, Baby-sitter

Room Facilities: Pool, Sauna, Hot tub, Tennis, Golf: Wailea; TV, Cable, Phone in rm., Crib-Hi-chair

Attractions: Golf, beaches, sightseeing, Wailea, Haleakala, Kihei Village, sailing, entertainment

Shops & Restaurants: Azeka shopping center-banks, grocery, clothing; International House of Pancakes

Comfortable suites with color TV, microwave, ceiling fans, washer and dryers. Spacious living and dining areas. Lanais with ocean or garden views. Weekly pool party, scuba and windsurfing lessons. Pool, hot tub, sauna and tennis are on the property, with golf and the beaches close by.

Leinaala Condominiums
998 S. Kihei Rd.
Kihei, Maui, HI 96753
808-879-2235 800-367-8047

Studio $, 1 Bedroom $$, 2 Bedrooms $$
1 Bedrm/week 5$, 2 Bed/week 7$
Min. Stay 5 Nights, Dep. Req'd. •
25 condos, Hi-rise, H-yes

Location: Beach front

General Facilities: Kitchen, Linens

Room Facilities: Pool, Tennis, TV, Cable, Phone in rm., Ind. AC Ctl.

Off the beaten path, but only a 20 minute drive from Kahului Airport and a half mile from shopping. Palm trees and green lawns lead to the beach for ocean sports. Frequent barbecues and pupu parties. Views of West Maui mountains and Haleakala.

─────────────────── KIHEI, MAUI ───────────────────

Luana Kai
940 S. Kihei Rd.
Kihei, Maui, HI 96753
808-879-1268 800-367-7042

1 Bedroom $$, 2 Bedrooms $$, 3 Bedrooms $$$
1 Bedrm/week 4$, 2 Bed/week 5$
AmEx/Visa/MC, Dep. 1 Night •
114 condos, Lo-rise, Key at Front desk
H-yes

Location: Airport: 15 Min-Kahalui; Downtown: ½ mile; Need car; Beach front
General Facilities: Kitchen, Linens, Baby-sitter
Room Facilities: Pool, Sauna, Hot tub, Putting green, TV, Phone in rm., Crib-Hi-chair
Attractions: Water sports, IAO Valley, entertainment
Shops & Restaurants: Kihei town, Azekas Place, Dolphin Center; Stouffer's Raffles

Vacationer's paradise with tropical style furnishings amidst warm and friendly people. Barbecue area for cook-outs, morning coffee, orientation, aerobic classes, snorkeling lessons, hula lessons and a dive clinic. Garden and ocean views from your balconies.

Maalaea Surf Resort
12 South Kihei Road
Kihei, Maui, HI 96753
808-879-1267 800-423-7953

1 Bedroom $$$, 2 Bedrooms $$$$
Min. Stay 3 Nights, Dep. Req'd. •
59 condos, Lo-rise, Key at Office
H-yes

Location: Airport: 8 miles; Downtown: 2½ miles; Need car
General Facilities: Daily maid, Kitchen, Linens, Baby-sitter
Room Facilities: Pool, Tennis, TV, Cable, Phone in rm., Ind. AC Ctl.
Attractions: Snorkel and dinner cruises, luaus, windsurfing, golf within 2½ miles
Shops & Restaurants: Azeka shopping center, Kahului shopping centers; Azeka's Ribs-Pancake House

Truly luxurious accommodations in one-or two-story townhouses amid tall palms. South Seas furnishings. Two swimming pools, two tennis courts, and several shuffleboards. Golden sand beach and gorgeous sunsets. A very private resort on peaceful Maui.

Mana Kai-Maui
2960 S. Kihei Rd.
Kihei, Maui, HI 96753
808-879-1561 800-525-2025

Studio $$, 1 Bedroom $$$, 2 Bedrooms $$$
AmEx/Visa/MC, Dep. 1 Night •
124 condos, Hi-rise, Key at Front office
H-yes

Location: Airport: 11 miles; Downtown: 3 miles; Need car; Beach front
General Facilities: Full serv., Conf. rm. cap. 125, Daily maid, Kitchen, Linens, Restaurant on prem., Bar on prem., Lounge, Baby-sitter
Room Facilities: Pool, Center on property, Golf: Silver Sword/Wailea; TV, Cable, Phone in rm., Crib-Hi-chair
Attractions: Activity desk, snorkeling, scuba, luaus, boat cruises
Shops & Restaurants: Dolphin Mall, Azeka Shopping, Kihei Town center; Ocean Terrace/seafood

A lovely resort located on a secluded mile-long beach. The large swimming pool is under palm trees and tropical flowers, as is the open air Terrace Restaurant. Lounge, beauty shop, gift and apparel shop and general store are all on the property. Mana Kai includes a complimentary car with unlimited mileage with each unit. Your choice of lanai views, the beach and blue Pacific, or upcountry Maui and Haleakala Mountain.

──────────── KIHEI, MAUI ────────────

Maui Hill   1 Bedroom $$$, 2 Bedrooms $$$, 3 Bedrooms
2881 S. Kihei Rd. $$$
Kihei, Maui, HI 96753   AmEx/Visa/MC, Dep. 2 Nights •
808-879-6321 800-922-7866   49 condos, Lo-rise, Key at Front desk

Location: Airport: 15 minutes; Downtown: 15 min.; Need car

General Facilities: Full serv., Daily maid, Kitchen, Linens

Room Facilities: Pool, Hot tub, Tennis, TV, Cable, Phone in rm., Ind. AC Ctl.

Attractions: Close to Haleakala, near Lahaina and whale watching cruises

A quiet hideaway with panoramic ocean views. Close to Haleakala Crater and Maui's finest beaches. Weekly Mai Tai party. Spacious rooms with tropical appointments, and suite resort convenience. Tennis court, pool, jet spa, and cable TV.

Nani Kai Hale   Studio $, 1 Bedroom $$, 2 Bedrooms $$
73 N. Kihei Rd.   Min. Stay 3 Nights, Dep. Req'd. •
Kihei, Maui, HI 96753   46 condos, Hi-rise, Key at Office or Apt. 405
808-879-9120 800-367-6032   H-yes

Location: Airport: 9 miles; Downtown: 2 miles; Need car; Beach front

General Facilities: Kitchen, Linens, Baby-sitter

Room Facilities: Pool, TV, Crib-Hi-chair

Attractions: Dinner cruises, snorkeling cruises, windsurf rentals, entertainment

Shops & Restaurants: Shell, grocery, clothing stores; Waterfront/fish-prime rib-veal

Spacious condominiums in central Maui on an excellent, uncrowded coral-free beach. For snorkelers and skin divers there are coral reefs to explore outside the surf. Coffee and donuts on Saturday morning and potlucks let you meet your fellow vacationers. Enjoy the pool or use the gas barbecue on the grounds of this sunny resort area with the most moderate climate in the islands.

Royal Mauian   1 Bedroom $$, 2 Bedrooms $$, 3 Bedrooms $$$
2430 South Kihei Road   Min. Stay 5 Nights, Dep. Req'd. •
Kihei, Maui, HI 96753   107 condos, Hi-rise, Key at Front desk
808-879-1263 800-367-8009

Location: Airport: 12 miles; Downtown: 2 miles; Need car; Beach front

General Facilities: Kitchen, Linens, Baby-sitter

Room Facilities: Pool, Golf: Silver Sword 3 miles; TV, Cable, Phone in rm., Crib-Hi-chair

Attractions: Sun, beach, golf, tennis, Haleakala Crater, winter whale watching

Shops & Restaurants: Lahaina shops; Steak-seafood in Lahaina

Tastefully furnished units for island living. Large pool where complimentary coffee and tea are served each morning. Carpeted Roof Garden with refrigerated bar, and gas grills for daytime sunning or evening cocktails. Snorkel to lava reefs to watch exotic fish, swim, tan or stroll on the beach.

Sand & Surf Condominium Apts.
145 N. Kihei Rd.
Kihei, Maui, HI 96753
206-845-8560

──────────────── KIHEI, MAUI ────────────────

Shores of Maui
2075 S. Kihei Rd.
Kihei, Maui, HI 96753
808-879-9140 800-367-8002

1 Bedroom $, 2 Bedrooms $$
1 Bedrm/week $$$$, 2 Bed/week 4$
Min. Stay 3 Nights, Visa/MC •
50 condos, Lo-rise, Key at Front desk

Location: Airport: 20 minutes; Downtown: 1 block; Beach front

General Facilities: Kitchen, Linens

Room Facilities: Pool, Hot tub, Tennis, Golf: Silver Sword 1 mile; TV, Cable, Phone in rm., Crib-Hi-chair, Ind. AC Ctl.

Attractions: Ocean activities, lava flow-Haleakala Volcano, entertainment

Shops & Restaurants: Star, Foodland, ABC, Dolphin Center, Rainbow Mall; Kihei Prime Rib-Stoffer Hotel

Clean, comfortable, brightly decorated condominiums across the street from snorkeling. Pool, hot tub, tennis, winter whale watching. Brightly decorated condominiums with Hawaiian style furniture, kitchen microwaves and washer/dryers.

Sugar Beach Resort
145 N. Kihei Rd.
Kihei, Maui, HI 96753
808-879-2778 800-367-5242

1 Bedroom $$, 2 Bedrooms $$$
1 Bedrm/week 4$, 2 Bed/week 8$
Min. Stay 4 Nights, Dep. Req'd. •
240 condos, Hi-rise, Key at Front office

Location: Airport: 8 miles; Downtown: 2 miles; Need car; Beach front

General Facilities: Kitchen, Linens, Restaurant on prem., Bar on prem., Baby-sitter

Room Facilities: Pool, Sauna, Hot tub, Tennis, Golf: Silver Sword 2 miles; TV, Cable, Phone in rm., Crib-Hi-chair, Ind. Heat Ctl.

Attractions: Scuba, snorkeling, fishing, surfing, windsurfing, luaus, jet ski, parasailing, entertainment

Shops & Restaurants: Tourist shops; Chinese

Oceanfront one-and two-bedroom units located on a five-mile stretch of white sandy beach in north Kihei. Fully furnished with color cable TV, central air conditioning and full kitchens. Polynesian dancing once a month in the winter.

──────────────── KIHEI ────────────────

Hale Kamaole Condominiums
2737 South Kihei Road
Kihei, HI 96753
808-879-2698 800-367-2970

1 Bedroom $$, 2 Bedrooms $$

One bedroom and split-level two-bedroom/two-bath units across from beach park. Telephone, ceiling fans, T.V.'s, two pools, tennis court on landscaped grounds.

Haleakala Shores Condominiums
2619 S. Kihei Road
Kihei, HI 96753
808-879-1218 800-367-8047

2 Bedrooms $$
Pool, Daily maid, Kitchen, Phone in rm.

Hawaiian-style buildings with elevators in a Polynesian garden setting. Relax on the sun deck by the pool, barbecue at the poolside lanai, play shuffleboard. Kamaole Park is across the road for beach swimming. Five minutes to golf and tennis.

─────────────── KIHEI ───────────────

Kauhale Makai
938 S. Kihei Road
Kihei, HI 96753
808-879-8888 800-367-2954

1 Bedroom $$, 2 Bedrooms $$, Hi-rise
Pool, Phone in rm.

Attractions: Snorkeling, windsurfing, beachcombing, Shuffleboard, volleyball, tennis, golf

300 feet of grass in front of the pool and jacuzzi leads to the sandy beach. Units with kitchenettes, color TV's and balconies. Outdoor barbecues, shuffleboard, volleyball and mini-golf.

Kihei Kai Nani
2495 South Kihei Road
Kihei, HI 96753
808-879-9088 800-367-8047

1 Bedroom $$
Min. Stay 7 Nights, Dep. Req'd. •
185 condos, Lo-rise, Key at Main office

Location: Airport: 11 miles; Downtown: 3 miles; Need car

General Facilities: Kitchen, Linens

Room Facilities: Pool, Shuffleboard, Golf: Nearby; TV, Cable, Phone in rm., Crib-Hi-chair

Attractions: All water sports, golf, tennis, beach

Shops & Restaurants: Kai Nani Village convenience market, shops; Prime Rib House

Across the road from Kamaole Beach II, low-rise condominiums in a Polynesian garden environment with palms and pulmeria. Owner-furnished units have lanais with varying views and comfortably accommodate four persons. Spend the sunny days at the beach, swimming, snorkeling, windsurfing, sailing, fishing or sunbathing. Outdoor barbecues and a garden pavilion for private meetings and entertainment.

─────────────── KOHALA ───────────────

Mauna Lani Point
HCR 2, Box 4600, Kohala Coast
Kohala, HI 96743
808-885-5022 800-642-6284

1 Bedroom $$$, 2 Bedrooms $$$$, 3 Bedrooms $$$$
Min. Stay 3 Nights, AmEx/Visa/MC,
  Dep. 3 Nights •
116 condos, Lo-rise, Key at Front office

Location: Airport: 20 miles; Downtown: 30 miles; Need car

General Facilities: Full serv., Bus. fac., Conf. rm. cap. 60, Daily maid, Kitchen, Linens, Baby-sitter, Child planned rec.: Summer day camp

Room Facilities: Pool, Sauna, Hot tub, Tennis, Recreation area, Golf: Francis H. I'i Brown; TV, Cable, Phone in rm., Crib-Hi-chair, Ind. AC Ctl.

Attractions: Deep-sea marlin fishing, scuba diving, historic royal fishponds, jogging

Shops & Restaurants: Mauna Lani Bay Hotel shops, art galleries; Gallery Restaurant/nouvelle

Spacious, sophisticated rattan furnished units with postcard views of the golf course and ocean. The pool has its own waterfall surrounded by spectacular exotic flowers, as well as a jacuzzi and sauna. Recreation area pavilion has barbecue and cooking facilities. Go to the Racquet Club for tennis, steam room and exercise work-out and stay for lunch or dinner. The Mauna Lani Beach Club lets you laze on the white sand cove in quiet, beautiful surroundings.

―――――――――――――― KOHALA ――――――――――――――

Shores at Waikoloa
5200 Kohala Coast
Kohala, HI 96743
808-885-5001 800-922-7866

1 Bedroom $$$$, 2 Bedrooms $$$$
AmEx/Visa/MC, Dep. 1 Night •
40 condos, Lo-rise, Key at Front desk

Location: Airport: 30 minutes; Need car
General Facilities: Full serv., Daily maid, Kitchen, Linens, Baby-sitter
Room Facilities: Pool, Hot tub, Tennis, Golf: Waikoloa Resort Course; TV, Cable, Phone in rm., Crib-Hi-chair, Ind. AC Ctl.
Attractions: The varied terrain on the Big Island lends to lots of sightseeing.

World class luxury and style on the prestigious Kohala Coast. Nearby beach for water activities, or take a trip around the Island.

―――――――――――――― KOLOA, KAUAI ――――――――――――――

Aston Poipu at Makahuena
1661 Pe'e Road
Koloa, Kauai, HI 96756
808-742-9555 800-922-7866

1 Bedroom $$$, 2 Bedrooms $$$, 3 Bedrooms $$$$
AmEx/Visa/MC, Dep. 1 Night •
43 condos, Lo-rise, Key at Front desk

Location: Airport: 30 minutes; Downtown: 30 min.; Need car
General Facilities: Full serv., Daily maid, Kitchen, Linens, Baby-sitter
Room Facilities: Pool, Hot tub, Tennis, Snorkeling, Golf: Kiahuna Golf Course-near; TV, Cable, Phone in rm., Crib-Hi-chair
Attractions: Near famous Poipu Beach, a distance from Waimea Canyon and Wailua Falls, entertainment

On a dramatic promontory on Kauai's sunny southern shore, tropically furnished l, 2 and 3 bedroom condominium suites. A spectacular setting with magnificent views near famous Poipu Beach. Hiking, sightseeing, relaxing and exploring.

Kiahuna Beachside
P.O. Box 369
Koloa, Kauai, HI 96756
808-742-7262

Kiahuna Condominium Apts.
P.O. Box 369
Koloa, Kauai, HI 96756
808-742-7262 800-367-7040

1 Bedroom $$, 2 Bedrooms $$$$
Min. Stay 2 Nights, AmEx/Visa/MC,
Dep. 1 Night •
80 condos, Lo-rise, Key at Front desk

Location: Airport: 11 miles; Downtown: 1 mile; Need car; Beach front
General Facilities: Full serv., Daily maid, Baby-sitter
Room Facilities: Pool, Sauna, Hot tub, Tennis, Golf: Kiahuna; TV, Cable, Phone in rm., Crib-Hi-chair
Attractions: Poipu, Kilohana, Waimea Canyon, Hanalei Bay
Shops & Restaurants: Kiahuna and Koloa Town; Keoki's

Kiahuna, meaning "Special Place," is a tropically decorated condominium resort located on the best stretch of Poipu Beach on the sunny south shore of Kauai. Relaxed pace as you view the acres of beautifully landscaped grounds aand beach from your private lanai. If sports are on your schedule, there is golf, tennis, snorkeling and surfing. Kiahuna is also convenient to dining, nightlife, and shopping.

—————————— KOLOA, KAUAI ——————————

Kiahuna Plantation
2253 Poipu Road
Koloa, Kauai, HI 96756
808-742-6411 800-367-7052

1 Bedroom $$$, 2 Bedrooms $$$$
Min. Stay 2 Nights, AmEx/Visa/MC,
Dep. Req'd. •
272 condos, Lo-rise, Key at Front desk
H-yes

Location: Airport: 14 miles; Downtown: 1 mile; Need car; Beach front

General Facilities: Full serv., Daily maid, Kitchen, Linens, Restaurant on prem., Bar on prem., Baby-sitter, Child planned rec.: Lagoon fishing-hula

Room Facilities: Tennis, Horses, surfing, Golf: Kiahuna-1 mile; TV, Phone in rm., Crib-Hi-chair

Attractions: Scenic attractions-Waimea Canyon (hiking), Spouting Horn, Fern Grotto, Kokee State Park, entertainment

Shops & Restaurants: Liberty House, Sears; Plantation Gardens/seafood

Condominiums on sunny south shore of Kauai with garden or ocean views. Kiahuna Shopping Village is across the street, and Old Koloa Town, a showpiece of Kauai's plantation past is two miles away. Rent boogie boards, snorkeling gear or surfboards. White sand beach. Pool at tennis complex. Surfing, tennis and scuba lessons available. Golf and honeymoon packages.

Lawai Beach Resort
5017 Lawai Road
Koloa, Kauai, HI 96756
808-742-9581 800-367-6046

On Kauai's sunny south shore facing a world-famous surfing beach. Two pools, two tennis courts, minutes to Kiahuna Golf Village.

Makahuena at Poipu
1661 Pe'e Road
Koloa, Kauai, HI 96756
808-742-7474 800-367-5124

2 Bedrooms $$$
2 Bedrms/week 8$
Min. Stay 4 Nights, Dep. Req'd.
78 condos, Lo-rise
H-yes

Location: Airport: 20 miles; Need car; Beach front

General Facilities: Kitchen, Linens, Baby-sitter

Room Facilities: Pool, Hot tub, Tennis, Golf: ½ mile Kiahuna; TV, Cable, Crib-Hi-chair

Attractions: Snorkeling, scuba diving, helicopter rides, deep-sea fishing, boat tours, beaches

Built on cliff-side with dramatic ocean views to the east and south. Two-bedroom units with swimming pool, jacuzzi, barbecue area and two tennis courts.

The Makahuena
RR 1, Box 103
Koloa, Kauai, HI 96756
808-742-7474

KOLOA, KAUI

Manualoha at Poipu Kai
RR 1
Koloa, Kauai, HI 96756
808-742-7555 800-367-8022

1 Bedroom $$
1 Bedrm/week 5$
Lo-rise
H-yes

Location: Airport: 20 miles; Need car

General Facilities: Kitchen, Linens, Restaurant on prem., Bar on prem., Baby-sitter

Room Facilities: Pool, Hot tub, Tennis, Golf: ½ mile Kiahuna; TV, Cable, Phone in rm., Crib-Hi-chair

Attractions: Helicopter rides, tours of Waimea Canyon, boat tours, deep-sea fishing

Shops & Restaurants: Three separate shopping villages; Keoki's/seafood-continental

Tropically furnished, beautifully appointed units built along the Greenbelt of Poipu Kai Resort leading to the Maunaloha pool and on to Brennecke's Beach for body surfing.

Sea Village

———————————— KOLOA, KAUAI ————————————

Nihi Kai Villas
1870 Hoone Road
Koloa, Kauai, HI 96756
808-742-6458 800-3318076

2 Bedrooms $$$
2 Bedrms/week 7$
Min. Stay 2 Nights, AmEx/Visa/MC,
Dep. 2 Nights •
70 condos, Lo-rise, Key at Office
H-yes

Location: Airport: 20 miles; Downtown: 15 miles; Need car; Beach front

General Facilities: Full serv., Daily maid, Kitchen, Linens, Baby-sitter

Room Facilities: Pool, Tennis, Paddle tennis, Golf: ½ block Kiahuna; TV, Cable, Phone in rm., Crib-Hi-chair

Attractions: Waimea Canyon, beaches, snorkeling, scuba diving, helicopter rides, boat tours, fishing

Shops & Restaurants: Three separate shopping villages; Keoki's/seafood-continental

This complete resort complex is located 20 yards from Brennecke Beach, famous for body surfing. One block further is Poipu Beach Park with safe swimming for everyone. These condominiums are furnished with complete kitchens, washer/dryer, lanais, televisions and telephones. Balconies with garden or ocean views. Two tennis courts, paddle tennis and pool.

———————————————————————————————

Poipu Crater Resort
RR 1, Box 101
Koloa, Kauai, HI 96756
808-742-7400 800-367-8020

2 Bedrooms $$
2 Bedrms/week 6$
30 condos, Lo-rise
H-yes

Location: Airport: 20 miles; Need car

General Facilities: Kitchen, Linens, Game room, Baby-sitter

Room Facilities: Pool, Sauna, Hot tub, Tennis, Golf: 1/2 mile Kiahuna; TV, Cable, Phone in rm., Crib-Hi-chair

Attractions: Waimea Canyon, deep-sea fishing, boat tours, snorkeling, helicopter rides, scuba diving

Shops & Restaurants: Three separate shopping villages; Keoki's/seafood-continental

These two-story, townhouse style units are built entirely in the caldera of an extinct volcanic crater. Swimming beaches are within walking distance. Tropically furnished with lanais.

--- KOLOA, KAUAI ---

Poipu Kai
R.R. 1 Box 173
Koloa, Kauai, HI 96756
808-742-6464 800-367-6046

1 Bedroom $$$, 2 Bedrooms $$$$, 3 Bedrooms
$$$$
AmEx/Visa/MC, Dep. 1 Night
240 condos, Lo-rise, Key at Administration
H-yes

Location: Airport: 17 miles; Downtown: 2 miles; Need car; Beach front

General Facilities: Full serv., Conf. rm. cap. 150, Daily maid, Kitchen, Linens, Restaurant on prem., Bar on prem., Lounge, Baby-sitter

Room Facilities: Pool, Hot tub, Tennis, Golf: ½ mile-Kiahuna; TV, Cable, Phone in rm., Crib-Hi-chair

Attractions: Spouting horn, Waimea Canyon, Poipu Beach Park, boat excursions from Kukuiula Harbor, entertainment

Shops & Restaurants: Kiahuna shopping village, Old Koloa Town Center; House of Seafood

Luxuriously appointed vacation suites covering over 100 acres, anchored at one end by Brennecke Beach and the other end by Keoniloa Bay. Nine tennis courts with daily tennis activities. Five swimming pools and ₁ mile from Kiahuna Golf Village.

Poipu Kapili
2827 Poipu Road
Koloa, Kauai, HI 96756
808-742-6449 800-443-7714

1 Bedroom $$$, 2 Bedrooms $$$$
1 Bedrm/week 8$, 2 Bed/week 10$
Min. Stay 4 Nights, AmEx/Visa/MC,
Dep. 2 Nights •
60 condos, Lo-rise, Key at Front office
H-yes

Location: Airport: 25 mimutes; Need car

General Facilities: Kitchen, Linens, Baby-sitter

Room Facilities: Pool, Tennis, Golf: Kiahuna-1 mile; TV, Cable, Phone in rm., Crib-Hi-chair

Attractions: Waimea Canyon, Napali Coast, mountains, valleys, gardens, beaches and views all around

Shops & Restaurants: Old Koloa Town, Kiahuna Village, Kukui Grove Cntr.; Plantation Gardens/seafood

A classic, architecturally designed condominium resort. Louvered wood sliding doors, high ceilings, tropical fans and private lanais. Pool, tennis and l mile from golf. Morning rainbows and golden sunsets. 3 minute walk to Poipu Beach and fine restaurants. A good base for sightseeing the island's many attractions.

KOLOA, KAUAI

Prince Kuhio Resort
P.O. Box 1060, 5160 Lauai Road
Koloa, Kauai, HI 96756
808-742-1409 800-722-1409

Studio $, 1 Bedroom $$
Min. Stay 5 Nights, Dep. Req'd. •
69 condos, Lo-rise, Key at Office on premises

Location: Airport: 14 miles; Need car

General Facilities: Kitchen, Linens

Room Facilities: Pool, Golf: 2 blocks; TV, Cable, Crib-Hi-chair, Ind. AC Ctl.

Attractions: Tours to any place on the island. Horseback, sailing, helicopter, kayaking, scuba

Shops & Restaurants: Liberty House, Andrade's, Koloa Town shops; Beach House-Koala Broiler

Three-story garden resort overlooking Prince Kuhio Park and the ocean. Three lovely beaches within 1.5 miles, plus a little lagoon a block away for sunning and swimming. The pool is surrounded by tropical plants and there is also a barbecue area. Golf, tennis, shopping, dining and dancing are not far away. Centrally located for sightseeing, 44 miles to the end of the road each way.

Sunset Kahili Condo Apt.
R.R. 1, Box 96, 1763 Pe'e Road
Koloa, Kauai, HI 96756
808-742-1691 800-367-8047

1 Bedroom $$, 2 Bedrooms $$$
1 Bedrm/week 5$
Min. Stay 3 Nights, Visa/MC, Dep. 3 Nights •
36 condos, Hi-rise, Key at Office
H-yes

Location: Airport: 13 miles; Downtown: 3 miles; Need car; Beach front

General Facilities: Daily maid, Kitchen, Linens, Lounge, Baby-sitter

Room Facilities: Pool, Golf: ¼ mile Kiahuna; TV, Cable, Phone in rm., Crib-Hi-chair

Attractions: Beaches and water sports on sunny Poipu

Shops & Restaurants: Kiahuna, Koloa Town stores; Beach House-Keoki's-Plantation

Lower floor views of ocean, plumeria, pool; upper floor ocean and Poipu Beach. Join the surfers, sunbathers, fishermen and swimmers, or be a spectator watching the porpoise, turtles and whales. Located midway between Waimea Canyon and the Na Pali Cliffs, Sunset Kahili is a 25-minute drive amidst rural sugar cane plantation from Lihue Airport. Walk to Brennecke body surfing beach and Poipu State Park.

Wailkomo Stream Villas
Poipu Road
Koloa, Kauai, HI 96756
808-742-7220 800-325-5701

1 Bedroom $$

Extensive greenery, tropical flowers, large lanais, ceiling fans. Walk to beach. Tennis court and pool. Adjacent to golf.

─────────────── KOLOA ───────────────

Kahala at Poipu Kai
2827 Poipu Road
Koloa, HI 96756
808-742-7555 800-367-8022

1 Bedroom $$
1 Bedrm/week 5$
Min. Stay 4 Nights, Visa/MC, Dep. Req'd. •
82 condos, Lo-rise
H-yes

Location: Airport: 20 miles; Need car; Beach front

General Facilities: Kitchen, Linens, Restaurant on prem., Bar on prem., Baby-sitter

Room Facilities: Pool, Hot tub, Tennis, Golf: Kiahuna— ½ mile; TV, Cable, VCR, Phone in rm., Crib-Hi-chair

Attractions: Tours of Waimea Canyon, beaches, snorkeling, scuba diving, helicopter rides, fishing

Shops & Restaurants: Three separate shopping villages; Keoki's, House of Seafood

Tropically furnished one bedroom condominiums directly adjacent to the 8 court Racquet Club. Garden and ocean views, and an easy walk to Poipu Beach Park.

─────────────────────────────────

Kuhio Shores Condominiums
Lawai Road
Koloa, HI 96756
808-742-6120 800-367-8022

1 Bedroom $$, 2 Bedrooms $$$
1 Bedrm/week 5$, 2 Bed/week 7$
Min. Stay 4 Nights, Dep. Req'd.
76 condos, Lo-rise
H-yes

Location: Airport: 20 miles; Need car; Beach front

General Facilities: Kitchen, Linens, Restaurant on prem., Bar on prem., Baby-sitter

Room Facilities: TV, Cable, Phone in rm., Crib-Hi-chair

Attractions: Helicopter sightseeing, fishing, boating, beach activities, Spouting Horn

Shops & Restaurants: Kiahuna, Old Koloa Town shops; Beachhouse Restaurant

Each unit in this four-story condominium has beautiful ocean views. Located on the rocky shoreline, just 15 feet from the Pacific Ocean. Relax, read, sunbathe and enjoy the playful waves of the crescent beaches.

─────────────────────────────────

Makanui at Poipu Kai
Koloa, HI 96756

1 Bedroom $$, 2 Bedrooms $$$
1 Bedrm/week 5$, 2 Bed/week 8$
Min. Stay 4 Nights, Dep. Req'd.
22 condos, Lo-rise
H-yes

Location: Airport: 20 miles; Need car

General Facilities: Kitchen, Linens, Restaurant on prem., Bar on prem., Baby-sitter

Room Facilities: Pool, Hot tub, Tennis, Golf: Kiahuna ½ mile; TV, Phone in rm., Crib-Hi-chair

Attractions: Many beautiful beaches, snorkeling, scuba diving, deep-sea fishing, boat tours

Shops & Restaurants: Local shops; Restaurant on premises

These large, beautifully appointed units have access to all the amenities of Poipu Kai. Fantastic panoramic mountain and ocean views, and, of course, easy walking distance to two sandy beaches. On-site pool and hot tub.

—————————— KOLOA ——————————

Poipu Makai Condominiums
Hoone Road
Koloa, HI 96756

2 Bedrooms $$$
2 Bedrms/week 8$
Min. Stay 4 Nights, Dep. Req'd.
13 condos, Lo-rise
H-yes

Location: Airport: 20 miles; Need car; Beach front

General Facilities: Kitchen, Linens, Baby-sitter

Room Facilities: Pool, Golf: Kiahuna ½ mile; TV, Cable, Phone in rm., Crib-Hi-chair

Attractions: Helicopter sightseeing, charter boats, Polynesian entertainment, beaches

Shops & Restaurants: Three shopping villages; Plantation Gardens

Building is on the Pacific Ocean enjoying a western view of the south coastline toward the sunset. All units are two-bedroom, two-bath with washers and dryers, television and telephone. A small pool is on the property for a change from the beach.

Poipu Palms Condominiums
Hoone Road
Koloa, HI 96756

2 Bedrooms $$$
2 Bedrms/week 7$
Min. Stay 4 Nights, Dep. Req'd.
12 condos, Lo-rise
H-yes

Location: Airport: 20 miles; Need car; Beach front

General Facilities: Kitchen, Linens, Baby-sitter

Room Facilities: Pool, Golf: Kiahuna ½ mile; TV, Cable, Phone in rm., Crib-Hi-chair

Attractions: Tours of Waimea Canyon, boat tours, Kokee Lodge & Museum, horseback riding

Shops & Restaurants: Kiahuna shopping Village, Koloa Town; The Aquarium Restaurant

Small 12 unit, three story building, is located on cliffs immediately above the Pacific Ocean. The complex has a sun deck and swimming pool and is within easy walking distance to beaches.

Poipu Sands at Poipu Kai
Poipu Road
Koloa, HI 96756

1 Bedroom $$$
2 Bedrms/week 12$
Min. Stay 4 Nights, Dep. Req'd.
72 condos, Lo-rise
H-yes

Location: Airport: 20 miles; Need car; Beach front

General Facilities: Kitchen, Linens, Restaurant on prem., Bar on prem., Lounge, Baby-sitter

Room Facilities: Pool, Hot tub, Tennis, Golf: Kiahuna ½ mile; TV, Cable, Phone in rm., Crib-Hi-chair

Attractions: Beach activities, deep-sea fishing, scuba diving, snorkeling

Shops & Restaurants: Local shops; House of Seafood

Sandy Shipwreck Beach is immediately adjacent to the Poipu Sands Condominiums. Tropically furnished with private lanais. These luxury units have microwaves and ceiling fans. Large swimming pool and nearby barbecue area. Brennecke's body surfing beach for the more adventurous is close, as is Poipu Beach Park with safe sandy swimming for everyone.

KOLOA

Whalers Cove
2640 Puuholo Road
Koloa, HI 96756
808-742-7272 800-367-7040

2 Bedrooms $$$$
Min. Stay 2 Nights, AmEx/Visa/MC,
Dep. 1 Night •
34 condos, Lo-rise, Key at Front desk

Location: Airport: 12 miles; Downtown: 1 mile; Need car
General Facilities: Full serv., Daily maid, Kitchen, Linens, Lounge, Baby-sitter
Room Facilities: Pool, Sauna, Golf: Kiahuna; TV, Cable, Phone in rm., Crib-Hi-chair, Ind. AC Ctl.
Attractions: Koloa Town, Waimea Canyon, Kilohana
Shops & Restaurants: Kiahuna shopping center; Keoki's

Oceanfront extra-spacious units, master bedroom features jacuzzi tub, deluxe furniture, and ocean views in a private location.

LAHAINA, MAUI

Aston Kaanapali Shores
3445 Honoapiilani Highway
Lahaina, Maui, HI 96761
808-667-2211 800-922-7866

Studio $$$, 1 Bedroom $$$, 2 Bedrooms $$$$
AmEx/Visa/MC, Dep. 1 Night •
410 condos, Hi-rise, Key at Front desk

Location: Airport: Less than 10 minutes; Downtown: 10 min.; Need car; Beach front
General Facilities: Full serv., Conf. rm., Daily maid, Kitchen, Linens, Restaurant on prem., Bar on prem., Lounge, Baby-sitter, Child planned rec.: Camp Kaanapali
Room Facilities: Pool, Sauna, Hot tub, Tennis, Snorkeling, TV, Cable, Phone in rm., Crib-Hi-chair, Ind. AC Ctl.
Attractions: Kaanapali beach, historic Lahaina, whale watching cruises (Dec. to April), Haleakala Park, entertainment
Shops & Restaurants: Lahaina shops; Aston Beach Club restaurant

Located on Kaanapali Beach, comfortable, spacious studio, one-and two-bedroom units featuring luxury baths, family-size lanais and gourmet kitchens. Four championship golf courses nearby. Guest activities program and summer children's activities program including nature walks, arts, crafts, hula lessons, lei-tying classes and treasure hunts.

Hale Kai
3691 Honoapiilani Rd.
Lahaina, Maui, HI 96761
808-669-6333

1 Bedroom $$, 2 Bedrooms $$$
1 Bedrm/week 5$, 2 Bed/week 6$
Min. Stay 3 Nights, Dep. Req'd.
40 condos, Lo-rise, Key at front desk, H-yes

Location: Airport: Maui Airport 30 Mi.; Downtown: 6 miles; Need car; Beach front
General Facilities: Kitchen, Linens, Baby-sitter
Room Facilities: Pool, TV, VCR, Phone in rm., Crib-Hi-chair
Attractions: Charter fishing boats, helicopter sightseeing, whale watching, horseback riding, entertainment
Shops & Restaurants: Supermarket, Lahaina Cannery Shopping Center; Erik's/seafood-Charthouse/stks

Two-story Polynesian style garden condominiums amid lush tropical foliage. A private retreat close to championship golf and tennis. On the beach for ocean activities. Joggers will like Honokowai Beach Park, hikers, the trails of Haleakala Crater, or bicycle enthusiasts will enjoy exploring the island.

————————————— LAHAINA, MAUI —————————————

Hale Mahina Beach Resort   1 Bedroom $$
3875 Lower Honoapiilani Rd.
Lahaina, Maui, HI 96761
808-669-8441 800-367-8047

At the "House of the Pale Moon" relax at the beachfront pool, jacuzzi or beach. Barbecue your dinner, walk on the beach, then let the sound of the surf lull you to sleep.

Hale Ono Loa
3823 Lower Honoapiilani Rd.
Lahaina, Maui, HI 96761
808-669-6362 800-367-2927

All of these cool, airy, spacious apartments are oriented to the trade winds. Lanais, pool. Shop Whaler's Village, golf at Kapalua or Kaanapali. Carefree living.

Hololani Resort Condo   1 Bedroom $$, 2 Bedrooms $$$
4401 Honoapiilani Rd.   Min. Stay Ask, Dep. Req'd. •
Lahaina, Maui, HI 96761   62 condos, Hi-rise, Key at Office
808-669-8021 800-367-5021   H-yes

Location: Airport: Maui/Kapalua 5 min.; Downtown: 6 miles; Need car; Beach front
General Facilities: Kitchen, Linens, Baby-sitter
Room Facilities: Pool, Golf: Kapalu-Kaanapali near; TV, Cable, Phone in rm., Crib-Hi-chair
Attractions: Many aquatic attractions. Historic area. Humpback whales play close to shore in winter, entertainment
Shops & Restaurants: Neighborhood grocery store, Whalers Village shops; Erik's/ seafood-Grill & Bar

Fully equipped two-bedroom, two-bath units with color TV and double lanai for winter whale watching. A mile of swimming beach, pool, not far from tennis and golf. A short drive brings you to Lahaina for shopping, dining or harbor activities.

Hono Koa Resort   2 Bedrooms $$
3801 Lower Honoapiilani Rd.   2 Bedrms/week 5$
Lahaina, Maui, HI 96761   AmEx/Visa/MC, Dep. 1 Night •
808-669-0979 800-367-7042   28 condos, Hi-rise, Key at Front desk, H-yes

Location: Airport: Kapalua—4 miles; Downtown: 10 min.; Need car
General Facilities: Daily maid, Kitchen, Linens, Baby-sitter
Room Facilities: Pool, Hot tub, Golf: Royal Kaanapali 4 miles; TV, Phone in rm., Crib-Hi-chair
Attractions: Fishing, sailing, scuba diving, parasailing, beaches, golf, tennis, entertainment
Shops & Restaurants: Lahaina shops, supermarket nearby, Kapalua; Leilani's/fine dining

Recently completed resort condominiums with lanai ocean or garden views. Swimming pool with entertainment and barbecue areas in the center of tropical trees and plants. A short walk to two beaches, large park for picnics and supermarket. All two-bedroom, two-bath units have oak and tile kitchens and tropical furnishings.

Kappa Sands

LAHAINA, MAUI

Honokeana Cove
5255 Lower Honoapiilani Road
Lahaina, Maui, HI 96761
808-669-6441 800-237-4948

1 Bedroom $$, 2 Bedrooms $$$, 3 Bedrooms $$$
1 Bedrm/week 5$, 2 Bed/week 7$, 3 Bed/week 9$
Min. Stay 5 Nights, Dep. 5 Nights •
38 condos, Lo-rise, Key at Office

Location: Airport: 5 minutes; Downtown: 7 miles; Need car; Beach front
General Facilities: Kitchen, Linens, Baby-sitter
Room Facilities: Pool, Golf: Kapalua near; TV, Cable, Phone in rm., Crib-Hi-chair
Attractions: Parasailing, golf, tennis, cruises, sunset sails, surfing, snorkeling, entertainment
Shops & Restaurants: Kapalua shops; Kapalua Grill & Bar/fish-steak

In the Napili section of West Maui, on a private, picturesque cove offering some of the best snorkeling on Maui. Napili Bay's crescent beach is reached in a 5 minute walk along a shoreline path. Lanais, ocean views, barbecues, and some with VCR's and radios. When you tire of the pool and beach, Lahaina is within easy reach. Weekly mai-tai or pu-pu parties at this romantic hideaway.

─────────────── LAHAINA, MAUI ───────────────

Hoyochi Nikko
3901 Lower Honoapiilani Rd.
Lahaina, Maui, HI 96761
808-669-8343

1 Bedroom $$
Min. Stay 5 Nights, Dep. Req'd. •
18 condos, Lo-rise, Key from manager
H-yes

Location: Airport: 2 miles; Downtown: 10 miles; Need car; Beach front

General Facilities: Daily maid, Kitchen, Linens, Baby-sitter

Room Facilities: Pool, Tennis, Surfing, snorkeling, Golf: Kapalu-Kaanapali near; TV, Cable, Phone in rm., Crib-Hi-chair

Attractions: Lahaina Town, Haleakala, Hana beaches, entertainment

Shops & Restaurants: Lahaina shops; Kapalua Grill & Bar

A small, friendly spot with a great view, oriental in design. Low density units face the ocean with the pool surrounded by a large lawn and attractive tropical garden. Bay protected barrier reef makes for safe ocean swimming and snorkeling. Golf, tennis, shopping and restaurants within a few miles. Soak up the sun and scenery and view the incredible sunsets.

───────────────────────────────────────

Hyatt Regency Maui
200 Kohea Kai Drive
Lahaina, Maui, HI 96761
808-667-7474

───────────────────────────────────────

Kaanapali Plantation
150 Puukolii Rd.
Lahaina, Maui, HI 96761
808-661-4446

───────────────────────────────────────

Kaanapali Royal
2560 Kekaa Drive
Lahaina, Maui, HI 96761
808-667-7200 800-367-7040

1 Bedroom $$$, 2 Bedrooms $$$
AmEx/Visa/MC, Dep. 1 Night •
36 condos, Villas, Key at Front desk

Location: Airport: 45 minutes; Downtown: 2 miles; Need car

General Facilities: Full serv., Daily maid, Kitchen, Linens, Baby-sitter

Room Facilities: Pool, Sauna, Hot tub, Tennis, Golf: Royal Kaanapali; TV, Cable, Phone in rm., Crib-Hi-chair, Ind. AC Ctl.

Attractions: Lahaina, whaling port, Kaanapali Resort, beaches

Shops & Restaurants: Kaanapali; Kimos

Kaanapali Royal condominiums are nearly twice the size of many typical units. Sunken living rooms and spacious master bedroom suites with tropical furniture. Seven acres of lush tropical landscape adjacent to Kaanapali North Golf Course. Pool, spa, sauna, tennis on the water's edge.

───────────────────────────────────────

Kaanapali Shores Resort
100 Kaanapali Shores Place
Lahaina, Maui, HI 96761
714-497-4253 800-854-8843

─────────────── LAHAINA, MAUI ───────────────

Kahana Reef
4471 Honoapiilani Road
Lahaina, Maui, HI 96761
808-669-6491

Kahana Sunset   1 Bedroom $$$
P.O. Box 10219
Lahaina, Maui, HI 96761
808-669-8011 800-367-8011

One-bedroom apartments, two-bedroom townhouses with trellised lanais upstairs and down set among exotic plants, flowers and shrubs. Reef-protected beach safe for children, windsurfing, pool, patios, barbecues. Grocery stores and restaurants.

Kahana Village   2 Bedrooms $$$, 3 Bedrooms $$$
4531 Honoapiilani Road   Min. Stay 5 Nights, Dep. Req'd. •
Lahaina, Maui, HI 96761   42 condos, Lo-rise, Key at Office on site
808-669-5111 800-824-3065

Location: Airport: West Maui 1 mile; Downtown: 6 miles; Need car; Beach front
General Facilities: Kitchen, Linens, Baby-sitter
Room Facilities: Pool, Snorkeling, TV, Cable, VCR, Phone in rm., Crib-Hi-chair
Attractions: Close to four of the best snorkeling beaches on Maui, golf and tennis, entertainment
Shops & Restaurants: Hotel area shopping, Safeway, The Cannery; Eric's Seafood-China Boat

You know you're in Hawaii when you stay at Kahana Village situated at the foot of pineapple and sugar cane fields. The white sand beach is set in a picturesque reef-protected cove. 40-foot-diameter pool with an oversize deck, private entertainment center with jacuzzi and barbecue. The open air beachhouses in early missionary style architecture have large lanais with island views. Vaulted ceilings and skylights in 2nd story units, sunken tubs in ground level units.

Kahana Villas   Hi-rise
4242 Lower Honoapiilani Rd.   Pool, Daily maid, Kitchen
Lahaina, Maui, HI 96761
808-669-5613 800-367-6046

Attractions: Tennis

Two-story, two-bedroom villas for your home away from home. Complimentary play at the tennis court. Pool, jacuzzi and 2 saunas. On-site convenience store and restaurant. 10 minutes to Old Lahaina. Across from Kahana Beach.

―――――――――――――――――― LAHAINA, MAUI ――――――――――――――――――

Kaleialoha Resort Condominium
3785 Lower Honoapiilani Rd.
Lahaina, Maui, HI 96761
808-669-8197 800-222-8688

Studio $$, 1 Bedroom $$
1 Bedrm/week 4$
Min. Stay 3 Nights, Visa/MC, Dep. 3 Nights •
35 condos, Hi-rise, Key at Office on property
H-yes

Location: Airport: 5 Min.; Downtown: 5 miles; Need car; Beach front

General Facilities: Kitchen, Linens, Baby-sitter

Room Facilities: Pool, TV, Cable, Phone in rm., Crib-Hi-chair

Attractions: Kaanapali Resort area, Old Lahaina Town

Shops & Restaurants: Kaanapali-Liberty House and specialty shops; Grill & Bar-casual dining

Hawaiian style living by the ocean. The beach is inside a protected outer reef. An interior courtyard shelters the pool. Five minutes from this peace and quiet is Kaanapali Resort area which features great entertainment, restaurants, shopping and golf course. "Old Lahaina Town" is ten minutes away. Bus service available.

Kapalua Villas
One Bay Drive
Lahaina, Maui, HI 96761
808-669-0244 800-367-8000

1 Bedroom $$$$, 2 Bedrooms $$$$
AmEx/Visa/MC, Dep. 1 Night •
180 condos, Villas, Key at Kapalua Bay Hotel
H-yes

Location: Airport: 4 miles; Downtown: 11 miles; Beach front

General Facilities: Full serv., Conf. rm. cap. 200, Daily maid, Kitchen, Linens, Restaurant on prem., Bar on prem., Lounge, Baby-sitter, Child planned rec.: Children's programs

Room Facilities: Pool, Tennis, Water sports, Golf: Bay Course-Village Course; TV, Cable, Phone in rm., Crib-Hi-chair, Ind. Heat Ctl.

Attractions: Historic whaling town of Lahaina, museums, galleries, Haleakala downhill bike ride, entertainment

Shops & Restaurants: Kapalua shops, jewelry, art, clothing, Market Cafe; The Bay Club/seafood-continent

Contemporary styling in soft colors to complement the harmonious, lush tropical landscaping. Artfully tucked into its surroundings, this resort offers the ultimate in privacy, luxury and tranquility. A children's program is offered in summer, and at Christmas and Easter. Live dinner music in the restaurants.

Konokeana Cove
5255 Lower Honoapiilani Rd.
Lahaina, Maui, HI 96761
808-669-6441

---------------------------- LAHAINA, MAUI ----------------------------

Kulakane
3741 Lower Honoapiilani Rd.
Lahaina, Maui, HI 96761
808-669-6119 800-367-6088

1 Bedroom $$, 2 Bedrooms $$$
1 Bedrm/week 5$, 2 Bed/week 8$
Min. Stay 3 Nights, Visa/MC, Dep. Req'd. •
42 condos, Lo-rise, Key at Rental office

Location: Airport: Kapalua 1 mile; Downtown: 7 miles; Need car; Beach front
General Facilities: Kitchen, Linens, Child planned rec.: Hula lessons
Room Facilities: Pool, Golf: Kaanapali & Kapalua near; TV, Cable, Phone in rm., Crib-Hi-chair
Shops & Restaurants: Walher's Village, Lahaina Cannery shopping center; Kapalua Bay Club, Seahouse

Six miles from the old whaling port of Lahaina, ten minutes to championship golf courses. Townhouse units with private lanais and ocean views. Surf, snorkel, swim and sunbathe.

Kuleana Maui
3959 Lower Honoapiilani Road
Lahaina, Maui, HI 96761
808-669-8080 800-367-5633

1 Bedroom $$, 2 Bedrooms $$$
1 Bedrm/week 4$, 2 Bed/week 6$
Min. Stay 3 Nights, Visa/MC, Dep. 3 Nights •
40 condos, Lo-rise, Key at Manager's office
H-yes

Location: Airport: West Maui-5 Min.; Downtown: 10 min.; Need car; Beach front
General Facilities: Kitchen, Linens, Game room, Lounge, Baby-sitter
Room Facilities: Pool, Tennis, Shuffleboard, Snorkel, TV, Cable, Phone in rm., Crib-Hi-chair
Attractions: Valleys and mountains of Maui, Haleakala Crater, Falls/pool at Hana, Lahaina whaling port
Shops & Restaurants: Whaler's Village, Liberty House; Kimo's/cont-Longhi's/Itali,P

Colorful tropical color scheme and furnishings in these condominiums, all with ocean view from private lanais. The grounds are filled with lush tropical foliage and you can walk along the lighted pathway at night. A private snorkeling area lets you view colorful tropical fish. Large pool, tennis and barbecues while you view the rocky coastline. Minutes to sandy beaches, shopping and golf.

Lahaina Roads
1403 Front Street
Lahaina, Maui, HI 96761
808-661-3166 800-624-8203

1 Bedroom $$, 2 Bedrooms $$
Min. Stay 3 Nights, Dep. Req'd. •
42 condos, Hi-rise, Key at Office on property

Location: Airport: 45 minutes; Downtown: 1 mile; Need car; Beach front
General Facilities: Daily maid, Kitchen, Linens
Room Facilities: Pool, TV, Cable, Phone in rm., Crib-Hi-chair
Attractions: Scuba, snorkeling, surfing, trip to Hana, Haleakala Crater, glass bottom boat, luaus, entertainment
Shops & Restaurants: Safeway, Longs Drug, shopping mall with boutiques; Seafood-Steak-French/5 star

Comfortable, well-equipped condos with panoramic views from private lanais. Rattan furniture in soundproof condos. Reef protected beach for water sports, and park and swimming beach minutes away. 5 minute walk to shopping, golf and tennis. Pool overlooks beach and the islands of Lanai and Molokai.

---------------------------------- LAHAINA, MAUI ----------------------------------

Lahaina Shores Hotel
475 Front Street
Lahaina, Maui, HI 96761
808-661-4835 800-367-2972

Studio $$, 1 Bedroom $$$
1 Bedrm/week 6$
AmEx/Visa/MC, Dep. 1 Night •
199 condos, Hi-rise, Key at Front desk, H-yes

Location: Airport: Kapalua—4 miles; Downtown: 2 blocks; Need car; Beach front

General Facilities: Full serv., Daily maid, Kitchen, Linens, Baby-sitter

Room Facilities: Pool, Hot tub, Golf: 5 miles; TV, Cable, Phone in rm., Crib-Hi-chair, Ind. AC Ctl., Ind. Heat Ctl.

Attractions: Water sports, tennis, historic Lahaina Town, whale watching, IAO Needle Park

Shops & Restaurants: Lahaina Town shops; Swan Court/Longhi's/La Bretone

Newly renovated with tropical furnishings in pastel colors. Spacious lanais with incredible views of the ocean and mountains. Two blocks from the center of town. Water sports and activities at the harbor. Tennis across the street, luau feast next door. Take time out to watch the special sunset before you begin your evening.

Lokelani
3833 Lower Honoapiilani Hiway
Lahaina, Maui, HI 96761
808-669-8110 800-367-2976

1 Bedroom $$, 2 Bedrooms $$$, Lo-rise
Pool, Kitchen, Linens, Phone in rm.

Attractions: Whale watching, swimming, golf, tennis, scuba diving, snorkeling

No schedules to keep here. Be as active or inactive as you like. Spend your day at the beach or sunbathing by the pool. Enjoy your fresh Hawaiian pineapple on the lanai overlooking the islands of Molokai and Lani. Listen to the surf and feel the cooling winds at night.

Mahana at Kaanapali
110 Kaanapali Shores Place
Lahaina, Maui, HI 96761
808-661-8751 800-922-7866

Studio $$$, 1 Bedroom $$$, 2 Bedrooms $$$$
Min. Stay 3 Nights, AmEx/Visa/MC,
Dep. 1 Night •
127 condos, Hi-rise, Key at Front desk

Location: Airport: Less than 10 minutes; Downtown: 10 min.; Need car; Beach front

General Facilities: Full serv., Daily maid, Kitchen, Linens

Room Facilities: Pool, Sauna, Tennis, Shuffleboard, snorkel, Golf: Nearby; TV, Cable, Phone in rm., Crib-Hi-chair, Ind. AC Ctl.

Attractions: Kaanapali beach, Lahaina Town, whale watching cruises (Dec. to April), Haleakala Park, entertainment

Shops & Restaurants: Gourmet sundry store

The only Kaanapali Beach resort where every guest has a beachfront condominium suite. Tastefully appointed units. Beachfront pool. Gourmet kitchens.

The Mahana
110 Kaanapali Shores Place
Lahaina, Maui, HI 96761
808-922-3368 800-367-5124

1 Bedroom $$$

Stunning suites with ocean views. Beachfront restaurant and bar, gourmet sundry store, tennis, shuffleboard, pool and sun deck. Activities program and weekly get-acquainted party.

LAHAINA, MAUI

Mahina Surf
4057 Lower Honoapiilani Road
Lahaina, Maui, HI 96761
808-669-6068 800-367-6086

Makani Sands   1 Bedroom $$, 2 Bedrooms $$$, Lo-rise
3765 Honoapiilani Rd.   Pool, Kitchen, Phone in rm.
Lahaina, Maui, HI 96761
808-669-8223 800-227-8223

Attractions: Scuba, snorkeling, surfing, golf

A wide range of individully furnished accommodations with private lanais. 2 miles to the Tennis Ranch and 5 miles to golf. Colorful tropical landscaping, sparkling pool, and golden beach make this a real Hawaiian retreat.

Maui Kaanapali Villas   Studio $$, 1 Bedroom $$$, 2 Bedrooms $$$$
P.O. Box 11295, 2805 Honoapiilani   Min. Stay 2 Nights, AmEx/Visa/MC,
Lahaina, Maui, HI 96761   Dep. 1 Night •
808-661-8687 800-367-7040   140 condos, Hi-rise, Lo-rise, Key at Front desk

Location: Airport: 27 miles; Downtown: 2 miles; Need car; Beach front

General Facilities: Full serv., Daily maid, Kitchen, Linens, Restaurant on prem., Bar on prem., Lounge, Baby-sitter

Room Facilities: Pool, Sauna, Hot tub, Golf: Kaanapali; TV, Cable, Phone in rm., Crib-Hi-chair, Ind. AC Ctl.

Attractions: Tours to Haleakala Crater, Hana Village or IAO Needle Park

Shops & Restaurants: Historic Lahaina Town; Gerard's, Longhi's/continental

All condos have beige carpet, twin or queen beds and spacious lanais. Tennis across the street, 5 miles to golf, luau feast next door. Ideal location, excellent weather, near harbor for sport fishing, scuba or snorkel dives. Pool and whirlpool.

Maui Kai Resort Condominium   Studio $$, 1 Bedroom $$, 2 Bedrooms $$$
106 Kaanapali Shores Place   1 Bedrm/week 5$, 2 Bed/week 9$
Lahaina, Maui, HI 96761   Min. Stay 2 Nights, Visa/MC, Dep. 2 Nights •
808-661-0002 800-367-5635   79 condos, Hi-rise, Key at Office on property
                                     H-yes

Location: Airport: 25 miles; Downtown: 5 miles; Need car; Beach front

General Facilities: Full serv., Kitchen, Linens, Game room, Baby-sitter

Room Facilities: Pool, Hot tub, TV, VCR, Phone in rm., Crib-Hi-chair, Ind. AC Ctl.

Attractions: Royal Kaanapali Golf Course, horseback riding, tours to Hana/Haleakala Crater-condo pickup

Shops & Restaurants: Whalers Village Museum/shopping, Lahaina Village; Beach Club-American

Family atmosphere and reasonable rates in this resort condominium right on the beach. After you have savored the many beach activities, relax in the hot therapy pool, use the barbecue pits to cook dinner, or the cabana with its kitchen, paperback library and ping pong. Private lanais with unobstructed ocean view.

---------------------------- LAHAINA, MAUI ----------------------------

Maui Sands
3559 Lower Honoapiilani Rd.
Lahaina, Maui, HI 96761
808-669-4811 808-367-5037

Napili Bay   Studio $$
33 Hui Drive   AmEx/Visa/MC, Dep. 1 Night •
Lahaina, Maui, HI 96761   35 condos, Lo-rise, Key at Front desk
808-669-6044 800-367-7042   H-yes

Location: Airport: Kapalua—2 miles; Downtown: 5 miles; Need car; Beach front
General Facilities: Daily maid, Kitchen, Linens
Room Facilities: TV, Crib-Hi-chair
Attractions: Lahaina Town, golf at Kapalua, Napili Bay and Kaanapali hotels
Shops & Restaurants: Lahaina Town; Hyatt Hotel's Swan Court

An ideal vacation hideaway with old-fashioned wood decor in beige and brown colors. Premier beach covered with white sand, wide lanais that offer ocean views and views of Molokai Island. A quiet, relaxing atmosphere for your low-key vacation.

Napili Point   1 Bedroom $$$, 2 Bedrooms $$$$
5295 Honoapiilani Hwy.   AmEx/Visa/MC, Dep. 1 Night •
Lahaina, Maui, HI 96761   103 condos, Lo-rise, Key at Front desk
808-669-9222 800-367-5124

Location: Airport: 15 minutes; Downtown: 15 min.; Need car
General Facilities: Full serv., Daily maid, Kitchen, Linens
Room Facilities: Pool, Snorkeling, TV, Cable, Phone in rm., Crib-Hi-chair
Attractions: Whale watching cruises, visits to Lahaina aand Haleakala Crater
Shops & Restaurants: Lahaina

Beautifully decorated and conveniently furnished condominiums with breathtaking views of Lanai and Molokai from your private lanai. Two-bedroom suites are split level. Complimentary manager's get-acquainted party. Experience all the comforts and space of a condominium with all the services and amenities of a fine resort.

Napili Shores Resort   Studio $$, 1 Bedroom $$$
5315 Honoapiilani Rd.   AmEx/Visa/MC, Dep. 1 Night •
Lahaina, Maui, HI 96761   152 condos, Lo-rise, Key at Front desk
808-669-8061 800-367-6046

Location: Airport: 3 miles Kapalua; Downtown: 9 miles; Need car; Beach front
General Facilities: Full serv., Daily maid, Kitchen, Linens, Restaurant on prem., Bar on prem., Baby-sitter
Room Facilities: Pool, Hot tub, Shuffleboard, TV, Cable, Phone in rm., Crib-Hi-chair
Attractions: Haleakala National Park, snorkeling, diving, entertainment
Shops & Restaurants: Orient Express/Thai-Chinese

Secluded hideaway on the leeward side of West Maui with enchanting garden estate landscaping. Two freshwater pools, one with jacuzzi, shuffleboard, croquet and nearby golf. Friday night mai-tai parties, gazebo on the pool terrace and an excellent restaurant overlooking the gardens. Free scuba lessons, snorkeling or just soak up the sun.

─────────────────── LAHAINA, MAUI ───────────────────

Napili Village Hotel
5425 Honoapiilani Hwy.
Lahaina, Maui, HI 96761
808-669-6228 800-336-2185

Studio $$, 1 Bedroom $$
1 Bedrm/week 4$
Min. Stay 3 Nights, Visa/MC, Dep. 3 Nights •
30 condos, Lo-rise, Key at Office
H-yes

Location: Airport: 2 miles; Downtown: 8 miles; Need car
General Facilities: Daily maid, Kitchen, Linens
Room Facilities: Pool, Golf: Kapalua— ½ mile; TV, Cable, Crib-Hi-chair
Attractions: Luaus, dinner cruises, fishing charters, surfing, tours, entertainment
Shops & Restaurants: Whalers Village, Lahaina Village; American

Napili Village Hotel consists of a few low-rise buildings in Polynesian style clusters with wall-to-wall carpeting and tropical furnishings. Private lanais, pool, barbecue, village store and beauty shop. Set on an uncrowded beach for full family fun. Pool party once a week with live entertainment.

Noelani
4095 L. Honoapiilani
Lahaina, Maui, HI 96761
808-669-8374 800-367-6030

Studio $$, 1 Bedroom $$, 2 Bedrooms $$$,
3 Bedrooms $$$
Min. Stay 3 Nights, AmEx/Visa/MC,
Dep. 3 Nights •
50 condos, Lo-rise, Key at Office

Location: Airport: 35 minutes; Downtown: 6 miles; Need car
General Facilities: Bus. fac., Daily maid, Kitchen, Linens, Baby-sitter
Room Facilities: Pool, Picnic area, Golf: 2 miles; TV, Cable, Phone in rm., Crib-Hi-chair
Attractions: Oceanfront beach activities available nearby, good snorkeling in front of property, entertainment
Shops & Restaurants: All Kaanapali stores, Whalers Village—3 miles; Kapalua Grill

Oceanfront condominiums with lanais, pastel tropical furnishings, on the waterfront with glorious views of Molokai and Lanai. 2 heated pools and barbecue picnic area. Sandy cove beach adjacent to the property with snorkeling along the reef directly in front of the property. Frequent mai tai parties hosted by the managers. Enjoy the peace, tranquility and Aloha spirit of Old Hawaii among the swaying palms.

Nohonani
3723 Lower Honoapiilani Road
Lahaina, Maui, HI 96761
808-669-8208

1 Bedroom $$, 2 Bedrooms $$
Min. Stay 4 Nights •
25 condos, Lo-rise, Key at Office

Location: Airport: Maui Kapalua-1 mile; Need car; Beach front
General Facilities: Kitchen, Linens, Baby-sitter
Room Facilities: Pool, Golf: Kapalua/Kaanapali-close; TV, Phone in rm., Crib-Hi-chair
Attractions: Haleakala, IAO Valley, Seven Sacred Pools, cruises, sailing, windsurfing
Shops & Restaurants: Lahaina Village; 50 fine restaurants

A small condominium complex, with spacious lanais, oceanfront living room and bedroom. Golden sand beaches, sparkling surf, plumeria and ginger on nicely landscaped grounds which include picnic tables, large pool and barbecues. A grocery store and post office are located one block away, as well as a public park and playground. Enjoy the fiery sunsets and star-studded nights from the comfort of your lanai.

Pono Kai

LAHAINA, MAUI

Paki Maui Resort
3615 Lower Honoapiilani Hwy.
Lahaina, Maui, HI 96761
808-669-8235 800-922-7866

Studio $$, 1 Bedroom $$, 2 Bedrooms $$$
AmEx/Visa/MC, Dep. 2 Nights •
80 condos, Hi-rise, Key at Front desk
H-yes

Location: Airport: 10 minutes; Downtown: 10 min.; Need car; Beach front

General Facilities: Full serv., Daily maid, Kitchen, Linens, Baby-sitter

Room Facilities: Pool, Hot tub, Tennis, Snorkeling, Golf: Nearby; TV, Cable, Phone in rm.

Attractions: Lahaina, Haleakala Crater, whale watching cruises, chartered sails, helicopter sightseeing

Shops & Restaurants: Lahaina Village

Oceanfront between Kaanapali and Kapalua. Tastefully appointed units with easy access to local recreation and restaurants. Pack a picnic and leave early to watch the spectacular sunrise at Haleakala Crater, or toast a Maui sunset from the lanai of your own private suite. Superb accommodations, gracious service, and good value for your vacation dollar.

Be sure to call the condo to verify details and prices and to make your reservation.

―――――――――――― LAHAINA, MAUI ――――――――――――

Papakea Beach Resort
3543 Honoapiilani Highway
Lahaina, Maui, HI 96761
808-669-4848 800-367-5637

Studio $$$, 1 Bedroom $$$, 2 Bedrooms $$$$
AmEx/Visa/MC, Dep. 1 Night •
364 condos, Lo-rise, Key at Front desk
H-yes

Location: Airport: West Maui-10 minutes; Downtown: 10 min.; Need car; Beach front
General Facilities: Full serv., Daily maid, Kitchen, Baby-sitter
Room Facilities: Pool, Sauna, Hot tub, Tennis, TV, Cable, Phone in rm., Crib-Hi-chair
Attractions: Lahaina Town, Kaanapali and Kapalua golf courses, entertainment
Shops & Restaurants: Sundry and grocery stores adjacent to property; Beach Club/continental

Your island home framed by coconut palms with all the conveniences of home. Three lighted tennis courts, 2 18-hole putting greens, two pools, saunas. Lahaina is just down the road when you tire of beach sun and fun. Some units have VCR's. Tennis clinics, round robins and swimmercize classes.

Polynesian Shores
3975 Honoapiilani Road
Lahaina, Maui, HI 96761
808-669-6065 800-433-6284

1 Bedroom $$, 2 Bedrooms $$, 3 Bedrooms $$$
1 Bedrm/week 5$, 2 Bed/week 7$,
  3 Bed/week 10$
Min. Stay 3 Nights, Visa/MC, Dep. Req'd. •
52 condos, Lo-rise, Key at Office, H-yes

Location: Airport: 5-45 minutes; Downtown: 6 miles; Need car; Beach front
General Facilities: Kitchen, Linens, Baby-sitter
Room Facilities: Pool, TV, Cable, VCR, Phone in rm., Crib-Hi-chair
Attractions: Snorkel, sail, luaus, Haleakala Crater, dinner and island cruises, Hana Waterfall, entertainment
Shops & Restaurants: Kapalua & Kaanapali shopping, Lahaina Village; Eric's Seafood Grotto

Airy, Polynesian-style condominiums stressing rattan, glass and pastels on two tropical oceanfront acres. Pupu party on ocean deck, pool and barbecues. Relaxed, carefree atmosphere for your vacation, but only minutes away from Lahaina, Kaanapali and Kapalua resort areas with golf, tennis, sailing, sport fishing, shopping and restaurants.

Puamana
P.O. Box 515
Lahaina, Maui, HI 96761
808-667-2551 800-367-5630

1 Bedroom $$$, 2 Bedrooms $$$, 3 Bedrooms
  $$$$
Min. Stay 3 Nights, Visa/MC, Dep. 3 Nights •
230 condos, Lo-rise, Key at Pumana Clubhouse
No S-yes

Location: Airport: 25 miles; Downtown: ¾ mile; Beach front
General Facilities: Daily maid, Kitchen, Linens, Lounge
Room Facilities: Pool, Sauna, Tennis, TV, Cable, Phone in rm., Crib-Hi-chair
Attractions: Haleakala Crater, IAO Valley, Hana, beaches, fishing, authentic luaus
Shops & Restaurants: Cannery Mall, fine shops, local shops; Gerards/European

Casual low-rise townhouses in a private neighborhood, once part of a sugar plantation. The plantation manager's residence is now the clubhouse with card room, saunas, reading room and lending library. Scenic grounds with tropical birds, flowers and fountains. Tennis, paddle tennis, badminton, ping pong, 3 pools.

──────────────── LAHAINA, MAUI ────────────────

Royal Kahana Resort
4365 Honoapiilani Highway
Lahaina, Maui, HI 96761
808-669-5911 808-421-0767

Studio $$, 1 Bedroom $$, 2 Bedrooms $$$
AmEx/Visa/MC, Dep. 2 Nights •
205 condos, Hi-rise, Key at Front desk

Location: Airport: Kapalua, W. Maui; Downtown: 5 miles; Need car; Beach front

General Facilities: Full serv., Bus. fac., Conf. rm. cap. 50, Daily maid, Kitchen, Linens, Baby-sitter

Room Facilities: Pool, Sauna, Tennis, Shuffleboard, Golf: Kapalua 1½ miles; TV, Cable, Phone in rm., Crib-Hi-chair, Ind. AC Ctl.

Attractions: Windsurfing, golf, tennis, Sugar cane train, Hana

Shops & Restaurants: Variety & convenience store, market, sundries; Eric's Seafood Grotto/fish

Enter the inviting Hawaiian style lobby and enter one of the three high-speed elevators to your comdominiums with sweeping views of the ocean. Beach, pool, his and hers saunas, tennis, putting green and volleyball courts. Meet new friends by the pool, or reserve the poolside cabana for a private party.

───

Sands of Kahana
4299 Honoapiilani Hwy.
Lahaina, Maui, HI 96761
808-669-0400 800-922-7866

1 Bedroom $$$, 2 Bedrooms $$$$, 3 Bedrooms $$$$
AmEx/Visa/MC, Dep. 1 Night •
182 condos, Hi-rise, Key at Front desk

Location: Airport: Less than 10 minutes; Downtown: 10 min.; Need car; Beach front

General Facilities: Full serv., Daily maid, Kitchen, Linens, Restaurant on prem., Bar on prem., Lounge, Child planned rec.: Crafts-hula-nature

Room Facilities: Pool, Hot tub, Tennis, Putting green, Golf: Nearby; TV, Cable, Phone in rm., Crib-Hi-chair

Attractions: Haleakala Crater and whale watching tours from Mid-December to late April, entertainment

Shops & Restaurants: Lahaina Village; Aston Beach Club

Uncommon in their sumptuous luxury, these condominiums are exquisitely decorated. Private lanais overlooking a magnificent ocean channel and the islands of Lanai and Molokai in the distance. Camp Kahana for the children offering arts, crafts, hula, tennis, pool, nature activities and Hawaiiana classes. With space, comfort and luxury, Sands of Kahana has to be experienced to be believed.

LAHAINA, MAUI

Valley Isle
4327 Lower Honoapiilani Rd.
Lahaina, Maui, HI 96761
808-669-4777 800-367-6092

Studio $$$, 1 Bedroom $$$, 2 Bedrooms $$$$
Min. Stay 5 Nights, Visa/MC, Dep. 5 Nights
Hi-rise, Key at Front desk

Location: Downtown: 7 miles; Need car; Beach front
General Facilities: Kitchen, Linens, Restaurant on prem., Lounge
Room Facilities: Pool, Golf: Minutes; TV, Cable, Phone in rm.
Attractions: Island tours, Lahaina, Kaanapali, scuba, snorkeling, golf, entertainment
Shops & Restaurants: On-site convenience store, boutique, Lahaina shops; Restaurant on property

Don't be surprised at the copper humpback whale in the lobby diving into the wishing pool. Maui is famous for whale watching. Completely furnished high-rise condominiums. Complimentary morning coffee, Tuesday night pupu party. Clothing, grocery, restaurant, cocktail lounge, 300 feet of beach, within minutes of 5 snorkeling beaches. Pool, barbecue area.

LIHUE, KAUAI

Banyan Harbor
3411 Wilcox Road
Lihue, Kauai, HI 96766
808-245-7333 800-422-6926

2 Bedrooms $$
Visa/MC,Dep. 1 Night •
148 condos, Lo-rise, Key at Front desk

Location: Airport: Lihue 2 Miles; Downtown: 2 miles; Need car
General Facilities: Kitchen, Linens
Room Facilities: Pool, Tennis, Shuffleboard, Golf: Kauai Hotel-Kauai Lagoons; Cable, Phone in rm., Crib-Hi-chair
Attractions: Boat tours, circle island plane/helicopter rides, luaus, scuba & snorkel tours, fishing, entertainment
Shops & Restaurants: Kukui Grove Center; Tempura Garden-Prince Bill's

Your home away from home, with rich decor and distinctive furnishings. Free scuba/snorkel lessons, cabana/BBQ, and adjacent to the Westin Kauai Hotel with 30 shops, 8 restaurants, carriage rides and nightlife. Cruise the Wailua River to the fern grotto, visit Waimea Canyon, the Grand Canyon of the Pacific, drive to Hanalei where "South Pacific" was filmed, or just stay by the pool, surrounded by tropical foliage and gently rolling grounds. Orientation presentation on the Island of Kauai, golf and tennis.

───────────────── LIHUE, KAUAI ─────────────────

Kauai Hilton Beach Villas
4331 Kauai Beach Dr.
Lihue, Kauai, HI 96766
808-245-1955 800-445-8667

1 Bedroom $$$, 2 Bedrooms $$$$
Dep. 1 Night •
150 condos, Lo-rise, Villas, Key at Hotel registr.
H-yes

Location: Airport: 4 miles; Downtown: 5 miles; Need car; Beach front

General Facilities: Full serv., Conf. rm., Daily maid, Kitchen, Linens, Restaurant on prem., Bar on prem., Lounge, Baby-sitter

Room Facilities: Pool, Hot tub, Tennis, Golf: Wailua Municipal close; TV, Cable, Phone in rm., Crib-Hi-chair, Ind. AC Ctl.

Attractions: Helicopter tours, Fern Grotto, luaus, Hawaiian Village, deep-sea fishing, scuba, entertainment

Shops & Restaurants: Plantation Marketplace, Kukui Grove Shopping Ctr.; Midori/Japan decor-continental

Conveniently located condominiums surrounding lagoons and pool. Beige carpet, mauve and peach color scheme, rattan furniture, tiled kitchen counters and laundry facilities. Children will find lots to do-hula lessons, fishing, lei-making, ukulele lessons and story-telling. Adults will also enjoy the hula lessons as well as the lounge cocktail music. Bathroom surprise—shampoo, mouthwash, shower cap, shoeshine cloth and sewing kit.

───────────────── MAALAEA VILLAGE, MAUI ─────────────────

Kanai A Nalu
R.R. 1, Box 389
Maalaea Village, Maui, HI 96793
808-244-5627 800-367-6084

2 Bedrooms $$
Pool, Kitchen, Linens

All units face the ocean in these specially designed condominiums. Lounge on the lawn under palms. Inner courtyard featuring waterfall, barbecue, swimming pool.

Makani A Kai
R.R. 1, Box 389
Maalaea Village, Maui, HI 96793
808-244-5627 800-367-6084

1 Bedroom $$, 2 Bedrooms $$
1 Bedrm/week 5$, 2 Bed/week 6$
Min. Stay 5 Nights, Dep. Req'd. •
95 condos, Hi-rise, Lo-rise, Key at Hono Kai
    Rental Office
No S-yes/H-yes

Location: Airport: 12 miles; Downtown: 12 miles; Need car; Beach front

General Facilities: Kitchen, Linens, Baby-sitter

Room Facilities: Pool, Golf: Nearby; TV, Cable, Phone in rm., Crib-Hi-chair, Ind. AC Ctl.

Attractions: Maalaea marina, sunset cruises, snorkeling trips, whale watching

Shops & Restaurants: Shopping center, Safeway, Lahaina; Waterfront

The last condominium in Maalaea with the beach outside your door. Pool, 2 restaurants, deli, store, fresh fish market at the harbor. Centrally located, yet secluded. Ocean and garden views, overhead fans and microwaves. Close to excellent golf courses and tennis.

MAALAEA VILLAGE

Maalaea Banyans
Hauoli Street
Maalaea Village, HI 96793
808-242-5668 800-367-5234

1 Bedroom $$, 2 Bedrooms $$, Lo-rise
Pool, Kitchen, Linens

Attractions: Swimming, snorkeling, scuba diving

Step outside your door to the pool surrounded by a wide green lawn, tropical plants, jacuzzi and barbecue. Below is the blue Pacific and nearby golden sand beach. Two-bedroom units have beamed ceilings and lofts. Sliding glass doors lead to your spacious lanai.

MAALAEA, MAUI

Hono Kai Resort
R.R. 1, Box 389 Maalaea Village
Maalaea, Maui, HI 96793
808-244-7012 800-367-6084

1 Bedroom $$

Completely furnished units, including linens & TV. Crescent-shaped pool at ocean's edge. Barbecue facilities, laundry facilities on every floor.

MAKAHA

Makaha Shores
85-265 Farrington Highway
Makaha, HI 96792
808-696-7121

Makaha Surfside
85-175 Farrington Hwy.
Makaha, HI 96792
808-695-9574

40 minutes from Waikiki in Hawaii's enchanted valley on the sunniest part of the island, uncrowded beaches away from traffic and noise. 2 pools, sauna, exercise room, picnic facilities.

MAKENA, MAUI

Makena Surf
96 Makena Alanui
Makena, Maui, HI 96753
808-879-1595 800-367-5246

1 Bedroom $$$$, Lo-rise

Hugging the coastline, Makena provides comfort, convenience and privacy. Daily maid and complete concierge services. Pools, tennis and minutes to golf, restaurants and shops.

Polo Beach Club
20 Makena Road
Makena, Maui, HI 96753
808-879-8847 800-367-6046

2 Bedrooms $$$$, Hi-rise
Pool, Daily maid, Kitchen, Linens

Attractions: Surfing, scuba diving, port of Lahaina, Hana's Seven Sacred Pools, sight-
    seeing, golf

A private resort with deluxe condominiums matching the outdoors with the indoors. Marble floored entrances and koa wood accents. 180-degree views from balconies with rattan chairs and table shaded by palms. Large free form pool and spa. 2 minutes to Wailea.

───────────────── MAUI ─────────────────

Puene Towers Condominium
1063 East Main
Maui, HI 96753
808-244-0564

Deluxe units with marble floored entrances, accented by rich koa wood. Secluded Pacific white sand beach. Free form pool, spa, sun deck overlooking the beach. Tennis, golf, shops and restaurants in Wailea.

───────────── MAUNALOA, MOLOKAI ─────────────

Ke Nani Kai   1 Bedroom $$, 2 Bedrooms $$
P.O. Box 126   AmEx/Visa/MC, Dep. 1 Night •
Maunaloa, Molokai, HI 96770   45 condos, Lo-rise, Key at Front desk
808-552-2761 800-922-7866

Location: Need car
General Facilities: Full serv., Daily maid, Kitchen, Linens
Room Facilities: Pool, Hot tub, Tennis, Golf: Kaluakoi; TV, Cable, Phone in rm.
Attractions: Pleasnt hiking trails and a donkey ride to Father Damien's Leper Colony
On the sunny west shore, surrounded by the championship Kaluakoi Golf Course, spacious, richly furnished units in Polynesian decor have fully equipped kitchens. Private lanais overlook 15 manicured acres and the unspoiled Molokai scenery. Sun on Hawaii's longest white sand beach or take to the pleasant hiking trails.

───────────────────────────────────────

Paniolo Hale   Studio $$, 1 Bedroom $$, 2 Bedrooms $$$
P.O. Box 146   Min. Stay 3 Nights, AmEx/Visa/MC,
Maunaloa, Molokai, HI 96770   Dep. 2 Nights •
808-552-2731 800-367-2984   77 condos, Lo-rise, Key at Office
                                         H-yes

Location: Airport: 12 Miles; Downtown: 22 miles; Need car
General Facilities: Kitchen, Linens, Baby-sitter
Room Facilities: Pool, Tennis, Water sports, Golf: Kaluakoi; Phone in rm., Crib-Hi-chair
Attractions: Snorkeling, Safari tour, other beaches, Father Damien's Leper Colony-Halawa Valley & Falls
Shops & Restaurants: 22 miles to variety of stores, 7 miles to grocery
Far from the hustle and bustle, undiscovered, unspoiled, the last of the Hawaiian Islands to be developed. Paniolo Hale, built in the true Hawaiian tradition, screened lanais, open beam ceilings, hardwood floors and ceiling fans. Molokai offers the serene tranquility of bygone years-the "do nothing island." Wild turkeys roam the golf course, deer take an evening stroll, and a wildlife safari is nearby. Pool, sandy beaches, picnic tables and barbecues. Molokai-The Friendly Island.

───────────────── MOLOKAI ─────────────────

Kaluakoi Golf Resort   Kitchen
P.O. Box 1977
Molokai, HI 96770
808-552-2555 800-367-6046

Attractions: Wildlife Park, kite factory, island tours, fishing, croquet, tennis, golf

------------------------------ NAPILI BAY, LAHAINA, MA ------------------------------

Napili Kai Beach Club
5900 Honoapiilani Road
Napili Bay, Lahaina, Maui, HI 96761
808-669-6271 800-367-5030

Studio $$$, 1 Bedroom $$$$, 2 Bedrooms $$$$
Dep. 2 Nights
180 condos, Lo-rise, Key at Lobby

Location: Airport: Kahului Airport; Downtown: 9 miles; Need car; Beach front

General Facilities: Full serv., Conf. rm. cap. 80, Kitchen, Linens, Restaurant on prem., Lounge

Room Facilities: Pool, Hot tub, Tennis, 18-hole putting green, Golf: Kapalua across the road; TV, Phone in rm.

Attractions: Lahaina Town, golf, water sports, West Maui Mountains, entertainment

Shops & Restaurants: Breezeway gift shop, Lahaina shops; Sea House & Sea Breeze Terrace

Your own steward available throughout your stay at these charming Polynesian condominiums scattered over 10 acres of private refuge. Private view lanais. Stroll or lounge on the beach after your complimentary coffee in the cabana. Swim in one of the 5 pools, use the large jacuzzi or recreation facilities with equipment supplied. Daily cabana coffee and tea party, weekly Mai Tai party and putting party, nightly entertainment and dancing at the Sea Horse. Warm and friendly staff makes you feel at home.

------------------------------ NAPILI BAY, MAUI ------------------------------

Napili Sunset
46 Hui Drive
Napili Bay, Maui, HI 96761
808-669-8083 800-447-9229

Studio $$, 1 Bedroom $$$, 2 Bedrooms $$$$
1 Bedrm/week 8$, 2 Bed/week 10$
Min. Stay 3 Nights, Dep. 3 Nights •
41 condos, Lo-rise, Key at Front desk

Location: Airport: 10 minutes; Downtown: 10 miles; Need car; Beach front

General Facilities: Daily maid, Kitchen, Linens, Baby-sitter

Room Facilities: Pool, TV, Phone in rm., Crib-Hi-chair

Attractions: Body surf, snorkel, surfing, swimming, entertainment

Shops & Restaurants: Whalers Village, Lahaina Cannery, Front Street

Clean, tropical furnishings in a quiet restful, family atmosphere. One-and two-bedroom units face the beach, while studio units are in the garden area among blooming flowers and near the pool. Just steps to the beach. Lots of Aloha spirit, friendly staff and Mai Tai parties.

Napili Surf Beach Resort
50 Napili Pt.
Napili Bay, Maui, HI 96761
808-669-8002

Studio $$, 1 Bedroom $$$
Min. Stay 5 Nights, Dep. Req'd. •
54 condos, Lo-rise, Key at Front desk

Location: Airport: Kapalua-3 miles; Downtown: 10 miles; Need car; Beach front

General Facilities: Full serv., Daily maid, Kitchen, Linens, Baby-sitter

Room Facilities: Shuffleboard, Golf: Kapalua-2 courses; TV, Crib-Hi-chair

Attractions: Haleakala Crater, Hana, entertainment

Shops & Restaurants: Kapalua shops, Kaanapali shops; Kapalua Hotel, The Bay Club

Modern decor in ocean or garden view units, off the highway at the end of a tree-lined country road. Two pools, three shuffleboards, two barbecues and outdoor lanais. The beach is on a secluded crescent bay. One mile to golf and tennis, close to Lahaina for fishing, boating, shopping. To ensure a truly relaxed, quiet vacation, there are no telephones in the rooms.

Poipu

NAPILI, MAUI

Coconut Inn
P.O. Box 10517, 181 Hui Road "F"
Napili, Maui, HI 96761
808-669-5712 800-367-8006

Studio $$, 1 Bedroom $$
Dep. 2 Nights •
40 condos, Lo-rise, Key at Front desk
H-yes

Location: Airport: Kapalua-25 miles; Downtown: 9 miles; Need car

General Facilities: Full serv., Daily maid, Kitchen, Linens, Game room, Baby-sitter

Room Facilities: Pool, Hot tub, Golf: Kapalua adjacent; TV, Cable, Phone in rm., Crib-Hi-chair

Attractions: Horseback riding, snorkeling, scuba diving, helicopter tours, entertainment

Shops & Restaurants: Lahaina Town—9 miles; Grill & Bar, fresh seafood

A lush tropical retreat tucked in the pineapple covered hills of West Maui. Early Hawaiian architecture, tropical cane and floral print furnishings in a cozy, homey atmosphere. Start your morning with a complimentary continental breakfast in the poolside breakfast room. After a day of swimming and sightseeing, enjoy the evening Mai Tai party. Snorkel classes available.

─────────────── PAHALA ───────────────

Colony One at Sea Mountain
P.O. Box 70
Pahala, HI 96777
808-928-8301 800-367-8047

Studio $$, 1 Bedroom $$, 2 Bedrooms $$
Min. Stay 2 Nights, Visa/MC, Dep. Req'd. •
35 condos, Lo-rise, Key at Office on site
H-yes

Location: Airport: Hilo—56 miles; Downtown: 5 miles; Need car; Beach front; Ski lift: Nearby

General Facilities: Conf. rm. cap. 100, Daily maid, Kitchen, Linens, Restaurant on prem., Bar on prem., Baby-sitter

Room Facilities: Pool, Hot tub, Tennis, Golf: Sea Mountain; TV, Phone in rm., Crib-Hi-chair

Attractions: 26 miles to Volcano National Park, 24 miles to southernmost point in the United States, entertainment

Shops & Restaurants: Basics only in village stores; Punalu'u Black Sands/beef-fish

Secluded, elegant condominiums, pale neutral walls, rattan, earth tone furnishings on the coast 30 minutes south of Volcano Park and the Big Island. Unhurried play on splendid 18-hole golf course. Black sand beach, tennis, restaurant, clubhouse, pool and jacuzzi.

Sea Mountain at Punalu'u Colon
Box 70
Pahala, HI 96777
808-928-8301 800-367-8047

─────────────── POIPU, KAUAI ───────────────

Poipu Shores Resort
R.R. 1 Box 95, 1775 Pee Road
Poipu, Kauai, HI 96756
808-742-7700 800-367-8047

1 Bedroom $$, 2 Bedrooms $$$, 3 Bedrooms $$$
Min. Stay 3 Nights, Visa/MC, Dep. 3 Nights •
39 condos, Lo-rise, Key at Front desk

Location: Airport: 15 miles; Need car

General Facilities: Daily maid, Kitchen, Linens, Baby-sitter

Room Facilities: Pool, Golf: Kiahuna-1 mile; TV, Cable, Phone in rm., Crib-Hi-chair

Attractions: Free tennis at Waiohai Tennis Club, golf at Robert Trent Jones course

Shops & Restaurants: Liberty House, Kiahuna Shopping Center; Beach House-Keoki's-P. Gardens

Discover the delights of vacationing at the secluded Poipu Shores Resort. Watch whales spout and dolphins frolic. Enjoy the magnificent sunsets over the Pacific Ocean. The beach, tennis, golf, surfing, and sailing are only minutes away. After dark, there is fine dining and entertainment in nearby restaurants and hotels. The ultimate vacation retreat, where there is no time but now.

─────────────── PRINCEVILLE, KAUAI ───────────────

Alii Kai II Hanalei
P.O. Box 3232
Princeville, Kauai, HI 96722
808-826-9988 800-648-9988

PRINCEVILLE, KAUAI

Mauna Kai
Country Club Drive, P.O. Box 3006
Princeville, Kauai, HI 96722
808-826-6855

2 Bedrooms $$, 3 Bedrooms $$
2 Bedrms/week 4$, 3 Bed/week 4$
Min. Stay 3 Nights, Dep. Req'd.
46 condos, Villas, Key at Manager's office

Location: Airport: 30 miles; Downtown: 30 miles; Need car

General Facilities: Kitchen, Linens

Room Facilities: Pool, Golf: Makai at Princeville; TV, Cable, Phone in rm., Crib-Hi-chair

Attractions: Boat cruises, helicopter sightseeing, fishing, snorkeling, beaches, golf, tennis

Shops & Restaurants: Princeville Center-grocery-gifts-post office-bank; Steak-Chinese-Mexican-Italian

Two-and three-bedroom condominiums with Hawaiian style furnishings, large open beams and cedar walls. Beautiful grounds highlighted by a large swimming pool. Property sits along the famous Princeville Makai Golf Course and there are 6 tennis courts a half mile away at the Princeville clubhouse. Shopping, restaurants and beaches are only a one minute drive away.

Pahio
P.O. Box 3099
Princeville, Kauai, HI 96722
808-826-6549

2 Bedrooms $$$$, Lo-rise
Pool, Kitchen

2300-square-foot, 2-bedroom vacation suites with fireplace, wet bar, spa and entertainment center complete with 67" TV, radio and cassette deck. Rattan furniture, ceiling fans, large lanais with deck furniture. Shopping, dining, golf at Princeville. Secluded beaches.

Sandpiper Village
P.O. Box 460, 4770 Pepelani Loop
Princeville, Kauai, HI 96722
808-826-1176   800-367-7040

2 Bedrooms $$, 3 Bedrooms $$
Min. Stay 2 Nights, AmEx/Visa/MC,
Dep. 1 Night •
30 condos, Lo-rise, Key at Front desk

Location: Airport: 33 miles; Downtown: 1 mile; Need car

General Facilities: Full serv., Daily maid, Lounge, Baby-sitter

Room Facilities: Pool, Sauna, Golf: Princeville; Cable, Crib-Hi-chair

Attractions: Golf, Hanalei Bay, Kalaulau Valley

Shops & Restaurants: Princeville shops; Nobel's

In the heart of master planned Princeville, commanding a scenic view of mountains and the ocean, Sandpiper Village's suites have all the necessities for easy living. Swimming pool, spa, sauna, golf and tennis, or drive to Hanalei for uncrowded beaches. After a day of rafting, snorkeling or surfing, relax in front of your TV or drive to Princeville for dinner, entertainment and shopping.

WAIANAE

Maili Cove
87-561 Farrington Hwy, Room 110
Waianae, HI 96792
808-696-4447

Pool, Daily maid, Kitchen, Linens, Phone in rm.

Exclusive year-round hideaway on Oahu's dry and sunny west coast. Peace and quiet with nothing to do but swim and lie in the sun. Access to golf, restaurants, shopping, horseback riding, deep-sea fishing.

─────────────── WAIANAE ───────────────

Makaha Shores
84-265 Farrington Hwy.
Waianae, HI 96792
808-696-7121

Makaha Valley Towers
84-740 Kili Dr.
Waianae, HI 96792
808-695-9055

─────────────── WAIKIKI, HONOLULU ───────────────

Monte Vista   Pool, Kitchen, Linens
320 Liliuokalani
Waikiki, Honolulu, HI 96815
808-923-4766

A few 2-bedroom units available for vacation rental with recreation areas, pool, roof sun deck and barbecue areas in a secured complex.

─────────────── WAILEA, KIHEI, MAUI ───────────────

Wailea Ekahi   1 Bedroom $$, 2 Bedrooms $$$
3300 Wailea Alanui   1 Bedrm/week 6$, 2 Bed/week 8$
Wailea, Kihei, Maui, HI 96753   Dep. Req'd., Lo-rise, H-yes

Location: Airport: l4 Miles; Downtown: 5 miles; Need car

General Facilities: Kitchen, Linens

Room Facilities: Pool, Tennis, Ocean activities, Golf: Nearby; TV, Cable, Phone in rm., Crib-Hi-chair

Attractions: Glass bottom boats, dinner cruises, snorkeling, biking, tennis, golf, lauas

Shops & Restaurants: Kaahumanu Shopping Center, resort shops; Stouffers Raffles

Luxury condominium homes offering pools, beaches, snorkeling, ocean activities, luaus. Tennis and golf discounts. Near restaurants, hotels and shopping. Tropical garden setting-pool, kiddie pool, jacuzzi, putting green.

─────────────── WAILEA, MAUI ───────────────

Wailea Elua Village   1 Bedroom $$$, 2 Bedrooms $$$, 3 Bedrooms
3600 Wailea Alanui Drive $$$$
Wailea, Maui, HI 96753   Min. Stay 5 Nights, Dep. 3 Nights •
808-878-4726 800-231-0611   152 condos, Lo-rise, Key at Rental office, H-yes

Location: Airport: 30 minutes; Need car; Beach front

General Facilities: Bus. fac., Daily maid, Kitchen, Linens, Lounge, Baby-sitter

Room Facilities: Pool, Hot tub, Paddle ball, Put. green, Golf: Wailea Blue & Orange; Cable, Phone in rm., Crib-Hi-chair

Attractions: Swimming, golf, beach, snorkeling

Shops & Restaurants: Grocery, complete shopping areas; Raffles-Stouffer

Casually elegant, completely furnished beachside condominiums with private lanais for an ocean view. Ceiling fans keep you cool when you come in from the beach or pool. Play paddleball or practice on the putting green.

WAILEA, MAUI

Wailea Villas
3750 Wailea Alanui
Wailea, Maui, HI 96753
808-879-1595 800-367-5246

Studio $$$, 1 Bedroom $$$$, 2 Bedrooms $$$$,
  3 Bedrooms 4$
Min. Stay 3 Nights, AmEx/Visa/MC,
Dep. 3 Nights •
140 condos, Villas, Key at Front desk
H-yes

Location: Airport: 20 miles; Downtown: 2 miles; Need car

General Facilities: Daily maid, Kitchen, Linens, Baby-sitter

Room Facilities: Pool, Tennis, Golf: Wailea golf; TV, Cable, Phone in rm., Crib-Hi-chair

Attractions: All water sports, helicopter rides, horseback riding, golf and tennis

Shops & Restaurants: Wailea shopping village, Kihei town; LePerouse/Fr.-Prince Court

Three distinctive low-rise condominiums set amid tropical gardens. Two swimming pools, putting green, jacuzzi, paddle tennis court, beach pavilion and barbecue grills. A two-minute drive to the Wailea beach with bath houses, showers and changing rooms. The villas are terraced into a 34-acre hillside with ocean or garden views.

WAILUA, KAUAI

Kaha Lani
4460 Nehe Road
Wailua, Kauai, HI 96766
808-822-9331 800-922-7866

1 Bedroom $$, 2 Bedrooms $$$, 3 Bedrooms
  $$$$
AmEx/Visa/MC, Dep. 1 Night •
55 condos, Lo-rise, Key at Front desk
H-yes

Location: Airport: 20 minutes; Need car; Beach front

General Facilities: Full serv., Daily maid, Kitchen, Linens, Baby-sitter

Room Facilities: Pool, Tennis, Snorkel, volleyball, Golf: Wailua Golf near; TV, Cable, Phone in rm., Crib-Hi-chair

Kaha Lani means "Heavenly Place" in Hawaiian. Spacious condominiums with tropical appointments and garden or ocean views. Tranquil, secluded setting on one of Kauai's loveliest beaches for a truly relaxed vacation.

WAILUKU

Island Sands Resort
RR 1, Box 391
Wailuku, HI 96793
808-244-0848 800-826-7816

Studio $, 1 Bedroom $$, 2 Bedrooms $$
1 Bedrm/week 4$, 2 Bed/week 5$
Min. Stay 3 Nights, Dep. Req'd. •
84 condos, Hi-rise, Key at Front office
H-yes

Location: Airport: 8 miles; Downtown: 5 miles; Need car; Beach front

General Facilities: Kitchen, Linens, Baby-sitter

Room Facilities: Pool, Golf: Close; TV, Cable, Phone in rm., Crib-Hi-chair, Ind. AC Ctl.

Attractions: Snorkel and diving cruises to Molokini crater, deep-sea fishing, dinner cruises, bicycles, entertainment

Shops & Restaurants: Many shopping malls; Waterfront/seafood

Beautiful grounds with spectacular view of Haleakala Crater and peaceful surroundings. Modern, Hawaiian-style furnishings. Watch the Humpback whales, snorkel in the blue coral water, relax and sun by the pool. Just a few steps from Maalaea Harbor for sailing and sport fishing. A quiet, unrushed area with central access to many popular areas.

Idaho

Sun Valley
Ketchum

--- KETCHUM ---

Alpine Villa
Box 456
Ketchum, ID 83340
208-726-8813

Stone Hill Condominiums   2 Bedrooms $$$
Valleywood Drive   Min. Stay 4 Nights, Dep. 1 Night •
Ketchum, ID 83340   9 condos, Lo-rise, Key at On arrival
208-726-5149

Location: Airport: 12 miles; Downtown: 1 mile; Need car

General Facilities: Kitchen, Linens

Room Facilities: Sauna, Hot tub, Cable, Phone in rm., Crib-Hi-chair, Ind. Heat Ctl.

Attractions: Skiing, rafting, hiking, fishing, golfing, biking, winter and summer ice skating

Shops & Restaurants: Small, unique specialty shops; French-Austrian-Continental

Professionally decorated townhouses overlooking the slopes of Baldy and the rugged Sawtooth Range. Wet rooms for skis and boots and whirlpool tub in each unit. Minutes from a winter and summer sports playground. Trout fishing, hiking, golfing and tennis. Shopping, restaurants and exciting nightlife, or bask in the sun on wide decks.

--- SUN VALLEY ---

Atelier   2 Bedrooms $$$
Sun Valley Co
Sun Valley, ID 83353
800-635-8261

The first condominiums built in Sun Valley. Convenient to Sun Valley shopping, dining, transportation and recreation facilities. Above Trail Creek trout stream.

──────────── SUN VALLEY ────────────

Bluff Condominium
P.O. Box 186
Sun Valley, ID 83353
208-726-0110

2 Bedrooms $$
2 Bedrms/week 7$
Min. Stay 7 Nights, Visa/MC, Dep. Req'd. •
90 condos, Lo-rise

Location: Airport: 12 miles; Downtown: 1 mile; Ski lift: Nearby

General Facilities: Daily maid, Kitchen, Linens, Baby-sitter, Child planned rec.: Children's activity

Room Facilities: Pool, Sauna, Hot tub, Tennis, Skiing, Golf: Elkhorn at Sun Valley; TV, Cable, Phone in rm., Crib-Hi-chair, Ind. Heat Ctl.

Attractions: Downhill and cross-country skiing, golf, tennis, river rafting, entertainment

Shops & Restaurants: All types; Evergreen

2-bedroom condominiums in Sun Valley with wonderful views. Summer and winter activities for children. Great skiing at Sun Valley Resort.

Dollar Meadows
Sun Valley Co
Sun Valley, ID 83353
800-635-8261

1 Bedroom $$$

Elkhorn Resort
Box 6009
Sun Valley, ID 83354
208-622-4511 800-635-9356

Studio $$, 1 Bedroom $$, 2 Bedrooms $$$,
3 Bedrooms $$$$
Dep. Req'd.
300 condos, Hi-rise, Key at Lobby

Location: Airport: Horizon Airlines; Ski lift: Sun Valley

General Facilities: Full serv., Conf. rm. cap. 400, Daily maid, Kitchen, Linens, Restaurant on prem., Bar on prem., Lounge, Child planned rec.: Recreation Center

Room Facilities: Pool, Tennis, Health club, Golf: 18-hole; TV, Ind. Heat Ctl.

Attractions: Hemingway haunts, Ketchum Ore Wagon Museum, ice skating, white water float trips, horses, entertainment

Shops & Restaurants: Elkhorn's shopping mall; Tequila Joe's, Papa Dino's

Year-round award-winning resort. 66 world-class ski runs at your doorstep. Return to a welcome fire and kitchen fully stocked according to your pre-arrival instructions. 5 swimming pools, 7 spas, tennis, golf, hayride, sleigh rides, constant activities during the year, movie tour. Children's playground, movies, video arcade, camps, day care. Continental breakfast, happy hour, live entertainment. Premier vacation resort for the whole family. Trout streams, biking trails. Visit Hemingway's haunts.

Copper Mountain Resort

──── SUN VALLEY ────

Knob Hill Ridge
Sun Valley, ID 83353
208-726-4340 800-251-3037

2 Bedrooms $$$$, 3 Bedrooms $$$$
Min. Stay 2 Nights, AmEx/Visa/MC, Dep. Req'd. •
200 condos, Lo-rise, Key at 380 Washington-#101
No S-yes/H-yes

Location: Airport: 15 miles; Downtown: 1 block; Ski lift: Nearby

General Facilities: Bus. fac., Conf. rm., Daily maid, Kitchen, Linens, Game room, Lounge, Baby-sitter, Child planned rec.: Local day care

Room Facilities: Pool, Sauna, Hot tub, Tennis, Ice skating, fly fishing, TV, Cable, VCR, Phone in rm., Crib-Hi-chair, Ind. Heat Ctl.

Attractions: Fly fishing guides, glider rides, helicopter skiing

Shops & Restaurants: Everything from grocery to sheepskin coats; International cuisine

Lovely surroundings amidst spectacular mountain views. Many activities, skiing, golf, tennis, shopping, dining and entertainment. Sun Valley for great skiing or summer adventures.

Mountain Resorts
Box 1710
Sun Valley, ID 83353
208-622-4511 800-635-4444

SUN VALLEY

River Run Lodge
P.O. Box 1298
Sun Valley, ID 83353
208-726-9086

1 Bedroom $$$, 2 Bedrooms $$, Lo-rise
Kitchen, Phone in rm.

Attractions: Skiing, golf, tennis, hiking, biking, horseback riding, fishing

All units with magnificent views, fully equipped and furnished. Outdoor jacuzzi hot pool. Welcome cocktail party every Sunday night. 200 yards from River Run Lift at the foot of Mt. Baldy. Warm., sunny climate for summer recreation.

Sun Valley Lodge
Sun Valley, ID 83354

Location: Downtown: 5 min.; Need car; Ski lift: Sun Valley

General Facilities: Kitchen, Restaurant on prem., Bar on prem.

Room Facilities: Pool, Tennis, Bikes, ice skating, Golf: 18-hole course

Attractions: Sun Valley wine auction, Ketchum rodeo, Wagon Days, skiing, bikes, ice skating

Shops & Restaurants: Ketchum galleries, shops, mall adjoining lodge; Lodge dining room

Stay in the condominiums of this family resort with top-notch facilities. Imposing Lodge conveying an air of genteel luxury and understated elegance. Several bars around the premises and wood paneled Lodge dining room. A Bavarian-looking mall adjoins the Lodge, offering irresistible shops and eateries. Hike in the Sawtooths, go white-water rafting, ride horseback, play tennis or use one of the three outdoor pools. Golf course on hilly terrain surrounded by aspen and evergreen. Free shuttle buses.

Warm Springs Resort
Box 228, 119 Lloyd Drive
Sun Valley, ID 83353
208-726-8274 800-635-4404

Studio $$, 1 Bedroom $$, 2 Bedrooms $$$, 3 Bedrooms $$$
1 Bedrm/week $$$$, 2 Bed/week 5$, 3 Bed/week 7$
Min. Stay 2 Nights, AmEx/Visa/MC, Dep. Req'd. •
150 condos, Lo-rise, Key at Front desk

Location: Airport: 12 miles; Downtown: 2 miles; Ski lift: Mt.Bald

General Facilities: Full serv., Bus. fac., Conf. rm. cap. 25, Daily maid, Kitchen, Linens, Baby-sitter

Room Facilities: Pool, Sauna, Hot tub, Tennis, tennis, ski, Golf: Near-Warm Springs; TV, Cable, Phone in rm., Crib-Hi-chair, Ind. Heat Ctl.

Attractions: Skiing on Mt. Baldy, all water sports nearby, fishing, mountain biking

Shops & Restaurants: All types, including various sporting goods shops; Peters/European

Warm Springs Resort at Sun Valley manages 150 completely equipped condominium packages with sizes ranging from convenient, economical studios to deluxe, spacious four bedroom units. All properties are located within easy walking distance of the Warm Spring lift. Unlimited winter activities, and diverse summertime activities, such as steelhead fishing, golf, horseback riding, windsurfing and rafting on the "River of No Return." Rodeo, arts and crafts festival and Wagon Days Parade.

———————————— SUN VALLEY ————————————

Wildflower
Sun Valley Co
Sun Valley, ID 83353
800-635-8261

———————————— SUN VALLEY (KETCHUM) ————————————

Spa Suite Hotel & Condominiums   1 Bedroom $$
P.O. Box 2771, 35l Second Ave
Sun Valley (Ketchum), ID 83353
208-726-0999   800-321-6447

Make these condominiums your Sun Valley vacation headquarters. Located at the base of Mt. Baldy, suites have ultra-modern kitchens, woodburning fireplaces and large spa master bath in deluxe suites. 4 season activities, such as ice skating, fishing, golf, and tennis.

Illinois

Galena

---------- GALENA ----------

Eagle Ridge Inn & Resort
Box 777
Galena, IL 61036
800-323-8421 800-892-2269

1 Bedroom $$, 2 Bedrooms $$$, 3 Bedrooms
$$$$
AmEx/Visa/MC, Dep. Req'd.

Location: Airport: Dubuque—20 miles; Downtown: 6 miles; Ski lift: x-country

General Facilities: Full serv., Bus. fac., Conf. rm. cap. 210, Daily maid, Kitchen, Linens, Restaurant on prem., Bar on prem., Game room, Lounge, Child planned rec.: Recreation programs

Room Facilities: Pool, Sauna, Hot tub, Tennis, Lake Galena, Golf: Eagle Ridge Golf Club; TV

Attractions: Historic Galena, Shenandoah Riding Center, Mississippi river cruises, Galena Wine Cellars, entertainment

Shops & Restaurants: Antique shops, Galena shops; Inn's restaurant/continental

Thick stands of trees, grassy meadows, careful landscaping greet you as you enter the main gates. Choose from golf course condominiums or townhouses overlooking the lake, all on 6,800 acres of hilly terrain. Cross-country skiing, Nordic ski center with rental equipment, hot food and bar. Two challenging golf courses, pro shop, lessons, practice fairway. Water sports, tennis, hay and sleigh rides, indoor pool, fishing, recreation programs, or simply sit back, enjoy the relaxed pace, sunsets, scenery.

Indiana

French Lick

============================ FRENCH LICK ============================

French Lick Spring Villas Pool
127 South Maple Street
French Lick, IN 47432
812-935-9381 800-457-4042

Attractions: Exercise room, golf

French Lick Springs Golf & Tennis Villas
French Lick, IN 47432 P-yes
812-936-9981 800-457-4042

General Facilities: Conf. rm., Kitchen, Restaurant on prem., Bar on prem., Game room, Baby-sitter

Room Facilities: Pool, Hot tub, Tennis, Croquet, skeet-trap, Golf: Two 18-hole courses

Attractions: Kimball Piano Factory tour, House of Clock Museum, steam train rides, West Baden tours, entertainment

Shops & Restaurants: Le Bistro, Mr. G's Pizzeria

Lobby with mosaic floor, seating areas overlooking the veranda and marble columns recalling an era of graciousness and quiet charm where high tea is served on Friday and Saturday afternoons. Five full service dining rooms. European mineral spa featuring complete beauty and health regimens. Game room with video games, pool tables, big screen TV. Top name entertainment. Variety of interesting packages. Two exciting golf courses.

Kentucky

Gilbertsville
Cadiz

CADIZ

Vacation Club International
Route 2
Cadiz, KY 42211
502-924-5814

1 Bedroom $, 2 Bedrooms $$, Lo-rise
Pool, Kitchen, Linens

Attractions: Lake Barkley State Resort Park, golf, beaches, boating, horses, trapshooting, exercise room, tennis

One-and two-bedroom villas with screened porches, wall-to-wall carpeting and paddle fans. Comfortably appointed with all household accessories. Rent a boat for fishing or skiing on Lake Barkely. Play tennis, pool, shuffleboard and video games.

GILBERTSVILLE

Ken-Bar Inn Resort and Club
Highway 641, P.O. Box 66
Gilbertsville, KY 42044
502-362-8652

1 Bedroom $$
Lo-rise

General Facilities: Conf. rm. cap. 500, Kitchen, Restaurant on prem., Game room, Child planned rec.: Playgrd.-pool-pond

Room Facilities: Pool, Sauna, Hot tub, Volley, basketball

Attractions: Empire Farms, Homeplace-1850, Environmental Education Center, hiking, jeep touring, fishin, entertainment

Shops & Restaurants: Harbor House/on-site

Set in the lakes region of southwestern Kentucky, known for its two parallel lakes, forming the world's largest man-made body of water. Half mile to the beach, but you may be too busy with the resort activities, such as indoor/outdoor pools, exercise room, hot tub, saunas, game room, volleyball, shuffleboard, horseshoes, basketball, aerobics, nature trail, picnic area and tennis. Younger guests enjoy their own pool, fishing pond and playground. Square or ballroom dancing, country entertainment often.

Louisiana

New Orleans

NEW ORLEANS

Hotel de la Monnaie
405 Esplanade
New Orleans, LA 70116
504-942-3700 800-945-3204

Studio $$$, 1 Bedroom $$$, 2 Bedrooms $$$$
1 Bedrm/week 7$, 2 Bed/week 9$
Dep. 1 Night •
53 condos, Lo-rise, Key at Front desk

Location: Airport: 18 miles; Downtown: ½ mile

General Facilities: Full serv., Bus. fac., Conf. rm. cap. 300, Daily maid, Kitchen, Linens, Baby-sitter

Room Facilities: Pool, Sauna, TV, Phone in rm., Crib-Hi-chair, Ind. AC Ctl., Ind. Heat Ctl.

Attractions: French Quarter attractions, entertainment

Shops & Restaurants: Gucci's, Saks, Macy's; Antoines/Commander's Palace

Explore the French Quarter from this award-winning property with continental elegance reminiscent of Nice, Monte Carlo and Cannes. Units are furnished with French and English antiques near lush, tropical courtyards. Walk to hot jazz, hotter cuisine and wonderful historic sights.

The Quarter House
129 Chartres Street
New Orleans, LA 70130
504-523-5906

1 Bedroom $$$, 2 Bedrooms $$$$
Pool, Daily maid, Kitchen, Phone in rm.

Attractions: French Quarter, Basin Street

One-and two-bedroom suites have whirlpool baths, color television and smoke detectors. Swimming pool, jacuzzi and tropical courtyard. Restaurant and tour reservation service. Accommodations noted for privacy, yet the location is excellent for sightseeing.

Maine

Carrabassett
Valley

Rockport

Kennenbunkport
Ogunquit

───────── CARRABASSETT VALLEY ─────────

Sugarloaf Mountain Resort　　　Kitchen
Carrabassett Valley
Carrabassett Valley, ME 04947
207-237-2000 800-457-0002

Attractions: Hartford Ballet Residency, nature walks, health spa, tennis, golf

───────── KENNEBUNKPORT ─────────

Nonantum Resort
P.O. Box 2626, Ocean Avenue
Kennebunkport, ME 04046
207-967-4050

───────── OGUNQUIT ─────────

Hillcrest Condominiums
Shore Rd, P.O. Box 2000
Ogunquit, ME 03907
207-646-7776

Please mention *Condo Vacations the Complete Guide* when you reserve
your condominium.

———————————— ROCKPORT ————————————

Samoset Resort
Box 78
Rockport, ME 04856
207-594-2511 800-341-1650

1 Bedroom $$, 2 Bedrooms $$$
1 Bedrm/week 5$, 2 Bed/week 7$
Min. Stay 3 Nights, AmEx/Visa/MC, Dep. 1
   Night
72 condos
No S-yes/H-yes

Location: Airport: Augusta 42 miles; Beach front; Ski lift: Camden

General Facilities: Bus. fac., Conf. rm., Kitchen, Restaurant on prem., Bar on prem., Game room, Lounge, Child planned rec.: Playground-Samo camp

Room Facilities: Pool, Sauna, Hot tub, Tennis, Croquet, volleyball, Golf: 18-hole ocean-side course; TV, Cable, Ind. AC Ctl., Ind. Heat Ctl.

Attractions: Lighthouses, Farnsworth Art Museum, Owls Head Transportation Museum, Shakespearean Theatre, entertainment

Shops & Restaurants: Rockport-Rockland-Camden shops, Maine shops, gifts; Marcel's/continental

Year-round resort on the rugged Maine coast. One-bedroom units with balconies, and two-level two bedrooms with whirlpools. Everything you want to do on a summer vacation, plus nearby boutiques and galleries for shopping, sightseeing and cultural entertainment. Winter skiing at Camden Snow Bowl, x-country ski trails, ice skating and sleigh rides. New England dining and nightly lounge entertainment. Keep in shape at the fitness center while the children enjoy the playground and video arcade.

Maryland

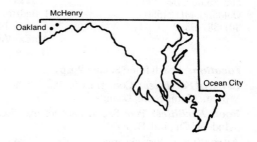

McHenry
Oakland
Ocean City

---------------------------- MCHENRY ----------------------------

Sunplace   2 Bedrooms 4$
P.O. Box 215
McHenry, MD 21541
301-387-7866 800-544-7754

Deep Creek Lake for summer fun, mountains for winter skiing. Cedar exteriors, master bath jacuzzi, garden tub, fireplace. Pool, community building, golf.

Villages of Wisp
P.O. Box 390
McHenry, MD 21541
301-387-4966

Colonial style modern townhouses on Deep Creek Lake along the slopes of Wisp Ski Resort. Serene retreat in beautiful West Maryland.

OAKLAND

Will O' Wisp
Star Route 1, Box 124
Oakland, MD 21550
301-387-5503

1 Bedroom $$, 2 Bedrooms $$$, 3 Bedrooms $$$$
1 Bedrm/week 5$, 2 Bed/week 8$, 3 Bed/week 10$
AmEx/Visa/MC, Dep. Req'd.
Hi-rise

Location: Beach front; Ski lift: Wisp Ski

General Facilities: Conf. rm. cap. 150, Kitchen, Linens, Restaurant on prem., Bar on prem., Game room, Lounge

Room Facilities: Pool, Sauna, Racquet, exercise, Golf: Wisp; TV, Cable, Phone in rm., Ind. AC Ctl., Ind. Heat Ctl.

Attractions: Wisp ski area, Deep Creek Lake

Shops & Restaurants: Four Seasons/continental

Just bring your food, clothes and beach towels. Individually decorated units with sliding glass doors and windows overlooking the lake, patios or balconies for lounging. Elevators, 4th floor washers and dryers. Allegheny mountain skiing. Torchlight ski parade at end of Winterfest weekend. Boat docks, lake cruises, protected swimming area, boat rentals. Indoor pool, full gym, game room, golf and gourmet restaurant. Special vacation plans available.

OCEAN CITY

Boardwalk One
First St. & Boardwalk, Box 762
Ocean City, MD 21842
301-289-3161

Pool, Kitchen

Attractions: Amusements, arcades, shops, ocean

Oceanfront efficencies with private balconies. Choice location on the Boardwalk for area amusements. Atlantic Ocean at your front door. Limited membership to Ocean City Health and Racquetball Club for weight room, aerobic dancing and indoor-heated pool.

The Quay
107th Street & Coastal Highway
Ocean City, MD 21842
800-437-7600

Hi-rise
Pool, Kitchen

Attractions: Miniature golf, tennis

Spacious two-and three-bedroom condominiums with panoramic views of both ocean and bay. 24-hour security, outdoor and indoor pools, nautical recreation area with billiards room.

Sea Watch
115th Street & Coastal Highway
Ocean City, MD 21842
800-437-7600

Hi-rise
Pool, Kitchen

Attractions: Basketball court, tennis

Everything you need within walking distance of these individually decorated apartments. Enjoy sunny days on the white sand beach. Take advantage of the lighted tennis courts, pool, game room, adult billiard room and the relaxing atmosphere of the green atrium.

Massachusetts

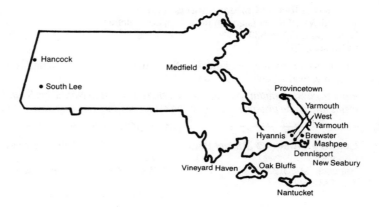

Hancock
South Lee
Medfield
Provincetown
Yarmouth
West Yarmouth
Hyannis • Brewster
Mashpee
Dennisport
Vineyard Haven • Oak Bluffs
New Seabury
Nantucket

―――――――――――――― BREWSTER ――――――――――――――

Brewster Green
South Pond Rd.
Brewster, MA 02631
617-896-5772

Ocean Edge Resort   1 Bedroom $$, 2 Bedrooms $$, Lo-rise
1 Village Dr., Route 6A   Pool, Kitchen, Linens
Brewster, MA 02631
508-896-2781 800-221-1837

Attractions: Melody Tent, Cape Cod Playhouse, Whale Watches, golf, tennis, Basketball, Drive range, tennis, golf

Private designer-decorated villas and townhouses with views of ponds, woods or golf course. Playground and structured activities for children. Golf, tennis lessons and tournaments. Play at the beach or pools, bicycle on the Cape Cod trail. Sunday evening cocktail.

―――――――――――――― DENNISPORT ――――――――――――――

Delray Beach Club   1 Bedroom $, 2 Bedrooms $$
188 Captain Chase Rd, Box 1247   Pool, Kitchen, Linens
Dennisport, MA 02639
508-398-3441

Attractions: One block to beach

Efficiency and one bedroom units one block from the beach. Heated outdoor pool, June to September. Outdoor gas grills.

DENNISPORT

Oceanside Resort Condominiums   Lo-rise
154 Old Wharf Rd. at Glendon Rd.   Pool, Kitchen
Dennisport, MA 02639
617-394-5359

Attractions: Nantucket Island, Martha's Vineyard, deep-sea fishing, National Seashore
hiking, fishing, golf

*Modern condominiums on a gentle rise, steps away from Nantucket Sound. Oceanfront
views and some private porches. In the center of Cape Cod's vacation wonderland.*

HANCOCK

Country Village @ Jiminy Peak   1 Bedroom $$$, 2 Bedrooms $$$$, 3 Bedrooms
Corey Rd. $$$$
Hancock, MA 01237   1 Bedrm/week 7$, 2 Bed/week 10$, 3 Bed/
413-738-5500   week 10$
                                                    Min. Stay 2 Nights, AmEx/Visa/MC,
                                                    Dep. 1 Night
                                                    20 condos, Lo-rise, Key at Front desk, H-yes

Location: Airport: 45 minutes; Downtown: 20 min.; Need car; Ski lift: Jiminy

General Facilities: Full serv., Conf. rm. cap. 200, Daily maid, Kitchen, Linens, Restau-
rant on prem., Bar on prem., Game room, Lounge, Baby-sitter, Child planned rec.: Ski
Wee, Patriot Pk.

Room Facilities: Pool, Sauna, Hot tub, Tennis, Alpine Slide, Golf: Waubeeka; TV, Cable,
Phone in rm., Crib-Hi-chair, Ind. AC Ctl., Ind. Heat Ctl.

Attractions: Williamstown Theatre Festival, Tanglewood, Jacob's Pillow, entertainment

Shops & Restaurants: Jardin/French

*Nestled in the scenic Jericho Valley, these units are furnished in old New England style with
neutral color schemes. Ski Wee and patriots program for the children, and planned win-
ter activities, plus bingo. Larger units have lofts, fireplaces and decks.*

Jiminy Peak Mountain Resort   1 Bedroom $$$, 2 Bedrooms $$$$
Hancock, MA 01237   Pool, Kitchen
413-738-5500

Attractions: Berkshire Museum, Norman Rockwell Museum, Tanglewood, Ioka Valley
Farm., Mt. Greylock, Health club, tennis, golf

*Condominiums with kitchens and sleeping accommodations, most of which include the
use of recreational facilities. Winter ski area in the Berkshires. Night skiing. Ski Wee Learn-
ing Center, supervised playroom and summer recreation activities for children.*

HYANNIS

Cape Winds Resort   Pool, Kitchen, Linens, Phone in rm.
657 West Main Street
Hyannis, MA 02601
617-778-4949

Attractions: Martha's Vineyard, Nantucket, Sandwich Village, Americana Museum &
Gardens, cruises

*Cape Cod condominiums. Clubhouse with video games and big screen television. Many
things to do in the area. Whale watching cruises, April through October, 3 hour canal
cruises, or pack a picnic lunch and spend a day at historic Sandwich Village.*

The Shores

HYANNIS

Hyannis Harborview Resort   1 Bedroom $$
213 Ocean Street
Hyannis, MA 02601
617-775-4420

Location: Downtown: 5 min.
General Facilities: Conf. rm. cap. 150, Restaurant on prem., Bar on prem., Lounge
Room Facilities: Pool, Sauna, Hot tub, Health spa, Ind. AC Ctl., Ind. Heat Ctl.
Attractions: Nantucket and Martha's Vineyard
Shops & Restaurants: Hyannis shops; Neptune Room

Courtesy van picks you up at the airport or bus terminal and brings you to this complete year-round resort. Spacious two-level units with everything you need for your vacation. Sun on the beach, lunch by the pool, watch the fishing boats and sailing ships. In winter walk through the hallways to the indoor pool oasis. Fine dining spots and Crow's Nest Lounge on the premises. 5 minutes to downtown Hyannis shops and attractions. Step out of the courtyard for a day trip to Martha's Vineyard or Nantucket.

HYANNIS

The Breakwaters
Box 118, 432 Sea Street
Hyannis, MA 02601
617-775-6831

1 Bedroom $$, 2 Bedrooms $$, 3 Bedrooms $$
1 Bedrm/week $$$$, 2 Bed/week 4$, 3 Bed/
week 5$
Min. Stay 3 Nights, Dep. Req'd.
18 condos, Lo-rise, Key at Office

Location: Airport: 2 miles; Downtown: l mile; Beach front
General Facilities: Daily maid, Kitchen, Linens, Baby-sitter
Room Facilities: Pool, Golf: 2 miles; TV, Cable, Crib-Hi-chair, Ind. Heat Ctl.
Attractions: Whale watching, fishing, excursions to Nantucket and Martha's Vineyard
Shops & Restaurants: Hyannis Center Shops; Marie Jeans-Up The Creek/fish

The Breakwater is on the beach of Nantucket Sound in a residential area one mile from town and docks. Charming, weathered, gray cottages, blue rugs, white wallpapers with country house furnishings in the Laura Ashley fashion. Swimming pool and decks with harbor views. Three diamond award rating from the American Automobile Association.

The Yachtsman Condominiums
P.O. Box 939, 500 Ocean Street
Hyannis, MA 02601
617-771-5454

2 Bedrms/week 9$, 3 Bed/week 9$
Min. Stay 7 Nights, AmEx/Visa/MC,
Dep. Req'd. •
125 condos, Villas, Key at Rental office

Location: Airport: 2 miles; Downtown: l mile; Need car; Beach front
General Facilities: Kitchen, Baby-sitter
Room Facilities: Pool, Cable, Phone in rm., Crib-Hi-chair, Ind. AC Ctl., Ind. Heat Ctl.
Attractions: Whale watching, Nantucket and Martha's Vineyard, Plymouth Rock
Shops & Restaurants: Cape Cod Mall, Filene's, Jordans; Chillingsworth/French

Multi-level townhouses, full kitchens with dishwashers, washers and dryers and decks. Views of Nantucket Sound. Private beach and heated pool, just minutes away from shopping, dining and sport activities. A convenient, elegant retreat.

MASHPEE

Southcape Resort & Club
Route 28, RFD l
Mashpee, MA 02649
617-477-3990

2 Bedrooms $$, Lo-rise
Pool, Kitchen, Linens

Attractions: Golf, fishing, Martha's Vineyard, Nantucket, Steam rooms, tennis

Pine scented land with country roads for jogging and quaint villages. Two-bedroom condominiums have entertainment areas with hi-fi, fireplaces or jacuzzis and living room big-screen color televisions. Seashore and park are five minutes away.

MEDFIELD

Ocean Watch
14 The Paddock Lane
Medfield, MA 02052
617-956-7640

NANTUCKET

Mariner House
30 Centre St.
Nantucket, MA 02554
617-228-3233

—————————————— Nantucket ——————————————

Monomoy Village
8 Federal Street
Nantucket, MA 02554
617-228-4449

1 Bedrm/week 8$, 2 Bed/week 9$
Min. Stay 7 Nights, Dep. Req'd.
8 condos, Villas

Location: Airport: 1 mile; Downtown: 1 mile; Need car

General Facilities: Kitchen, Linens

Room Facilities: ¼ mile to beach, TV, Cable, Phone in rm., Ind. Heat Ctl.

Attractions: The unique island of Nantucket, preserved as it was in the 19th century.

Shops & Restaurants: 21 Federal/The Boarding House

Newly renovated cottages with pine floors, Shaker furnishings and color coordinated fabrics. Fully equipped kitchens, fireplace, washer/dryer, cable TV, deck or courtyard with furniture and barbecue, all set in a landscaped private compound. Beach sports, art galleries, museums and historic sites.

———————————————————————————————

Tristram's Landing
Madaket
Nantucket, MA 02554
508-228-0359

Min. Stay 3 Nights, Visa/MC, Dep. Req'd.
Lo-rise, Villas, Key at Main office

Location: Airport: 5 miles; Downtown: 5 miles; Need car; Beach front

General Facilities: Daily maid, Kitchen, Linens, Game room, Baby-sitter, Child planned rec.: Play area

Room Facilities: Tennis, Sailing, Canoeing, Phone in rm., Crib-Hi-chair, Ind. Heat Ctl.

Attractions: Fabulous beaches, super ocean activities, sailing, swimming, Great Point excursions

Shops & Restaurants: Nantucket restaurants

Multi-level townhouses with sleeping quarters well separated from living areas. Almost snow-free winters, delightful, warm spring and fall days. Beach, swimming hole, tennis, recreation hall and outdoor play area. Fishing, nature trails, Nantucket Town.

—————————————— NEW SEABURY ——————————————

New Seabury Cape Cod
P.O. Box B
New Seabury, MA 02649
617-477-9111 800-222-2044

Villas

Location: Airport: Boston—1½ hours; Beach front

General Facilities: Conf. rm. cap. 125, Daily maid, Kitchen, Linens, Restaurant on prem., Bar on prem., Game room, Baby-sitter

Room Facilities: Pool, Tennis, Health spa, jogging, Golf: 2 championship courses

Attractions: Sandwich Glass Museum, Heritage Plantation, fishing excursions, jogging and bike trails

Shops & Restaurants: Boutiques, Popponesset Market Place; New Seabury Restaurant

Seaside villas with full housekeeping services on Cape Cod's southern tip. Decor ranges from 19th century Nantucket style with antiques, wide plank floors and French doors, to cool California contemporary. Something for every age, starting with three miles of sandy white beach. Numerous children's activities—movies, waterbug slalom race, beach blanket bingo. Tennis instruction and health spa with Nautilus equipment. Two championship golf courses.

OAK BLUFFS

Island Country Club Inn
P.O. Box 1585
Oak Bluffs, MA 02557
617-693-2002

Studio $$, 1 Bedroom $$, 2 Bedrooms $$
1 Bedrm/week 4$, 2 Bed/week 5$
AmEx/Visa/MC, Dep. Req'd. •
51 condos, Lo-rise, Key at Registr. office
H-yes

Location: Airport: 10 miles; Downtown: 1 mile; Need car

General Facilities: Conf. rm. cap. 200, Daily maid, Kitchen, Linens, Restaurant on prem., Bar on prem., Lounge, Baby-sitter

Room Facilities: Pool, Tennis, Golf: Farm Neck Golf adjacent; TV, Cable, Phone in rm., Crib

Attractions: Bus tours, fishing, charters, sailing

Shops & Restaurants: Anthony's

Informal resort-like property on Martha's Vineyard. Patios and decks with views of Nantucket Sound and Sengekontacket Pond. 24 post and beam suites with fireplaces. Beachcomb, swim, bicycle on scenic paths, fish, windsurf. Three Har-Tru tennis courts, pro shop, tennis pro, lessons. Relax in leisure in this island resort for all seasons.

PROVINCETOWN

Eastwood At Provincetown
324 Bradford St.
Provincetown, MA 02657
508-487-0760 800-462-1126

Kitchen, Linens

Attractions: First landing place of Pilgrims, playhouse, Boston ferry boat, Provincetown Heritage Museu, putting green, shuffleboard, tennis

Bright, airy, professionally decorated condominiums with coordinated carpeting, ceramic tiled kitchen and bathroom floors and custom designed draperies. Clubhouse with fireplace, wet bar, food preparation unit. Picnic tables, gazebo, lawns, shrubs and shade trees.

Fishermans Cove Condominiums
145 Commercial Street
Provincetown, MA 02657
516-487-1397

Sandcastle Condominiums
Route 6A, P.O. Box 576
Provincetown, MA 02657
617-487-9300

1 Bedroom $$

Kitchens, phones, TV's and balconies overlooking Cape Cod Bay. Beach, indoor and outdoor pools and tennis. Hike among the dunes or browse the shops and art galleries of quaint, historic Provincetown.

─────────────── SOUTH LEE ───────────────

Oak 'n Spruce Resort
P.O. Box 237, Meadow Street
South Lee, MA 01260
413-243-3500 800-341-5700

1 Bedroom $$$$, 2 Bedrooms $$$$
1 Bedrm/week 8$, 2 Bed/week 10$
Dep. Req'd.
Lo-rise

Location: Ski lift: x-country

General Facilities: Kitchen, Linens, Restaurant on prem., Bar on prem., Game room, Lounge, Child planned rec.: Supervised activity

Room Facilities: Pool, Sauna, Hot tub, Tennis, Health Club, Golf: 3 par 9-hole course

Attractions: Tanglewood, Norman Rockwell Museum, Jacob's Pillow Dance Festival, Beartown State Forest, entertainment

Shops & Restaurants: On-site restaurant/continental

Year-round resort in the Berkshires. Informal atmosphere with recreation department offering planned activities for children and adults. Have a snack in front of the game room fireplace, fish for trout in the nearby stream, participate in aerobics and water aerobics. Golf, tennis and x-c ski trails. Restaurant features special events, buffets and cookouts.

─────────────── VINEYARD HAVEN ───────────────

Causeway Harborview
Skiff Avenue, Box 450
Vineyard Haven, MA 02568
508-693-1606

Studio $$, 1 Bedroom $$, 2 Bedrooms $$,
3 Bedrooms $$
1 Bedrm/week $$$$, 2 Bed/week $$$$,
3 Bed/week $$$$
Dep. Req'd., 24 condos, Lo-rise, Key at Office

Location: Airport: 15 minutes; Downtown: 10 min.

General Facilities: Daily maid, Kitchen, Linens

Room Facilities: Pool, Water sports, harbor, TV, Crib-Hi-chair, Ind. Heat Ctl.

Attractions: Martha's Vineyard-beautiful scenery, beaches, boating

Shops & Restaurants: Small stores; Black Dog Tavern/New England

Comfortable, homey apartments and cottages in a hillside setting overlooking the beautiful harbor. Minutes walk to town and waterfront activities. The spacious, well-landscaped property has a large pool and picnic sites with barbecues.

─────────────── WEST YARMOUTH, CAPE COD ───────────────

The Englewood Townhouses
60 Broadway
West Yarmouth, Cape Cod, MA 02673
617-775-3900

Two-story townhouses, second-story balconies, first-floor patios. 100 yards to beach, outdoor and indoor pools, tennis, shuffleboard, barbecue area. Weekly rentals.

─────────────── YARMOUTH ───────────────

The Cove at Yarmouth
P.O. Box 1000, Route 28
Yarmouth, MA 02673
617-771-3666

1 Bedroom $$
Pool, Kitchen

Attractions: Hyannis Harbour tours, Kennedy Compound, Martha's Vineyard, Nantucket Island, health spa, racquetball, tennis

Townhouses in the heart of Cape Cod with stereo systems and whirlpool baths. Total recreation environment, area beaches, picnic and barbecue areas. Try windsurfing or deep-sea fishing, ride on the Cape Cod & Hyannis Railroad.

Michigan

Wakefield

Boyne Falls

Bellaire
Traverse City • • Acme
Thompsonville

ACME

Grand Traverse Resort Village
6300 North US-31
Acme, MI 49610
616-938-2100 800-678-1308

Studio $$, 1 Bedroom $$$, 2 Bedrooms $$$, 3
  Bedrooms $$$$
AmEx/Visa/MC, Dep. 1 Night •
293 condos, Hi-rise, Lo-rise, Key at Lobby area
No S-yes/H-yes

Location: Airport: Traverse 5 miles; Downtown: 6 miles; Beach front; Ski lift: 6 areas

General Facilities: Full serv., Bus. fac., Conf. rm. cap. 1750, Daily maid, Kitchen, Linens, Restaurant on prem., Bar on prem., Game room, Lounge, Baby-sitter, Child planned rec.: Crafts, recreation

Room Facilities: Pool, Sauna, Hot tub, Tennis, Health-Racquet Club, Golf: Nicklaus designed "Bear"; TV, Cable, Phone in rm., Crib-Hi-chair, Ind. AC Ctl., Ind. Heat Ctl.

Attractions: Cherry orchard tours, skiing, Winery tours, Sleeping Bear Dunes, Interlochen Music Camp, entertainment

Shops & Restaurants: Tower Gallery of shops, art, wines, clothes; Trillium, Hannah Lay Gourmet

For a carefree getaway, romantic escape or fun-filled family vacation, stay in these golf or lakefront condominiums. Cherry blossoms in the spring and golden leaves in the autumn surround the renowned golf course. Winter skiing, complete Nordic ski center. Charter fishing boats, private game reserve. Complete resort activities including children's programs, video games and pinball. Outdoor cooking facilities at the Beach Club. Casual to elegant dining and nightly entertainment, deli, homemade pizza.

———————————— BELLAIRE ————————————

Shanty Creek-Schuss Mtn. Resort
Bellaire, MI
Location: Beach front; Ski lift: Nearby
General Facilities: Conf. rm., Kitchen, Restaurant on prem., Child planned rec.:
Activity programs
Room Facilities: Pool, Tennis, Health Club, fishing, Golf: "Legend" and Schuss Mt.
Attractions: Canoes, paddleboats, skeet shooting, orchard tours, hayrides, fishing, Lake
Bellaire
Shops & Restaurants: Ivanhof
*These two resorts recently merged to form this complex on northern Michigan's Gold Coast.
Rolling wooded country dotted with natural lakes and streams. Wide variety of activities
for children, winter skiing, summer fishing, hiking and water sports. Private beach club
on the lake. Arnold Palmer and Billy Diddel designed golf courses.*

———————————— BOYNE FALLS ————————————

Boyne Mountain
P.O. Box 1
Boyne Falls, MI 49713
616-549-2441

———————————— THOMPSONVILLE ————————————

Crystal Mountain Resort
Route M-115
Thompsonville, MI 49683
616-378-2911 800-321-4637

Visa/MC, •
36 condos
No S-yes/H-yes

Location: Airport: Cherry Capital; Downtown: 30 min.; Ski lift: On-site
General Facilities: Conf. rm. cap. 225, Kitchen, Restaurant on prem., Bar on prem.
Room Facilities: Pool, Tennis, Canoeing, fishing, Golf: Crystal Mountain Resort; TV,
Cable, Phone in rm., Ind. AC Ctl., Ind. Heat Ctl.
Attractions: Sleeping Bear Dunes National Lakeshore, National Music Camp-Inter-
lochen, entertainment
Shops & Restaurants: Traverse City—30 minutes, antique shops; Brookside/
American
*This year-round resort and conference center offers fine dining, quality golf and tennis.
Sightseeing and water sports abound, with Lake Michigan and numerous inland lakes just
minutes away. A family resort with nightly activities for guests. Scenic rural location and
recreational amenities make it a popular vacation destination.*

---------------------------- TRAVERSE CITY ----------------------------

Pinestead Reef-Vip   1 Bedroom $$, 2 Bedrooms $$, Lo-rise
1265 U.S. 31 N   Kitchen
Traverse City, MI 49684
616-947-4010

Attractions: Sleeping Bear Sand Dunes, Interlochen Music Camp, Pt. Betsie Lighthouse, Shanty Creek, golf

On Grand Traverse Bay with 1,000' of beachfront, luxury resort villas furnished in earthtones. Sail, boat, swim or fish in the Bay. Pinestead-Reef has deep and shallow water docking facilities. Traverse City golf and tennis.

---------------------------- WAKEFIELD ----------------------------

Indianhead Mountain Resort   1 Bedroom $$
500 Indianhead Road
Wakefield, MI 49968
906-229-5181 800-346-3426

Nestled upon a mountain top in a photographers' paradise surrounded by rugged wilderness, quiet and whitewater and waterfalls. Fully equipped kitchens, fireplaces with complimentary wood. Indoor/outdoor recreation complex, golf and tennis.

Our goal is to provide as *complete* a listing of condo vacation properties as possible. If you know of a condo we don't list, please send us their name and address on the form at the back of this Guide.

Minnesota

Park Rapids • • Hill City • Lutsen
Grand Rapids
Detroit Lakes • • Breezy Point
Nisswa • • Deerwood
Brainerd
• Alexandria

Minnetonka •

ALEXANDRIA

Lake Carlos Villas   1 Bedroom $
R.R. #5, South Lake Carlos
Alexandria, MN 56308
612-846-1784

Sunshine or snow, an outstanding family fun region. Fireplaces with wood, TV, radio, decks with grill and furniture. Smowmobile and x-country ski trails. Clubhouse, indoor and outdoor pools, hot tub and sauna. In summer each unit is furnished a boat.

BRAINERD

Causeway On Gull   2 Bedrooms $$$
Route 6, Box 116
Brainerd, MN 56401
218-963-3510 800-247-1216

Room Facilities: Pool, Tennis, Lake, Golf: Gull Lake golf course

Attractions: Sailing, water skiing, fishing, windsurfing, speedboats, snowmobiles, x-country skiing

Rich in architectural design surrounded by more than an acre of wooded land, wooded nature trail outside your door. Tennis courts with ball machine, golf practice facility, 18-foot speedboat. Pool surrounded by plush gardens, stone waterfall and towering pines. Yamaha snowmobiles available for winter use. Four passenger golf cart for riding around.

BRAINERD

Cragun's Pine Beach Lodge
2001 Pine Beach Road
Brainerd, MN 56401
218-829-3591 800-272-4867

Alpine designed cottages and townhouses with fireplaces, in-house audio-visual equipment, smoke alarms and color TV. Sandy beaches, marina, indoor pool, fishing, hunting, tennis, golf, volleyball. Winter x-country skiing, dog and sleigh rides, and skating.

BREEZY POINT

Breezy Point International
HCR2, Box 70
Breezy Point, MN 56472
218-562-7811 800-328-2284

Studio $$, 1 Bedroom $$, 2 Bedrooms $$$$
AmEx/Visa/MC, Dep. Req'd. •
Lo-rise, Key at Front desk
H-yes

Location: Airport: Brainerd 20 miles; Downtown: 20 miles; Need car; Beach front; Ski lift: Ski Bull

General Facilities: Bus. fac., Conf. rm. cap. 750, Daily maid, Kitchen, Linens, Restaurant on prem., Bar on prem., Game room, Lounge, Baby-sitter, Child planned rec.: Full program

Room Facilities: Pool, Sauna, Hot tub, Tennis, Boating, bikes, hike, Golf: Breezy Point 36 holes; TV, Cable, Phone in rm., Crib-Hi-chair, Ind. AC Ctl., Ind. Heat Ctl.

Attractions: Lake, fishing, hiking, golf, skiing, tennis, boating, entertainment

Shops & Restaurants: Antiques and local boutiques, Nisswa Mall; Marina Dining Room/American

Deluxe resort set on the shores of Big Pelican Lake. Rustic elegance, blue, moss green and rust color schemes, fireplaces, jacuzzis and some VCRs. Top 40 band, easy listening music, adult and children recreation programs. Excellent food and entertainment. State-of-the-art convention and meeting facilities. An upbeat fun resort with something for everyone.

DEERWOOD

Ruttgers Bay Lodge & Conf. Center
Box 400
Deerwood, MN 56444
218-678-2885 800-328-0312

1 Bedroom $$, 2 Bedrooms $$$$
Dep. 1 Night
Key at Front desk

Location: Beach front; Ski lift: x-country

General Facilities: Bus. fac., Conf. rm., Daily maid, Kitchen, Linens, Restaurant on prem., Child planned rec.: Summer activities

Room Facilities: Pool, Sauna, Hot tub, Tennis, Volleyball, marina, Golf: Bay Lodge-two 9-hole; TV, Phone in rm., Ind. AC Ctl.

Attractions: Brainerd Lakes Area, summer theatre, historical museums, antique shows, regional festivals, entertainment

Shops & Restaurants: The Country Store, Pro Shop, Corner Sportswear; Colonial Room, on-site

Golf Course condominiums with walkouts overlooking the golf course, and villas adjoining the indoor pool. Modified American Plan packages with special activities available year-round. Marina has boat rentals, tackle and bait. Full range of dining from elegant to casual. Pine-scented forest, daily activity programs and summer Kid's Kamp. X-country ski trail and sleigh rides for winter vacationers. Townhomes, 1 mile from the Lodge, with dockage, launching, tennis court, pool, whirlpool and sauna.

DETROIT LAKES

Breezy Shores Resort
1275 West Lake Drive
Detroit Lakes, MN 56501
218-847-2695 800-346-4978

2 Bedrooms $$, Lo-rise
Pool, Kitchen, Linens

Attractions: Boating, golf, tennis, fishing, ice fishing, snowmobiling, skiing, ice skating, Activity Center, golf

Two-story townhouses with fireplaces-wood supplied-decks and balconies on 800 feet of private beach. Activity center has indoor pool, sauna, whirlpool, game room and social area. Summer boating and water sports, plus nearby golf and tennis.

Edgewater Beach Club
321 Park Boulevard
Detroit Lakes, MN 56501
218-847-1351

2 Bedrooms $$, Lo-rise
Pool, Kitchen, Phone in rm.

Attractions: Detroit Mt. skiing, Tamarac Wildlife Refuge, Soo-Pass "Dude Ranch," Itasca State Park, Marina, golf

Country life with the convenience of town living. Area ski slopes-6 tows. Indoor and outdoor pools and sauna. Lake sports. Beach, marina, tennis, miniature golf, park and playground adjacent. Tamarac Wildlife Refuge. Restaurants and entertainment nearby.

GRAND RAPIDS

Sugar Hills Resort
P.O. Box 369
Grand Rapids, MN 55744
218-326-9461 800-752-5263

1 Bedroom $, 2 Bedrooms $$, Lo-rise
Pool, Kitchen

Attractions: Golf, tennis, boating, skiing, fishing, windsurfing, paddleboats, sailing, Volleyball, hiking

Western ski style condominiums at the base of the hills near the indoor pool, or townhouses surrounded by trees on the golf course near beach, tennis courts and indoor pool. Supervised programs for 4 years and older. Clubhouse dining and cocktails.

HILL CITY

Quadna Mountain Vacation Club   1 Bedroom $$
100 Quadna Rd.
Hill City, MN 55748
218-697-8133 800-422-6649

Villas and townhouses for modern living in a rustic setting. Winter skiing, fall colors and superb hunting, spring and summer fishing and water sports. Indoor/outdoor pools-tennis, horseshoes, badminton, croquet, bocce, shuffleboard, dining, bar and entertainment.

Kana Lani

LUTSEN

The Village Inn and Resort
P.O. Box 26
Lutsen, MN 55612
218-663-7241 800-642-6036

1 Bedroom $$, 2 Bedrooms $$$, Lo-rise
Pool, Kitchen

Attractions: Boundary Waters Canoe Area, alpine slide, hiking, fishing, music festivals, art fairs, volleyball, lawn games, tennis, golf

Condominiums and townhouses on Lake Superior's North Shore and the Sawtooth Mountain Range. Breakfast rides, overnights and hay rides. Indoor pool, jacuzzi, tennis, volleyball, lawn games, Alpine Slide. Recreation programs for children and naturalist programs.

MINNETONKA

Breezy Point Resort
10560 Wayzata Boulevard
Minnetonka, MN 55343
218-562-7811 800-328-2284

Lo-rise
Kitchen

Attractions: Skiing, snowmobiling, fishing, boating, ice fishing, ice skating, Dockside-entertainment, Trapshooting, volleyball, tennis, golf

────────────────────── NISSOVA ──────────────────────

Grand View Lodge
134 Nokomis
Nissova, MN 56468
218-963-2234 800-432-3788

AmEx/Visa/MC •
16 condos
No S-yes/H-yes

Location: Airport: 17 miles—Brainerd; Downtown: 17 miles

General Facilities: Bus. fac., Conf. rm. cap. 350, Kitchen, Restaurant on prem., Bar on prem., Child planned rec.: Activities program

Room Facilities: Pool, Sauna, Hot tub, Tennis, Sailing, riding, TV, Cable, Phone in rm., Ind. AC Ctl., Ind. Heat Ctl.

Attractions: Grand View Gardens, entertainment

Shops & Restaurants: Sundries, gift shop; Kavanaughs/French

Located in northern Minnesota lake country, Grand View Lodge sits among tall pines, sandy beaches and deep blue waters. Exceptional dining, friendly service and a vacation with activities for the entire family. You'll especially enjoy the resort's famous flower gardens.

────────────────────── PARK RAPIDS ──────────────────────

North Beach Vacation Club
Niawa Star Route
Park Rapids, MN 56470
218-732-9708 800-362-3145

Townhouses with views of the lake. Winter skiing, summer sailing, canoeing, swimming. Jog or bike on scenic trails in the crystal clear air. Shipwreck Supper Club for dining and entertainment. Playground for the children.

Our listings—supplied by the managements—are as complete as possible. Many of the condos have more features than we list. Be sure to inquire when you book.

Mississippi

Gulfport

GULFPORT

Shoreline Oaks
30 East Beach Blvd, P.O. Box 6823
Gulfport, MS 39501
601-868-1916

1 Bedroom $$, 2 Bedrooms $$
1 Bedrm/week $$$$, 2 Bed/week 4$
Min. Stay 2 Nights, Visa/MC, Dep. Req'd.
10 condos, Lo-rise, Key will be arranged
H-yes

Location: Airport: 5 minutes; Downtown: 5 min.; Need car; Beach front

General Facilities: Kitchen, Linens

Room Facilities: Pool, Hot tub, TV, Cable, Ind. AC Ctl., Ind. Heat Ctl.

Attractions: Excursions to the islands, Marine life, water activities, Casino cruise ships, historical

Shops & Restaurants: Edgewater Mall and individual specialty stores; Cajun, Mexican, Italian

A five minute drive from the airport and you're in your Shoreline Oaks condominium. The beach is across the street, and should you tire of the water activities, take an island excursion, visit the many historical attractions, or board a casino cruise ship. Shaded grounds for a family picnic or barbecue, private patio or deck and even an ice bucket and corkscrew for the wine!

Missouri

Osage Beach
Lake Ozark

Joplin • Galena
Lakeview • • Branson
Kimberling City   Reeds Spring

BRANSON

Alpine Lodge
S.R. 1, Box 795 Indian Point
Branson, MO 65616
417-338-2514

1 Bedroom $, 2 Bedrooms $

Less than 1 mile from Silver Dollar City in Shepherd of the Hills country, individual Alpine lodges and two-bedroom A-Frame cottages overlooking Table Rock Lake and the Ozark hills. Each unit has picnic tables and grills. Spend the day at the pool with a slide.

Bentree Lodge
Indian Point Road, Box 967
Branson, MO 65616
417-338-2218 800-272-6766

1 Bedroom $$
AmEx/Visa/MC, Dep. 1 Night •
20 condos, Lo-rise, Key at Front desk

Location: Airport: 45 miles; Need car

General Facilities: Conf. rm. cap. 200, Daily maid, Kitchen, Linens, Restaurant on prem., Bar on prem., Game room, Lounge, Baby-sitter

Room Facilities: Pool, Sauna, Hot tub, Tennis, Fitness center, TV, Phone in rm., Crib-Hi-chair, Ind. AC Ctl., Ind. Heat Ctl.

Attractions: Boating, skiing, fishing, Silver Dollar City, music shows

Shops & Restaurants: Bentree Restaurant/continental

Set on 15 acres, 1.5 miles south of Silver Dollar City on Indian Point Road, overlooking beautiful Table Rock Lake. Two pools, jacuzzi, sauna, tennis courts, game room, restaurant and lounge. Elegantly furnished suites with color TV, queen-sized beds and direct dial phones.

BRANSON

Del Mar Resort on Lake Taneyco
Lakeshore Dr. S.R. 4, Box 2193
Branson, MO 65616
417-334-6241

1 Bedroom $, 2 Bedrooms $, Lo-rise
Pool, Kitchen, Linens

Attractions: Silver Dollar City, White Water, Shepherd of the Hills Farm., Country Music
shows, Horseshoes, badminton

On the shores of Lake Tanneycomo in the Ozark Mountains. Open acreage with trees, playground with horseshoes, tetherball, volleyball, badminton and plenty of room for softball and soccer. Fishing dock where boats, licenses, bait, tackle, gas and oil are available.

Happy Valley Lodge
S.R. 1, Box 849
Branson, MO 65616
417-338-2342

1 Bedroom $, 2 Bedrooms $, Lo-rise
Pool, Kitchen, Linens

Attractions: Car museum, trout hatchery, School of the Ozarks Museum, Sammy Lane
Pirate cruise, crafts, horseshoes

When you want to get away from city living into the serenity of the mountains. Pool with water slide, playground with swings and slide, games, ski and pontoon boat rentals. All fishing needs available for bass fishing in the clean, unpolluted lake.

Lakeshore Resort
P.O. Box 537
Branson, MO 65616
417-334-6262

Large air-conditioned, heated cottages with windows overlooking the lake. Family resort with playground, recreational and picnic areas with grills on tree lined grounds. Year-round fishing, lighted, covered steel boat dock and pool.

Ozarks Prime Resort
Star Route 4, Box 2668
Branson, MO 65616
417-334-6800

Pointe Royale Village
Box 1988
Branson, MO 65616
417-334-0079

1 Bedroom $$, 2 Bedrooms $$$
Pool, Kitchen, Linens

Attractions: Fishing, boating, tennis, golf

Vacation condominiums along the 18-hole golf course with patios or decks. Fine fishing, rental boats, supplies, guide. Scuba dive, sail or boat at Table Rock State Park Marina. Special golf and fishing packages with continental breakfast and complimentary wine.

BRANSON

Riverpoint Estates Luxury Condos   2 Bedrooms $$
Box 966   Pool, Kitchen
Branson, MO 65616
417-334-6721

Attractions: Silver Dollar City, country music shows, fish hatchery, pirate cruise, white water, playground, tennis

Two-and three-bedroom condominiums with fireplaces, caarpeted living rooms, 7-foot beds, pool and lake views. Club House lounge with wet bar and refrigerator-freezer. Excellent trout fishing, launching ramp, and private dock slips steps away from your front door.

GALENA

Lake Country Resort & Golf Club   1 Bedroom $$, 2 Bedrooms $$, 3 Bedrooms $$
Hwy. Y-18, Route 3, Box 91   1 Bedrm/week $$$$, 2 Bed/week $$$$, 3 Bed/
Galena, MO 65656   week $$$$
417-538-2291   Min. Stay 2 Nights, AmEx/Visa/MC, Dep. 2
Nights
16 condos, Lo-rise, Villas, Key at Infor. center
H-yes

Location: Airport: 1 hour; Downtown: 30 min.; Need car

General Facilities: Full serv., Bus. fac., Conf. rm. cap. 50, Daily maid, Kitchen, Linens, Restaurant on prem.

Room Facilities: Pool, Hot tub, Tennis, Hike, Bike, Water, Golf: On site; TV, Crib-Hi-chair, Ind. AC Ctl., Ind. Heat Ctl.

Attractions: Silver Dollar City, Shepherd of the Hills, music shows

Shops & Restaurants: Battlefield & Lakeview shopping, antiques & crafts; Wooden Nickel/steaks-ribs-fish

Super comfortable condominiums with views of the lake, golf course, or bluffs. There are numerous recreational and entertainment facilities within a short drive. Many guests prefer to stay at the Village condominiums with its wood and homey earth tones, electric fireplaces and cathedral ceilings, and just enjoy the quiet and privacy of the pool or 9-hole golf course.

JOPLIN

Loma Linda Estates & Country Club
Route 5, P.O. Box 1000
Joplin, MO 64801
417-781-2620

KIMBERLING CITY

Idyllwilde Reosrt
Route 3, Box 674
Kimberling City, MO 65686
417-739-4951

1 Bedroom $, 2 Bedrooms $$
Dep. 2 Nights •
13 condos, Lo-rise, Key at Office

Location: Airport: 45 minutes; Downtown: 5 miles; Need car; Beach front

General Facilities: Kitchen, Linens, Game room, Baby-sitter

Room Facilities: Pool, Putting green, Golf: 4 miles; TV, Crib-Hi-chair, Ind. AC Ctl., Ind. Heat Ctl.

Attractions: Shepherd of the Hills, golf, Talking Rocks Caverns, Lost Silver Mine Play

Shops & Restaurants: Shopping centers, antiques, crafts, pottery, gifts; All types

Nicely furnished apartments among oak and hickory trees on Table Rock Lake for active vactioners. Little ones will love fenced-in playground especially for them. Also a playground with climbing ropes and tree house. Covered boat dock with electrical hook-up, boat rentals, pool, shuffleboard, horseshoes, and miniature putting green. Game room, picnic area, grills.

Kimberling Inn Resort & Vacation
P.O. Box 159, Highway 13
Kimberling City, MO 65686
417-739-4311 800-833-5551

Studio $, 1 Bedroom $$, 2 Bedrooms $$$
Dep. 1 Night •
100 condos, Lo-rise, Key at Lobby
P-yes/H-yes

Location: Airport: 45 miles; Need car

General Facilities: Bus. fac., Conf. rm. cap. 200, Daily maid, Kitchen, Linens, Restaurant on prem., Bar on prem., Game room, Lounge, Baby-sitter, Child planned rec.: Games, golf

Room Facilities: Pool, Sauna, Hot tub, Tennis, Boat docks, Golf: Kimberling Hills CC near; TV, Cable, Phone in rm., Crib-Hi-chair, Ind. AC Ctl., Ind. Heat Ctl.

Attractions: Silver Dollar City, 1880's Theme Park, country music shows, Shepherd of the Hills

Shops & Restaurants: Pier Supper Club/steaks-fish

Lakefront condominiums adjacent to Kimberly Inn Resort, with full use of all resort amenities. Exclusive and private family vacation atmosphere, but within walking distance to Kimberling City for shopping, browsing and dining. Full fun opportunities on Table Rock Lake. Easy drive to area attractions.

LAKE OZARK

Holiday Shores
Hwy. 54, P.O. Box 812
Lake Ozark, MO 65049
314-348-3438

Pool, Kitchen

Attractions: Ha Ha Tonka Castle & Park, Bagnell Dam, Bridal Cave, Grand Glaize Bridge, Ozarks Watershow, Lake, fishing, golf

Two-bedroom loft units for six with large balconies. Some units have whirlpool tubs and lake views. Set on a wooded hillside above the Lake of the Ozarks with local marinas to provide your boating and fishing needs. Lake of the Ozarks Park is nearby.

———————————————— LAKE OZARK ————————————————

The Lodge of Four Seasons   2 Bedrooms $$$
P.O. Box 215, Lake Road HH   Villas
Lake Ozark, MO 65049
314-365-3000 800-365-3001

General Facilities: Bus. fac., Conf. rm. cap. 1000, Kitchen, Restaurant on prem., Bar
on prem., Lounge, Baby-sitter, Child planned rec.: Supervised activity

Room Facilities: Pool, Sauna, Tennis, Fitness Center, bikes, Golf: 18-hole R.T. Jones
course; TV

Attractions: Entertainment

Shops & Restaurants: Toledo Room-HK's/Fish Market

*Award-winning resort with a staff committed to warm and caring hospitality. Secluded
villas among the trees with lake views. Relax and be pampered at the Spa, dine at the four-
star restaurants, be entertained at The Fifth Season. The best equipment and facilities for
golf and tennis. Marina for boating, water sports, indoor-outdoor pools, supervised chil-
dren's programs, babysitting. Face-body massages, hair care, boutiques, cinema.*

———————————————— LAKEVIEW ————————————————

Notch Estates Condominiums   1 Bedroom $$, 2 Bedrooms $$
P.O. Box 2097   Min. Stay 2 Nights, AmEx/Visa/MC,
Lakeview, MO 65737   Dep. 1 Night
417-338-2941   36 condos, Lo-rise, Key at Registr. Lobby

Location: Airport: 45 miles; Downtown: 6 miless; Need car

General Facilities: Daily maid, Kitchen, Linens

Room Facilities: Pool, Hiking trail, TV, Ind. AC Ctl., Ind. Heat Ctl.

Attractions: Silver Dollar City, Shepherd of the Hills play, Music shows

Shops & Restaurants: Two miles to small shopping area; Wooden Nickel/steaks-
seafood

*All new units with walk-out decks overlooking scenic countryside located in the heart of
the Ozark Mountains, just one mile west of Silver Dollar City, yet away from the traffic.*

———————————————— OSAGE BEACH ————————————————

Lake Chalet Resort   AmEx/Visa/MC, Dep. Req'd.
Route 2, Box 3986   7 condos, Lo-rise, Key at Best Western Inn
Osage Beach, MO 65065   H-yes
314-348-4718

Location: Airport: 55 miles; Need car

General Facilities: Full serv., Kitchen, Linens, Restaurant on prem., Bar on prem.,
Game room, Lounge, Baby-sitter, Child planned rec.: Play area

Room Facilities: Pool, Shuffleboard, TV, Cable, VCR, Phone in rm., Crib-Hi-chair, Ind.
AC Ctl., Ind. Heat Ctl.

Attractions: Water Theme Park, caves, Ha-Ha Tonka State Park, fish, boating, music
shows, Bagnell Dam

Shops & Restaurants: Osage Village Factory, Merchant Mall, Oneida store; Blue
Heron/intercontinental

*Condominiums overlooking the Lake of the Ozarks, professionally decorated in blue tones.
Boating at your door, 2 outside swimming pools, swimming area and lakeside dock. Play
area with swings for children. Planned get-acquainted gatherings for adults.*

———————————————— OSAGE BEACH ————————————————

Lakewood Condominiums
RR #2, Box 59-401
Osage Beach, MO 65065
314-348-1721

Marriott's Tan-Tar-A Resort   Villas
State Road K.K.
Osage Beach, MO 65065
314-348-3131 800-392-5304

Location: Airport: St. Louis—30 min.

General Facilities: Kitchen, Restaurant on prem., Bar on prem., Game room, Lounge, Child planned rec.: Planned activities

Room Facilities: Pool, Hot tub, Tennis, Aerobics, bowling, Golf: One 9-hole, one 18-hole

Attractions: Bridal Cave and Ha Ha Tonka State Park, excursion boat rides, Stephens College Theatre

Shops & Restaurants: Outlet mall, antique shops; Wildrose on the Water

Water sports and golf are given top priority here. Lakefront villas with incredible views peek out of trees. Organized recreational programs for children 5 years and older, and special teen programs. Nightly, live entertainment and wide screen T.V. Full health spa, indoor and outdoor tennis, jogging trails, fishing, horseback riding and choice of two golf courses.

———————————————— REEDS SPRING ————————————————

Bar M Ranch   1 Bedroom $, 2 Bedrooms $, Lo-rise
HCR 4, Box 2990
Reeds Spring, MO 65737
417-338-2593

Off the beaten track, on a private road, spacious property with a Western atmosphere. Quiet walks, pool sunbathing, hot and cold whirlpool spas. Steel dock opening on a wide waterway for fishing, water skiing, swimming. Boat rentals. Woods for walking.

Montana

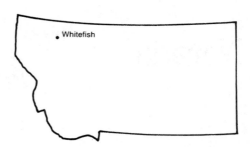

Whitefish

WHITEFISH

Bay Point Estates
300 Bay Point Drive, Box 35
Whitefish, MT 59937
406-862-2331

1 Bedroom $
Visa/MC •
50 condos

Location: Airport: Glacier—9 miles; Downtown: ¾ mile; Ski lift: Big Mtn.

General Facilities: Conf. rm. cap. 50, Kitchen, Child planned rec.: Summer program

Room Facilities: Pool, Sauna, Hot tub, Hiking, fishing, Golf: ¾ mile—Whitefish; TV, Cable, Phone in rm., Ind. Heat Ctl.

Attractions: 25 miles from Glacier Nat'l Park, Big Mountain Ski Resort, Whitefish Lake, Flathead Lake

Shops & Restaurants: Art galleries, clothing, sporting goods; Whitefish Lake Restaurant

Condominiums furnished in various styles on Whitefish Lake across from the 27-hole golf course. View decks with barbecues, 600' lake frontage and indoor pool. Summer program for children allows parents to enjoy their holiday. Relaxed homey atmosphere where memories are made—not just a place to sleep.

The Edelweiss
Box 55
Whitefish, MT 59937
406-862-3687 800-858-5439

1 Bedroom $$$, 2 Bedrooms $$$$
Kitchen, Phone in rm.

Attractions: Glacier National Park, skiing, sleigh rides, x-country skiing, Spa

Located in the heart of the Big Mountain Alpine Village. Units furnished with contemporary interiors, queen-size beds and patios. Ski all day and come home to a hot toddy in front of the fireplace, or a moonlit sleigh ride through the snow.

Nevada

Incline Village
Lake Tahoe
Zephyr Cove
Stateline

Las Vegas

INCLINE VILLAGE

All Seasons Resorts
P.O. Box 4268, 807 Alder Avenue
Incline Village, NV 89450
702-831-2311 800-322-4331

1 Bedroom $$, 2 Bedrooms $$
Pool, Daily maid, Kitchen, Linens

Attractions: Lake Tahoe, Diamond Peak ski area, casinos, golf, tennis, Weight Center

Condominiums with fireplaces, wood not provided, at Incline Village, a planned recreational community. On-site clubhouse with pool, spa-whirlpool, weight center and sun deck. Passes for Incline's private beaches are available at the front desk.

Club Tahoe
914 Northwood Boulevard, Box 4650
Incline Village, NV 89450
702-831-5750 800-527-5154

2 Bedrooms $$$, Lo-rise
Pool, Kitchen, Linens, Phone in rm.

Attractions: Reno, Tahoe and Carson City casinos, boating, swimming, fishing, hiking, skiing, gym, racquetball, tennis, golf

10,000-square-foot facility houses these two-bedroom condominiums with sleeping loft. Two TVs, multiplex stereo, washer/dryer, and fireplace. Workout in the universal gym and racquetball courts, lighted tennis courts, horseshoe pits and swimming pool.

Coeur du Lac Condominiums
Lakeshore Blvd. & Juanita
Incline Village, NV 89450
702-831-3318

1 Bedroom $$, 2 Bedrooms $$, Lo-rise
Pool, Kitchen, Linens

Attractions: Skiing, golf, water ski, fish, casinos, Recreation Center

Secluded condominiums 1 block from a private beach. Rustic, roomy interiors with beamed ceilings, redwood paneled walls and wood burning fireplaces. Recreation center with pool, jacuzzi and saunas. Ski a different area every day.

Popu Kapili

INCLINE VILLAGE

Forest Pines Condos
P.O. Box 4057
Incline Village, NV 89450
702-831-1307 800-458-2463

1 Bedroom $$, 2 Bedrooms $$, Lo-rise
Pool, Kitchen, Linens

Attractions: Lake Tahoe, casinos, skiing, tennis, golf, swimming, fishing, boating

Condominiums in a pine tree studded landscape with uncluttered views. Central parking and minimum interior roadways for less automobile noise. Recreation building with outdoor pool, indoor jacuzzi, sauna and game room. Close to Lake Tahoe beaches and winter skiing.

L'Ermitage
Southwood Blvd.
Incline Village, NV 89450
702-813-3318

Lo-rise
Kitchen

Attractions: Skiing, golf, boating, water sports, sailing, water skiing, jet skiing

Park-like setting with pines. Architecturally designed, decorator condominiums with wood burning fireplaces, fully equipped wet bar, master bedroom walk-in closet, trash compactor and barbecue on dining room deck. Walk to beaches, boat launch, pool and tennis.

INCLINE VILLAGE

Lakeside Tennis & Ski Resort
P.O. Box 5576, 987 Tahoe Blvd.
Incline Village, NV 89450
702-831-5258 800-222-2612

Studio $$, 1 Bedroom $$, 2 Bedrooms $$$,
3 Bedrooms $$$$
1 Bedrm/week 5$, 2 Bed/week 6$, 3 Bed/
week 9$
Min. Stay 2 Nights, AmEx/Visa/MC, Dep. 1
Night •
36 condos, Lo-rise, Key at Front desk, H-yes

Location: Airport: 45 minutes; Downtown: 3 min.; Need car; Ski lift: Incline

General Facilities: Full serv., Bus. fac., Conf. rm. cap. 20, Daily maid, Kitchen, Linens,
Restaurant on prem., Bar on prem., Baby-sitter

Room Facilities: Pool, Hot tub, Tennis, Golf: Incline Golf Course; TV, Cable, Phone in
rm., Crib-Hi-chair, Ind. Heat Ctl.

Attractions: M.S. Dixie dinner/dance on the lake, Ponderosa Ranch, Truckee raft rides,
water skiing

Shops & Restaurants: Le Petite Pier/French

*Contemporary furnishings to rustic and modern with varying color schemes. A five-minute
walk to the beach or drive to Ski Incline. Tennis packages and clinics are available. Water
sports in the summer or winter skiing in this beautiful Tahoe setting.*

McCloud At Incline Village
144 Village Boulevard
Incline Village, NV 89450
702-832-7170 800-841-7443

1 Bedroom $$, 2 Bedrooms $$$, Lo-rise
Kitchen, Linens, Phone in rm.

Attractions: Beaches, tennis, skiing, casinos, hiking, sailing, horseback riding, golf

*Condominium clusters among the pines. Wood exteriors, wood, glass, stone and light
colors in the interiors. Thermal windows, pathways to hot tub and sauna and separate
buildings for parking. Close to the lake and Incline Village. 20 ski areas within 45 minutes.*

Third Creek
929 Northwood Boulevard
Incline Village, NV 89450
702-831-9821

1 Bedroom $$$$, 2 Bedrooms $$$$, Lo-rise
Pool, Kitchen, Linens

Attractions: Skiing, horseback riding, tennis, golf, lake swimming, casinos, nightlife

*Solar condominiums with wood exteriors. Interiors have vaulted ceilings, rock fireplaces,
cedar decks and airy solariums. Well landscaped with stone-lined paths and wooden
bridges, among the pines, streams and flowers. Relax in the outdoor jacuzzi after skiing.*

LAKE TAHOE

Stillwater Cove
Incline Village
Lake Tahoe, NV 89450
702-831-5400

1 Bedroom $$$$, 2 Bedrooms $$$$, Lo-rise
Kitchen, Linens

Attractions: Skiing, beach, boats, trout fishing, sailing, windsurfing, water skiing,
tennis, golf

*One to five bedroom condominiums on 23 acres of wilderness with 2000 feet of lake front-
age. Granite steps to the Beach House and promenade deck. Steel pier with boats; buoys
for personal boats and Harbormaster to teach sailing, windsurfing and water skiing.*

LAS VEGAS

The Cage House   Pool, Daily maid, Kitchen, Linens
105 East Harmon Avenue
Las Vegas, NV 89109
702-798-1020

Ultra modern resort hotel. Large heated pool, spa, tennis court and sun deck. Complimentary service to the airport and local casinos. One-half block from The Strip-the heart of excitement and glamour.

Sheffield Inn   Pool, Daily maid, Kitchen
3970 Paradise Road
Las Vegas, NV 89109
712-796-9000

This gracious resort has suites with whirlpool tub-for-two and satellite TV. The tree-lined parkland area features a pool and jacuzzi. Manager's nightly reception and complimentary continental breakfast.

STATELINE

Ridge Tahoe   2 Bedrooms $$$
P.O. Box 5790, 400 Ridge Club Dr.   Min. Stay 2 Nights, Dep. Req'd.
Stateline, NV 89449   Key at Front desk
702-588-3553 800-648-3341

Location: Airport: Reno International; Downtown: 6 miles; Need car; Ski lift: 1 mile

General Facilities: Full serv., Conf. rm., Daily maid, Kitchen, Linens, Restaurant on prem., Bar on prem., Game room, Lounge

Room Facilities: Pool, Hot tub, Tennis, Weight room, racquet, TV, Cable, VCR

Attractions: Stateline Casinos, skiing, lake cruises, horseback riding, fishing, yachting

Shops & Restaurants: Ridge Club 5-star dining room

Elegant, casual rustic interiors in these suites perched on a mountain peak, minutes from Heavenly Valley, casinos and Tahoe's beaches. Enjoy the soothing rooftop spa beneath the stars, overlooking the mountains and valley. Spend the evening dining and dancing at the Ridge Club, after skiing or tennis. Summer lake activities and miles of trails to explore.

ZEPHYR COVE

Pine Wild   3 Bedrooms $$$
600 Highway 50, P.O. Box ll347   Min. Stay 2 Nights, Visa/MC, Dep. Req'd. •
Zephyr Cove, NV 89448   135 condos, Lo-rise, Key at Sales office/on site
702-588-2790 800-822-2790   No S-yes

Location: Airport: 10 miles; Downtown: 5 min.; Need car

General Facilities: Conf. rm. cap. 30, Daily maid, Kitchen, Linens, Baby-sitter

Room Facilities: Hot tub, Tennis, Boat dock, Golf: Edgewood Tahoe-2 miles; TV, Cable, VCR, Phone in rm., Crib-Hi-chair, Ind. Heat Ctl.

Attractions: South Shore casinos, skiing, snowmobiling, boating, horses, golf, tennis, star entertainment

Shops & Restaurants: Round Hill Mall, Safeway, specialty shops; Zackery's/Midnight Mine//Ricos

Spacious two-story townhouses with wood-burning fireplaces, cable color TV, and two private decks. Lake and beachfront units have a second fireplace in the master bedroom. Just 5 minutes from South Shore casinos. Security gate system and beautifully landscaped.

New Hampshire

Franconia
Lincoln • • Bartlett
Bretton Woods \ • Jackson
Woodstock
• Gilford
• Plymouth
Waterville Valley •
Weirs Beach •
Laconia •

• Weare

BARTLETT

Attitash Mountain Village
Route 302
Bartlett, NH 03812
603-374-6501 800-862-1600

Studio $$, 1 Bedroom $$, 2 Bedrooms $$$,
 3 Bedrooms $$$$
Min. Stay 2 Nights, AmEx/Visa/MC, Dep.
 Req'd. •
170 condos, Lo-rise, Key at Front desk
H-yes

Location: Airport: 65 miles; Downtown: 6 miles; Need car; Ski lift: Attitash

General Facilities: Full serv., Bus. fac., Conf. rm. cap. 100, Daily maid, Kitchen, Linens,
Restaurant on prem., Bar on prem., Game room, Lounge, Baby-sitter, Child planned
rec.: Playground

Room Facilities: Pool, Sauna, Hot tub, Tennis, Basketball, TV, Cable, Phone in rm.,
Crib-Hi-chair, Ind. AC Ctl., Ind. Heat Ctl.

Attractions: Skiing, hiking, sightseeing, amusement areas, snowmobiling, x-country
skiing, entertainment

Shops & Restaurants: Major factory outlet area; Doolittle/on-site, Bernerhof

*Surrounded by 750,000 acres of White Mountain National Forest, with snow covered
mountains for winter skiing, pond ice skating and sleigh rides. The rest of the year, relax
in the sparkling sunlight, swim in the pool or river, bike, hike and canoe. Children's play-
ground, tennis and 18-hole courses nearby. The spacious condominiums offer country
sophistication with modern conveniences, many with fireplaces, whirlpools, wood stoves
and loft bedrooms.*

———————— BRETTON WOODS ————————

Mount Washington   Location: Ski lift: Nearby
Route 302
Bretton Woods, NH 03575
603-278-1000 800-258-0330

General Facilities: Conf. rm. cap. 700, Kitchen, Restaurant on prem., Bar on prem.,
Baby-sitter

Room Facilities: Pool, Tennis, Croquet, hiking, Golf: 18-hole course

Attractions: Victorian stables for trail rides, lessons, complete tennis program

Shops & Restaurants: Antiques; Main dining room

This Spanish Renaissance inspired hotel has been designated a National Historic Landmark. Dining room has an extensive wine list and an orchestra to accompany your evening meal. Complete tennis program, riding stables and championship golf. Activities department always has something planned, rain or shine.

———————— FRANCONIA ————————

Mittersill Timeshare Resort
Route 18, Mittersill Rd.
Franconia, NH 03580
603-823-5511

———————— GILFORD ————————

Samoset at Winnipesaukee   2 Bedrooms $$, Lo-rise
2696 Lake Shore Road, Route 11   Pool, Kitchen
Gilford, NH 03246
603-293-8823 800-338-2163

Attractions: Tennis

Townhouses designed to blend into the white-pine wooded and lake surroundings. Well insulated with thermopane windows, fireplaces, carpeting and easy-care vinyl. Skiing, snowmobiling, sleigh rides, toboggan slides.

———————— JACKSON ————————

Nordic Village
Jackson, NH 03860
603-383-4265

———————— LACONIA ————————

Overlook at Winnipesaukee
257 Weirs Boulevard, Route 3
Laconia, NH 03246
603-528-2756

The best in four-season living on the shores of Paugus Bay on Lake Winnipesaukee. Large units with complete access to pool, hot tub, tennis, docks and mooring facilities.

─────────────── LACONIA ───────────────

Steele Hill, Phase 1
RFD #1, Box 190
Laconia, NH 03246
603-524-0500

Lo-rise
Pool, Kitchen

Attractions: Racquetball, tennis, golf

500 acres of unspoiled farmland and hardwood forests overlooking Lake Winnipesaukee. Pressure-free, comfortable vacation. Glass solarium surrounding the exterior of the wood-paneled dining room. Amenities building with bar, lounge, weight room and game room.

─────────────── LINCOLN ───────────────

Riverfront Condominiums
Kancanmagus Highway, Box 477
Lincoln, NH 03251
603-745-3441

Rivergreen
P.O. Box 696
Lincoln, NH 03251
603-745-6261   800-654-6183

Pool, Kitchen, Phone in rm.

Attractions: Exercise room, golf

Superior accommodations set alongside the Pemigewasset River. Suites include individual jacuzzis. Free shuttle service to Loon. Pools, sauna, library and enclosed barbecue area.

Village of Loon Mountain
P.O. Box 508
Lincoln, NH 03251
603-745-3401   800-258-8932

Studio $$, 1 Bedroom $$$, 2 Bedrooms $$$,
    3 Bedrooms $$$
Min. Stay 2 Nights, AmEx/Visa/MC,
    Dep. Req'd. •
220 condos, Key at Registr. office

Location: Airport: 75 mi. Manchester; Need car; Ski lift: Loon Mtn.

General Facilities: Bus. fac., Conf. rm. cap. 100, Restaurant on prem., Bar on prem., Game room, Lounge, Baby-sitter, Child planned rec.: Activities program

Room Facilities: Pool, Sauna, Hot tub, Tennis, Phone in rm., Ind. Heat Ctl.

Attractions: All major area attractions are within 5 miles. Across from a major ski area—41 trails, entertainment

Shops & Restaurants: Mill Front Mall, many small shops; Dickens/gourmet, Common Man

Loon Village is secluded on 240 wooded acres, surrounded by the White Mountain National Forest. A four-season resort with tennis courts, paddle tennis courts, two indoor and two outdoor pools, whirlpools, saunas, ice skating rink, downhill skiing and teen center. Scandinavian furnishings in this centrally located resort, with lounge and bingo. D.G. Wagoner's is the village nightspot with weekend entertainment. Grocery store on the premises.

———————————————— PLYMOUTH ————————————————

Cold Spring Resort 1 Bedroom $$, 2 Bedrooms $$, 3 Bedrooms $$
RR 3, Box 40 1 Bedrm/week $$$$, 2 Bed/week 4$, 3 Bed/
Plymouth, NH 03264 week 5$
603-536-4600 Dep. Req'd.

Location: Ski lift: Loon Mt.

General Facilities: Restaurant on prem., Lounge, Baby-sitter

Room Facilities: Pool, Sauna, Tennis, Kiddie Pool, Golf: 18-hole; TV, Cable, Phone in rm.

Shops & Restaurants: Terrace on the Green

Designed to blend into the lush foliage and Revolutionary heritage of Cold Spring with exquisite interior design and scenic views from every window. All winter and summer sports, exploding autumn colors, trout and salmon fishing. Covered bridges, old stone mills and gem mines and Revolutionary farmhouses for the history buff. The restored Club House, where you can play cards, sit by the fire, or enjoy a cocktail on the terrace, was originally built during colonial days. Terrace on the Green for dining.

———————————————— WATERVILLE VALLEY ————————————————

Black Bear Lodge 1 Bedroom $$
Box 357 1 Bedrm/week $$$$
Waterville Valley, NH 03223
603-236-8371 800-258-8988

Location: Ski lift: 10 min.

General Facilities: Kitchen, Game room

Room Facilities: Pool, Sauna, Tennis, Ice skating, TV, Cable, Phone in rm.

A good place for two couples wishing to share a vacation. Access to Sports Center, game room, indoor pool, sauna and jacuzzi. Fieldstone fireplace in the lobby for socializing. Children under 5 ski free. Get in shape at the fitness center, indoor tennis, racquetball and squash courts. Video arcade and soda fountain.

Golden Eagle Lodge Hi-rise
Condominiums Kitchen, Linens
Waterville Valley
Waterville Valley, NH 03223
603-236-4205 800-552-4767

Attractions: White Mountain attractions, covered bridges, N.H. Science Center, scenic drives, waterfall

Built to contemporary hotel standards with wood finish exteriors and decorator-furnished interiors offering views of Corcoran's Pond and White Mountain peaks. Within easy walking distance to beach and boating on the pond, indoor sports center, with pools.

─────────── WATERVILLE VALLEY ───────────

Inns of Waterville Valley
Snowbrook Road, P.O. Box 411
Waterville Valley, NH 03215
603-236-8366

1 Bedroom $$, 2 Bedrooms $$
1 Bedrm/week $$$$, 2 Bed/week 4$
Min. Stay 2 Nights, Visa/MC, Dep. Req'd.
19 condos, Lo-rise, Key at Next door

Location: Airport: 65 miles; Downtown: 22 miles; Need car; Ski lift: Nearby

General Facilities: Daily maid, Kitchen, Linens, Baby-sitter, Child planned rec.: Town program

Room Facilities: Pool, Sauna, Hot tub, Weight room, Golf: 9-hole adjacent; TV, Cable, Phone in rm., Crib-Hi-chair, Ind. Heat Ctl.

Shops & Restaurants: Limited; Carnevale's/Northern Italian

Well-appointed, comfortable condominiums decorated in earth tones. All units have kitchens with microwaves and in-room jacuzzis and some have hot tubs. In the heart of the White Mountains; numerous summer activities; winter skiing at Waterville Valley.

───

The Village Inn
P.O. Box 1
Waterville Valley, NH 03215

───

Windsor Hill Condominiums
Route 49
Waterville Valley, NH 03215
603-236-8321 800-343-1286

Studio $$$, 1 Bedroom $$$, 2 Bedrooms $$$$,
3 Bedrooms $$$$
1 Bedrm/week $$$$, 2 Bed/week 5$, 3 Bed/
week 5$
Min. Stay 2 Nights, AmEx/MC, Dep. Req'd. •
132 condos, Lo-rise, Key at On-site office

Location: Airport: 2 hours; Need car; Ski lift: Nearby

General Facilities: Daily maid, Kitchen, Linens, Baby-sitter, Child planned rec.: Town recreation ctr.

Room Facilities: Pool, Golf: Waterville Valley; TV, Cable, Crib-Hi-chair, Ind. Heat Ctl.

Attractions: White Mountain attractions, craft fairs, ski swaps, music festivals, ski competitions

Shops & Restaurants: Jugtown Country Store, Post Office, shops; Several fine restaurants

Each home has its own private entrance from the outside. Outdoor heated swimming pool with sun deck, several picnic areas with tables and grills throughout the 10-acre site. Alpine and cross-country skiing from Thanksgiving into April. 9-hole golf course, 18 clay tennis courts, 4.5 acre lake with sandy beach, climbing and hiking trails and trout fishing. Town sponsored recreation program for the whole family.

─────────────── WEARE ───────────────

Lake Shore Village Resort
744 Reservoir Dr.
Weare, NH 03281
603-529-1800

Lo-rise
Pool, Kitchen

Attractions: Dixfield Notch, Six Gun City, Old Man of the Mountain, The Flume, Lost River, Polar Caves, Volley Basketball, tennis, golf

Your warmly furnished cottage overlooks Lake Horace and has a private dock, boat & motor, fieldstone fireplace and sliding glass windows. Spring fishing, hiking, golf; summer lake swimming, waterskiing, tennis; fall hiking, hunting, and canoeing.

Kaanapili Shores

―――――――――――――――――― WEIRS BEACH ――――――――――――――――――

Cedar Lodge at Brickyard Mt.
Route 3, P.O. Box 5293
Weirs Beach, NH 03246
603-366-4316

Studio $$, 1 Bedroom $$$, 2 Bedrooms $$$$
1 Bedrm/week 6$, 2 Bed/week 7$
AmEx/Visa/MC, Dep. Req'd.
23 condos, Hi-rise, Key at Front desk

Location: Airport: Gilford 20 minutes; Downtown: 10 min.; Need car; Ski lift: Loon Mt.

General Facilities: Full serv., Daily maid, Kitchen, Linens, Child planned rec.: Playground

Room Facilities: Pool, Tennis, TV, Cable, Ind. AC Ctl., Ind. Heat Ctl.

Attractions: Boat cruise on Winnipesaukee, train rides, sea plane rides, horses, boating

Shops & Restaurants: K-Mart, Zayre, Star market, Hallmark gift shop; The Manor/American-French

Enjoy serenity, privacy and panoramic views of Lake Winnipeasaukee and mountains. Double beds in bedroom, sliding glass doors to balcony and full-size bathtubs. Lodge is set atop Brickyard Mountain to protect you from road noises. Inviting, homey, individually decorated units with pool, tennis, playground and lawn games. Many family activities in nearby Weirs Beach.

--------------------- WEIRS BEACH ---------------------

Village at Winnipesaukee   2 Bedrooms $$$
Route 3, P.O. Box 5276   Pool, Kitchen, Linens
Weirs Beach, NH 03246
603-366-4878

Attractions: Excursion boat trips, seaplane rides, parachute jumping, kite skiing, theatre, museums, volleyball, basketball

Two-and three-bedroom condominiums with patios or balconies. On-site tennis, picnic grounds and swimming. Short walk to private beach and dock. Winter skiing, summer water sports, fall harvest fairs and frosty days, spring flowering fruit trees and lake trout.

--------------------- WOODSTOCK ---------------------

Jack O'Lantern Resort   Pool, Kitchen
1-93 Route 3
Woodstock, NH 03251
603-745-8181

Attractions: Tennis, golf

Beautifully landscaped 250-acre resort along the Pemigewassset River. 6100 yard, par 70, 18-hole golf course and pro shop. Game room, snack bar, and lounge with entertainment.

Our listings—supplied by the managements—are as complete as possible. Many of the condos have more features than we list. Be sure to inquire when you book.

New Jersey

Atlantic City

ATLANTIC CITY

Park Lane
177 S. Illinois Ave.
Atlantic City, NJ 08401
609-344-8277

1 Bedroom $$
1 Bedrm/week 7$
Dep. Req'd.
44 condos, Hi-rise, Key at Office

Location: Airport: 3 miles; Downtown: walk

General Facilities: Full serv., Conf. rm. cap. 50, Daily maid, Kitchen, Linens, Lounge, Baby-sitter

Room Facilities: TV, Phone in rm., Crib-Hi-chair, Ind. AC Ctl.

Attractions: Casinos, shows, Boardwalk, boxing matches, horse racing, Ice Capades, Miss America Pageant

Shops & Restaurants: Downtown shops; Casino restaurants

Comfortable apartments in wicker and cane one block from the beach. Fish, swim, sunbathe, walk on the beach and Boardwalk, and try your hand at games of chance in the 12 casinos. Dine at the casinos and enjoy their nightly entertainment. Guest Services Department for free and discount show and restaurant tickets.

New Mexico

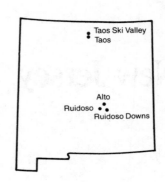

Taos Ski Valley
Taos

Alto
Ruidoso
Ruidoso Downs

ALTO

High Country Lodge
P.O. Box 137, Highway 37
Alto, NM 88312
505-336-4321

Lo-rise
Pool, Kitchen

Attractions: Recreation area, tennis

The closest lodging to New Mexico ski areas. Cozy units with fireplaces, covered porches and outdoor barbecue grills. For non-skiers, enclosed pool, spa, saunas, table tennis, video games and pinball machines. Tennis, playground, horseback riding and trout fishing.

RUIDOSO DOWNS

Champions Run
P.O. Box 601
Ruidoso Downs, NM 88346
505-378-8080

2 Bedrooms $$$, Lo-rise
Pool, Kitchen, Linens

Attractions: Golf, hiking, fishing, hunting, horseback riding, Ruidoso Downs Race
Track, skiing

Walk to the Ruidoso Downs Race Track from these townhome-style condominiums with terraced, spacious floor plans. Two-and three-bedroom homes have wood burning fireplaces, jacuzzis in master bath and microwaves. Ski from Thanksgiving through Easter.

RUIDOSO

Carrizo Lodge
P.O. Box 1371-M 513
Ruidoso, NM 88345
505-257-9131

1 Bedroom $$
Pool, Kitchen, Phone in rm.

Attractions: Skiing, golf, tennis, swimming, fishing, hiking, horseback riding, hunting, fitness center

Resort surrounded by the Lincoln National Forest with rustic lodging accommodations. Original lodge is listed on the National Register of Historic Places. Fish for trout in Carrizo Creek, which wanders through the property.

Crown Point Condominiums
P.O. Box 4179 HS
Ruidoso, NM 88345
505-257-9182

2 Bedrooms $$, Lo-rise
Pool, Kitchen, Linens

Attractions: Horse racing, nightclubs, stores, mountain hiking, racquetball, tennis

Fully furnished condominiums on top of a mountain overlooking Ruidoso with views of the valley. Enjoy a leisurely walk in the mountains among the tall trees. Relax in the library while the children play video games. Free laundry facilities.

Fairway Meadows Condos
Box 2428
Ruidoso, NM 88346
Kitchen

Two-bedroom, two-bath units with washer/ dryers, fireplaces and free firewood. Ski packages available.

High Sierra Condominiums
P.O. Box 4179 H.S.
Ruidoso, NM 88345
505-257-6913

1 Bedroom $$, 2 Bedrooms $$$, Lo-rise
Pool, Daily maid, Kitchen, Linens, Phone in rm.

Attractions: Space Museum, White Sands Nat. Monument, Valley of the Fires, summer racing, art galleries, basketball, tennis

High on Camelot Mountain, overlooking lake of the Inn of the Mountain Gods and surrounding hills. Condominiums with laundry rooms, wet bars and fireplaces in the middle of the woods. A hike in the woods may bring you glimpses of deer or wild turkeys.

The Springs Condominiums
1230 Mechem
Ruidoso, NM 88345
505-258-5056

2 Bedrooms $$, 3 Bedrooms $$$
2 Bedrms/week 5$, 3 Bed/week 7$
Visa/MC,Dep. Req'd. •, 22 condos,
Lo-rise, Key at Main office, P-yes/H-yes

Location: Airport: Ruidoso 30 minutes; Downtown: 3 miles; Need car; Ski lift: Apache
General Facilities: Daily maid, Kitchen, Linens, Baby-sitter
Room Facilities: Pool, Hot tub, Horseshoes, TV, Cable, Crib-Hi-chair, Ind. Heat Ctl.
Attractions: Flying J Ranch chuckwagon show, Ruidoso Downs Race Track, Ski Apache, Smokey Bear Natl. Forest
Shops & Restaurants: Art galleries, gift, ski shops, clothing boutiques

Tucked away like a village unto itself, the Springs offers a life-style of tall pines, cool, quiet nights and the warm glow of a roaring fire. Year-round attractions in the cool mountains of the Southwest desert and plains, where winter becomes a real wonderland.

─────────────────────── RUIDOSO ───────────────────────

Vantage Point
P.O. Box 356
Ruidoso, NM 88345
505-258-3100

1 Bedroom $$, 2 Bedrooms $$,
Lo-rise Kitchen

Attractions: Ruidoso Downs horse racing, fishing, horseback riding, swimming, tennis, golf

Fully carpeted units with rock fireplaces in a quiet, peaceful setting. Close to the ski area turnoff, and special shortcut to the race track. Sun decks on upper units, and lower units have enclosed courtyards with grills.

West Winds Lodge & Condos
208 Eagle Drive, P.O. Box 1458
Ruidoso, NM 88345
505-257-4031 800-421-0691

Studio $$, 1 Bedroom $$, 2 Bedrooms $$,
    3 Bedrooms $$$$
Visa/MC,Dep. 1 Night •
14 condos, Lo-rise, Key at Office
H-yes

Location: Airport: 20 miles; Downtown: 2 blocks; Ski lift: Nearby

General Facilities: Conf. rm. cap. 20, Daily maid, Kitchen, Linens

Room Facilities: Pool, Hot tub, Horse racing, Golf: Cree Meadows; TV, Cable, Crib-Hi-chair, Ind. Heat Ctl.

Attractions: Billy the Kid historic tours, Apache Indian Reservation, quarterhorse races, scenic tours

Shops & Restaurants: Art galleries, gift shops, jewelry and leather; La Lorraine-Fr./Cattle Baron

Two-story condominiums with upstairs loft, modern earth toned furnishings, in a quiet, restful setting. Indoor heated pool and hot tub, Cree Meadows Golf Course and Ski Apache. Horseracing from May to Labor Day, summer festival concert series in June, motorcycle festival, mule racing, street fair and chili cook-off. Space Hall of Fame, ghost towns, petroglyphs, and Valley of the Fires lava flows.

Whispering Bluff Condos
White Mountain Drive
Ruidoso, NM 88345

─────────────────────── TAOS SKI VALLEY ───────────────────────

The Kandahar
P.O. Box 72
Taos Ski Valley, NM 87525
505-776-2226

1 Bedroom $$, 2 Bedrooms $$$
Kitchen, Phone in rm.

Attractions: All levels of skiing, Health Spa

Mountain-style living in ski-in/ski-out condominiums. Health spa with weight training center, steam bath and jacuzzi. Entertainment and restaurants a few steps away. Sit in front of a crackling fire while you watch your favorite TV shows after a day of skiing.

─────────────── TAOS SKI VALLEY ───────────────

Sierra Del Sol
P.O. Box 84
Taos Ski Valley, NM 87525
505-776-2981 800-523-3954

Studio $$$, 1 Bedroom $$$$, 2 Bedrooms $$$$
1 Bedrm/week 10$, 2 Bed/week 10$
Min. Stay 3 Nights, AmEx/Visa/MC,
   Dep. Req'd. •
32 condos, Lo-rise, Key at Office on site
No S-yes

Location: Airport: 19 miles; Downtown: 19 miles; Need car; Ski lift: Taos
General Facilities: Conf. rm. cap. 30, Daily maid, Kitchen, Linens, Baby-sitter
Room Facilities: Skiing, TV, Crib-Hi-chair, Ind. Heat Ctl.
Attractions: Historic Taos, Taos Plaza, Wheeler Peak Wilderness Area, Carson Nat.
   Forest
Shops & Restaurants: Taos art galleries, Indian crafts, jewelry stores

Spacious condominiums with fireplaces only 70 yards away from Taos Ski Valley's main chair lifts, ski shops and ski rentals. In summer, there is trout fishing, nature walks in the forest, art festivals, and Pueblo Indian ceremonies. Raft the Rio Grande, listen to chamber music, or enjoy the hot tubs and saunas. Walking distance to all shops, restaurants and nightlife with on-site parking.

───

The Twining Condominiums
P.O. Box 696
Taos Ski Valley, NM 87525
505-776-8648 800-552-0070

2 Bedrooms $$$$
Kitchen, Linens, Phone in rm.

Attractions: Taos skiing, Taos art colony

Studio units with extensive kitchens and living area. Two-story, two-bedroom units with fireplaces, jacuzzi master baths and balconies in Taos Ski Valley. All lifts, lodges, restaurants and lounges are within walking distance. 19 miles to Taos Art Colony.

─────────────────── TAOS ───────────────────

Quail Ridge Inn
P.O. Box 707
Taos, NM 87571
505-776-2211 800-624-4448

Studio $$, 1 Bedroom $$$, 2 Bedrooms $$$,
   3 Bedrooms $$$$
AmEx/Visa/MC, Dep. Req'd. •
110 condos, Lo-rise, Key at Front desk

Location: Airport: Taos--5 miles; Downtown: 4 miles; Need car; Ski lift: Taos
General Facilities: Full serv., Conf. rm. cap. 125, Daily maid, Kitchen, Linens, Restaurant on prem., Bar on prem., Lounge, Baby-sitter, Child planned rec.: Shortie swatters
Room Facilities: Pool, Sauna, Hot tub, Tennis, Racquetball, TV, Cable, Phone in rm.,
   Crib-Hi-chair, Ind. Heat Ctl.
Attractions: Taos Ski Valley, Taos Indian Pueblo, Millicent Rogers Museum, Rio Grande
   Gorge, art gallery, entertainment
Shops & Restaurants: Arts and crafts, Indian artifacts, clothing; Carl's French Quarter/Cajun

Personal attention from the staff of this modern pueblo-style resort set in the unspoiled country of the Sangre de Cristo Mountains. Southwest adobe condominiums with fireplaces for the cool nights. Tennis and racquetball clinics, instruction and tournaments. Taos area not only has year-round activities from water sports to skiing but also offers art and music festivals, theatres, lectures and art exhibitions for a true Southwestern vacation experience.

New York

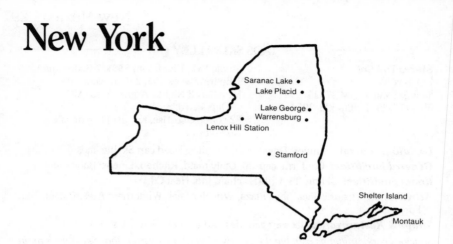

Saranac Lake •
Lake Placid •

Lake George •
• Warrensburg •
Lenox Hill Station

• Stamford

Shelter Island

Montauk

LAKE GEORGE

Depe Dene
Lake Shore Dr, Rt. 9N, Box 2422
Lake George, NY 12845
518-668-2788

Lo-rise
Pool, Kitchen, Linens

Attractions: Saratoga Racetrack, Great Escape, Waterslide, Fort William Henry, amusement parks, canoes, shuffleboard, golf

Two-story townhouses located directly on the shoreline of Lake George. All the conveniences of home in a mountain setting. Sit on the beach and watch the activity or use one of the resort's rowboats, kayaks or canoes. Rivers and streams for spring fishing.

Top of the World Townhouses
RR #1, Box 1390
Lake George, NY 12845
518-668-5716

LAKE PLACID

Wildwood on the Lake
88 Saranac Avenue
Lake Placid, NY 12946
518-523-2624

LENOX HILL STATION

Club Getaway
Box 606
Lenox Hill Station, NY 10021
212-935-0222

Pool, Daily maid, Kitchen, Linens

Attractions: Covered bridges, Tanglewood, vineyards, antiques, crafts, Torys Cave, archery, fitness center, tennis

Prepaid getaway vacations which include meals, wine, sports, instructions, entertainment and lodging. Set in the lawns and woodland meadows of the Berkshires, surrounded by mountains and overlooking a private lake.

———————————— MONTAUK, LONG ISLAND ————————————

Gurney's Inn Resort & Spa
Old Montauk Highway
Montauk, Long Island, NY 11954
516-668-2345 800-832-1131

2 Bedrooms $$$, Lo-rise
Pool, Daily maid, Kitchen, Linens, Phone in rm.

Attractions: Montauk Point lighthouse, golf, tennis, fishing, boating, Marino therapeutic spa

Beach cottages featuring large decks and glass-enclosed sunporches. Custom designed in soft, relaxing sea and sky colors, Italian floor tiles. Convertible sofa bed and fireplace in living room. Adult Health & Beauty Spa with separate male and female pavilions.

———————————— SARANAC LAKE ————————————

Ampersand Bay Resort
Saranac Lake
Saranac Lake, NY 12983
518-891-3001

1 Bedroom $$, 2 Bedrooms $$$, Lo-rise
Kitchen, Linens

Attractions: Olympic arena, summer ski jumping, chamber music, theatre, climbing, Whiteface Mtn., lake activities

Rustic Adirondack log cabins for four to six people. Carefree vacationing on wilderness rivers and lakes. Motor boats and canoes to rent or bring your own boat for a trip to one of the many islands for a secluded picnic. Fantastic fishing.

Mahana

SARANAC LAKE

Castle Point Resort
Condominiums
1 Will Rogers Drive
Saranac Lake, NY 12983
518-891-2220

SHELTER ISLAND

Pridwin Resort (The)　　　　Pool, Kitchen
Crescent Beach
Shelter Island, NY 11946
516-749-0476

Attractions: Golf, charter boats, open boat fishing, charter sailing, billiards, ping-pong, tennis

Comfortable housekeeping cottages in a rural atmosphere between the eastern tips of Long Island. Woodlands, meadows, flowers, wildlife and sandy beaches for sunning and water sports. Electronic indoor games. Summer buffets, cookouts, dancing and entertainment.

STAMFORD

Deer Run Resort　　　　　　Studio $$$, 1 Bedroom $$$, 2 Bedrooms $$$$
Route 10, P.O. Box 251　　　　AmEx/Visa/MC, Dep. Req'd.
Stamford, NY 12167　　　　　　45 condos, Villas, Key at Front desk-deposit
607-652-2001 800-252-7317　　H-yes

Location: Airport: Albany—1-¼ hours; Downtown: 3 miles; Need car; Ski lift: Deer Run

General Facilities: Conf. rm., Daily maid, Kitchen, Linens, Restaurant on prem., Bar on prem., Game room, Lounge, Baby-sitter, Child planned rec.: Button Buck Ski Sch.

Room Facilities: Pool, Sauna, Hot tub, Tennis, Skiing, boating, Golf: Stamford Country Cl. near; TV, Phone in rm., Crib-Hi-chair, Ind. AC Ctl., Ind. Heat Ctl.

Attractions: Baseball and Soccer Halls of Fame, James Fenimore Cooper House, Howe Caverns, game farm, entertainment

Shops & Restaurants: Oneonta Mall, Penney's, Jamesway, Nichols, Ames DS; Hidden Inn/seafood steaks

Beautiful lakefront villas in the scenic Catskill Mountains, modern furniture in earth tones, mirrored walls and natural wood paneling around fireplace. On-site Antler Lodge offers fine dining. Day trips to the many area attractions, sports programs, indoor/outdoor heated pools, fishing in two lakes, hiking, camping, canoeing, sailing and bowling.

WARRENSBURG

Green Mansion Country Club　　1 Bedroom $$, 2 Bedrooms $$$$, Lo-rise
Estate　　　　　　　　　　　Kitchen
Box 370, Green Mansions Road
Warrensburg, NY 12885
516-494-3721

Attractions: Adirondacks, Pack Forest, sporting events

Summer and winter resort in the Adirondacks, adjacent to Pack Forest with tall pines and a spring-fed lake. Fully equipped condominiums with fireplaces, continuous-clean ovens and dishwashers. Many units have stereos and washer/dryers.

North Carolina

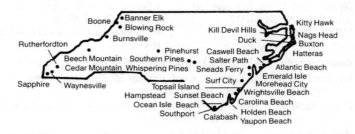

ATLANTIC BEACH

A Place At The Beach
Fort Macon Rd, P.O. Box 1140
Atlantic Beach, NC 28512
919-247-2636 800-334-2667

2 Bedrooms $$, Villas
Pool, Kitchen

Attractions: Tennis

Near Fort Macon State Park on beautifully landscaped grounds with a full range of recreational facilities. The pool has a waterslide and hot tub. Playground area, tennis and sport courts.

Fairfield Resorts
E. Fort Macon Rd., P.O. Box 1140
Atlantic Beach, NC 28512
919-247-2636 800-334-2667

Peppertree Resort
Salterpath Rd.
Atlantic Beach, NC 28512
919-247-2092

Sands Villa Resort
P.O. Box 1140, Fort Macon Road
Atlantic Beach, NC 28512
919-247-2636 800-334-2667

1 Bedroom $$, 2 Bedrooms $$, Hi-rise
Pool, Daily maid, Kitchen, Linens

Attractions: Sports court, tennis

Villas on 25 acres of landscaped grounds with washer/dryer, microwave, balcony and whirlpool in master bath. Water oriented recreation on the beach, pier, indoor and outdoor pools. Lighted tennis courts. Visit the old port town of Beaufort for antique shops.

---------------------------- ATLANTIC BEACH ----------------------------

Whaler Inn Beach Club   1 Bedroom $$, 2 Bedrooms $$$
3600 Slater Path Rd, P.O. Box 220   1 Bedrm/week 5$, 2 Bed/week 6$
Atlantic Beach, NC 28512   Visa/MC,Dep. 1 Night
919-247-4169   46 condos, Hi-rise, Key at Front desk
                                     H-yes

Location: Airport: 30 miles; Downtown: 5 miles; Need car; Beach front

General Facilities: Full serv., Conf. rm. cap. 50, Daily maid, Kitchen, Linens, Game room, Child planned rec.: Supervised games

Room Facilities: Pool, Sauna, Hot tub, Basketball, Volleyball, Golf: Bogue Country Club; TV, Cable, Crib-Hi-chair, Ind. AC Ctl., Ind. Heat Ctl.

Attractions: Dinner and harbor cruises, outer banks still untouched by man, ocean, dining, sightseeing.

Shops & Restaurants: Food Lion, Eckerds, Rose's Department Store; Beaufort House, Blackbeards

Luxurious condominiums at affordable prices on the ocean. Tuesday night dinners for guests, lock-in on Thursday nights for teenagers, sand castle sculpture contests on Fridays. Basketball and volleyball on the property with fine dining and shopping nearby. Supervised games for the children—a real family vacation.

---------------------------- BANNER ELK ----------------------------

Adams Apple   1 Bedroom $$, 2 Bedrooms $$
Route l, Box 298   Kitchen, Linens
Banner Elk, NC 28604
704-963-4950 704-963-6325

Attractions: Basketball, tennis

An abundance of peace and quiet in these condominiums on the western slope of Grandfather Mountain. Stone fireplaces and private decks. Hiking and fishing, mountain living.

The Highlands at Sugar   1 Bedroom $$, 2 Bedrooms $$, Hi-rise
P.O. Box 892, Highland Drive   Pool, Kitchen
Banner Elk, NC 28604
704-898-9601

Attractions: Grandfather Mountain, hiking, mile-high swinging bridge, Linville Falls, Linville Caverns, weight room, spa, golf

Maagnificent scenery high in the Blue Ridge Mountains. Units with jacuzzis, fireplaces, picture windows, and wet bars. Free shuttle to Sugar Mountain ski slopes. Tennis and horseback riding available on Sugar Mountain.

Mossy Creek at Sugar Mountain
Sugar Mountain Resort, Hwy. 184
Banner Elk, NC 28604
704-898-6311

BANNER ELK

Pinnacle Inn
P.O. Box 1136
Banner Elk, NC 28604
704-387-4276 800-438-2097

Studio $, 1 Bedroom $$, 2 Bedrooms $$
1 Bedrm/week $$$$, 2 Bed/week 4$
Min. Stay 2 Nights, AmEx/Visa/MC,
Dep. 1 Night •
242 condos, Lo-rise, Key at Front office

Location: Airport: 2 hours; Downtown: 3 miles; Need car; Ski lift: Ski Beech

General Facilities: Conf. rm. cap. 75, Daily maid, Kitchen, Linens

Room Facilities: Pool, Sauna, Hot tub, Tennis, Shuffle, steam room, TV, Cable, Phone in rm., Crib-Hi-chair, Ind. Heat Ctl.

Attractions: Grandfather Mountain, Linville Caverns, Tweetsie RR, Mystery Hill, Linn Cove Viaduct, entertainment

Shops & Restaurants: Fred's General Mercantile, Mast general store; Teaberrys/steak-seafood-fowl

Four-season resort. Minutes to Ski Beech, the highest ski area east of the Rockies. Brilliant autumns, cool, green summers, and an abundance of wild flowers in the spring. The All Seasons Centre has an indoor pool, sauna, steam, exercise and game room. For non-swimmers, there's a viewing deck. In the summer, there are weekly activities programs, daily health and fitness routines. Bridge and bingo nights. Tennis-shuffleboard complex. Summer welcome cocktail party and restaurant night each week.

Sugartop Resort & Country Club
Rt. 1, Box 397, Hwy. 184
Banner Elk, NC 28604
704-898-6211 800-438-4555

2 Bedrooms $$$, Hi-rise
Pool, Kitchen, Linens

Attractions: Golf, tennis, hiking, skiing, Spring Fling, New Year's Eve Torchlight Parade, exercise room

Mountain condominiums with fireplaces, wet bars and covered balconies. Sugar Mountain skiing with several slopes suited for racing. Ski school for children 5 to 10. Well-planned recreational programs in summer, as well as golf, tennis, and hiking.

BEECH MOUNTAIN

Four Seasons at Beech
Rt. 2, Box 56F, Beech Mt. Parkway
Beech Mountain, NC 28604
704-387-4211

Studio $, 1 Bedroom $$
1 Bedrm/week $$$$
AmEx/Visa/MC, Dep. Req'd. •
35 condos, Lo-rise, Key at Front desk
H-yes

Location: Airport: 56 miles; Need car; Ski lift: Nearby

General Facilities: Conf. rm. cap. 125, Daily maid, Linens, Restaurant on prem., Bar on prem., Baby-sitter, Child planned rec.: Skiwee, summer camp

Room Facilities: Skiing, Golf: Beech Mountain-near; TV, Cable, Crib-Hi-chair, Ind. Heat Ctl.

Attractions: 5 ski areas, 6 golf courses, Gorge and Grandfather Mt. scenic areas, Tweetsie RR Park

Shops & Restaurants: Crafts, Boone Mall, furniture outlet stores; Teaberry's-/American

One-and two-room condominiums in a Tudor-style lodge atop Beech Mountain, directly across from ski area, in America's highest town. Summers are cool with light breezes to help make the most of the many recreational activities and sightseeing opportunities.

──────────────── BEECH MOUNTAIN ────────────────

The Pinnacle Inn
Beech Mtn. Pkwy.
Beech Mountain, NC 28604
704-387-4276 800-438-2097

──────────────── BLOWING ROCK ────────────────

Chetola Resort
North Main Street, P.O. Box 205
Blowing Rock, NC 28605
704-295-9301 800-243-8652

1 Bedroom $$, 2 Bedrooms $$
1 Bedrm/week 4$, 2 Bed/week 5$
Min. Stay 2 Nights, AmEx/Visa/MC,
  Dep. Req'd. •
60 condos, Villas, Key at Chetola Lodge

Location: Airport: 90 miles; Downtown: 3 blocks; Need car; Ski lift: Nearby

General Facilities: Full serv., Bus. fac., Conf. rm. cap. 75, Kitchen, Linens, Restaurant on prem., Bar on prem., Child planned rec.: Summer day camp

Room Facilities: Pool, Sauna, Hot tub, Tennis, Racquet, fitness center, TV, Cable, Phone in rm., Crib-Hi-chair, Ind. AC Ctl., Ind. Heat Ctl.

Attractions: Waterfalls, hiking, crafts, plays, cultural events, family attractions, entertainment

Shops & Restaurants: Local craft guilds; Claire's-S.C. low country

Set in the mountains adjacent to Blue Ridge Parkway and surrounded by a National Park. Recreation Center with daily planned activities and children's summer day camp. Tennis, racquetball, indoor pool, fitness center, and a lake for trout fishing and canoeing.

───

Hound Ears Club   P-yes
Box 188
Blowing Rock, NC 28605
704-963-4321

Location: Ski lift: Nearby

General Facilities: Conf. rm. cap. 60, Kitchen, Restaurant on prem., Bar on prem., Baby-sitter

Room Facilities: Pool, Tennis, Golf: Hound Ears Club

Attractions: Tweetsie Railroad, Glendale Springs, Roan Mountain, entertainment

Shops & Restaurants: Antiques, arts and crafts; Hound Ears Club Dining Room

A rather small, four-season resort, remote and secluded, yet offering an atmosphere where service and comfort are at a premium. Intimate dining room done in sea-greens and warm garden colors where Gene Fleri plays the organ. Brown Bagg Lounge with dance floor. The hard-to-find swimming pool is adjoined by a rock grotto and pavilion creating a setting of unsurpassed natural beauty. Stables and bridle trails a few miles away. Scenic golf course.

BLOWING ROCK

Swiss Mountain Village
Flat Top Road, Rt. 2, Box 86
Blowing Rock, NC 28605
704-295-3373

Studio $, 1 Bedroom $$, 2 Bedrooms $$
1 Bedrm/week $$$$, 2 Bed/week $$$$,
3 Bed/week $$$$
Min. Stay 2 Nights, Dep. 1 Night •
40 condos, Villas, Key at Office on site
H-yes

Location: Airport: 35 miles; Downtown: 1.5 mile; Need car; Ski lift: Nearby
General Facilities: Daily maid, Kitchen, Linens, Bar on prem., Baby-sitter
Room Facilities: TV, Cable, Crib-Hi-chair, Ind. Heat Ctl.
Attractions: Golf, tennis, horseback, white water rafting, Appalachian Ski Mountain
Shops & Restaurants: Crafts & outlet, chain store, groceries; Many types

Log cabins built of natural materials with rough hewn log walls and native stone fireplaces. Chalets with stairway to the loft over the stone fireplace. Hiking in the forest filled with rhododendron and laurel, and trout fishing with no license required. Attractions in the vicinity include hang gliding, canoe trips, sleigh riding, picnic grounds, outdoor amphitheater, Scottish games, art show, crafts fair, Linville Caverns and Tweetsie Railroad.

Village at Green Park
Goforth Road
Blowing Rock, NC 28605
704-295-9861 800-255-9861

2 Bedrooms $$
2 Bedrms/week 7$
Min. Stay 2 Nights, Dep. Req'd.
12 condos, Villas
No S-yes/P-yes

Location: Airport: 1-2 hours; Downtown: 1.5 mile; Need car; Ski lift: 4 miles
General Facilities: Kitchen, Linens, Restaurant on prem., Bar on prem., Lounge, Baby-sitter
Room Facilities: Pool, Golf: Blowing Rock Golf; TV, Cable, Phone in rm., Crib-Hi-chair, Ind. AC Ctl., Ind. Heat Ctl.
Attractions: Appalachian Summer hosted by Appalachian State U, summer host for NC symphony
Shops & Restaurants: Antique, jewelry, unique shops; The Best Cellar/international

Beautiful villas, tastefully appointed and furnished, overlooking Blowing Rock Golf and Country Club. Adjacent to historic Green Park Inn. Attend the local cultural activities and escape the summer heat.

BOONE

Smoketree Lodge
P.O. Box 3407
Boone, NC 28607
704-963-6505

1 Bedroom $$, 2 Bedrooms $$

Located 12 miles south of Boone, central to all major ski slopes. Fully furnished condos with HBO and Cinemax. Lobby with stone fireplace and wide-screen TV. Amenities include indoor pool, jacuzzi, saunas and workout area.

---------------- BOONE ----------------

Willow Valley Resort
P.O. Box 1782
Boone, NC 28607
704-963-6551

1 Bedroom $$, 2 Bedrooms $$
Pool, Kitchen

Attractions: Skiing, fishing, mile-high hiking, theater, tennis, golf

Modern living in a rustic setting at this all-season resort set in the Appalachian highlands. Away from the hustle and bustle of the city, close to nature with diverse leisure activities. All units are fully equipped and some have washer/dryers and dishwashers.

---------------- BURNSVILLE ----------------

Alpine Village
200 Overlook Dr.
Burnsville, NC 28714
704-675-4103

1 Bedroom $$, 2 Bedrooms $$
1 Bedrm/week $$$$, 2 Bed/week 5$
Min. Stay 2 Nights, Visa/MC, Dep. Req'd.
21 condos, Lo-rise, Villas, Key at Office in Clubhouse
H-yes

Location: Airport: 1½ hours; Downtown: 16 miles; Need car

General Facilities: Daily maid, Kitchen, Linens, Game room, Lounge, Baby-sitter

Room Facilities: Pool, Hot tub, Tennis, Hiking, trout fishing, Golf: Mount Mitchell; TV, Phone in rm., Crib-Hi-chair, Ind. Heat Ctl.

Attractions: Blue Ridge Parkway (2 mi.), Biltmore estate, T. Wolfe home, local crafts, Grandfather Mt, entertainment

Shops & Restaurants: Small shops featuring local craftsmen; Albert's-Ger. Beam's-Chinese

Luxurious townhouses with fabulous views from each deck; tennis and heated pool on property. Hiking trails, trout fishing and discounted golf on great Mount Mitchell course; small, quiet and secluded. Surrounded by a national forest, the ideal place for relaxing in the cool mountain air.

Mount Mitchell Lands & Golf Club Lo-rise
7590 Hwy. 80 S.
Burnsville, NC 28714
704-675-4923

Surrounded by the Pisgah National Forest, an hour drive from Asheville, these fully equipped townhouses overlook the golf course. Cool summer days and nights in elevations over 3,000 feet. South Toe River winds through the golf course. Clubhouse and dining room.

---------------- BUXTON ----------------

Cape Hatteras Beach Club
Rt. 12 & Old Lighthouse, POB 550
Buxton, NC 27920
919-995-4115

---------------- CALABASH ----------------

Carolina Shores Resort
Rt. 179, P.O. Box 2220
Calabash, NC 28459
919-579-7001 800-533-3396

———————————— CAROLINA BEACH ————————————

Atlantic Towers
1615 South Lake Park Blvd.
Carolina Beach, NC 28428
919-458-8313

Visa/MC,Dep. Req'd. •
137 condos, Hi-rise, Key at Front desk
No S-yes/H-yes

Location: Airport: 20 minutes; Downtown: 20 min.; Need car; Beach front

General Facilities: Full serv., Bus. fac., Conf. rm. cap. 25, Daily maid, Kitchen, Linens, Bar on prem., Game room, Lounge, Baby-sitter, Child planned rec.: At times

Room Facilities: Pool, TV, Cable, VCR, Phone in rm., Crib-Hi-chair, Ind. AC Ctl., Ind. Heat Ctl.

Attractions: Historic Wilmington, Battleship N.C, Fort Fisher Historical Site, aquarium, ocean

Shops & Restaurants: Major chain stores, outlets & specialty shops; All types

With the Atlantic Ocean as the front yard, these delightful condominiums are a full-service, guest-oriented property. Relax with your family on the sandy beach or by the pool, or visit the many sights in historic Wilmington.

———

Beach Harbour Resort
302 Canal Dr, P.O. Box 1749
Carolina Beach, NC 28428
919-458-4185

———

Carolina Beach Realty
307 N. Lake Park Blvd.
Carolina Beach, NC 28428
919-458-4444   800-222-9752

———

Paradise Tower Resort
901 S. Lake Park Blvd., Hwy 421
Carolina Beach, NC 28428
919-458-7946

Dep. 1 Night •
37 condos, Hi-rise, Key at Tower lobby area
No S-yes/H-yes

Location: Airport: 20 miles; Downtown: 20 Min.; Need car; Beach front

General Facilities: Full serv., Daily maid, Kitchen, Linens, Baby-sitter

Room Facilities: Pool, Golf: Nearby; TV, Cable, VCR, Phone in rm., Crib-Hi-chair, Ind. AC Ctl., Ind. Heat Ctl.

Attractions: Historic Wilmington, Battleship N.C, Fort Fisher, Aquarium, University of North Carolina

Shops & Restaurants: Major chain stores, specialty shops, outlet stores; All types

Two-bedroom, two-bath, completely furnished oceanfront condominiums with daily maid service. Rest and relax by the pool or sun and swim in the Atlantic Ocean. For the more ambitious, golf and tennis are nearby. Children are welcome in this family resort.

────────────────── CAROLINA BEACH ──────────────────

Spinnaker Point
400 Virginia Ave, P.O. Box 1888
Carolina Beach, NC 28428
919-458-4554 800-334-0454

2 Bedrooms $$, 3 Bedrooms $$
2 Bedrms/week 5$, 3 Bed/week 6$
Min. Stay 2 Nights, Visa/MC, Dep. Req'd. •
42 condos, Lo-rise, Key at Office

Location: Airport: 18 miles; Downtown: 15 miles; Need car; Beach front

General Facilities: Kitchen, Linens, Baby-sitter

Room Facilities: Pool, Hot tub, Tennis, Marina, Golf: Cape Golf—5 miles; TV, Cable, Crib-Hi-chair, Ind. AC Ctl., Ind. Heat Ctl.

Attractions: Charter and cruise boats, live theatre, buggy rides, amusement parks, movies

Shops & Restaurants: Independence Mall, specialty shops, souvenirs; The Steeple-seafood, steaks

The colorful Cape Fear area is fun for the whole family. Villas in mauve and grey or seafoam and cream. Chrome furniture with glass coffee tables, private balconies and bay windows in a colorful setting of natural cypress. 85-acre resort on a peninsula. Plentiful boating, fishing and golf. Huge expanse of preserved marshland, crossed by a boardwalk to the oceanfront. Private marina on the Intracoastal Waterway for convenient boat access.

────────────────── CASWELL BEACH ──────────────────

Caswell Dunes
44 Pinehurst Drive
Caswell Beach, NC

3 Bedrooms $$
3 Bedrms/week 4$
Min. Stay 2 Nights, Dep. Req'd.
32 condos, Lo-rise

Location: Airport: 35 miles; Downtown: 30 miles; Need car

General Facilities: Daily maid, Kitchen, Linens

Room Facilities: Pool, Hot tub, Golf: Oak Island Country Club; TV, Cable, VCR, Crib-Hi-chair, Ind. AC Ctl., Ind. Heat Ctl.

Shops & Restaurants: Local beach shops, nautical and clothing

You'll like the bright cool colors of the contemporary beach furnishings in these exquisitely decorated units complete with covered decks and garage. Take the walkways to the beach or pool.

Southern Shore Villas
S.E. 58th Street
Caswell Beach, NC

Min. Stay Ask, Dep. Req'd.
27 condos, Lo-rise

Location: Airport: 35 miles-Wilmington; Downtown: 30 miles; Need car

General Facilities: Daily maid, Kitchen, Linens

Room Facilities: Pool, Hot tub, TV, Cable, Crib-Hi-chair, Ind. AC Ctl., Ind. Heat Ctl.

Shops & Restaurants: Local shops

Condominiums delightfully decorated in mint green and mauve wicker style beach furnishings. Quiet, secluded villas, yet close to shopping, restaunts and island activities.

─────────────── CEDAR MOUNTAIN ───────────────

Sherwood Forest
P.O. Box 156, Hwy. 276
Cedar Mountain, NC 28718
704-885-2091

Villas
Pool, Kitchen

Attractions: Great Smoky Mountains Nat. Park, Pisgah Nat. Forest, Biltmore House and
Gardens, boating, fishing, tennis, golf

New villas in the woods, on a trout stream, overlooking the golf course. Woodburning fire-
places, screened porches, open decks, grills, washers and dryers.

─────────────── DUCK ───────────────

Barrier Island Station
State Route 1200
Duck, NC 27949
919-261-3525 800-261-3825

2 Bedrooms $$, 3 Bedrooms $$$
2 Bedrms/week 9$, 3 Bed/week 9$
Min. Stay 3 Nights, AmEx/Visa/MC,
   Dep. Req'd.
134 condos, Villas, Key at Guard Gate H-yes

Location: Airport: 60 miles; Downtown: ½ mile; Need car; Beach front

General Facilities: Daily maid, Kitchen, Linens, Restaurant on prem., Bar on prem.,
Game room, Lounge, Baby-sitter

Room Facilities: Pool, Sauna, Hot tub, Tennis, TV, Cable, Phone in rm., Crib-Hi-chair,
Ind. AC Ctl., Ind. Heat Ctl.

Attractions: Wright Bros. Memorial Museum, Lost Colony outdoor drama, fishing, wind
surfing, sailing, entertainment

Shops & Restaurants: Small shops; Barrier Island Inn/Steak-fish

While the architecture is Victorian, the furnishings are ultra-modern. Ocean and Sound
views, wet bars and jacuzzis, located in a quiet setting. Full-time activities director. A short
distance to the ocean for sunning and swimming. Enjoy tennis, windsurfing and sailing.

Maui Kaanapali Villas

―――――――――――――――――― DUCK ――――――――――――――――――

Ocean Pines
S.R. 275
Duck, NC 27949
919-261-4181

―――――――――――――――――― EMERALD ISLE ――――――――――――――――――

Pebble Beach Resort
9000 Coast Guard Rd.
Emerald Isle, NC 28557
919-354-3040 800-682-7810

―――――――――――――――――― HAMPSTEAD ――――――――――――――――――

Belvedere Plantation Golf Club   1 Bedroom $$, 2 Bedrooms $$, 3 Bedrooms $$
P.O. Box 400, Coastal Hwy. 17 N.   1 Bedrm/week $$$$, 2 Bed/week 4$, 3 Bed/
Hampstead, NC 28443   week 5$
919-270-2761 800-334-8126   Visa/MC,Dep. Req'd. •
                                          84 condos, Villas, Key at Belvedere Plantation
                                          H-yes

Location: Airport: 22 miles; Downtown: 25 miles; Need car

General Facilities: Kitchen, Linens, Restaurant on prem., Lounge

Room Facilities: Pool, Sauna, Tennis, Golf: Belvedere on property; TV, Cable, Phone in rm., Ind. AC Ctl., Ind. Heat Ctl.

Attractions: Beaches, marina, saltwater fishing, hunting, Marine Resources Center, Fort Fisher Park

Shops & Restaurants: Grocery, drug, beauty salon, outlet mall, Penney's; Bridge Tender/st.-Fraziers

Villas in a plantation setting with spacious grounds, shaded leisure areas and boardwalk promenade on a championship golf course. Privacy gate and a 200-slip marina, plus 3 nine-hole golf courses, putting green, driving range, tennis courts and swimming pool. 15-minute drive to the ocean, or 5 minute boat ride. Surf casting, pier and deep-sea fishing and indoor trolling. Clubhouse includes dining room, lounge, lockers and showers.

―――――――――――――――――― HATTERAS ――――――――――――――――――

Hatteras Inn Cabanas   1 Bedroom $
P.O. Box 387   1 Bedrm/week $$$$
Hatteras, NC 27943   Min. Stay 2 Nights, Visa/MC, Dep. Req'd.
919-986-2241 800-338-4775   40 condos, Lo-rise, Key at Office
                                   P-yes

Location: Airport: 2 miles; Downtown: 1 mile; Need car; Beach front

General Facilities: Kitchen, Baby-sitter

Room Facilities: TV, Cable, Crib-Hi-chair, Ind. AC Ctl., Ind. Heat Ctl.

Attractions: Deep-sea fishing, surf fishing, sail boarding, surfing, lighthouses, Lost Colony

Shops & Restaurants: Gift, specialty, tackle, boating shops, groceries; Channel Bass-Frog Dog-Tides

Comfortable, rustic one-room oceanfront condominiums. Surf and pier fishing, near charter fleet to the Gulf Stream. Swimming, shelling and sail boarding in this historic maritime area of uncrowded beaches.

—————————————— HOLDEN BEACH ——————————————

Ocean Palms   3 Bedrooms $$$
769 Ocean Blvd. West   3 Bedrms/week 8$
Holden Beach, NC 28462   Min. Stay 3 Nights, Dep. Req'd.
919-842-7443   8 condos, Lo-rise

Location: Airport: 38 miles; Downtown: 35 miles; Need car; Beach front

General Facilities: Daily maid, Kitchen, Baby-sitter

Room Facilities: Pool, Golf: Lockwood Folly 4 miles; TV, Cable, VCR, Phone in rm., Crib-Hi-chair, Ind. AC Ctl., Ind. Heat Ctl.

Attractions: N.C. Battleship Memorial, Orton Plantation, Waccamaw pottery, cruises, fishing, golf

Shops & Restaurants: 45 minutes to Wilmington and Myrtle Beach; Calabash/ seafood

Three large bedrooms in townhouse condominiums with pastel colors in modern beach decor on the ocean. Family atmosphere for beach and pool fun.

———

Water's Edge
427 Ocean Boulevard, West
Holden Beach, NC 28462

—————————————— KILL DEVIL HILLS ——————————————

The Golden Strand
P.O. Box 2011
Kill Devil Hills, NC 27948
919-441-7808

———

Sea Ranch II
1710 North Virginia Dare Trail
Kill Devil Hills, NC 27948
919-441-4445

—————————————— KITTY HAWK ——————————————

Heron Cove   3 Bedrooms $$
5507 S. Virginia Dare Trail   3 Bedrms/week 6$
Kitty Hawk, NC 27949   Min. Stay 2 Nights, Dep. Req'd.
919-441-8070 800-543-9232   12 condos, Lo-rise
                                        H-yes

Location: Airport: 2 hours; Downtown: 2 hours; Need car; Beach front

General Facilities: Daily maid, Kitchen, Linens

Room Facilities: Pool, Golf: Nags Head Links; TV, Cable, Phone in rm., Crib-Hi-chair, Ind. AC Ctl., Ind. Heat Ctl.

Attractions: Wright Memorial, Elizabeth II, Lost Colony, Cape Hatteras National Seashore, entertainment

Shops & Restaurants: Gift shops, shell shops; By Georges/seafood, steaks

Luxury and leisure in these 3-bedroom, 2-bath units with elevator access. Balconies overlook the pool. Join in the weekly barbecues.

KITTY HAWK

Ocean Dunes Condominiums
P.O. Box 387
Kitty Hawk, NC
919-986-2241 800-338-4775

Studio $
Min. Stay 2 Nights, Visa/MC, Dep. Req'd.
40 condos, Lo-rise, Key at Office on premises
P-yes

Location: Airport: 2 miles; Downtown: 1 mile; Beach front

General Facilities: Kitchen

Room Facilities: TV, Cable, Crib-Hi-chair, Ind. AC Ctl., Ind. Heat Ctl.

Attractions: Lighthouse, Wright Brothers, Lost Colony/Roanoke Island, Ocracoke Island

Shops & Restaurants: Local shops, groceries, Red & White; Channel Bass/seafood Pilot Hse

Oceanfront condos near fishing pier and gulf stream charter fleet, clean, tranquil beaches, shopping and restaurants nearby.

Sea Scape Beach & Golf Villas
P.O. Box 276
Kitty Hawk, NC 27949
919-261-3881 800-843-9451

2 Bedrooms $$
2 Bedrms/week $$$$
Min. Stay 2 Nights, Visa/MC, Dep. Req'd. •
84 condos, Lo-rise, Villas, Key at On-site property
H-yes

Location: Airport: 80 miles; Downtown: 5 miles; Need car

General Facilities: Kitchen, Linens, Restaurant on prem., Bar on prem., Game room, Lounge, Baby-sitter

Room Facilities: Pool, Hot tub, Tennis, Mini golf, volleyball, Golf: On 10th fairway; TV, Cable, VCR, Phone in rm., Crib-Hi-chair, Ind. AC Ctl., Ind. Heat Ctl.

Attractions: Deep sea, surf and pier fishing, Wright Brothers Memorial, hang gliding, wind surfing.

Shops & Restaurants: Sidneys Galleon Esplanade, Outer Banks Mall; Owens Seafood

Plush contemporary furnishings in these two-bedroom, two-bath condominiums. Balconies with pool, tennis and golf course views. Many local attractions. The area is a fisherman's dream. 36 holes of golf per day are included. Perfect for a quiet weekend getaway or a fun-filled vacation with the kids.

MOREHEAD CITY

The Breakers
P.O. Box 736
Morehead City, NC 28557
919-247-2400 800-334-3157

Lo-rise
Pool, Kitchen, Linens, Phone in rm.

Attractions: Fort Macon, Cape Lookout, Hampton Mariners Museum, Beaufort, charter fishing, marina, tennis, golf

Oceanfront condominiums with private walkways to the beach, observation decks and screened balconies. 190 beautiful acres and two miles of sandy beach. High dunes covered by a dense maritime forest to the ocean's edge. Located in the town of Pine Knoll Shores.

MOREHEAD CITY

Notch Estates
P.O. Box 128
Morehead City, NC 28557
417-338-2941

Studio $, 1 Bedroom $$, 2 Bedrooms $$,
  3 Bedrooms $$
1 Bedrm/week 4$, 2 Bed/week 5$, 3 Bed/
  week 6$
Min. Stay 2 Nights, AmEx/Visa/MC,
  Dep. 1 Night
Lo-rise, Key at Notch Inn Office
H-yes

Location: Airport: 50 miles; Downtown: 13 miles; Need car

General Facilities: Conf. rm. cap. 360, Daily maid, Kitchen, Linens, Restaurant on prem., Lounge, Baby-sitter

Room Facilities: Pool, TV, Ind. AC Ctl., Ind. Heat Ctl.

Attractions: Silver Dollar City, Shepherd of the Hills, Table Rock Lake

Shops & Restaurants: Service Merchants Mall, Banister, Carters; Notch/family, Wooden Nickel

150 secluded scenic acres with hiking trails and a private lake. Units decor varies from modern to country. Views of valleys and trees. On-site restaurant and lounge, and minutes away from Music Show and Silver Dollar City.

Sand Castles
Morehead City, NC
919-579-3535

Studio $$, 1 Bedroom $$, 2 Bedrooms $$, 3 Bedrooms $$
1 Bedrm/week $$$$, 2 Bed/week 4$, 3 Bed/
  week 4$
Min. Stay 2 Nights, Dep. Req'd.
156 condos, Lo-rise, Key at Office
H-yes

Location: Airport: Wilmington 45 min.; Downtown: 1 block; Need car; Beach front

General Facilities: Bus. fac., Kitchen, Baby-sitter, Child planned rec.: Play area

Room Facilities: Pool, Sauna, Hot tub, Tennis, Boat docks, fishing, TV, Cable, Phone in rm., Crib-Hi-chair, Ind. AC Ctl., Ind. Heat Ctl.

Attractions: 70 golf courses within 1 hr., fishing, clamming, crabbing, charter fishing, tours

Shops & Restaurants: Gift, liquor, grocery, Myrtle Beach shopping; Twin Lakes/seafood, Calabash

Wide choice of tastefully furnished modern condominiums located on a small family beach. Over a dozen golf courses and restaurants within 10 minutes. A family vacation for those who want an uncrowded and unspoiled beach.

NAGS HEAD

Ocean Villas
Mile Post 16-¼, P.O. Box 67
Nags Head, NC 27959
919-441-3405

—————————————— OCEAN ISLE BEACH ——————————————

Brick Landing Plantation
Rt. 2, off Hwy. 179
Ocean Isle Beach, NC 28459
919-754-4373 800-438-3006

2 Bedrooms $$, Lo-rise, Villas
Pool, Kitchen, Linens, Phone in rm.

Attractions: Golf

Master planned community built around a golf course on a 22-foot bluff. Hardwood forests, lakes, ponds and Sauce Pan Marsh. Swimming pool outside your window, beach minutes away. Away from tourist congestion, yet close enough to drive to Myrtle Beach.

The Winds Beach and Golf Resort
310 E. First Street
Ocean Isle Beach, NC 28459
919-579-6275 800-334-3581

1 Bedroom $$, 2 Bedrooms $$
1 Bedrm/week $$$$, 2 Bed/week $$$$
AmEx/Visa/MC, Dep. Req'd. •
44 condos

Location: Downtown: 2.5 miles

General Facilities: Conf. rm. cap. 45, Kitchen

Room Facilities: Pool, Sauna, Hot tub, Tennis, Shuffleboard, Golf: 40 nearby courses; TV, Cable, Phone in rm., Ind. AC Ctl., Ind. Heat Ctl.

Attractions: Colonial rice plantation, Confederate fort, aquarium, Brookgreen Gardens, cruises

Shops & Restaurants: Independence Mall, Cotton Exchange, pottery; The Courtyard/international

Pure white powdered sand, gentle surf, sheltered from storms and rough seas, The Winds Resort is on a seven-mile island with seven miles of beach unshared by any other hotel. The mild climate makes for year-round golf and tennis, fabulous fishing. Relaxed, country feeling away from the crowds, yet 20 minutes away from nightlife. Island restaurants, pool, exercise and recreation rooms, cookout areas. The friendly staff can assist you in planning day trips to nearby attractions.

—————————————— PINEHURST ——————————————

Foxfire Resort & Country Club
P.O. Box 711
Pinehurst, NC 28374
919-295-5555 800-334-9540

1 Bedroom $, 2 Bedrooms $$$
1 Bedrm/week $$$$, 2 Bed/week 5$
AmEx/Visa/MC, Dep. Req'd. •
80 condos, Villas, Key at Front Desk

Location: Airport: 80 miles; Need car

General Facilities: Conf. rm. cap. 200, Daily maid, Kitchen, Linens, Restaurant on prem., Bar on prem., Lounge

Room Facilities: Pool, Tennis, Golf: 2 golf courses; TV, Cable, Phone in rm., Crib-Hi-chair, Ind. AC Ctl., Ind. Heat Ctl.

Attractions: Located in the heart of the North Carolina Sandhills, exciting two-bedroom, bi-level quad

Located in the heart of the North Carolina Sandhills, architecturally designed two-bedroom, bi-level quad villas, with two outdoor decks among the pines near the first tees. Ranch-style Club Villas have fireplaces, garage and screened porches. Pro shop, clubhouse, pool, tennis. Excellent cuisine in the dining room, cocktail lounge, and 36-hole architect-designed championship golf course for the perfect golfing vacation.

─────────────── PINEHURST ───────────────

Pinehurst Hotel & Country Club   Lo-rise
Carolina Vista, POB 4000   Pool, Kitchen, Linens, Phone in rm.
Pinehurst, NC 28374
919-295-6811

Attractions: Gun Club, Riding Club, croquet, lawn bowling, biking, walking tours, trap
and skeet, tennis, golf

*Comfortable furnished condominiums, tastefully decorated. 28 tennis courts amid the
pines, 7 golf courses. Horse-drawn carriages, equestrian facility and Gun club with instructor, Annie Oakely. True Southern hospitality in a year-round resort.*

─────────────── PLEASURE ISLAND ───────────────

The Sands   2 Bedrooms $, Villas
Wilmington Beach   Kitchen
Pleasure Island, NC 27948
919-441-6993

Tastefully decorated villas with private balconies on a wide sandy beach.

─────────────── RUTHERFORDTON ───────────────

Cleghorn Plantation Golf Club
Rt. 4, Box 69, Cox Rd.
Rutherfordton, NC 28139
704-287-2091 800-334-1068

─────────────── SALTER PATH ───────────────

Summer Winds   2 Bedrooms $$$, Hi-rise
Hwy. 58, P.O. Box 100   Pool, Kitchen, Linens
Salter Path, NC 28575
919-247-2104 800-334-6866

Attractions: Exercise room, tennis

*Open airy beach condominiums, views, ceramic tile bath floors, quarry tile in foyer and
kitchen, carpeting, pass-through bar to dining area, sound and weather insulated. Sports
complex, four pools, two lighted tennis courts.*

SAPPHIRE

Fairfield Sapphire Valley
4000 Hwy. 64 W.
Sapphire, NC 28774
704-743-3341 800-438-3421

Studio $$, 1 Bedroom $$$, 2 Bedrooms $$$$,
  3 Bedrooms $$$$
1 Bedrm/week 6$, 2 Bed/week 8$, 3 Bed/
  week 8$
Min. Stay 2 Nights, AmEx/Visa/MC,
  Dep. Req'd. •
200 condos, Lo-rise, Key at Guest Registr.
H-yes

Location: Airport: 55 miles; Need car; Ski lift: Nearby

General Facilities: Full serv., Bus. fac., Conf. rm. cap. 80, Daily maid, Kitchen, Linens, Restaurant on prem., Game room, Baby-sitter, Child planned rec.: Sunburst Program

Room Facilities: Pool, Sauna, Hot tub, Tennis, Golf: Holly Forest Golf Course; TV, Cable, VCR, Phone in rm., Crib-Hi-chair, Ind. AC Ctl., Ind. Heat Ctl.

Attractions: Biltmore House & Gardens, rafting, Indian reservation, gem mining, Carl Sandburg Home, entertainment

Shops & Restaurants: Antique, craft, specialty and dress shops; Holly Forest Country Club

A four-season resort in the Blue Ridge Mountains. Country setting, contemporary furnishings in browns, blues, mauves and greens. Recreation Department, Wednesday night B-B-Q, 3 lakes on the property. 8 lighted tennis courts, recreation complex for children, indoor and outdoor swimming pools. Four ski slopes for winter fun and well-equipped ski shop. Scenic mountain trails for horseback riding, hiking or jogging.

SNEADS FERRY

Chicora Beach Holiday, Inc.
North Topsail Shores, POB 778
Sneads Ferry, NC 28460
800-682-3460 800-222-1536

North Topsail Shores
P.O. Box 778
Sneads Ferry, NC 28460
919-328-0335 800-222-1536

SOUTHERN PINES

Hyland Hills
4100 U.S. #1 North
Southern Pines, NC 28387
919-692-4434

Two-bedroom, two-bath condominiums ideal for golfers with discounts at 8 sandhills courses. On-site restaurant.

Napili Point

SOUTHPORT

Bald Head Island Mgmt.
P.O. Drawer 10999, 704 E. Moore St.
Southport, NC 28461
919-457-5000 800-443-6305

Studio $$$, 1 Bedroom $$$, 2 Bedrooms $$$,
  3 Bedrooms $$$
1 Bedrm/week 6$, 2 Bed/week 6$, 3 Bed/
  week 8$
Min. Stay 3 Nights, AmEx/Visa/MC,
  Dep. Req'd. •
90 condos, Lo-rise, Key at Front desk

Location: Airport: 40 minutes; Downtown: 20 min.; Beach front

General Facilities: Conf. rm. cap. 50, Daily maid, Kitchen, Linens, Restaurant on prem., Bar on prem., Lounge, Baby-sitter, Child planned rec.: Summer day camp

Room Facilities: Pool, Tennis, Croquet, canoeing, Golf: Bald Head Island Course; TV, Phone in rm., Crib-Hi-chair, Ind. AC Ctl., Ind. Heat Ctl.

Attractions: Orton Plantation, Wilmington, Wacamaw Pottery outlet, Myrtle Beach, entertainment

Shops & Restaurants: Island Chandler-gourmet items, videos, beach toys; The Inn, Peli Deli

Condominiums on a 2,000-acre private island community accessible only by private passenger ferry. No cars allowed on the island, but electric vehicles are available to rent. Various condominiums to rent in this traditional, family beach community. Tennis, golf, pool, 14 miles of beach, croquet, clamming, crabbing, fishing, biking and canoeing.

──────────────── SUNSET BEACH ────────────────

Oyster Bay Plantation
900 Shoreline
Sunset Beach, NC 28459
919-579-7181 800-222-1524

Studio $$, 1 Bedroom $$, 2 Bedrooms $$,
3 Bedrooms $$$
1 Bedrm/week 4$, 2 Bed/week 5$, 3 Bed/
week 7$
Visa/MC,Dep. Req'd. •
130 condos, Lo-rise, Villas, Key at Office
H-yes

Location: Airport: 35 miles; Downtown: 20 min.; Need car

General Facilities: Bus. fac., Conf. rm. cap. 125, Daily maid, Kitchen, Linens, Baby-sitter

Room Facilities: Pool, Hot tub, Golf: O. Bay & Bricklanding; TV, Cable, VCR, Phone in rm., Crib-Hi-chair, Ind. AC Ctl., Ind. Heat Ctl.

Attractions: Golfing, boating, deep-sea fishing, dining (seafood capital of the world), shopping

Shops & Restaurants: Waccamaw Pottery, Myrtle Square & Briarcliff Malls; Parson's Table/seafood-beef

Truly close to it all, but a true feeling of island living and tranquility amidst a canvas of awesome natural beauty. The Colony at Oyster Bay has 1200 sq. ft. condominiums, 2-bedroom, 2 ceramic tile baths and quarry tile floor kitchens. The Fairway Villas are large with informal and functional floor plans. Lush landscaping and access to the Intracoastal Waterway for boat owners. One mile from the beach.

──────────────── SURF CITY ────────────────

Surf
Highway 210
Surf City, NC 28445
919-328-2511 800-255-2233

1 Bedroom $, 2 Bedrooms $$
1 Bedrm/week $$$$, 2 Bed/week $$$$
Min. Stay 2 Nights, Dep. Req'd.
180 condos, Lo-rise, Key at Century 21-Hwy. 50

Location: Airport: 45 minutes; Downtown: 30 min.; Need car; Beach front

General Facilities: Daily maid, Kitchen

Room Facilities: Pool, Golf: 20 minutes; TV, Cable, Crib-Hi-chair, Ind. AC Ctl., Ind. Heat Ctl.

Attractions: Fishing piers, Cotton Exchange, Airlee Gardens, Orton Plantation, USS-N.C.

Shops & Restaurants: Local gift and craft shops, malls; Fish

An exciting resort community on one of the last undeveloped beaches in North Carolina. The beaches can only be reached by bridges across the Intercoastal Waterway. Color-coordinated beach style furnishings. Natural landscaped setting with free form-pool, shaded sitting areas and clubhouse.

TOPSAIL ISLAND

Topsail Dunes
North Topsail
Topsail Island, NC
919-328-0639

1 Bedroom $$, 2 Bedrooms $$$, 3 Bedrooms $$$
1 Bedrm/week 4$, 2 Bed/week 5$, 3 Bed/week 7$
Dep. Req'd.
224 condos, Lo-rise, Key at Albert Realty
H-yes

Location: Airport: 35 minutes; Downtown: 30 miles; Need car; Beach front

General Facilities: Kitchen

Room Facilities: Pool, Sauna, Hot tub, Tennis, Golf: North Shore Country Club; TV, Cable

Attractions: Deep-sea fishing, pier fishing, surf fishing, air tour of the island, beaches

Shops & Restaurants: Food Lion, regular shopping mall in Wilmington; Saratoga/steak and seafood

Topsail Island is for those individuals who want to enjoy the sun, surf, pool and tennis for a quiet laid-back vacation.

WAYNESVILLE

Ithilien Lodge Condominium
Upper Walker Road, Box 987
Waynesville, NC 28786
704-452-2466

1 Bedroom $, Lo-rise
Pool, Kitchen

Attractions: White-water rafting, mountain trails, lakes, Ghost Town, Cherokee Indian Reservation, exercise room, golf

Large, beautifully furnished units with mountain and valley view from the windows and decks. A real vacation retreat, high in the Great Smoky Mountains.

WHISPERING PINES

Whispering Pines Resort
263-B Pine Ridge Drive
Whispering Pines, NC 28327
919-949-3777 800-334-9536

1 Bedroom $$, 2 Bedrooms $$
Pool, Kitchen

Attractions: N.C. Motor Speedway, horse, harness racing, North Carolina State Zoo, tennis, golf

Located in North Carolina's majestic sandhills, this country club is conceived, designed and built for golfers, but offers other activities as well—all-weather tennis, pool, lake boating and sailing, and fine fishing. The perfect setting for a refreshing vacation.

──────────── WRIGHTSVILLE BEACH ────────────

Cordgrass Bay
527 Causeway Dr, P.O. Box 1040
Wrightsville Beach, NC 28480
919-256-4516 800-992-6503

Lo-rise
Pool, Kitchen

Attractions: Tennis

On Shell Island Sound where $_2$ of the land is committed to the conservation of natural landscape and open space. Atlantic on the east, intercoastal waterway on the west and Wrightsville Beach to the south.

One South Lumina
P.O. Box 1040
Wrightsville Beach, NC 28480
919-256-9100

1 Bedroom $$, Hi-rise
Pool, Daily maid, Kitchen

Imaginatively designed exteriors, designer decorated interiors on professionally landscaped grounds. When you're not at the beach, you'll be in the freshwater pool. Ocean views, furnished balconies, covered parking and elevator service.

──────────── YAUPON BEACH ────────────

Oak Island Beach Villas
1000 Caswell Beach Road
Yaupon Beach, NC

1 Bedroom $$, 2 Bedrooms $$, 3 Bedrooms $$
1 Bedrm/week 4$, 2 Bed/week 4$, 3 Bed/
   week 5$
Min. Stay 2 Nights, Dep. Req'd.
Lo-rise

Location: Airport: 35 miles; Downtown: 30 miles; Need car; Beach front

General Facilities: Daily maid, Kitchen, Linens

Room Facilities: Pool, Hot tub, Golf: Oak Island adjacent; TV, Cable, Crib-Hi-chair, Ind. AC Ctl., Ind. Heat Ctl.

Attractions: Historical attractions, fishing, beach activities

Shops & Restaurants: Local shops

Each unit is beautifully decorated with wicker furniture in bright fabrics. Units conveniently located to the pool and jacuzzi.

Oklahoma

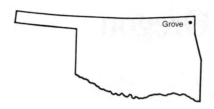

Grove

GROVE

Meghan Coves
P.O. Box 1868
Grove, OK 74344
918-786-4444

2 Bedrooms $$
Pool, Daily maid, Kitchen, Linens

Attractions: Bowling, movie theater, Cherokee Queen party barge, racquetball, tennis

Cape Cod village townhouses on the wooded shoreline of a 60,000-acre lake with private boat slips. Tennis courts, pools, clubhouse with racquetball courts, fitness center, jogging and walking trails. Fish off the air conditioned, heated fishing dock.

We want to hear from you—any comments regarding the condos or our publication may be noted on the form at the end of the book.

Oregon

Gleneden Beach
• Lincoln City
⚡ Welches
Bend
• Sunriver

BEND

The Inn of the Seventh Mountain
P.O. Box 11207
Bend, OR 97709
503-382-8711

1 Bedroom $$$$, 2 Bedrooms $$$$, Lo-rise
Pool, Daily maid, Kitchen, Linens, Phone in rm.

Attractions: Skiing, white water rafting, patio boat tours, canoe float trips, fishing, mt. bike tours, ice skating

Comfortably decorated units with fireplaces in a beautiful alpine setting. 14 miles from Mt. Bachelor with its Outback Super Express chair. Shuttle service to mountain. Warm., friendly staff to make your vacation experience complete. Full range of summer activities.

GLENEDEN BEACH

Beachcombers Haven Vacation
7045 N.W. Glen
Gleneden Beach, OR 97388
503-764-2252

Studio $, 2 Bedrooms $, 3 Bedrooms $$
2 Bedrms/week $$$$, 3 Bed/week 5$
Min. Stay 2 Nights, Visa/MC, Dep. 1 Night •
12 condos, Lo-rise, Key at Office
H-yes

Location: Airport: 100 miles; Downtown: 3 miles; Need car; Beach front

General Facilities: Daily maid, Kitchen, Linens

Room Facilities: TV, Phone in rm., Crib-Hi-chair

Attractions: 20 minutes south to Newport, a quaint seaport. Marina Science Center, tidepools

Shops & Restaurants: Art colony, glass blowing, kite festival, Mall; Chez Jeanette-French

Spend your family vacation in these large, roomy apartments in quiet Gleneden Beach, overlooking seven miles of the beautiful Pacific Ocean, close to golf and tennis. Off-shore salmon fishing, and rivers for steelhead fishing. Oil and water color paintings from Lincoln City's art colony.

GLENEDEN BEACH

Cavalier By The Sea
P.O. Box 58
Gleneden Beach, OR 97388
503-764-2352

2 Bedrooms $$
Min. Stay 2 Nights, AmEx/Visa/MC,
    Dep. 1 Night
25 condos, Lo-rise, Key at Front office
No S-yes

Location: Airport: 2 miles; Downtown: 6 miles; Need car; Beach front

General Facilities: Daily maid, Kitchen, Linens, Game room

Room Facilities: Pool, Sauna, Golf: Salishan—nearby; TV, Cable, Phone in rm., Crib-Hi-chair, Ind. Heat Ctl.

Attractions: De Pae Bay boat basin, charter ocean fishing, whale watching, golf, tennis, museums

Shops & Restaurants: Salishan Marketplace, De Pae Bay City, Lincoln; Salishan restaurants

Ocean view units with private patios and saunas. Indoor pool, game room, direct beach access. Enjoy a romantic sunset and cozy fire in these elegant rooms. A place to escape everyday cares and responsibilities.

LINCOLN CITY

Ocean Terrace Condominium
4229 S.W. Beach Avenue
Lincoln City, OR 97367
503-996-3623 800-648-2119

1 Bedroom $$
AmEx/Visa/MC, Dep. Req'd. •
41 condos, Lo-rise, Key at Office
No S-yes

Location: Airport: 90 miles; Need car; Beach front

General Facilities: Daily maid, Kitchen, Linens

Room Facilities: Pool, Golf and tennis near, TV, Cable, Crib-Hi-chair, Ind. Heat Ctl.

Attractions: Ocean activities, whale watching, surf fishing, horseback riding, beach-combing

Shops & Restaurants: Gift shops

Individually owned and decorated condominium units, some with oceanfront view, with an indoor swimming pool. Located near four golf courses, top-rated restaurants, art galleries and wine tasting facilities. Try surf or deep-sea fishing, beachcombing, kite flying or go on a picnic.

SUNRIVER

Sunriver Lodge and Resort
P.O. Box 3609
Sunriver, OR 97707
503-593-1221 800-547-3922

2 Bedrooms $$$
Pool, Kitchen, Linens, Phone in rm.

Attractions: Oregon High Desert Museum, Lava Lands River Caves, Lava Cast Forest, Pine Mt. Observatory, Nature Center, tennis, golf

15 miles south of Bend, 300 days of sunshine, snowcapped Mt. Bachelor, lush forests, golf, tennis, skiing, kids klub, nature center, fishing guide, shopping mall, 2 pools, restaurants, all at the Sunriver Resort. Daily ski shuttle, ski and rental shop.

---------------------------------- WELCHES ----------------------------------

Rippling River
68010 E. Fairway Ave.
Welches, OR 97067
503-622-3101 800-547-8054

1 Bedroom $$, 2 Bedrooms $$$
Pool, Kitchen

Attractions: Skiing, golf, tennis, fishing, bicycling, hiking

Come and enjoy the clean mountain air, fantastic scenery and year-round activities. All the comforts of home with all the vacation amenities you'd ever want. Lounges for beverages and entertainment, casual to elegant dining rooms. Easy access to three skiing areas.

Pennsylvania

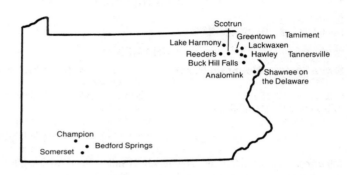

Scotrun
Greentown   Tamiment
Lake Harmony   Lackwaxen
Reeders   Hawley   Tannersville
Buck Hill Falls
Analomink   Shawnee on
the Delaware

Champion
Bedford Springs
Somerset

ANALOMINK

Alpine Village
Analomink, PA 18320
800-233-8240

2 Bedrooms $$$, Villas
Kitchen

Attractions: Mineral & Gem Museum, Mine Replica, 1867 Chapel, Petrified Gardens

Ski to the slopes from your charming Swiss chalet. Slopeside chalets with indoor pools, steam and whirlpool baths. "Just for Kids" programs at Alpine Mountain. Separate trails for advanced and beginner skiers. Year-round ice skating at Penn Hills.

Penn Estates
In the Poconos
Analomink, PA 18320
717-424-8795 800-233-4122

2 Bedrooms $$$$, Villas
Pool, Kitchen, Linens

Attractions: Roller skating, horse racing, bowling, horseback riding, golf, gym, spa, hiking, tennis, golf

Villas offering indoor pool with whirlpool in a tropical setting. Microwaves, trash compactors, Thermasol steam and whirlpool baths. Restaurant with take-out service. Live entertainment in Reflections Nite Club. So much to do you'll never want to leave.

---------------------------- BEDFORD SPRINGS ----------------------------

Bedford Springs Hotel
Bedford Springs, PA 15522

---------------------------- BUCK HILL FALLS ----------------------------

Buck Hill Inn
Buck Hill Falls, PA 18312

---------------------------- CHAMPION ----------------------------

Seven Springs Mountain Resort
R.D. #1
Champion, PA 15622
814-352-7777   800-458-2313

Studio $$$, 1 Bedroom 3$, 2 Bedrooms 4$,
    3 Bedrooms 5$
1 Bedrm/week 4$, 2 Bed/week 5$, 3 Bed/
    week 7$
Min. Stay 2 Nights, Dep. Req'd.
500 condos, Villas, Key at Lodge front desk
H-yes

Location: Airport: 75 miles; Downtown: 17 miles; Need car; Ski lift: 1 mile

General Facilities: Bus. fac., Conf. rm. cap. 1500, Daily maid, Kitchen, Linens, Restaurant on prem., Bar on prem., Game room, Lounge, Baby-sitter, Child planned rec.: Animal walk/minigolf

Room Facilities: Pool, Sauna, Hot tub, Tennis, Mini-golf, bowling, TV, Cable, Phone in rm., Crib-Hi-chair, Ind. AC Ctl., Ind. Heat Ctl.

Attractions: Fallingwater, white water rafting, Fort Ligonier, state parks, "whoola" hoop contest, darts, entertainment

Shops & Restaurants: 12 shops—boutiques on-site, drug, grocery, K-Mart; Helen's/French, Amer., Italian

Modern contemporary villas and townhouses situated among the scenic Laurel Highland Mountains. Activities Staff offers varying activities each day, dining, dancing and entertainment. Indoor pool, mini golf, bowling alleys, racquetball & health spa, petting zoo, game rooms, sports massage, water sports, beauty parlor and roller skating. Summer or winter there's always something to do, or you can do nothing but enjoy the relaxed family atmosphere.

---------------------------- GREENTOWN ----------------------------

White Beauty Lakeview Resort
Route 507
Greentown, PA 18426
717-857-0234   800-233-4130

1 Bedroom $$$, Lo-rise
Pool, Kitchen, Phone in rm.

Attractions: Cruiser boat rides, moonlight cruise, hiking, hunting, autumn flaming foliage, archery, rifle range, tennis, golf

All in one, all-season resort. Social staff providing a variety of activities for children and adults. Recreation area and lighted sports area. Sandy beach, diving raft and picnic area. Don't forget to bring your boat for water skiing.

——————————————— HAWLEY ———————————————

Tanglewood Lakes, Inc.
P.O. Box 257
Hawley, PA 18428
717-226-3000

1 Bedroom $$, 2 Bedrooms $$$
Pool, Kitchen, Linens

Attractions: Skiing, rec. room, tennis

High quality accommodations with a friendly staff to assist you. Skiing in season at property slopes. Daily planned activities, docks for your boat, recreation room, snack bar and ski lodge.

——————————————— LACKWAXEN ———————————————

Country Squire Lakeshore Club
Box 1A59
Lackwaxen, PA 18435
717-685-7400

Villas
Pool, Kitchen, Linens

Attractions: Trout fishing, nature walks, ice skating, trap and rifle ranges, skiing, archery-trap shooting, tennis

Individually decorated modern villas with decks, fireplaces and grills. Year-round activities—skiing, private stable with indoor and outdoor riding arenas, hunting preserve, mountain wilderness trails, Delaware River rafting, boat launch and Recreation Center.

——————————————— LAKE HARMONY ———————————————

Split Rock Lodge
Westwood Villas at Split Rock
Lake Harmony, PA 18624
717-722-9111   800-255-7625

Pool, Kitchen

Attractions: Pocono Mountains, Lake Harmony, boating, racquetball, volleyball

Contemporary designed villas set in unspoiled woodlands. Sit back and enjoy the clear mountain air and impeccable service. Relax at the tropical indoor pool, saunas or whirlpool. Water sports on Lake Harmony, workout room and recreation area.

——————————————— REEDERS ———————————————

Mountain Springs Lake
Mountain Springs Drive
Reeders, PA 18352
717-629-0251

——————————————— SCOTRUN ———————————————

Caesars Brookdale on the Lake
Brookdale
Scotrun, PA 18355
717-226-2101   800-233-4141

——————————————— SHAWNEE-ON-THE-DELAWARE ———————————————

Shawnee Village
Phase I & II Box 93
Shawnee-on-the-Delaware, PA 18356
717-424-5731

―――――――――― SHAWNEE-ON-THE-DELEWARE ――――――――――

Shawnee Inn Villas
P.O. Box 178   Pool, Kitchen, Linens
Shawnee-on-the-Delaware, PA 18356
717-424-1300 800-742-9633

Attractions: Delaware Water Gap National Recreation Area, Pocono Raceway, Bushkill
  Falls, Van Campen In, Fitness/Racquet Club, tennis, golf

*Villas, chateaus and bi-level townhouses through the resort with various views. So much
for everyone to do and enjoy. Children's playground, water slides, pony rides, electronic
game center, snack bar and Play and Water Park.*

―――――――――――――――― SOMERSET ――――――――――――――――

Hidden Valley Resort Lo-rise
RD 4, Box 243, 1 Craighead Drive Pool, Kitchen, Linens
Somerset, PA 15501
800-443-6454 800-458-0175

Attractions: Frank Lloyd Wright's Fallingwater, Laurel Caverns, Ft. Ligonier, Storybook
  Forest, Fitness trail, tennis, golf

*Villas and townhouses with beautifully appointed rooms designed for maximum con-
venience. Fresh mountain air, rural environment. Four-seasons resort with planned children's activities, workshops, theme parties, dances, swimming and boat races, and sport
clinics.*

―――――――――――――――― TAMIMENT ――――――――――――――――

Wayne Newton's Tamiment Pool, Kitchen, Linens, Phone in rm.
Tamiment Resort & Country Club
Tamiment, PA 18371
717-588-6652 800-233-8105

Attractions: Skiing, boating, fishing, special events, golf, tennis, volleyball, basketball

*One-and two-bedroom condominiums in this all-year, all-occasion resort in the scenic
Pocono Mountains. Whether you're looking for relaxation or recreation, you'll find it here.
90-acre private lake, indoor/outdoor pools, adult recreation programs.*

――――――――――――――― TANNERSVILLE ―――――――――――――――

Ski Side Village Villas
Big Pocono Rd., P.O. Box 154 Kitchen, Linens
Tannersville, PA 18372
717-629-2939

Attractions: Golf, skiing, alpine slide, Pretzel Factory

*Two-and three-bedroom condominiums in the Poconos with saunas and whirlpool baths,
fireplaces and two televisions.*

Rhode Island

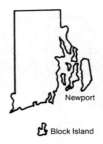

Newport

Block Island

BLOCK ISLAND

Island Manor Resort
Chapel St, Box 400
Block Island, RI 02807
401-466-5567

1 Bedroom $$, Lo-rise
Daily maid, Kitchen, Linens

Attractions: Settler's Rock and North Light, The Maze, Clay Head Cliffs, Lapham wildlife estate, Bicycles

A nature lover's island paradise. Trails through pines, flowers and ponds, rolling hills, stone fences, wildlife, view cliffs and crescent beach. Efficiency units with kitchettes, and one bedroom suites. Run by the McCabe family who will be happy to help you.

NEWPORT

The Newport Bay Club
America's Cup Avenue, Box 1440
Newport, RI 02840
401-849-8600

1 Bedroom $$$, 2 Bedrooms $$$$, Hi-rise
Kitchen, Phone in rm.

Attractions: Nearby health club, racquetball, swimming, Nautilus, waterfront, docks, antiques, museums

You are in the heart of Newport Bay, on the waterfront, and within walking distance to shops, antiques, museums, restaurants and nightclubs when you stay here. Suites with deluxe marble baths and jacuzzis, or two-level townhouses with balconies on both levels.

Newport Onshore
379 Thames
Newport, RI 02840
401-849-8553 800-842-2480

1 Bedroom $$, 2 Bedrooms $$, Hi-rise
Pool, Kitchen

Attractions: Newport Harbor, marina

On Thames Street, directly on Newport Harbor with its seventy-five slip marina. Classic, contemporary outside architecture, landscaped quadrangle and pool with harborfront lawn. All units have two private sun decks, fireplaces, and double whirlpool tubs.

Paki Maui

NEWPORT

The Wellington Yacht Club
543 Thames at Wellington
Newport, RI 02840
401-849-1770

Studio $$, 1 Bedroom $$$, 2 Bedrooms $$$$
1 Bedrm/week 10$, 2 Bed/week 10$
Min. Stay 2 Nights, AmEx/Visa/MC,
   Dep. Req'd.
50 condos, Lo-rise, Key at Office
H-yes

Location: Airport: 45 minutes; Downtown: 2 blocks

General Facilities: Kitchen, Linens, Baby-sitter, Child planned rec.: Pool parties

Room Facilities: Pool, Sauna, Tennis, Health club, Golf: Several courses nearby; TV, Cable, VCR, Phone in rm., Crib-Hi-chair, Ind. AC Ctl., Ind. Heat Ctl.

Attractions: Mansion tours, antique shopping, beaches, boating, music festival, shows, trolley tours, entertainment

Shops & Restaurants: Benettons, Brick Market shops, Bannisters Wharf; Clare Cooke House-Black Pearl

Harborfront condominiums with water view. Enjoy the excitement of Newport's nightlife or the leisurely atmosphere of Newport's historical sites, sailing, shopping, and antiquing. Children's splash parties, barbecues, sailing charters, cocktail parties, and complimentary continental breakfast.

South Carolina

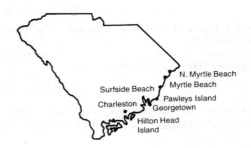

N. Myrtle Beach
Myrtle Beach
Surfside Beach
Pawleys Island
Charleston
Georgetown
Hilton Head
Island

CHARLESTON

Seabrook Conference Resort
P.O. Box 32099
Charleston, SC 29417
800-922-2401 800-845-2475

1 Bedroom $$, 2 Bedrooms $$$, 3 Bedrooms $$$
1 Bedrm/week 4$, 2 Bed/week 5$, 3 Bed/ week 7$
Min. Stay 2 Nights, AmEx/Visa/MC, Dep. Req'd.
338 condos, Villas, Key at Seabrook Reception
No S-yes/H-yes

Location: Airport: Charleston 30 miles; Downtown: 23 miles; Need car; Beach front

General Facilities: Full serv., Bus. fac., Conf. rm. cap. 250, Daily maid, Kitchen, Linens, Restaurant on prem., Bar on prem., Game room, Lounge, Baby-sitter, Child planned rec.: Planned programs

Room Facilities: Pool, Tennis, Horses, fishing, Golf: 2 golf courses; TV, Cable, Phone in rm., Crib-Hi-chair, Ind. AC Ctl., Ind. Heat Ctl.

Attractions: Equestrian center, bicycles, sailboats, deep-sea charters, fishing & crabbing equipment, entertainment

Shops & Restaurants: Seabrook Shoppe, Village Market, Village Spirits; Island House-Seaview-Capt Sams

Oceanfront resort near Charleston on a 2,200-acre private island. Variety of colorful birds, flowers, trees and rain forest. 20 lighted tennis courts, 2 72-par golf courses, pro shop and private lessons. Recreation staff plans children's activities, puppet shows-pony rides-treasure hunts-nature exploration-ice cream making-movies-dances. Fine dining on Carolina seafood, evening entertainment in Bohicket's Lounge.

---------------------------- CHARLESTON ----------------------------

Wild Dunes—Charleston's Island 1 Bedroom $$, 2 Bedrooms $$$, 3 Bedrooms
P.O. Box 1410 $$$$
Charleston, SC 29402   1 Bedrm/week 5$, 2 Bed/week 6$, 3 Bed/
803-886-6000 800-845-8880   week 8$
                                  AmEx/Visa/MC, Dep. 1 Night
                                  Lo-rise, Villas

Location: Airport: Charleston 35 min.; Downtown: 15 miles; Beach front

General Facilities: Daily maid, Kitchen, Linens, Restaurant on prem., Child planned rec.: Activity programs

Room Facilities: Pool, Tennis, Yacht Harbor, Golf: 2 courses; TV, Phone in rm., Ind. AC Ctl., Ind. Heat Ctl.

Attractions: Deep-sea fishing, harbor cruises, creek fishing, tennis, golf

Shops & Restaurants: General store, Mt. Pleasant and Charleston shops; Island House/seafood, The Club

Luxuriously furnished, extremely spacious villas by the ocean, golf course, tennis courts, or lagoon. Convenient to all sports activities. Canoe trips, swimming lessons, story telling for children. Beachside cabana with snacks and beverages. Floats, chairs, umbrellas, sailboats and windsurfer rentals. Stocked freshwater lagoons for fishing, or yacht harbor private charters. Restaurants with specialty menus and family cookouts at the beach.

---------------------------- GEORGETOWN ----------------------------

DeBordieu   Villas
P.O. Box 1746   Pool, Kitchen, Phone in rm.
Georgetown, SC 29442
803-546-4176

Attractions: Wildlife preserve, ocean, pool, tennis, golf, marshes, creeks, beach club

Luxury villas on 2,700 acres of woodlands, bordered by 25,000 acres of protected wildlife preserve. Unspoiled beauty and isolation in this year-round fishing heaven. All villas are oceanfront or around the pool. Boat ramp, golf and tennis. Security gate.

---------------------------- HILTON HEAD ISLAND ----------------------------

Adventure Inn Beach & Golf Club 1 Bedroom $, 2 Bedrooms $$
Box 5646   Kitchen
Hilton Head Island, SC 29938
803-785-5151 800-845-9500

Attractions: Bicycling

Large spacious villas with balconies overlooking the ocean, where the sound of the surf will soothe you to sleep. Located so you can participate in all the Hilton Head has to offer—tennis, golf, fishing, forests and wooded paths for walking or bicycling.

Brigantine Quarters   Villas
Shipyard Plantation, P.O. Box 6658   Pool, Kitchen
Hilton Head Island, SC 29928
803-785-6446 800-845-6446

Attractions: Tennis

Spacious and bright interiors giving an "island" feeling. An easy walk to the beach and Shipyard Racquet Club. Outdoor area for family picnics.

HILTON HEAD ISLAND

Continental Club
12 South Forest Beach Drive
Hilton Head Island, SC 29928
803-842-3224 800-367-8211

1 Bedroom $, 2 Bedrooms $$, Lo-rise
Pool, Daily maid, Kitchen, Linens, Phone in rm.

Attractions: 13 award-winning golf courses, Sunday polo, marinas, equestrian centers, tennis, golf

Located on the southern end of an 18-mile-long island, these 16 townhomes are designer decorated with private landscaped courtyards. Swimming pool is just outside your door, and you are right across from the beach. Play tennis at Van der Meer Tennis Center.

Cottages at Shipyard Plantation
P.O. Box 7528
Hilton Head Island, SC 29938
803-686-4424 800-255-2471

1 Bedroom $, 2 Bedrooms $$, Lo-rise
Pool, Daily maid, Kitchen, Linens

Attractions: Golf courses, tennis, shops, restaurants, Fitness Center

New townhomes designed in the Low Country manner, clustered in a private park with shady porches overlooking the lagoons and fairways. Reception center with indoor/outdoor pool, fitness center and racquetball. Immediate access to Shipyard golf, tennis and the beach.

Hilton Head Island Beach Club
40 Folly Field Road
Hilton Head Island, SC 29928
803-842-4402 800-845-9508

1 Bedroom $$, 2 Bedrooms $$, Villas
Pool, Kitchen, Linens

Attractions: Swimming, tennis, golf, beach

Balcony villas bordered by the beach. Jog, beachcomb, swim or simply take a before dinner stroll on the wide beach. Oceanfront pool, poolside bar, restaurant and lounge.

Island Club
85 Folly Field Rd.
Hilton Head Island, SC 29928
803-785-5221 800-528-9336

1 Bedroom $$, 2 Bedrooms $$, Hi-rise
Pool, Kitchen, Linens, Phone in rm.

Attractions: Theaters, marinas, nightspots, golf, exercise room, tennis

Villas in a small, exclusive family resort, individually decorated with ocean or lagoon views. Unwind on the beach or by one of three terraced pools. Lighted tennis and pro shop with whirlpool, saunas and exercise room.

Monarch At Sea Pines
Beach Lagoon Rd, P.O. Box 6959
Hilton Head Island, SC 29938
803-785-2040 800-527-3490

Villas
Pool, Kitchen, Linens

Attractions: Golf, tennis, fishing, horseback riding, jogging, biking, shelling

Indulge yourself in these two-bedroom, two-bath villas with private master suites and whirlpools in the master bath. Two swimming pools and three open-air whirlpools set among tropical gardens.

—————————————— HILTON HEAD ISLAND ——————————————

Palmetto Dunes
P.O. Box 5606
Hilton Head Island, SC 29938
803-785-1161   800-845-6130

1 Bedroom $$$, 2 Bedrooms $$$$, Lo-rise, Villas

One to four bedroom fully equipped villas in various locations. Large living and dining areas, patios and decks. Private access to three miles of beach, tennis, golf, bicycle and boat rentals. 25 pools in the resort, and kiddie pools for the children.

Player's Club—Hilton Head
DeAllyon Rd.
Hilton Head Island, SC 29938
803-785-8000

1 Bedroom $$, 2 Bedrooms $$, Villas
Pool, Kitchen

Attractions: Golf, tennis, boating, bicycles, surf fishing, sailing, arcades, fitness center

Practical, beautiful villas, some with floor to ceiling glass greenhouse enclosures, whirlpools and saunas. Comfortable and stylishly attractive. 14 tennis courts with tennis instructor. Fitness center with 14 nautilus machines, lap pool and racquetball courts.

Sea Crest Surf & Racquet Club
3 N. Forest Beach Dr.
Hilton Head Island, SC 29928
803-842-4210

Sea Pines Resort
Box 7000
Hilton Head Island, SC 29938
803-758-3333   800-845-6131

1 Bedroom $$, 2 Bedrooms $$, 3 Bedrooms $$$
1 Bedrm/week 4$, 2 Bed/week 5$, 3 Bed/ week 6$
Dep. Req'd.
500 condos, Villas, Key at Welcoming Center

Location: Airport: Savannah, GA 1 hour; Downtown: close; Beach front

General Facilities: Conf. rm. cap. 500, Daily maid, Kitchen, Linens, Restaurant on prem., Bar on prem., Lounge, Child planned rec.: Fun for Kids

Room Facilities: Pool, Tennis, Marina, Golf: 3 championship courses; TV, Cable

Attractions: Ancient Indian grounds, forest preserve, dinner cruises, carriage tours, art galleries, entertainment

Shops & Restaurants: Harbour Town antiques, specialty shops, gifts; Overlook/Port Royal Resort

Red and white lighthouse welcomes you as you enter Sea Pines Plantation. Excellent to elegant furnishings in 500 villas in a variety of locations—water, wooded or fairway—yet centrally located to resort amenities. Mild year-round temperatures for all-season enjoyment. Championship golf, tournament tennis. 90-slip yatch basin, marina charters, 12 pools, 15 miles of trails, crabbing, fishing and miles of beach. Summer "Fun for Kids" and free concerts, playground. 12 restaurants and outdoor cookouts.

─────────────── HILTON HEAD ISLAND ───────────────

Sea Pines Villas
P.O. Box 6959
Hilton Head Island, SC 29938
803-785-2040 800-527-3490

Villas
Pool, Kitchen, Linens

Attractions: Tennis, golf, deep-sea fishing, sailing, horseback riding, jogging, bird-watching

Privacy and relaxed comfort at various locations within Sea Pines Plantation.

───

Spinnaker & Southwind at Shipyard
25 Bow Circle, P.O. Box 6899
Hilton Head Island, SC 29938
803-785-4881 800-336-3224

2 Bedrms/week 6$, 3 Bed/week 8$
Min. Stay 7 Nights, Dep. Req'd. •
70 condos, Lo-rise, Key at Poolhouse

Location: Airport: 10 Min./Hilton Head; Need car

General Facilities: Kitchen, Linens, Game room, Lounge

Room Facilities: Pool, Sauna, Hot tub, Tennis, Bikes, playground, TV, Cable, VCR, Phone in rm., Crib-Hi-chair, Ind. AC Ctl., Ind. Heat Ctl.

Attractions: 12 miles of sugar sand beach, 25 golf courses, 300 tennis courts, fishing, boating, horses, entertainment

Shops & Restaurants: 30 shopping plazas, two outlet malls-A. Klein; Harbourmaster/cont. & seafood

Delicate summer colors of light pinks, greens & blues accent the designer decorated beauty of each unit. All villas have either golf or lagoon views and are located inside private gates. Free golf and tennis, two blocks to the beach, weekly family cookouts at the pool, children's playground, steam room and nautilus. Many elegant shops and restaurants as well as numerous recreational activities.

─────────────── HILTON HEAD ───────────────

Heritage Club at Harbour Town
P.O. Box 6959
Hilton Head, SC 29938
803-785-2040 800-527-3490

Villas
Pool, Kitchen, Linens

Attractions: Golf, tennis, deepsea fishing, sailing, horses, bikes, jogging, beach, exercise equipment

Sophisticated accommodations in luxury villas with two master suites, each with whirlpool baths. Gas log fireplace, formal dining area and three color TV's. Clubhouse with health and exercise equipment. Harbour Town yatch basin and lighthouse to visit.

─────────────── MYRTLE BEACH ───────────────

Jade Tree Cove
200 75th Avenue
Mrytle Beach, SC 29577
803-449-9455

Phone in rm.

Attractions: Tennis

———————————————— MYRTLE BEACH ————————————————

Beach Colony Resort
5308 North Ocean Boulevard
Myrtle Beach, SC 29577
803-449-4010 800-222-2141

Studio $, 1 Bedroom $, 2 Bedrooms $$,
   3 Bedrooms $$
1 Bedrm/week $$$$, 2 Bed/week 4$,
   3 Bed/week 5$
AmEx/Visa/MC, Dep. 1 Night •
154 condos, Hi-rise, Key at Front desk
H-yes

Location: Airport: 6½ miles; Downtown: 3 miles; Need car; Beach front

General Facilities: Full serv., Conf. rm. cap. 60, Daily maid, Kitchen, Linens, Restaurant on prem., Bar on prem., Lounge, Baby-sitter, Child planned rec.: Summer months only

Room Facilities: Pool, Sauna, Hot tub, Racquet, exercise room, Golf: Pine Lakes; TV, Cable, Phone in rm., Crib-Hi-chair, Ind. AC Ctl., Ind. Heat Ctl.

Attractions: Brookgreen Gardens, deep-sea fishing, dinner cruises, Carolina Opry, Georgetown tours, entertainment

Shops & Restaurants: Waccamaw Pottery outlet, Briarcliffe Mall; Fusco's, Mayor's House/cont.

Oceanfront accommodations conveniently located. Three outdoor and one indoor pool, playing privileges at Pine Lakes Country Club and free tennis at Myrtle Beach Tennis & Swim Club. Summer games and prizes for the children. Ocean setback, complemented by native flora, hibiscus, sea oats and palm fronds, and a boardwalk across the dunes. Outdoor pool bar and grill.

———

Beach House Golf & Racquet Club
6800 North Ocean Boulevard
Myrtle Beach, SC 29577
803-449-7484

1 Bedroom $, 2 Bedrooms $, Hi-rise
Pool

Attractions: Golf

Condominiums with balcony views of Myrtle Beach and pool. Free tennis at Myrtle Beach Racquet Club, and 25 area golf courses. Restaurant row to the north. Five minutes to the downtown hub.

———

Bluewater Resort
P.O. Box 3000
Myrtle Beach, SC 29578
803-626-8345 800-845-6994

1 Bedroom $, 2 Bedrooms $$, Hi-rise
Pool, Kitchen

Attractions: Myrtle Beach Pavillion, water parks & slides, Brookwood Gardens, Wildlife Park, mini golf, racquet-exercise room, golf

Vast array of apartments, suites, condominiums and villas on Myrtle Beach. Five indoor and outdoor whirlpools, 5 outdoor pools, extra large indoor pool with glass covered removed in summer and a special private pool for children.

Sands of Kahana

MYRTLE BEACH

Caribbean Chelsea House Villas
30th Avenue North
Myrtle Beach, SC 29577
803-448-7181 800-845-0883

2 Bedrooms $$, Lo-rise
Pool, Kitchen

Attractions: Amusement Parks, tennis, fishing, golf, theaters, charter fishing, shuffleboard

You and the children come home relaxed and contented after your vacation at the Caribbean. Swim in the pool and sun on the large wooden deck where you can get lunch and drinks from the poolside bar. Build sandcastles and hunt for shells on the beach.

Carolina Winds
200 76th Ave. N, Drawer 7518
Myrtle Beach, SC 29578
803-449-2477 800-523-4027

1 Bedroom $, Hi-rise
Pool, Kitchen

Attractions: Pavilion, water slides, water sports park, miniature golf, golf, tennis, exercise room

On the beach with an oceanfront pool, one bedroom suites and three bedroom condominiums. Indoor and outdoor whirlpools and indoor pool. Exercise room and large kiddie pool. Free tennis at Myrtle Beach Racquet Club and world famous golf courses. On-site restaurant.

———————————— MYRTLE BEACH ————————————

Four Seasons Beach Resort
5801 N. Ocean Blvd.
Myrtle Beach, SC 29577
803-449-6441

1 Bedroom $, 2 Bedrooms $
Kitchen

Attractions: Grand Strand, Myrtle Beach, water sports, golf

Attractive, comfortable units on the quiet cabana section of the Grand Strand. Lifeguard on duty at the beach, or swim and play water games in the pool. Shops and restaurants nearby in the Myrtle Beach area.

Holiday Towers Condominiums
P.O. Box 3072
Myrtle Beach, SC 29578
803-626-9012

Kingston Plantation Resort
9770 Kings Road
Myrtle Beach, SC 29577
800-449-0006 800-876-0010

1 Bedroom $$, 2 Bedrooms $$, 3 Bedrooms $$$
Min. Stay 1 Night, AmEx/Visa/MC,
     Dep. 1 Night •
150 condos, Hi-rise, Lo-rise, Villas, Key at Radisson Hotel desk
No S-yes/H-yes

Location: Airport: 12 miles; Downtown: 8 miles; Need car; Beach front

General Facilities: Full serv., Conf. rm., Daily maid, Kitchen, Linens, Restaurant on prem., Bar on prem., Game room, Lounge, Baby-sitter, Child planned rec.: Full and half day

Room Facilities: Pool, Sauna, Hot tub, Tennis, Sport & Health Club, Golf: Nearby; TV, Cable, Phone in rm., Crib-Hi-chair, Ind. AC Ctl., Ind. Heat Ctl.

Attractions: Brookgreen Gardens, deep-sea fishing, golf, tennis, entertainment

Shops & Restaurants: Waccamaw Pottery, Outlet Mall, Belk; Carolinas-southern regional

This is an oceanside 145-acre resort, featuring high-rise, low-rise, and villa condominiums with lake and wooded views. Most units have sofa-beds with contemporary furnishings in pastel colors. The resort has a four million dollar sport and health club.

Ocean Forest Villa Resort
5601 North Ocean Blvd.
Myrtle Beach, SC 29577
803-449-9661 800-845-0347

2 Bedrooms $$
2 Bedrms/week 7$
AmEx/Visa/MC, Dep. 1 Night •
165 condos, Lo-rise, Key at Registr. desk

Location: Airport: 14 miles; Downtown: 3 miles; Need car; Beach front

General Facilities: Full serv., Daily maid, Kitchen, Linens, Baby-sitter, Child planned rec.: Summer activities

Room Facilities: Pool, Hot tub, TV, Cable, Phone in rm., Crib-Hi-chair, Ind. AC Ctl., Ind. Heat Ctl.

Attractions: 45 championship golf courses nearby, sightseeing tours, 60 miles of beach

Shops & Restaurants: Sears, J.C. Penney, Waacawaw pottery; Fresh seafood and steaks

Family vacation resort with pool or beach views. Situated in Pine Lakes residential area. 10 acres, 1100 feet of sandy beach across Ocean Boulevard. All condominiums are two-bedroom, one queen bed, two twins and a sleeper sofa. Two outdoor pools and whirlpools.

─────────────── MYRTLE BEACH ───────────────

Ocean Park Condominiums
1905 S. Ocean Blvd, Drawer 3967
Myrtle Beach, SC 29578
803-448-1915   800-624-8539

1 Bedroom $, 2 Bedrooms $$, Hi-rise
Pool, Kitchen, Linens

Attractions: Myrtle Waves Water Park, Amusement Park, golf, sailing, surfing, fishing, tennis, exercise room

Large variety of floor plans in new luxury units. Kitchens with microwaves and self-defrosting refrigerators. Glass enclosed indoor pool overlooking the Atlantic and outside free-form pool. Exercise room with tanning lounge.

───

Ocean Villas Beach Club
7509 N. Ocean Blvd.
Myrtle Beach, SC 29577
803-449-0837

1 Bedroom $, Villas
Pool, Kitchen

Spacious one-bedroom, 1½ bath villas with private balconies. Health club privileges.

───

Ramada Ocean Forest Resort
5523 North Ocean Blvd, Box 3090
Myrtle Beach, SC 29578
803-497-0044   800-522-0818

AmEx/Visa/MC, Dep. 1 Night •
193 condos, Hi-rise, Key at Front desk
No S-yes/P-yes/H-yes

Location: Airport: 8 miles; Downtown: 3 miles; Need car; Beach front

General Facilities: Full serv., Conf. rm. cap. 100, Daily maid, Kitchen, Linens, Restaurant on prem., Bar on prem., Lounge

Room Facilities: Pool, Sauna, Hot tub, Health club, Golf: 50 courses in area; TV, Cable, Phone in rm., Crib-Hi-chair, Ind. AC Ctl., Ind. Heat Ctl.

Attractions: Carolina Opry, Brookgreen Gardens, Sculpture Garden, Myrtle Beach Pavilion, water park

Shops & Restaurants: Waccamaw pottery, Briarcliffe & Myrtle Square Mall; Gullyfield/seafood

Luxury oceanfront accommodations in full service hotel. Condominiums have pastel decor, 2 double beds and private balcony with ocean view. Complimentary airport van.

───

Sands Beach Club
1000 Shore Drive
Myrtle Beach, SC 29577
803-449-1531   800-845-6999

1 Bedroom $$, 2 Bedrooms $$$
1 Bedrm/week 5$, 2 Bed/week 9$
AmEx/Visa/MC, Dep. 1 Night •
225 condos, Hi-rise, Villas, Key at desk, H-yes

Location: Airport: 17 miles; Downtown: 7 miles; Need car; Beach front

General Facilities: Full serv., Bus. fac., Conf. rm. cap. 225, Daily maid, Kitchen, Linens, Restaurant on prem., Bar on prem., Baby-sitter, Child planned rec.: Summer activities

Room Facilities: Pool, Hot tub, Tennis, Racquet, basketball, TV, Cable, Phone in rm., Crib-Hi-chair, Ind. AC Ctl., Ind. Heat Ctl.

Attractions: 45 championship golf courses, shopping, beach, entertainment

Shops & Restaurants: Sears, J.C. Penney, Waccawaw pottery; Fresh seafood, steaks

Oceanfront and ocean view condominiums located on exclusive Shore Drive. Family oriented, free summer children's activity program, indoor/outdoor pool and whirlpool. Live music in the lounge in the evenings. Two tennis courts, racquetball and basketball.

────────── MYRTLE BEACH ──────────

Sands Ocean Club
500 Shore Dr.
Myrtle Beach, SC 29577
803-449-6461

Studio $, 1 Bedroom $$, 2 Bedrooms $$, 3 Bedrooms $$$
AmEx/Visa/MC, Dep. Req'd.
Hi-rise

Location: Airport: 8 miles; Downtown: 3 miles; Beach front

General Facilities: Kitchen, Restaurant on prem., Bar on prem., Game room, Lounge, Child planned rec.: Seasonal program

Room Facilities: Pool, Sauna, Hot tub, Tennis, Fitness Center, Golf: Pawleys Plantation; TV, Cable, Ind. AC Ctl.

Attractions: Carolina Opry, Brookgreen Gardens, Mt. Olympus Waterslide, Myrtle Beach Pavilion, entertainment

Shops & Restaurants: Myrtle Square Mall, Waccamaw pottery, gift shop; Windows-on-site/seafood-steaks

Suites overlooking the Atlantic Ocean and Grand Strand beaches where you'll soon be swimming or sunbathing. Fully equipped fitness center for working out or resting in heated whirlpools. Glass enclosed indoor pool. After a hard day playing tennis or golf, sit back and relax at Sandals Lounge with its happy hour, complimentary hors d'oeuvres and nightly entertainment. Also popular is Ocean Annie's beach bar with its pool parties, bikini contests and live entertainment. Special honeymoon packages.

──────────────────────────────

Schooner Beach and Racquet Club
7100 N. Ocean Blvd.
Myrtle Beach, SC 29577
803-449-6431

1 Bedroom $$, 2 Bedrooms $$
Dep. 1 Night
Hi-rise

Location: Airport: 8 miles; Downtown: 3 miles; Beach front

General Facilities: Kitchen, Bar on prem., Child planned rec.: Activities

Room Facilities: Pool, Hot tub, Health club, bikes, Golf: Myrtlewood Golf Club; TV, Cable, VCR, Crib-Hi-chair

Attractions: Carolina Opry, Ripley's Believe It Or Not, Mt. Olympus Waterslide, Pavilion, entertainment

Shops & Restaurants: Myrtle Square Mall, Waccamaw pottery; Carolina seafood

Condominiums with whirlpool tubs, natural wood, mirrored walls and oceanfront balconies. Something for everyone with planned week activities, free transportation to off-site attractions, complimentary tennis and membership golf privileges. Poolside gazebo bar for drinks and sandwiches, well-designed children's playground. Free transportation to and from the airport. Indoor games, books and in-house video library should the weather turn cold, although you can still use the heated, covered pool.

────────── N. MYRTLE BEACH ──────────

Links Golf & Racquet Club
1004 Hwy. 17 S
N. Myrtle Beach, SC 29582
803-272-7181

—————————————— N. MYRTLE BEACH ——————————————

Maritime Beach Club
400 N. Ocean Blvd.
N. Myrtle Beach, SC 29582
803-249-3414

1 Bedroom $$, 2 Bedrooms $$, Hi-rise
Pool, Kitchen, Phone in rm.

Attractions: Swim, shell, sail, fish, jog, golf, tennis

Condominiums with full ocean views, ceramic tile entries and baths with raised tubs, private dressing rooms and designer kitchens, in a professionally landscaped setting. A great vacation for children—private exits to beach.

Tilghman Beach & Racquet Club
P.O. Box 315
North Myrtle Beach, SC 29597
803-249-3457 800-334-5061

Lo-rise
Pool, Kitchen

Attractions: Beach, surfing, golf, amusements, fishing pier, tennis

On-site pier and shell-covered beach for fishing, beachcombing or long walks. Oceanfront condominiums with screened porch and balcony off the master bedroom. Children's pool and family picnic area. Lie quietly on the beach and be soothed by the sun and sound of waves.

—————————————— PAWLEYS ISLANDS ——————————————

Litchfield By The Sea
U.S. Hwy. 17, P.O. Drawer 320
Pawleys Islands, SC 29585
803-237-4225 800-845-1897

2 Bedrooms $$, Hi-rise, Lo-rise, Villas
Pool, Kitchen, Linens

Attractions: Swim, bicycle, sail, fish, Brookgreen Gardens, colonial plantation tours, health club, racquetball, tennis, golf

Wide range of villas and townhomes with varying views and amenities. Each condominium group has its own pool and beach access. Guests may use the Waccamaw House facilities—indoor and outdoor pools, health club, racquetball courts, jacuzzi, lounge and movie theaters.

Please mention *Condo Vacations the Complete Guide* when you reserve your condominium.

--------------------------- SURFSIDE BEACH ---------------------------

Myrtle Beach Resort
P.O. Box 14428, 5905 Frontage Rd.
Surfside Beach, SC 29587
803-828-8000 800-845-0359

Studio $$, 1 Bedroom $$, 2 Bedrooms $$$
1 Bedrm/week $$$$, 2 Bed/week 4$,
3 Bed/week 6$
AmEx/Visa/MC, Dep. Req'd. •
300 condos, Hi-rise, Lo-rise, Key at Rental office

Location: Airport: 3 miles; Downtown: 6 miles; Need car; Beach front

General Facilities: Full serv., Bus. fac., Conf. rm. cap. 50, Daily maid, Kitchen, Linens, Restaurant on prem., Bar on prem., Game room, Child planned rec.: Peak season activity

Room Facilities: Pool, Sauna, Tennis, 2 exercise rooms, Golf: Deertrack; TV, Phone in rm., Crib-Hi-chair, Ind. AC Ctl., Ind. Heat Ctl.

Attractions: Tennis, golf, beach, Myrtle Beach amusements, Carolina Opry, Brookgreen Gardens, entertainment

Shops & Restaurants: General store, Waccamaw Pottery, Outlet Park; Local seafood restaurants

A 44-acre family resort among woods and lagoons with windswept dunes and sandy beach. Attractive wood bridges and walkways, 6 day and night tennis courts, 5 outdoor pools, oceanfront cabana bar and indoor atrium pool. For real relaxing, spend your time basking in the sun at the beach, watching the children play in the surf. Seasonal nightly entertainment and dancing under the stars. 24-hour security.

Plantation Resort
1250 U.S. Highway 17 North
Surfside Beach, SC 29577
803-238-3556 800-845-5039

Studio $, 1 Bedroom $$, 2 Bedrooms $$, 3 Bedrooms $$
1 Bedrm/week 4$, 2 Bed/week 5$, 3 Bed/week 6$
AmEx/Visa/MC
Lo-rise

Location: Airport: M. Beach Jetport; Downtown: minutes

General Facilities: Full serv., Bus. fac., Conf. rm. cap. 120, Daily maid, Kitchen, Linens

Room Facilities: Pool, Sauna, Hot tub, Tennis, Fitness Center, Golf: Deer Track Golf 36-holes; TV, Cable, Phone in rm.

Attractions: The Grand Strand, 40 championship golf courses, beach, tennis

Shops & Restaurants: Myrtle Beach malls, unique low country stores; 1000 area restaurants

Villas with hotel-style amenities and 36 championship holes of golf at your doorstep. Hop on the free beach shuttle bus for your day at the beach. Year-round recreation at the Health and Swim Club with a 70-foot heated, enclosed pool with retractable roof, tennis courts and exercise area where you can take classes in aerobics, water aerobics and weight training. Free jetport pickup and drop-off service.

Tennessee

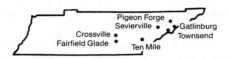

--- CROSSVILLE ---

Thunder Hollow
P.O. Box 1289
Crossville, TN 38557
615-484-9566

--- FAIRFIELD GLADE ---

Fairfield Glade—Kensington W.   1 Bedroom $$$, 2 Bedrooms $$$$, Villas
P.O. Box 1500   Pool, Kitchen, Linens
Fairfield Glade, TN 38555
619-484-7521

Attractions: Opryland, Dollywood, Catoosa Wildlife Management Area, Lake St. George
   marina, tennis, golf

*A self-contained year-round resort. Two championship golf courses, three pools, Lake St.
George marina and swimming, tennis complex, Dorchester Riding Stables, and hiking on
12,000 acres. Comfortable accommodations for an unhurried life-style.*

--- GATLINBURG ---

Club Chalet Inn of Gatlinburg
4105 Ski Mountain Road
Gatlinburg, TN 37738
615-436-5536

GATLINBURG

Cobbly Nob
Route 3, Box 619
Gatlinburg, TN 37738
615-436-5298

1 Bedroom $$, 2 Bedrooms $$, 3 Bedrooms $$
1 Bedrm/week 5$, 2 Bed/week 6$
Min. Stay 2 Nights, Dep. Req'd. •
50 condos, Lo-rise, Key at Rental office
H-yes

Location: Airport: 1 hour; Downtown: 10 min.; Need car; Ski lift: Ober

General Facilities: Full serv., Kitchen, Linens, Restaurant on prem., Bar on prem., Lounge

Room Facilities: Pool, Sauna, Hot tub, Tennis, Golf: Cobbly Nob; TV, Cable, VCR, Phone in rm., Ind. AC Ctl., Ind. Heat Ctl.

Attractions: Surrounded by Great Smoky Mtn. National Park, trout fishing, horses, Dollywood, hiking

Shops & Restaurants: Arts & crafts community, mall, Pigeon Forge; Burning Bush/gourmet

Country furnishings in log cabins with jacuzzi, skylights and stone fireplaces, or golf course condominiums with patios and charcoal grills, or King of the Mountain chalets that accommodate 22 persons, with enclosed spa room with 6-person hot tub. This is a 1,000-acre resort surrounded by the Great Smoky Mountains National Park, minutes from downtown Gatlinburg and ski slopes. 4 pools, tennis, golf course and fishing.

Condo Villas of Gatlinburg
201 Parkway
Gatlinburg, TN 37738
615-436-4121 800-223-6264

Studio $$, 1 Bedroom $$, 2 Bedrooms $$
1 Bedrm/week 5$, 2 Bed/week 5$, 3 Bed/
   week 6$
Min. Stay 2 Nights, AmEx/Visa/MC,
   Dep. Req'd. •
60 condos, Villas, Key at 201 Parkway
No S-yes

Location: Airport: 35 miles; Downtown: 3 miles; Need car; Ski lift: Nearby

General Facilities: Kitchen, Linens

Room Facilities: Pool, TV, Cable, Phone in rm., Crib-Hi-chair, Ind. AC Ctl., Ind. Heat Ctl.

Attractions: Ski slopes, Dollywood, Great Smoky Mtn. National Park

Shops & Restaurants: Factory Merchants Mall; 50 to 100 restaurants

Log homes in early American surrounded with trees and views of the Great Smokies, or chalet villas in contemporary styling. Large heated pool with waterfall, picnic areas and hiking trails. Villas have cathedral ceilings with wood beams and whirlpool tubs in the bathroom. Security guards on duty day and night. Winter ski packages available.

─────────────── GATLINBURG ───────────────

Deer Ridge Mountain Resort
Route 3, Box 849
Gatlinburg, TN 37738
615-436-2325 800-631-3379

1 Bedroom $$, 2 Bedrooms $$, 3 Bedrooms $$$
1 Bedrm/week 4$, 2 Bed/week 5$, 3 Bed/
   week 7$
Min. Stay 2 Nights, AmEx/Visa/MC,
   Dep. Req'd. •
84 condos, Lo-rise, Key at Reception Center
H-yes

Location: Airport: 60 miles; Downtown: 11 miles; Need car; Ski lift: 13 miles

General Facilities: Full serv., Bus. fac., Conf. rm. cap. 50, Daily maid, Kitchen, Linens, Child planned rec.: Playground Equipment

Room Facilities: Pool, Sauna, Hot tub, Tennis, hiking, skiing, Golf: Bent Creek; TV, Cable, Phone in rm., Crib-Hi-chair, Ind. AC Ctl., Ind. Heat Ctl.

Attractions: Great Smoky Mt. Nat. Park, Dollywood, Dixie Dinner Theater, Passion Play

Shops & Restaurants: Factory Merchants Mall, Smoky Mountain Crafts

Beautiful, fully equipped large suites with private balconies for a spectacular 180-degree view of the Great Smoky Mountains. Relax in the swimming pool, jacuzzi, sauna or steam room, or exercise on the tennis court or the nearby 18-hole golf course.

Gatlinburg Summit
Top of Ski View Drive
Gatlinburg, TN 37738
615-436-2600 800-848-4148

Gatlinburg Town Square
P.O. Box 887
Gatlinburg, TN 37738

Greenbrier Valley Resorts
US 321, Rt. 3, Box 920
Gatlinburg, TN 37738
615-436-2015 800-641-7457

Min. Stay 1 Night, AmEx/Visa/MC,
   Dep. 1 Night •
20 condos, Key at Office
No S-yes/H-yes

Location: Airport: 1 hour 15 minutes; Downtown: 10 miles; Need car; Ski lift: Nearby

General Facilities: Full serv., Bus. fac., Conf. rm., Kitchen, Linens

Room Facilities: Pool, Sauna, Hot tub, Tennis, Golf: Bent Creek; TV, Cable, VCR, Phone in rm., Crib-Hi-chair, Ind. AC Ctl., Ind. Heat Ctl.

Attractions: Great Smoky Mt. National Park, Gatlinburg, Ober Gatlinburg, Dollywood, Pigeon Forge

Shops & Restaurants: Gatlinburg, Outlet malls in Pigeon Forge; Burning Bush/ Teagues/Peddler

Chalets, condos and log cabins surrounded by the unparalleled beauty of the Great Smoky Mountains. A year-round resort offering swimming, tenis, golf, downhill skiing and the entire playground of Great Smoky Mountains National Park. For the adventure-minded there is white-water rafting or tubing or skip stones among the many bubbling brooks.

─────────────── GATLINBURG ───────────────

High Alpine Resort
Upper Alpine Way, Rt. 2 Box 786
Gatlinburg, TN 37738
615-436-6643 800-666-6643

Studio $$, 1 Bedroom $$$, 2 Bedrooms $$$$
Min. Stay 2 Nights, AmEx/Visa/MC,
Dep. 1 Night •
36 condos, Lo-rise, Villas, Key at Office
on property
No S-yes/H-yes

Location: Airport: 1 hour; Downtown: 3 miles; Need car; Ski lift: Nearby

General Facilities: Conf. rm., Kitchen, Linens

Room Facilities: Pool, Cable, Phone in rm., Crib-Hi-chair, Ind. AC Ctl., Ind. Heat Ctl.

Attractions: Bus tours of Great Smoky Mountains, Dollywood, Cherokee Reservation

Shops & Restaurants: Several of the largest and best-known outlet malls; Old Heidelberg Castle/German

Located high upon Mount Harrison, half-mile from Ober Gatlinburg, a year-round attraction and ski resort. Condominiums are furnished in earth tones, some with whirlpool tubs and hot tubs. Large decks have views of Mount LeConte and ski slopes. Away from the noise and congestion of downtown, yet convenient to dining pleasures and area attractions.

Highland Condominiums
Campbell-Lead Rd, Rt. 4 Box 369
Gatlinburg, TN 37738
615-436-3547 800-233-3947

1 Bedroom $$, 2 Bedrooms $$$, Lo-rise
Pool, Kitchen, Linens

Attractions: Great Smoky Mountains National Park, Gatlinburg entertainment, tennis

Space, comfort and privacy with the Great Smoky Mountains at your doorstep. One-, two-and three-bedroom condominiums with a bath for every bedroom, wood-stocked fireplace, private entrance and balcony and a whirlpool bath.

Mountain Place Resort
Route 3, Box 756
Gatlinburg, TN 37738

Oak Square at Gatlinburg
990 River Road
Gatlinburg, TN 37738
615-436-7582 800-423-5182

1 Bedroom $$, 2 Bedrooms $$$
Pool, Daily maid, Kitchen, Linens

Attractions: Winter skiing, sledding, Dollywood, ice skating, Great Smoky Mountains National Park

One-and two-bedroom condominiums with wood burning fireplaces and kitchenettes with elevator service. Close proximity to the slopes, walk to restaurants and Aerial Tramway. Gatlinburg Trolley stops at the door to take you on a shopping trip or to Dollywood.

GATLINBURG

Oak Square
990 River Road
Gatlinburg, TN 37738
615-436-7582 800-423-5182

1 Bedroom $$, 2 Bedrooms $$$
1 Bedrm/week 4$, 2 Bed/week 6$
Dep. 1 Night •
60 condos, Hi-rise, Key at Office

Location: Airport: 45 miles; Downtown: 1 block; Ski lift: Ober
General Facilities: Full serv., Conf. rm. cap. 85, Daily maid, Linens
Room Facilities: Pool, Hot tub, TV, Cable, Phone in rm., Crib-Hi-chair, Ind. AC Ctl., Ind. Heat Ctl.
Attractions: Ski lodge, Dollywood, Smoky Mountains National Park

Oak Park is ideally located in downtown Gatlinburg and offers a wide variety of accommodations. Gatlinburg Trolley transports you around the village and to Dollywood. Indoor pool for winter swimming, easy access to the slopes and Aerial Tramway. Suites have wood-burning fireplaces and kitchenettes.

The Summit
Top of Ski View Drive, Box 649
Gatlinburg, TN 37738
615-436-4222 800-231-2701

1 Bedroom $$, 2 Bedrooms $$, Hi-rise
Pool, Kitchen

Attractions: Fishing, swimming, golf, tennis, golf

Winter snow and skiing, summer swimming and fishing, spring hiking and horseback riding along the dogwood, tiger lilies and wildflowers, fall foliage colors, backpacking and fishing, something to do year-round. Condominiums with fireplaces and ski slope views.

Hatteras Inn Cabanas

GATLINBURG

Town Square Resort Club
Gatlinburg, TN 37738

Tree Tops Resort of Gatlinburg   1 Bedroom $$, 2 Bedrooms $$, Hi-rise
Roaring Fork Rd, P.O. Box 1009   Pool, Kitchen, Linens
Gatlinburg, TN 37738
615-436-6559

Attractions: Great Smoky Mountain National Park, fishing, Dollywood, fitness center, golf

Condominiums with jacuzzis and fireplaces totally tree surrounded and naturally blended into the mountains. 3 blocks from the national park. Nature trails, unspoiled picnic areas, and trout stocked mountain streams where you can forget the pace of everyday life.

PIGEON FORGE

Mountain Meadows Resort   2 Bedrooms $$, Lo-rise
850 Rolling Hills Dr, P.O. Box 929   Pool, Kitchen
Pigeon Forge, TN 37863
615-428-2897

Attractions: Dollywood, golf, Great Smoky Mountains National Park

Convenience and beauty in a quiet mountain setting surrounded by the Great Smoky Mountains and grassy meadows. Two-bedroom view townhouses with kitchens. Close to Dollywood, six miles of family entertainment, music and crafts.

Oakmont Resort of Pigeon Forge   1 Bedroom $$, 2 Bedrooms $$, Lo-rise
555 Middle Creek Road   Pool, Kitchen, Linens
Pigeon Forge, TN 37863
615-453-3240

Attractions: Dollywood, Gatlinburg Country Club, Old Mill, fishing, Water Circus, exercise room, golf

New, luxury condominiums with private aqua-jet therapeutic whirlpools in the master bath. Hilltop location, half-mile from Dollywood. Join new friends in the recreation room with its kitchenette and stone fireplace, or swim in the indoor/outdoor pool.

Pinecrest Townhomes   Lo-rise
P.O. Box 130, 300 Plaza Way   Kitchen
Pigeon Forge, TN 37863
615-453-6500

Attractions: Dollywood, Great Smoky Mountaind National Park, Old Mill, golf

Two-bedroom townhomes with 2.5 baths, king and queen size beds, balconies and mountain stone fireplaces for romantic evenings. Located among tall pines and minutes from Great Smoky Mountains National Park in a peaceful, scenic setting.

SEVIERVILLE

Riveredge Village Condominiums
953 Dolly Parton Parkway
Sevierville, TN 37862
615-453-3333

───────────────── TEN MILE ─────────────────

The Landing   1 Bedroom $$, 2 Bedrooms $$, Villas
Rt. 2 Box 120   Pool, Kitchen, Linens
Ten Mile, TN 37880
615-334-9600 800-225-5896

Attractions: Tennessee River, Watts Bar Lake, boating, water sports, pontoon boats

Two-bedroom log chalets and one-bedroom modern stone villas on the waterfront. All have porch with spa, wood burning fireplace and outdoor grills. 95-mile lake with pontoon boats. Relaxed gourmet dining in the Yacht Club or floating Sunset Deck.

───────────────── TOWNSEND ─────────────────

Riveredge Village Condominiums 2 Bedrooms $$
Townsend, TN 37882   2 Bedrms/week 4$
615-448-6036   Min. Stay 2 Nights, Dep. Req'd.
                                    8 condos, Lo-rise, Key at Office
                                    H-yes

Location: Airport: 30 minutes; Downtown: 2 blocks; Need car; Beach front; Ski lift: 18 miles

General Facilities: Kitchen, Linens

Room Facilities: Pool, Sauna, Hot tub, Biking, Jogging, TV, Cable, Crib-Hi-chair, Ind. AC Ctl., Ind. Heat Ctl.

Attractions: Great Smoky Mt. Nat. Park, Cades Cove

Shops & Restaurants: Pigeon Forge Factory Outlet, Townsend Crafts Mall; Family style

Elegantly decorated two-bedroom suites on the peaceful side of the Smokies. Balconies overlook the Little River and view the mountains. Fish, hike, view wildlife, or relax in the whirlpool or swimming pool.

Our goal is to provide as *complete* a listing of condo vacation properties as possible. If you know of a condo we don't list, please send us their name and address on the form at the back of this Guide.

Texas

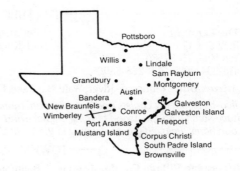

Pottsboro
Willis • • Lindale
Sam Rayburn
Grandbury • • Montgomery
Austin
Bandera •
New Braunfels •• Galveston
• Conroe Galveston Island
Wimberley Freeport
Port Aransas
Mustang Island Corpus Christi
South Padre Island
Brownsville

AUSTIN

Lakeway on Lake Travis
18 B Schooner Cove
Austin, TX 78734
800-252-3473 800-826-1841

Lo-rise
Pool, Kitchen, Linens

Attractions: Golf, tennis, water sports, fishing, boating

Texas Hill Country location on Lake Travis. Choice of condominiums set in the rolling hills, by the lake or pool. Family recreation among the oaks. Perfect for lazy days on the lake, yet minutes from Austin excitement.

Texas Timeshare in Lakeway
18-B Schooner Cove
Austin, TX 78734
512-261-6663 800-826-1841

2 Bedrooms $$$
2 Bedrms/week 4$
Min. Stay 2 Nights, AmEx/Visa/MC,
  Dep. 1 Night •
18 condos, Villas, Key at Office

Location: Airport: 30 miles; Downtown: 20 mi.; Need car

General Facilities: Daily maid, Kitchen, Linens, Bar on prem., Lounge, Child planned rec.: Summer day camp

Room Facilities: Pool, Hot tub, Tennis, Marina, boat rental, Golf: Live Oak & Yaupon; TV, Cable, Phone in rm., Crib-Hi-chair, Ind. AC Ctl., Ind. Heat Ctl.

Attractions: Hill Country, highland lakes, Sea World of Texas, Capitol Bldg., LBJ Ranch

Shops & Restaurants: Specialty shops, Frost Brothers; Barbara Ellens/homestyle

Contemporary furnished villas for resort living overlooking Lake Travis and Lakeway Marina. Hill Country or pool side settings. Abundant recreational opportunities for the whole family. Great restaurants nearby.

BANDERA

The Bandera Homestead
R.R. #2, P.O. Box 150
Bandera, TX 78003
512-796-3051

1 Bedroom $$, 2 Bedrooms $$, Lo-rise
Pool, Kitchen

Attractions: Historic Bandera, Cowboy Capital of the World, horse racing, Sea World, Camp Verde, volleyball, horseshoe, golf

Rustic log cabin condos on the 1,800-acre River Ranch. Pools under shade trees, lounge chairs and observation deck. Pavilion for outdoor barbecues overlooking the pools and river. Bandera County is a paradise for nature lovers.

BROWNSVILLE

Rancho Viejo Resort Country Club
P.O. Box 3918, Hwy. 77 North 83
Brownsville, TX 78520
512-350-4000 800-292-7263

Studio $$, 1 Bedroom $$, 2 Bedrooms $$$$,
   3 Bedrooms $$$$
AmEx/Visa/MC, Dep. 1 Night •
Villas, Key at Hotel front desk

Location: Airport: 30 minutes; Downtown: 15 min.

General Facilities: Full serv., Bus. fac., Conf. rm. cap. 900, Daily maid, Linens, Restaurant on prem., Bar on prem., Lounge, Child planned rec.: Swimming-tennis-golf

Room Facilities: Pool, Hot tub, Tennis, Golf: 2 championship courses; TV, Cable, Crib-Hi-chair, Ind. AC Ctl., Ind. Heat Ctl.

Attractions: South Padre Island-30 minutes, shopping in Mexico-20 minutes, zoo, Air Force Museum, entertainment

Shops & Restaurants: Sunrise & Amigo-Land Mall, Valley Vista; Casa Grande Supper Club

Rancho Viejo Resort and Country Club has two championship golf courses, tennis, swimming and fine dining at the Casa Grande Supper Club which has entertainment Thursday through Saturday in season. South Padre Island is 30 minutes away, or be in Mexico in twenty minutes. Swimming pool with waterfall and swim-up bar amidst semi-tropical landscaping. Golf packages available.

CONROE

April Sound Country Club
P.O. Box 253
Conroe, TX 77301
409-588-1101

1 Bedroom $$, 2 Bedrooms $$, Lo-rise
Pool, Daily maid, Kitchen, Linens

Attractions: Lake Conroe, golf, tennis, water sports, aquatic driving range

Individually decorated condominiums in the pines. Resort geared to tennis and golf. Family pool, two adult pools, outdoor mini-restaurant. Inland Marina for fishing or ski boats.

CORPUS CHRISTI

El Constante
14802 Windward Drive
Corpus Christi, TX 78418
512-949-7088

1 Bedroom $$, 2 Bedrooms $$, Lo-rise
Pool, Daily maid, Kitchen

Attractions: Country Club privileges

One-bedroom units with one bath, two-bedroom with 2.5 baths with completely equipped kitchens.

—————————————— CORPUS CHRISTI ——————————————

Fairway Villas
14401 Commodore
Corpus Christi, TX 78418

1 Bedroom $$, 2 Bedrooms $$, Villas
Pool, Kitchen

Attractions: Bayfront Arts & Science Park, Art Museum, Artesian Park, Heritage Park (historic homes), fishing, tennis, golf

Luxuriously furnished condominiums adjacent to Padre Island Country Club. A short walk and you're at the beach.

Puente Vista
14300 Aloha
Corpus Christi, TX 78418
512-933-7081

2 Bedrooms $$, Lo-rise
Pool, Kitchen, Phone in rm.

Attractions: Tennis, golf, sightseeing boats, surfing, fishing, boat facilities

All units have waterside decks, and deck or patio overlooking the courtyards and land-scaped grounds. Area has observation towers for an extended bird's-eye view. 30 feet from your door are canals for boat docking.

The Gulfstream
14810 Windward Drive
Corpus Christi, TX 78418
512-949-8061 800-542-7368

2 Bedrooms $$$
2 Bedrms/week 4$
Min. Stay 2 Nights, AmEx/Visa/MC,
  Dep. 2 Nights •
131 condos, Hi-rise, Key at Front desk
H-yes

Location: Airport: 20 Miles; Downtown: 15 miles; Need car; Beach front

General Facilities: Full serv., Conf. rm. cap. 40, Daily maid, Kitchen, Linens, Game room, Child planned rec.: Game room

Room Facilities: Pool, Hot tub, Shuffleboard, Golf: Country Club 2 miles; TV, Phone in rm., Crib-Hi-chair, Ind. AC Ctl., Ind. Heat Ctl.

Attractions: Fishing, national seashores

Shops & Restaurants: Dillards, Jeskes, Penney's, Sears, Mervyns; Wayward Lady-Country Line BBQ

Each unit is spacious, tastefully decorated and a short walk across and down the stepped seawall to the Gulf of Mexico. A large swimming pool, game room for the children, jacuzzi and shuffleboard. Guest privileges are available on request for the nearby Padre Isles Country Club for golf, tennis, swimming, dining, drinking and dancing.

Villa Del Sol
3938 Surfside Blvd.
Corpus Christi, TX 78402
512-883-9748 800-242-3291

1 Bedroom $$, Villas
Pool, Daily maid, Kitchen

Attractions: Aransas Wildlife Refuge, ballet, symphony, Art Museum, Museum of Oriental Cultures, golf

Beautifully landscaped grounds with palms, flowering shrubs, tropical plants and bedding plants. Your one-bedroom condominium sleeps 4 adults and 2 children. Satellite TV, spec-travision, pay premium movies and stereo tape deck. Balconies look out over the Bay.

---------------------------------- FREEPORT ----------------------------------

Inverness At San Luis Pass
Route #2, Box 1270
Freeport, TX 77541
409-239-1433

Studio $$, 1 Bedroom $$
2 Bedrms/week 5$
Min. Stay 2 Nights, AmEx/Visa/MC, Dep. Req'd.
40 condos, Lo-rise, Key at Front office

Location: Airport: 68 miles; Downtown: 20 miles; Need car; Beach front

General Facilities: Kitchen, Linens

Room Facilities: Pool, TV, Crib-Hi-chair, Ind. AC Ctl., Ind. Heat Ctl.

Attractions: TEXSUN sightseeing cruise tours

Shops & Restaurants: Brazos Mall, Penney's, Dillards, Sears; Windswept/steaks and seafood

Located on Follet's Island, Inverness has beautiful beaches in a quiet and isolated area. Within an hour and a half drive are Houston, Galveston and Lake Jackson, all of which offer a variety of dining and entertainment. For the fisherman, there are good locations for Gulf or bay fishing.

------------------------------ GALVESTON ISLAND ------------------------------

Seaside Point
7820 Seawall Blvd
Galveston Island, TX 77551
409-744-6200 800-992-1187

---------------------------------- GALVESTON ----------------------------------

Casa Del Mar
6102 Seawall
Galveston, TX 77551
409-740-2431 800-392-1205

1 Bedroom $$
Pool, Daily maid, Kitchen, Linens, Phone in rm.

Attractions: Tall ship Elissa, Seawolf Park, Stewart Beach, Ashton Villa, Bishop's Palace, RR Museum

Clean-lined buildings with driftwood and white stucco exteriors. Decorator furnished interiors, view balconies and two hallway bunks for the "wee ones." Oleanders around the two pools. Cookout grills and picnic tables. You'll be minutes away from the beach.

Four Seasons On The Gulf
4000 Seawall Blvd.
Galveston, TX 77550
713-763-7138

Pool, Kitchen, Phone in rm.

Attractions: Galveston Island State Park-Sea Arama Marine World-Tour Train-Bishop's Palace-Railroad Museum, shuffleboard, tennis, golf

Two-bedroom units with 2.5 baths, sleep 6, and have all your vacation needs, including food processors, microwaves, stereos, fireplaces and hair dryers. Three miles to water sports, and fishing across the street. Rods, bicycles and tennis equipment are supplied.

────────────── GALVESTON ──────────────

Inverness by the Sea
7600 Seawall Blvd.
Galveston, TX 77551
409-740-4066

2 Bedrooms $$, Hi-rise
Pool, Kitchen, Linens

Attractions: Point Bolivar Lighthouse, Galveston Island State Park, Dollhouse Museum, Colonel Paddleboa, exercise room, tennis

Completely furnished two-bedroom suites down to ice makers and stereos. Beachfront property with tennis, exercise room, saunas, pool, rec. room and ll miles of continuous sidewalk. 30 miles of beach for a real family vacation.

The Victorian Condotel
6300 Seawall Blvd.
Galveston, TX 77551
409-740-3555 800-392-1215

1 Bedroom $, 2 Bedrooms $$
1 Bedrm/week $$$$, 2 Bed/week 4$
Min. Stay 2 Nights, AmEx/Visa/MC,
Dep. Req'd. •
330 condos, Lo-rise, Key at Front desk

Location: Airport: Hobby 45 miles; Need car; Beach front

General Facilities: Full serv., Bus. fac., Conf. rm. cap. 200, Daily maid, Kitchen, Linens, Game room, Child planned rec.: Playground

Room Facilities: Pool, Hot tub, Tennis, Playground, TV, Cable, VCR, Crib-Hi-chair, Ind. AC Ctl., Ind. Heat Ctl.

Attractions: Railroad Museum, Marineworld, 1894 Opera House, NASA, Moody Gardens, Sea-arama

Shops & Restaurants: The Strand, Houston/Galleria; Gaidos-seafood

Texas history is at your doorstep in these fully accessorized Victorian suites complete with private balconies overlooking the Gulf. Convenient beaches, fishing pier, shopping and gourmet dining pleasures are nearby.

────────────── GRANDBURY ──────────────

The Ridge Chalets
Route 9, Box 47
Grandbury, TX 76048
817-573-7148

1 Bedroom $, 2 Bedrooms $$, Lo-rise
Kitchen

Attractions: Water sports, tennis

Condominiums on Lake Granbury for full enjoyment of water sports and fishing.

─────────────── HORSESHOE BAY ───────────────

**Horseshoe Bay Country Club
Resort**
Box 7766
Horseshoe Bay, TX 78654
512-598-8561 800-252-9363

Location: Beach front

General Facilities: Conf. rm. cap. 250, Kitchen, Restaurant on prem., Bar on prem.,
    Game room

Room Facilities: Pool, Tennis, Sailing, water ski, Golf: 3 golf courses

Attractions: LBJ home, Longhorn Caverns, Falls Creek Winery

Shops & Restaurants: The Captain's Table, Keel Way

Two-and three-bedroom condominiums in this private country club resort with its spring-fed streams, ancient rocks, exotic gardens and miles of shoreline and coves. Fully equipped marina for the boater, and two-tiered pool fed by a waterfall for swimmers. Tennis complex with fitness program consisting of body shape-up classes and aqua aerobics, Equestrian Center and three Robert Trent Jones' designed golf courses.

─────────────── LINDALE ───────────────

Garden Valley Resort
Route 2, Box 501
Lindale, TX 75771
214-882-6107

─────────────── MONTGOMERY ───────────────

Inverness Condominium
13151 Walden Road
Montgomery, TX 77356
409-582-4477 713-353-9671

1 Bedroom $$, 2 Bedrooms $$
1 Bedrm/week $$$$, 2 Bed/week 4$
Min. Stay 2 Nights, AmEx/Visa/MC
86 condos, Lo-rise, Key at Inverness PR office

Location: Airport: 1 hour 15 Min.; Downtown: 1 hour; Need car

General Facilities: Bar on prem., Game room, Lounge

Room Facilities: Pool, Sauna, Hot tub, Lake, Golf: Walden Golf on Lake; TV, Cable,
    Phone in rm., Crib-Hi-chair, Ind. AC Ctl., Ind. Heat Ctl.

Attractions: Walden Golf Club, Yacht Club, Crews Nest Night Club, Lake Conroe, tennis,
    raquetball

Shops & Restaurants: Galleria, Houston, 1½ hours away; Yacht Club, Cafe on the
    Green

Championship golf package includes green fees at Walden golf course on Lake Conroe. Beautiful yacht club with Friday night seafood buffet. Condos are on the first fairway, and there are two swimming pools.

MONTGOMERY

Walden on Lake Conroe
14001 Walden Rd.
Montgomery, TX 77356
409-582-6441

Location: Airport: Houston—1 hour

General Facilities: Conf. rm. cap. 350, Kitchen, Restaurant on prem.

Room Facilities: Pool, Tennis, Yacht harbor, Golf: 72 par course

Attractions: Lake Conroe water sports, Reflections III-70' yacht for charters, Sam Houston Nat. Park

Shops & Restaurants: Ship's store; Commodore Rm-Cafe on the Green

Resort with seven contemporary complexes of one-, two-and three-bedroom spacious, fully equipped condominiums overlooking the yacht harbor, lagoons or wooded East Texas terrain. Each cluster has its own pool. 16 tennis courts. Full service marina with rental sail and power boats. Try the driving range across from the golf clubhouse before tackling the par 72 course with a slope rating of 126 from the middle tees.

MUSTANG ISLAND, PORT ARANSAS

Sandpiper Condos-Mustang Island
Park Rd 53, P.O. Box 1268
Mustang Island, Port Aransas, TX 78373
512-749-6251

1 Bedroom $$, 2 Bedrooms $$, Hi-rise
Pool, Kitchen, Linens, Phone in rm.

Attractions: Fishing, beach, tennis

A covered porte cochere entry welcomes you upon arrival at this high-rise condominium complex. Suites are individually decorated for a pleasant, relaxing vacation. Elevated boardwalk to the Gulf beach, pool, whirlpool, lanai area, sun decks and tennis courts.

MUSTANG ISLAND

Casa Del Cortes
Hwy. 53
Mustang Island, TX

NEW BRAUNFELS

Comal River Condominiums
Comal Street
New Braunfels, TX 78130

2 Bedrooms $$

Quiet, relaxing atmosphere under the shade of native trees yet close to all New Braunfels' activities. Wood burning fireplaces and T.V.

Inverness at New Braunfels
401 W. Lincoln
New Braunfels, TX 77541
409-239-1433

1 Bedroom $$, 2 Bedrooms $$
Pool, Kitchen, Phone in rm.

Attractions: Deep-sea excursions, historic Galveston, swimming, beach, volleyball, shuffleboard

Family beach vacation. Be sure and bring beach toys and lots of beach towels. It's wise to pick up your supplies before you come since the nearest grocery is 15 miles away. Fishing in the Gulf or Christmas Bay. Board and card games in the office.

---------------------- NEW BRAUNFELS ----------------------

Woodlands Condominiums
New Braunfels, TX 78138

Walk out your back door to the 18-hole golf course or the nearby boat ramp to beautiful Canyon Lake.

---------------------- PORT ARANSAS ----------------------

Angler's Courts
403 N. Alister Box 218
Port Aransas, TX 78373
512-749-5327

Aransas Princess   2 Bedrooms $$$, Hi-rise
On the Beach, Acc. Rd. 1A, Box 309   Pool, Kitchen
Port Aransas, TX 78373
512-749-5117

Attractions: Gulf of Mexico, Corpus Christi Bay, intercoastal canal, beach, boating, tennis, golf

Palatial condominiums on the Texas Riviera. Watch the boats go through the channel as you await the sunset from your private balcony. Tennis, two pools, jacuzzi and dry sauna. Glass enclosed elevators take you to your condominium after a day at the beach.

Bay Tree Condominium
1125 N. Station Drawer A
Port Aransas, TX 78373
512-749-5859

Beachgate   Lo-rise
On the Beach, Box 116   Kitchen
Port Aransas, TX 78373
512-749-5900

Four one-bedroom apartments on Mustang Island Beach in a natural setting of sand dunes, sea oats and beach morning glories. Resident manager to see to your needs and tell you about island activities.

Beachhead Resort   2 Bedrooms $$
1319 S. 11th St, Box 1577   2 Bedrms/week $$$$
Port Aransas, TX 78373   Visa/MC,Dep. 1 Night •
512-749-6261   34 condos, Lo-rise, Key at Front desk

Location: Airport: 50 miles; Need car; Beach front

General Facilities: Full serv., Conf. rm. cap. 70, Daily maid, Kitchen, Linens, Game room, Lounge

Room Facilities: Pool, Tennis, TV, Cable, Phone in rm., Crib-Hi-chair, Ind. AC Ctl., Ind. Heat Ctl.

Attractions: Fishing, boating, beach

Shops & Restaurants: Local shops; Pelican Landing-Seafood

Comfortable, clean, lovely grounds on the beach. Peaceful, serene, close to shopping, fine dining, boating and fishing. A special place for special people who are given special attention.

Victorian Condotel

PORT ARANSAS

Buccaneer Courts
713 Mustang Isl. Rd., Box 507
Port Aransas, TX 78373
512-749-5566

Casa Del Mar
104 Dunes Drive, P.O. Box 488
Port Aransas, TX 78373
512-749-6996

2 Bedrooms $, Lo-rise
Kitchen, Linens

Attractions: Seashore, Horace Caldwell Pier, Port Aransas docks, deep-sea fishing, "Old Mexico"'

Small project with two-bedroom units within the Mustang Island dunes seashore, in a natural setting. No phones, no pool, no pets, just the relaxation of the dunes and beach. Near pier and docks for deep-sea fishing and sailing.

Casadel Beach Hotel & Racquet
P.O. Box 1149
Port Aransas, TX 78373
512-749-6942

1 Bedroom $$, 2 Bedrooms $$$, Hi-rise
Pool, Kitchen

Attractions: Port Aransas fishing village, golf, tennis, water sports, deep-sea, bay and surf fishing, exercise room

On the beach at Mustang Island, beautifully furnished suites with Gulf or pool views from balconies with outdoor furniture. Concrete boardwalk to the beach. 5 miles to Port Aransas for the sport fisherman; trout, flounder and redfish for the bay and surf fisherman.

-------------------- PORT ARANSAS --------------------

Casadel Beach Racquet Club
Box 1149
Port Aransas, TX 78373
512-749-6942

Channelview Condominium
423 Channelview, Box 776
Port Aransas, TX 78373
512-749-6156

1 Bedroom $$, 2 Bedrooms $$, 3 Bedrooms $$
Min. Stay 2 Nights, Visa/MC, Dep. 1 Night •
36 condos, Lo-rise, Key at In the office
H-yes

Location: Airport: 45 minutes; Downtown: 1 minute; Need car; Beach front
General Facilities: Daily maid, Kitchen
Room Facilities: Sauna, Private fishing pier, TV, Cable, Phone in rm., Crib-Hi-chair, Ind. AC Ctl., Ind. Heat Ctl.
Attractions: Private lighted fishing pier, boat slips, peaceful environment
Shops & Restaurants: Shell shops, Pat Magee's, Things; Seafood & Spaghetti Works
Unique location with a peaceful and pleasant atmosphere. Especially attractive to families.

Cline's Landing Condominium
1000 N. Station St, Box 1628
Port Aransas, TX 78373
512-749-5275

2 Bedrooms $$$, 3 Bedrooms $$$$
2 Bedrms/week 7$, 3 Bed/week 10$
Dep. Req'd.
108 condos, Hi-rise, Key at Mgt. office

Location: Airport: Port Aransas; Downtown: minutes
General Facilities: Full serv., Conf. rm. cap. 200, Kitchen, Game room, Lounge, Child planned rec.: Playground
Room Facilities: Pool, Hot tub, Marina
Attractions: Boating, fishing excursions, duck hunting, boat and beach tours, tennis
Shops & Restaurants: Quaint Port Aransas shops; Port Aransas restaurants
Enter the lobby and be impressed with the seven-story atrium graced with trailing philodendron. 1,450 sq. ft. two-bedroom units. Three-bedroom units are 2,075 sq. ft. with walk-in closets, master bathrooms with skylights and jacuzzis. Let the children enjoy the playground while you barbecue your catch of the day at the picnic area. Bristol class marina for Gulf access with slip rentals. Walk for miles on the beach before you settle down to relax on the sand. 24 hr. security and area camera scanning.

Coral Cay Condominium
1321 S. 11th St., Box 448
Port Aransas, TX 78373
512-749-5111 800-221-4981

1 Bedroom $$, 2 Bedrooms $$, Lo-rise
Pool, Daily maid, Kitchen, Linens, Phone in rm.

Attractions: Port Aransas fishing village, deep-sea fishing, jazz, country music, beach
Choose your condominium size and location, beachfront, Gulf view or poolside. Native grasses and wild flowers among the landscaped grounds. Just a few blocks away from Port Aransas fishing village with its shops, restaurants and entertainment.

——————————— PORT ARANSAS ———————————

Dunes Condominium
1000 Lantana Box 1238
Port Aransas, TX 78373
512-749-5155 800-288-3863

1 Bedroom $$, 2 Bedrooms $$
Min. Stay 2 Nights, AmEx/Visa/MC,
   Dep. 1 Night •
86 condos, Hi-rise, Key at Front desk, H-yes

Location: Airport: 20 miles; Downtown: 1 mile; Need car; Beach front

General Facilities: Full serv., Bus. fac., Conf. rm. cap. 100, Daily maid, Kitchen, Linens, Lounge

Room Facilities: Pool, Hot tub, Tennis, Shuffleboard, fishing, TV, Cable, Phone in rm., Crib-Hi-chair, Ind. AC Ctl., Ind. Heat Ctl.

Attractions: Charter fishing of all kinds, surf, pier, jetty fishing, entertainment

Shops & Restaurants: Local stores; Pelican's Landing/seafood

Individually decorated condominiums with 200 sq. ft. of Gulf viewing space balconies. The pool is screened from the wind and surrounded with tropical vegetation. Covered lanai area. Steps to the beach and tennis. Port Aransas marina for charter fishing boats.

El Cortes Villas
Mustang Island, Box 1266
Port Aransas, TX 78373
512-749-6206

1 Bedroom $, 2 Bedrooms $$, Villas
Pool, Daily maid, Kitchen

Attractions: Deepsea fishing, surf fishing, beach, tennis, golf

Modern villas behind the sand dunes with private walking acess to the beach. Just a few miles to the fishing port of Aransas.

Executive Keys
Box 1087
Port Aransas, TX 78373
512-749-6272

2 Bedrooms $$, Lo-rise
Pool, Daily maid, Kitchen, Linens, Phone in rm.

Attractions: Fishing, swimming, beach sports, crabbing, volleyball

Comfortable, individually decorated suites for the vacationing family. Three picnic areas with grills. Large pots for boiling crabs/shrimp are available. Two-story townhouse units can also be rented with special weekly rates. A place to get away and enjoy the beach.

Gulf Beach Courts
506 E. Ave. G, Box 778
Port Aransas, TX 78373
512-749-5416

Gulf Shores Condominium
Park Rd. 53, Box 1298
Port Aransas, TX 78373
512-749-6257

Haney's Cottages
225 E. Oakes, Box 171
Port Aransas, TX 78373
512-749-5792

PORT ARANSAS

Island Retreat Condominium
700 Island Retreat Court, Box 637
Port Aransas, TX 78373
512-749-6222

1 Bedroom $, 2 Bedrooms $, 3 Bedrooms $$
2 Bedrms/week $$$$, 3 Bed/week $$$$
Min. Stay 3 Nights, Visa/MC, Dep. 1 Night •
148 condos, Lo-rise, Key at Office
P-yes

Location: Airport: Corpus Christi; Downtown: 1.5 mile; Need car; Beach front

General Facilities: Full serv., Conf. rm. cap. 100, Daily maid, Kitchen, Linens

Room Facilities: Pool, Tennis, TV, Cable, Phone in rm., Ind. AC Ctl., Ind. Heat Ctl.

Attractions: Texas Gulf Beach and Corpus Christi for big city life

Shops & Restaurants: Surf shops, shell shops and tourist shops; Water Front/seafood

Family-size condominiums decorated in earth tones with wood paneling, accented with Mediterranean styles. Two walkways to the sandy beach on the Gulf of Mexico or the sands of Mustang Island. Swimming pool, spacious parking, and the privacy of your own patio-balcony.

Marine Courts
411 N. Alister, Box 76
Port Aransas, TX 78373
512-749-5509

Mayan Princess Condominium
Park Rd. 53, Box 156
Port Aransas, TX 78373
512-749-5183 800-542-7368

1 Bedroom $$$, 2 Bedrooms $$$
1 Bedrm/week 7$, 2 Bed/week 10$
Min. Stay 2 Nights, Visa/MC, Dep. 2 Nights •
60 condos, Hi-rise, Key at Front desk
H-yes

Location: Airport: 30 miles; Downtown: 25 miles; Need car; Beach front

General Facilities: Full serv., Conf. rm. cap. 50, Daily maid, Kitchen, Linens

Room Facilities: Pool, Hot tub, Tennis, Golf: 8 miles; TV, Phone in rm., Crib-Hi-chair, Ind. AC Ctl., Ind. Heat Ctl.

Attractions: Surf, pier and deep-sea fishing, shelling, beachcombing, boating and sailing, charter boat

Shops & Restaurants: Corpus Christi shops and Port Aransas shops; Numerous seafood restaurants

Nestled in the dunes along Mustang Island, The Mayan Princess is just ten miles from Port Aransas and Corpus Christi. There are three swimming pools and a hot tub outdoors. The beach is only a few yards away. Play golf or tennis or get up early for bird watching.

---------------------------------- PORT ARANSAS ----------------------------------

Merrimac Cottages
Station & White, Box 172
Port Aransas, TX 78373
512-749-5360

Mustang Island Beach Club   2 Bedrooms $$
Park Rd. 53   2 Bedrms/week 4$
Port Aransas, TX 78373   Min. Stay 2 Nights, Visa/MC, Dep. 1 Night •
512-749-5446   16 condos, Villas, Key at Reception center

Location: Airport: 30 miles; Need car

General Facilities: Daily maid, Kitchen, Linens

Room Facilities: Pool, Hot tub, TV, Cable, Phone in rm., Crib-Hi-chair, Ind. AC Ctl., Ind. Heat Ctl.

Attractions: Charter fishing, beaches, water sports, shelling, crabbing, bikes, dune buggies

Shops & Restaurants: Seafood Cajun style

Mustang Island Beach Club condominiums are furnished in rattan, glass, and earth tones of mauve and blues. Vacation activity centers around the beaches and water sports, especially year-round fishing. Many historical sights to visit, or rent three-wheel bikes and dune buggies to explore the undeveloped coastline.

Mustang Isle Apartments   1 Bedroom $, 2 Bedrooms $$, Lo-rise
2100 S. 11th St., Box 37   Kitchen, Linens
Port Aransas, TX 78373
512-749-6011

A small condominium complex on Mustang Isle. All-electric kitchens, air conditioning and cable TV. A short walk through the dunes takes you to the beach.

Mustang Towers   2 Bedrooms $$, 3 Bedrooms $$
Park Rd. 53, Box 1870   2 Bedrms/week 4$, 3 Bed/week 5$
Port Aransas, TX 78373   Visa/MC,Dep. 1 Night •
512-749-6212 800-343-2772   56 condos, Hi-rise, Key at Office
                                      H-yes

Location: Airport: 35 miles; Downtown: 6 miles; Need car; Beach front

General Facilities: Full serv., Bus. fac., Daily maid, Kitchen, Linens, Game room

Room Facilities: Pool, Hot tub, Tennis, Volleyball, horseshoes, TV, Phone in rm., Crib-Hi-chair, Ind. AC Ctl., Ind. Heat Ctl.

Attractions: Deep-sea fishing, scenic boat cruises, Aransas Wildlife Refuge, 3½ hrs. from Mexico, entertainment

Shops & Restaurants: 2 shopping malls, Penney's, Sears, Foleys, K-Mart; Seafood & Spaghetti Works

A special place where you mark your time by the spectacular sunsets over the Gulf and sunsets over the Bay. Contemporary furnishings with sea motif, 2 sliding glass doors lead to Gulf view balcony. Miles of sandy beach unspoiled by man. An island retreat. Bi-level pool with waterfall, sun decks, cabanas, and activity room.

PORT ARANSAS

Port Royal Ocean Resort
Park Rd. 53, Box 336
Port Aransas, TX 78373
512-749-5011 800-847-5659

1 Bedroom $$, 2 Bedrooms $$, 3 Bedrooms $$$
Dep. 1 Night
Hi-rise

Location: Downtown: 30 min.; Beach front

General Facilities: Conf. rm. cap. 700, Daily maid, Kitchen, Linens, Restaurant on prem., Bar on prem., Game room

Room Facilities: Pool, Tennis, Shuffleboard volleyball, Golf: Padre Isle Golf Course

Attractions: Port Aransas for deep-sea fishing and charters, Fisherman's Wharf, Marine Science Lab

Shops & Restaurants: Lobby level boutique, gift shop, convenience store; Royal Beachcomber

Professionally decorated with spacious living rooms, sun deck terraces, built-in stereo, whirlpool and steam baths in master suites. 500-foot Royal Blue Lagoon Pool with waterfalls, hidden grottoes, swim-up cabana bars, four whirlpool spas and huge dune water slide. Beach for surfing, swimming and shelling. Royal Beachcomber restaurant and lounge for an evening out.

Sand & Surf Condominium
1423 11th Street, Box 1439
Port Aransas, TX 78373
512-749-6001

1 Bedroom $
Kitchen, Linens

One-bedroom units with two double beds, fully equipped kitchens, dishwasher, disposal, separate bath dressing areas, large linen closet and walk-in closet. Upstairs units have private view balconies. Small room set aside for recreation.

Sandcastle Condominium
Sandcastle Rd. On Beach, Box 1688
Port Aransas, TX 78373
521-749-6201 800-727-6201

1 Bedroom $$, 2 Bedrooms $$$, Hi-rise
Pool, Kitchen, Linens

Attractions: Tennis

View units with sliding glass doors to the balcony. Attractively decorated in rattan and glass with ceiling fans. Wooden walkway to the beach. Pool with lounges and umbrella tables surrounded by lawn, palms and colorful flowers.

Be sure to call the condo to verify details and prices and to make your reservation.

––––––––––––––––––––– PORT ARANSAS –––––––––––––––––––––

Sea Gull Condominium
Park Rd. 53, Box 1207
Port Aransas, TX 78373
512-749-4191

1 Bedroom $$, 2 Bedrooms $$, 3 Bedrooms $$$
Min. Stay 2 Nights, AmEx/Visa/MC,
    Dep. 1 Night
105 condos, Hi-rise, Key at Front desk
H-yes

Location: Airport: 45 minutes; Downtown: 8 miles; Need car; Beach front

General Facilities: Full serv., Conf. rm. cap. 100, Daily maid, Kitchen, Linens, Child planned rec.: Playground

Room Facilities: Pool, Tennis, Basketball, horseshoes, TV, Cable, Phone in rm., Crib-Hi-chair, Ind. AC Ctl., Ind. Heat Ctl.

Attractions: Beach, trips to Mexico, deep sea and bay fishing

Shops & Restaurants: Groceries, clothes, souvenirs; Spaghetti Works/pasta-seafood

The Sea Gull is an 11-story high-rise located directly on the beach. All units overlook the Gulf of Mexico and are furnished in a luxurious manner. Beach boys set up chaises and umbrellas at no charge—tipping is forbidden. Basketball, volleyball, horseshoes and children's playground are all available at Sea Gull.

––

Sea Isle Village
1129 S. 11th St., Box 1686
Port Aransas, TX 78373
512-749-6281

1 Bedroom $, 2 Bedrooms $$, Lo-rise
Pool, Daily maid, Kitchen, Linens

Attractions: Beach, fishing

Complex with efficiency to three bedroom apartments. Satellite TV. Pool, boardwalk to beach.

––

Sea Sands Condominium
1377 S. 11th St., Box 537T
Port Aransas, TX 78373
512-749-6246

1 Bedroom $, 2 Bedrooms $, Lo-rise
Pool, Kitchen, Linens

Attractions: Fishing, beachcombing, swimming

Attractively furnished apartments with living room white brick walls. Lounge around the pool. One block to the Gulf of Mexico for beachcombing, swimming and relaxing.

––

Spanish Village
200 N. Alister, Box 578
Port Aransas, TX 78373
512-749-5253

––

Sunday Villas
1900 S. 11th St., Box 1213
Port Aransas, TX 78373
512-749-6480

2 Bedrooms $$, Villas
Pool, Daily maid, Kitchen, Linens

A colony of uniquely designed unattached condominiums in Port Aransas. The beach is a short walk away over the dunes. Pool.

PORT ARANSAS

Teal Harbor Condominium
200 W. Cotter St., P.O. Box F
Port Aransas, TX 78373
512-749-4131

2 Bedrooms $$$, Hi-rise
Pool, Kitchen, Linens

Attractions: Crabbing, surf-fishing, charter boat fishing-touring, boating, beaches, marina

Beautifully designed condominiums along the Texas coast. Unit access is by key-operated elevators serving two units, monitored by closed circuit TV. Marina with boatslips 23' x 70', and resident Harbor Master.

The Pelican
1107 S. 11th St., Box 1690
Port Aransas, TX 78373
512-749-6226

2 Bedrooms $, 3 Bedrooms $$
2 Bedrms/week $$$$, 3 Bed/week $$$$
Visa/MC,Dep. 2 Nights •
65 condos, Lo-rise, Key at Office, H-yes

Location: Airport: 1 mile; Downtown: ⅓ mile; Need car; Beach front

General Facilities: Daily maid, Kitchen, Linens, Baby-sitter

Room Facilities: Pool, Sauna, Golf: 18 miles; TV, Cable, Phone in rm., Ind. AC Ctl., Ind. Heat Ctl.

Attractions: Horseback riding, fishing tournaments, sunset cruises, wildlife refuge, Lighthouse, entertainment

Shops & Restaurants: Islander-gifts, souvenirs, Pat Magees, sun wear; Spaghetti Works, Tortuga Flats

A family-style condominium complex in a sleepy little fishing village accessed from Aransas Pass by free auto ferries. Playground, badminton court and swimming pool are enclosed in a large, privately fenced yard. Everything for the fisherman, or just spend your time on the beach, collecting shells, sunning, and swimming. Water aerobics from June to August, playground and badminton court. Spacious surroundings for kite flying or frisbee throwing, or just enjoying the view.

POTTSBORO

Tanglewood on Texoma Resort Hotel
Highway 120
Pottsboro, TX 75076
800-833-6569

Visa/MC, •
120 condos

Location: Airport: DFW Airport; Downtown: 5 miles

General Facilities: Conf. rm. cap. 135, Kitchen, Restaurant on prem., Bar on prem.

Room Facilities: Pool, Tennis, Riding, boating, Golf: 18-hole course; TV, Phone in rm., Ind. AC Ctl., Ind. Heat Ctl.

Attractions: President Eisenhower's birthplace, Lake Texoma, entertainment

Shops & Restaurants: Midway Mall, Kelly Square, The Depot; The Point/cont.- Pompanos

On tree-covered hills, situated on the shore of beautiful Lake Texoma, Tanglewood on Texoma offers the perfect setting for that perfect vacation. Lake recreational activities, fine cuisine in the Commodores Room, cocktails in the Yacht Club or high atop the nine-story tower overlooking the lake in the Moonraker. Dance floor and planned holiday activities.

━━━━━━━━━━━ SAM RAYBURN ━━━━━━━━━━━

Rayburn Country Resort 1 Bedroom $$, 2 Bedrooms $$, Villas
P.O. Box 36 Pool, Kitchen
Sam Rayburn, TX 75951
409-698-2444

Attractions: Jones Country Music Shop, water sports, fishing, sailing, badminton, horseshoes, tennis, golf

*Recreational development among pines, dogwoods, magnolias and azaleas with water
sports and fishing on clear Sam Rayburn Lake. Robert Trent Jones designed golf course,
and four all-weather, lighted tennis courts.*

━━━━━━━━━━━ SOUTH PADRE ISLAND ━━━━━━━━━━━

Bahi'a Mar Resort Hi-rise
Park Road 100, P.O. Box 2280 Pool, Kitchen
South Padre Island, TX 78578
512-943-1343

Attractions: 30-minute drive to Matamoros, Mexico, tennis

*Bahi'a Mar Resort on the "top of Texas" offers two-and three-bedroom condominiums for
weekly or monthly rental. On a subtropical island near the beach, with a lagoon, pool,
tennis and Gulf fishing.*

Island Estates Condominium
112 Oleander St.
South Padre Island, TX 78597

Padre South Resort 2 Bedrooms $$, Hi-rise
1500 Gulf Blvd, P.O. Box 2338 Pool, Kitchen, Linens
South Padre Island, TX 78597
512-761-4951

Attractions: 30 minutes to Old Mexico, Confederate AFB with WWII planes, golf

*Full-service vacation resort with efficiencies or two-bedroom suites. Balconies with Gulf
and Laguna Madre Bay views. Mild surf for getting your feet wet, white sand beach for sun-
ning. Barbecue area, patio/deck area with gazebos, indoor/outdoor bars.*

South Padre Hilton Resort 2 Bedrooms $$$$
500 Padre Blvd, P.O. Box 2081
South Padre Island, TX 78597
512-761-6511 800-292-7704

Location: Beach front
General Facilities: Kitchen
Room Facilities: Tennis

*Two-bedroom condominiums on a quarter mile of sparkling beachfront. Year-round pack-
age values.*

――――――――――――――――――― WILLIS ―――――――――――――――――

Landing At Seven Coves
700 Kingston Cove
Willis, TX 77378
713-222-6865

――――――――――――――――― WIMBERLEY ―――――――――――――――

Woodcreek Resort   Lo-rise
No. 1 Woodcreek Drive   Pool, Kitchen
Wimberley, TX 78676
512-847-2221 800-252-9303

Attractions: Boating, canoeing, fishing, hiking, biking, hayrides, bonfires, barbecues,
health spa, tennis, golf

*Texas hill country townhomes for nature lovers. Swim, play tennis, golf, or use the health
spa. Marina for paddle boating and canoeing. Explore the area by foot, bicycle or horseback. For a special dinner, dine in the Sam Houston Dining Room in a teepee or jail.*

Enter your favorite condo in our "Condo of the Year" contest (entry form is
in the back of the book).

Utah

Salt Lake City ● Park City
△ Alta
Snowbird

ALTA

Black Jack Condominium Lodge
Alta
Alta, UT 84092
801-742-3200

1 Bedroom $$$$, 2 Bedrooms $$$$
Kitchen, Linens

Attractions: Skiing

Midway between Alta and Snowbird. Mountain view living rooms, fireplaces with wood provided and kitchens with trash compactors. Lodge with fireplace and sunken hearth, ski locker room. Four-wheel drive to take you to ski areas in the morning.

PARK CITY

Acclaimed Lodging
P.O. Box 3629
Park City, UT 84060
801-649-3736 800-552-9696

2 Bedrooms $$$, 3 Bedrooms $$$
Min. Stay 4 Nights, AmEx/Visa/MC,
Dep. 1 Night •
18 condos, Lo-rise, Key at Park City Central
P-yes

Location: Airport: 30 miles; Downtown: 25 miles; Need car

General Facilities: Full serv., Kitchen, Linens, Restaurant on prem., Bar on prem., Baby-sitter

Room Facilities: Pool, Sauna, Hot tub, Tennis, Ski, hike, fish, Golf: Park Meadows Golf; TV, Cable, Phone in rm., Ind. Heat Ctl.

Attractions: 3 ski areas within a 3-mile radius, snowmobiles, backpacking, fishing, entertainment

Shops & Restaurants: Historic Main Street in Park City; Deer Valley Cafe, Mariposa

Fully equipped two-level townhouses within the Park City Racquet Club complex. Dinner/sleigh rides available on the premises, cross-country skiing tours, just one mile from Park City ski lifts on the City bus route.

———————————— PARK CITY ————————————

Acorn Chalet Lodging
1314 Empire
Park City, UT 84060
801-649-9313 800-443-3131

1 Bedroom $$, 2 Bedrooms $$, Lo-rise
Kitchen, Linens

Attractions: Park City skiing

Chalets 80 yards from the gondola. Access to free pool and jacuzzi near chalets.

Blue Church Lodge & Townhouses
P.O. Box 1720
Park City, UT 84060
801-649-8009

Studio $$, 1 Bedroom $$$, 2 Bedrooms $$$,
3 Bedrooms $$$$
1 Bedrm/week $$$, 2 Bed/week $$$,
3 Bed/week $$$$
Min. Stay 3 Nights, Visa/MC, Dep. Req'd. •
12 condos, Hi-rise, Key at Prior instructions

Location: Airport: 40 minutes; Downtown: 30 min.; Ski lift: Park City
General Facilities: Daily maid, Kitchen, Linens, Game room, Lounge
Room Facilities: Hot tub, TV, Cable, Phone in rm., Crib-Hi-chair, Ind. Heat Ctl.
Attractions: Downhill and cross-country skiing, snowmobiling, ice skating, ballooning
Shops & Restaurants: Main Street shopping located 1 street from lodge; Mr. Hunan/
  Chinese

*The Blue Church Lodge offers quaint country charm with some antique replicas, located
in the heart of Park City's historic district within walking distance of Main Street with its
shops, restaurants and nightlife. Indoor spa and table tennis in the game room. Golfing
and other outdoor sports in summer. Winter brings skiing, snowmobiling, ice skating,
sleigh rides, helicopter skiing and cross-country skiing on groomed tracks.*

Budget Lodging
P.O. Box 3813, 1940 Prospector Ave.
Park City, UT 84060
801-649-2526 800-522-7669

Studio $$, 1 Bedroom $$
AmEx/Visa/MC, Dep. Req'd. •
50 condos, Hi-rise, Key at Front desk

Location: Airport: 38 miles; Downtown: 3 miles; Ski lift: Park City
General Facilities: Full serv., Daily maid, Kitchen, Linens
Room Facilities: Pool, Hot tub, TV, Phone in rm., Crib-Hi-chair, Ind. Heat Ctl.
Attractions: Skiing, snowmobiling, ballooning, fishing, sailing, windsurfing, old-time
  steam train
Shops & Restaurants: Mrs. Fields, Main Street Mall; Adolph's/Swiss

*Modern condominium units, comfortably furnished including outdoor swimming pool and
hot tub. Park City ski area is three-quarters of a mile away. Free public transportation.
Restaurants and shops within walking distance.*

─────────────── PARK CITY ───────────────

Coalition Lodge
P.O. Box 75, 1300 Park Avenue
Park City, UT 84060
801-649-8591

2 Bedrooms $$$
2 Bedrms/week 7$
AmEx/Visa/MC, Dep. Req'd.
5 condos, Lo-rise, Key at Office #6

Location: Airport: 35 minutes; Downtown: 1 mile; Ski lift: Park City

General Facilities: Daily maid, Kitchen, Linens

Room Facilities: Sauna, TV, Crib-Hi-chair, Ind. Heat Ctl.

Attractions: Hot air ballooning, snowmobiling, skiing, hiking, fishing, hunting, golf, tennis

Shops & Restaurants: Old town major shopping zone; 39 excellent restaurants

Large size, designer furnished condominiums in an old west mining town. Warm., friendly atmosphere. 3 minutes from Park City ski area. Free bus service in front of the lodge to all ski areas, outside ski lockers. Fine restaurants and shops on a free bus route.

───────────────────────────────────────

Courchevel
P.O. Box 680128
Park City, UT 84068
801-649-9598 800-453-5789

1 Bedroom $$
3 Bedrms/week $$$$
Min. Stay 2 Nights, AmEx/Visa/MC, Dep. 1
Night •
26 condos, Lo-rise, Key at Park City Central

Location: Airport: SLC 35 miles; Downtown: 1 mile; Ski lift: Nearby

General Facilities: Daily maid, Kitchen, Linens, Child planned rec.: Local child care

Room Facilities: Alpine skiing, TV, Cable, Phone in rm., Crib-Hi-chair, Ind. Heat Ctl.

Attractions: Park City, historic silver mining town, gambler's trips to Nevada, steam train.

Shops & Restaurants: Unique shops and boutiques in Park City; Huggery-seafood buffet

Units are decorated with a French accent to create a warm cozy atmosphere. Free city-wide bus route to Park City, walk to ski lifts. U.S. Film Festival at Park City in January followed by celebrity ski races and snow sculpture contest. Fall Oktoberfest and hot air balloon festival in the Fall. Park City nightlife with dance bands and folk singers.

───────────────────────────────────────

Edelweiss Haus
P.O. Box 495, 1482 Empire Ave.
Park City, UT 84060
801-649-9342 800-438-3855

1 Bedroom $$, 2 Bedrooms $$
1 Bedrm/week 4$, 2 Bed/week 5$
AmEx/Visa/MC, Dep. Req'd. •
45 condos, Hi-rise, Key at Front office

Location: Airport: 35 miles; Downtown: 1 mile; Ski lift: Park City

General Facilities: Conf. rm. cap. 30, Kitchen, Linens

Room Facilities: Pool, Sauna, Hot tub, Winter-summer sports, TV, Cable, Phone in rm., Crib-Hi-chair, Ind. Heat Ctl.

Shops & Restaurants: Local resort shops; All types

Located 250 yards from Park City ski area, these condominiums are decorated in earth tones, brown and white. Outdoor heated swimming pool and jacuzzi. Close to market, ski shops and restaurants.

PARK CITY

Intermountain Lodging
P.O. Box 3803
Park City, UT 84060
801-649-2687 800-221-0933

Studio $, 1 Bedroom $, 2 Bedrooms $$, 3 Bedrooms $$$
Min. Stay 3 Nights, AmEx/Visa/MC, Dep. Req'd. •
150 condos, Lo-rise, Key at At complexes
No S-yes/H-yes

Location: Airport: 26 miles; Downtown: 1 mile; Ski lift: Park City

General Facilities: Full serv., Bus. fac., Conf. rm. cap. 25, Daily maid, Kitchen, Linens, Baby-sitter, Child planned rec.: Ski school-day care

Room Facilities: Pool, Skiing, mtn. sports, TV, Cable, VCR, Phone in rm., Crib-Hi-chair, Ind. Heat Ctl.

Attractions: Nordic and alpine skiing, boating, golf, tennis, ballooning, sleigh and hay rides, entertainment

Shops & Restaurants: Alex's/French

Comfortable, deluxe condominium units centrally located to all activities. Balconies overlooking mountains and ski resort. Fine accommodations at reasonable rates located in America's best mountain resort area.

Tamarron

─────────────── PARK CITY ───────────────

Park Meadows Racquet Club
P.O. Box 680128
Park City, UT 84068
801-649-9598 800-453-5789

2 Bedrooms $$, 3 Bedrooms $$$
2 Bedrms/week 4$, 3 Bed/week 5$
Min. Stay 2 Nights, AmEx/Visa/MC,
    Dep. 1 Night •
180 condos, Lo-rise, Key at 1700 Park Avenue
P-yes

Location: Airport: SLC 35 miles; Downtown: 2 miles; Ski lift: Nearby

General Facilities: Daily maid, Kitchen, Linens, Restaurant on prem., Bar on prem., Lounge

Room Facilities: Pool, Sauna, Hot tub, Tennis, Aerobics classes, Golf: Park Meadows Golf-near; TV, Cable, Phone in rm., Crib-Hi-chair, Ind. Heat Ctl.

Attractions: 3 golf courses within 6 miles, Park City, Mormon Tabernacle, Nevada gambling trips

Shops & Restaurants: Unique shops and boutiques in Park City; Alex's/French-continental

Traditional style, 3 levels, sliding doors to deck and lots of grassy area for play. Sauna, swimming pool and hot tub available for a fee. On-site Park City Racquet Club public facilities. Approximately 1.5 miles from Jack Nicklaus-designed Park Meadow Golf Course. Horseback riding, windsurfing, riding the rapids and helicopter skiing.

───

Park Plaza/Park Regency
P.O. Box 3988
Park City, UT 84060
800-553-1818 801-649-0870

───

Park Station Condominium Hotel
P.O. Box 1360
Park City, UT 84060
801-649-7717 800-367-1056

Studio $$, 1 Bedroom $$, 2 Bedrooms $$$,
    3 Bedrooms $$$$
AmEx/Visa/MC, Dep. Req'd. •
80 condos, Hi-rise, Key at Front desk
H-yes

Location: Airport: 40 minutes; Downtown: 2 blocks; Ski lift: Nearby

General Facilities: Full serv., Conf. rm. cap. 50, Daily maid, Kitchen, Linens, Babysitter

Room Facilities: Pool, Sauna, Hot tub, Tennis, TV, Cable, VCR, Phone in rm., Crib-Hi-chair, Ind. AC Ctl., Ind. Heat Ctl.

Attractions: Alpine & cross-country skiing, water skiing, swimming, sailing, hiking, golf, tennis

Shops & Restaurants: Clothing, gifts, art, liquor, food, ski equipment; Philippes-French

Located next to Park City ski area's town lift. Within easy walking distance of the restaurants, shops and nightlife of the historic Main Street district. Finest hotel services in a luxurious condominium environment.

PARK CITY

Powderwood Resort
6975 N. 2200 W.
Park City, UT 84060
801-649-2032 800-223-7829

1 Bedroom $, 2 Bedrooms $$
Min. Stay 3 Nights, AmEx/Visa/MC, Dep. 1
Night •
192 condos, Lo-rise, Key at Rental office
No S-yes

Location: Airport: 30 miles; Downtown: 25 miles; Ski lift: Nearby

General Facilities: Full serv., Kitchen, Linens, Game room, Lounge, Baby-sitter

Room Facilities: Pool, Sauna, Hot tub, Tennis, Gym, jogging trail, Golf: 5 minute drive; TV, Cable, Phone in rm., Crib-Hi-chair, Ind. Heat Ctl.

Attractions: Arnold Palmer Golf Course, horses, helicopter tours, ballooning, fishing, hiking, entertainment

Shops & Restaurants: Shopping centers, supermarkets,; Cisero's-Italian

All units have gas log fireplaces, sliding glass doors to private balconies, and queen-sized beds in the master bedroom. Continental breakfast and wine and cheese parties. This 3 year-old project has a clubhouse with a 40" color TV, electronic organ, pool table, card-backgammon table and two fireplaces. Whirlpool in a covered gazebo, steam room fitness room and volley ball and badminton court. Shuttle buses to ski resorts. Both summer and winter activities at this total resort.

Prospector Square Hotel
2200 Sidewinder Dr, Box 1698
Park City, UT 84060
801-649-7100 800-453-3812

1 Bedroom $$$, 2 Bedrooms $$$$, 3 Bedrooms
$$$$
Hi-rise, Key at Office

Location: Airport: SLC 30 minutes; Downtown: minutes; Ski lift: Park City

General Facilities: Full serv., Bus. fac., Conf. rm. cap. 330, Daily maid, Kitchen, Linens, Restaurant on prem., Child planned rec.: Ski area ski school

Room Facilities: Pool, Sauna, Hot tub, Tennis, Athletic Club, Golf: Two courses Park City; TV, Cable, Phone in rm.

Attractions: Park City, Deer Valley and Park West Ski areas, music, climbing, golf, tennis alpine slide, entertainment

Shops & Restaurants: Park City's 80 unique shops and galleries; Grub Steak-on-site/seafood/stk

1890's mining town atmosphere in the Wasatch Mountains, Prospector Square Hotel features three-bedroom condominiums which sleep eight. Outstanding ski vacation for all abilities. Athletic club, in-room movies, Grub Steak restaurant with Sunday Buffet Brunch Extravaganza, live entertainment and bar, and complimentary bus service to Park City resorts. Tennis, racquetball and volleyball courts.

──────────────── PARK CITY ────────────────

Resort Center Lodging
P.O. Box 3449
Park City, UT 84060
801-649-0800 800-824-5331

Studio $, 1 Bedroom $$, 2 Bedrooms $$, 3 Bedrooms $$$$
AmEx/Visa/MC, Dep. 1 Night •
91 condos, Lo-rise, Key at Resort Center Lodge
H-yes

Location: Airport: 35 miles; Downtown: ¾ mile; Ski lift: Nearby

General Facilities: Full serv., Conf. rm. cap. 385, Daily maid, Kitchen, Linens, Restaurant on prem., Bar on prem., Lounge, Baby-sitter, Child planned rec.: Ski instruction 3 yr

Room Facilities: Pool, Sauna, Hot tub, Tennis, Volleyball, skiing, TV, Phone in rm., Crib-Hi-chair, Ind. Heat Ctl.

Attractions: Ballooning, 3 golf courses within 10 miles, steam train, biking, fishing, brewery tours

Shops & Restaurants: Historic Main St. with boutiques, antiques, gifts; Columbine-fish, seafood

Resort Center offers accommodations with ski-in/ski-out access. Light woods, brass, glass decor with cathedral ceilings and gas fireplaces. Indoor/outdoor pool, sauna, hot tub, steam room fitness center and underground parking. Skater's Center, cross-country and downhill skiing. Summer recreation includes water sports, golf, tennis, hiking and fishing. Unique shops, nightclubs and great dining.

───

Resort Village Plaza
P.O. Box 680128
Park City, UT 84068
801-649-9598 800-453-5789

1 Bedrm/week $$$$, 2 Bed/week 4$
Min. Stay 2 Nights, AmEx/Visa/MC,
Dep. 1 Night •
160 condos, Lo-rise, Key at 1700 Park Avenue

Location: Airport: SLC 35 miles; Downtown: 1 mile; Ski lift: Nearby

General Facilities: Daily maid, Kitchen, Linens, Restaurant on prem., Bar on prem., Child planned rec.: Child care facility

Room Facilities: Hot tub, On-site skiing, Golf: Nearby; TV, Cable, Phone in rm., Crib-Hi-chair, Ind. Heat Ctl.

Attractions: 50 miles to horse racetrack in Evanston, WY, Park City, Mormon Tabernacle

Shops & Restaurants: Unique shops and boutiques in Park City; Columbine/prime rib-stir fry

At the base of the Park City ski area lifts for ski-in, ski-out accessibility. Year-round outdoor heated pool and within walking distance of shops, movie theatres, restaurants, supermarket and ice skating rink. Arrangements can be made for car rentals, lift tickets, ski equipment rentals, baby sitting and "First-Nighter" food packages. Something for everyone from winter skiing to summer activities.

─────────────────── PARK CITY ───────────────────

Ridgepoint
P.O. Box 680128
Park City, UT 84068
801-649-9598 800-453-5789

2 Bedrooms $$$, 3 Bedrooms $$$
3 Bedrms/week 6$
Min. Stay 2 Nights, AmEx/Visa/MC,
Dep. 1 Night •
42 condos, Lo-rise, Key at 1700 Park Avenue

Location: Airport: 35 miles Salt Lake; Downtown: 2 miles; Need car; Ski lift: Nearby
General Facilities: Daily maid, Kitchen, Linens, Child planned rec.: Local care facility
Room Facilities: Pool, Hot tub, Tennis, Alpine skiing, Golf: 3 within 10 miles; TV, Cable, Phone in rm., Crib-Hi-chair, Ind. Heat Ctl.
Attractions: Museums, shops, 3 ski areas within 5 miles, Mormon Tabernacle, genealogy resources
Shops & Restaurants: Park City boutiques, Salt Lake City mall stores; Glitretind-international

Sumptuous condominiums exuding warmth and an alpine ambience. Ski bridge to Deer Valley Resort. Mountain and valley views. 2 miles away, Park City offers many unique shops and restaurants. Summer days are clear and cool and the area is framed by pines, aspen and wildflowers. Outdoor concerts and the Utah Symphony Series and August arts festival at Park City.

───

Shadow Ridge Resort Hotel
50 Shadow Ridge Street, Box 1820
Park City, UT 84060
801-649-4300 800-451-3031

Studio $$, 1 Bedroom $$, 2 Bedrooms $$
Min. Stay 7 Nights, AmEx/Visa/MC,
Dep. 2 Nights •
48 condos, Hi-rise, Key at Front desk

Location: Airport: SLC Airport-34 miles; Downtown: 8 blocks
General Facilities: Full serv., Bus. fac., Conf. rm. cap. 250, Daily maid, Kitchen, Linens, Restaurant on prem., Bar on prem., Lounge, Baby-sitter
Room Facilities: Pool, Sauna, Hot tub, Skiing, golf, Golf: Park City Municipal Golf; TV, Cable, VCR, Phone in rm., Crib-Hi-chair, Ind. AC Ctl., Ind. Heat Ctl.
Attractions: Tours-Mrs. Fields Cookie Factory & Schirf Brewery, Timpanogos Cave, Temple Square, skiing, entertainment
Shops & Restaurants: Resort center, Main St. Mall, specialty stores

Four-story brick condominium development with rust, tan and forest green color schemes. Balconies off each sleeping room and private jacuzzi. Weekend entertainment in the lounge. Ski lockers, tuning and hot wax available, and walk to ski runs and Alpine Slide. Water sports in the summer with 3 reservoirs within a half-hour's drive, hayrides and flyfishing in secluded mountain streams, plus four championship golf courses within 15 minutes.

───

Silver Cliff Village
1485 Empire Avenue, P.O. Box 2818
Park City, UT 84060
801-649-5500 800-331-8652

2 Bedrooms $$, Lo-rise
Kitchen

Attractions: Alpine, x-country skiing-ballooning-golf-tennis-bike tours-sailing-fishing-hiking

Spacious, comfortable condominiums adjacent to Park City ski area. Woodburning fireplace, spa tub in master bedroom, washer/dryer and kitchen microwave. Staff will happily arrange your vacation activities.

─────────────── PARK CITY ───────────────

Silver King Hotel
P.O. Box 2818
Park City, UT 84060
801-649-5500 800-331-8652

Studio $$, 1 Bedroom $$, 2 Bedrooms $$
Min. Stay 3 Nights, AmEx/Visa/MC,
Dep. Req'd. •
85 condos, Hi-rise, Key at Front desk
H-yes

Location: Airport: 1 mile; Downtown: 35 min.; Need car; Ski lift: Nearby

General Facilities: Full serv., Conf. rm. cap. 150, Daily maid, Kitchen, Linens, Lounge

Room Facilities: Pool, Sauna, Hot tub, Golf: Park City Municipal; TV, Phone in rm., Crib-Hi-chair, Ind. AC Ctl., Ind. Heat Ctl.

Attractions: Skiing, snowmobiling, hot air ballooning, golf, tennis, swimming

Shops & Restaurants: Historic Main Street area, Resort Center Mall; Cafe Mariposa-Cont., Adolphs

Silver King Hotel is located at the base of the Park City ski area. Fully equipped studios, one-and two-bedroom suites, and two-bedroom penthouse suites with all the amenities and services.

───────────────────────────────────

Silvertown Condominiums
1505 Park Avenue, P.O. Box 1090
Park City, UT 84060
801-649-9022

1 Bedroom $$, 2 Bedrooms $$$, 3 Bedrooms $$$
AmEx/Visa/MC, Dep. 1 Night •
13 condos, Key at Office

Location: Airport: 45 minutes; Downtown: 10 blocks; Ski lift: Park City

General Facilities: Kitchen, Linens

Room Facilities: Sauna, Hot tub, Golf: Park City—2 blocks; TV, Phone in rm., Crib-Hi-chair, Ind. Heat Ctl.

Attractions: Skiing, golf, alpine-slide, recreation water within 1 hour drive

Shops & Restaurants: Grocery store, Main Street shops-10 blocks; Adolfs/Swiss, Glitretend/fish

Tastefully decorated units in Park City, Utah. Walk to ski lifts.

───────────────────────────────────

Snowflower Condominiums
P.O. Box 957, 400 Silver King Dr
Park City, UT 84060
801-649-6400 800-852-3101

Studio $$$, 1 Bedroom $$$$, 2 Bedrooms $$$$, 3 Bedrooms $$$$
Min. Stay 7 Nights, AmEx/Visa/MC,
Dep. Req'd. •
142 condos, Lo-rise, Key at Front desk
H-yes

Location: Airport: 45 minutes; Ski lift: Park City

General Facilities: Bus. fac., Conf. rm. cap. 70, Daily maid, Kitchen, Baby-sitter

Room Facilities: Hot tub, Tennis, TV, Cable, Phone in rm., Crib-Hi-chair

Attractions: Skiing, snowmobiling, hot air ballooning, sleigh rides, ice skating, x-country skiing

Shops & Restaurants: Local shops; Over 42 restaurants

Summer or winter, something for everyone. Skiers' access to 82 designated trails. On-site tennis, close to golf, racquetball, swimming, hiking and horses, Park City special events, shops and restaurants. Units have jetted hot tubs and fireplaces.

--- PARK CITY ---

Stag Lodge
P.O. Box 3000, 8200 Royal St. East
Park City, UT 84060
801-649-7444   800-453-3833

3 Bedrooms 7$
Min. Stay 7 Nights, AmEx/Visa/MC,
   Dep. Req'd. •
34 condos, Lo-rise, Key at Front desk
No S-yes/H-yes

Location: Airport: 35 miles; Downtown: 3 miles; Need car; Ski lift: Nearby

General Facilities: Full serv., Conf. rm. cap. 40, Daily maid, Kitchen, Linens, Restaurant on prem., Lounge, Baby-sitter

Room Facilities: Pool, TV, Cable, Phone in rm., Crib-Hi-chair, Ind. Heat Ctl.

Attractions: Ballooning, x-c, Mormon Tabernacle, steam railroad, theatre, sleigh rides

Shops & Restaurants: Main Street shopping; Philippe's/contintental

Luxury units done in a southwestern motif with private hot tubs. On the slopes of Deer Valley Resort for ski-in/ski-out access. Lodge features a highly regarded full-service restaurant.

The Innsbruck
1201 Norfolk, P.O. Box 222
Park City, UT 84060
801-649-9829

1 Bedroom $$, 2 Bedrooms $$$
1 Bedrm/week 5$, 2 Bed/week 7$
Min. Stay 2 Nights, Dep. Req'd. •
8 condos, Lo-rise, Key at On premises

Location: Airport: 35 miles; Downtown: bus 1 mile; Ski lift: Park City

General Facilities: Kitchen, Linens

Room Facilities: Pool, Sauna, Hot tub, Golf: Park City, Park Meadows; TV, Crib-Hi-chair, Ind. Heat Ctl.

Attractions: Skiing, ice skating, golf, tennis, hiking, Alpine Slide

Shops & Restaurants: Park City Main Street unique shops; Baja Cantina/Mexican

A-frame one-bedroom chalets with rough wood walls, conversation pit and gas-burning Franklin stove fireplace. Modern apartments with spiral wrought iron staircases and large sleeping lofts. Mt. Metro shuttle bus takes you to Main Street, Deer Valley ski area and Park City Racquet Club.

The Stein Eriksen Lodge
7400 Lake Flat Road, Box 3779
Park City, UT 84060
801-649-3700   800-453-1302

1 Bedroom $$$$, 2 Bedrooms $$$$, 3 Bedrooms
   4$
1 Bedrm/week 5$
AmEx/Visa/MC, Dep. Req'd. •
120 condos, Lo-rise, Key at Front desk, H-yes

Location: Airport: Salt Lake City; Downtown: 30 miles; Ski lift: Deer Vlly

General Facilities: Full serv., Conf. rm. cap. 180, Daily maid, Kitchen, Linens, Restaurant on prem., Bar on prem., Lounge, Baby-sitter

Room Facilities: Pool, Sauna, Tennis, Health club, Golf: Two courses in town; TV, Cable, Phone in rm., Ind. Heat Ctl.

Attractions: Historic Main Street, Alpine slide, Ontario Mine, hiking, tennis, sail boarding, fishing, entertainment

Shops & Restaurants: 86 shops & boutiques on Main Street; Glitretind/European

Overstuffed down comforters and Norwegian pine furniture, gold plated fixtures and terry cloth robes, oversize whirlpool bathtub, fireplace and custom European kitchen. Friendly and informal service, mountain scenery and rustic Norwegian elegance.

---------------------- SALT LAKE CITY ----------------------

Chamonix Group
3865 S. 3500 E., Suite 206
Salt Lake City, UT 84109
801-262-1299

2 Bedrooms $$$, Lo-rise
Kitchen

Attractions: Gondola, outdoor/indoor tennis, hayrides, mine train ride, Alping Slide, fishing, swimming, skiing, golf

Charming two-story alpine chalets have wood walls and cathedral ceilings for a real mountain feeling. View the mountains from your private sun deck. Private ski room, parking for four vehicles and upstairs loft.

---------------------- SNOWBIRD ----------------------

The Lodge At Snowbird
Snowbird Resort, Entry 3
Snowbird, UT 84092
801-521-6040

Studio $$$, 1 Bedroom $$$$, 2 Bedrooms 4$
AmEx/Visa/MC, Dep. Req'd. •
120 condos, Hi-rise, Key at Front desk

Location: Airport: 45 minutes; Downtown: 35 min.; Ski lift: Alta

General Facilities: Full serv., Conf. rm., Daily maid, Kitchen, Linens, Restaurant on prem., Bar on prem., Lounge, Baby-sitter, Child planned rec.: Ski season programs

Room Facilities: Pool, Sauna, Hot tub, Tennis, Ski resort, TV, Cable, Phone in rm., Crib-Hi-chair, Ind. Heat Ctl.

Shops & Restaurants: Trolley Square, Shopping malls

Full-size kitchen, fireplace and specially designed sofa beds. Non-ski season rates are less than half the ski season rates.

Please mention *Condo Vacations the Complete Guide* when you reserve your condominium.

Vermont

Stowe
Smugglers Notch ••
East Burke
• Bolton Valley
Bolton
Fairlee
Warren •
Waitsfield

Killington
•

• Plymouth
• Rutland

Manchester
Center
•• Stratton Mt.
Rawsonville • • •
• West Dover
Wilmington • •

BOLTON VALLEY

Bolton Valley Resort
Bolton Valley, VT 05477
802-434-2131 800-451-3220

1 Bedroom $$$, 2 Bedrooms $$$$, 3 Bedrooms $$$$
1 Bedrm/week 6$, 2 Bed/week 7$, 3 Bed/week 10$, Min. Stay 2 Nights, 108 condos

Location: Airport: Burlington-19 miles; Downtown: 19 miles; Ski lift: B.Valley

General Facilities: Bus. fac., Conf. rm. cap. 50, Daily maid, Kitchen, Linens, Restaurant on prem., Bar on prem., Lounge, Baby-sitter, Child planned rec.: Nursery, Pied Piper

Room Facilities: Pool, Sauna, Tennis, Sports club-aerobics, Golf: Nearby; TV, Phone in rm., Crib-Hi-chair

Attractions: Shelburne Museum, Champlain Shakespare festival, Barre granite quarries, tours, cruises, entertainment

Shops & Restaurants: On-site country store, gift shop, Burlington shops; Lindsays/nouveau cuisine

Casually decorated in early American style with fireplaces and decks, located in a self-contained village steps from ski slopes. Restaurants, indoor sports club, tanning bed, masseuse, gift shops. Winter programs for children under 6, including 3 evenings of games, movies and crafts. The only major resort in Vermont offering night skiing. Summer fishing and hiking. The on-site naturalist can take you on a guided nature tour, or get in shape with aerobic and stretch classes.

BOLTON

Trailside Condominiums
Bolton Valley
Bolton, VT 05477
802-434-2769 800-451-5025

1 Bedroom $$$, 2 Bedrooms $$$$, 3 Bedrooms
$$$$
1 Bedrm/week 6$, 2 Bed/week 7$, 3 Bed/
week 10$
Min. Stay 2 Nights, Visa/MC, Dep. Req'd.
Lo-rise

Location: Airport: Burlington; Downtown: walk; Ski lift: Bolton V.

General Facilities: Kitchen, Linens, Restaurant on prem., Bar on prem., Lounge, Child planned rec.: Ski lessons/programs

Room Facilities: Pool, Sauna, Hot tub, Tennis, B. Valley sports club, TV, Phone in rm.

Attractions: Novice to expert skiing, cross-country skiing, telemark skiing, Honey Bear day/night care, entertainment

Shops & Restaurants: Bolton Village unique shops, grocery market; Lindsay's/nouvelle cuisine

Condominiums within the Village area, on or near ski trails, with fireplaces and decks/patios. Bolton Valley Sports Club for pre-ski, after-ski and non-skiers. 7 restaurants and cafes with varied menus. James Moore Tavern for an after-ski hot cider and nightly entertainment. Especially for children, Bear's Den ski center, terrain garden for outdoor play, Pied Piper, dinner, movies, games, crafts, and nursery. MAP packages.

EAST BURKE

Burke Mountain Condominiums
Box 247
East Burke, VT 05832
802-626-3305 800-541-5480

1 Bedroom $$$, 2 Bedrooms $$$$, Lo-rise
Kitchen

Attractions: Skiing, windsurfing, swimming, lake fishing

Choice of 5 slopeside and trailside condominiums with kitchens and TV. Fun ski instruction and races for children and teens. Short drive to area lakes for rest-of-the-year swimming, windsurfing and fishing.

FAIRLEE

Eagle's Nest Inn & Resort
Lake Shore Road, P.O. Box 308
Fairlee, VT 05045
802-333-4302

AmEx/Visa/MC, Dep. Req'd. •
36 condos, Lo-rise, Key at Lobby front desk
No S-yes/P-yes/H-yes

Location: Airport: 20 miles; Downtown: 2 miles; Beach front; Ski lift: 20 min.

General Facilities: Conf. rm. cap. 100, Daily maid, Kitchen, Linens, Restaurant on prem., Bar on prem., Game room, Lounge, Baby-sitter

Room Facilities: Pool, Sauna, Hot tub, Tennis, Boating, fishing, Golf: 18-hole championship; Phone in rm., Crib-Hi-chair, Ind. AC Ctl., Ind. Heat Ctl.

Attractions: Maple sugar making, antiquing, foliage, Queechee balloonfest, Dartmouth Col, Octoberfest, entertainment

Shops & Restaurants: West Lebanon Shopping Center, J.C. Penny's; Water's Edge/continental

Cozy townhouses with picturesque Vermont scenery, located on Lake Morey. Townhouses are two-story, contemporary to traditional Vermont furnishings, with kitchenettes. Centrally located Lodge for dining, library reading and card or board games. Crystal clear lake makes fishing and water activities a must. Fall foliage, winter skiing, bicycling, horseback riding and ping-pong. Local auctions, antique shops and flea markets.

---------------------------- KILLINGTON ----------------------------

Killington Townhouses
R.R. 1, Box 10-A
Killington, VT 05751
802-773-4488 800-822-5011

1 Bedroom $$, 2 Bedrooms $$
1 Bedrm/week 4$, 2 Bed/week 6$
AmEx/Visa/MC, Dep. Req'd.
16 condos, Lo-rise, Key at Greenbrier Inn-Rt. 4

Location: Airport: Rutland-15 miles; Need car; Ski lift: Nearby

General Facilities: Kitchen, Linens

Room Facilities: Sauna, Hot tub, Tennis, Badminton, volleyball, Golf: Nearby; TV, Phone in rm., Crib-Hi-chair, Ind. Heat Ctl.

Attractions: Pico Alpine Slide, Wilson Castle, museums, galleries, Killington gondola, summer theatre

Shops & Restaurants: Bridgewater Mall, outlets, Rutland stores; Hemingways/nouvelle-Jasons/It.

Luxurious vacation living in decorator-furnished, fully appointed townhouse units. 4 bedroom chalet with wood paneling and ski house decor. Rental includes free use of Cortina Inn Health Spa: indoor pool, sauna, whirlpool, exercise room and 8 tennis courts. Killington Gondola has a view that extends into 5 states and Canada. 6 mountains for skiing, golf, fishing, horses and entertainment within minutes.

Killington Village
712 Killington Road
Killington, VT 05751
802-422-3101 800-343-0762

---------------------------- MANCHESTER CENTER ----------------------------

Bromley Village Condominiums
Box 1130
Manchester Center, VT 05255
802-824-5458

1 Bedroom $$$$, 2 Bedrooms $$$$, Lo-rise
Pool, Kitchen, Linens

Attractions: Skiing, Tater Hill Country Club (golf, tennis, swimming), Green Mountain Nat'l Forest

Slopeside accommodations at Bromley Village or Magic Mountain. Ski to lifts and come back to a warm fire and soothing whirlpool tub. Two mountains offering 15 lifts and over 100 trails for beginner to expert. Weekend entertainment in the Magicside Lodge.

─────────── PLYMOUTH ───────────

Hawk Inn & Mountain Resort
Route 100, P.O. Box 64
Plymouth, VT 05056
802-672-3811 800-451-4109

2 Bedrooms $$$$, 3 Bedrooms $$$$
Min. Stay 2 Nights, AmEx/Visa/MC,
Dep. Req'd.
Lo-rise

Location: Airport: Burlington; Downtown: nearby; Ski lift: Nearby

General Facilities: Full serv., Daily maid, Kitchen, Linens, Restaurant on prem., Child planned rec.: Day program

Room Facilities: Pool, Sauna, Hot tub, Tennis, Spa, boats, horses, Golf: Woodstock golf

Attractions: Sailing, canoeing, stables, squash, racquetball, jogging, fishing

Shops & Restaurants: Quaint villages, antiques, crafts, maple syrup; Hawk's River Tavern Restaurant

Spectacular award-winning resort with townhouses tucked away in private, wooded sites where you can enjoy the changing Vermont seasons. Ski Killington's six mountains, explore the forest on x-country skis or snowshoes. Skate at the lighted rink, then to the glass-enclosed spa. Lake Amherst for boating and 300-acre Nature Preserve for riding, hiking and picnicking. Maple syrup in the spring, apple cider in the fall. Nouvelle cuisine at Hawk's River Tavern. Forget your problems, refresh your spirit.

─────────── RAWSONVILLE ───────────

Bear Creek Condominiums
Route 30, Box 100
Rawsonville, VT 05155
802-297-1700

2 Bedrooms $$$$, Lo-rise
Kitchen, Linens, Phone in rm.

Attractions: Alpine and x-country skiing, golf, tennis, hiking, riding, board sailing

Condominiums in southern Vermont with fine dining, fireside lounge and entertainment on the property. Free shuttle service takes you to Stratton Mountain for alpine and nordic skiing. Then take a romantic sleigh ride in the cool, crisp mountain air.

─────────── RUTLAND ───────────

Pico Resort Hotel
P.O. Box 2365, Sherburne Pass
Rutland, VT 05701
803-773-4464 800-447-1505

1 Bedroom $$, 2 Bedrooms $$$$, Lo-rise
Pool, Kitchen, Linens, Phone in rm.

Attractions: Alpine slide, miniature golf, Pico Sports center, golf, tennis, hiking, fishing, health club, weight

Cozy, attractively furnished units with the lifts at your doorstep so children have no trouble finding their way home. New Pico Sports Center with aerobic classes, weight training equipment, saunas, hot tub, indoor pool and nursery.

Jackson Hole Ski Area

SMUGGLERS NOTCH

The Village At Smugglers Notch
Route 108
Smugglers Notch, VT 05464
802-644-8851   800-451-8752

AmEx/Visa/MC, Dep. Req'd. •
279 condos, Lo-rise, Villas, Key at Front desk
H-yes

Location: Airport: 28 miles; Ski lift: Nearby

General Facilities: Full serv., Conf. rm. cap. 300, Kitchen, Linens, Restaurant on prem., Bar on prem., Game room, Lounge, Baby-sitter, Child planned rec.: Camps for kids

Room Facilities: Pool, Sauna, Hot tub, Tennis, Skiing, Golf: Stowe Country Club; TV, Phone in rm., Crib-Hi-chair, Ind. Heat Ctl.

Attractions: Stowe Alpine slide, Ben & Jerry's ice cream factory, Shelburne Museum, Montreal day trips, entertainment

Shops & Restaurants: Antiques & specialty craft stores, Factory outlets; Ilse De France/Crown & Anchor

Self-contained resort village with fully equipped condominium homes in a peaceful mountain setting. Ski resort in winter, summer tennis, family and children's programs. Live entertainment, dancing and movies in the lounge. All day ski camps, summer discovery and adventure camps for children, as well as Alice's Wonderland child care.

―――――――――――――――――― STOWE ――――――――――――――――――

Golden Eagle Resort
P.O. Box 1090, Mountain Road
Stowe, VT 05672
802-253-4811 800-626-1010

2 Bedrooms $$
2 Bedrms/week 6$
AmEx/Visa/MC, Dep. 1 Night •
8 condos, Lo-rise, Key at Front office
H-yes

Location: Airport: 40 Miles; Downtown: ½ mile; Ski lift: Stowe

General Facilities: Conf. rm. cap. 60, Daily maid, Kitchen, Linens, Restaurant on prem., Bar on prem., Game room, Lounge, Baby-sitter

Room Facilities: Pool, Sauna, Hot tub, Tennis, Skiing, fishing, hike, Golf: Stone Country Club-near; TV, Cable, Phone in rm., Crib-Hi-chair, Ind. AC Ctl., Ind. Heat Ctl.

Attractions: Concerts-theatre-tennis-golf-horse & dog shows-antique car rally-craft fairs-auctions, entertainment

Shops & Restaurants: Small shops with unique products; Alpine/Bavarian-Partridge/fish

Quiet, scenic Vermont resort, beautifully landscaped gardens and grounds, trout ponds, walking trails, tennis, heated pools, health spa with indoor pool, whirlpool and sauna. Stowe is the ski capital of the East, but also has many summer activities. Visit Morgan Horse Farm., Trapp Family Gardens, the world's largest granite quarry or Shelburne Museum. Movies, Monday night winter wine and cheese parties, summer poolside barbecues, picnic tables and lawn games. Package plans are also offered.

―――

Mount Mansfield Townhouses
Mountain Road
Stowe, VT 05672
802-253-7311 800-253-4754

AmEx/Visa/MC, Dep. 1 Night •
100 condos, Lo-rise, Key at Front desk
H-yes

Location: Airport: 40 minutes; Downtown: 6 miles; Ski lift: Stowe

General Facilities: Full serv., Bus. fac., Conf. rm. cap. 200, Daily maid, Kitchen, Linens, Restaurant on prem., Bar on prem., Game room, Lounge, Baby-sitter, Child planned rec.: All season programs

Room Facilities: Pool, Sauna, Tennis, Fitness Center, Golf: Stowe Country Club 4 mi; TV, Cable, Phone in rm., Crib-Hi-chair, Ind. Heat Ctl.

Attractions: Morgan Horse Farm., granite quarry, Lake Champlain, Shelburne Museum, antique car rally, entertainment

Shops & Restaurants: Unique, family or individually owned shops; Toll House-Cliff House-C. Club

Contemporary, slopeside townhouses in a wooded setting in a quaint New England village. Summer water activities on nearby lakes, concerts, theaters, trails, trout streams and ballooning to name a few activities. Fantastic world-class skiing for all levels. Three on-site restaurants and over 30 in Stowe Village to satisfy every taste. Apres-ski entertainment, Fireside Tavern and special events. Special children's programs with nature walks, crafts and ski school. Golf, tennis and resort packages.

——————————————————— STOWE ———————————————————

Mountainside Resort at Stowe   1 Bedroom $$, 2 Bedrooms $$$, 3 Bedrooms
930 Cottage Club Rd, Box A-9 $$$
Stowe, VT 05672   1 Bedrm/week 4$, 2 Bed/week 6$, 3 Bed/
802-253-8610 800-458-4893   week 7$
                                  Visa/MC, Lo-rise, Key at Cottage Club Rd.

Location: Downtown: 3 miles; Ski lift: Stowe
General Facilities: Kitchen, Linens
Room Facilities: Pool, Sauna, Hot tub, TV, Cable, Phone in rm.
Attractions: Skiing, snowboards, Winter carnival, cross-country challenge, ice skating
Shops & Restaurants: Ski shop, convenience store

Individually decorated, fully equipped, firewood provided. Indoor pool, sauna, whirlpool, lounge, wet bar, lighted tennis courts. 3 miles to shopping, entertainment, ice rink, horses. Recreation field has swings, horseshoes, barbecues, picnic tables. Quiet, hillside setting.

Scandinavia Inn & Chalets   Lo-rise
Mountain Road, Box 1470NS   Kitchen, Phone in rm.
Stowe, VT 05672
802-253-8555

Attractions: Indoor tennis at Top Notch, Village Health Club, Ice Skating arena, Horse-driven sleighs

---

Stoweflake Resort Townhouses   Studio $$$, 1 Bedroom $$$$, 2 Bedrooms $$$$
Box 369   Lo-rise, Key at Reception desk
Stowe, VT 05672
802-253-7355 800-782-9009

Location: Airport: Burlington 45 min.; Ski lift: Stowe
General Facilities: Conf. rm. cap. 250, Kitchen, Restaurant on prem., Bar on prem., Lounge
Room Facilities: Pool, Sauna, Tennis, Badminton, Golf: Stowe Country Club; TV
Attractions: Horseback riding, skiing, Lake Elmore, jogging, ice skating, movies, antiques and crafts, entertainment
Shops & Restaurants: Stowe Villages shops, antiques, crafts; Winfield's/Cont-Amr.

Four-season resort hosted by the Baraw family. Secluded, luxury units with fireplaces and ski rooms. Step out of your door to cross-country trails. Two mountains for the downhill skier with ski schools and nursery. Two-story Nordic suites and cottage apartments also available. Spring flowers and lush summer valleys for picnicking beside mountain streams. Vivid fall colors. Light snacks at Charlie B's Vermont decorated bar and lounge with frequent entertainment, romantic candelit dinner at Winfield's.

The Village Green at Stowe   2 Bedrooms $$$
Cape Cod Rd, RR #1, Box 2975   Lo-rise
Stowe, VT 05672
802-253-9705 800-451-3297

Contemporary furnishings, tastefully laid out units among grassy fields blending with Stowe's pristine New England atmosphere. Indoor pool, tennis. Shuttle to ski lifts. Summer biking, jogging, mountain climbing and lake activities.

─────────────── STOWE ───────────────

Topnotch At Stowe
P.O. Box 1260
Stowe, VT 05672
802-253-8585 800-451-8686

1 Bedroom $$, 2 Bedrooms $$$, 3 Bedrooms
$$$$

Location: Airport: Burlington 45 min.; Downtown: walk; Need car; Ski lift: Stowe

General Facilities: Full serv., Conf. rm. cap. 200, Kitchen, Linens, Restaurant on prem., Game room, Lounge

Room Facilities: Pool, Sauna, Hot tub, Tennis, Exercise room, horses, Golf: Stowe Country Club

Attractions: Ice skating, tobogganing, country bazaars, auctions, flea markets, craft shows, entertainment

Shops & Restaurants: Stowe Village boutiques; Topnotch restaurant

Concierge greets you in the library when you arrive. Retire to your condominium where you'll find a private library, imported soaps, bath gels and fluffy towels. Be ready for a great ski vacation. Ice-skate, toboggan or snowshoe for a change of pace. The rest of the year is equally exciting with tennis, equestrian center, exercise room, swimming, games, putting green and lawn croquet. After a long hike in the woods, dine on the terrace and dance at the Buttertub Bar.

Trapp Family Lodge
Stowe, VT 05672
802-253-8511 800-826-7000

Pool, Kitchen, Phone in rm.

Attractions: Golf, tennis, swimming, concerts, trout fishing, mountain gondola rides, Sports Center

Units on the hillside, steps away from the Lodge with view decks. Over 40 miles of groomed cross-country trails and a complete Touring Center, plus Mt. Mansfield for downhill skiing in the winter.

─────────────── STRATTON MOUNTAIN ───────────────

Stratton Mountain Resort
Stratton Mountain, VT 05155
802-197-2200 800-843-6862

AmEx/Visa/MC
110 condos, Villas

Location: Airport: Albany, NY 81 miles; Downtown: 18 miles; Ski lift: Nearby

General Facilities: Conf. rm. cap. 225, Kitchen, Restaurant on prem., Bar on prem.

Room Facilities: Pool, Sauna, Hot tub, Tennis, Sports center, Golf: Stratton Mt. Country Club; TV, Cable, Phone in rm., Ind. Heat Ctl.

Attractions: Charming Vermont towns, biking, fishing, skiing, entertainment

Shops & Restaurants: Stratton Mt. Village, Manchester retail outlets; Mulligans-Sage Hill-Tenderloin

An award-winning, four-season mountain vacation center in Southern Vermont. All year long it serves as the favorite location for skiers, golfers, tennis players and sports enthusiasts. 27-hole of golf surrounded by dramatic mountain scenery, and Lake, Mountain and Forest nines. Fully-equipped pro shop and practice range. Seven restaurants on the mountain offer a variety of fare and some have dancing and entertainment.

———————————————— WAITSFIELD ————————————————

Eagles at Sugarbush
Route 100, P.O. Box 180
Waitsfield, VT 05673
802-496-5700

2 Bedrooms $$
2 Bedrms/week 7$
Visa/MC,Dep. Req'd.
16 condos, Villas, Key at Clubhouse Office
H-yes

Location: Airport: Burlington-50 min.; Downtown: ½ mile; Need car; Ski lift: Nearby

General Facilities: Full serv., Kitchen, Linens, Game room, Lounge, Baby-sitter

Room Facilities: Pool, Sauna, Tennis, Racquet/game room, Golf: Sugarbush-near; TV, Cable, Phone in rm., Crib-Hi-chair, Ind. AC Ctl., Ind. Heat Ctl.

Attractions: Skiing, tennis, golf, swimming, fishing, Grand Prix Horse Show, 4th of July fun, entertainment

Shops & Restaurants: Antique and specialty shops, grocery stores; The Common Man-European

Custom-built, individual, contemporary two-thousand-square-foot residences with individual saunas. Backwoods trails and streams for fishing, riding, canoeing or bird-watching, country walks through covered bridges and pastures. Clubhouse with pool, tennis and racquetball, plus multi-million dollar sports center. Some of the finest and most challenging ski runs in the U.S. from novice to professional. Privacy and relaxation in unspoiled Vermont.

———————————————— WARREN ————————————————

The Battleground
Route 17, Sugarbush
Warren, VT 05674
802-496-2288

Pool, Kitchen, Linens, Phone in rm.

Attractions: Skiing at Sugarbush, tennis, Sugarbush Sports Center, swimming, paddle tennis

Arrive at this luxury four-season resort through a rustic covered bridge. Townhouses on 60 wooded acres. Step out on your deck and watch picturesque brooks meander along the valley. Ledgestone fireplace, washer/dryer and color cable TV in your two-bath unit.

Sugarbush Inn
Sugarbush Access Road
Warren, VT 05674
802-583-2301 800-451-4320

Location: Ski lift: x-country

General Facilities: Conf. rm. cap. 225, Kitchen, Restaurant on prem., Bar on prem.

Room Facilities: Pool, Sauna, Hot tub, Tennis, Hiking, fishing, Golf: Sugarbush Golf Course

Attractions: Skiing, hiking, fishing, soaring, polo

Shops & Restaurants: Montpelier shopping; Onion Patch, Main dining room

One-, two-and three-bedroom condominiums in a luxurious, isolated retreat in the Green Mountains. Trout-filled streams, wooden bridges, tennis, indoor and outdoor pools, and outstanding golf course. Nightly seafood bar on the front lawn of the Inn. Winter cross-country skiing.

--------------------------------- WEST DOVER ---------------------------------

Dover Watch at Mount Snow   2 Bedrooms $$$$
Country Club Rd., Rt. 100, Box 535   Kitchen, Linens, Phone in rm.
West Dover, VT 05356
802-464-2270

Attractions: Marlboro Music Festival, historic Wilmington, Lake Whitingham, skiing, wildlife, boating, golf

More than 1200 feet of living space in these designer decorated townhouses. Each unit has its own parking and private entrance, sauna, whirlpool tub, breakfast bar and fireplaces with wood provided. Ski to your heart's content at Mt. Snow.

--------------------------------- WILMINGTON ---------------------------------

Crafts Inn   1 Bedroom $$, Lo-rise
West Main St.   Pool, Kitchen
Wilmington, VT 05363
802-464-2344

Attractions: Skiing, swimming, Lake Whitingham, Gym, racquetball

One-bedroom condominiums with fully equipped kitchens for a hearty breakfast before skiing. Movie theater, restaurant and videotape library on property. Workout in the gym, swim in the lake or pool, tour the Wilmington shops or just enjoy Vermont.

Spyglass Hill Condominiums
Mann Road
Wilmington, VT 05363
802-464-7458

Virginia

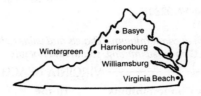

─────────────── BASYE ───────────────

Bryce Resort
P.O. Box 3
Basye, VA 22810
703-856-2121

Chalet High   2 Bedrooms $$$, Lo-rise
P.O. Box 12   Kitchen
Basye, VA 22810
703-856-2126

Wood exteriors and beautifully furnished interiors in townhouses at the northern end of Bryce Resort. Two-bedroom unit with Jacuzzi, steam shower, fireplace and remote control VCR. Three-bedroom units have jacuzzis, saunas, Jenn-Aire grills and fireplaces.

The Pine Villas   1 Bedroom $$$, 2 Bedrooms $$$
P.O. Box 76   Kitchen, Linens
Basye, VA 22810
703-856-2111

Attractions: Fishing, golf, tennis, horses, skiing, Endless caverns, Orkney Springs

Chalets, condos and townhouses that sleep 4 to 10 persons. Short walk to amenities, or just off the ski slopes. Recreation room with sauna and jacuzzi. Try grass skiing or windsurf on Lake Laura. Lakes, rivers and national forest to explore.

―――――――――――― HARRISONBURG ――――――――――――

Massanutten Village
Box 1227
Harrisonburg, VA 22801
703-289-9441

Lo-rise
Pool, Kitchen, Linens

Privately owned condominiums, chalets and villas right on the mountain. Indoor sports complex, Le Club for swimming, sauna and hot tub.

――――――――――――― VIRGINIA BEACH ―――――――――――

The Colony Condominiums
1301 Atlantic Ave.
Virginia Beach, VA 23451
804-425-8689

Hi-rise
Pool, Kitchen, Linens

Fully furnished units accommodating six people. Contemporary furnishings. Pool overlooks the ocean.

――――――――――――― WILLIAMSBURG ――――――――――――

Kingsmill Resort
1010 Kingsmill Road
Williamsburg, VA 23185
804-253-1703 800-832-5665

1 Bedroom $$$, 2 Bedrooms $$$$, 3 Bedrooms
$$$$
AmEx, Dep. 1 Night
Villas

Location: Airport: Norfolk-Newport News; Downtown: 5 minutes

General Facilities: Conf. rm. cap. 300, Daily maid, Kitchen, Linens, Restaurant on prem., Bar on prem., Game room, Lounge

Room Facilities: Pool, Sauna, Hot tub, Tennis, Sports Club, Golf: 2 courses; TV

Attractions: Busch Gardens, The Old Country entertainment center, Jamestown, Yorktown, Williamsburg

Shops & Restaurants: Colonial Williamsburg shops; Riverview Room/Bray Dining Rm.

Tastefully furnished villas overlooking the James River, golf course fairways or tennis courts. Sports Club, Nautilus exercise room, billards-card room, pools, casual bar and grille. 2 challenging golf courses, 10 tennis courts. Explore colonial Williamsburg, Jamestown and Yorktown. Have fun with your children at The Old Country entertainment center with rides, shows and exhibits, set in eight authentic European-style villages. Choice of elegant or casual dining.

———————————— WINTERGREEN ————————————

Wintergreen
Route 664
Wintergreen, VA 22958
804-325-2200 800-324-2200

Studio $$$, 1 Bedroom $$$, 2 Bedrooms $$$$
AmEx/Visa/MC, Dep. 1 Night •
350 condos, Hi-rise, Lo-rise, Villas, Key at Front
    desk
H-yes

Location: Airport: Charlottesville; Downtown: 16 miles; Need car; Ski lift: Nearby

General Facilities: Full serv., Bus. fac., Conf. rm. cap. 450, Daily maid, Kitchen, Linens, Restaurant on prem., Bar on prem., Game room, Lounge, Baby-sitter, Child planned rec.: Program & activities

Room Facilities: Pool, Sauna, Hot tub, Tennis, Spa, equestrian center, Golf: 18-hole championship; TV, Phone in rm., Crib-Hi-chair, Ind. AC Ctl., Ind. Heat Ctl.

Attractions: Gypsy Hill Park, Michie Tavern Museum, Castle, Stonewall Jackson House, Goshen Pass area, entertainment

Shops & Restaurants: Market, Factory Outlet, Virginia metalcrafters; Mitchie Tavern/Amer., 5 on-site

Mountain villa accommodations with fireplaces for warm., cozy evenings. Mountain setting for golf, tennis, hiking and spa sports facility. Valley setting for swimming, tennis, golf, horseback riding and Lake Monocan. Spring Wildflower Symposium, summer cool mountain air, fall guided hiking through brilliant colors, and winter skiing. Kids in Action program with different events each day, including "Kids in the Kitchen," fully equipped playground and playroom. Picnics, buffets & lounge entertainment.

Washington

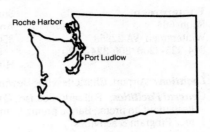

Roche Harbor

Port Ludlow

PORT LUDLOW

The Resort at Port Ludlow
60M #3 Paradise Bay Road
Port Ludlow, WA 98365
206-437-2222 800-732-1239

General Facilities: Conf. rm. cap. 125, Kitchen, Restaurant on prem., Bar on prem., Game room, Child planned rec.: Supervised game room

Room Facilities: Pool, Sauna, Hot tub, Tennis, Bikes, Croquet, Golf: Port Ludlow Golf Course

Attractions: Victorian homes tours, Port Townsend, Hurricane Ridge, sailing on Puget Sound, entertainment

Shops & Restaurants: Harbormaster / seafood

Comfortable condominiums ranging from one bedroom and bath combinations to four-bedroom, four-bath suites, most with a bird's-eye view of the water and hills. Designed for family enjoyment, recreational activities include pools, squash court, tennis courts, saunas, pitch and putt area, and bicycles. Rent a sailboat on Puget Sound or join a sightseeing tour at the 30-slip marina. Relax in the solitude of the 3500 acres, or participate in nature hikes, raft trips and charter fishing.

ROCHE HARBOR

Roche Harbor Resort
P.O. Box 4001
Roche Harbor, WA 98250
206-378-2155

1 Bedroom $$, 2 Bedrooms $$$
Pool, Kitchen

Attractions: Whale Museum, cruises, English & American Camps, UofW Marine Laboratories, Limekiln Park, volleyball, horseshoes, tennis

Arrive at the island via a two-hour ferry ride for rural charm and romantic escape any time of the year. Mild spring and fall temperatures. Whales return in spring, summer boating, fall salmon fishing and winter scuba diving and beachcombing.

West Virginia

Morgantown

Canaan Valley, Davis

White Sulphur Springs

CANAAN VALLEY, DAVIS

Land of Canaan Vacation Resort
Route 1, Box 291
Canaan Valley, Davis, WV 26260
304-866-4425

2 Bedrooms $$
Min. Stay 2 Nights, MC, Dep. Req'd.
Villas, Key on-site

Location: Airport: 30 miles; Need car

General Facilities: Bus. fac., Daily maid, Kitchen, Linens, Game room, Baby-sitter, Child planned rec.: Activities Director

Room Facilities: Pool, Hot tub, Tennis, Golf: Canaan Valley Resort Park; TV, Cable, VCR, Phone in rm., Crib-Hi-chair, Ind. Heat Ctl.

Attractions: National forest, two state parks, primitive wilderness, Blackwater falls, white water, hunting, entertainment

Shops & Restaurants: None; Oriskany Inn/continental

Modern Broyhill furnishings with oak trim, two-bedrooms with jacuzzi, and tennis, pool and hot tub on the property. Recreation and activities director to help plan your vacation fun. A national forest, two state parks and a primitive wilderness area are minutes away. Canaan Valley State Park boasts ice skating, skiing, golfing, hiking, & bird watching. Enjoy the wildflowers of spring, warm mountain beauty of summer, and fall hunting season. Vacation time is always here.

――――――――――――――― MORGANTOWN ―――――――――――――――

Lakeview Resort Club
Route 6, Box 88-A
Morgantown, WV 26505
304-594-1111 800-624-8300

2 Bedrooms $$$$
2 Bedrms/week 7$
AmEx/Visa/MC, Dep. 1 Night •
72 condos, Villas, Key at Sheraton Lakeview

Location: Airport: 8 miles; Downtown: 10 miles; Need car; Ski lift: WHISP Ski

General Facilities: Full serv., Bus. fac., Conf. rm. cap. 300, Daily maid, Kitchen, Linens, Restaurant on prem., Bar on prem., Game room, Lounge, Baby-sitter, Child planned rec.: Games/arts/stories

Room Facilities: Pool, Sauna, Hot tub, Tennis, Fitness Center, Golf: 2 courses on property; TV, Cable, Phone in rm., Crib-Hi-chair, Ind. AC Ctl., Ind. Heat Ctl.

Attractions: White water, summer theatre, state parks, forests, glassmaking, sports & cultural events, entertainment

Shops & Restaurants: Shopping mall and outlet glass factory mall; Reflections on the Lake/Amer.

Contemporary or traditional townhouses done in soft shades of blue, beige, or salmon with cedar and stone exteriors. Complete activities program with activities staff, and games, arts & crafts, stories, movies and entertainment for the children. Two 18-hole golf courses, indoor/outdoor swimming pools, tennis, hot tubs and gourmet dining. A four-season resort for privacy, excitement, and relaxation set in West Virginia's wooded hills.

――――――――――――― WHITE SULPHUR SPRINGS ―――――――――――――

The Greenbrier
White Sulphur Springs, WV

General Facilities: Kitchen, Restaurant on prem.

Room Facilities: Pool, Sauna, Hot tub, Tennis, Shuffleboard, Golf: 3 golf courses

Attractions: Horse-drawn carriage rides, Droop Mountain, Organ Caves, Pearl Buck's birthplace

Shops & Restaurants: Ryder Cup Grille/Golf Club

Condominiums surrounded by 6500 acres of broad lawns, a profusion of gardens, and acres of eastern deciduous forests. Plethora of activities available, such as horseback riding, jogging, fishing, golf, tennis, shuffleboard, table tennis, lawn bowling, bicycling, swimming and hiking.

Be sure to call the condo to verify details and prices and to make your reservation.

Wisconsin

St. Germain
Minocqua Eagle River
Sturgeon Bay
Nekoosa Mishicot
Wisconsin Dells
Oconomowoc
Lake Geneva

─────────── EAGLE RIVER ───────────

7-Mile Pinecrest Resort
P.O. Box 1148
Eagle River, WI 54521
715-479-8118

1 Bedroom $, 2 Bedrooms $$, Lo-rise
Kitchen

Attractions: 7 Mile Lake, boating, fishing, swimming

Cottages in the wilderness with water, woods and wildlife. Forest atmosphere for complete rest and relaxation. Aluminium fishing boat included for trying to catch musky and walleye.

─────────────────────────────────────

The Braywood Resort
1084 Catfish Lake Road
Eagle River, WI 54521
715-479-6494

1 Bedroom $, Lo-rise
Daily maid, Kitchen, Linens

Attractions: Catfish Lake, fishing, boating, biking, hunting, riding, downhill and x-country skiing, volleyball, shuffleboard, golf

Completely furnished units with decks, barbecue grills and picnic tables. You'll enjoy the many water activities on the lake in the natural beauty of the Eagle River Chain of Lakes region. Winter skiing and snowmobiling.

─────────────────────────────────────

Eagle Waters Resort
Box 1509
Eagle River, WI 54521
715-479-4411

1 Bedroom $$, Lo-rise
Pool, Daily maid, Kitchen, Linens

Attractions: Eagle River Chain of Lakes water skiing, fishing, sailing, golf, tennis, Eagle Lake, marina

One-bedroom suites with kitchenettes and lakefront view patios. Peace and quiet in the north woods air. Lay back and relax by the pool, take to the lake for water fun and fishing, hike or bike in the woods with the wildlife along the nature trail.

─────────────── EAGLE RIVER ───────────────

Lake Forest Recreation Area
3801 Eagle Waters Road
Eagle River, WI 54521
715-479-7843

2 Bedrooms $$, Lo-rise, Villas
Pool, Kitchen, Linens

Attractions: 28 lakes, beach, golf, tennis, marina, x-country skiing, ice skating, toboganing, fitness room

Treehouse Village condominiums are unique, two-level, 1250-square-foot, round units with whirlpool baths and stereos. Lake Forest condominiums are also two-story with a 14' aluminum fishing boat.

───────────────────────────────

Safer's Gypsy Villa Resort
950 Circle Drive
Eagle River, WI 54521
715-479-8644

1 Bedrm/week $$$$, 2 Bed/week $$$$, 3 Bed/week 7$
Min. Stay 2 Nights, Visa/MC, Dep. Req'd. •
21 condos, Lo-rise, Key at Office
P-yes

Location: Airport: 5 miles; Downtown: 4½ miles; Need car; Beach front

General Facilities: Full serv., Conf. rm., Kitchen, Linens, Game room, Baby-sitter, Child planned rec.: Games

Room Facilities: Sauna, Hot tub, Golf: Lake Forest-near; TV, Crib-Hi-chair, Ind. Heat Ctl.

Attractions: Longest freshwater chain of lakes in the world, gateway to the Nicolet National Forest, entertainment

Shops & Restaurants: Eagle River-Three River shopping; Persian Paradise, Everetts/Fr.

Ultra-modern villas with living room cathedral ceilings on beachfront. Buildings far apart for privacy, with private docks and free scheduled pontoon boat service to and from the island. Campfire cookouts, music, dancing, treasure hunts, private lakefront and beach with slides, swings, swimming float with spring board. Marina with boat rentals. Year-round activities of all types.

─────────────── LAKE GENEVA ───────────────

Americana Lake Geneva Resort
Hwy. 50
Lake Geneva, WI 53147
414-248-8811

1 Bedroom $$$, 2 Bedrooms $$$$
Pool, Kitchen

Attractions: Skeet and trap shooting, boating, miniature golf, tennis, skiing, horseback riding, fitness centre

Resort among 1,400 acres of rolling hills and countryside in Wisconsin's Kettle Morraine area. Many year-round recreational and amusement facilities, including skeet and trap shooting, indoor/outdoor tennis, winter skiing, guided trail horseback riding, and canoes.

─────────────── MINOCQUA ───────────────

Island City Point Resort
P.O. Box 313M
Minocqua, WI 54548
715-356-5101

Lookout Village

—————————————— MINOCQUA ——————————————

The Pointe Resort and Club
P.O. Box 1066
Minocqua, WI 54548
715-356-4431

1 Bedroom $$, 2 Bedrooms $$, Lo-rise
Pool, Kitchen

Attractions: Golf, fishing, lake recreation, x-country skiing, snowmobiling, ice fishing, exercise room

Lakeside condominiums with fireplaces and jacuzzis. Recreation Center has lap pool, exercise room, steam room and whirlpool. Try x-country skiing or ice fishing right outside your door. 1 hour to downhill skiing. Moonlight ski tours, sleigh rides, and festivals.

—————————————— MISHICOT ——————————————

Fox Hills Resort
P.O. Box 129
Mishicot, WI 54228
414-755-2376

1 Bedroom $$$, 2 Bedrooms $$$$, Villas
Pool, Daily maid, Kitchen, Linens

Attractions: Downhill and x-country skiing, charter fishing, horseback riding, tennis, exercise trail, Health Club, golf

Something for everyone all year round. Condominiums feature cathedral ceilings, jacuzzi baths tubs, fireplaces and view patios or balconies. All summer and winter sports. Five minutes to Lake Michigan for sport fishing.

398 Wisconsin

Fairway Townhomes
463 Tomahawk Trail
Nekoosa, WI 54457
715-325-3141

2 Bedrooms 6$
Pool, Kitchen

Attractions: Tennis, golf

Located on the tenth fairway, a few hundred feet from the Lake Arrowhead Clubhouse Bar and Restaurant, heated pool and lighted tennis courts. Townhouses with jacuzzi, washer/dryer and fireplace.

─────── OCONOMOWOC ───────

Olympia Village Resort & Spa
135 Royale Mile Road
Oconomowoc, WI 53066
414-567-0311 800-558-9573

Villas
Pool, Kitchen, Linens

Attractions: Summer pool matches, Olympia Stables, water sports, twin movie theaters, fishing, Professional Spa, tennis, golf

Villas with golf, pool, lake or ski views in a forest and lake setting. All the year-round activities you could ever want. Restaurants, cocktail lounges, nightclub entertainment and dancing. Private, sandy beach on Silver Lake.

─────── ST. GERMAIN ───────

Ed Gabes Lost Lake Condominiums
P.O. Box 24
St. Germain, WI 54558
715-542-3079

Lo-rise
Pool, Kitchen, Linens

Attractions: Fishing, boating, tennis, waterskiing, seaplane rides, x-country skiing, dog sled Races, badminton, shuffleboard

Comfortable units with fully equipped kitchens, barbecues and aluminium boats. Ramp and pier space if you prefer to bring your own boat for water skiing and fishing. Swings and slides for the children.

─────── STURGEON BAY ───────

The Rushes
Longerquist Rd, 1309 N. 14th Ave
Sturgeon Bay, WI 54235
414-839-2730

Lo-rise
Pool, Kitchen, Linens

Attractions: Peninsula Players, sightseeing, golf, Washington Island, fishing, sailing, Exercise room, badminton, tennis

Decorator furnished with private sun deck and natural Door County fieldstone fireplace and patio. Each unit has two TV's and a VCR. 2,800 feet of shore frontage and 8,000-square-foot recreation center. Walk and jog on the woodland trails, practice on the putting green.

──────────── WISCONSIN DELLS ────────────

Villas At Christmas Mountain
S-944 Christmas Mountain Drive
Wisconsin Dells, WI 53965
608-253-1000

2 Bedrooms $$
2 Bedrms/week 6$
Min. Stay 2 Nights, AmEx/Visa/MC, Dep.
  Req'd. •
150 condos, Villas, Key at Hotel lobby
H-yes

Location: Airport: 50 miles; Downtown: 4½ miles

General Facilities: Full serv., Bus. fac., Conf. rm. cap. 250, Daily maid, Kitchen, Linens, Restaurant on prem., Bar on prem., Game room, Lounge, Baby-sitter, Child planned rec.: Activities Directors

Room Facilities: Pool, Sauna, Hot tub, Tennis, Skiing, horses, TV, Cable, Phone in rm., Crib-Hi-chair, Ind. AC Ctl., Ind. Heat Ctl.

Attractions: Many attractions in the area. Crane Foundation, House on the Rock, ski show, boat trips, entertainment

Shops & Restaurants: Craft and goods stores; Many fine restaurants

Modern luxury villas, two fireplaces, whirlpool in master bedroom, Jenair grills on all porches. Resort atmosphere with many local attractions, such as golf, skiing, horseback riding, restaurants, pools and Recreation Center available on-site. Wisconsin's finest four-season resort.

Wyoming

Jackson Hole
Jackson

JACKSON HOLE

Teton Shadows
Jackson Hole, WY 83001
800-325-8605

3 Bedrooms $$$
3 Bedrms/week 5$
Dep. Req'd.
Lo-rise

Location: Ski lift: 16 miles

General Facilities: Kitchen, Linens

Room Facilities: Tennis, Golf: Jackson Hole golf; TV, Cable, Phone in rm., Crib-Hi-chair, Ind. Heat Ctl.

Shops & Restaurants: Art galleries, shops

Beautiful wood walls and furniture. 10 miles to Jackson, 5 minutes to Grand Teton National Park. Hiking, cross-country ski trails and abundant wildlife.

―――――――――――――――― JACKSON ――――――――――――――――

Jackson Hole Racquet Club Resort
Star Rt. Box 3647
Jackson, WY 83001
307-733-3990 800-443-8616

Studio $$, 1 Bedroom $$$, 2 Bedrooms $$$,
3 Bedrooms $$$$
1 Bedrm/week 7$, 2 Bed/week 9$, 3 Bed/
week 10$
Min. Stay 2 Nights, AmEx/Visa/MC,
Dep. 1 Night •
120 condos, Lo-rise, Key at At front desk
No S-yes/H-yes

Location: Airport: 22 miles; Downtown: 8 miles; Need car; Ski lift: Nearby

General Facilities: Bus. fac., Conf. rm. cap. 120, Daily maid, Kitchen, Linens, Restaurant on prem., Bar on prem., Lounge, Baby-sitter, Child planned rec.: Kinderschuleskiarea

Room Facilities: Pool, Sauna, Hot tub, Tennis, Health Club, Golf: Teton Pines; TV, Cable, Phone in rm., Crib-Hi-chair, Ind. Heat Ctl.

Attractions: Tours to Yellowstone/Grand Teton Parks. Horses, white water rafting.

Shops & Restaurants: Numerous art galleries, Ralph Lauren, outlets; Stigler's-Austrian/US cuisine

Nestled at the foot of the Teton Mountains; full service, year-round resort; fully equipped kitchens, washer and dryers; fireplace and sun deck. 4 miles from Jackson Hole Ski area; 50 miles south of Yellowstone National Park, adjacent to the new Arnold Palmer 18-hole championship golf course at Teton Pines. Free delivery from the on-property grocery and liquor store. Wood and stone units with western decor.

―――――――――――――――――――――――――――――――――――――

Spring Creek Ranch
Box 3154
Jackson, WY 83001
307-733-8833 800-443-6139

1 Bedroom $$, 2 Bedrooms $$$
Pool, Kitchen, Linens

Attractions: Wildlife sanctuary, Grand Teton Nat. Park, horses, mountain climbing, white-water, fishing, tennis, golf

Spring Creek Ranch is just north of Jackson, with cattle ranches to the west and National Elk Refuge on the east. Condominiums in this unhurried resort feature fireplaces in both living room and master bedroom. Detailed, comfortable furnishings with view balconies.

Puerto Rico

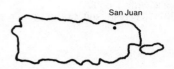

San Juan

SAN JUAN

Point Pleasant Resort
Smith Bay Estate
San Juan, PR
809-775-7200 800-524-2300

AmEx/Visa/MC, Dep. Req'd. •
149 condos, Villas, Key at Front desk

Location: Airport: 8 miles; Downtown: 5 miles; Need car; Beach front

General Facilities: Full serv., Bus. fac., Conf. rm. cap. 60, Daily maid, Kitchen, Linens, Restaurant on prem., Bar on prem., Lounge, Baby-sitter

Room Facilities: Pool, Tennis, Phone in rm., Crib-Hi-chair, Ind. AC Ctl.

Attractions: Nature trail on property, Coral World, St. John Ferry, all marine activities, entertainment

Shops & Restaurants: Gift shop on-site, duty-free shopping in town; Agave Terrace/con.-West Indian

Tropically furnished condominiums on 15 hillside acres with tropical gardens on a small secluded beach. Breathtaking views. Adjacent to Pineapple Beach. Complimentary cars four hours daily. The perfect honeymoon hideaway for nature lovers.

Please mention *Condo Vacations the Complete Guide* when you reserve your condominium.

Virgin Islands

St. Thomas

St. Croix

ST. CROIX

Sugar Beach
Est. Golden Rock, Christiansted
St. Croix, VI 00820
809-773-5345 800-524-2049

Studio $$, 1 Bedroom $$, 2 Bedrooms $$$,
3 Bedrooms $$$
1 Bedrm/week 6$, 2 Bed/week 7$, 3 Bed/
week 9$
Min. Stay 3 Nights, Visa/MC, Dep. Req'd. •
46 condos, Lo-rise, Key at On site

Location: Airport: 8 miles; Downtown: 2 miles; Need car; Beach front

General Facilities: Conf. rm. cap. 30, Daily maid, Kitchen, Linens, Baby-sitter

Room Facilities: Pool, Tennis, TV, Crib-Hi-chair, Ind. AC Ctl.

Attractions: Water sports, snorkeling, Buck National Island Underwater Park, Seaplane island hopping, entertainment

Shops & Restaurants: Duty-free liquor-tobacco-crystal-jewelry-Java Wrap; Serendipity Inn/continental

Enjoy the luxury and comfort of lovely tropical beachfront homes. Minutes from historic downtown Christiansted, tennis, and 200-year-old sugar mill. Weekly barbecue on beautifully landscaped grounds overlooking the Caribbean.

ST. THOMAS

Anchorage Beach Villas
c/o Prop. Mgmt. Caribbean, Rt. 6
St. Thomas, VI 00802
800-524-2038

2 Bedrooms $$$$, Hi-rise
Pool, Daily maid, Kitchen, Linens

Attractions: Snorkeling, scuba diving, sailing, fishing, tennis, sightseeing, tennis

On the beach overlooking Cowpet Bay and Great St. James, adjacent to the St. Thomas Yacht Club. Suites with washer/dryers and private balconies. Fine sailing and fishing. St. Thomas nightlife and international dining.

--------------------- ST. THOMAS ---------------------

Cowpet Bay Village
c/o Prop. Mgmt. Caribbean, Rt. 6
St. Thomas, VI 00802
800-524-2038

2 Bedrooms $$$$
Daily maid, Kitchen, Linens

Attractions: Beach activities, tennis

Located on a palm-fringed crescent beach with a deep-water anchorage. Condominiums with Mediterranean flavor. Beach bar and water sports center. Rental cars and sightseeing tours available.

Crystal Cove
Property Management, Route 6
St. Thomas, VI 00802
800-524-2038

1 Bedroom $$$, 2 Bedrooms $$$$, Lo-rise
Pool, Daily maid, Kitchen, Linens

Attractions: Beach, snorkeling, scuba, boat rentals, fishing, tennis, golf

Sapphire Beach condominiums with terrace or balcony overlooking the beach. Saltwater swimming pool with sunning deck. Water sports at your doorstep.

Fairway Village at Mahogany
c/o Prop. Mgmt. Caribbean, Rt. 6
St. Thomas, VI 00802
800-524-2038

1 Bedroom $$$, Hi-rise
Daily maid, Kitchen, Linens

Attractions: Golf, beach, scuba, snorkeling, sailing, sport fishing, windsurfing

Villas with fully equipped kitchens built on the terraced side of a mountain. Golf course views. Wooden tanning deck around the freshwater pool. Island trails for slow walks through the foliage to Magens Bay Beach. Airport Hospitality Office for arrival assistance.

Harbour House Villas
% Prop. Mgmt. Caribbean, Route 6
St. Thomas, VI 00802
800-524-2038

1 Bedroom $$$, 2 Bedrooms $$$$, Villas
Pool, Daily maid, Kitchen, Linens, Phone in rm.

Attractions: Tennis, fishing, sailing, beach sports

Intimate studios and spacious one-and two-bedroom suites with oceanview balconies. Walk to the beach where there's a water sports center for equipment rental, sailing and deep-sea fishing excursions. Waterfront cocktail pavilion and restaurant.

Mahogany Run Villas
% Prop. Mgmt. Caribbean, Route 6
St. Thomas, VI 00802
800-524-2038

1 Bedroom $$$$, 2 Bedrooms $$$$, Lo-rise
Pool, Daily maid, Kitchen, Linens

Attractions: Golf, beach, tennis, swimming

Tastefully furnished condominiums on a 315 acre estate. Enjoy your favorite sun and water sports at Magen's Beach. Pool, tennis and golf on the property.

ST. THOMAS

Pineapple Villas
Box 11783
St. Thomas, VI 00801
809-775-0275

Studio $$$
Dep. 3 Nights •
7 condos, Lo-rise, keys in open room

Location: Beach front

General Facilities: Daily maid, Kitchen, Linens, Restaurant on prem., Bar on prem., Baby-sitter

Room Facilities: Pool, Tennis, Windsurfing school, TV, Cable, Phone in rm., Crib-Hi-chair, Ind. AC Ctl.

Attractions: Swimming, scuba diving, windsurfing

Shops & Restaurants: Diving shop, boutiques; Stouffer Resort restaurants

One bedroom villas on the same property as Stouffer Grand Beach Resort with private patio entrances.

Sapphire Village
c/o Prop. Mgmt. Caribbean, Rt. 6
St. Thomas, VI 00802
800-524-2038

1 Bedroom $$$, 2 Bedrooms $$$$, Hi-rise
Pool, Daily maid, Kitchen, Linens

Attractions: Swimming, sailing, snorkeling, scuba diving, windsurfing, golf, tennis

Resort condominium comfort overlooking Sapphire Beach with its blue Caribbean waters. Tropically furnished units with combination living/dining rooms and dressing areas. Two freshwater pools.

Watergate Villas
c/o Prop. Mgmt. Caribbean, Rt. 6
St. Thomas, VI 00802
800-524-2038

1 Bedroom $$$, 2 Bedrooms $$$, Villas
Pool, Daily maid, Kitchen, Linens

Attractions: Tennis, golf, swimming, water sports

Enjoy your Caribbean vacation in the comfort and privacy of your own condominium home. Prepare dinner as the sunsets over Bolongo Bay, or choose to eat out in the award-winning Watergate Villas restaurant.

Tourism Information

Every state has a great deal of free information available for tourism. Write and ask for their general packet and be sure to mention specific areas you are interested in.

ALABAMA
Alabama Bureau of Tourist & Travel
532 S. Perry St.
Montgomery, AL 36104
800-252-2262

ALASKA
Alaska State Division of Tourism
Department of Economic
Development
P.O. Box E
Juneau, AK 99811
907-465-2010

ARIZONA
Arizona Office of Tourism
1100 W. Washington
Phoenix, AZ 85007
602-255-3618

ARKANSAS
Arkansas Department of Parks &
Tourism
1 Capitol Mall
Little Rock, AR 72201
800-643-8383

CALIFORNIA
California Office of Tourism
Department of Commerce
1121 L Street, Suite 103
Sacramento, CA 95814
916-322-1396 or 800-862-2543

COLORADO
Colorado Tourism Board
1625 Broadway, Suite 1700
Denver, CO 80202
303-592-5410

CONNECTICUT
Connecticut Department of
Economic Development
210 Washington Street
Hartford, CT 06106
203-566-3385

DELAWARE
Delaware Tourism Office
99 Kings Highway
P.O. Box 1401
Dover, DE 19903
302-736-4271

DISTRICT OF COLUMBIA
Washington D.C. Convention &
Visitors Association
1575 Eye Street N.W., Suite 250
Washington, DC 20005
202-789-7000

FLORIDA
Florida Division of Tourism, Visitor
Inquiry Section
101 E. Gaines Street, Fletcher
Building, Room 422
Tallahassee, FL 32399-2000
904-487-1462

GEORGIA
Georgia Department of Industry &
Trade
Box 1776
Atlanta, GA 30301
404-656-3590

HAWAII
Hawaii Visitors Bureau
Waikiki Business Plaza
2270 Kalakaua Avenue
Honolulu, HI 96815
808-023-1811
also 50 California Street, Suite 450
San Francisco, CA 94111
415-392-8173

IDAHO
Idaho Travel Council
Hall of Mirrors, Second Floor
700 W. State Street
Boise, ID 83720
800-635-7820

ILLINOIS
Illinois Department of Commerce &
Community Affairs
Illinois Travel Information Center
310 South Michigan Avenue, Suite
108
Chicago, IL 60604
312-793-2094

INDIANA
Indiana Department of Commerce,
Tourism Development Division
1 N. Capitol, Suite 700
Indianapolis, IN 46204
800-292-6337

IOWA
Iowa Development Commission,
Tourism & Travel Division
200 East Grand Avenue
Des Moines, IA 50309
515-281-3100

KANSAS
Kansas Department of Commerce,
Travel & Tourism
400 W. Eighth Street, Fifth Floor
Topeka, KS 66603-3957
913-296-2009

KENTUCKY
Kentucky Department of Travel
Development
Capital Plaza Tower, 22nd Floor
Frankfort, KY 40601
502-564-4930

LOUISIANA
Louisiana Office of Tourism
Box 94291 Capitol Station
Baton Rouge, LA 70804-9291
800-334-8626

MAINE
Maine State Division of Tourism
189 State Street
Augusta, ME 04333
207-289-5710

MARYLAND
Maryland Office of Tourist
Development
Redwood Tower
217 E. Redwood Street
Baltimore, MD 21202-3316
301-333-6611

MASSACHUSETTS
Massachusetts Department of
Commerce & Development
Division of Tourism
100 Cambridge Street
Boston, MA 02202
617-727-3201

MICHIGAN
Michigan Department of
Commerce, Travel Bureau
P.O. Box 30226
Lansing, MI 48909
800-543-2937

MINNESOTA
Minnesota Travel Information
Center
375 Jackson Street
St. Paul, MN 55101
800-328-1461

MISSISSIPPI
Mississippi Department of
Economic Development
Division of Tourism
Box 849
Jackson, MS 39205
800-847-2290

MISSOURI
Missouri Division of Tourism
Truman Office Building
Box 1055
Jefferson City, MO 65102
314-751-4133

MONTANA
Montana Chamber of Commerce
1424 Ninth Avenue
Helena, MT 59620
800-548-3390

NEBRASKA
Nebraska Department of Economic
Development
Division of Travel & Tourism
301 Centennial Mall S., Box 94666
Lincoln, NE 68509
800-228-4307

NEVADA
Nevada Commission on Tourism
800 East Williams, Suite 207
Carson City, NV 89710
800-237-0774

NEW HAMPSHIRE
New Hampshire Office of Vacation
Travel
Box 856
Concord, NH 03301
603-271-2343

NEW JERSEY
New Jersey Division of Travel &
Tourism
CN 826
Trenton, NJ 08625
609-292-2470

NEW MEXICO
New Mexico Tourism & Travel
Division
Economic Development & Tourism
Department
Bataan Memorial Building
Santa Fe, NM 87503
800-545-2040

NEW YORK
New York State Department of
Commerce
Division of Tourism Development
1 Commerce Plaza
Albany, NY 12245
800-225-5697
New York Convention & Visitors
Bureau Inc.
2 Columbus Circle
New York, NY 10019-1823
212-397-8222

NORTH CAROLINA
North Carolina Travel & Tourism
Division
Department of Commerce
430 North Salisbury Street
Raleigh, NC 27611
800-847-4862

NORTH DAKOTA
North Dakota Tourism Promotion
Liberty Memorial Building
Capitol Grounds
Bismark, ND 58505
800-437-2077

OHIO
Ohio Office of Travel & Tourism
P.O. Box 1001
Columbus, OH 43216
800-282-5393

OKLAHOMA
Oklahoma Tourism & Recreation
Department
500 Will Rogers Building
Oklahoma City, OK 73105
405-521-2409

OREGON
Oregon State Tourism Division
595 Cottage Street, N.E.
Salem, OR 97310
800-547-7842

PENNSYLVANIA
Pennsylvania State Bureau of Travel
Marketing
Department of Commerce
Room 453 Forum Building
Harrisburg, PA 17120
800-847-4872

PUERTO RICO
Puerto Rico Tourism Company
301 San Justo St.
Old San Juan, PR 00905
809-721-2400

RHODE ISLAND
Rhode Island Tourism Division
Department of Economic
Development
7 Jackson Walkway
Providence, RI 02903
401-277-2601

SOUTH CAROLINA
South Carolina Department of
Parks, Recreation & Tourism
1205 Pendleton St.
Columbia, SC 29202
803-253-6318

SOUTH DAKOTA
South Dakota State Department of
Tourism
Capitol Lake Plaza
Pierre, SD 57501
800-843-1930

TENNESSEE
Tennessee Department of Tourism
Development
320 Sixth Avenue N
Nashville, TN 37202
615-741-2169

TEXAS
Texas Tourist Agency
First City Center
P.O. Box 12008
Austin, TX 78711
512-462-9191

UTAH
Utah State Travel Council
Council Hall Capitol Hill
Salt Lake City, UT 84114
801-553-5681

VERMONT
Vermont Travel Division
134 State Street
Montpelier, VT 05602
802-838-3236

VIRGINIA
Virginia Division of Tourism
202 N. Ninth Street, Suite 500
Richmond, VA 23219
804-786-4484 or 800-847-4882

WASHINGTON
Washington State Travel
Development Division
101 General Administration
Building
Olympia, WA 98504
800-544-1800

WEST VIRGINIA
West Virginia State Travel
Development Division
Office of Economic & Community
Development
2101 Washington Street E., Third
Floor
Charleston, WV 25305
800-225-5982

WISCONSIN
Wisconsin State Division of Tourism
P.O. Box 7606
Madison, WI 53707
608-266-2161 or 800-432-8747

WYOMING
Wyoming State Travel Commission
Frank Norris Jr. Travel Center
Cheyenne, WI 83002
800-225-5996

Index

———————— GEORGIA ————————

———————— HAWAII ————————

VOTE

FOR YOUR CHOICE OF
CONDO OF THE YEAR

To the editors of **Condo Vacation, The Complete Guide.**

I cast my vote for "Condo of the Year" for:

Name of Condo _____

Address _____

_____

Phone _____

Reasons _____

_____

_____

I would also like to (please check one):

____ Recommend a new Condo   ____ Comment

____ Critique   ____ Suggest

Name of Condo _____

Address _____

_____

Phone _____

Comment _____

_____

_____

Please send your entries to:
Condo Vacations, The Complete Guide
P.O. Box 20429
Oakland, CA 94620

Free Subscription to Mondo Condo Newsletter™

From time to time we will send you a free copy of our Mondo Condo News-letter that will keep you posted about special Condo travel offers, air and Condo packages, and golf Condo resort packages and family travel specials. This free subscription is available for a limited time only. Subscribe now!

Name _____

Address _____

City _____ State _____ ZIP _____

Are you planning a Condo Vacation within the next year? If so, how many adults _____ children _____ ?

Are you interested in receiving information regarding Condos for sale? If so, where? Northeast _____ Southeast _____ Midwest _____ West _____ Hawaii _____ Which special areas? _____

Are you golfers? _____ Do you ski? _____

When taking a vacation, do you generally travel by car _____ rail _____ or air _____ ?

Lanier Travel Guides have set the standard for the industry:

All necessary information about facilities, prices, pets, children, amenities, credit cards and the like. Like France's Michelin... —New York Times

Provides a wealth of the kinds of information needed to make a wise choice. —American Council on Consumer Interest

AVAILABLE IN BOOK STORES EVERYWHERE

Golf Resorts — The Complete Guide

The first ever comprehensive guide to over 500 golf resorts coast to coast. Includes complete details of each resort facility and golf course particulars. As an added bonus, there is a guide within the guide of over 1,800 public golf courses with full details. Introduction by Fuzzy Zoeller.

All-Suite Hotel Guide — The definitive directory

"They appeal to every segment - individual, corporate travellers, long time stays, and meetings." —Corporate and Incentive Travel. "One of the hottest trends in the industry." —Time.

The only guide to the all-suite hotel industry features over 800 hotels nation-wide and abroad. There is a special bonus list of temporary office facilities. A perfect choice for business travellers and much appreciated by families who enjoy the additional privacy provided by two rooms.

The Complete Guide to Bed & Breakfast Inns & Guesthouses in the United States and Canada

Annually revised, and the most complete directory with over 5,000 listings in over 50 states. This classic volume provides full details and special lists identifying inns noted for gourmet cuisine, antiques, conference facilities and more. "Contains all necessary information about facilities, prices, particulars, children, and amenities, credit cards and more. Like France's Michelin." —New York Times. A national best seller!

Bed & Breakfast Cookbook

This beautiful book offers recipes from some of America's finest inns. First prize winner in the Philadelphia Book Fair and a cook book best seller. This lovely book, printed on parchment, makes a great gift!

Elegant Small Hotels — A Connoisseur's Guide

This selective guide for discriminating travellers describes over 200 of America's finest hotels characterized by exquisite rooms, fine dining, and perfect service par excellence. "Elegant Small Hotels makes a seductive volume for window shopping." —Chicago Sun Times. "If elegant small hotels are your thing - and whose aren't they? - check out Elegant Small Hotels. . .complete with celebrity comments on many of them." —Elle. Introduction by Peter Duchin.

22 Days in Alaska

Your on-the-road guide to the wonders of Alaska and Northwestern Canada. Travelling this vast area requires careful planning and our 22-day itinerary takes you on a tour of the best and most fascinating that the north country has to offer, with lots of options. Part of the famed 22-day series.

Travel Notes

Travel Notes

Travel Notes

Travel Notes

Travel Notes